REVIEW OF RESEARCH IN EDUCATION

Review of Research in Education is published annually on behalf of the American Educational Research Association, 1430 K St., NW, Suite 1200, Washington, DC 20005, by SAGE Publications, 2455 Teller Road, Thousand Oaks, CA 91320. Send address changes to AERA Membership Department, 1430 K St., NW, Suite 1200, Washington, DC 20005.

Member Information: American Educational Research Association (AERA) member inquiries, member renewal requests, changes of address, and membership subscription inquiries should be addressed to the AERA Membership Department, 1430 K St., NW, Suite 1200, Washington, DC 20005; fax 202-238-3250; e-mail: members@aera.net. AERA annual membership dues are $150 (Regular and Affiliate Members), $110 (International Affiliates), and $40 (Graduate and Undergraduate Student Affiliates). **Claims:** Claims for undelivered copies must be made no later than six months following month of publication. Beyond six months and at the request of the American Educational Research Association, the publisher will supply missing copies when losses have been sustained in transit and when the reserve stock permits.

Subscription Information: All non-member subscription inquiries, orders, back-issue requests, claims, and renewals should be addressed to SAGE Publications, 2455 Teller Road, Thousand Oaks, CA 91320; telephone (800) 818-SAGE (7243) and (805) 499-0721; fax: (805) 375-1700; e-mail: journals@sagepub.com; http://www.sagepublications .com. **Subscription Price:** Institutions: $306; Individuals: $62. For all customers outside the Americas, please visit http://www.sagepub.co.uk/customercare.nav for information. **Claims:** Claims for undelivered copies must be made no later than six months following month of publication. The publisher will supply missing copies when losses have been sustained in transit and when the reserve stock will permit.

Abstracting and Indexing: Please visit http://rre.aera.net and, under the "More about this journal" menu on the right-hand side, click on the Abstracting/Indexing link to view a full list of databases in which this journal is indexed.

Copyright Permission: Permission requests to photocopy or otherwise reproduce copyrighted material owned by the American Educational Research Association should be submitted by accessing the Copyright Clearance Center's Rightslink® service through the journal's website at http://rre.aera.net. Permission may also be requested by contacting the Copyright Clearance Center via its website at http://www.copyright.com, or via e-mail at info@copyright.com.

Advertising and Reprints: Current advertising rates and specifications may be obtained by contacting the advertising coordinator in the Thousand Oaks office at (805) 410-7763 or by sending an e-mail to advertising@sagepub.com. To order reprints, please e-mail reprint@ sagepub.com. Acceptance of advertising in this journal in no way implies endorsement of the advertised product or service by SAGE or the journal's affiliated society(ies). No endorsement is intended or implied. SAGE reserves the right to reject any advertising it deems as inappropriate for this journal.

Change of Address: Six weeks' advance notice must be given when notifying of change of address. Please send old address label along with the new address to ensure proper identification. Please specify name of journal.

International Standard Serial Number ISSN 0091-732X
International Standard Book Number ISBN 978-1-4833-58758 (Vol. 38, 2014, paper)
Manufactured in the United States of America. First printing, March 2014.
Copyright © 2014 by the American Educational Research Association. All rights reserved.

Printed on acid-free paper

REVIEW OF RESEARCH IN EDUCATION

Language Policy, Politics, and Diversity in Education

Volume 38, 2014

Kathryn M. Borman, Editor
University of South Florida

Terrence G. Wiley, Editor
Center for Applied Linguistics

David R. Garcia, Editor
Arizona State University

Arnold B. Danzig, Editor
San José State University

AMERICAN
EDUCATIONAL
RESEARCH
ASSOCIATION

SAGE

Review of Research in Education

Language Policy, Politics, and Diversity in Education

Volume 38

EDITORS

KATHRYN M. BORMAN
University of South Florida

DAVID R. GARCIA
Arizona State University

TERRENCE G. WILEY
Center for Applied Linguistics

ARNOLD B. DANZIG
San José State University

AMERICAN EDUCATIONAL RESEARCH ASSOCIATION

Tel: 202-238-3200 Fax: 202-238-3250
http://www.aera.net/pubs

FELICE J. LEVINE
Executive Director

JOHN NEIKIRK
Director of Publications

Contents

II. International Context

Cover image © iStockphoto.com

Introduction

Language Policy, Politics, and Diversity in Education

TERRENCE G. WILEY
Center for Applied Linguistics

DAVID R. GARCIA
Arizona State University

ARNOLD B. DANZIG
San José State University

MONICA L. STIGLER
Arizona State University

*R*eview *of Research in Education: Vol. 38, Language Policy, Politics, and Diversity in Education* explores the role of educational language policies in promoting education as a human right. There are an estimated nearly 7,000 living languages in the world. Yet, despite the extent of language diversity, only a small number of the world's languages are used as mediums of instruction. Even in English-dominant countries, such as the United States, it is important to understand the role of educational language policies (ELPs) in promoting educational access through the dominant language, and its impact on educational equity, achievement, and students' sense of identity.

The United Nations Declaration on Rights of Persons Belonging to National or Ethnic Minorities, Article 4 (1991) affirms, "States should take appropriate measures so that, whenever possible, persons belonging to National or Ethnic minorities may have adequate opportunities to learn their mother tongue or to have instruction in their mother tongue" (cited in Spring, 2000, p. 31). Presently and historically, a growing minority of children in the United States and a majority in many countries around the world attend schools where there is a difference between the language or variety of language spoken at home and the language of instruction in school. As a result, to learn in school, language minorities must learn the language of schooling, which requires some type of accommodation (Wiley, 2013).

Review of Research in Education
March 2014, Vol. 38, pp. vii-xxiii
DOI: 10.3102/0091732X13512984
© 2014 AERA. http://rre.aera.net

Educational access, equity, and achievement vary widely both across and within nation states. In the 21st century, however, few would argue that education should be a human right. This principle was endorsed in Article 26 of the 1948 Universal Declaration of Human Rights (Spring, 2000). Despite this endorsement, many of those from language minority backgrounds in the United States and around the world often fail to perform as well as children who speak the dominant language.

In the U.S. context, the principle of the right to linguistic accommodation was first recognized by the Supreme Court in 1974 in *Lau v. Nichols*. The *Lau* decision, however, did not address the question of whether language minority children have a right to learn the language of their family or community. For the English-only–speaking majority in the United States, that question of one's right to one's native language, when it is other than English, is generally weighed against the perceived need to promote English as the common national language. Similar beliefs in the need to promote a national language are widely held in other countries, such as France, where the promotion of French is seen as requisite for the promotion of a national identity (Wiley, 2013).

A central question of importance taken up by the authors in this volume is whether language minorities should have a right not only to linguistic accommodation but also to the promotion of their languages as a means for developing a positive identification with their languages and cultures. This approach was supported in a UNESCO resolution six decades ago. The resolution held that every child should have a right to attain literacy in his or her mother tongue. The case for minority language rights in education remains contested but has been strongly defended (see May, Chapter 9). Joel Spring (2000) provided a detailed argument and proposal for universal rights to education, which emphasized the importance of cultural and language rights as a central component. His focus demonstrated particular sensitivity to the educational position of indigenous peoples, many of whose languages and cultures often face depreciation or even extinction from the expansion of the power of nation states and the economics of globalization, which have disrupted their sociocultural and economic ecologies (McCarty & Nicholas, Chapter 5; Wiley, 2013). Spring (2000, p. 159) contended that all people should have a right to an education in their own language and in the methods of teaching and learning appropriate to their own culture, and a right to an education that teaches the following:

1. An understanding of their own culture and their relation to it
2. Their mother tongue
3. The dominant or official language of the country
4. An understanding of the effect of the world culture and economy on their own culture and economy

The first two points raised by Spring (2000) are predicated on the supposition that children need to develop a positive identity with their home cultures and mother tongues(s) to learn effectively by building on the resources they bring to school. The third point recognizes the pragmatic need to access and participate in the dominant society. The final point, the right of understanding the effects of world culture, is seen as being necessitated by the intrusion of the global economy and dominant languages that threaten the ecology of indigenous cultures and traditional economies (Spring, 2000; Wiley, 2013).

Other questions about the impact of educational policies relate to the differential statuses of language minorities and the failure to recognize speakers of minority languages. Many countries attempt to neutralize linguistic diversity by promoting a "common" or "national" language. This strategy can have negative consequences for both minorities and speakers of the dominant language if the majority population disassociates itself from language minorities or uses minority languages to stigmatize minority populations.

The role of English as the world's dominant language or lingua franca also poses challenges (see Shohamy, Chapter 11). In many countries around the world, English is a required subject in school and increasingly for university admission (Jenkins, 2013). It is also increasing as a medium of instruction, especially in mathematics and science instruction. Thus, the impact of English language educational policies as well as that of other dominant languages in a global context are subjects worthy of consideration (see Tollefson, 2013; Tollefson & Tsui, Chapter 8).

Another focus of this volume addresses the importance of other major languages within the context of global economic, political, and cultural contexts. Given the large number of speakers of Spanish in both global and U.S. contexts, it is also important to consider the implications for ELPs (see the chapters by García, Chapter 3, and Macías, Chapter 2). Despite the presence of over 35 million Spanish speakers in the United States, Spanish continues to be taught primarily as a "foreign" language. As Macías (Chapter 2) notes in his chapter, the historical role of Spanish in the United States is complex but the case may be made for its status as a conational language of the United States.

Finally, within most countries and increasingly within the United States, there are many languages that play an important role as heritage and thriving languages of immigrant and indigenous communities. Thus, this volume also addresses the importance of considering policies related to these languages and their speakers.

DEMOGRAPHIC BACKGROUND

To capture the global language landscape, we turned to Ethnologue (2013a, 2013b, 2013c, 2013d, 2013e), a comprehensive reference work that catalogs all of the world's known living languages into summaries of languages by country, numbers of speakers, language size, language status, and language family (www.ethnologue.com/statistics). Our review of these statistics highlights two contrary trends. First, there is tremendous language diversity around the world. Second, the majority of the world's languages are endangered as a relatively few number of dominant languages maintain

TABLE 1
Distribution of World Languages by Area of Origin

Area	Living Languages		Speakers			
	Count	%	Total	%	M	*Mdn*
Africa	2,146	30.2	789,138,977	12.7	367,726	27,000
Americas	1,060	14.9	51,109,910	0.8	48,217	1,170
Asia	2,304	32.4	3,742,996,641	60.0	1,624,565	12,000
Europe	284	4.0	1,646,624,761	26.4	5,797,975	61,150
Pacific	1,311	18.5	6,551,278	0.1	4,997	950
Total	7,105	100.0	6,236,421,567	100.0	877,751	7,000

Source. Used by permission, © SIL International, Lewis, M. Paul, Gary F. Simons, and Charles D. Fennig (eds.). 2013. *Ethnologue: Languages of the World, Seventeenth edition.* Dallas, Texas: SIL International. Online version: http://www.ethnologue.com (http://www.ethnologue.com/statistics/size).

and expand their national and international presence. These divergent trends illustrate the challenge faced by many students worldwide who encounter languages in school that differ from their mother tongue. Likewise, there are many teachers who may not be familiar with or speak the languages of the children they teach.

Table 1 presents the approximate number of living languages worldwide, organized by five areas: Africa, the Americas, Asia, Europe, and the Pacific. The count includes the number of living languages that originate in a specified area and the number of speakers of that language, regardless of where in the world those persons actually live. Ethnologue defines a living language "as one that has a least one speaker for who it is their first language." The results highlight the tremendous language diversity across the globe, particularly in Africa and Asia where 63% of the world's living languages are found. In addition, the results put the magnitude of our language diversity in perspective given that 60% of the world's population lives in Asia, the most linguistically diverse region of the world.

Table 2 provides information on the distribution of languages in the world by the number of first-language speakers. From this perspective, the concentration of first-language speakers into a few dominant languages becomes evident. Worldwide, only eight languages (0.1% of the total number of living languages) account for just over 40% of speakers.

Table 3 lists the 24 most spoken languages of the world in descending order along with the country in which the primary entry for the language is found. The italicized languages are macro languages, defined as "multiple, closely related individual languages that are deemed in some usage contexts to be a single language" (Ethnologue, 2013e, para. 7). Macro languages are summarized as a single group. This analysis highlights two additional findings of note with regard to English. Some may find it surprising that English is the third most spoken language in the world behind both

TABLE 2
Distribution of World Languages by Number of First-Language Speakers

Population Range	Living Languages			Speakers		
	Count	%	Cumulative %	Total	%	Cumulative %
100,000,000–999,999,999	8	0.1	0.1	2,528,029,108	40.5	40.5
10,000,000–99,999,999	77	1.1	1.2	2,381,969,581	38.2	78.3
1,000,000–9,999,999	308	4.3	5.5	962,536,721	15.4	94.2
100,000–999,999	928	13.1	18.6	294,564,660	4.7	98.9
10,000–99,999	1,798	25.3	43.9	61,216,188	1.0	99.9
1,000–9,999	1,984	27.9	71.8	7,628,190	0.1	100.0
100–999	1,054	14.8	86.7	463,621	0.0	100.0
10–99	340	4.8	91.4	12,947	0.0	100.0
1–9	134	1.9	93.3	551	0.0	100.0
0	188	2.6	96.0	0	0.0	100.0
			100.0			
Unknown	286	4.0				
Total	7,105	100.0		6,236,421,567.0	100.0	

Source. Used by permission, © SIL International, Lewis, M. Paul, Gary F. Simons, and Charles D. Fennig (eds.). 2013. *Ethnologue: Languages of the World, Seventeenth edition.* Dallas, Texas: SIL International. Online version: http://www.ethnologue.com (http://www.ethnologue.com/statistics/size).

TABLE 3
Languages With at Least 50 Million First-Language Speakers

Rank	Language	Primary Country	Total Countries	Speakers (Millions)
1	Chinese (zho)	China	33	1197.0
2	Spanish (spa)	Spain	31	406.0
3	English (eng)	United Kingdom	101	335.0
4	Hindi (hin)	India	4	260.0
5	Arabic (ara)	Saudi Arabia	59	223.0
6	Portuguese (por)	Portugal	11	202.0
7	Bengali (ben)	Bangladesh	4	193.0
8	Russian (rus)	Russian Federation	16	162.0
9	Japanese (jpn)	Japan	3	122.0
10	Javanese (jav)	Indonesia	3	84.3
11	German, standard (deu)	Germany	18	83.8
12	Lahnda (lah)	Pakistan	7	82.7
13	Telugu (tel)	India	2	74.0
14	Marathi (mar)	India	1	71.8
15	Tamil (tam)	India	6	68.8
16	French (fra)	France	51	68.5
17	Vietnamese (vie)	Vietnam	3	67.8
18	Korean (kor)	South Korea	6	66.4
19	Urdu (urd)	Pakistan	6	63.4
20	Italian (ita)	Italy	10	61.1
21	Malay (msa)	Malaysia	13	59.4
22	Persian (fas)	Iran	29	56.6
23	Turkish (tur)	Turkey	8	50.7
24	Oriya (ori)	India	3	50.1

Source. Used by permission, © SIL International, Lewis, M. Paul, Gary F. Simons, and Charles D. Fennig (eds.). 2013. *Ethnologue: Languages of the World, Seventeenth edition.* Dallas, Texas: SIL International. Online version: http://www.ethnologue.com (http://www.ethnologue.com/statistics/size).

Chinese and Spanish. But its global impact is evident given that it is spoken in more countries than any other language.

Table 4 provides the distribution of languages in the world by their status, in terms of language development or language endangerment. According to the Ethnologue website, "The Status element of a language includes . . . an estimate of the overall development versus endangerment of the language . . . (and) categorization of the official recognition given to a language within the country (http://www.ethnologue.com/about/language-status). The Expanded Graded Intergenerational Disruption Scale levels are defined and assigned on a 13-level scale. Table 4 uses only ranges from 0 to 9 (0 = *International*—the language is widely used between nations in trade, knowledge exchange, and international policy; 9 = *Dormant*—the language serves as

TABLE 4
Distribution of World Languages by Status of Development or Endangerment

EGIDS	Living Languages			Number of Speakers					
	Count	%	Cumulative %	Total	%	Cumulative %	M	Mdn	
0: International	6	0.1	0.1	1,818,381,088	29.2	29.2	303,063,515	334,800,758	
1: National	95	1.3	1.4	1,917,448,972	30.7	59.9	20,183,673	6,915,000	
2: Provincial	70	1.0	2.4	702,091,474	11.3	71.2	10,029,878	1,152,735	
3: Wider communication	166	2.3	4.7	520,850,402	8.4	79.5	3,137,653	697,200	
4: Educational	345	4.9	9.6	240,886,147	3.9	83.4	698,221	100,000	
5: Developing	1,534	21.6	31.2	587,368,282	9.4	92.8	382,900	26,000	
6a: Vigorous	2,502	35.2	66.4	382,441,032	6.1	98.9	152,854	10,000	
6b: Threatened	1,025	14.4	80.8	53,902,649	0.9	99.8	52,588	2,700	
7: Shifted	456	6.4	87.2	12,053,328	0.2	100.0	26,433	1,080	
8a: Moribund	286	4.0	91.3	922,885	0.0	100.0	3,227	260	
8b: Nearly extinct	432	6.1	97.4	75,308	0.0	100.0	174	18	
9: Dormant	188	2.6	100.0	0	0.0	100.0	0	0	
Total	7,105	100.0		6,236,421,567	100.0				

Source. Used by permission, © SIL International, Lewis, M. Paul, Gary F. Simons, and Charles D. Fennig (eds). 2013. *Ethnologue: Languages of the World, Seventeenth edition.* Dallas, Texas: SIL International. Online version: http://www.ethnologue.com (http://www.ethnologue.com/statistics/size).

Note. EGIDS = Expanded Graded Intergenerational Disruption Scale. Information about the EGIDS can be found at http://www.ethnologue.com/about/language-status

a reminder of heritage identity for an ethnic community, but no one has more than symbolic proficiency). The final level on the scale, *Extinct*, is not included in Table 4.

This insightful view of language trends reinforces previous findings and pinpoints the importance of programs and policies in language maintenance. The challenge is one of both maintaining languages and building on the linguistic and cultural foundations of the linguistic family and community resources that children bring to school. The dominance of dominant languages is evident in the relatively few languages that are considered *International* or *National*, less than 2% of languages worldwide. Likewise, nearly 20% of the world's languages are regarded as *Shifted* to *Extinct*. The most striking point of the distribution is the percentage of languages that vary from *Developing* to *Threatened*. A total of 71% of the world's languages fall in this range. The common thread among the categorization of these languages is that they are all in states of transition. It is precisely in these mutable states that policies and programs can have the greatest impact, a point that underscores the timeliness and importance of this volume (for a definition of the Expanded Graded Intergenerational Disruption Scale, see http://www.ethnologue.com/about/language-status).

Finally, Table 5 summarizes the distribution of languages for a select group of countries (for a full listing, see http://www.ethnologue.com/statistics/country). This table is ordered according to the Diversity Index, a measure that indicates the probability that any two people selected at random in a given country would have a different mother tongue. The values range from 1.0, indicating total diversity or that no two people have the same mother tongue, to a value of 0, indicating language heterogeneity or that the population shares the same mother tongue. This view underscores the language diversity in regions such as Africa and Asia. It also places U.S. language diversity in context with its North American neighbors. Canada is more diverse linguistically than the United States, so it is likely that two Canadian residents do not share the same mother tongue. In the United States, more residents share the same mother tongue than in Canada. But the U.S. population is more linguistically diverse than Mexico, a finding that is largely attributable to the prevalence of Spanish in the United States.

DISCUSSION

In light of these trends, Volume 38 of *Review of Research in Education* presents new research and deeper explorations of key research themes by a distinguished group of international scholars of language policy. The individual chapters provide readers with insight into the local and national contexts for language policies along with discussing the international forces that frame the contours of present-day tensions created by the dominance of a few dominant languages.

In our review of this impressive collection of chapters, a number of major themes arise in our minds from across the chapters. This introduction is intended as a reference guide to explicate those themes but we also invite readers to experience the volume's content for themselves to discover insight to guide their own inquiry and practice.

TABLE 5
Linguistic Diversity of Countries in the World, Select Countries (From Highest to Lowest)

Country	Diversity Index	Coverage %	Living Languages				Speakers		
			Total	%	Indigenous	Immigrant	Count	M	Mdn
Kenya	0.93	96	72	1.01	67	5	37,577,462	544,601	175,905
India	0.92	95	454	6.39	447	7	1,092,380,631	2,534,526	34,200
South Africa	0.87	84	44	0.62	28	16	44,637,399	1,206,416	18,000
Philippines	0.85	96	192	2.7	181	11	96,367,126	520,903	20,000
Afghanistan	0.79	98	41	0.58	39	2	22,964,800	574,120	8,000
Iraq	0.73	88	26	0.37	22	4	25,922,820	1,127,079	40,000
Belgium	0.70	72	29	0.41	10	19	13,300,500	633,357	63,600
Israel	0.67	84	50	0.7	35	15	8,672,175	206,480	42,500
Canada	0.60	89	173	2.43	87	86	32,882,232	213,521	6,535
China	0.51	98	301	4.24	298	3	1,211,899,138	4,108,133	26,800
Italy	0.48	91	43	0.61	36	7	77,535,830	1,988,098	50,600
United States	0.33	84	420	5.91	214	206	278,640,074	787,119	435
Panama	0.27	68	19	0.27	14	5	3,752,843	288,680	6,800
Finland	0.14	75	20	0.28	12	8	5,066,660	337,777	3,100
Mexico	0.11	99	288	4.05	282	6	110,118,349	387,741	4,725
Brazil	0.05	95	228	3.21	215	13	192,255,839	885,972	200
Japan	0.03	75	16	0.23	15	1	122,680,863	10,223,405	4,100
North Korea	0.00	100	1	0.01	1	0	20,000,000	20,000,000	20,000,000

Source. Used by permission, © SIL International, Lewis, M. Paul, Gary F. Simons, and Charles D. Fennig (eds.). 2013. *Ethnologue: Languages of the World, Seventeenth edition*. Dallas, Texas: SIL International. Online version: http://www.ethnologue.com (http://www.ethnologue.com/statistics/size).

The chapters that comprise *Review of Research in Education: Vol. 38. Language Diversity, Policy, and Politics in Education* examine language policies, rights, and activism from different countries and cultures around the world. In each case, it is important to situate language and education in the local sociohistorical context in order to make meaning of present-day educational realities faced by the multitude of language minority populations around the globe. For example, one must understand the historic racism and segregation of Hispanics in U.S. schools to interpret the backlash to present day policies such as Structured English Immersion, where Hispanic students are segregated by language ability. Or in Wales, one must know the hegemonic nature of Western European Imperialism to appreciate the current interest in and strength of Welsh language revitalization.

Despite the contextual differences, the impact of colonialism is a common theme across the chapters because of the devastating and lasting impact of these policies on indigenous languages. Colonial education policies maintained the power and dominance of the colonizers while simultaneously eroding the social cohesion and cultural capital of the indigenous population. In her chapter "Overcoming Colonial Legacies," Ramanathan (Chapter 12) recalls,

This one colonial policy [Divide and Rule] took root and went very deeply into the South Asian ideological space to where [English-medium] education was deemed as having more cultural capital and symbolic power than an education in the vernaculars. (p. 292)

The lasting effects of such policies continue to reproduce social and economic inequalities long after colonial rule. Therefore, many of the chapters examine present-day policies and practices that are intended to remedy historic inequalities.

As such, Freire's (2011) reminder that without critical consciousness, there is always a risk of oppressed persons becoming oppressors also resonates throughout the volume. For example, in the chapter, "Justifying Educational Language Rights," May (Chapter 9) points out that "in many postcolonial countries, small English-speaking elites have continued the same policies as their former colonizers in order to ensure that (limited) access to English language education acts as a crucial distributor of social prestige and wealth" (p. 218).

It is important to acknowledge that while the policies during colonial rule served to silence indigenous voices, colonialism was an encompassing system of domination rooted in racism and greed. May (Chapter 9) keenly points out,

African Americans have been speaking English for 200 years in the United States and yet many still find themselves relegated to urban ghettos. Racism and discrimination are far more salient factors here than language use. Likewise, English is almost as inoperative with respect to Latino social mobility in the United States as it is with respect to Black social mobility. Twenty-five percent of Latinos currently live at or below the poverty line, a rate that is at least twice as high as the proportion of Latinos who are not English speaking. (p. 219)

Powers (Chapter 4) asserts, "Language, like race, has been an important marker of social status and is a significant aspect of individuals' social identities" (p. 81). Thus, present-day language education policies continue to reject the funds of knowledge of minority students opting instead for English-only instruction. It appears that progressive gains made in the 1960s and 1970s toward more inclusive, multicultural and bilingual education practices have been largely retracted. The impact of such subtractive policies can have a broad impact with rippling effects that extend beyond the classroom into the fabric of indigenous communities. For example, McCarty and Nicholas (Chapter 5) document the difficult social conditions faced by Native American communities, linking such conditions to restrictive language education policies that "have had cascading negative consequences for Indigenous children and youth, who experience some of the lowest rates of educational attainment and the highest rates of poverty, depression, and teen suicide" (p. 107). Despite the overwhelming empirical evidence that suggests the efficacy of multicultural and bilingual education, structural inequalities, Nativist sentiments, and a climate of anti-immigration delimit opportunities for minoritized students to excel in school and raise their socioeconomic status.

Many languages were marginalized or nearly obliterated through the sociohistorical practices of colonialism. In an effort to build on the language resources that children bring to school "mother tongue medium" ELPs have been adopted in countries such as Tanzania, Ethiopia, and South Africa. These policies have had a positive impact on student learning and participation and have opened access to educational opportunities that were not afforded to minoritized students when colonial languages were used as the medium of instruction. Tollefson and Tsui (Chapter 8) note, "there is widespread evidence internationally that mother-tongue [medium of instruction policies] can significantly reduce barriers to educational access and equity" (p. 190).

As an alternative response to colonial language policies, several authors focus on heritage language (HL) policies and programs, which are a central theme throughout this volume. HL policies are also termed *community language* (CL) policies, because as Lee and Wright (Chapter 6) note, the term *heritage language* "has been criticized for evoking images of the past and relegating languages to a powerless position" (p. 138), and García (Chapter 3) adds that the term *heritage language* further contributes to "the silencing of U.S. bilingualism" (p. 69).

HL/CL programs are predominately an outgrowth of sustained community action and advocacy on the part of parents, activists, and progressive educators to "speak back" to colonial powers in the reclamation and affirmation of the value of native languages, "linguistically encoded knowledges," and cultural traditions. "Community-based HL/CL programs are driven by the desire to transmit language and culture intergenerationally so that connections within families and ethnic communities through socialization into cultural values and practices can be maintained" (Lee & Wright, p. 139).

Most HL/CL programs take place in nonformal learning centers where "vernacular resources—typically seen as 'backward' become a most valuable well of resources for reconstructing lives and communities." Lee and Wright (Chapter 6) maintain that "community-based HL/CL programs open up possibilities for learning and working in multiple languages, exploring alternative educational possibilities, and promoting multiple linguistic identities in this current climate of English-only and anti-immigration policies" (p. 158).

Nonformal learning centers are important spaces for language preservation and positive cultural identity formation. In most contexts, schools serve only as secondary spaces for HL learning. Examples of government and school-supported HL programs, such as those in Wales, Hawaii, and some Indigenous communities detailed in this volume, constructed in a rights-based, cultural, and historical framework exist but only in conjunction with and as a result of strong community and parental advocacy and activism.

The support for HL and diverse language programs and education policies in the United States comes from many camps. For example, support can be constructed in a national security and economic competiveness framework. Bale (Chapter 7) documents the waxing and waning support, both ideologically and financially, for HL programs and notes that significant support is offered during times of war and economic expansion. Governments rarely take the lead on signaling the positive value of HL learning or supporting programs for such learning when not explicitly connected to national security efforts. Furthermore, Lee (Chapter 6) notes that higher education programs to promote language capacity in the national interest ironically focus on nonnative speakers, ignoring the value of HLs "spoken by many young immigrant and American born students when they first enter school" (p. 144).

Finally, García (Chapter 3) also addresses a response to HL from a national security standpoint. In her chapter, "U.S. Spanish and Education: Global and Local Intersections," García states, "In the 21st century, as globalization and its new technologies have spurred the movement of people, information, and goods across the world, nation-states are caught simultaneously in acts of interrelationship and acts of self-protection" (p. 59). In an attempt to maintain English as the lingua franca, García asserts that U.S. language education policies "[impose] English on Latinos by constructing Spanish-speakers as inferior subaltern subjects" (p. 59). At the same time, García suggests "the Spanish state exploits the great number of Spanish-speakers in the United States to bolster the sociolinguistic situation of Spanish within its own national borders and abroad" (pp. 58-59).

VOLUME OVERVIEW

Terrence Wiley's chapter "Diversity, Super-Diversity, and Monolingual Language Ideology in the United States" looks at language diversity and language policy in the United States. Wiley questions some basics of the taken-for-granted assumptions about language and language diversity that are part of popular culture. He uses a question from the popular game show "Jeopardy," which asks "What is the oldest American city?" as an opportunity to explore more deeply into issues related to language and language policy, migration, and globalization. In a thoughtful analysis, Wiley follows how English became the dominant language during the Colonial era and was established as the "common language" prior to the American Revolution. Unlike Lawrence Cremin's (1972) classic work on the history of American education, which focuses primarily on the transit of high (i.e., university) culture, Wiley's research expands our understanding of what counted as knowledge and learning. He illustrates how language is itself related to the transit of culture, often used to understand the American Colonial experience. His research and data analysis provide explanations of and appreciation for the forces that contribute to current conditions, and what he terms ethnolinguistic *super-diversity*.

Reynaldo Macías's chapter on Spanish as the second national language of the United States provides important historical and legal contexts for understanding the official and unofficial status of Spanish at local, state, and national levels. With data that underscore the historical growth in the number of Spanish speakers over the past 150 years, Macías points out trends toward sustainability and vitality of not only Spanish but also the community structures that use language. Macías documents the unique history of Spanish in the United States and proposes a unique status with consideration for political recognition as a "second national language."

Ofelia García's research points to the continued failure of Spanish language education policies in the U.S. policies for educating both Latinos and non-Latino students. She argues that failure is the result of three irreconcilable positions: (a) characterization of English as unique and lingua franca by U.S. educational authorities, (b) definition of language authorities in Spain and Latin America of Spanish as a global language of influence, and (c) the lived experiences of bilingual Latino speakers. In this way, García provides vivid illustration of the relationship between ideology and education practice. García provides the historical foundation for understanding how education policies that shape the teaching of Spanish have promoted standardization and the spread of Spanish to its global position today in the United States and elsewhere. She examines ways the Spanish language education policy is implemented by federal, state, and local U.S. educational agencies, as well as the influence of external agencies concerned with language policy and teaching controlled by Spain. Both approaches ignore the lived experiences of bilingual Latinos. García concludes by arguing for "translanguaging," the complex discourse of practices of bilinguals and the pedagogies that use these practices, as a way to promote authentic language practices.

Jeanne Powers provides a foundational overview and historical background for English Learner rights and ELP in the United States, with direct reference to language minorities. Her chapter focuses on the legal opinions issued by federal and state courts, and her research provides an overview of the topic, with an important update based on the most recent *Flores* cases. Powers discusses language rights in the context of the judiciary and analyzes court cases affecting language minority students. She includes in-depth analyses of precedent-setting cases such as *Brown v. Board* and expands on the history of race and language in court cases affecting minority students. Her review highlights the reluctance of courts to extend civil rights law, with the result that major decisions about language policies in schools are taken by state and local officials, and the imprecise or indeterminate federal education policy.

Language reclamation projects or policies may take place in many community institutions. McCarty and Nicholas examine language policies and the roles and responsibilities of a community institution of particular interest to educators: schools. They begin by exploring the important links among language and educational equity, Indigenous self-determination, and community well-being, with deep appreciation for the cultural practices and language-rich experiences of Native peoples. They view language reclamation, revitalization, regeneration, and regenesis, as part of the larger issue of language rights. McCarty and Nicholas argue that "the project of language reclamation is not merely or even primarily a linguistic one but is profoundly linked to issues of educational equity, Indigenous self-determination, and the (re)construction of community well-being via culturally distinctive worldviews, identities, and life orientations" (p. 107). In their chapter, they examine four cases to illustrate the language regenesis processes across various settings, and detail different aspects of school-based revitalization and language reclamation. In the Hawaiian case study, for example, they point to not only revitalization of Indigenous language but also outstanding academic results for students on high school graduation, college attendance, and academic honors. Despite the many challenges, they conclude that schools, school personnel, and school-based programs are agents of language reclamation and have a responsibility for school-based practices and family language policies in support of these goals.

Jin Sook Lee and Wayne Wright's chapter outlines the relevant contexts and issues for understanding the many benefits of HL/CL for linguistic minority children, with particular focus on community-based programs. The authors begin by defining HLs/CLs in a broader connection of individuals to families through language. In outlining the history of HL/CL family connections, they also point to a pattern where language restriction–oriented policies allowances and loopholes open up spaces for community-based-program agency within the limits of federal and state policies. The chapter then addresses challenges and needs of HL/CL programs, including the need for more appropriate curriculum, materials, and instruction; recruitment and professional development of teachers; and recruitment and retention of students. To illustrate their points, they provide case examples of community-based language programs in Korean and Cambodian Khmer-speaking communities, which have contributed to language diversity in the U.S. context. They conclude on an optimistic note, suggesting that HL/CL programs open up spaces for learning and promote linguistic diversity.

Jeff Bale's chapter "Heritage Language Education and the 'National Interest'" focuses on U.S. domestic policy and the promotion of HL education. He examines federal education policy and funding streams that have responded to geopolitical crises over the past 60 years. Bale adopts a policy-driven approach that focuses more on domestic issues and language rights. He categorizes the research literature into three approaches: technocratic, pragmatic, and critical, which assists readers in understanding the significant issues raised in this domain.

James Tollefson and Amy Tsui explore language diversity and language policy across many countries, with reference to educational access and equity. The chapter begins by exploring the principles that are part of the "Education for All" concept, which is an entryway for understanding worldwide efforts to improve educational access and equity. They examine the ways that globalization in the economy and politics have profound consequences for language policies in education. Specifically, they argue that migration, urbanization, and changes in the nature of work result in language policies in education, which shape language learning. By examining specific illustrative cases in Asia and Europe, they argue that language policies affect access and equity in education. The chapter concludes with suggestions for how language policies may be used to open access and reduce inequalities in education.

Stephen May's chapter "Justifying Educational Language Rights" provides a broad overview of the many arguments (normative and empirical) that are potentially useful to support educational language rights. May reports communication problems in the context of the dominance of English as a worldwide language and language of wider communication, from the perspective of individual and group rights. His analysis provides a rights-based perspective, which references the protection of English to serve the elite and marginalize the majority of the population. May's literature review yields a conceptual framework of tolerance-oriented and promotion-oriented language rights, as a way to analyze different national and international approaches to educational language rights. Drawing on educational research and international law, he suggests that although international legal doctrine seems to support promotion-oriented rights, in practice, it seldom goes beyond the more limited provision of tolerance-oriented rights to language minority communities. Implicitly, this suggests that rights-based approaches have largely been ineffective.

Colin Williams's description of language revitalization in Wales examines the nexus of historical roots, community development, public education, and local government, needed for understanding the complexities in the process of language revitalization. He provides readers a detailed case study of the Welsh experience, local concerns, and wider considerations. In contrast to other examples in this volume, the case in Wales provides an example of central government policies supporting language initiatives, constitutional reform, and local community engagement. His examples include the establishment of the Welsh television channel, Welsh national curriculum, and Welsh Language Board providing a statutory framework for treating English and Welsh "on the basis of equality." At the same time, he illustrates the power of community development and the challenges sustaining local community organizations and local efforts to develop/increase the use of Welsh. In the end, Williams concludes that community collective action stimulates government language policy.

Elana Shohamy's chapter "The Weight of English in Global Perspective: The Role of English in Israel" emphasizes that countries are not homogenous entities and that understanding effects on English on other languages and people requires analysis and interpretation within different sociolinguistic realities. Her research points to the deeper connections among languages, communities, and spaces, which are embedded in complex realities associated with history, geography, politics, religion, economics, education, and ideology. The chapter interrogates the complexities of English in Israel, its global language status, and the ways in which these complexities interact with local issues. Her analysis follows the role and importance of English in Israeli Jewish schools and at universities; she points to a different pattern in Arab schools, in which Arabic is the language of instruction and a vital community language, and English is a third or fourth language. She concludes that categorizing languages as global or national does not capture the complexity of factors associated with language engagement and that it is the responsibility of language policy experts to document trends and challenge resulting inequalities.

Vaidehi Ramanathan's chapter explores the South Asian context and account of English and vernacular literacy practices from a postcolonial perspective in India. She is a socio/applied linguist and offers sociohistorical background from which it is possible to view current policies and practices in language teaching and learning. Her chapter provides descriptions of educational sites, processes, and practices (i.e., textbooks, medium of instruction, tracks of schooling) through which policy-related inequities are reproduced. At the same time, she documents ways in which individual teachers and multiple institutional domains (formal and informal) engage in ways that make conditions more just and equal. Ramanathan concludes with discussion of the ways in which a postcolonial research framework explicates inequities around language policies and illustrates how human beings enhance vernaculars in ways that promote civic engagement and move people to more equal footings.

CONCLUSION

Similar to the changes we are experiencing in the natural world, language diversity is in flux due to large-scale trends with widespread implications that affect every nation. This timely volume arrives at a crossroads in the course of these global shifts. The authors' perspectives provide a solid intellectual grounding from which to inform the consequential policies and programs that will shape the educational and social environments for millions of students worldwide.

ACKNOWLEDGMENTS

The editors would like to express appreciation to the contributing authors for their original scholarship and diligence in meeting deadlines, to the consulting editors for their time and and editorial guidance, and to the members of the editorial board for providing feedback on the overall volume coherence. We wish to thank John Neikirk, Felice Levine, and the AERA publications committee for their support throughout the publication process. A special acknowledgment is extended to Monica Stigler, our editorial assistant, for keeping us on track and monitoring all communications throughout the preparation of the volume. We also want to thank Sara Sarver at Sage, who was extraordinarily helpful in moving us through the publication process. Finally, we would like to acknowledge our colleague and friend, Kathryn M. Borman, who initially brought our editorial team together. Her dedication to high-quality educational research and professional encouragement ultimately made this volume possible, and we wish her good fortune in the future.

REFERENCES

Cremin, L. (1972). *American education: The colonial experience 1607-1783*. New York, NY: HarperCollins.

Ethnologue. (2013a). *Distribution of world languages by area of origin* [data file]. Retrieved from http://www.ethnologue.com/statistics

Ethnologue. (2013b). *Distribution of world languages by number of first-language speakers* [data file]. Retrieved from http://www.ethnologue.com/statistics

Ethnologue. (2013c). *Distribution of world languages by status of development or endangerment* [data file]. Retrieved from http://www.ethnologue.com/about/language-status

Ethnologue. (2013d). *Languages with at least 50 million first-language speakers* [data file]. Retrieved from http://www.ethnologue.com/statistics

Ethnologue. (2013e). *The problem of language identification*. Retrieved from http://www.ethnologue.com/about/problem-language-identification#MacroLgsID

Freire, P. (2011). *Pedagogy of the oppressed* (30th anniversary ed.). New York, NY: Continuum International.

Jenkins, J. (2013). *English as a lingua franca in the international university: The politics of academic English language policy*. London, England: Routledge.

Spring, J. (2000). *The universal right to education: Justification, definitions, and guidelines*. Mahwah, NJ: Lawrence Erlbaum.

Tollefson, J. (Ed.). (2013). *Language policies in education: Critical issues* (2nd ed.). London, England: Routledge.

United Nations. (1991). *Declaration on the rights of persons belonging to national or ethnic, religious and linguistic minorities* (A/RES/47/135). Retrieved from http://www.un.org/documents/ga/res/47/a47r135.htm

Wiley, T. G. (2013). A brief history and assessment of language rights in the United States. In J. W. Tollefson (Ed.), *Language policies in education: Critical issues* (2nd ed., pp. 61–90). London, England: Routledge.

I. United States Context

Chapter 1

Diversity, Super-Diversity, and Monolingual Language Ideology in the United States: Tolerance or Intolerance?

TERRENCE G. WILEY
Center for Applied Linguistics

Each new demographic shift and economic or social change bring seemingly new issues into popular and political focus—questions, debates, and policies about the role of language in education and society and the recent claims that transnational migrations and globalization are resulting in unprecedented forms of ethnolinguisic "super-diversity."

This chapter addresses issues related to language diversity, policy, and politics within the U.S. context and notes recent trends and future projections. The first section takes as a point of departure a seemingly simple question from a popular television game show to illustrate some of the complexity in posing seemingly simple historical questions. The second major section considers how ethno-racial labeling and linguistic diversity have been constructed through time in U.S. Census data and considers their implications for claims regarding the allegedly unprecedented super-diversity of the present. The third part addresses how English became dominant during the colonial period, thereby establishing its position as the common language prior to the American Revolutions. The fourth section revisits issues and themes addressed in some of my work on the history of language policy, politics, rights, and ideologies (Ovando & Wiley, 2007; Wiley, 1998, 1999a, 1999b, 2005, 2007, 2010, 2013a, 2013b; Wiley & Lukes, 1996). In particular, it focuses on the evolution of English-only ideology and how it became hegemonic during the World War I era. This final section is largely based on Wiley (2000) as it looks in relation to language policies in the United States at the differential impact of language policies on various ethnolinguistic groups in the United States.

WHEN TO BEGIN? HISTORY IN JEOPARDY

In considering the evolution of language ideologies and policies in the United States, one of the first decisions in framing the discussion is determining where to

Review of Research in Education
March 2014, Vol. 38, pp. 1-32
DOI: 10.3102/0091732X13511047
© 2014 AERA. http://rre.aera.net

1

begin. A common approach is to focus on their genesis within the paradigm of the United States as a nation-state. To delimit focus to that paradigm is consistent with some prior treatments (Kloss, 1977/1998; Tatalovich, 1995). The primary focus on the national period, however, lends itself to an ideological interpretation that tends to equate the nation and national identity with one language, with the construct of "mother tongue" and of what Bonfiglio (2010) calls the "invention of the native speaker," wherein there is an assumed "imagined community" (Anderson, 1991) of speakers of a common language in geographical space where language and territory are united as one. State-serving scholars of the Third Reich would carry this logic even further by basing national unity on not only the alleged congruence of territory and language but also more insidiously the unity of nation and blood (Hutton, 1999).

Within the context of what ultimately became the United States, there is a need to begin much earlier than the national period, by giving consideration to indigenous peoples and the broader context of colonization (see Macías, 2014). This antecedent history involves the indigenous peoples and the initial, and ongoing, clashes between the colonizers; "the settlers"; the imperial rivalries between Spanish, English, French, Portuguese, and Russian empires in the Americas; and the subsequent clashes among some of the nations derived from former colonizers. Even when delimiting the focus to the national period of the United States, the history and evolution of language and racial policies must be seen within the context of expansionist wars and annexations as well as within the context of immigration.

Within these contexts, notions of heritage, national, and local identities compete for recognition and legitimacy. A simple question from a popular television game show helps illustrate the challenge of getting the past "right." On a "Jeopardy" television game show (aired April 11, 2013), the final jeopardy question, under the category of "world cities," asked contestants to name the purported oldest city in what is now part of U.S. territory, which was "founded" in 1521. One contestant guessed Santa Fe, New Mexico. The winner identified San Juan, Puerto Rico. The question and the answers reflected a way of thinking about the United States and its antecedent history, in which the English "founding" of Jamestown (in 1607) and the failed attempt at Roanoke, Virginia (in 1583), were trumped by a prior Spanish colonization of areas that only later came under U.S. control as a result of the Spanish–American War (1898–1901).

The case of Puerto Rico, and of San Juan itself, is complex, originally populated by the Ortoiroid people. Columbus encountered the Taíno, who were conquered, exploited, and depleted by Spain during the 16th century. The island was an important Spanish outpost against European rivals. It was invaded by the United States during the Spanish–American War (1898–1901) and surrendered to the United States in 1898. After years of U.S. territorial administration, it became a U.S. "commonwealth" in 1952. Puerto Rico also receives immigrants of Puerto Rican ancestry from the mainland (see Language Policy Task Force, 1992; Wiley, 1999a). Thus, Puerto Rico's ethnic, racial, and linguistic heritage is very complex and not easily categorized by conventional schemes. Today, there is a larger Puerto Rican origin population on the U.S. mainland than on the island. Kloss (1971) made a distinction between *external* and *internal* immigrants in an effort to differentiate between various types of immigrant language minorities. By his definition, Puerto Ricans might be considered "internal" immigrants.

The "Jeopardy" contestant's choice of Santa Fe might be defended, however, based on evidence that Pueblo peoples had settled in what was called Ogapoge around 900 A.D. The area was later colonized, or "founded," as Santa Fe by the Spanish (Hazen-Hammond, 1988). It is not clear whether the popular source Wikipedia inspired or was consulted by the "Jeopardy" question about San Juan being the oldest city that is now part of the United States, but it provides the following perspective about Santa Fe:

Don Juan de Oñate led the first effort to colonize the region in 1598, establishing Santa Fé de Nuevo México as a province of New Spain. Under Juan de Oñate and his son, the capital of the province was the settlement of San Juan de los Caballeros north of Santa Fe near modern Ohkay Owingeh Pueblo. New Mexico's second Spanish governor, Don Pedro de Peralta, however, founded a new city at the foot of the Sangre de Cristo Mountains in 1610, which he called *La Villa Real de la Santa Fé de San Francisco de Asís*, the Royal Town of the Holy Faith of Saint Francis of Assisi. In 1610, he made it the capital of the province, which it has almost constantly remained, making it the oldest state capital in what is the modern United States. (Jamestown, Virginia, is of similar vintage (1607) but is no longer a capital, while San Juan, Puerto Rico is older (1521) but is a territorial, rather than a state, capital.) Santa Fe is at least the third oldest surviving U.S. city in the 50 states that was founded by European colonists, behind the oldest St. Augustine, Florida (1565). (Although Santa Fe is not one of the oldest continuously occupied cities, as between 1680–1692 it was abandoned due to Indian raids.) ("Santa Fe," 2013)

Focusing on Santa Fe prior to its absorption into the United States provides informative perspectives about the diversity of areas and populations later incorporated. The 17th century saw major efforts by Spanish colonizers to convert the native peoples in proximity to Santa Fe and as well as the suppression of indigenous religious practices. According to Spicer (1962), "[T]he intensified forceful suppression of the kachinas seems to have been the feature of the Spanish program" (p. 168), but it met with resistance culminating in the Pueblo Rebellion of 1680. This period of "abandonment" resulted briefly in "complete freedom from Spanish control" (p. 168). This was followed by greater repressive efforts by the Spanish resulting in population disruption and decline with the "surviving communities . . . [being] without exception smaller than the largest villages when the Spanish came" (p. 169).

Other forms of competition between groups continued through the 18th century and during the period of Mexican control. The Pueblo Indian communities "and the Spanish settlements as well, were subjected to increased raiding" (Spicer, 1962, p. 169) by Navajos and Apaches. Internal strife involving native peoples continued long after Mexico lost Texas, which also briefly claimed the territory, until well into the period of American control, which resulted from conquest during the Mexican–American War (1845–1848; Spicer, 1962).

During the Spanish and Mexican periods of control, many of the indigenous Tiwa inhabitants had acquired Spanish and Catholicism. Moreover, through the encounter with the initial and subsequent colonizers, the local population came to reflect the intermingling of the diverse peoples in contact.

[A] complex pattern of social interactions between Spanish colonists and Indians developed, too. Some Spaniards married Indians, and many Spanish men had children by Indian women, creating a new ethnic group. As the lives of Spaniards and Indians intertwined, most Pueblo Indians learned to speak at least some Spanish and, in some cases, Spaniards learned to speak one or more of the Indian languages. When they didn't intermarry, the two groups often lived in close intimacy, in a complex relationship which included Spanish dependency on Indians for the economic well-being. Yes this system exploited a people who . . . had lived free of external control for many thousands of years before the Spanish came. (Hazen-Hammond, 1988, p. 27)

Reflecting the super-diversity that results from conquest, colonization, and frequent contact and interaction, a complex system for describing the diversity among the population emerged consisting of over 70 terms.

Although these designations were inconsistently applied in practice, some of the most common words usages included: Gachupin or Peninsular = European-born Spanish; Criollo = American-born Spanish; Mestizo = mixed Spanish and Indian; Mulato = mixed Spanish and black; Lobo = mixed Indian and black or Indian and Oriental [*sic*]; Coyote = Indian and mestizo or Indian mulato. (Hazen-Hammond, 1988, p. 28)

One group that emerged and prospered as farmers for a time came to be called Hispanos, of Mexican descent. During the late 19th century, they came under increasing competition for land from English-speaking Americans from the east, who "in less than a generation after 1865 populated thousands of areas" that were used "for grazing with sheep or cattle" and logging (Spicer, 1962, p. 171). All this quickly resulted in environmental damage. "Lands along the Rio Grande River and its tributaries which the Indians had farmed for centuries were washed away in floods" (p. 171). The destructive land use practices were not corrected until the 20th century. "The old story of encroachment on Indian lands, so familiar to other parts of the United States . . . was being re-enacted" (p. 172).

Following the establishment of the state of New Mexico in 1912, immigration increased rapidly, posing a threat to the Pueblos. North of Santa Fe, Taos village lost a major portion of its land. New waves on English-speaking immigrants arrived after World War II.

Until the 1940s, the Hispanics of Santa Fe had managed to preserve their language and culture more or less intact. But by the late 1950s, the disruptions of war, the advent of increasing numbers of Anglos from outside the state, and other factors had seriously weakened the collective impetus to pass the Spanish language and Spanish cultural practices on to following generations. In the post war era the first generation of Spanish Santa Feans in three-and-a-half centuries grew up not speaking Spanish. (Hazen-Hammond, 1988, p. 118)

As for the Pueblo Indians in proximity to Santa Fe, they had different status from other Indians as a result of their brief status as Mexican citizens (Spicer, 1962). Pueblo Indians of the nearby Taos Pueblo had to struggle to reassert their indigenous status and associated claims to sacred sites in legal struggles that lasted through the late 20th century.

In the late 1980s, Hazen-Hammond (1988) noted that 1.5 million tourists per year were visiting the city of Santa Fe to experience the "authentic" heritage of the city as represented by its art galleries and museums, while at the same time "unwittingly placing a further barrier between the people of Santa Fe and their heritage" (p. 117).

This paradoxical conflict between the old and the new, between longtime Santa Feans and newcomers, in which newcomers seek the old, and oldtimers are forced into the new, lies at the heart of seemingly unresolvable (sic.) stresses in the city . . . . To people who have lived in the City of Holy Faith all their lives, and to the people whose ancestors built this city on the ruins of Ogapoge, Santa Fe is simply no longer Santa Fe. (Hazen-Hammond, 1988, p. 117)

The case of Santa Fe illustrates that the question of who writes history and what history counts is not a trivial one (Wiley, 2006). Any historical framing of the founding of North American towns and cities with reference to only English or European conquerors or colonizers erases the antecede experience of indigenous peoples as those without written history. With conquest and colonization comes erasure through the promotion of what Blaut (1993) called the "myth of emptiness" that presumes that conquered lands contain nothing of worth until "settled" by those who possess higher civilization and, therefore, more human worth. The imposition of the colonizer's lens in writing history as analyzed by Mignolo (2003) and Blaut (1993) led to the suppression of the local knowledge of the colonized in the Americas (see also Mignolo, 2000). The idea that English provides the common national bound of the United States parallels other popular ideologies involving the social construction of the allegedly homogenous nation-state (Anderson, 1983). These use the invention of the "native speaker" and the myth of common language as a basis for national unity and identity (Bonfiglio, 2010). Thus, within the context of U.S. history, it is useful to dig deeper into notions of diversity present and past and to understand how notions of the alleged super-diversity of the present diversity depend in large part on how notions of diversity in the past have been constructed.

CONSTRUCTING DIVERSITY PAST, PRESENT, AND FUTURE THROUGH THE U.S. CENSUS

As Blommaert (2013) has noted, a number of scholars (e.g., Vertovec, 2010) have been promoting the notion of an unprecedented degree of linguistic super-diversity that has resulted from increased global migration and been promoted by technologies that facilitate social networking. These forces have ushered in a litany of labels such as "languaging, polylanguaging, transidiomatic practices, metrolingualism, super-vernacularization, and so forth" (Blommaert, 2013, p. 192; see also Blommaert &

TABLE 1

Those Living in Households Where a Language Other Than English Is Spoken, Age 5 and Older

1980, *n* (%)	1990, *n* (%)	2000, *n* (%)	2011, *n* (%)[a]
23.1 (11)	31.8 (13.8)	46.9 (17.9)	78.4 (25.6)

Source. U.S. Census 1980, 1990, 2000, as cited in Wiley (2005).
a. American Community Survey 2006 and 2011 (2007–2011 5-year sample).

Rampton, 2011, for further discussion). With the proliferation of new labels by the current generation of scholars, it would be helpful to see more analysis of the phenomena to which the new labels are being ascribed and the extent to which they offer more explanatory power than more conventional terminology. Leaving this concern aside, the contention here, again, is that the extent to which present configurations of diversity are "super" and unprecedented depends on how notions of past diversities are constructed and how they relate to presumed antecedent majority, "mainstream," or dominant reference groups and similar constructions of minority statuses. Using U.S. Census data as a point of reference, this section provides examples of how language and ethno-racial diversity have been constructed, reconstructed, and projected.

Although the specific focus of self-reported survey questions has varied over time and is not consistent through time, the U.S. Census and more recent samples such as the American Community Survey have collected data related to race (as constructed by the census's own categories), national origin, literacy (primarily English literacy), English "oral" proficiency, and the use of languages other than English in households (although the 2010 decennial census has dropped this question, it continues to be asked in the American Community Survey; see Wiley, 2005, particularly Chap. 4, for discussion and elaboration regarding U.S. Census data).

Despite their limitations, what can we learn from census data currently and through time? Table 1 focuses on the presence of languages other than English over the past three decades and visibly indicates that language diversity, if taken as an indicator of diversity within the United States, is clearly increasing when 1980 is taken as the base year.

Table 2 identifies the most languages other than English that are spoken in U.S. households by U.S. Census ethno-racial categories. Focusing on Table 1, the trend over the past three decades demonstrates substantial increases in Spanish and non-European languages, with the exception of Russian, which surged after the collapse of the former Soviet Union. The shift to Spanish and non-European languages, however, reflects changes in immigration patterns related largely to a liberalization in U.S. immigration policies initiated during the Johnson administration (1963–1968). In 1965, racially based national-origin policies that had been in existence since the early 1920s were replaced by more inclusive policies (Wiley, 1998, 2007). The shift toward Spanish gained speed as the 20th century progressed. It represents increased

TABLE 2

Those Living in Households Where a Language Other Than English Is Spoken, Age 5 and Older, by Census Ethno-Racial Categories

Languages Most Spoken in the Home	American Community Survey Categories of Race							
	White	Black	American Indian/ Alaska Native	Chinese	Japanese	Other Asian/ Pacific Islander	Other Race	Two Major Races	Three or More Major Races
1. English	182,761,761	32,697,368	1,670,274	564,331	419,483	2,450,313	2,492,065	4,718,401	438,186
2. Spanish	22,501,304	850,912	275,560	18,025	10,006	76,548	11,544,779	832,915	47,847
3. Chinese	39,571	5,601	453	2,448,166	1,813	100,410	1,813	25,612	930
4. Hindi	58,285	17,500	4,190	1,876	752	1,881,857	41,924	55,586	2,171
5. French	950,857	994,621	6,696	2,584	555	15,979	16,191	36,354	3,295
6. Filipino/Tagalog	27,173	4,149	473	5,320	1,904	1,608,200	1,827	43,870	2,819
7. Vietnamese	11,380	1,140	184	13,272	710	1,288,916	972	13,954	485
8. German	1,160,598	27,516	3,419	630	246	3,804	3,817	17,689	1,639
9. Korean	21,531	4,285	501	2,253	6,081	1,068,907	780	16,435	1,403
10. Russian	841,599	2,557	554	107	61	2,915	975	6,876	370
11. Arabic	713,451	63,672	391	30	161	7,279	7,539	40,077	795
12. Italian	727,446	6,857	711	316	36	1,846	2,499	5,979	536
13. Portuguese	558,001	34,499	698	1,074	1,712	2,617	60,545	21,993	1,544
14. Polish	598,723	1,238	120	113	0	150	308	1,905	105
15. Dravidian	5,182	1,244	1,649	647	30	549,929	9,196	11,298	387
16. Sub-Saharan African	9,436	482,802	616	418	0	6,181	1,449	3,859	129
17. Japanese	60,297	8,610	661	3,252	314,945	23,790	2,214	36,568	2,495
18. Persian, Iranian, Farsi	319,806	1,876	48	70	66	9,776	897	37,959	283
18. Greek	308,620	1,749	149	39	0	259	241	1,778	49
20. Thai, Siamese, Lao	11,515	1,209	125	3,301	287	280,448	397	8,014	296

Source. American Community Survey 2007–2011. Analysis by A. Kapashesit, Center for Applied Linguistics.

7

immigration, particularly from Mexico, which began to increase following anti-Asian immigration policies of the late 19th century and the anti–eastern and southern European policies of the 1920s. European immigrants, in particular, of the late 19th-century and early 20th-century Europe, had previously provided major sources of "cheap" labor for U.S. industrialization (Wiley, 1998).

In looking at present language diversity compared with that of the early 20th century, major shifts in the linguistic composition of the country are apparent (compare Table 2 with Table 3). Whereas European languages—particularly German—previously dominated among U.S. languages other than English until 1970, Spanish and non-European languages now reflect the new diversity. But does this mean that the present configuration is more super-diverse in comparison to the 20th century, or merely a new configuration? Note also that the data for 1910 and 1940 were limited to the "White" population, which indicated a prior preoccupation of looking at linguistic diversity primarily for those of European origin. It is apparent that all of these periods could be construed as representing super-diversities within their own times.

If we look further back to the period of the American Revolution and the founding of the United States using census data, it is not possible to ascertain language data; however, some data are available related to race and national origin as constructed through the categories of the time. Tables 4, 5, and 6 provide information regarding the composition within the three major colonial regions (the New English, Middle, and Southern Colonies, of the British American colonies) around 1776. Several patterns emerge; first, those of English origin were the largest group in two of the three colonial regions (New England and the Middle colonies). There was, however, a substantial but undifferentiated African population in the Middle and, particularly, in the Southern colonies, where they were the largest group. There were also others of European origin, who included speakers of other languages, and a small, but undifferentiated, "indigenous" population, which represented only a small part of those counted (Parrillo, 2009).

Not included, however, were the vast populations to the West, as yet not incorporated. The lack of differentiation among the African population is noteworthy since there was significant diversity among its many peoples, who had been subjected to involuntary incorporation and forced to use oral English, while suppressing their own African tongues. They were simultaneously also prohibited from acquiring English literacy (Weinberg, 1995). Nevertheless, there is evidence of the linguistic diversity that African peoples brought with them as well as, in some cases, of the literacy in languages other than English among the newly enslaved (Lepore, 2002).

Table 7 provides data based on the first U.S. Census of 1790. As Parrillo (2009) notes, there has been a strong Eurocentric bias, particularly in early census data (see Table 8):

When we move past the Eurocentric presentation of the 1790 census data to include non-Whites, we acquire a more complete understanding of the extensive diversity in America at that time. By doing so, we not only find a smaller proportion of society of dominant Anglo-Saxon groups, but also further dispel mistaken assumptions about our past . . . [that] affect past-present comparisons. (p. 68)

TABLE 3
Major Languages of the U.S. Foreign-Born Population 1910, 1940, 1970

Language	White Only[a]		All Races[b]
	1910	1940	1970
German	3,963,624	2,648,080	1,788,286
English	3,362,792	2,506,420	1,743,284
Yiddish[c]	2,759,032	1,589,040	1,201,535
Italian	2,267,009	2,475,880	3,301,184
Russian	1,690,703	1,671,540	921,330
French	1,365,110	1,561,100	1,025,994
Swedish	1,272,150	778,200	283,991
Dutch	1,051,767	924,440	438,116
Slovak	943,781	801,680	419,912
Danish	683,218	423,200	131,408
Spanish	528,842	359,520	410,580
Hungarian	382,048	389,240	325,074
Portuguese	258,131	428,360	1,696,240
Polish	228,738	159,640	70,703
Norwegian	183,844	122,180	58,218
Bulgarian	166,474	171,580	82,561
Lithuanian	140,963	122,660	95,188
Flemish	126,045	102,700	127,834
Basque	119,948	97,080	38,290
Albanian	118,379	165,220	193,745
Slovene	105,669	70,600	83,064
Romanian	72,649	83,780	140,299
Ukrainian	57,926	356,940	149,277
Greek	42,277	43,120	26,055
Czech	25,131	35,540	96,635

Source. Adapted from U.S. Census Bureau, Population Division (Authors Campbell Gibson and Emily Lennon). Maintained by Information and Research Services Internet Staff (Population Division). Retrieved from http://www.census.gov/population/www/documentation/twps0029/tab06.html
a. Data for 1910 and 1940 are for the White population only.
b. The term *race* was used by the U.S. Census during this period as if ethnolinguistic labels and race were equivalent.
c. Hebrew is included with Yiddish for 1910–1940.

TABLE 4
Ethno-Racial Diversity in New England Around 1776

English	70.5%
Unassigned	16.9%
Scots	4.0%
Dutch, French German, and Irish	2.9%
Scots-Irish	2.8%
African	2.3%
Indigenous	0.6%

Source. U.S. Bureau of the Census (1976; *Historical Statistics of the United States*, Part II, Series Z; cited in Parrillo, 2009, p. 46).

TABLE 5
Ethno-Racial Diversity in the Middle Colonies Around 1776

English	40.6%
German	15.2%
African	12.4%
Scots	6.7%
Scots-Irish	6.5%
Irish	3.4%
French and Swedish	3.2%
Indigenous	2.9%
Unassigned	2.7%

Source. U.S. Bureau of the Census (1976; *Historical Statistics of the United States*, Part II, Series Z; cited in Parrillo, 2009, p. 47).

Thus, despite the fact that early census data point to high levels of diversity in the former colonial and new national populations, they tend to underrepresent the actual diversity of those living in the country. The majority of Native Americans lived apart from those counted in the census; thus, most were neither included "nor protected by the Constitution, nor even then considered part of American society" (Parrillo, 2009, p. 68). Chinese and other Asian peoples, though increasingly present following the first Opium War (1839–1842) between Britain and the Qing Dynasty, and particularly after the Taiping Rebellion (1850–1864), with the massive social and economic dislocations in southern China, had no presence in U.S. Census data until 1870 (Parrillo, 2009). Beginning in the 1880s, first the Chinese, and subsequently other Asians, would face various immigration-exclusionary acts by Congress.

TABLE 6
Ethno-Racial Diversity in Southern Colonies Around 1776

African	39.2%
English	37.4%
Scotts	7.0%
Indigenous	3.9%
Scots-Irish	3.8%
German	3.5%
Irish	3.5%
Dutch, French, Swedish, and Others	2.1%

Source. U.S. Bureau of the Census (1976; *Historical Statistics of the United States*, Part II, Series Z; cited in Parrillo, 2009, p. 49).

TABLE 7
Ethnic and National-Origin Diversity Among the "White" Population Around 1776

Dutch	3.4%
English	60.9%
German	8.7%
Scots-Irish	6.0%
Swedish and French	2.4%
Unassigned	6.6%

Source. U.S. Bureau of the Census (1976; *Historical Statistics of the United States*, Part II, Series Z; cited in Parrillo, 2009, p. 67).

The first half of the 19th century saw increased immigration from Ireland, particularly as a result of the Potato Famine (1845–1852). Various waves of German migration have occurred since the late 17th century. Following the American Civil War (1861–1865), however, large numbers of Germans entered the country. Through colonial and U.S. history, they frequently established German and German–English bilingual schools (Toth, 1990). From the second part of the 19th century into the early decades of the 20th century, there were also unprecedented levels of immigration, initially from western Europe but increasing from eastern and southern Europe.

To what extent was this super-diversity of the time appreciated as such? In 1907, the U.S. Congress, responding to rising Nativist sentiments, established the United States Immigration Commission, also known as the Dillingham Commission, which was named after the senator who chaired it, to do fact finding on the origins and

TABLE 8
U.S. Early National Population 1790

African	18.9%
Dutch	2.7%
English	48.3%
Irish	2.9%
Native American	1.8%
Scots-Irish	4.8%
Swedish and French	1.8%
Unassigned	6.6%

Source. Parrillo (2009, p. 69).

consequences of the unprecedented immigration that the United States had been experiencing since the 1870s.

The extent of immigration was unprecedented in terms of sheer numbers and in terms of the percentage of the population that was of immigrant origin. Immigrants migrated not only to the cities in response to the demand for "cheap" labor in cities but also to the mining towns of the west and the farmlands of the Midwest. Again, however, although immigration to major cities was unprecedented, immigration in the interior of the country, despite steadily increasing in raw numbers of immigrants, failed to keep pace with the growing population over the course of the 100 years between 1870 and 1970 as the percentages of population declined (see Table 9).

Another characteristic of census data are their tendency to contrast a dominant group with minority groups. Labeling distinctions between the dominant group or "mainstream" population (see Table 10) have shifted over time, but the basic representation of the relationship as noted by Parrillo (2009, Chap. 8, "Intergenerational Comparisons") remains relatively stable. Whereas "English" was considered the dominant or mainstream group in 1790 census data, "British" was in 1890. By 1920, the focus was on "Northwestern Europeans," and by 2000, "White non-Hispanic." Although the mainstream labels change, the pattern persists of dominant group contrasted with others (see Parrillo, p. 147) In more recent data and projections, note that the major census categories are not parallel given that African American and Asian American are quasi-geographical origin in reference, whereas White, non-Hispanic is racial, although "Hispanic" is more of an ethnic or cultural designation (see also Rumbaut, 2011). Also, note that there is no parallel category for "White Hispanic."

TABLE 9
Percentage of Immigrant Population in Selected Midwestern States 1870–1970

Year	State	Count	Percentage
	Minnesota		
1870		439,706	36.5
1890		1,301,826	35.9
1910		2,075,708	26.2
1930		2,563,953	15.2
1950		2,982,483	7.0
1970		3,804,971	2.6
	Iowa		
1870		1,194,020	17.1
1890		1,911,986	16.9
1910		2,224,771	12.3
1930		2,470,939	16.8
1950		2,621,073	3.2
1970		2,824,376	1.4
	Nebraska		
1870		122,993	25.0%
1890		1,058,910	19.1%
1910		1,192,214	14.8%
1930		1,377,963	8.7%
1950		1,325,510	4.3%
1970		1,482,414	1.9%
	Kansas		
1870		364,399	13.6%
1890		1,427,096	10.4%
1910		1,690,949	8.0%
1930		1,880,999	4.3%
1950		1,905,299	2.0%
1970		2,246,578	1.2%

Source. U.S. Census, cited by Watkins (1980, pp. 62–64).

TABLE 10
2000 U.S. Population and Future Projection

Census Ethno-Racial Categories	2000, %	2050, %
African American	12.5	14.6
Asian American	4.0	8.0
Hispanic American	12.5	24.4
Native American	1.0	1.0
Non-Hispanic White	70.0	50.1
Other		1.9

Source. U.S. Census, cited in Parrillo (2009, pp. 193, 195).

EXPLAINING THE EARLY DOMINANCE OF ENGLISH

English achieved its status of the dominant language before the founding of the United States during the British American colonial period. Languages can achieve status through either official designation or unofficial means such as market forces (Weinstein, 1979, 1983). Languages can achieve hegemony through following what Gramsci (1971) called the *manufacture of consent*, which is achieved through willing acceptance of dominant ideologies rather than through *force*. Thus, it is more subtle and effective in achieving dominance and social control (see also Fairclough, 1989; Tollefson, 1991).

In the case of the United States, the spread of English through the English colonies in the Americas resulted from what Heath (1976) concluded was its *status achievement*, facilitated by factors other than official decree. Among the factors Heath noted was the antecedent status of the conquerors in their countries of origin. Castilian achieved prestige and was being promoted in Spain over competing vernaculars (Illich, 1979), and English had rebounded in status following the end of Norman rule. Heath (1976) also considered social organizations of the indigenous peoples under colonial rule and the rule of influential agents and interests groups in the colonies and their influence on informal practice. Importantly, she noted that language practices were based largely on the perceptions of those in the colonial populations rather than on a received formal language policy through the presence or absence of official designations or sanctions as a policy (Heath, 1976; see also Wiley, 1999a).

In the British colonies, the language status achievement of English legitimated governmental "decisions regarding acceptable language for those who are to carry out the political, economic, and social affairs of the political process" and that "the process by which the chosen language achieves this status is the result of the interaction of political and socio-economic forces" (Heath, 1976, p. 51) between the colonizer and colonized.

CHARACTERIZING THE IDEOLOGICAL CLIMATE OF LANGUAGE POLICIES IN THE UNITED STATES: LANGUAGE TOLERANCE HYPOTHESIS REVISITED[1]

This final section reassesses the *language tolerance hypothesis* (Kloss, 1977/1998) within the context of U.S. history and its prior English colonial history through the lens of the English-only ideology that has been used to rationalize policy prescriptions for the assimilation and subordination of various groups into the United States. It is based largely on revisiting Wiley (2000), with permission, and subsequent related work cited herein.

Throughout much of U.S. history, there has been a high degree of consistency in the overt prescriptions that disparate ethnolinguistic groups should assimilate. In particular, *linguistic assimilation* into English has been a dominant theme and dictate for most speakers of languages other than English. Weiss (1982), however, noted that it is important to make a distinction between mere *behavioral assimilation* and *structural incorporation*. In other words, a distinction can be made between education for domestication and education for full economic participation. Historically, the dominant, English-only ideology has prescribed linguistic assimilation for all groups, with far less emphasis on structural incorporation, which would imply social and economic integration and full participation. Throughout U.S. history, the typical ideological prescription for English linguistic assimilation has been advanced as a singular approach for achieving very different ends.

One of the most comprehensive analyses of formal language policies in the United States was conducted by the German-born historian and language demographer, Heinz Kloss. In his best-known work, *The American Bilingual Tradition* (1977/1998), he concluded that the dominant policy orientation throughout U.S. history has been *tolerance*. Kloss, however, noted one period of exception, the World War I era. During this period, there were widespread restrictions that were imposed not only on German but also on other European immigrant languages (Wiley, 1998). With the exception of the World War I period, Kloss argued that a policy climate of linguistic tolerance was prevalent over the course of most of U.S. history. He concluded that it "is justified to speak of an American bilingual tradition must not be understood to imply that it was the prevailing, let alone the American, tradition with regard to language policy" (p. 285).

Kloss acknowledged, but also downplayed, the role of the dominant monolingual ideology, which he called the "powerful tradition upholding the merits and desirability of "one country, one language . . ." (p. 285). From his perspective, the challenge of maintaining immigrant languages fell on the desire and agency of language minorities themselves. Thus, if language minorities became "Anglicized" it was not because of the imposition of laws unfavorable to them but "*in spite of* nationalities laws relatively *favorable* to them. Not by legal provisions and measures of the authorities, not by governmental coercion did the nationalities become assimilated, but rather by the absorbing power of the highly developed American society" (Kloss, 1977/1998, p. 283). The notion of "absorbing power" was not explicated—more on this later.

Again, Kloss's (1977/1998) evidence relied on the analysis of formal policies, and more specifically on specific types of language policies, which he called "language laws." He made a point of not focusing on "racial" laws and not confounding the two (Macías & Wiley, 1998; Wiley, 2002). Kloss (1977/1998) also concentrated on "nationality" laws—as in those related to national origin—that might have relevance for immigrant languages. By so doing, his work can be seen largely as relevant to an immigrant paradigm. Given that the major source of immigration up through the early 20th century had been European, his work and conclusions take on a more Eurocentric focus. His attempt to disconnect language policies from ethnic and racial policies as a matter of methodology is extremely questionable because it failed to analyze the goals and intentions underlying the formation and implementation of policies and how they intersect with other agendas related to the treatment of racial and ethnic minorities, who may also be language minorities (see Leibowitz, 1969, 1971, 1974). Deviations from a policy climate of tolerance, such as during the World War I period, which ushered in a wave of restrictive language policies (Tatalovich, 1995; Wiley, 1998), were "*only isolated instances* of an oppressive state policy aiming at the elimination of non-English languages," according to Kloss (1977/1998, p. 285).

So how did Kloss (1977/1998) explain the reasons for language shift? He pointed to two factors: the "absorbing power" of the dominant Anglo society and "unofficial moral pressure." Regarding "absorbing power," the notion is not explicated. Others, such as Veltman (1983), have also alluded to it, also without delineation. Thus, a more thorough explication of the construct is warranted. Regarding "unofficial moral pressure," Kloss (1977/1998) noted,

[T]here were, however, a great many instances in which individuals (including public school teachers) and groups exerted *unofficial moral pressure* [italics added] upon members of the minority groups, especially children, so as to make them feel that to stick to a "foreign" tongue meant being backward or even un-American (p. 285).

Thus, although Kloss (1977/1998) did not seem to recognize or analyze linguistic discrimination and seemed aware of linguistic stigma and prejudice, he chose to delimit his data and analysis to "formal" laws and policies. Thus, by focusing mostly on formal language and nationality laws that affected mostly European immigrants, Kloss's analysis failed to make connections between racially motivated ideologies and agendas and the use of language policies as instruments of social, economic, and political control.

In summary then, the "tolerance hypotheses" applied to the United States is limited because of its narrow focus on formal policies and its lack of focus on *implicit* or *covert* policies and practices. Second, it is Eurocentric in that it is mostly focused on European immigrants rather than on involuntarily relocated African and indigenous peoples. Moreover, the social contexts were those in which "unofficial moral pressure" achieved the same results as—or possibly even more thoroughgoing results than—formal coercive policies would have. Language ideologies and practices coexist with racial, ethnic, religious, and other forms of social domination within the context of competition between groups; thus, the analytical challenge is to ascertain the relationship among these ideologies (Leibowitz, 1969, 1971; Wiley, 2000; see also Macías, 1992).

In noting these problems in Kloss's (1977/1998) approach, it is also important to add that interpreting his scholarship on the United States, and his intellectual contributions, is further complicated by the fact that he began his work as a scholar in Germany, prior to World War II, under the Third Reich. Although Kloss denied association with the Nazi Party, Hutton (1999) has identified a number of important issues that make the connection plausible, with implications for the interpretation of his later work on the language policy in the United States. As noted in Wiley (2002), the fact that Kloss's work remains indexical to the study of historical language policy in the United States underscores the need for a new generation of scholars to expand the boundaries of the field.

To go beyond the explanatory limitations of the tolerance theme, it is necessary to broaden the scope of historical inquiry by analyzing implicit and covert policies as well as formal or explicit policies, comparing the experiences of immigrant language minorities with those of indigenous groups and involuntary immigrants, and analyzing the language ideologies within the context of intergroup competition and conflict.

Initial Modes of Contact, and Subsequent Treatment of Language Minority Groups

The initial modes of contact interaction between Europeans and native peoples included conquest, conversion, annexation, enslavement, and removal. U.S. expansionism during the 19th century was rationalized by a self-fulfilling ideology of "Manifest Destiny" (Wiley, 2000). Kloss (1971) had narrow definitions of groups that were potentially affected by language laws. *Immigrant groups* comprised "every linguistic minority and majority of whose adult members are foreign born or the children of foreign born" and *indigenous groups* consisted of "a majority of whose adult members are natives of native parentage" (p. 253). By this definition, those from Africa could have been included, but they are excluded from Kloss's analyses. Thus, the immigrant category excludes the enslaved who were forcibly brought to the United States. The notion of *indigenous* groups also needs further explication (Wiley, 2000; Wiley & Lukes, 1996; see also Macías, 2014).

First, it may include those peoples residing in the Americas prior to European exploration, conquest, encroachment, and displacement. There is also a second connotation that has relevance for languages that were originally colonial but subsequently became indigenized, such as Spanish in what ultimately became part of the southwestern United States. Thus, Macías (1999) contends that "[i]ndigenous groups are those who occupied an area that is now the United States prior to the national expansion into that area, and those groups who have a historical/cultural tie to the "Americas" prior to European colonization" (p. 63; see also Macías, 2014). Based on these considerations, the question of whether the historical context of U.S. language policies have been largely tolerant or intolerant toward ethnolinguistic minorities is better answered contextually, based on the initial mode of incorporation of each group and its subsequent treatment in formal law as well as in informal social, educational, economic, and political contexts.

Based on these considerations of involuntary immigrants and *indigenous* peoples, source populations for language diversity in the United States and its territories would include the following: (1) indigenous peoples residing in what became the 13 colonies and subsequently became the United States; (2) immigrant peoples from Europe, who migrated to the colonies that subsequently became United States; (3) peoples in Africa forcibly abducted, enslaved, and brought to the territories that subsequently became the United States; (4) peoples in Africa who were forcibly brought here until the end of the U.S. slave trade in 1808; (5) immigrant peoples who have migrated into the United States and its territories after 1789; (6) peoples residing in lands west of the Appalachians and east of the Mississippi, transferred in the Treaty of Paris in 1783; (7) peoples residing in the immense territory (contiguous to the Mississippi and Missouri rivers) acquired through the Louisiana Purchase in 1803; (8) peoples residing in Florida and parts of what are now southern Alabama, Mississippi, and Louisiana prior to 1820; (9) peoples residing in Oregon Country, which included present-day Washington and Idaho, prior to its acquisition in 1846; (10) peoples residing in Texas and other territories north of the Rio Grande prior to 1848; (11) peoples residing in the Mexican Cession, including California, Nevada, Utah, and parts of what are now Arizona, New Mexico, and Colorado, prior to 1848; (12) peoples residing in territory acquired in the Gadsden Purchase of 1853, comprising what are now southern Arizona and New Mexico; (13) peoples residing in Alaska prior to its purchase in 1867; (14) peoples residing in Hawaii prior to its annexation in 1896; (15) peoples residing in Puerto Rico, the U.S. Virgin Islands, and Guam prior to 1898; (16) peoples residing in the Philippines prior to its conquest in 1898 and peoples residing in various island territories in the Pacific prior to 1945; (17) peoples legally allowed to immigrate to the United States after 1965, with the relaxation of racial quotas as a basis for immigration; (18) peoples previously with undocumented status who have subsequently been allowed to seek amnesty; (19) peoples who voluntarily or involuntarily entered the United States and stayed without legal authorization; and (20) refugees and asylum seekers who legally were granted entry to the United States (updated from Wiley, 2000; see also Wiley, 2013a).

The Intersection of the Ideologies of Racism, Monoculturalism/Nativism, and Linguicism

Attempts to establish a hierarchical distribution of privileges and obligations on the basis of race have been called *racialization*. Miles (1989) defined racialization as an ideological "process of delineation of group boundaries and an allocation of persons within those boundaries by primary reference to purportedly inherent and/or biological (typically phenotypical) characteristics" (p. 74). Weinberg (1990) has further noted that racism is a *systematic, institutional procedure* for excluding some while privileging others; thus, it involves more than simple prejudice since it has the power to advantage and the power to disadvantage. Racism is premised on the belief that some are inherently superior to others. From an ideological perspective, racism promotes *monoculturalism*, which Haas (1992) defines as "the practice of catering to the dominant or mainstream culture, providing second class treatment or no special consideration at all to persons of non-mainstream cultures" (p. 161). Correspondingly, linguistic discrimination, or *linguicism*, according to Phillipson (1988), uses language "ideologies to legitimate, effectuate and reproduce an unequal division of power and resources (both material and non-material) between groups" (p. 339).

The ideological underpinnings of discriminatory racial policies, thus, have affinities in that they both promote subordination through restriction. In terms of establishing legal claims, however, they differ in one fundamental way, because, unlike race, language is assumed to be *mutable* (Del Valle, 2003). Unlike Kloss, who stringently tried to separate language laws from racial laws, Leibowitz (1969, 1971, 1974) concluded that policies focused on language restriction have often been aligned with economic and political agendas to discriminate against racial and national-origin ethnic groups. Thus, the similarities among linguicism, racism, and other inhumanities need to consider the relationships among them (Wiley, 2000).

As noted in the discussion of U.S. Census data, race has always played a more significant role in delineating group boundaries than language. Likewise, Nativist and neo-Nativist ideologies have been used to demarcate group boundaries even among European immigrants, for example, between Nordics and southern Europeans (Wiley, 2005). This was apparent in the work of the Dillingham commission (1907–1911), whose findings reinforced a *two-tiered* system of racialization: one that defined boundaries *within* the European-origin population, largely on the basis of religion, culture, social class, and language. To this were added distinctions that defined racial boundaries *between* European-origin peoples and all others primarily on the basis of perceived physical differences (Wiley, 1998). As European-origin linguistic minorities assimilated into the English-speaking Anglo-dominant milieu, color and other physical differences persisted as the primary determinants of group boundaries between those of European origin and all others (Wiley, 1998, 2000).

Race and National Origin

Until changes in immigration laws in 1965 that largely resulted from the Civil Rights Movement, race was one of the principle determinants of citizenship in the United States. Following the ratification of the U.S. Constitution in 1789, the newly established Congress passed the Nationalization Act of 1790, which effectively limited citizenship to Whites and those of European origin only (Wiley, 2000). As Spring (1996) notes, the Nationalization Act was compatible with dominant racial ideologies of the time and the colonial past:

English belief in their own cultural and racial superiority over Native Americans and, later, enslaved Africans, Mexican Americans, Puerto Ricans, and Asians, was not born on American soil. It was part of the cultural baggage English colonists brought to North America. English beliefs in their cultural and racial superiority were used to justify the occupation of Native American lands. North America acted as a hothouse for the growth of white racism and chauvinism. Again, it is important to stress, that this phenomenon was not unique to North America, but it followed the English flag around the world. (p. 35)

Although there were instances of negative sentiment against some European ethnolinguistic minorities, such as Germans or Scott-Irish in some areas prior to the passage of the act, notions of racial and cultural superiority were generally more salient considerations than language as criteria for citizenship for immigrants (Wiley, 2000).

The status of indigenous peoples was more problematic. In 1831, the Supreme Court asserted the novel conclusion that Indian peoples were *domestic foreigners*:

domestic dependent nations . . . [who] . . . occupy a territory to which we assert a title independent of their will . . . in a state of pupilage. Their relationship to the United States resembles that of a ward to his guardian. ("Cherokee Nation v. Georgia," 1990, p. 59)

The notion that they were in a state of "pupilage" was consistent with both racial ideologies and what Blaut (1993) called the "colonizer's model," in which native peoples were seen as being in need of receiving tutelage or mentorships by their conquerors. Also, by being labeled "occupants," their rights to ownership could be more easily challenged (Wiley, 2000).

Linguistic Acculturation and Deculturation

As has been noted, within the context of U.S. history and its antecedent colonial history, racism and language discrimination have been closely aligned. From the perspective of social control, linguistic assimilation has been championed as a means for assimilation. Recalling again Weiss's (1982) distinction between structural and behavioral assimilation, the latter has frequently involved deculturation, without structural incorporation. Ideologies of the alleged racial, cultural, and linguistic superiority of English-speaking or Anglo-dominant groups have long histories. Early examples include what became the British Isles through English efforts, for example, to subordinate the Irish (Spring, 1994, 1996; Takaki, 1993). Similar notions of racial superiority and inferiority toward African peoples were common in England throughout the colonial period and used to justify the slave trade (Jordan, 1974). Schmidt (1995) argues that by the 19th century, linguistic and racist ideologies in the United States had converged into Anglo-Saxon and Germanic chauvinism. "Anglo-Saxon racialist thought focused on the superiority of the English language as a derivative of German culture" (p. 4). Schmidt concludes that language has "played an important role in both the ideology and practice of the system of racial domination that held sway in the U.S. prior to the Second Reconstruction of the 1960s" (p. 4). Thus, language ideologies manifested in various historical contexts need to be scrutinized in terms of their relationship to racial ideologies as instruments of social control (Leibowitz, 1971, 1974; Wiley, 2000).

"Indigenous Occupants": From Initial Appeasement to Removal and Subsequent Coercive Domestication

Prior to resolving the legal status of *indigenous occupants*, there was the larger issue of *appeasement*. European intruders had long attempted to use Indians as pawns in their colonial conflicts, and Indians had learned the value of playing the Europeans against themselves. It should come as little surprise that the first federal expenditure by the revolutionary Continental Congress, in 1775, was for Indian education. A sum of $500 was allocated to Dartmouth College to promote education for appeasement. Thus, from its inception, Indian education was linked to pacification and the acquisition of more Indian lands in the west (Weinberg, 1995). Even so, official rationalizations for civilizing Indians exhibited ambivalence regarding the extent to which Indians were potentially more victims than a threat. It was frequently argued that Indian contact with Whites had to be regulated in order to protect the Indians from exploitation, moral corruption, and eventual extinction. Anxiety for Indian well-being and longevity notwithstanding, the concern was frequently linked to opportunism, and schemes to "civilize" Indians were hedged with ominous threats to remove them, should the Indians fail to heed opportunities to join civilization. President Jefferson's explanation in an 1803 letter to William Henry Harrison is particularly revealing:

[O]ur settlement will gradually circumscribe and approach the Indians, and they will in time either incorporate with us as citizens of the United States or remove beyond the Mississippi. The former is certainly the termination of their history most happy for themselves; but in the whole, it is essential to cultivate their love. (Jefferson, 1990, pp. 21–22)

Through the acquisition of superior civilization, Indians were to experience "the termination of their history" as a "happy" event. Should they fail to become enraptured by that process, they were to be *removed*—as they ultimately were. Initial plans for Indian tutelage in White civilization called for federal regulation of trading posts. Jefferson strategized that Indians would be more willing to surrender their lands if they could be weaned into agricultural production, including the domestication of animals, and into the manufacturing of domestic wares. Through trade Jefferson hoped to inculcate an appetite for "civilized" goods that would alter the lifestyles of Indian peoples, making them dependent on their conquerors.

In the early decades of the 18th century, the U.S. government became increasingly interested in using education and Christian conversion as the primary means of appeasing and domesticating Indians, particularly in those areas where they increasingly had contact with the encroaching White population. In 1819, Congress passed the Civilization Fund Act (1819/1990), which authorized funds for the encouragement of schooling among the Indians. The Act's overt purpose was to protect against the further decline and extinction of the Indians by promoting schools among them. The plan called for instruction in the "arts of civilization" (p. 33) as well as the promotion of basic literacy skills and training in agriculture. In keeping with Jefferson's vision, the plan would help convert the Indians into an economy requiring much less land. From the perspective of their conquerors, trade fostered economic change and dependency. Christianity and instruction in basic English literacy were prescribed as the principal means for pacification, a process that Hernández-Chávez (1994) likened to *cultural genocide*. According to the plan, Indians were to be weaned into civilization, divested of most of their lands, and thereby *saved from extinction*. Some government strategists, however, were less benevolently focused in their support for the Civilization Act. Secretary of War John C. Calhoun, for example, "viewed the schools as auxiliary to the government policy of removal" because they could be used to inculcate "the desirability of emigration [i.e., removal]" (Weinberg, 1995, p. 181).

Despite the intention of their conquerors to use education and English as tools for deculturation, Indians saw the obtainment of these devices in a pragmatic sense. They were necessary tools in the struggle for survival. Some tribal leaders in the southeast, many themselves bicultural and biracial, realized the value of literacy—both in English *and* in their native languages—as essential for self-preservation and effective competition with the encroaching White population. As Weinberg (1995) observes, when the education of the conquerors "did not compromise their own self-respect and ethnic identity . . . the Cherokee and sister tribes . . . were able to retain both, their educational achievements outstripped those of the conquerors themselves" (p. 178).

The first Anglo attempts at schooling the Cherokee were solely in English, with predictably unspectacular results. Because teachers had no knowledge of Indian languages, instruction was conducted only in English. However, since most students were unable to comprehend English, "reading became a matter of memory without meaning; writing, of copying without comprehension; and arithmetic, an exercise in misunderstanding. Small wonder that the 'scholars' were addicted to running away" (Weinberg, 1995, p. 184).

Although initial English-only literacy education was largely a failure, with the invention of the Cherokee syllabary, by Sequoyah in 1822, there was a remarkable turn of events (Lepore, 2002). The Cherokee script allowed for the development of bilingual education and for the circulation of *Cherokee Phoenix*, a weekly bilingual newspaper published by the Cherokees themselves. The *Phoenix* became a major instrument in the expression of opposition to the removal of the Cherokee in Georgia (Weinberg, 1995).

Indian Removal

Through the promotion of Cherokee literacy/English biliteracy in the early decades of the 19th century, the Cherokee of the southeast had been able to successfully coexist and/or compete with the encroaching White population. By 1833, missionaries estimated that 60% of the Cherokee were literate in their native language and that about 20% were English literate (Weinberg, 1995). From the perspective of U.S. expansionist policies, English education as a tool of pacification and deculturation had fallen short of its goal of facilitating both domestication and removal. Thus, the decisive solution was to order the physical removal of the Cherokee from the southeast to a region west of the Mississippi. Through an infamous saga known as the "Trail of Tears" (Ehle, 1988), Indian removal was accomplished during the decade of the 1830s. During this period, the federal government imposed a series of fraudulent treaties that resulted in the forced uprooting of 125,000 Indians (Weinberg, 1995). This exodus constituted the largest forced migration of indigenous peoples in modern history (Spring, 1994). Many resisted, and thousands perished due to starvation and disease during the compelled exodus (see Ehle, 1988).

Despite their removal, treaty provisions allowed for the expansion of education among the Cherokee, who, by 1852, had established a schooling system under their own administration. Observers during the period concluded that the Cherokee educational system was superior to those in the neighboring states of Arkansas and Missouri. Educational gains were also made among the Choctaw, especially after their removal from the east. Roman script had been adapted to their language by missionaries, who had more of an influence on Choctaw education than on Cherokee education. In 1842, the Choctaw developed their own tribal schools. The tribal schools were conducted in English, but Sabbath schools, which continued to be popular for basic literacy education, were conducted in Choctaw (Weinberg, 1995).

Subsequent Coercive Assimilation

Following the Civil War, the United States became more aggressive in forcing English and Anglo culture on Indians. A policy of *coercive assimilation* was implemented to hasten deculturation and domestication of Indians in order to wrench away the autonomy of tribal governance and authority. The policy was implemented during the 1880s when the Bureau of Indian Affairs established a system of English-only boarding schools that were fundamental to this purpose (Crawford, 1995b; Spicer, 1962, 1980; Weinberg, 1995; Wiley, 1999a). As with prior deculturation efforts, native languages were to be replaced by English and Indian customs were to be destroyed. In addition, Indians were to undergo indoctrination for patriotic allegiance to the U.S. government. To ensure the goal of total indoctrination, Indian children were physically removed from their families at a young age so as best to reduce the influence of their parents, grandparent, and tribes (see Spring, 1994).

Reflecting on the brutality of the plan, Weinberg (1995) observed that a large number of Indian children resisted their indoctrination through English because "[t]hey had been taught from earliest childhood to despise their conquerors, their language, dress, customs—in fact everything that pertained to them" (p. 206). Spicer (1962) notes that during the early stages of coercive assimilation, fewer than a dozen native languages died out (p. 117), and the program failed to produce significant "numbers of Indians who actually became bilingual" (p. 440). Undeterred, the schools steadfastly attempted to teach Indian children to shun their native languages and cultures. In many schools there was an absolute prohibition on speaking native languages. Punishments were harsh, with offenders being humiliated or beaten or having had their mouths washed with lye soap (Norgren & Nanda, 1988). One of the more effective devices used to advance English and exterminate native languages involved mixing students who spoke different Indian languages. Although this measure was effective in discouraging native language use; it was often counterproductive for promoting English literacy (Spicer, 1962). As noted, by the 1850s, the Cherokee had attained high levels of native language literacy and biliteracy. However, following the imposition of English-only instruction in the 1880s, their overall literacy rates plummeted in both Cherokee and English (Weinberg, 1995). "[O]ver time . . . the English Only policy did take a toll on the pride and identity of many Indians, alienating them from their cultural roots and from their tribes, giving them little or nothing in return" (Crawford, 1995b, p. 27).

Less restrictive policies were not implemented until the 1930s when, under Commissioner of Indian Affairs John Collier (appointed 1932), there was a shift in federal policy from coercive assimilation to experimentation with cultural maintenance (Szasz, 1974). By the late 1960s, many Indian parents, who recalled their own prior educational experiences, met the newly enacted bilingual policies with considerable skepticism. Crawford (1995b) notes, "Among Indians who vividly remember the pain they suffered in school and who hope to shield their children and grandchildren from the same experience [federally imposed programs]" (pp. 27–29; see also Crawford, 1995a, chap. 9; Ruíz, 1995).

In assessing on the impact of English-only ideologies on Indian peoples and of the policies derived from them, it is clear that the aim was deculturation through behavioral assimilation but *not* structural integration. Thus, the imposition of English-only policies was more a means than an end. From the perspective of Indian peoples, however, the issue was not merely one of whether to replace their native languages with English and English literacy. Rather, the situation was more complex. Leaders among the five so-called civilized tribes, some of them bilingual and of dual heritage, recognized the necessity for English literacy given their disadvantaged position in treaty and other legal transactions without it. At stake were the negotiations and the retention of their rights to continue to occupy their ancestral lands. Within the context of increasing contact with the intruders, Indian peoples sought to compete with them by gaining knowledge of their devices, including some of the most barbarous, that is, chattel slavery.

Despite their efforts at self-preservation and resistance, Indian peoples were forcibly removed in one of the largest forced relocations of Native peoples in modern history (Spring, 1994). Once firmly established in Indian Territory, they again established their own schools and successfully competed with White settlers in adjacent areas. This again resulted in policies aimed at the removal of their autonomy through deculturation, based on English monolingual ideological justification, which was not reversed until the 1930s and has left a legacy to the present (Wiley, 2000).

Colonial Period Antecedents of Nativism

In contrast to the underlying agendas for the imposition of English on Indian peoples, for European immigrants the emphasis on English represented an attempt to amalgamate them. It was largely motivated by the desire for *both* behavior assimilation and structural incorporation of peoples who were deemed worthy of amalgamation. The theme of a new *American race* emerging from a blending of European immigrant peoples was prevalent at the outset of the early national period. Crevecoeur (1782/1974) applauded the mixture of "English, Scotch, Irish, French, Germans, and Swedes. From this promiscuous breed, that race now called Americans have arisen" (p. 813). During both the late colonial and early nationalist periods, English and Christian Education—meaning *Protestant* education—was emphasized as the principal means for achieving this purpose.

Antecedents of linguicism were prevalent, however, even during the latter period of English colonization. Among the better known examples are Benjamin Franklin's protestations against Germans and their language: "Instead of Learning our Language, we must learn theirs, or live as in a foreign country" ("Benjamin Franklin on the German Immigration to Pennsylvania," Franklin, 1751/1974). Franklin's expressed concerns included fear of economic competition with the Germans and a distrust of their loyalty and willingness to fight in defense of the English colony. He prescribed English education as a cure for removing their "prejudices." In a reply to Franklin's concerns, William Smith (1754/1974) concurred proposing that a society be founded in London for the purpose of propagating "Christian knowledge and the English Language among the Germans of Pennsylvania" (pp. 631–632) adding that "the method of education should be calculated rather to make good citizens than what is called good school" (p. 632).

Language as a Marker of Difference in the Insipient Nativism in the Early National Period

As the newly established national government sought rapid expansion westward, the theme of amalgamation persisted. Even before the establishment of organized Nativists activities such as those of the Know Nothing movement, antiforeign sentiment expressed in the popular press linked language with religious intolerance. For example, in 1836 the *American Protestant Vindicator*—an influential newspaper—attacked Catholics, noting that "the 'papists' were aliens, immigrants with foreign accents or language" (Bennett, 1995, p. 39).

Increasingly, the promotion of English through the common schools was prescribed as the panacea for the perceived foreign threat to the emerging national identity. In 1836, teachers were admonished to teach the children of immigrants "and educate them in the same schools with our own, and thus *amalgamate them* with our community" ("Concerns for Americanization of the Immigrant in the West," 1836, p. 991). Urgency was added by the conclusion:

It is altogether essential to our national strength and peace, if not to our national existence, that foreigners who settle on our soil should cease to be Europeans and become Americans; as our national language is English, and as our literature, our manners, and our institutions are of English origin, and whole foundation of our English society, it is necessary that they become subsequently Anglo-American . . . and to acquire uniformity, it must be subjected to the crucible, and the schoolmaster is the chemist. ("Concern for Americanization of the Immigrant in the West," 1836/1974, p. 992)

The theme of the English language and the promotion of a common Anglo-American culture imposed through a uniform education was a major motif in the 19th century (see, e.g., The President of Middlebury College (VT) on Schools and the Immigrant, 1848/1974; Stowe, 1836/1974). It continues to be a mantra that persists to the present. Nevertheless, ethnicity and religion were often more overt targets than language in anti–European immigrant diatribes of the 19th century. For example, Massachusetts teachers were warned midcentury that amalgamation with the English-speaking Irish population would contaminate the general population unless the negative cultural traits of the group were eliminated through education ("An Editorial in *The Massachusetts Teacher* on the Irish Immigrant," 1851/1974). Nevertheless, in Nativisit reasoning, the imposition of English education was often linked to anti-immigrant agendas ("A Nativist Insists on 'America for the Americans,'" 1848/1974).

Nativists and neo-Nativists promoted a more reactionary Anglo-Protestant ideology in response to religious, ethnic, and linguistic differences among European immigrants. These differences were being used to racialize immigrants deemed less worthy of structural assimilation and to thereby provide a rational for restrictive immigration policies. Nativism became more prevalent in the decades of the 1840s and 50s under the auspices of the Know-Nothing Movement. It subsided during the Civil War and reconstruction but reemerged in the last decades of the 19th century.

Late 19th and Early 20th Centuries: Language Differences Gain Salience as Markers of Difference Among the European Majority

Although religion and ethnicity were the primary targets of Nativism among the European-origin population during most of the 19th century, language, as a marker of the same, became a more overt target of Nativism. As early as 1889, several ballot measures to restrict German instruction were passed in the Midwest. Although these actions attempted to restrict the use of the German language in schools, they were primarily anti-Catholic and anti-immigrant in intent, and they were subsequently reversed at the polls (Kloss, 1977/1998; Wiley, 1998).

Nativist attacks on foreign languages peaked between the World War I era and the early 1920s. During the war, German Americans were demonized, and their patriotism was questioned. Wartime superpatriotism led to hasty passage of official English policies in 34 states by 1922. Most of these statutes required overt restrictions on the use of German and other languages in schools, churches, and the press. The attack on German spilled over to other European immigrant languages. By the end of the war, restrictive policies had accentuated the importance of foreign language and accent as identifiers of "un-American" sympathies. The impact on German instruction in schools was devastating. In only 7 years (1915–1922), German instruction in high schools was reduced from a high of 324,000 students to fewer than 14,000. More important, German failed to recover, despite *Meyer v. Nebraska*, 1923, which simultaneously guaranteed the right to foreign language teaching and legitimized the official use of English as the common medium of instruction (Wiley, 1998).

The World War I Era's Impact on Subsequent Language Ideologies and Policies: When English-Only Became Hegemonic

What has been the legacy of the climate of repression of the World War I era? What significance does it have for today? Some scholars (e.g., Kloss, 1977/1998) interpret these events as brief digressions from a more typical climate of tolerance for bilingualism and accommodation of other languages. If these were digressions, they were ones from which the dominant culture never found its way back to a more tolerant course. In hindsight, the World War I era climate of repression definitely accelerated the monocultural and monolingual assimilation of many European-origin peoples into the dominant Anglo culture and accentuated the salience of English as a defining characteristic of the America identity.

Although the process of linguistic assimilation had been going on steadily before World War I (Conzen, 1980), until that time there had been a higher tolerance for bilingualism and biculturalism as well as tolerance for those not prepared to make the transition to Anglo conformity. Thus, the World War I era attack on German was an assault on bilingualism, biculturalism, and any attempt to accommodate those who did not speak English. By the war's end, the national shift toward the imposition of official and restrictive English-only policies represented an alteration in the dominant national ideology away from tolerance of language diversity toward an even more rigid monolingualism and monoculturalism. The dominant ideology had, in effect, absorbed several of the long-held tenets of nativism, which, until then had represented the extremist views of a reactionary minority within the Anglo-dominant group (Wiley, 1998).

Conclusion

If we were to accept Kloss's (1977/1998) conclusion that language tolerance has generally been the operative principle in the evolution of U.S. language policies, then recent attempts to restrict languages other than English, and even certain dialects of English, could be interpreted as breaking with the presumably tolerant traditions of the past. The more compelling conclusion, however, is that through U.S. history there has always been an expectation of linguistic assimilation into English. For indigenous peoples, this expectation was designed to facilitate behavioral assimilation and structural subordination. For European immigrants, it was designed to facilitate both behavioral and structural assimilation. Bilingualism and biculturalism for both populations have been conditionally tolerated but never endorsed, and at times been severely attacked. African Americans were the first to experience the full brunt of native-language erasure (Weinberg, 1995; Wiley, 2005). This forced shift to English had unintended outcomes, however, reflecting creative cultural resiliency that resulted in a unique, Creolized variety of African American vernacular English (AAVE, popularly called Ebonics).

If recent efforts at language restrictionism (Wiley, 2000, 2010, 2013b) are viewed from the perspectives of prior Nativist ideology, there is considerable consistency over time. The issue then becomes one of the extent to which Nativism has been a minor current or a central part of the ideology of what it means to be an *American*, that is, a citizen of the United States who is behaviorally assimilated. What appears to have changed in the mix among the ideologies of inhumanity over time is acceptability of overt prejudice and discrimination on the basis of language, whereas other prejudices, particularly on the basis of ethnicity and race, have became expressed more covertly. Thus, in recent decades, the acceptability of prejudice on the basis of language allows it to function as a surrogate for other forms of prejudice.

The ideology of *English monolingualism* as the principal defining characteristic of the U.S. American identity among peoples of European origin did not became hegemonic until the World War I era, with the rise of the Americanization movement. That movement was largely a Nativist response to unprecedented levels of immigration of non–English speaking peoples from eastern and southern Europe. Envenomed by wartime hysteria, xenophobia, and jingoistic zealotry, a rash of official English policies placed restrictions on the use of other languages, and the widespread persecution of speakers of German and other languages followed (Leibowitz, 1971; Ricento, 1998; Tatalovich, 1995; Wiley, 1998). However, its most blatant precursors were clearly apparent prior to the Civil War in the anti-immigrant Know-Nothing movement and the subsequent Nativist and neo-Nativists movements (Bennett, 1995). Thereafter, the linguistic homogeneity component of Nativism went mainstream. It has been reflected in the anti–bilingual education movements that continue to hold sway in those states that have succumbed to restrictive, English-only educational policies (see Arias & Faltis, 2012; Arias & Wiley, 2013; Lillie, Markos, Arias, & Wiley, 2012; Wiley, 2010, 2013a, 2013b, for analyses of current manifestations).

As we consider why the United States has been losing ground in foreign-language education, has restricted bilingual education in some states, and has failed in education to tap and channel the rich linguistic resources among its multilingual population (Macías, 2014; see also Garcia, 2014), the hegemony of the English-only ideology linked to a narrow conceptualization between the relationship between language and notions and citizenship prevails. Unlike Kloss (1977/1998), who underscored the legacy of linguistic intolerance unleashed during the World War I era, the late U.S. Senator Paul Simon (1988) got it right when he lamented in the *Tongue-Tied American,* "There is more than one reason for the lack of emphasis on foreign languages in the United States, but one word, *Americanization*, explains the major part of it" (pp. 11–12). It also explains the ideological basis of the persistent attacks on bilingualism, bilingual education, and the denial of the *ongoing* multilingual and multicultural "super-diversity" of the United States to which all of its many antecedent histories contribute.

NOTE

[1]This section is based on Wiley (2000). The presentation here involves a partial revision and reprinting of the prior piece, with permission.

REFERENCES

Anderson, B. (1983). *Imagined communities: Reflections on the origin and spread of nationalism.* New York, NY: Verso.

Anderson, B. (1991). *Imagined communities: Reflections on the origin and spread of nationalism.* London, England: Verso.

Arias, M. B. & Faltis, C. J. (2012). (Eds.). *Implementing educational language policy in Arizona legal, historical and current practices in SEI.* Bristol, England: Multilingual Matters.

Arias, M. B., & Wiley, T. G. (2013). Language policy and teacher preparation: The implications of a restrictive language policy on teacher preparation. *Applied Linguistics Review, 4,* 83–104

Bennett, D. H. (1995). *The party of fear: The American far right from Nativism to the Militia movement* (2nd ed.). New York, NY: Vintage Books.

Blaut, M. (1993). *The colonizer's model of the world: Geographical diffusionism and eurocentric history.* New York, NY: Guilford.

Blommaert, J. (2013). *The sociolinguistics of globalization.* Cambridge, England: Cambridge University Press.

Blommaert, J., & Rampton, B. (2011). Language and superdiversity. *Diversities, 13*(2), 1–22.

Bonfiglio, T. P. (2010). *Mother tongues and nations: The invention of the native speaker.* New York, NY: De Gruyter.

Cherokee Nation v. Georgia. (1990). In F. P. Prucha (Ed.), *Documents of United States Indian policy* (2nd ed., pp. 57–59). Lincoln: University of Nebraska Press.

Civilization Fund Act. (1990). In Prucha, F. P. (Ed.), *Documents of United States Indian policy* (2nd ed., p. 33). Lincoln: University of Nebraska Press.

Concerns for Americanization of the immigrant in the West. (1974). In S. Cohen (Ed.), *Education in the United States: A documentary history* (Vol. *2*, pp. 991–992). New York, NY: Random House.

Conzen, K. N. (1980). Germans. In S. T. Thernstrom, A. Orlov, & O. Handlin (Eds.), *Harvard Encyclopedia of American ethnic groups* (pp. 404–425). Cambridge, MA: Belknap Press of Harvard University Press.

Crawford, J. (1995a). *Bilingual education: History, politics, theory, and practice* (3rd ed.). Los Angeles, CA: Bilingual Education Services.

Crawford, J. (1995b). Endangered Native American languages: What is to be done, and why? *Bilingual Research Journal, 19,* 17–38.

Crevecoeur, M.-G. J. de. (1974). Crevecoeur describes the new American man. In S. Cohen (Ed.), *Education in the United States: A documentary history* (Vol. *2*, pp. 812–817). New York, NY: Random House.

Del Valle, S. (2003). *Language rights and the law in the United States: Finding our voices.* Clevedon, England: Multilingual Matters.

An editorial in *The Massachusetts Teacher* on the Irish immigrant. (1974). In S. Cohen (Ed.), *Education in the United States: A documentary history,* Vol. *2,* pp. 995–997). New York, NY: Random House.

Ehle, J. (1988). *Trail of tears: The rise and fall of the Cherokee Nation.* New York, NY: Anchor.

Fairclough, N. (1989). *Language and power.* London, England: Longman.

Franklin, B. (1974). Benjamin Franklin on the German immigration to Pennsylvania. In S. Cohen (Ed.), *Education in the United States: A documentary history* (Vol. *1*, pp. 630–631). New York, NY: Random House.

García, O. (2014). U.S. Spanish and education: Global and local intersections. *Review of Research in Education, 38,* 58-80.

Gramsci, A. (1971). *Selections from the prison notebooks.* (Eds. & Trans.) Q. Hoare & G. Nowell-Smith. London: Lawrence & Wishart.

Haas, M. (1992). *Institutional racism: The case of Hawaii.* Westport, CT: Praeger.

Hazen-Hammond, S. (1988). *A short history of Santa Fe.* San Francisco, CA: Lexikos.

Heath, S. B. (1976). Colonial language status achievement: Mexico, Peru, and the United States. In A. Verdoodt & R. Kjolseth (Eds.), *Language and sociology* (pp. 49–91). Leuven, Belgium: Peeters.

Hernández-Chávez, E. (1994). Language policy in the United States: A history of cultural genocide. In T. Skutnabb-Kangas & R. Phillipson (Eds.), *Linguistic human rights: Overcoming linguistic discrimination* (pp. 141–158). Berlin, Germany: Mouton de Gruyter.

Hutton, C. M. (1999). *Linguistics and the Third Reich: Mother-tongue fascism, race, and the science of language.* London, England: Routledge.

Illich, I (1979). Vernacular values and education. *Teacher's College Record, 81,* 31–75.

Jefferson, T. (1990). President Jefferson on Indian Trading Houses. In F. P. Prucha (Ed.), *Documents of United States Indian policy* (2nd ed., pp. 21–22. Lincoln: University of Nebraska Press:

Jordan, W. (1974). *The White man's burden: Historical origins of racism in the United States.* New York, NY: Oxford.

Kloss, H. (1971). Language rights of immigrant groups. *International Migration Review, 5,* 250–268.

Kloss, H. (1998). *The American bilingual tradition.* Washington, DC: Center for Applied Linguistics. (Reprinted from *The American bilingual tradition* by H. Kloss, 1977, Rowley, MA: Newbury House)

Language Policy Task Force. (1992). English colonialism in Puerto Rico. In J. Crawford (Ed.), *Language loyalties: A source book on the official English controversy* (pp. 63–71). Chicago, IL: University of Chicago Press. (Reprinted excerpts from "Language Policy in the Puerto Rican Community," *Bilingual Review/La La Revista Bilingüe, 5,* 1–39)

Leibowitz, A. (1969). English literacy: Legal sanction for discrimination. *Notre Dame Lawyer, 45,* 7–67.

Leibowitz, A. H. (1971). *Educational policy and political acceptance: The imposition of English as the language of instruction in American schools.* Washington, DC: Center for Applied Linguistics. (ERIC Document Reproduction Service No. ED047321)

Leibowitz, A. H. (1974). *Language as a means of social control.* Paper Presented at the VIII World Congress of Sociology, Toronto, Ontario, Canada.

Lepore, J. (2002). *A is for American: Letters and other characters in the newly United States.* New York, NY: Alfred A. Knopf.

Lillie, K. E., Markos, A., Arias, M. B., & Wiley, T. G. (2012). Separate and not equal. The implementation of SEI in Arizona classrooms. *Teachers College Record, 114*(9), 6–7.

Macías, R. F. (1992). *Cauldron-boil & bubble—United States language policy towards indigenous language groups.* Unpublished manuscript, Linguistic Minority Research Institute, University of California at Santa Barbara.

Macías, R. F. (1999). Language policies and the sociolinguistics historiography of Spanish in the United States. In J. K. Peyton, P. Griffin, & R. Fasold (Eds.), *Language in action* (pp. 52–83). Creskill, NJ: Hampton Press.

Macías, R. F. (2014). Spanish as the second national language of the United States: Fact, future, fiction, or hope? *Review of Research in Education, 38,* 33-57.

Macías, R. F., & Wiley, T. G. (1998). Introduction. In H. Kloss (Ed.), *The American bilingual tradition* (pp. vii–xiv). Washington, DC: Center for Applied Linguistics.

Mignolo, W. (2000). *Local histories/global designs: Coloniality, subaltern knowledge and border thinking.* Princeton, NJ: Princeton University Press.

Mignolo, W. (2003). *The darker side of the renaissance: Literacy, territoriality, & colonization* (2nd ed.). Chicago, IL: University of Chicago Press.

Miles, R. (1989). *Racism*. London, England: Routledge.

A Nativist insists on "America for the Americans."(1974). In S. Cohen (Ed.), *Education in the United States: A documentary history* (Vol. 2, pp. 997–999). New York, NY: Random House.

Norgren, J., & Nanda, S. (1988). *American cultural pluralism and the law*. New York, NY: Praeger.

Ovando, C. J., & Wiley, T. G. (2007). Language education in the conflicted United States. In R. Joshee & L. Johnson (Eds.), *Multicultural education policies in Canada and the United States: Symbol and substance* (pp. 107–119). Vancouver, British Columbia, Canada: University of British Columbia Press.

Parrillo, V. N. (2009). *Diversity in America* (3rd ed.). Los Angeles, CA: Pine Forge Press.

Phillipson, R. (1988). Linguicism: Structures and ideologies in linguistic imperialism. In T. Skutnabb-Kangas & J. Cummins (Eds.), *Minority education: From shame to struggle* (pp. 339–358). Clevedon, England: Multilingual Matters.

The president of Middlebury College (VT) on schools and the immigrant. (1974). In S. Cohen (Ed.), *Education in the United States: A documentary history* (Vol. 2, p. 995). New York, NY: Random House.

Ricento, T. (1998). National language policy in the United States. In T. Ricento & B. Burnaby (Eds.), *Language and politics in the United States and Canada: Myths and realities* (pp. 85–112). Mahwah, NJ: Lawrence Erlbaum.

Ruíz, R. (1995). Language planning considerations in indigenous communities. *Bilingual Research Journal, 19*, 71–81.

Rumbaut, R. (2011, April). *Pigments of our imagination: The racialization of the Hispanic-Latino category*. Washington, DC: Migration Policy Institute.

Santa Fe. (2013, August 18). *Wikipedia*. Retrieved from http://en.wikipedia.org/wiki/Santa_Fe,_New_Mexico

Schmidt, R. (1995, March). *Language policy and racial domination: Exploring the linkages*. Paper presented at the annual conference of the American Association for Applied Linguistics, Long Beach, CA.

Simon, P. (1988). *The tongue-tied American: Confronting the foreign-language crisis*. New York, NY: Continuum.

Smith, W. (1974). William Smith to Benjamin Franklin. In S. Cohen (Ed.), *Education in the United States: A documentary history* (Vol. 1, pp. 631–632). New York, NY: Random House.

Spicer, E. H. (1962). *Cycles of conquest: The impact of Spain, Mexico, and the United States on the Indians of the southwest, 1533-1960*. Tucson: University of Arizona Press.

Spicer, E. H. (1980). American Indians, federal policy toward. In S. T. Thernstrom, A. Orlov, & O. Handlin (Eds.), *Harvard encyclopedia of American ethnic groups* (pp. 114–122). Cambridge, MA: Belknap Press of Harvard University Press.

Spring, J. (1994). *Deculturation and the struggle for equality: A brief history of the education of dominated cultures in the United States*. New York, NY: McGraw-Hill.

Spring, J. (1996). *The American School: 1642-1996* (3rd ed.). New York, NY: McGraw-Hill.

Stowe, C. (1974). Calvin Stowe on the Americanization of the immigrant. In S. Cohen (Ed.), *Education in the United States: A documentary history* (Vol. 2, pp. 993–994). New York, NY: Random House.

Szasz, M. C. (1974). *Education and the American Indian: The road to self-determination since 1928*. Albuquerque: University of New Mexico Press.

Takaki, R. (1993). *A different mirror: A history of multicultural America*. Boston, MA: Little, Brown and Company.

Tatalovich, R. (1995). *Nativism reborn? The official English language movement and the American states*. Lexington: University Press of Kentucky.

Tollefson, J. W. (1991). *Planning language, planning inequality: Language policy in the community.* New York, NY: Longman.

Toth, C. (1990). *German-English bilingual schools in America.* Bern, Switzerland: Peter Lang.

Veltman, C. (1983). *Language shift in the United States.* Berlin, Germany: Mouton.

Vertovec, S. (2010). Towards post-multiculturalism? Changing communities, contexts, and conditions of diversity. *International Social Science Journal, 199,* 83–95.

Watkins, D. K. (1980). Danes and Danish on the Great Plains. In P. Schach, (Ed.), *Languages in conflict: Linguistic acculturation on the Great Plains* (pp. 58–76). Lincoln: University of Nebraska Press.

Weinberg, M. (1990). *Racism in the United States: A comprehensive classified bibliography.* Westport, CT: Greenwood.

Weinberg, M. (1995). *A chance to learn: A history of race and education in the United States* (2nd ed.). Long Beach: California State University.

Weinstein, B. (1979). Language strategists: Rethinking political frontiers on basis of linguistic choices. *World Politics, 31,* 344–64.

Weinstein, B. (1983). *The civic tongue: Political consequences of language choices.* New York, NY: Longman.

Weiss, B. J. (Ed.). (1982). *American education and the European immigrant: 1840-1940.* Urbana: University of Illinois Press.

Wiley, T. G. (1998). The imposition of World War I era English-only policies and the fate of German in North America. In T. Ricento & B. Burnaby (Eds.), *Language and politics in the United States and Canada* (pp. 211–241). Mahwah, NJ: Lawrence Erlbaum.

Wiley, T. G. (1999a). Comparative historical perspectives in the analysis of US language policies. In T. Heubner & C. Davis (Eds.), *Political perspective on language planning and language policy* (pp. 17–37). Amsterdam, Netherlands: John Benjamins.

Wiley, T. G. (1999b). What happens after English is declared the official language of the United States? Lessons from case histories. In E. Kibbee (Ed.), *Language legislation and language rights* (pp. 179–195). Amsterdam, Netherlands: John Benjamins.

Wiley, T. G. (2000). Continuity and change in the function of language ideologies in the United States. In T. Ricento (Ed.), *Ideology, politics, and language policies: Focus on English* (pp. 67–85). Amsterdam, Netherlands: John Benjamins.

Wiley, T. G. (2002). Accessing language rights in education: A brief history of the U.S. context. In J. Tollefson (Ed.), *Language policies in education: Critical readings* (pp. 39–64). Mahwah, NJ: Lawrence Erlbaum.

Wiley, T. G. (2005). *Literacy and language diversity in the United States.* Washington, DC: Center for Applied Linguistics.

Wiley, T. G. (2006). The lessons of historical investigation: Implications for the study of language policy and planning. In T. Ricento (Ed.), *Language policy: Essential readings* (pp. 136–152). London, Netherlands: Blackwell.

Wiley, T. G. (2007). Immigrant minorities: USA. In M. Hellinger & A. Pauwels (Eds.), *Handbooks of applied linguistics: Vol. 9. Language and communication: Diversity and change* (pp. 53–85). Berlin, Germany: Mouton de Gruyter.

Wiley, T. G. (2010). The United States. In J. A. Fishman & O. Garcia (Eds.), *Handbook of language and ethnic identity* (pp. 302–322). Oxford, England: Oxford University Press.

Wiley, T. G. (2013a). A brief history and assessment of language rights in the United States. In J. W. Tollefson (Ed.), *Language policies in education: Critical issues* (2nd ed., pp. 61–90). London, England: Routledge.

Wiley, T. G. (2013b). Constructing and deconstructing "illegal" children. *Journal of Language, Identity, and Education, 12,* 167–172.

Wiley, T. G., & Lukes, M. (1996). English-only and standard English ideologies in the United States. *TESOL Quarterly, 30,* 511–535.

Chapter 2

Spanish as the Second National Language of the United States: Fact, Future, Fiction, or Hope?

REYNALDO F. MACÍAS

University of California, Los Angeles

Bestow great attention on Spanish and endeavor to acquire an accurate knowledge of it. Our future connections with Spain and Spanish America will render that language of valuable acquisition. The ancient history of that part of America, too, is written in that language. I am sending you a dictionary.

—Thomas Jefferson, in a letter to his nephew, Peter Carr, in 1787.

INTRODUCTION

The status of a language is very often described and measured by different factors, including the length of time it has been in use in a particular territory, the official recognition it has been given by governmental units, and the number and proportion of speakers. Spanish has a unique history and, so some argue status, in the contemporary United States based on these and other criteria. At least eight arguments have been identified that would promote this unique status:

1. Spanish was spoken in North "America" as a colonial language over 100 years before the establishment of the first permanent English-speaking colonies at Jamestown and Plymouth.
2. Two thirds of what is now the United States was at one time under an official Spanish language polity.
3. The principal mode of initial incorporation of large numbers of Spanish speakers to the nation was through war, including peace treaties providing various civil rights, guaranteeing liberties, and the granting of citizenship en masse to those conquered populations.

Review of Research in Education
March 2014, Vol. 38, pp. 33-57
DOI: 10.3102/0091732X13506544
© 2014 AERA. http://rre.aera.net

4. In the past and present, the United States has recognized the official status of the Spanish language at the federal, state, and local levels of government, including outlying polities within the jurisdiction of the nation, either as a recognition of the prior sovereign in those territories (Spain, Mexico) or as a recognition of large numbers of Spanish speakers.

5. The number of people who can speak Spanish, either monolingually or bilingually, has steadily increased in the United States, and in North America, since the founding of the United States.

6. The futures of Spanish in the United States are for continued growth, trailing the numerical and proportional growth of Chican@s, Puerto Ricans, and other Latin@s in the country.

7. Spanish is the most popular "foreign" (as in non-English) language taught in the schools and colleges of the United States.

8. Spanish is a world language, widely spoken throughout the globe, and the official language of more than 22 countries and international organizations and the United States is one of the largest Spanish-speaking countries in the world.

Some authors argue that this is a history and status unlike other indigenous, colonial, or immigrant languages and that these points argue for an exceptionalism for Spanish in the United States, even to the extent of recognizing and accepting it as a second national language. For example, Alonso (2006), in promoting six institutional responses of college Spanish departments to the increased and increasing enrollments in Spanish classes, indicated that "only then will Spanish be ready to assume the role *demanded* [italics added] of it *by historical circumstance* [italics added] as the second national language of the United States" (p. 20). It is important to recognize the additive nature of this call for recognizing and accepting Spanish as a second national language, not as a substitute for English—a point that I address below. Yet Spanish and its status, its use in schooling, and its use in other educational and public situs have often been a contentious public policy issue, especially when reflecting intergroup social relations between Anglos (most often White Euro-Americans but occasionally African-descended Anglophones) and Chican@s and other Latin@s (see Crawford, 1993; Huntington, 2004). Where there was a community or polity with a monolingual, English-speaking majority or dominance, the public policy issue of recognizing or using Spanish was often framed by local policy makers as anti-"American" (meaning United States), foreign, and in and of itself self-defeating for those who spoke the language (Leibowitz, 1971, 1976). These controversies provided for episodic periods during which the language issues (e.g., the language of instruction in the schools) was the basis for the politics of social control of the Spanish-speaking peoples on the one hand and self-determination by and for the Spanish-speaking peoples on the other. So other than as a descriptor of the number of Spanish speakers in the country, what does it mean to identify or ascribe the status to Spanish as a second national language?

Part of the "American lore" or ideology regarding language diversity in civil society is that this diversity comes primarily, if not exclusively, from immigrants. Kloss (1971) addressed this connection and how it was reflected in public policies, and the basis of those policies, by identifying four "theories": tacit compact theory, take and give theory, antighettoization theory, and national unity theory. The first two theories reflect the belief that immigrants gain something coming to the United States and, therefore, must give up their language, culture, and any claims or rights to them in return. The second two theories associate the continuation of immigrant languages with social, political, and economic isolation, and the lack of progress of the immigrant, and as a disruptive force to the national unity. However, as we see below, the history of Spanish does not fit neatly into these theories identified by Kloss (1971). These theories much better reflect what we have come to identify as ideologies of language (see Leeman, 2004; Wiley & Lukes, 1996). The dominant and popular U.S. view reflected here is that the principal, if not exclusive, source of the linguistic diversity within the nation is immigration and can be influenced or controlled primarily through immigration laws; secondarily, through naturalization and citizenship policies conditioned on demonstrated English language abilities; and third, through required "Americanization" in the schools (the forced English-only and cultural socialization under the guise of civic and government education, and "instillation" of patriotism; see Leibowitz, 1984).

The history and political economy of the various groups and languages as socioeconomic context are important for exploring language status, rights, and their manifestation in educational policies (Macías, 2000a; Wiley, 1999, 2006). Several of these above-stated arguments demand that territorial expansion, economic development, immigration and population growth, and political consolidation within a country are a more substantive frame of reference for analyses of the question of the exceptionality of Spanish in the United States. This study, then, explored whether the claims that Spanish indeed has a unique status within what is now the United States are warranted. It explored the aforementioned arguments for Spanish language exceptionalism, and the "fit" with some of these various "theories" or paradigms underlying language status and educational policies, more generally, to explore its status as the second national language in the United States.

IS SPANISH DIFFERENT OR EXCEPTIONAL FROM OTHER LANGUAGES IN THE UNITED STATES?

Each of the eight arguments identified here has been proposed by others as a rationale for the recognition of Spanish in some official status, either singly, or in various combinations. The exposition below is limited to an initial exploration of the first five, with a brief annotation of the future of Spanish to the discussion of its growth in the United States. There is no attention to the last three arguments, some of which are partly addressed elsewhere in this volume.

Spanish Was Spoken in North "America" Over 100 Years Before the Establishment of the First Permanent English-Speaking Colonies at Jamestown and Plymouth

It is fairly common knowledge that Spain chartered Genoan Christopher Columbus in 1492, to sail West to establish trade relations with Asia and India and that he encountered "new" lands and peoples in the Caribbean and mainlands of what has become known as the Western hemisphere of the globe. It is useful, especially for our purposes, to explore how Spanish gets learned, spoken, and spread throughout these "new" lands; the colonial ownership claims to these new "discoveries"; and how this relates to what is now the United States.

In 1959, the noted anthropologist Eric Wolf described this initial encounter with this background related to the "Spanish" language:

> In 1519, Middle America witnessed the coming of the Spaniards, who brought with them to the New World their Romance language, historically the linguistic legacy of Roman rule in Spain. The Roman Empire yielded to pressures from within and without, but the population of the Peninsula continued to speak in Iberian Latin dialects in the face of conquest and occupation by Vandal, Goth, and Arab. When the Christian principalities of the Spanish north rallied to drive out the Arab invaders again, one of the north Spanish dialects, Castilian, spoken in the narrow confines of the kingdom of Oviedo in the Cantabrian Mountains, became the idiom of the Reconquest. As the Reconquest led to the political consolidation and hegemony of the kingdom of Castile, this dialect of the northern marches became the language of the new Spanish state. The year 1492 marked the victory of the Spanish armies over the Arabs in Spain and the expansion of Castile overseas, into the New World beyond the Atlantic. But 1492 also marked the appearance of the first Castilian grammar, the *Gramática de la lengua castellana*, by Antonio de Nebrija (1444-1532), written with the express purpose of acquainting future subject populations speaking other languages with the new language of command. (p. 43)

Recognizing this new land mass and its various peoples as previously unknown to the Europeans, and certainly not Christian, Christopher Columbus, and the Spaniards with him, claimed the new areas for the Royals of Spain under the Doctrine of Discovery. The Doctrine established the right of Christian kings to claim for God and country undiscovered lands, that is, lands that were not already claimed by other Christian monarchs and in which the population was not already Christian for purpose of expansion and Christianization, under penalty of slavery, torture, or death. This policy was set out in three papal bulls issued in 1452 (*Papal Bull Dum Diversas*) and 1455 (*Bull Romanus Pontifex*), both by Pope Nicholas V, and in 1493 (*Bull Inter Caetera*) by Pope Alexander VI, extending the reasoning used earlier to justify the Crusades in the "Holy Lands" in the 11th, 12th, and 13th centuries. This Doctrine became the foundation of what is known today as the Law of Nations (or modern international law), because it set the rules by which different Christian monarchs could competitively claim these lands.

France, England, the Netherlands, and other European monarchies soon followed Spain and Portugal in seeking to "discover" new lands, peoples, and resources, to conquer and exploit, albeit by respecting the prior claims of the peninsular powers. Thus, began the period Western historians have named the Age of Discovery, or the Colonial Period (because these "discovered" lands became colonies of these European royals, establishing empires beyond kingdoms).

The found territories were well populated throughout the continents. In meso-America alone, "Estimates put the indigenous Mexican population at approximately 25.3 million in 1519, 16.8 million in 1523, 2.6 million in 1548, 1.3 million in 1595, and 1 million in 1605" (Terborg, García Landa, & Moore. 2007, p. 119). Some authors claim that this decline led to the extinction of more than 100 languages. The population recovery was accompanied by considerable mixing of peoples of various ethnic backgrounds, although Indians always comprised the majority of the population of New Spain, or colonial Mexico; people solely African or European constituted a very small subpopulation. By the end of the 16th century, Spanish speakers were primarily the Spanish elite colonials and their American-born progeny (*criollos*).

The second largest group was of mixed European and Indian stock raised in a Spanish environment (*euromestizos*); mixed stock of Indians and Europeans raised in an indigenous environment (*indomestizos*); and Spanish-speaking mixed groups with an African component (*afromestizos*) who also made up a considerable fraction of the population. (Hidalgo, 2006, p. 5)

Wolf (1959) contended, "If the Amerinds had maintained their pre-conquest level of population, 300,000 Spaniards and 250,000 African Negroes could probably not have affected the Amerind gene pool appreciably" (p. 30). By the end of the 18th century, he guestimated,

On the basis of the returns for the Spanish census of 1793, . . . Indians and Indo-mestizos (mestizos in whose outward appearance Indian physical characteristics dominate) made up 70 percent of the Middle American population. Afro-mestizos (or mestizos in whom Negroid characteristics were dominant) accounted for 10 percent. Whites and Euro-mestizos (mestizos in whom European physical characteristics were dominant) accounted for 20 percent. (pp. 31–32)

The racial and language policies adopted by Spain were significant in establishing a hierarchy of languages and in eventually supporting the acquisition and spread of Spanish by the local colonized population. The language of administration was Castellano throughout the colonial period. The language diversity among the indigenous population was addressed in various ways by Royal decisions in the first 100 years of colonial administration: supporting the languages of the various indigenous groups; selecting Nahuatl as the "language of the Indians," with the encouragement of the Crown, resulting in the publication of 80 books in Nahuatl by 1600; and promoting the teaching and learning of Latin through schooling and religious education (see Gray, 1999; Gray & Fiering, 2000; Heath, 1972). These colonial policies of Spain were applied even as the indigenous populations were being diminished and the indigenous societies were being colonially restructured. When New Spain became independent Mexico (and many other new, decolonized, polities in Central America), in 1821, the new governments received Spanish as their political-linguistic legacy. After independence, Mexico adopted literacy and language policies that promoted a single nationalism through Castellanization, especially through the establishment of schools, although ideologically doting on the diverse indigenous roots of the native population.

The beginning of the Age of Discovery attracted many of the European monarchs. The King of England, Henry VII, in 1496, authorized the Venetian John Cabot to investigate, claim, and possess lands. Under the Discovery Doctrine, Cabot was obliged to avoid lands already claimed by the Christian monarchs of Spain and

Portugal. England explored and sought such lands and was principally restricted to the northern areas of the Western hemisphere. Permanent settlements, that is, occupation, were not successful in what became the United States, until 1607 at Jamestown. The English approach to colonization through discovery was more mercantilistic, commercially organized, and settler based than that of the Spanish. Settler populations established colonies and towns with the intent to develop commerce between England and the new areas of occupation. Settler contacts with the indigenous populations of the northeastern coastal part of the continent were less about discovery claims to large swaths of territory for the King, or colonial control of the indigenous populations, and more about a practice of "measured distance," establishing clear areas of settler occupation and movement, with reestablishment (removal) of the local AmerIndian populations to other areas further West, through agreement, force, or happenstance (Lepore, 1998).

The practice of measured distance was also the basis for "tolerance" of religious and other differences. Religious refugees were often Reformed Christians considered cults and heretics by the new Church of England, and thus persecuted in the metropole. As they settled in New England, they established their separate towns and churches where they could practice their religions without interference from other varieties of Christians, and without the contact of the indigenous non-Christians, nonbelievers. An exception to this measured distance practice was the enslaved African population that arrived in the English colonies very soon after they were permanently settled. Regarding this population there was a "socially" measured distance through a repression of their indigenous African languages, an imposition of limited oral English (to understand commands and facilitate control), and a prohibition of teaching reading, writing, and general schooling, although they were in close physical contact with English colonists.

There was no specific language policy for the English colonies formulated by England during the colonial period. Heath (1976) characterized the language attitude of England toward the colonies as one of deferral, so long as the language policies of the colonial-settlers did not conflict with any of the nonlanguage policies of the Crown. According to Heath, language choice and style was a matter of individual choice in England, something not to be legislated by the state. These attitudes toward language use were paralleled in the colonies. Locally, occasional attempts were made, primarily by religious groups, to change the language and culture of the Indians. These schools, according to Heath, were short-lived because of the lack of institutional support and the lack of centralized broad policy formulation on the part of the English. As Heath sums up, "They failed to intermarry with the Indians or provide social structures which would promote culture and language shifts outside formal policy decisions" (p. 81).

Competition between the northern European powers over their "discoveries," and wars between the European colonial monarchies, left England the winner of the prior claims made by Sweden, Holland, and France. In the Treaty of Paris of 1763, between France and England, which concluded the French and Indian Wars, or what is also known as the Seven Years War, France ceded its discovery claim to Canada, Quebec, and the claims east of the Mississippi river to the Appalachian mountain range to England. France's claims west and southwest of the Mississippi river were granted to Spain. The colonial dominion of the "new world" changed between the colonial powers until the period of colonial independence (decolonization) began with the rebellion of the northern mid-Atlantic British colonies (1776). This was followed by those in the rest of the continent and the Caribbean against Spain and France in the first quarter of the 19th century (most dated to 1821). The independence movements established the modern nation-state of constitutional republics throughout the continent with the mirror of self-government, initiating a new period of political relationships between the peoples of the Western hemisphere. The legacy of colonial competition over lands and resources was visited on the behaviors between these new nation-states. The colonial languages of these areas continued as the language of government and administration of the new states, with little recognition of the continued linguistic diversity contributed by indigenous groups. Spanish became the dominant language in nearly two dozen countries, English, French, Dutch, and Portuguese in less than six each in the Western hemisphere.

Broadly, Spain and Britain were the last two "standing" colonial empires in the Western hemisphere in the middle of the 1700s (Portugal holding its own with its Southern Cone colony of Brazil). With different approaches to the development and administration of their colonies and empire building, they remained political siblings under the color of authority of the Doctrine of Discovery, when it came to the lands and the indigenous diversity.

There were at least three types of colonialism in the world: (a) a small colonizer elite with a large indigenous, colonized population; (b) a settler colonization, where settler-colonizers geographically and demographically displaced the indigenous populations (an English pattern of colonialism in the North American context); and (c) a small colonizer elite, with large colonized native populations characterized by a racial mixture between colonizer and colonized and an incomplete cultural imposition from the colonizer to the colonized (a Spanish pattern in much of the Western hemisphere). Although Spanish became a colonial language in this period, the predominant speakers of the language in the colonies became the detribalized mestizos with a majority demographic basis in the indigenous peoples of the hemisphere. The notion here of an incomplete cultural imposition, then, is based primarily on the spread of language (Castellano) and adoption of religion (Catholic Christian) and not on the daily life, diet, or other popular practices of the majority colonized population, which tended to continue local, indigenous life, beliefs, and practices. Keep in mind the Indianization of the Spanish language (Parodi, 2006) and the adaptation to the local indigeneity of the Catholic Church and Christian religion.

The Spanish language spread over the colonies in New Spain, New Granada, and its other overseas possessions to the extent that on independence from Spanish colonialism (1810–1821) in much of middle America, the overwhelming majority of the political and social elites were Spanish speaking and Spanish became the official language of the new republics. At the beginning of the 21st century, Spanish was the first language for 90% of the Mexican population and a lingua franca for many of the indigenous language speakers (Terborg et al., 2007). In 2010, Mexico was also the largest Spanish-speaking country in the world with over 100 million Spanish speakers (Hidalgo, 2006).

What Are the Important Points to Note From This Brief Review?

How does this rationalize Spanish as a second national language in the United States today? Its basic premise is that Spanish was "here" first, and that ought to count for something. Appeals to historicity are common in status discussions.

Second, although the English language was the legacy of the British empire in what became the United States, we should note that it exercised a very permissive, if not tolerant, approach to official language policies, leaving such decisions to local jurisdictions and civil society. Some might stretch these notions to be included in the liberties and freedoms espoused in the Enlightenment and that undergirded the principles of revolution and government in the Declaration of Independence.

A third point to be made from this brief review is that Spanish is spoken in the Western hemisphere in the majority by detribalized indigenous populations. The rights of indigenous peoples, of colonized populations, are implicated here. Although Spanish is classified as a colonial language, the majority of its speakers are not colonial-settlers, immigrants, or strictly their progeny, as is the case with English speakers in the United States.

Two Thirds of What Is Now the United States Was at One Time Under an Official Spanish Language Polity

After gaining independence from Britain, one of the first issues the newly independent United States needed to determine was territorial integrity. Under the Treaty of Paris (1783) between the Continental Congress and England, which ended the war for independence, the former British colonies were recognized as individually separated from England and independent states incorporating not only their colonial jurisdictional territories but also an emancipation of the British colonial territory west of the Appalachian mountains to the Mississippi river, but not to the north into Canada. The territory between the Mississippi and the Appalachians was reserved for their Indian occupants (as defined in the Royal Proclamation of 1763). The British claims in the south (west Florida) were ceded back to Spain not the United States (Spain also continued to claim former British territory as far north as the Ohio and Tennessee rivers from 1783 until 1820; Cox, 1976). The newly independent states even left open the possibility of gaining more British colonial territory, Canada, as a new state, if it so desired (Article XI, Articles of Confederation; see Spaeth & Smith, 1991).

Controversy continued as to conflicting claims to boundaries between states, to the nature of "clear title" to these territories with regard to the AmerIndian occupation of these lands and the legal nature of their landownership. The new nation generally recognized other "first discovery" claims of colonial control and ownership, primarily of Spain to the west, and to the south, and federal control and ownership of national territory not otherwise part of a sovereign member-state.

Constitution of the United States of America (effective March 4, 1789)

Article IV, Section 3. New States may be admitted by the Congress into this Union; but no new State shall be formed or erected within the Jurisdiction of any other State; nor any State be formed by the Junction of two or more states, or parts of States, without the Consent of the Legislatures of the States concerned as well as Congress;

The Congress shall have the Power to dispose of and make all needful Rules and Regulations respecting the Territory or other Property belonging to the United States; and nothing in this Constitution shall be so construed as to Prejudice any Claims of the United States or of any particular State.

Section 4. The United States shall guarantee to every State in this union a Republican Form of Government, and shall protect each of them against invasion. (Spaeth & Smith, 1991, p. 207)

Much of the early work of the new nation was spent on adjudicating the conflicting claims of jurisdictional boundaries between member-states. All of the land in the jurisdiction of the new republic that was not part of a sovereign member-state was under the control and authorization of the federal government. Lands occupied by indigenous peoples were defined as part of the United States, with recognition of a prior and continuing *occupancy* of the land by the indigenous population, with a federal government right of first option to buy. Sale of Indian lands to private hands was soon prohibited (see *Johnson v. McIntosh*, 1823, on U.S. ownership of Indian lands within its jurisdiction, claimed by the prior colonial sovereign, based on a recognition of the Doctrine of Discovery; and identification of the Indian nations as "domestic dependent nations"). The new republic adopted the "measured distance" policy of relations with Indians and the use of treaties between the domestic dependent nations and the federal government, as a way of official engagements and interactions.

Territorial expansion of the United States is another critical dimension in providing an adequate socioeconomic-historical context for examining the status of Spanish in the United States. Nineteenth-century U.S. territorial expansion included over 2 million square miles of land that was previously under either Spain, Mexico, or some form of government that included Spanish as an official language and, thus, part of the Spanish language heritage of the United States. This territorial expansion included the following: (a) the 1 million square miles of the Louisiana Purchase (initially explored by the Spanish, under French colonial administration between 1699 and 1763, and then again under Spanish rule between 1763 and 1803); (b) the 38,700 square miles of territory east of the Mississippi (east and west Florida) that Spain ceded to the United States, along with its rights to Oregon, in 1819; (c) the nearly 1 million square miles of land taken in the U.S.–Mexican war (1846–1848); (d) the Gadsen Purchase of 45,000 square miles in 1853; and (e) the occupation of Cuba, Puerto Rico, and the Philippines in 1898, as the result of the U.S. intervention into what is called the Spanish–American war. In the 45 years between 1803 and 1848, the United States expanded across the continent, acquiring 2.3 million square miles, two thirds of its present land area, most of which was under an official Spanish language sovereign, with processes of territorial administration and political conversion to statehood in place.

How Does This Argument Inform Us Regarding the Status of Spanish?

The principal understanding of this argument is that the United States has a colonial heritage beyond the British and that this should be recognized. Nearly two thirds of the country was previously under Spanish colonial rule, and more than half did not include any prior English claims. So, if we are to recognize the language legacy of the British in the new United States, we should likewise recognize the language legacy of the Spanish in the additional territory acquired postindependence. Note that the Spanish had explicit policies regarding the language diversity of indigenous populations and the adoption of Spanish as the official language of the independent republics realized in decolonization from Spain. England did not. The argument raises issues of the history of the language and its speakers in an area (historicity; geo-linguistic demography), the nature of the language contact, and the integration of disparate language communities into a new, common polity.

The Principal Mode of Initial Incorporation of Large Numbers of Spanish Speakers to the Nation Was Through War, Concluding With Peace Treaties Providing Various Civil Rights and the Granting of Citizenship En Masse to Those Conquered Populations

The initial incorporation of Mexicans, Filipinos, Cubans, Puerto Ricans, and other Spanish speakers in significant numbers was through war, conquest, and territorial expansion in the 19th century. Their postincorporation treatment as vanquished peoples greatly affected the official policies and popular attitudes toward them and the Spanish language. The Spanish-speaking and other indigenous populations were incorporated into the U.S. social system at different times and in different ways. American Indian nations were absorbed, militarily conquered, relocated, or otherwise "terminated."

The war with Mexico ended in 1848, and the ceded lands were occupied by an estimated 100,000 Mexicans and a similar number of indigenas, with a network of towns, commercial centers, and transportation routes (Martínez, 1975). The Treaty of Guadalupe Hidalgo recognized this demography and to some extent this political economy.

Some have argued that the Treaty also guaranteed language rights to the conquered resident population of Mexicans. Language rights in the Treaty of Guadalupe Hidalgo, however, were not explicitly mentioned. The understanding of the protection of cultural and language rights apparently was based on that in the 1803 Treaty for the purchase of the Louisiana Territory between France and the United States (Klotz, 1968), for which there was an understanding of such protection. France raised the question of protecting its Catholic, French-speaking population from the Protestant, English-speaking United States. Language, culture, and religion were much intertwined in expression and practice. It is maintained that the "liberties" referred to in the 1803 Treaty reflected the French cultural and language rights and, along with properties and religion of the persons remaining in the sold territory, were to be respected (Klotz, 1968). The subsequent concessions by the U.S. government on language in the Louisiana territory, like language competencies required for elected officials, or the translation of laws into both English and French, have been identified as expressions of the Treaty protections "in the free enjoyment of their liberty, property, and the religion which they profess."

According to the Treaty of Guadalupe Hidalgo, the Mexicans that remained in the ceded territory "shall be maintained and protected in the free enjoyment of their liberty and property, and secured in the free exercise of their religion without restriction." The continuity of definitions between the Treaty of 1803 and the Treaty of Guadalupe Hidalgo is of interest if "liberty" and "religion" were understood to include not only unfettered use of the (non-English) language but also public access and support for its use (Griswold del Castillo, 1990). The debates during the California Constitutional conventions imply that the use of interpreters and the publication of the Constitution and laws in English and Spanish were a recognition of the spirit of the Treaty of Guadalupe Hidalgo (Lozano, 2011).

Attention to the Treaty of Guadalupe Hidalgo was renewed and increased during the Chican@ movement of the 1960s and 1970s, owing to its legal protections of property rights of land grants in the ceded Mexican territories and as a basis for claimed cultural and language rights. Claims by the Hopi and other Pueblo natives regarding their prewar status as Mexican citizens and their subsequent civil and property rights in the United States under the Treaty have also brought new attention to the Treaty. A collaboration between Chican@s and other indigenous groups (through the International Indian Treaty Council) has also appealed and filed claims with international organizations, like the United Nations, on protections of their human rights and their right to self-determination (Griswold del Castillo, 1990). "Today the Treaty of Guadalupe Hidalgo gives Mexican Americans a special relationship to the majority society. As a conquered people, Mexicans within the United States have been given a special consideration under an international Treaty" (Griswold del Castillo, 1990, p. 173).

At the end of the 19th century, the United States intervened in the Cuban war of independence from Spain (the Spanish–American war) and in the process gained the former Spanish colonies of Cuba, Puerto Rico, the Philippines, and Guam. Under the Teller Amendment (1898), the United States was forbidden to annex Cuba, but it acquired Puerto Rico and occupied the Philippine Islands in the south Pacific, until it gave the latter their qualified political independence as of July 4, 1946. The incorporation of Puerto Rico alone added over 950,000 Spanish speakers to the United States population, with limited U.S. citizenship granted en masse in 1917, through an act of Congress, known as the Jones Act (Álvarez-González, 1999; Castro, 1977). The United States still includes Puerto Rico and Guam within its jurisdiction, having changed its political relation with Puerto Rico from colony to commonwealth in 1952.

The common nature of incorporation into the United States of the Mexicans and Puerto Ricans, the two largest groups who speak Spanish, was war, then occupation. The political status of the areas postincorporation varied for Puerto Rico, which is outside the continental United States, and the territory ceded by Mexico, which was contiguous with the country prior to the war, and became the "Southwestern" part of the nation, and which has been divided into nearly a dozen states.

How Does the Review of This Argument Give Us a Better Understanding of Spanish as a National Language?

This argument outlines, in principle, that a legally binding agreement continues to officially recognize the language practices of a group, the state ought not interfere with those practices, and there should have been a promotive bilingual government administration of these lands as they were incorporated into U.S. jurisdiction. These populations were incorporated into the U.S. body politic involuntarily.

The United States Has Recognized the Official Status of the Spanish Language at the Federal, State, and Local Levels of Government, Including Outlying Polities Within the Jurisdiction of the Nation

What does it mean to officially recognize a language when there is no national, constitutional official language in the United States? It is important to understand the organization of government to put these language policy issues within the context of the area's legal relationship to the governmental structure of the United States, for example, as a state, territory, federal district, commonwealth, or "domestic dependent nation." The United States is also a complex set of centralized and decentralized political relations, with a separation of powers and a check and balance on the distribution of power, authority, and scope of activity. The federal government, as a whole, is also constrained as to its duties and actions by the Constitution, leaving all else as the responsibility and authority of the sovereign constituent states. Each of these jurisdictions has certain exclusive rights and responsibilities in establishing, promoting, and implementing policies.

With two thirds of the national jurisdiction having been under earlier Spanish rule, one can predict there are many states that were successfully created by Congress from these territories. If we look into the history of some of these states, we can get exemplars of official Spanish, keeping in mind there are other jurisdictions with similar histories and profiles, and even some with official languages other than Spanish.

California

California came under U.S. jurisdiction in 1848, as a result of the U.S.–Mexican War, as part of the land ceded by Mexico to the United States in the Treaty of Guadalupe Hidalgo. It became a state, without going through a Territorial phase, in 1850, as the 31st of the Union (Belz, 2001). In the California Constitutional Convention in 1849, the 8 Spanish-surnamed delegates and the immediate history of the area wielded much linguistic influence on the proceedings and the other 40 delegates (Lozano, 2011). Article XI, Miscellaneous Provisions, §21, of the California Constitution of 1849, provided, "All laws, decrees, regulations, and provisions, which from their nature require publication, shall be published in English and Spanish." According to Fedynskyj (1971), this provision was made part of the California Constitution in the spirit of the Treaty of Guadalupe Hidalgo of 1848, which assured Mexicans residing in all the occupied territory the protection of person and property guaranteed by the Constitution and laws of the Republic.

To effect this official bilingualism, the first California legislature established the office of State Translator, provided for the printing of 1,050 copies in English and 350 copies in Spanish of all the laws of California passed at that session of the Legislature, and provided for distribution of the journals, laws, supreme court reports, and other documents. An act of April 29, 1852, Chap. 50, maintained,

> The distribution of the laws in Spanish shall be made by the Secretary of State, as follows: one copy to each Justice of the Supreme Court, to each District Judge, to each County Clerk, to each Senator and member of the Assembly in the counties of Sonoma, Marin, Mendocino, Contra Costa, Santa Clara, Monterey, San Luis Obispo, Santa Barbara, San Diego, and Los Angeles, and to each county judge in said counties. The residue shall remain in the State Library until otherwise disposed of by law. (Fedynskyj, 1971, pp. 472–473)

A joint legislative committee was appointed to designate the laws and resolutions to be translated and to decide on the qualifications of translators. Spanish editions of California session laws before 1863 were abridged editions of the original English volumes. The ratio between English and Spanish contents oscillated between 3:1 and 3:2. The last Spanish edition was published in 1878 for the 1877–1878 session (Fedynskyj, 1971).

Many legal notices were also published in Spanish and English by the state and local governments in newspapers throughout California. The extant robust Spanish language press was a principal vehicle for this bilingual publication. As the English language newspapers began to develop, they often included "Spanish pages" in order to qualify for the money for the Spanish language notices as well. It was apparently the margin of profit for a number of struggling English language printers and publishers as well, who printed the Spanish language sections to gain the public subsidies and not necessarily to inform the people (Gutiérrez, 1977). When the California government suspended this practice, the Spanish language press was dealt a strong economic blow, while the English language press dropped the Spanish pages. According to Ruiz (1972) the laws requiring the bilingual publication continued on the books until 1878.

At the time of statehood for California, 18% of all schooling in the state was private and Catholic (Ewing, 1918; Leibowitz, 1971). These schools were usually taught in Spanish, and, of course, consisted mostly of Mexican origin students (Sappiens, 1979). The Catholic schools were initially state supported. In 1852, the state prohibited religious schools from receiving state funds (Leibowitz, 1971).

The State Bureau of Public Instruction, in 1855, stipulated that all schools must teach exclusively in English (Leibowitz, 1971). The Catholic Church initially led the fight opposing the imposition of English in California Schools, even by partially encouraging bilingual schooling, but soon after 1855, under the direction of the Baltimore Diocese, it was a primary proponent of assimilation (Leibowitz, 1971). In 1870, the California State legislature enacted a statute providing that all the schools in the state (religious and public) be taught in the English language (Leibowitz, 1971). This law superseded the State Bureau of Public Instruction's similar regulation of 1855.

After gold was discovered in 1849, a large number of Anglo, European, Latin American, and Asian sojourner workers and immigrants flooded to the northern California mountains to look for their fortune, quickly displacing in numbers the indigenous populations (Pitt, 1966). Southern California remained "Mexican" in population well into the 1870s. The state laws, however, were made in the north and not always favorable to what was perceived as the Mexican south. The English-only agitation continued, culminating in the Constitution of 1879 provision that prohibited the use of any other language for the publication of laws. Laws authorizing the publication of Spanish editions of session laws were formally repealed in 1897 (Fedynskyj, 1971).

California remained a predominantly English-only state until the 1960s and 1970s, when a liberal revision of the laws created an opening of sorts. In 1967, Senate Bill 53 allowed the use of other languages beside English as media of instruction in California public schools. This bill overturned the 1872 law requiring English-only instruction and opened the way for the 1974 Chacón-Moscone Bilingual-Bicultural Education Act, which established transitional bilingual education programs to meet the needs of students who could not speak English (who happened to be overwhelmingly of Mexican origin). Also, the California Supreme Court determined that Spanish literacy could satisfy the literacy requirement for voting in California under an equal protection standard (*Castro v. State of California*, 1970). California also adopted the Bilingual Services Act in 1974, to guide the provision of bilingual state government workers to meet the needs of constituents who spoke a language other than English and were limited in their English (Valdés, 2006; Valdés, Fishman, Chávez, & Pérez, 2006). Although the execution of the law has been much criticized, it was used as a blueprint for President Clinton's Executive Order 13166 (2000), which directed the federal government to seek the same goals by requiring departments and agencies to develop plans to serve limited English-proficient Americans. This liberalization of the language policies and recognition of Spanish was challenged in two policy areas in the 1980s and 1990s, when English became the symbolic official language of the state through popular initiative in 1986, and the California bilingual education law was similarly changed in 1998 to a "structured English immersion" program as the default treatment for public school students not proficient in English.

What Do We Take Away From This Truncated Summary of Official Recognitions of Spanish?

There is no question that Spanish has been an official language in the United States, and is such today. Not only California but also New Mexico, Colorado, Puerto Rico (see Álvarez-González, 1999; Language Policy Task Force, 1978), and other states and territories officially recognized languages other than English (Kloss, 1977), especially Spanish, for official purposes. It has been recognized at multiple levels of government as a recognition of the former sovereign in the area and as a recognition of substantial numbers of Spanish-speaking constituents in those jurisdictions.

Agreements with prior sovereigns of respecting, protecting, and even promoting the language of their former populations implicate the notion of involuntary "immigrants" but more specifically the creation of national minorities rather than immigrant minorities. These jurisdictions have used a territorial principle, and a proportionality principle, in executing these official Spanish policies, especially at the local level and the state level. Conflicts in legal authority by language have been worked out in various ways in different places. Additional costs for translations, interpretations, or administration in multiple languages have been rejected as not being sufficient for the state to prohibit Spanish language freedoms.

The consequences of these recognitions and uses of official Spanish include a better representative democracy between citizens and government. Neither civil society nor the state was harmed in recognizing official Spanish, whereas, often, State intervention prohibiting or restricting the use of non-English languages has caused harm, and maintained White privilege.

The Number of People Who Can Speak Spanish Has Steadily Increased in the United States and in North America, Since the Founding of the United States

The number of Spanish speakers has increased for over 150 years in the United States at a rate faster than the national population, the ethnic base of the Spanish-speaking population has become bilingual, and there is every indication the growth of Spanish speakers will continue into the near future.

Numbers and Distribution of Languages

The 118,000 Spanish speakers of 1850 represented about 0.5% of the total national population of about 23 million (see Table 1). In 2011, there were 34.7 million Spanish speakers in the country, representing 12.3% of the total national population of 308.7 million. Not only was there an increase in absolute numbers but a proportionate increase to the national population as well.

One should take note, however, that these languages may be grossly undercounted in the earlier years (see Macías, 2000b) as a result of identifying only onetime contributions to the national linguistic diversity. Another reason for a severe undercount in other sources is that they often do not include the population of Puerto Rico in

TABLE 1
Growth of the Spanish-Speaking Population in the United States, 1850–2011

| | | | | Total Spanish Speakers | |
| | | | | | |
Year	Total U.S. Population	Spanish Speakers on Mainland United States	Population of Puerto Rico	*N*	% (Of Total Population)
1850	23,191,876	118,000	—	118,000	0.5
1900	75,994,575	562,000	953,200	1,515,200	2.0
1960	178,464,236	3,336,000	2,349,500	5,685,500	3.2
2000	281,421,906	28,101,052	3,008,567	31,109,619	11.1
2011	308,745,538	34,745,940	3,323,245	38,069,185	12.3

Source. This table is a shortened version of Macías (2000b), Table 1, updated with data for 2011. Data for 2011 come from the American Community Survey estimates for that year.

these estimates, post 1898. A third reason for this undercount is that the U.S. Census reports language data in the first half of the 20th century limited to foreign White and native White of foreign or mixed parentage on the mainland (also see Leeman, 2004). The noninclusion of island Puerto Ricans and the racial qualifications of the records seriously distorts the linguistic diversity of the late 19th century and early 20th century, at least when it comes to the Spanish language. Again, the focus on the "immigrant" population in the early 20th century tends to distort the size and language character of indigenous racial/linguistic groups. The limits of mother tongue questions for "Whites" in 1910 and 1920 distort the figures, especially as Mexicans were not so classified.

Comparatively, the growth rate of Spanish speakers was also greater than the total number of speakers of other non-English languages. Between 1980 and 2007, the percentage of Spanish speakers increased 211%, all non-English speakers (not including Spanish) increased 140%, whereas the total national population grew by only 34%. Spanish speakers constituted 62.3% of the non-English language speakers in the United States in 2007, an increase from 48% in 1980. On the flip side, the population speaking only English in the United States went from 89% in 1980 to 80% in 2007. Lieberson and Curry (1971) echoed a conclusion from *Language Loyalty*, the major study on language shift in the first half of the 20th century (Fishman, 1966), that summarizes much of the history and exceptionality of Spanish language demography.

Compared with the situation in many nations, a staggering number of immigrants and their descendents in the United States have given up their ancestral languages and shifted to a new mother-tongue. Nearly two-thirds of the 35 million immigrants between 1840 and 1924 were native speakers of some other tongue. *Except for such groups as the Spanish-speaking residents of the Southwest* [italics added], the Pennsylvania Dutch, the French-speaking residents of New England, and the Creoles in the Louisiana Bayous, the shift to an English mother-tongue was both rapid and with relatively little inter-group conflict. (p. 125)

It is not possible to report on what has happened in the future, so confidently describing whether this past growth will continue into the future is a difficult task. Projections, trend analyses, and scenario building have all been used for strategic planning and extrapolating what may and what probably will happen in the future.

TABLE 2
Self-Reported Bilingualism, Latin@s in the United States, 1975, 1992, 2000, 2011

Year	Group, Age (Data Source)	% English Monolingual	% Bilingual	% Non-English Monolingual
1975	Spanish origin, 4 years + (Current Population Survey Supplement)	21.9	66.6	11.2
1992	Total Hispanic (National Adult Literacy Survey)	25.0	50.0	25.0
2000	Hispanic or Latin@, 5 years+ (Census)	21.4	54.5	23.6
2011	Hispanic or Latin@, 5 years+ (American Community Survey)	22.9	54.0	20.2

Source. See Estrada (1985), p. 385, Table 5; Greenberg, Macías, Rhodes, and Chan (2001) p. 31, Table 2.3; and U.S. Census Bureau, American Fact Finder website, Table PCT011 for the year 2000 data, and Table B16006 for the year 2011 data.

In predicting the future of Spanish, the most often used technique has been statistical projections. These language projections, however, have often been piggybacked, or based on ethnicity. The 2012 Census Bureau projections of the national population tell us several things regarding the composition of our nation's population and its possible future components through 2060 that are useful in projecting Spanish language futures. The numerical dominance of the White population will continue to decrease and may be less than half of the total school age population in a little more than one generation. Net immigration may continue with an 80% non-White contribution to the population growth. After 2020, within one generation, Latin@s may contribute more net growth to the U.S. population than all other groups combined. In effect, the United States is projected to become a more diverse nation.

According to the Census report, the White (not including Hispanic) population is projected to peak in 2024, at 199.6 million, up from 197.8 million in 2012. Unlike other race or ethnic groups, however, its population is projected to slowly decrease thereafter, falling by nearly 20.6 million from 2024 to 2060. Meanwhile, the Hispanic population would more than double, from 53.3 million in 2012 to 128.8 million in 2060. Consequently, by the end of the period, nearly one in three U.S. residents would be Hispanic, up from about one in six today. The United States is projected to become a majority-minority nation for the first time in 2043. Although the White (not including Hispanic) population will remain the largest single group, no group will make up a majority of the national population. This is a phenomenal prediction, even though it mirrors the minority status of Whites in the world population. That is, the U.S. national population will be more like the rest of the hemisphere, if not the rest of the world, than it has been in the dominant American imaginary. Minorities were 37% of the U.S. population in 2012 and are projected to comprise 57% of the population in 2060 (more than double, from 116.2 million to 241.3 million over the period).

If we assume a similar language distribution among Latin@s as in 2011 (74% spoke Spanish; see Table 2), then the number of Spanish speakers may be as large as 96 million in 2060, nearly tripling in size from 34.7 million in 2011.

TABLE 3
Self-Reported Oral Fluency and Literacy by Hispanic Subgroup, 1992

	English				Non-English		
Group	% Monolingual	% Monoliterate	% Bilingual	% Biliterate	% Monolingual	% Monoliterate	% Nonliterate
Total Hispanic	25.0	33.0	50.0	35.0	25.0	27.0	6.0
Mexican origin	25.0	34.0	48.0	30.0	27.0	29.0	7.0
Puerto Rican	20.0	27.0	66.0	51.0	13.0	16.0	6.0
Cuban	3.0	9.0	55.0	45.0	41.0	42.0	4.0
Central/South American	11.0	14.0	52.0	42.0	37.0	38.0	6.0
Hispanic Other	49.0	58.0	38.0	28.0	13.0	13.0	1.0

Source. Greenberg, Macías, Rhodes, and Chan (2001), Table 2.3, p. 31, and Table 2.4, p. 32.

Bilingualization of the Population

Even with the growth of the Spanish-speaking population in the United States, there are studies concluding that Chican@s, Puerto Ricans, and other Latin@s are shifting to English at an even greater rate than earlier European immigrants. These studies question the vitality of the Spanish language in the United States and its sustainability into the future without the contributions of new Spanish-speaking immigrants (see Porcel, 2011, for a discussion of the complexity of factors influencing language maintenance and shift). For our purpose in exploring this argument, the predictability of these studies is not controlling. That is, that even with the growth of Latin@ English speakers (monolinguals and bilinguals), the number of Spanish speakers continues to grow. The growth in numbers of the Spanish-speaking population has been appreciable in absolute terms and comparative terms, and it has spread to more areas of the country than the prior Mexican or Spanish colonial territories.

In the recent current language data sets, however, we can construct a category of bilinguals and of English and Spanish monolinguals, among Latin@s (see Tables 2 and 3), to explore this reality of acquiring and even shifting to English. The data cover a short period of time—between 1975 and 2011—but reflect a rather striking similarity across this time period, with a bit more than half the Latin@ population as bilinguals and 20% to 25% each as monolingual English or (presumably) Spanish.

There does not seem to be much variation in the bilingualization of the individual national origin groups. Cubans retain a high degree of Spanish monolingualism, whereas Other Hispanics reflects the opposite—a low Spanish monolingualism and nearly half as English monolinguals (see Table 3). We can still say that three quarters of the Latin@ population speak Spanish, and three quarters of the Latin@ population speak English, and be consistent and not contradictory. One can even argue that Latin@s in the United States have come to "own" English as well as Spanish as a speech community. Is this a stable situation in which more Latin@s learn English, become bilingual or English monolingual, but are refreshed with monolingual Spanish-speaking immigrants? Or will we find that as much as a quarter of the Spanish monolinguals are U.S. born, as we saw in 1976 (Estrada, 1985; Macías, 1985)? What is the role of Spanish language recovery and revival (beyond the teaching of Spanish for heritage speakers) for these English-speaking individuals after a lifetime of interacting with English-dominant schools and workplaces?

Another usual indicator of the stability of the language abilities among these populations is literacy in Spanish (see Table 3). We saw in the 1992 data (possibly) about a 15% lower rate of biliteracy overall than bilingualism (Greenberg, Macías, Rhodes, & Chan, 2001). It seemed that there were oral bilinguals who were literate only in English (about 7% or 8%), and a smaller number who were literate only in Spanish (about 2%), with a 4% to 7% nonliteracy rate across the groups. Of course, this data were from a single point in time, but it is the only nationally representative information we have on biliteracy in the United States.

Underlying the growth in the number of Spanish speakers is the stability of community structures within which to use the language, both a legacy of the prior sovereign's settlement in a good part of the country. There is an "opportunity structure" for Spanish that is stable and internal to the United States and external to the United States (neighboring Mexico is the largest Spanish-speaking country in the world with 110 million people; Lewis, Simons, & Fennig, 2013). Puerto Rico has a population that is 98% Spanish speaking. The United States is in the northern crown of a continent that has over 300 million speakers of Spanish (Godenzzi, 2006). This does not mean there are no counterforces promoting language shift or attempting to discourage or prohibit the use of the language (García, 2011; Mar-Molinero & Paffey, 2011). It does mean that, overall, Spanish speakers in the United States have increased in number despite them.

What Does This Argument Tell Us About the Status of Spanish?

This argument is about the size of the Spanish-speaking population in the United States, but it is also about sustainability and vitality, across time (historicity). Part of the question is whether the growth needs to continue or has the past growth been enough for a recognition of exceptional status? From a language policy perspective, does there need to be a guarantee of a speech community's size or continued growth for address? This argument makes the case that the growth over 150 years should count for something.

DISCUSSION

If we return to the eight arguments of Spanish as a second national language in the United States that we started with at the beginning of this essay and ask the question again as to whether Spanish has an exceptional status in the United States, how can we answer? In exploring only some of the arguments, we find logic, fact, if not merit, in them. We have seen that Spanish in the United States does not have a strictly immigrant status, nor can it simply be accepted as a colonial language, implying those who speak it to be descendants of colonial-settlers, ignoring the base of an indigenous gene pool among the majority of Spanish speakers in the country, if not the world. Spanish was planted more than 500 years ago in, and spread among the peoples of, the Western continent, and survives. It continues to grow in numbers of speakers and spreads more widely within the U.S. national territory and is being revived in places and newly spoken in other places. There is at least an appeal to Treaty protections regarding language and cultural liberties against a tide of dominant ideologies of assimilation and Anglo-Euro cultural parochialism. Factually, Spanish has had and has official status. Is this enough or do these arguments demand more? Must it be recognized, given an appropriate status of exceptionalism broadly, as the "second national language" of the country?

As we remember the rationales for various public policies attendant to language status and educational practice, at the beginning of this essay, we perforce return to the notion of language rights, with the freedoms, as well as the duties and obligations, inherent in the notion of rights, as a result of the political organization of communities and collectivities for (self-) governance of those communities.

More recently, in the past half century, the development of international linguistic and human rights has developed more robustly by reflecting on these issues. Language diversity was recognized in many of these discussions, even if language was not initially central to many of the documents that reflected the developing global consensus on the common bases for relationships between nations, and then, more specifically, the relationship between governments and those governed within whatever polity they might be (Macías, 1979). In 1996, the Universal Declaration of Linguistic Rights was completed by a nongovernmental organization, in collaboration with UNESCO, and has yet to be adopted by national governments. It expressed several principles or arguments regarding the rights to language that are useful to point out here—the different notions of a linguistic right and the notion of a linguistic community as a human collectivity.

The Declaration aims to be applicable to a great diversity of linguistic situations. It has therefore given special attention to the definition of the conceptual apparatus on which its articles are based. Thus, it considers as axes of a linguistic community: historicity, territoriality, self-identification as a people and the fact of having developed a common language as normal means for communication between its members. (Universal Declaration of Linguistic Rights Follow Up Committee, 1998)

This exploration of the facts and futures of Spanish in the United States certainly covers these four axes in the affirmative. If Spanish speakers are more specifically the Spanish-speaking linguistic community, then what might be its rights under this Universal Declaration? In a 15-year follow-up meeting (in 2011) of the groups involved in the development and adoption of the Universal Declaration of Linguistic Rights, a manifesto of the principles that should guide the implementation of the Declaration was developed and adopted (PEN International, 2011). It distilled 10 principles described as central for equitable linguistic human rights, reflecting a different set of values regarding language diversity than we saw above in Kloss's (1971) four "theories" and that bear on the status of Spanish in the United States.

1. Linguistic diversity is a world heritage that must be valued and protected.
2. Respect for all languages and cultures is fundamental to the process of constructing and maintaining dialogue and peace in the world.
3. All individuals learn to speak in the heart of a community that gives them life, language, culture, and identity.
4. Different languages and different ways of speaking are not only means of communication; they are also the milieu in which humans grow and cultures are built.
5. Every linguistic community has the right for its language to be used as an official language in its territory.
6. School instruction must contribute to the prestige of the language spoken by the linguistic community of the territory.
7. It is desirable for citizens to have a general knowledge of various languages, because it fosters empathy and intellectual openness, and contributes to a deeper knowledge of one's own tongue.
8. The translation of texts, especially the great works of various cultures, represents a very important element in the necessary process of greater understanding and respect among human beings.
9. The media is a privileged loudspeaker for making linguistic diversity work and for competently and rigorously increasing its prestige.
10. The right to use and protect one's own language must be recognized by the United Nations as one of the fundamental human rights. (PEN International, 2011)

Some countries have adopted new language and cultural policies based more closely on these values, recognizing the language diversity within their borders as part of their national linguistic patrimony. The United States recognized some of these values in adopting the Native American Languages Act in 1990. Mexico adopted Constitutional changes in 2001, recognizing all indigenous languages as coequal in status with Spanish and as part of their national cultural patrimony (Althoff, 2006). These documents, laws, and constitutional changes reflect a different set of ideas regarding language diversity and sociopolitical organization from those on which many language policies are now based in the United States and abroad of one nation one language. Some even argue that there is a new emerging national political linguistic norm in Europe—that bastion, nay root, of one nation one language—that is, national bi- and multilingualism (de Varennes, 2004). Single nation-language nationalism is giving way to additive multilingualism through the construction of the European Union (Mar-Molinero & Stevenson, 2006). Equitable language rights are being discussed and litigated and charters of protection drawn up (Vollebaek, 2010).

Given the Universal Declaration of Linguistic Rights, it would seem that there can be equitable rights for all linguistic communities within each polity, whether based on proportionality, personality, territoriality, historicity, or other principles. Using the Declaration as a guide to "given" status, what would this look like in the United States (for a different rationale and view of the possible futures, or hopeful ones, see Fishman, 2006)?

- Official recognition and use of Spanish (along with English) in all jurisdictions in which there is a historical and significant presence of Spanish speakers
- The end to anti-Spanish language legislation—including English-only policies and English-restrictive policies, especially those that impede the exercise of fundamental human and civil rights
- Affirmatively support the official recognition and use of Spanish, along with English, in the public schools in those areas where there are concentrations of Spanish speakers, or heritage speakers for language recovery purposes
- No condition for statehood for Puerto Rico on an English-speaking majority
- Establish interpreter and translation services, even multilingual tracks, in public services, courts, health, and communications
- Establish a respect for language diversity; recognition and support of all languages especially at local levels where concentration, continuity, historicity, and desire provide a threshold for its recognition and use

With these changes in approach, values, policies, and practices, then Spanish would definitely have a given status as a second national language in the United States. But if our response is based on the ideologies of the past, which supported language imposition and were a mechanism of maintaining White privilege, then this status as a second national language will be merely a descriptor of the language diversity of the country and little more, until democratic demands to the contrary.

REFERENCES

Alonso, C. (2006). Spanish: The foreign national language. *ADFL Bulletin, 37*(2–3), 15–20.

Althoff, F. D. (2006). Centralization vs. local initiatives: Mexican and U.S. legislation of Amerindian languages. In M. Hidalgo (Ed.), *Mexican indigenous languages at the dawn of the twenty-first century* (pp. 167–191). Berlin, Germany: Mouton de Gruyter.

Álvarez-González, J. (1999). Law, language and statehood: The role of English in the great state of Puerto Rico. *Law and Inequality, 17,* 359–443.

Belz, H. (2001). Popular sovereignty, the right of revolution, and California Statehood. *Nexus. 6,* 3–22.

Castro v. State of California, 2 Cal. 3d 223 (1970).

Castro, R. (1977). The Bilingual Education Act—A historical analysis of Title VII. In R. F. Macías (Ed.), *Perspectivas en Chicano Studies I. Papers presented at the Third Annual Meeting of the National Association of Chicano Social Science, 1975* (pp. 81–122). Los Angeles, CA: National Association of Chicano Social Science and UCLA Chicano Studies Center.

Cox, R. (1976). Spain and the founding fathers. *Modern Language Journal, 60*(3), 101–109.

Crawford, J. (1993). *Hold your tongue: Bilingualism and the politics of "English only."* Reading, MA: Addison-Wesley.

de Varennes, F. (2004, May). *Pax lingua, pax humanus: Linguistic rights as a foundation for peace.* Keynote speech at the Linguistic Diversity and Sustainability Forum, Barcelona, Spain.

Estrada, L. (1985). The extent of Spanish/English bilingualism and language loyalty in the United States. *Aztlán, 15,* 379–392.

Ewing, J. A. (1918). Education in California during the pre-statehood period. *Annual Publication of the Historical Society of Southern California, 11,* 51–59.

Fedynskyj, J. (1971). State session laws in non-English languages: A chapter of American legal history. *Indiana Law Journal, 46*, 463–478.

Fishman, J. (1966). *Language loyalty in the United States: The maintenance and perpetuation of non-English mother tongues by American ethnic and religious groups.* The Hague, Netherlands: Mouton.

Fishman, J. (2006). Imagining linguistic pluralism in the United States. In G. Valdés, J. A. Fishman, R. Chávez, & W. Pérez (Eds.), *Developing minority language resources: The case of Spanish in California* (pp. 273–288). Clevedon, England: Multilingual Matters.

García, O. (2011). Planning Spanish: Nationalizing, minoritizing, and globalizing performances. In M. Díaz-Campos (Ed.), *Handbook of Hispanic sociolinguistics* (pp. 667–685). Malden, MA: Wiley-Blackwell.

Godenzzi, J. (2006). Spanish as a lingua franca. *Annual Review of Applied Linguistics, 26*, 100–122.

Gray, E. (1999). *New world Babel: Languages and nations in Early America.* Princeton, NJ: University of Princeton Press.

Gray, E., & Fiering, N. (Eds.). (2000). *The language encounter in the Americas, 1492-1800.* New York, NY: Berghahn Books.

Greenberg, E., Macías, R. F., Rhodes, D., & Chan, T. (2001). *English literacy and language minorities in the United States* ([NCES 2001-464). Washington, DC: U.S. Department of Education, National Center for Educational Statistics.

Griswold del Castillo, R. G. (1990). *The Treaty of Guadalupe Hidalgo: A legacy of conflict.* Norman: University of Oklahoma Press.

Gutiérrez, F. (1977). Spanish language media in America: Background, resources, history. *Journalism History, 4*(2), 34–41.

Heath, S. (1972). *Telling tongues: Language policy in Mexico, colony to nation.* New York, NY: Teachers College Press.

Heath, S. (1976). Colonial language status achievement: Mexico, Peru and the United States. In A. Verdoodt & R. Kjolseth (Eds.), *Language in sociology* (pp. 49–92). Louvain, Belgium: Institute de Linguistique de Louvain & Éditions Peeters.

Hidalgo, M. (Ed.). (2006). *Mexican indigenous languages at the dawn of the twenty-first century.* Berlin, Germany: Mouton de Gruyter.

Huntington, S. (2004). The Hispanic challenge. *Foreign Policy, March-April*, 30–45.

Johnson v. McIntosh, 1823, 21 US (8 Wheat.) 543, 5 L.Ed. 681.

Kloss, H. (1971). Language rights of immigrant groups. *International Migration Review, 5*, 250–268.

Kloss, H. (1977). *The American bilingual tradition.* Rowley, MA: Newbury House.

Klotz, E. (1968). The honest and the glorious. In *El Tratado de Guadalupe Hidalgo, 1848* (pp. 10–28). Sacramento, CA: Telefact Foundation.

Language Policy Task Force. (1978). Language policy and the Puerto Rican community. *Bilingual Review/La Revista Bilingüe, 5*, 1–39.

Leeman, J. (2004). Racializing language: A history of linguistic ideologies in the US census. *Journal of Language and Politics, 3*, 507–534.

Leibowitz, A. (1971). *Educational policy and political acceptance: The imposition of English as the language of instruction in American schools.* Washington, DC: ERIC Clearinghouse for Linguistics, Center for Applied Linguistics. (ERIC Document Reproduction Service No. ED 047321).

Leibowitz, A. (1976). Language and the law: The exercise of power through official designation of language. In W. O'Barr & J. O'Barr (Eds.), *Language and politics* (pp. 449–466). The Hague, Netherlands: Mouton.

Leibowitz, A. (1984). The official character of English in the United States: Literacy requirements for immigration, citizenship, and entrance into American life. *Aztlán, 15*, 25–70.

Lepore, J. (1998). *The name of war: King Philip's war and the origins of American identity.* New York, NY: Vintage Books.

Lewis, M. P., Simons, G. F., & Fennig, C. D. (Eds.). (2013). *Ethnologue: Languages of the world* (17th ed.). Dallas, Texas: SIL International. Retrieved from http://www.ethnologue.com.

Lieberson, S., & Curry, T. (1971). Language shift in the United States: Some demographic clues. *International Migration Review, 5,* 123–137.

Lozano, R. (2011). Translating California: Official Spanish usage in California's constitutional conventions and state legislature, 1848-1894. *California Legal History, 6,* 321–355.

Macías, R. F. (1979). Language choice and human rights in the U.S. In J. Alatis (Ed.), *Georgetown University round table on languages and linguistics, 1979. Language in public life* (pp. 86–101). Washington, DC: Georgetown University Press.

Macías, R. F. (1985). National language profiles of the Mexican origin population in the U.S. In W. Connor (Ed.), *Mexican Americans in comparative perspective* (pp. 283–308). Washington, DC: The Urban Institute Press.

Macías, R. F. (2000a). Language politics and the sociolinguistic historiography of Spanish in the United States. In P. Griffin, J. Peyton, W. Wolfram, & R. Fasold (Eds.), *Language in action: New studies of language in society* (pp. 52–83). Cresskill, NJ: Hampton Press.

Macías, R. F. (2000b). The flowering of America: Linguistic diversity in the United States. In S. McKay & S. Wong (Eds.), *New immigrants in the United States* (pp. 11–57). Cambridge, England: Cambridge University Press.

Mar-Molinero, C., & Paffey, D. (Eds.). (2011). Linguistic imperialism: Who owns global Spanish? In M. Díaz-Campos (Ed.), *Handbook of Hispanic sociolinguistics* (pp. 747–764). Malden, MA: Wiley-Blackwell.

Mar-Molinero, C., & Stevenson, P. (Eds.). (2006). *Language ideologies, policies and practices: Language and the future of Europe.* Basingstoke, England: Palgrave Macmillan.

Martínez, O. (1975). On the size of the Chicano population: New estimates, 1850-1900. *Aztlán, 6,* 43–68.

Parodi, C. (2006). The indianization of Spaniards in New Spain. In M. Hidalgo (Ed.), *Mexican indigenous languages at the dawn of the twenty-first century* (pp. 29–52). Berlin, Germany: Mouton de Gruyter.

PEN International. (2011). *Girona [Spain] Manifesto on Linguistic Rights.* Retrieved from http://pen-international.org/who-we-are/translation-linguistic-rights/girona-manifesto/girona-manifesto-on-linguistic-rights/

Pitt, L. (1966). *The decline of the Californios: A social history of the Spanish-speaking Californians, 1846-1890.* Berkeley: University of California Press.

Porcel, J. (2011). Language maintenance and language shift among US Latinos. In M. Díaz-Campos (Ed.), *Handbook of Hispanic sociolinguistics* (pp. 623–645). Malden, MA: Wiley-Blackwell.

Ruiz, M. (1972). *Mexican American legal heritage in the southwest.* Los Angeles, CA: Author.

Sappiens, A. (1979). Spanish in California. *Journal of Communication, 29*(2), 72–83.

Spaeth, H., & Smith, E. (1991). *The Constitution of the United States* (13th ed.). New York, NY: HarperPerennial.

Terborg, R., García Landa, L., & Moore, P. (2007). Language planning in Mexico. In R. Baldauf & R. Kaplan (Eds.), *Language planning and policy: Latin America: Vol. 1. Ecuador, Mexico and Paraguay* (pp. 115–217). Clevedon, England: Multilingual Matters.

Universal Declaration of Linguistic Rights Follow-Up Committee. (1998). *Universal declaration of linguistic rights.* Barcelona, Spain: Author. Retrieved from http://www.linguistic-declaration.org/llibre-gb.htm

U.S. Census Bureau. (2012, December 12). *US Census Bureau projections show a slower growing, older, more diverse nation a half century from now (Press Release CB12-243)*. Washington, DC: Author.

Valdés, G. (2006). The Spanish language in California. In G. Valdés, J. A. Fishman, R. Chávez, & W. Pérez (Eds.), *Developing minority language resources: The case of Spanish in California* (pp. 24–53). Clevedon, England: Multilingual Matters.

Valdés, G., Fishman, J., Chávez, R., & Pérez, W. (2006). *Developing minority language resources: The case of Spanish in California*. Clevedon, England: Multilingual Matters.

Vollebaek, K. (2010, February). *Languages in social integration: Balancing the unbalanceable?* Plenary address by the High Commissioner on National Minorities, Organization for Security and Co-operation in Europe, Bratislava, Slovak Republic. Retrieved from http://www.osce.org/hcnm/41837

Wiley, T. (1999). Comparative historical perspectives in the analysis of U.S. language policies. In T. Heubner & C. Davis (Eds.), *Political perspectives on language planning and language policy* (pp. 17–37). Amsterdam, Netherlands: John Benjamins.

Wiley, T. (2006). The lessons of historical investigation: Implications for the study of language policy and planning. In T. Ricento (Ed.), *Language policy: Essential readings*, (pp. 136–152). London, England: Blackwell.

Wiley, T., & Lukes, M. (1996). English-only and standard English ideologies in the United States. *TESOL Quarterly, 30*, 511–535.

Wolf, E. (1959). *Sons of the shaking earth—People of Mexico and Guatemala: Their land, history and culture*. Chicago, IL: University of Chicago Press.

Chapter 3

U.S. Spanish and Education: Global and Local Intersections

OFELIA GARCÍA

City University of New York

Spanish, as we know it today, made its debut as "a world language" at the very end of the 15th century in a highly heterogeneous languagescape—the newly constructed nation-state of Spain and the newly found Americas.[1] Spanish grappled with bringing together the many forms of Romance spoken in Castile and Aragon at the same time when it was brought to new shores where people spoke in other ways. Thus, what we know as Spanish today emerged from contact with people who languaged very differently, both within the Iberian Peninsula and in the overseas colonies. Interestingly, the spread of "Spanish" was not simply imposed by the Crown on its subjects by coercion but was rather a product of hegemony. It was the authority gained by the wealth in the colonies, its coloniality (Mignolo, 2000), that gave Spanish its power and prestige and the impetus to spread in the Peninsula itself. From its very beginning, Spanish became the language of Empire as a result of its colonial condition.

In much the same way, Spanish today has achieved global status[2] precisely because of its coloniality. It is the colonial relationship that Latin America has maintained with the United States that has resulted in the presence of 50.6 million Latinos in the United States, representing 16% of the U.S. population (U.S. Census Bureau, 2010). And it is the buying power of subaltern subjects, now in one of the most powerful countries in the world, that is giving Spanish its authority as it positions itself globally. However, as in the 16th century, it is not the *languaging* of colonial subjects— that is, their language practices—that are favored. As we will see, the language planning agencies of Spain, and those operating in Latin America, continue to attempt to impose certain language regimes on those they still consider colonial subjects. As the Spanish state exploits the great number of Spanish speakers in the United States to bolster the sociolinguistic situation of Spanish within its own national borders and

Review of Research in Education
March 2014, Vol. 38, pp. 58-80
DOI: 10.3102/0091732X13506542
© 2014 AERA. http://rre.aera.net

abroad, the United States imposes English on Latinos by constructing Spanish speakers as inferior subaltern subjects.

Much distance separates the 16th century from the 21st century. In the 21st century, as globalization and its new technologies have spurred the movement of people, information, and goods across the world, nation-states are caught simultaneously in acts of interrelationship and acts of self-protection. The diasporic people who are Spanish speaking today show, more than ever, the effects of dynamic and changing sociopolitical arrangements. Despite much early movement of people and transgression of borders (see, e.g., the Inca Garcilaso's *Comentarios Reales*), from the 16th century until the 20th century the language diversity of Spain and of what became Latin America was contained within political borders. Today, however, space itself has lost its territorial boundaries. It is individuals that embody space, and their interactions contain features associated with what we have learned to call different languages (see Blommaert, 2010; Makoni & Pennycook, 2007; Pennycook, 2010). In the past, the language diversity of Spain, Latin America, and the United States could be "hidden" from public view because the discourse was controlled by a single national power with a monoglossic discourse against diverse and heterogeneous practices. Today, however, language practices neither correspond to official national borders nor respond to a single center of power or express a unitary identity.

In the 21st century there has been increased recognition of a new sociolinguistic arrangement of mobile linguistic resources (Blommaert, 2010; Canagarajah, 2013). And yet there is little recognition of these new ways of languaging in education. It is precisely the clash between educational systems that have been designed to protect or promote the nation-state as the preferred form of political organization and its nationalist linguistic identity, and the ways in which speakers, now in mobile interactions across spaces use and embody language practices to break out from the control of nation-states, that results in much educational failure and the resulting academic inequity among groups.

This chapter will argue that the failure of Spanish language education policies in the United States to educate both Latinos and non-Latinos has to do with the clash between three positions—(a) the English language, characterized by U.S. educational authorities as the unique and powerful lingua franca; (b) the Spanish language, as defined by the language authorities in Spain and Latin America as a global language of influence; and (c) language as lived and practiced by bilingual Latino speakers. U.S. educational policies treat the "Spanish" of its Latino students as a problem to be eradicated because of negative attitudes toward bilingualism. At the same time, U.S. educational policies also view the "English" of "nonnative" Latinos as a problem, guaranteeing that monolingual English speakers conserve advantages (for a critique of the concept of "native," see especially Bonfiglio, 2010). The language authorities of Spain and Latin America also see U.S. "Spanish" as a problem, needing remediation. Yet, at the same time, Spain needs U.S. Spanish to bolster the status of Spanish as a global language. It is U.S. Spanish, as spoken in one of the most powerful nations in the world, that is the dagger in the heart of global Spanish as constructed by Spain, as well as the motor driving what may be a global use of Spanish. It is also U.S. Spanish that pierces the bubble of U.S. English. The result of these irreconcilable positions has been the failure of Spanish language education policies in the United States to educate U.S. Latinos and promote their bilingualism.

Recently, there has been a marked increase in all Spanish language education programs in the United States. But as we will see in this article, Spanish language education programs in the United States have not been very successful. This chapter will argue that the failure of these Spanish as a "foreign" language programs also lies in their insistence that Spanish, the "target" language, be kept separate from English, which is linked tightly to a U.S. monolingual identity. Spanish is promoted as a global language of authority outside the United States, and at the same time, it distances itself from the practices of bilingual subaltern subjects. The result, as we will see, is the failure of Spanish language education in the United States for all.

Because language education policy is the purview of nation-states as they organize educational programs and curricula, this chapter starts by offering a historical perspective of how Spanish was linguistically constituted. It does so to help us understand the role that teaching Spanish, and in Spanish, has had in promoting the standardization and spread of Spanish from its origins in Castile to its global position today, especially in the United States.

The chapter then focuses on the teaching of Spanish in the United States and the relationship of ideologies and practices on Spanish language education policy, as carried out internally by federal, state, and local U.S. educational agencies, as well as by external agencies controlled by Spain. In bringing all these perspectives together, the chapter contributes to the understanding that the future of successful Spanish language teaching and learning in the United States, as well as the academic success of Latinos in U.S. schools, rests on the acceptance of practices that honor their fluid bilingual languaging—their *translanguaging* (García, 2009a). As we will see, teaching U.S. Latinos today without including their Spanish language practices restricts their voices, knowledge, opportunities, and imagination. But teaching Spanish today as *a* language without taking into account translanguaging does not support bilingual students' advancement in the globalized world of the 21st century. The chapter ends with a description of how translanguaging in education can be used to create a U.S. bilingual trans-subject, able to appropriate Spanish language practices into their entire linguistic repertoire.

CONSTRUCTING A SPACE FOR "SPANISH": SPAIN, LATIN AMERICA, AND THE UNITED STATES

Spanish was linguistically constituted slowly. During the 10th and 11th centuries, the variety spoken in northern Old Castile and Burgos grew in importance, spurred by the military success of Castile in the *Reconquista* against the Moors (718–1492). Hall (1974) explains, "Concomitantly with the *Reconquista*, the Castilian dialect became the standard for the regions which came under Castilian rule, gradually over-laying the other regional koinés such as Asturian, Leonese, Aragonese, and the conservative Mozarabic spoken in the central area" (p. 121). López-García (1985) has argued that Castilian emerged as a koiné, as a way to ensure that those who spoke Basque and Romance would understand each other. In the 13th century Alfonso X The Wise (1221–1284) compiled Castile's legal tradition in his *Siete Partidas* (1265) and codified the orthography of Castilian, modeled on the speech of the upper class of Toledo. It was this orthography that became the expected medium in courtly writing during this time (R. Wright, 1997).

With the marriage of the Catholic Monarchs, Isabella I of Castile and Ferdinand of Aragon in 1469, the crowns of Aragon/Catalonia and Castile/Leon/Galicia were united. Through that political union, the dialectal group that became known as Castilian gained power and authority. In 1492, as the Moorish kingdom of Granada surrendered, Antonio de Nebrija published his *Gramática de la Lengua Castellana*, the first grammar of any Romance language. Nebrija dedicates the grammar to Queen Isabella: "*Siempre la lengua fue compañera del imperio*" ["Language always was the companion of empire"]. A single "Spanish" language was needed to rule its subjects.

It was the nascent Spanish of the 16th century that was used by missionaries in the *catequización* of the indigenous population to Catholicism (Briceño Perozo, 1987). On June 7, 1550, Charles V issued an edict that Spanish be used in evangelization in the Viceroyalty of New Spain, including most of what is today the United States west of the Mississippi River, and the Floridas. A great number of pedagogical material in Spanish, including textbooks, dictionaries, and grammars (called *artes*), were shipped to the Americas. But the failure of teaching Catholicism in a language that was not understood led to a change in policy. In 1570, King Phillip II authorized the use of the indigenous languages of vast territories, what became known as *lenguas generales*, to evangelize. And in 1596, he formalized the diglossic compartmentalized arrangement between the languages of its territories that was to remain in force until the 21st century—Spanish for administration and for the elite, and the local indigenous languages for daily communication within indigenous communities and for evangelization (García, López, & Makar, 2010; Hamel, 1994).

Although Castilian remained the language of White European *conquistadores* in the dominions of the Spanish Empire and was not taken up by most of the indigenous population during the 16th and 17th century, a similar sociolinguistic situation existed within Spain. When the border with Portugal was drawn in 1640, and the one with France in 1659 after the Thirty Years War, Castilian was not, by any means, the language of the territory among all social classes. Promoting Castilian became a priority of the state (S. Wright, 2004).

In 1713, the Real Academia Española was founded on instructions of Philip V, the first Bourbon ruler of Spain, to guarantee a Spanish norm and to "*velar por que los cambios que experimente [. . .] no quiebren la esencial unidad que mantiene en todo el ámbito hispánico*" ["to watch that the changes that it undergoes [. . .] do

not disrupt the essential unity that it maintains in the entire Hispanic context"]
(http://noticias.juridicas.com/base_datos/Admin/rd1109-1993.html#a1). That is,
the Academy's principal task was to ensure the unity of Spanish throughout a highly
multilingual Spanish-speaking world. Thus, the motto of the Academy was "*limpia,
fija y da esplendor*" ["cleans, fixes, and gives splendor"]. A year later, in 1714, Castilian
was declared the language of the state, and in 1768, King Charles III of Spain decreed
that there should be one language and one currency in his kingdom, including its
colonies. At that time, 78% of the population of New Spain spoke indigenous languages (Cifuentes & del Consuelo Ros, 1993). Monolingual education for indigenous minorities in the dominions of the Spanish Empire became the policy and has
remained so today, for the most part.

After four centuries of colonial relations, Spain lost much of the territories that
had been part of its Empire, as King Charles IV abdicated to Napoleon Bonaparte,
bringing an end to Spain's "sovereign power." As we will see, the democratic discourses
of Enlightenment thinking were produced as part of new relations of power, which
included the growing imperialist designs of the newly constituted United States and
the independence of Latin American countries.

The weakened status of the Spanish state led, on one hand, to the aggressive
moves of the United States to acquire what had been part of the Spanish Empire
and, on the other, to the independence movement of Latin American countries.
In 1803, the United States purchased Louisiana from France, and in 1819, it
acquired Florida under the Adams–Onís treaty, renouncing claims to Texas. As
the Spanish Empire crumbled in the early 19th century, Latin American countries
gained independence.

In 1845, the United States annexed Texas. This led to the Mexican American War,
which resulted in the Treaty of Guadalupe Hidalgo (February 2, 1948), by which
Mexico ceded territory amounting to 500,000 square miles that today encompasses
California, Nevada, New Mexico, Utah, most of Arizona and Colorado, and parts of
Texas, Oklahoma, Kansas, and Wyoming, beside giving the United States undisputed
control of Texas (Rives, 1918).

To carry out the policy of Manifest Destiny, the United States adopted an attitude
of Protestant superiority, arguing that its imperialist designs improved the lives of
those who were "ignorant" and "backward" (García, 2011a). Only Mexicans considered to be White were permitted citizenship and allowed to attend schools with
Anglo Whites in the Southwest territories.

Almost from the beginning of the creation of independent Latin American states,
as well as the annexation of Spanish-speaking territories to the United States, the
Spanish language and its teaching in schools was a topic of great concern. In the
newly formed Latin American countries, Spanish, spoken by the ruling elite of
European descent, served to form a sense of nation, ignoring the many other languages (del Valle & Stheeman, 2002). The affirmation of American Spanish, continued from Castilian despite some differences, became an important consideration.

In 1847, Andrés Bello (1781–1865), born in Caracas before independence, published his *Gramática de la lengua castellana destinada al uso de los americanos* [Castilian Grammar Intended for Use by Americans]. In the prologue, Bello argues that the Spanish language should conserve what he calls "*su pureza*" ["its purity"] so as to ensure a common language between the two continents. And yet Bello argues that Latin American countries have as much right as regions of Spain to have their own differences but adds that this is so only "*cuando las patrocina la costumbre uniforme y auténtica de la gente educada*" ["when it is sponsored by the regular and authentic use of people who are well educated"]. A diglossic relationship was once more established between the Spanish of the White European-descent elite and the languages of the indigenous groups or African slaves. Only the Spanish of the White elite was accepted for use in government and education, with the languages of the Others remaining outside of official domains.

In 1870, the Real Academia Española authorized the establishment of what became known as *Academias Correspondientes* in the Americas. The agreement talked about "*repúblicas americanas españolas, hoy independientes, pero siempre hermanas nuestras por el idioma*" ["American republics of Spain, independent today, but always our sisters because of the language"] because "*una misma lengua hablamos*" ["we speak one language"] (quoted in Lázaro, 1994). It warned that unless there was a strong defense of the Castilian language, "*llegará la lengua en aquella tan patria como la nuestra a bastardearse . . .*" ["the language will become bastardized in that which is as much fatherland as ours"]. The *Academias Correspondientes* were finally able to "*oponer un dique, más poderoso tal vez que las bayonetas mismas, al espíritu invasor de la raza anglo-sajona en el mundo por Colón descubierto*" ["oppose a dike, perhaps more powerful than even the bayonets, to the invading spirit of the Anglo-Saxon race in the world that was discovered by Columbus"]. And perhaps it is this last statement that better reveals the difficulties of teaching Spanish in the Americas, with Spanish seen as a bayonet that must divide languages into hierarchical camps and as a dike that stops the flows not only between Spanish and the languages of Indigenous peoples but also between Spanish and the language of the great U.S. Empire––English. As a result, 19 *Academias Correspondientes* were established after 1871 in Latin America. As Spanish spread in the Americas north of the Rio Grande and beyond its original territories, the Spanish of the United States also had to be reined in. Thus, in 1973, the *Academia Norteamericana de La Lengua* was established in New York. As we will see, maintaining the dike between Spanish and English so as to stop the flow from English became an obsession in U.S. Spanish language teaching, the subject of the next section.

THE ROLE OF SPANISH TEACHING IN NATIONAL CONSTRUCTIONS

A standardized Spanish, referred to as "Castilian" in most of Spain and "Spanish" in most of the Americas (with the exception of the Southern Cone), was upheld with a heavy hand in schools in Spain and Latin America and imposed in the few spaces in the United States where Spanish was taught, always in an inferior position to English. The Black Legend, promoting tales of cruelty of the *conquistadores* and the Inquisition to justify the U.S. imperialistic designs, meant that the learning of Spanish was never much valued.

Spanish for trade, and as spoken by White Europeans, was judged positively at the beginning of U.S. history. For example, Thomas Jefferson suggested to his nephew: "Bestow great attention on Spanish and endeavor to acquire an accurate knowledge of it. Our future connections with Spain and Spanish America will render that language of valuable acquisition" (quoted in García, 1993, p. 73).

Spanish was first introduced in U.S. higher education at Harvard University in 1816, but it was only taught through reading-translation, and mostly as a way to develop linguistic discipline in English. The Modern Language Association, which came into being in 1883, paid little attention to the Spanish spoken in the Southwest territories (García, 1993). The American Association of Teachers of Spanish and Portuguese (AATSP) was established in New York in 1917, to counteract the teaching of German in secondary schools, now the enemy in World War I. But "foreign" language study was not in any way encouraged in elementary schools, and the position of AATSP was that "the best modern Spanish . . . is that spoken by the educated people of Old and New Castile" (Espinosa, 1923, p. 244). The Modern Foreign Language Study of 1929 recommended that language study be limited to 2 years and that students be taught only to read (Huebener, 1961).

The late 19th and early 20th centuries were years of restriction of languages other than English in the United States. However, these were years of intensive immigration, especially from southern and eastern Europe. Theodore Roosevelt recommended that immigrants who had not learned English after 5 years should be returned to their countries (García, 2009a) and in 1915 said,

We have room for but one language here, and that is the English language, for we intend to see that the crucible turns our people out as Americans, of American nationality, and not as dwellers in a polyglot boarding house. (quoted in Edwards, 1994, p. 166)

The melting pot, the metaphor made popular in Israel Zangwill's 1908 play, was in full force, and U.S. schools reacted accordingly.

By 1923, 34 states had passed laws requiring that English be the sole language of instruction in U.S. public schools. In 1855 in California, English had been declared the only language of instruction (Castellanos, 1983), and in New Mexico an 1891 statute required all schools to teach in English. The tide, however, started to turn in 1923 when the U.S. Supreme Court struck down language-restrictive laws in Nebraska, Idaho, and Ohio in *Meyer v. Nebraska*. But in 1949, the report *What the High Schools Ought to Teach* characterized foreign-language study as useless and time-consuming. And Harvard's *General Education in a Free Society* report declared that foreign-language study was only useful "to improve one's English" (Huebener, 1961, p. 14).

In the meantime, the Mexican American community in the southwest became more excluded from Spanish language education, and those who continued to arrive were placed in segregated schools where the focus was the learning of English. In 1942, the Bracero program allowed the entry of short-term Mexican contract laborers for agricultural work. They joined not only other Mexican Americans but also the growing number of Puerto Ricans who, as U.S. citizens since the Jones Act of 1917, were headed to the factories of the northeast. Spanish was increasingly seen as the language of conquered or dominated people of color. These Spanish-speaking Latinos were now coming into a depressed U.S. economy that was rapidly changing, and the public schools that were meant to educate the population were failing Latinos in large numbers. In the early 1940s, Texas, New Mexico, and Florida introduced Spanish into some elementary classrooms to help Latino children. In 1953, the New York City Board of Education commissioned a study, "Teaching Children of Puerto Rican Background in New York City Schools," which recommended that the Spanish language be used in the education of Puerto Rican children. Increasingly schools started to experiment with using Spanish in the education of Latino children with the purpose of ensuring not only their comprehension of academic content but also their shift to English (García, 2009a).

KEEPING IT SEPARATE

The two positions—one reluctantly favoring the teaching of Spanish as a "foreign language" to White Anglo students and the other grudgingly supporting the use of Spanish to teach Spanish-speaking children—came to the forefront during the 1960s, although they remained strictly separate. On the one hand, Russia's launch of Sputnik resulted in considering "foreign" language study as a possible instrument for defense. The National Defense and Education Act, passed in 1958, provided financial assistance for the teaching of foreign languages. For the first time, language education programs were introduced into elementary schools (Foreign Language in the Elementary Schools), countering attitudes held in the early part of the century. On the other hand, the Civil Rights Era brought to the forefront the racial and language discrimination that Latino students were experiencing in U.S. schools. Mexican Americans and Puerto Ricans joined African Americans in demanding equal rights, and during this brief period, Latinos were effective in asserting the importance of the use of Spanish in their education. Many bilingual education programs were established. In 1963, the Coral Way Elementary School started a two-way bilingual education program that included Cuban American children whose parents wanted to ensure that they continued to develop academic Spanish, as they acquired English, as well as Anglo-Miamians who wanted their children to learn Spanish to deal with the growing Cuban population. Mexican American communities also established bilingual education programs to maintain and develop the Spanish of their children in Texas, New Mexico, California, and Arizona (Castellanos, 1983, García, 2009a). For the first time, in 1965, the American Association of Teachers of Spanish and Portuguese acknowledged that U.S. Latinos might make good Spanish teachers (García, 1993). But despite the greater acknowledgement of the importance of Spanish language teaching both for Anglos and Latinos, the two traditions remained separate.

As a result of much lobbying by civil rights groups and Latino advocacy groups, the Bilingual Education Act (Title VII of the Elementary and Secondary Education Act) was passed in 1968, granting federal funds to school districts that had a large number of students who were not proficient in English—mostly, at that time, Spanish speakers and Native Americans. In 1965, the Immigration and Naturalization Act was amended, abolishing national-origin quotas and ushering in immigration especially from Latin America but also from Asia and other non-Western nations.

By the time the Bilingual Education Act was reauthorized in 1974, it limited the use of Spanish (and other languages other than English) in education until children learned English. That is, bilingual education was defined as transitional, with the explicit goal being the "mainstreaming" of children into English-only classrooms. In 1974, the U.S. Supreme Court ruled in *Lau v. Nichols*: "There is no equality of treatment merely by providing students with the same facilities, textbooks, teachers and curriculum; for students who do not understand English are effectively foreclosed from any meaningful education." Something had to be done for Latino students.

Although the federal U.S. bilingual education policy was now transitional, Latino educators continued to organize "developmental maintenance bilingual education" for their children in which interactive language practices were used. Because of the suspicion of the so-called stigmatized code-switching, bilingual teachers were not taught to use these linguistic interactions strategically. Although some early efforts were made to call attention to the possible value of using languages flexibly (what Jacobson, 1981, called "concurrent translation"), the educational authorities started to call for language separation, valuing educational success only from a monolingual perspective.

In the meantime, the "foreign-" language profession was progressing without much contact with the bilingual education field. Teachers of Spanish as a "foreign" language continued to be mostly Anglos. In 1979, President Carter established a Presidential Commission to study the status of foreign-language study in the United States. The recommendations of the Commission of Foreign Languages and International Studies pointed to the "scandalous incompetence in foreign languages" of the United States and recommended more study abroad programs, international exchanges, and overseas experiences. Little mention, however, was made of the language resources of the ethnic community. The U.S. Spanish "foreign-" language education profession entered a period of increased isolation, precisely as globalization was moving the dike that had kept Spanish and English, as well as the foreign language and the bilingual education professions, separate and distinct. The United States reacted to the greater number of Spanish speakers in their midst and their greater multilingualism by drawing tighter its linguistic borders, using English only, especially in education, as its instrument of Empire.

U.S. ENGLISH RESTRICTIONS OF U.S. SPANISH

In 1981, Senator Hayakawa introduced a Constitutional Amendment to make English the official language of the United States. The perfect storm was now enveloping the U.S. language education field itself—on one hand, there was a call to learn "foreign" languages made by a Presidential Commission, but on the other, there was a strong demand that schools pay attention only to English and that Spanish as a U.S. language be restricted. Caught in the eye of this storm were the many U.S. Latinos, with much needed bilingual expertise but enveloped in an English-only climate.

During this time, the bilingual education profession struggled with reauthorizations of the Bilingual Education Act every 4 years, attempting to protect the spaces for using Spanish in the education of those Latino children whom the federal government called "limited English proficient." With the 1984 reauthorization, bilingual education funds became available for the first time for programs known as Special Alternative Instructional Programs where English only was used. Programs that became known as "structured immersion" or "sheltered English" were developed during this time. Although only 4% of the funding was reserved for these kinds of programs, the 1988 reauthorization expanded the funding of these English-only programs to 25% of the total. The last time the Bilingual Education Act was reauthorized, in 1994, the quota for these English-only programs was lifted, although, as we will see, under the guise of bilingual education, another attempt to distance Spanish as a sign of identity of the Latino community was begun—the so-called dual-language programs.

As English-only was given more attention, there were more Latino students entering middle schools, high schools, and universities. In this anti-Spanish climate, and spearheaded by Guadalupe Valdés, the movement to teach Spanish to Latinos in secondary and tertiary programs in ways that differed from teaching Spanish as a foreign language to monolinguals started to gain ground (Valdés, 1997; Valdés, Lozano, & García Moya, 1981). Spanish language classes were now full of Latino students in whose homes Spanish was spoken. The communicative language approach followed in "foreign-" language classes was simply not adequate for these students. Very little, however, was done by educational authorities to advance these programs.

In 2001, the Bilingual Education Act (Title VII of the Elementary and Secondary Education Act) was repealed. In its place, Title III of the No Child Left Behind Act (Pub. L. No. 107-110) was now titled "Language Instruction for Limited English Proficient and Immigrant Students." The No Child Left Behind Act turned attention toward the teaching and assessment of English proficiency and academic standards met through English only. Although "Hispanic students" was one of the categories of attention under No Child Left Behind, Latino students were only deemed to do well depending on their English language proficiency. Attention was turned from the teaching of Spanish to raising standards in English only. Economic resources were taken from Spanish language education to strengthen the teaching of English and Math (Dillon, 2010). If in 1979 the U.S. competencies in languages other than English were "scandalous," they now became increasingly absent, as globalization made full entry.

ENGLISH MONOLINGUALISM OVER SPANISH LANGUAGE EDUCATION AND BILINGUAL EDUCATION

Despite the ubiquitous presence of Spanish in U.S. society today, the quality of Spanish language education, for both non-Latinos and Latinos, has not improved substantially. It is true that the teaching of Spanish is faring better than the teaching of other languages. In 2008, 93% of high schools that taught "foreign" languages taught Spanish. And even though in 1960 there were only 178,689 Spanish language students in U.S. universities, in 1998 there were 656,590, and by 2006 there were 822,985 students of Spanish (Furman, Goldberg, & Lusin 2007). The same can be said of the growth of Spanish language students in secondary schools. In 2000, there were 4,057,608 students of Spanish in high school, compared to 1958 when there were only 691,024 students of Spanish (Draper & Hicks, 2002). But in 2000, there were only 699,765 Spanish language students in intermediate schools (seventh and eighth grades) and 304,882 students in elementary schools (K–6). Eighty percent of Spanish students in 2000 were in secondary schools, and these programs continue to focus on academic skills that have little to do with the language practices of U.S. Latinos. In 1997 at the elementary level, 79% of schools offering language programs taught Spanish, and this figure increased to 88% in 2008 (Rhodes & Pufahl, 2010). But the Spanish language programs at the elementary level are mostly of the language experience type, not truly focusing on Spanish language development. Spanish language education programs have more students than ever, but are they making a difference in promoting bilingual Americans?

Today Spanish language teaching in the United States continues an elitist tradition, taught mostly at the secondary and tertiary levels, with an academic emphasis, and not in relationship with the Spanish spoken by the 50.6 million Latinos in the United States. Spanish taught in secondary and tertiary institutions continues to be billed as a "foreign" language, the language of Spain and of Latin American countries, kept separate from the Spanish of the Other, of subaltern minorities who continue to be relegated to inferior positions. Many would agree with Dame Edna, the character created by the comedian Barry Humphries who, when asked if Spanish should be learned, replied,

Forget Spanish. There's nothing in that language worth reading except Don Quixote . . . There was a poet named García Lorca, but I'd leave him on the intellectual back burner if I were you. As for everyone's speaking it, what twaddle! Who speaks it that you are really desperate to talk to? The help? Your leaf blower? (Dame Edna, 2003, p. 116)

Although Spanish classes for bilingual Latinos have proliferated in both universities and secondary schools, they have not gone far enough in developing Latino bilinguals. In the year 2000, only 141,212, that is, 1.9% of secondary school students who took Spanish were in Spanish classes for Spanish speakers (Draper & Hicks, 2002). Compared to the 4 million Latino students who were between 15 and 17 years of age in 2000, this number is clearly insufficient (see Valdés, Fishman, Chávez, & Pérez, 2006). Beaudrie (2012) estimates that in 2010, 40% of Spanish language programs at the secondary level had some program of Spanish for Spanish speakers. This is a remarkable growth from 1997 when only 9% of schools offered such courses (Rhodes & Branaman, 1999). But the quality of these programs differs, and the number of programs is insufficient for the many Latino secondary school students.

Rather than recognizing that the students in these programs are Spanish speaking or bilingual, the field has recently taken up the term *heritage language*. Spanish is now relegated to a past that is "foreign," the Spanish of Latin American countries or Spain, but not recognized as an indigenous language practice of the United States. In addition, the term *heritage language* contributes to the silencing of U.S. bilingualism (for this critical perspective, see García, 2005).

The "heritage" language movement has done little to stop the erasure of the bilingualism of the Latino community. Although English-only constitutional amendment efforts were abandoned at the federal level, English-only laws were passed by 28 states as of this writing, and 3 states have banned bilingual education (California, Proposition 227, 1998; Arizona, Proposition 203, 2000; Massachusetts, Question 2, 2002; García, 2009a). The word *bilingual*, what Crawford (2004) has called "the B-word" (p. 35) has been progressively silenced (García, 2008; Wiley, 2005; Wiley & Wright, 2004). Every federal office with the word *bilingual* in its name has been renamed, substituting *bilingual* with *English language acquisition*. At the same time that bilingual education programs of the transitional and the developmental kind have been eliminated in state after state, one type of bilingual education has grown—the so-called dual-language programs.

As with the term *heritage language* program, the phrase "dual language" says something about the silencing of bilingualism in the United States and the distancing of these programs from the Latino community. Early on, Guadalupe Valdés (1997) warned about the lack of attention that "dual-language" education paid to Latino students. Many others have since become critics of the language separation, the "parallel monolingualism" found in these programs (Cummins, 2008; Fitts, 2006; García, in press-a; Gort, 2012; Palmer, 2007). "Dual-language" programs protect an authoritative standardized "Spanish" from "U.S. English." These "dual-language" programs in no way give any space to the language practices of the bilingual Latino community, stigmatizing their practices and compartmentalizing English and Spanish strictly. On one hand, Spanish and English are separated rigorously, with one language used at different times or spaces, or by different teachers and for different subjects; on the other hand, children who speak Spanish and English are brought together. But although children are recognized as "English language learners" or "speakers of English," no one is recognized as "bilingual"; and yet the majority of these students are bilingual (García, 2011b). Lee, Hill-Bonnet, and Gillispie (2008) suggest that in these "dual-language" programs, children experience "thickening identities" as either speakers of English or speakers of Spanish that may not lead to development as bilingual speakers. In the compartmentalized monolingual programming of "dual-language" education programs, bilingualism as a possibility is erased, with teachers, and even children, reminding others, "Speak English here" or "Speak Spanish here" (Angelova, Gunawardena, & Volk, 2006).

Even in their naming as "dual," these programs shy away from bilingualism, promoting instead a monoglossic view of bilingualism, an outdated additive conception of $1 + 1 = 2$ (García, 2009a). Instead of promoting a dynamic bilingualism more in tune with 21st-century practices, these "dual-language" programs continue the old tradition of compartmentalizing the two languages, enforcing a diglossic relationship that keeps the hierarchy of English over Spanish and that keeps Spanish away from the bilingual practices that characterize Spanish speakers in the United States. Standardized exams continue to insist on English only, and Spanish is robed with Otherness, alienating it, therefore, from a position of being part of U.S. language practices.

To minoritize Spanish, U.S. educational authorities insist on the needs and poverty of Spanish-speaking Latinos, highlighting, for example, that the median income of U.S. Latinos was $36,000, compared to $50,000 for White non-Latinos in 2005. But U.S. educational authorities hardly ever speak about the fact that bilingual Latinos actually do better than those who are English monolinguals. Linton (2003), for example, found a "positive relationship between upward mobility and bilingualism" (p. 24). Bilingualism in education only enters the picture officially when Latino children are still acquiring English. That is, once Latino students learn English and become bilingual, there is never any use of bilingualism as a resource in their education (García & Kleifgen, 2010). Latino students' bilingual language practices at home are much more complex than those in U.S. monolingual schools; and yet these practices are stigmatized and ignored by schools, intent on teaching "English," separately from language practices associated with "Spanish," and intent on teaching "Spanish," separately from "academic English."

The Swiss economist, François Grin (2003) has explained that if one language is promoted to prominent status, then its "native" speakers will have social and economic advantages precisely because of their competence in the prestigious language. By constructing Spanish as a language of poverty, silencing the bilingualism of U.S. Latinos, and insisting that English is Latinos' "second" language, White English monolinguals enjoy privilege. At the same time that U.S. schools insist on devaluing the Spanish of Latino students, other political hegemonic forces have started to promote Spanish as a global language. The next section considers how this shift has been constructed, so that we can later analyze the repercussions that this new position has had in U.S. Spanish language education policy.

GLOBAL SPANISH AND U.S. SPANISH

What is global about Spanish today, and what is it that business interests in Spain and Latin America want from U.S. Latinos? Language, as we have seen, has always been a marker of national and ethnic identity, as well as a form of economic and social capital (Bourdieu, 1991), but in the 21st century, global languages have been commodified more than ever. Ammon (2003) has determined that to be a global language, a language not only has to be spoken by many, but it must also have economic, political, and cultural power. The 16th edition of *Ethnologue* (M. P. Lewis, 2009) reports that Spanish is spoken "natively" by 329 million people. Of these, 28 million live in Spain, accounting for 11% of the Spanish-speaking population worldwide. As the French sociolinguist Louis-Jean Calvet (1999) has said, without Latin America—and Spanish speakers in the United States—Spanish would be considered only a regional language in Spain. Moreno-Fernández and Otero (2008) are more optimistic in their estimates, indicating that there are 359 million speakers in countries where Spanish is official or national and 41 million "native" speakers in places where Spanish is not official, bringing the total of Spanish "native" speakers to almost 400 million. If we add those whom Moreno-Fernández and Otero claim speak Spanish as a "second" language (24 million) and others who are learning Spanish (15 million), there are 439 million potential users of Spanish, making Spanish one of the most widely spoken languages, after English and Chinese.

Spanish is also the official or national language of 20 countries. Only English, French, and Arabic are spoken in more nation-states than Spanish. And Spanish is the official language in many international bodies, including the United Nations, UNESCO, and the European Union.

The economic power of Spanish comes, interestingly enough, mostly from Latinos in the United States, in what is the fourth-largest Spanish-speaking country. U.S. Latinos numbered 50.6 million in 2010, comprising 16% of the entire U.S. population. Of these, 34 million spoke Spanish at home in 2010 (U.S. Census Bureau, 2010). Eighty-nine percent of those who speak Spanish at home are bilingual, speaking English very well, well, or not well. Only 11% do not speak English.

The U.S. Latino market of $951 billion in 2008 was larger than that of the economies of all but 13 countries in the world. Humphreys (2008) estimates that the Latino economic clout will be $1.4 trillion in 2013, having risen from $212 billion in 1990. In 2008, Latinos accounted for 8.9% of all U.S. buying power, up from 5% in 1990. The U.S. Latino consumer power is 3 times that of the rest of the Spanish-speaking world (Carreira, 2002; Villa, 2000). The economic volume produced by Spanish in U.S. television, radio, movies, newspapers, and magazines is superior to that of any other Spanish-speaking country in the world (Marcos Marín, 2006). The words of David Graddol (2006) may be instructive in this regard:

Spanish has grown to be roughly the same size as English in terms of its native-speaker base, and may overtake it. Spanish is challenging English in some parts of the USA, where a number of towns have predominantly Spanish-speaking populations. The language is growing in economic importance in both Latin America and the USA. Spain is active in promoting itself as the global centre of authority for the language. (p. 61)

According to De Swaan (2001), languages that can detach themselves from specific territories raise their Q-value (communication value), with the possibility of becoming a lingua franca. Thus, Spain has mounted a campaign to make visible the fact that Spanish users live beyond Spain and Spanish-speaking Latin America, especially as the financial crisis broadens. To raise the Q-value of Spanish, Spain has adopted an aggressive policy of Spanish language promotion, accompanied with a more flexible attitude toward the Spanish spoken elsewhere.

On May 11, 1990, Spain's Ministry of Foreign Affairs created the Instituto Cervantes with a clear mission: *"agrupar y potenciar los esfuerzos en la defensa y promoción del español en el extranjero"* ["to group and build capacity for the efforts in the defense and promotion of Spanish outside of Spain"] (Sánchez, 1992). The Instituto Cervantes offers Spanish language courses and professional development for teachers of Spanish and certifies teachers of Spanish as a foreign language through its DELE (*Diploma de español como Lengua Extranjera*). It also maintains a virtual Spanish language classroom, which claims to use *"el español peninsular central"* ["central peninsular Spanish"] (www. cervantes.es). To promote and defend this "central peninsular Spanish," 77 centers have been established to date, 5 of them in the United States: in Albuquerque, Boston, Chicago, Seattle, and New York.

To promote Spanish as a global language, a language that is "fashionable," a chic language of "Latinidad," trendy singers, actors, and fashions, as well as promising financial returns in an expanding market (García, 2008, 2009b; Mar-Molinero, 2008), an ideology of *Hispanofonía* is being constructed (del Valle, 2006; "Interview With Rainer Enrique Hamel," 2004). About this ideology, Hamel says that it is

basado en una política de diversidad piramidal. [España] ya no intenta exportar, como en sus primeros años, el *español con la "zeta." Admite la diversidad del español* [based on politics of pyramidal diversity. [Spain] doesn't try to export, as it did during its first years, Spanish with the "zed." It allows the diversity of Spanish.]

With peninsular Castilian at the top of the pyramid, at the top of the "orders of indexicalities," as Blommaert (2010) would say, the diverse national Spanish varieties are given entry. García Canclini (2001) has called this process of Spain's linguistic imperialism *"rehispanización,"* a rehispanization that claims Latin Americans and U.S. Latinos as speakers of Spanish but does not quite acknowledge their bilingual language practices.

Another example of the growing attention to global Spanish has been the fact that since 1997, with the support of the Instituto Cervantes and of the Real Academia Española, there have been international conferences on behalf of Spanish, the so-called *Congreso Internacional de Lengua*. The third conference took place in Rosario, Argentina, in 2004, and was accompanied by a counterconference organized mostly by indigenous Latin Americans that called for the recognition of multilingual identities. The last *Congreso Internacional de Lengua* took place in Cartagena, Colombia, in 2007. Significantly, there were no contributions from the U.S. Spanish-speaking community. The complicity of Latin American cultural agencies and governments, as José del Valle (2009) has argued, has been of paramount importance in the Hispanofonía ideological construct.

In 2004, the Real Academia Española issued their new language policy for the Pan-Hispanic world. *La Nueva Política Lingüística Panhispánica* says, in part, that its policy had been in the past to maintain language purity, based on the linguistic habits of a very small number of its speakers. It adds the following, however:

En nuestros días, las Academias, en una orientación más adecuada y también más realista, se han fijado como tarea común la de garantizar el mantenimiento de la unidad básica del idioma, que es, en definitiva, lo que permite hablar de la comunidad hispanohablante, haciendo compatible la unidad del idioma con el reconocimiento de sus variedades [In our days, the Academies, with a more adequate and realistic orientation have agreed to guarantee the basic unity of the language; that is, in reality, what allows us to speak about the Spanish-speaking community, making the unity of the language compatible with the recognition of its varieties]. (del Valle, 2008, p. 11)

This statement already shows the Academies' linguistic strategies—expanding the idea of global Spanish, ensuring that Latin American varieties patronized by nation-states are recognized, while holding the reins on the practices of bilinguals, whether they are indigenous Latin Americans or U.S. Latinos. What has been the consequence of the construction of Spanish as a global language on U.S. language education policies? The next section considers this.

U.S. SPANISH AND TEACHING LATINOS FOR SOCIAL JUSTICE

The language practices of U.S. Latino communities have little to do with the global image of Spanish projected by the language authorities in Spain or Latin America, and also little to do with the English-only emphasis in U.S. schools or even with many programs to teach "Spanish" to both Anglos and Latinos. U.S. Latinos, living in social, cultural, and linguistic *fronteras* or *borderlands*, populate their discourse with practices that some may identify as "English" or "Spanish" but, seen from their perspective as bilingual speakers, are simply different features of their linguistic repertoire that they use to perform appropriately in their homes and community as well as in their schools (see García & Otheguy, in press). As Paris (2010) has remarked, there are centrifugal forces (Bakhtin, 1981) pulling Latinos of all backgrounds toward more prestigious Spanish language practices and centripetal forces pushing them toward more dominant English practices. The result is the flexible language practices that U.S. Latino students perform every day to meet their communicative and academic needs.

The flexible language practices of Latino bilinguals are further stigmatized as, on one hand, simply "Spanglish"[3] and, on the other, English "fossilization." The flexible language practices of U.S. Latino bilinguals are not validated, relegating them to an inferior position below the Spanish or English of those who are said to speak these languages "natively." Diasporic Latino communities, communicating through dynamic technologies and with more agency than in the past, do not have linguistic systems that are unique and separate, as nation-states would wish. Bilingual Latinos are not simply two monolinguals in one (Grosjean, 1982). Rather, their bilingualism is dynamic (García, 2009a), and they use their entire linguistic repertoire to signify and construct meaning. I have referred to the dynamic bilingual use that guarantees that Latino bilinguals learn and lead their lives with dignity and justice as "translanguaging" (García, 2009b). To educate bilingual Latino students, U.S. educators would have to stop treating the interdependent practices of their bilingual Latinos as those of racialized, subaltern "Others," separating them into two untouchable "global" languages that schools then evaluate as "incomplete." Instead, schools would have to recognize Latino translanguaging as a discursive practice of true bilingual North Americans, in order to extend their language practices to those recognized as "standard academic language," whether "English" or "Spanish."

Translanguaging refers not only to the complex discourse practices of bilinguals but also to the pedagogies that use these practices to release ways of speaking, of being, and of knowing of subaltern peoples. The term *translanguaging* was coined in Welsh (*trawsieithu*) by Cen Williams (1997) to refer to a bilingual approach in which one language is used as input and the other as output. Many have now extended the term to mean all flexible bilingual use, especially in language teaching (Blackledge & Creese, 2010; Creese & Blackledge, 2010; García, 2009a, 2011b; Hornberger & Link, 2012; G. Lewis, Jones, & Baker, 2012a, 2012b; Wei, 2011). Used as pedagogy, translanguaging has the potential to release ways of speaking of Latinos that have been constrained by national languages and ideologies of the modern/colonial world system in which both the United States and Spain participate. In so doing, translanguaging as pedagogy can redress the power of "English" and "Spanish," as constructed by the United States, Spain, and Latin America, at the same time that it denounces the "coloniality of power and knowledge" (Mignolo, 2000, p. 231) and enacts a bilingual subjectivity. Many other scholars have recently called for a flexible translanguaging pedagogy to educate Latino students (García, in press-b; Sayer, 2013), although many are still using old terms such as *code-switching* in order to refer to what amounts to this flexible language use (see, e.g., Martínez, 2010; Sayer, 2008).

In conceptualization, translanguaging differs from code-switching in that it refers not simply to a shift between two languages but to the use of complex discursive practices that cannot be assigned to one or another code and that gives voice to oppressed and minoritized language practices (for more on translanguaging, see García & Li Wei, in press). Bilingual students use these complex and fluid discursive practices to perform their learning—reading, writing, listening, discussing, taking notes, writing reports and essays, and taking exams. By incorporating languaging and cultural practices familiar to Latino bilingual students, a translanguaging pedagogical approach reduces the risk of alienation and "Otherness" that monolingual education systems create. Instead, it validates the translanguaging practices of Latino students as those of bilingual North Americans who have a more expanded linguistic repertoire than that of monolingual students.

Although U.S. language education policies have become more restrictive than ever (Arias & Faltis, 2012; Gándara & Hopkins, 2010), it turns out that teachers, anxious to meet the needs of the growing Latino bilingual population in schools, many times negotiate the English-only education policies by incorporating translanguaging into their pedagogical practices. This is something we have observed again and again, especially in schools that are successful with Latino students (see, e.g., García, Flores, & Woodley, 2012). Despite the silencing of bilingualism, and of Spanish in the face of English, both students and teachers in classrooms are, more than ever, using translanguaging as a resource to both learn and teach. This is especially so as the Common Core State Standards, adopted by 45 of the 50 states and the District of Columbia as of this writing, demand more complex language use. Translanguaging is needed more than ever, recognized as a discursive ability of Latino bilinguals, a pedagogical approach to academically challenge the growing number of bilingual Latino students, and a way to extend their use of standard academic "English" as well as standard academic "Spanish." In classrooms with bilingual students (see García, Zakharia, & Otcu, 2013) translanguaging is being used to also extend Latino's use of "Spanish," going beyond the static definitions of "Spanish" assigned by some Spanish language educators who do not accept the bilingual language practices of U.S. Latinos. To teach Spanish as U.S. Spanish, as the language of Latinos, and not simply as a hegemonic global language, Spanish language educators, as well as bilingual educators, must build on the flexible translanguaging of bilingual Latinos.

CONCLUSION

This chapter has reviewed the language education policies that have contributed to the continued failure of Spanish language education in the United States, and of U.S. Latinos in the nation's schools. As the review shows, both English and Spanish were constructed as instruments of nation-states to protect their Empires and exercise power. The construction of "academic English" and "academic Spanish" is used in the same way today. Educational systems today are enmeshed in the movement of people that globalization has brought and in the dynamism of information that new technologies have produced. The result is a clash between the rigidity with which schools approach language, both "English" and "Spanish," and the practices of the increasingly bilingual Latinos that make up the United States.

U.S. Latinos, caught between the imperial designs of the United States and Spain, have much to show the world, for increasingly their translanguaging gives them a social advantage in an increasingly multilingual U.S. society, enabling them to negotiate multiple interactions. Educational authorities would do well to build on this translanguaging, rather than stigmatize it and attempt to extinguish it. In taking up translanguaging as a pedagogy, educators would have a better chance of developing U.S. Latinos as confident users of standard English and standard Spanish, as they learn from their students about the complexity and richness of bilingual language practices. The success of teaching Spanish in the United States resides precisely on recognizing U.S. Spanish practices as important locally for Latinos and non-Latinos, as well as for the global success of "Spanish" throughout the world. Rather than keeping "Spanish" and "English" separate, it is time for educators to understand that only the interrelationship of new and old language practices will sustain a future in which Spanish is not billed as "heritage," but recognized as an authentic "American" language practice.

ACKNOWLEDGMENTS

I'm grateful to José del Valle for his very thoughtful comments on an earlier version of this chapter, and to Kate Seltzer for her careful reading.

NOTES

[1]The first attempts to standardize Spanish can be traced to Alfonse the Sage's work on the development of *castellano drecho*.

[2]Referring to Spanish as a "global language" and not merely an "international language" focuses not simply on the number of Spanish speakers in different countries but on its colonial condition, which has in turn enabled its ability to compete in global markets because of economic, political, and cultural power.

[3]The term *Spanglish* is contested. Whereas some Latino scholars actively defend it as a way to appropriate a derogatory term (see, e.g., Rosa, 2010; Zentella, 1997), Otheguy and Stern (2010) have argued against its use on the grounds that it prevents Latinos from sustaining Spanish language practices.

REFERENCES

Ammon, U. (2003). The international standing of the German language. In J. Maurais & M. A. Morris (Eds.), *Languages in a globalizing world* (pp. 231–249). Cambridge, England: Cambridge University Press.

Angelova, M., Gunawardena, D., & Volk, D. (2006). Peer-teaching and learning: Co-constructing language in a dual language first grade. *Language and Education, 20*, 173–190.

Arias, B. M., & Faltis, C. (Eds.). (2012). *Implementing educational language policy in Arizona: Legal, historical and current practices in SEI*. Bristol, England: Multilingual Matters.

Bakhtin, M. (1981). *Dialogic imagination: Four essays*. Austin: University of Texas Press.

Beaudrie, S. (2012). Research on university-based Spanish heritage language programs in the United States: The current state of affairs. In S. Beaudrie & M. Fairclough (Eds.), *Spanish as a heritage language in the US: State of the field* (pp. 203–222). Washington, DC: Georgetown University Press.

Blackledge, A., & Creese, A. (2010). *Multilingualism*. London, England: Continuum.

Blommaert, J. (2010). *The sociolinguistics of globalization*. Cambridge, England: Cambridge University Press.

Bonfiglio, T. P. (2010). *Mother tongues and nations: The invention of the native speaker*. Berlin, Germany: Walter de Gruyter.

Bourdieu, P. (1991). *Language and symbolic power.* Cambridge, MA: Harvard University Press.

Briceño Perozo, M. (1987). *La obligación de enseñar el castellano a los aborígenes de América* [The obligation to teach Spanish to the Indigenous peoples of the Americas]. Caracas, Venezuela: Colección Logos.

Calvet, L. J. (1999). *La guerre des langues et les politiques linguistiques* [The war of languages and language policies] (2nd ed.). Paris, France: Hachette.

Canagarajah, S. (2013). *Translingual practice: Global Englishes and cosmopolitan relations.* London, England: Routledge.

Carreira, M. (2002). The media, marketing and critical mass: Portents of linguistic maintenance. *Southwest Journal of Linguistics, 21,* 37–54.

Castellanos, D. (1983). *The best of two worlds: Bilingual-bicultural education in the U.S.* Trenton: New Jersey State Department of Education.

Cifuentes, B., & del Consuelo Ros, M. (1993). Oficialidad y planificacion del español: Dos aspectos de la politica del lenguaje en Mexico en el siglo XIV [Officialdom and the planning of Spanish: Two aspects of language policy in Mexico in the XIV century]. *Iztapalapa, 13*(29), 135–146.

Crawford, J. (2004). *Educating English learners: Language diversity in the classroom* (5th ed.). Los Angeles, CA: Bilingual Educational Services.

Creese, A., & Blackledge, A. (2010). Translanguaging in the bilingual classroom: A pedagogy for learning and teaching? *Modern Language Journal, 94,* 103–115.

Cummins, J. (2008). Teaching for transfer: Challenging the two solitudes assumption in bilingual education. In J. Cummins & P. Corson (Eds.), *Encyclopedia of language and education: Vol. 5. Bilingual education* (2nd ed., pp. 65–75). New York, NY: Springer.

Dame Edna (Barry Humphries). (2003). Ask Dame Edna. *Vanity Fair, February,* 116.

De Swaan, A. (2001). *Words of the world.* Malden, MA: Polity.

del Valle, J. (2006). US Latinos, la hispanofonía, and the language ideologies of high modernity. In C. Mar-Molinero & M. Stewart (Eds.), *Globalization and language in the Spanish-speaking world: Macro and micro perspectives* (pp. 27–46). Hampshire, England: Palgrave.

del Valle, J. (2008). The Pan Hispanic community and the conceptual structure of linguistic nationalism. *International Multilingual Research Journal, 2,* 5–26.

del Valle, J. (2009). Total Spanish: The politics of a Pan-Hispanic grammar. *PMLA, 124,* 880–887.

del Valle, J., & Stheeman, L. G. (Eds.). (2002). *The battle over Spanish between 1800 and 2000: Language ideologies and Hispanic intellectuals.* London, England: Routledge.

Dillon, S. (2010, January 20). Foreign languages fail in class, except Chinese. *New York Times,* p. A18.

Draper, J., & Hicks, J. H. (2002). *Foreign language enrollments in public secondary schools, Fall 2000.* Retrieved from http://www.actfl.org/sites/default//files/pdfs/public/Enroll2000.pdf

Edwards, J. (1994). *Multilingualism.* London, England: Routledge.

Espinosa, A. (1923). Where is the best Spanish spoken? *Hispania, 6,* 244–246.

Fitts, S. (2006). Reconstructing the status quo: Linguistic interaction in a dual-language school. *Bilingual Research Journal, 30,* 337–365.

Furman, N., Goldberg, D., & Lusin, N. (2007). *Enrollment in languages other than English in United States institutions of higher education, Fall 2006.* New York, NY: Modern Language Association of America. Retrieved from http://www.lpri.coh.arizona.edu/classes/ariew/slat583/enrollmentsurvey_final.pdf

Gándara, P., & Hopkins, M. (Eds.). (2010). *Forbidden language: English learners and restrictive language policies.* New York, NY: Teachers College Press.

García, O. (1993). From Goya portraits to Goya beans: Elite traditions and popular streams in U.S. Spanish language policy. *Southwest Journal of Linguistics, 12,* 69–86.

García, O. (2005). Positioning heritage languages in the United States. *Modern Language Journal, 89,* 601–605.

García, O. (Ed.). (2008). Spanish as a global language [Special issue]. *International Multilingual Research Journal, 2*(1).

García, O. (2009a). *Bilingual education in the 21st century: A global perspective.* Malden, MA: Wiley-Blackwell.

García, O. (2009b). Livin' and teachin' la lengua loca: Glocalizing U.S. Spanish ideologies and practices. In R. Salaberry (Ed.), *Language allegiances and bilingualism in the United States* (pp. 151–171). Clevedon, England: Multilingual Matters.

García, O. (2011a). Planning Spanish: Nationalizing, minoritizing and globalizing performances. In M. Díaz-Campos (Ed.), *The handbook of Hispanic sociolinguistics* (pp. 665–685). Malden, MA: Wiley-Blackwell.

García, O. (with Makar, C., Starcevic, M., & Terry, A.). (2011b). Translanguaging of Latino kindergarteners. In K. Potowski & J. Rothman (Eds.), *Bilingual youth: Spanish in English speaking societies* (pp. 33–55). Amsterdam, Netherlands: John Benjamins.

García, O. (in press-a). Dual or dynamic bilingual education? Empowering bilingual communities. In R. Rubdy & L. Alsagoff (Eds.), *The global-local interface: Language choice and hybridity.* Bristol, England: Multilingual Matters.

García, O. (with Leiva, C.). (in press-b). Theorizing and enacting translanguaging for social justice. In A. Creese & A. Blackledge (Eds.), *Heteroglossia as practice and pedagogy.* New York, NY: Springer.

García, O., Flores, N., & Woodley, H. H. (2012). Transgressing monolingualism and bilingual dualities: Translanguaging pedagogies. In A. Yiakoumetti (Ed.), *Harnessing linguistic variation for better education* (pp. 45–76). Bern, Germany: Peter Lang.

García, O., & Kleifgen, J. (2010). *Educating emergent bilinguals. Policies, programs and practices for English Language Learners.* New York, NY: Teachers College Press.

García, O., López, D., & Makar, C. (2010). Language and identity in Latin America. In J. A. Fishman & O. García (Eds.), *Handbook of language and ethnic identity* (pp. 353–373). Oxford, England: Oxford University Press.

García, O., & Otheguy, R. (in press). Hispanic bilingualism. In M. Lacorte (Ed.), *The Routledge handbook of Hispanic applied linguistics.* New York, NY: Routledge.

García, O., & Li Wei (in press). *Translanguaging: Implications for language, bilingualism and education.* Basingstoke, England: Palgrave McMillan.

García, O., Zakharia, Z., & Otcu, B. (Eds.). (2013). *Bilingual community education and multilingualism: Beyond heritage languages in a global city.* Bristol, England: Multilingual Matters.

García Canclini, N. (2001). *Consumers and citizens: Globalization and multicultural conflicts.* Minneapolis: University of Minnesota Press.

Gort, M. (2012). Code-switching patterns in the writing-related talk of young emergent bilinguals. *Journal of Literacy Research, 44,* 45–75.

Graddol, D. (2006). *English next: Why global English may mean the end of "English as a foreign language."* London, England: British Council. Retrieved from http://www.britishcouncil.org/learning-research-englishnext.htm

Grin, F. (2003). *Language policy evaluation and the European charter for regional or minority languages.* Basingstoke, England: Palgrave.

Grosjean, F. (1982). *Life with two languages.* Cambridge, MA: Harvard University Press.

Hall, R. (1974). *External history of the romance languages.* New York, NY: Elsevier.

Hamel, R. E. (1994). Linguistic rights for Amerindian peoples in Latin America. In T. Skutnabb-Kangas & R. Phillipson (Eds.), *Linguistic human rights: Overcoming linguistic discrimination* (pp. 289–303). Berlin, Germany: Mouton de Gruyter.

Hornberger, N., & Link, H. (2012). Translanguaging and transnational literacies in multilingual classrooms: A bilingual lens. *International Journal of Bilingual Education and Bilingualism, 15,* 261–278.

Huebener, T. (1961). *Why Johnny should learn foreign languages.* Philadelphia, PA: Chilton.

Humphreys, J. M. (2008). The multicultural economy 2008. *Georgia Business and Economic Conditions, 68*(3), 1–16.

Interview with Rainer Enrique Hamel. (2004, November 15). *Reforma.* Retrieved from http://www.hamel.com.mx/Archivos-PDF/Work%20in%20Progress/2004%20Hamel%20Entrevista%20Reforma.pdf

Jacobson, R. (1981). The implementation of a bilingual instructional model: The new concurrent approach. In P. Gonzalez (Ed.), *Proceedings of the Eighth Annual International Bilingual Bicultural Education Conference at Seattle.* Rosslyn, VA: National Clearinghouse for Bilingual Education.

Lázaro, F. (1994). *La Real Academia y la unidad del idioma: Actas del congreso de la lengua Española de 1992* [The Royal Academy and language unity: Proceedings of the Conference on the Spanish Language of 1992]. Madrid, Spain: Instituto Cervantes. Retrieved from http://cvc.cervantes.es/obref/congresos/sevilla/apertura/Aper_Laz_Car.htm

Lau v. Nichols, 414 U.S. 563, 39 L. E.D. 2d 1 (1974).

Lee, J. S., Hill-Bonnet, L., & Gillispie, J. (2008). Learning in two languages: Interactional spaces for becoming bilingual speakers. *International Journal of Bilingual Education and Bilingualism, 11,* 75–94.

Lewis, G., Jones, B., & Baker, C. (2012a). Translanguaging: Developing its conceptualisation and contextualisation. *Educational Research and Evaluation, 18,* 655–670.

Lewis, G., Jones, B., & Baker, C. (2012b). Translanguaging: Origins and development from school to street and beyond. *Educational Research and Evaluation, 18,* 641–654.

Lewis, M. P. (Ed.). (2009). *Ethnologue: Languages of the world* (16th ed.). Dallas, TX: SIL International.

Li Wei (2011). Moment analysis and translanguaging space: Discursive construction of identities by multilingual Chinese youth in Britain. *Journal of Pragmatics, 43,* 1222–1235.

Linton, A. (2003). *Is Spanish here to stay? Contexts for bilingualism among U.S.-born Hispanics.* University of California, San Diego, Center for Comparative Immigration Studies. Retrieved from http://escholarship.org/uc/item/4rf0c6k7

López-García, A. (1985). *El rumor de los desarraigados. Conflicto de lenguas en la peninsula Ibérica* [The rumor of the uprooted: Conflict of languages in the Iberian Peninsula]. Barcelona, Spain: Anagrama.

Makoni, S., & Pennycook, A. (2007). *Disinventing and reconstituting languages.* Clevedon, England: Multilingual Matters.

Marcos Marín, F. (2006). *Los retos del español* [The challenges of Spanish]. Madrid, Spain: Iberoamericana/Vervuert.

Mar-Molinero, C. (2008). Subverting Cervantes: Language authority in global Spanish. *International Multilingual Research Journal, 2,* 27–47.

Martínez, R. A. (2010). Spanglish as literacy tool: Toward an understanding of the potential role of Spanish-English code-switching in the development of academic literacy. *Research in the Teaching of English, 45,* 124–149.

Mignolo, W. D. (2000). *Local histories/global designs.* Princeton, NJ: Princeton University Press.

Moreno-Fernández, F., & Otero, J. (2008). The status and future of Spanish among the main international languages: Quantitative dimensions. *International Multilingual Research Journal, 2,* 67–83.

Otheguy, R., & Stern, N. (2010). On so-called "Spanglish." *International Journal of Bilingualism, 15,* 85–100.

Palmer, D. (2007). A dual immersion strand programme in California: Carrying out the promise of dual language education in an English-dominant context. *International Journal of Bilingual Education and Bilingualism, 10,* 752–768.

Paris, D. (2010). The second language of the United States: Youth perspectives on Spanish in a changing multiethnic community. *Journal of Language, Identity, and Education, 9,* 139–155.

Pennycook, A. (2010). *Language as a local practice.* London, England: Routledge.

Rhodes, N. C., & Branaman, L. E. (1999). *Foreign language instruction in the United States. A national survey of elementary and secondary schools.* McHenry, IL: Delta Systems.

Rhodes, N. C., & Pufahl, I. (2010). *Foreign language teaching in US schools: Results of a national survey.* Washington, DC: Center for Applied Linguistics.

Rives, G. L. (1918). *The United States and Mexico, 1821-1848: A history of the relations between the two countries from the independence of Mexico to the close of the war with the United States* (Vol. 2). New York, NY: Scribner.

Rosa, J. D. (2010) *Looking like a language, sounding like a race: Making Latin@ panethnicity and managing American anxieties* (Unpublished doctoral dissertation). University of Chicago, Chicago, IL.

Sánchez, A. (1992). Spanish language spread policy. *International Journal of the Sociology of Language, 95,* 51–69.

Sayer, P. (2008). Demistifying language mixing: Spanglish in school. *Journal of Latinos and Education, 7,* 94–112.

Sayer, P. (2013). Translanguaging, TexMex, and bilingual pedagogy: Emergent bilinguals learning through the vernacular. *TESOL Quarterly, 47,* 63–88.

U.S. Census Bureau. (2010). *The Hispanic population: 2010* (2010 Census Brief). Washington, DC: Author.

Valdés, G. (1997). Dual-language immersion programs: A cautionary note concerning the education of language-minority students. *Harvard Educational Review, 67,* 391–429.

Valdés, G., Fishman, J. A., Chávez, R., & Pérez, W. (2006). *Developing minority language resources: The case of Spanish in California.* Clevedon, England: Multilingual Matters.

Valdés, G., Lozano, A., & García-Moya, R. (1981). *Teaching Spanish to the Hispanic bilingual: Issues, aims, and methods.* New York, NY: Teachers College Press.

Villa, D. (2000). Languages have armies, and economies, too: The presence of U.S. Spanish in the Spanish-speaking world. *Southwest Journal of Linguistics, 19,* 143–154.

Wiley. T. (2005). *Literacy and language diversity in the United States* (2nd ed.). Washington, DC: Center for Applied Linguistics.

Wiley, T., & Wright, W. (2004). Against the undertow: Language minority education policy and politics in the "age of accountability." *Educational Policy, 18,* 142–168.

Williams, C. (1994). *Arfarniad o ddulliau dysgu ac addysgu yng nghyd-destun addysg uwchradd ddwyieithog* [An evaluation of teaching and learning methods in the context of bilingual secondary education] (Unpublished doctoral dissertation). University of Wales, Bangor, Wales.

Wright, R. (1997). Linguistic standardization in the Middle Ages in the Iberian peninsula: Advantages and disadvantages. In S. Gregory & D. A. Trotter (Eds.), *De mot en mot: Aspects of medieval linguistics: Essays in honour of William Rothwell* (pp. 261–275). Cardiff, Wales: University of Wales Press.

Wright, S. (2004). *Language policy and language planning: From nationalism to globalization.* New York, NY: Palgrave.

Zentella, A. C. (1997). *Growing up bilingual.* Malden, MA: Blackwell.

Chapter 4

From Segregation to School Finance: The Legal Context for Language Rights in the United States

JEANNE M. POWERS

Arizona State University

In this chapter, I review the legal trajectory of language rights in public schooling in the United States and how language has been intertwined with other policy issues in court cases aimed at expanding access and equity for minority students: desegregation and school finance. Most of these cases originated in the Southwestern United States where there were and continue to be critical masses of Latino students—largely Spanish speakers of Mexican descent—attending public schools. As an organizing frame for the chapter, I expand Ruiz's (1984) framework for analyzing orientations[1] in language policy. My goal is to document and analyze the assumptions in legal arguments marshaled in these cases about how English language learners (ELLs) attending public schools should learn and be taught English and how students' home languages fit into those processes.[2]

I focus on the legal opinions issued by federal and state courts because although courts do not create policy, they play an important role in the policymaking process (Bosworth, 2001; Horowitz, 1977). Courts can reject a policy by declaring it unconstitutional and set the parameters for policymaking by legislatures. Likewise, when courts rebuff plaintiffs' claims, they uphold and often reinforce the status quo. Moreover, as critical race theorists have observed, legal decisions play an important cultural role in legitimizing and institutionalizing racial inequality. Language, like race, has been an important marker of social status and is a significant aspect of individuals' social identities (Lippi-Green, 2011; Perea, 1992). Language is also a key medium for participation in social settings (Rodriguez, 2006). Language and race are not interchangeable, but the legal framework for language rights in the United States was an extension of civil rights era policies aimed at addressing racial discrimination

Review of Research in Education
March 2014, Vol. 38, pp. 81-105
DOI: 10.3102/0091732X13506550
© 2014 AERA. http://rre.aera.net

81

(Skrentny, 2002). Many contemporary decisions that address language rights have been brought by plaintiffs that courts have also identified as racial minorities or by their national origins. However, because of its central role in human interaction, language also differs from race in important ways that may not be adequately addressed by civil rights policies aimed at limiting the role of race in society (Rodriguez, 2006).

I also address federal education policies where relevant because in the mid-1960s, legal decisions about desegregation and language rights were often shaped by federal legislation and regulations. My review highlights how courts have been reluctant to extend civil rights law beyond the thinnest conceptualization of language rights, preferring instead to leave major decisions about language policies in schools to state and local officials and the vagaries of federal education policy.

CONCEPTUAL FRAMEWORK

Ruiz (1984) identified two dominant orientations in language policy: (a) language-as-problem and (b) language-as-right. Ruiz also described a third orientation toward language planning that he saw as more emergent: language-as-resource. As I explain below, my review suggests that there is a fourth orientation evident in court opinions and policy documents: language-as-barrier. Whereas Ruiz characterized these as "competing but not incompatible approaches" (p. 18), in this chapter I propose that to understand how courts and federal policies have addressed language education for ELLs in U.S. public schools, these orientations can be arranged within the fields created by two intersecting continua: (a) the goals of the language policy and (b) the use of the home language in instruction (see Figure 1).

In the language-as-problem orientation, language issues are viewed as so tightly coupled to social and policy problems such as poverty, dropping out of school, and low educational attainment that the minority language becomes an indicator of these conditions (Ruiz, 1984). The home language is viewed as both a problematic characteristic of students and as indexing other disadvantages. In general, the language-as-problem orientation implies language policies and practices that exclusively focus on teaching students English. In the most robust instantiation of the language-as-resource orientation, students' home languages are understood as an integral part of supporting students to learn English *and* a skill that ELL students should continue to develop alongside becoming proficient in English.[3] Moreover, speakers of a second language, particularly native speakers, are considered assets because they are able to translate and mediate between cultural groups that are separated by language differences within or across societies. A thinner version of the language-as-resource orientation views the home language as a tool to more effectively teach students English without addressing students' skills in their home languages or seeing speakers of multiple languages as having advantages over monolingual speakers.

There is also evidence of a language orientation that occupies a middle ground between the language-as-problem orientation and the language-as-resource orientation, the language-as-barrier orientation. In the language-as-barrier orientation, language is a

FIGURE 1
Language Orientations in Education Policy

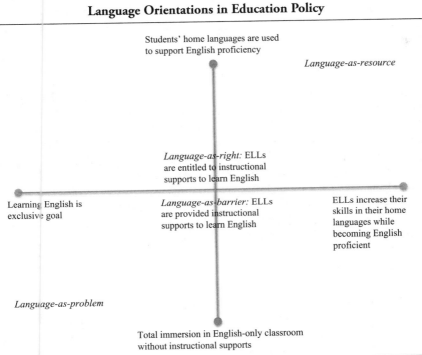

Students' home languages are used
to support English proficiency

Language-as-resource

Language-as-right: ELLs
are entitled to instructional
supports to learn English

Learning English is
exclusive goal

Language-as-barrier: ELLs
are provided instructional
supports to learn English

ELLs increase their
skills in their home
languages while
becoming English
proficient

Language-as-problem

Total immersion in English-only classroom
without instructional supports

problem to be solved, but school practices are a central concern. That is, schools must help ELL students develop skills in English that will enable them to access the content of the curriculum.[4] This is a qualitative shift from the language-as-problem orientation in which ELL students are viewed as presenting difficulties for schools and school practices are not deeply scrutinized.[5] The language-as-barrier orientation reflects shifts in how educational inequality was viewed by some policymakers as civil rights law was elaborated (Skrentny, 2002). Yet within a civil rights framework, the legal status of ELLs is a function of their inability to speak English: "Once the language barrier has been overcome the language minority ceases to have status as a language minority" (Rodriguez, 2006, p. 706).

The language-as-right orientation may inform the other orientations depending on the role of students' home languages in instruction. That is, court decisions or policies may imply that students' rights are limited to ameliorating the barriers their insufficient skills in English pose for participating in and benefiting from English-dominant educational programs, or the right to access, which might not include the use of the home language in instruction (Wiley, 2002). Conversely, language policies might suggest that ELLs are entitled to become fluent speakers of English *and* their home languages simultaneously.[6] I view these as ideal types that help us clarify the assumptions about language that have shaped legal and policy arguments on how ELLs should learn and be taught English and the role of their home languages in those processes.

SEGREGATION

The first set of opinions that addressed how ELLs should be taught in public schools, albeit indirectly, were the Mexican American segregation cases that predated *Brown v. Board of Education* (1954): *Romo v. Laird* (1925), *Roberto Alvarez v. the Board of Trustees of the Lemon Grove School District* (1931), *Independent School District v. Salvatierra* (1930), *Mendez v. Westminster* (1946), *Delgado v. Bastrop* (1948), and *Gonzales v. Sheely* (1951).[7] In all of these cases, Mexican American parents prevailed in their challenges of their school districts' extralegal segregation practices (see Alvarez, 1986; Arriola, 1995; Donato & Hanson, 2012; Gross, 2007; Powers & Patton, 2008; Powers, 2008; San Miguel, 1987; Strum, 2010; Valencia, 2005, 2008; Wollenberg, 1976). Adopting the language-as-problem orientation, district officials claimed that "Spanish-speaking students" had to be taught in separate classrooms and schools because they lacked the English language skills they needed to learn alongside their Anglo peers, although most evidence suggests that students were placed in Mexican schools regardless of their English proficiency.

Romo and *Alvarez* were heard in state trial courts and had little influence beyond their local contexts. In *Salvatierra*, the Texas Court of Appeals held that although segregation based on national origins was unconstitutional, school districts could segregate students if it was necessary to address students' language deficiencies. The *Salvatierra* court also determined that the school district did not intentionally discriminate against Mexican American students. Clearly convinced by district officials' claims that they had developed a reasonable plan to address students' needs—the court reproduced extensive portions of the superintendent's testimony in its opinion—it dismissed the testimony of two witnesses that suggested that all Mexican students, regardless of language ability, were required to attend the district's Mexican school. The Supreme Court declined to grant certiorari in 1931.

Fifteen years later, *Mendez v. Westminster* (1946) was a clear victory for Mexican American parents with far more significance. In *Mendez*, Mexican American parents charged that four Orange County school districts' policies requiring their children to attend separate Mexican schools were unconstitutional. In his decision for the U.S. District Court, Judge Paul McCormick ruled that although the school facilities and other resources allocated to the schools for "children of Mexican ancestry or descent" or "Spanish-speaking children" were equal to or exceeded those for "English-speaking" children, the districts' segregation practices violated state law and "unmistakably disregard rights secured by the supreme law of the land" (*Mendez v. Westminster*, 1946, p. 549). Although McCormick's decision did not challenge the doctrine of segregation because the core of the opinion was based on a legalistic reading of California's education code, it was a remarkable decision for its time given the narrow parameters of existing civil rights law.[8] In *Delgado v. Bastrop* (1948), the parties reached an agreement without going to trial. Finally, in *Gonzales v. Sheely* (1951), the court declared that segregation "because of racial or national origins" violated the equal protection clause of the Fourteenth Amendment (p. 1008).

These cases differ from the National Association for the Advancement of Colored People's (NAACP's) lawsuits that culminated in *Brown v. Board of Education* (1954) in significant ways, one of which was the use of language as a proxy for race (Powers, 2012). There were no formal laws that empowered school districts to segregate Mexican American students (Donato & Hanson, 2012). The legal arguments marshaled by the plaintiffs did not challenge the language-as-problem orientation. Starting with *Mendez*, a key strategy the plaintiffs' lawyers used was to document how Mexican American students' English skills were not systematically assessed prior to their placements in Mexican schools and that their initial placements were not reevaluated (Powers, 2008; Powers & Patton, 2008). The plaintiffs did not address students' right to learn their home language. All of the parties—plaintiffs, districts, lawyers, and judges—assumed that students should be taught in English. Yet the *Mendez* court also conceded that it was permissible for school officials to place elementary school students with "foreign language handicaps" in separate classrooms after "credible examination of each child whose capacity to learn is under consideration" (*Mendez v. Westminster*, 1946, p. 550; see also G. A. Martinez, 1994).

Another important feature of Mexican American segregation cases was that Mexican Americans were considered White by courts and other state actors. Yet Mexican American civil rights organizations and lawyers for Mexican American plaintiffs also used the argument that Mexican Americans were White to challenge segregation and other forms of racial discrimination. An extensive literature has explored the origins and consequences of this legal Whiteness (see, e.g., Behnken, 2011; Blanton, 2006; Foley, 1998, 2010; Gross, 2007; Haney López, 1997; Romero, 2005; Sheridan, 2003; Wilson, 2003), which had important implications for desegregation cases in the Southwest in the late 1960s and early 1970s.

In the post-*Brown* era, Mexican American plaintiffs continued to use the legal system in efforts to compel districts to desegregate. In Texas, the plaintiffs' legal victory in *Delgado* did not result in desegregation. State officials resisted desegregating Mexican schools by gerrymandering attendance zones, allowing freedom of choice for Anglo students, and maintaining segregation in the lower grades (Valencia, 2008). *Hernandez v. Driscoll* (1957) challenged the segregation of Mexican American classrooms in the early elementary grades. Prior to *Delgado v. Bastrop* (1948), Mexican American students were segregated in separate buildings and schools through the sixth grade. *Hernandez* followed the legal trajectory of the *Mendez* cases; the Texas courts did not extend the Supreme Court's holding in *Brown* to Mexican American segregation. Wilson (2003) observed that the lawyer for the Mexican American plaintiffs only briefly invoked *Brown* in his legal arguments. Likewise, the *Hernandez* court did not cite *Brown* in its opinion, relying on *Independent School District v. Salvatierra* (1930), *Mendez v. Westminster* (1946), and *Delgado v. Bastrop* (1948). As in these earlier cases, the court found that students' placements were not based on their English proficiency and as a result the district was engaging in "unreasonable race discrimination against all Mexican children as a group throughout the first two grades" (*Hernandez v. Driscoll*, 1957, p. 14).

In the late 1960s, racial discrimination tended to be the focal issue of segregation cases in the Southwest, many of which had Black and Latino/Latina plaintiffs. Language issues played a less central role in these cases than in *Salvatierra* (1930), *Mendez* (1946), and the cases the latter inspired. During this period, federal legislation, regulations, and judicial opinions were redefining the federal government's approach to segregation. In 1964, Congress passed the Civil Rights Act, which authorized the Attorney General to initiate desegregation lawsuits, prohibited racial discrimination in any program that was supported by federal funds, and empowered federal agencies to enforce the antidiscrimination requirement (Stone, Seidman, Sunstein, Tushnet, & Karlan, 2005). The Department of Health Education and Welfare (HEW) issued desegregation guidelines in 1965 and 1966 that banned school districts from creating attendance zones and freedom of choice plans that would maintain segregation. The Fifth Circuit Court affirmed the HEW guidelines in a series of decisions and declared that the Supreme Court's decisions in *Brown I* and *II* required school districts to take "affirmative action" to desegregate (*United States v. Jefferson County Board of Education*, 1966, p. 845). In *Green v. County School Board of New Kent County* (1968), the Supreme Court ruled that offering students the freedom to choose the schools they wished to attend in a context where segregation was deeply entrenched was not sufficient to create "a unitary system in which racial segregation was eliminated root and branch" (p. 438).

Federal agencies also began to broaden official definitions of discrimination beyond the Black–White binary paradigm of race (Perea, 1997; Skrentny, 2002). Although the Civil Rights Act prohibited discrimination based on "race, color, religion or national origin" (78 Stat. 241, Section 401(b)), HEW and the Justice Department initially did not use the new legislation to address the segregation of Mexican American students because they considered them White for desegregation purposes (Bowman, 2010; San Miguel, 1987). In the mid-1960s, Mexican American activists demanded that the federal government address discrimination against Mexican Americans and appoint Mexican American representatives to the agencies and commissions charged with implementing federal civil rights legislation (San Miguel, 1987; Wilson, 2005). In 1968, the Mexican American Legal Defense Fund was founded with a grant from the Ford Foundation to fund civil rights litigation. Some of the Mexican American Legal Defense Fund's early cases were desegregation lawsuits aimed at forcing HEW to take action against the discrimination against Mexican American students the latter had extensively documented in the wake of the Civil Rights Act.

By the late 1960s, the U.S. Commission on Civil Rights (1971) embarked on a series of studies addressing the "educational deprivations faced by Mexican American students," focusing primarily on the Southwest (p. 7). The federal government and Black and Mexican American plaintiffs were challenging school segregation plans in the Southwest because districts were using Mexican Americans' legal status as White—the argument that the lawyers for Mexican American plaintiffs had used in earlier cases to successfully challenge segregation—to maintain segregation. If Mexican Americans were White, district officials could claim that a predominantly Black and Mexican American school was integrated. In 1968, 3 months before the Supreme Court announced its decision in *Green*, HEW took action against a school district in Texas for its efforts to preserve segregation by allowing White families to transfer into its schools in order to avoid attending a desegregated school and attempting to annex a White residential area (Schott, 1982). An investigation by HEW and the Justice Department uncovered evidence that many districts had engaged in similar strategies. In 1970, the Department of Justice sued school districts throughout Texas and the Texas Education Agency to force them to desegregate. Although many of the original actions focused on Black students, federal agencies expanded some of these to address the segregation of Mexican American students (*United States v. Texas Education Agency*, 1970).

In a parallel development, in late 1968 steelworker Jose Cisneros initiated a lawsuit against the Corpus Christi Independent School District with the support of his union when the school district rebuffed parents' and HEW's requests to address poor conditions in predominantly Mexican American schools (Valencia, 2008; Wilson, 2003). In his decision for the plaintiffs, Judge Seals held the following: (a) the Supreme Court's holding in *Brown* applied to Mexican Americans because they comprised an "identifiable ethnic minority" that had experienced segregation and discrimination and *Brown* forbids both practices; (b) Black students had been segregated by law and as a result Corpus Christi operated as a dual school system; and (c) the school district's administrative practices, which used existing patterns of residential segregation to maintain segregated schools, were a form of de jure segregation (*Cisneros v. Corpus Christi ISD*, 1970, p. 607). In holding that *Brown* applied to Mexican Americans, the court cited the government studies and reports that had been generated under the auspices of the Civil Rights Act. Although *Cisneros* was relitigated over the next decade, Seal's decision provided the legal foundation for courts to address the segregation of Mexican American students in the Justice Department's cases. In 1973, the Supreme Court drew on these cases and documents to reach similar conclusions in *Keyes v. Denver School District No. 1* (1973).

LANGUAGE RIGHTS

In the late 1960s, federal agencies and courts began to directly address the needs of ELLs. As I explain below, the most influential and enduring of these efforts reflected the language-as-barrier orientation. Unlike desegregation, these language policies are not grounded in constitutional principles but the guarantees provided by federal legislation that expanded civil rights laws to include language as a protected category (San Miguel, 2004). The most well known of these is the Supreme Court's decision in *Lau v. Nichols* (1974), which is best understood in the context of the federal legislation and regulations that preceded and followed it (Gándara, Moran, & Garcia, 2004).

In 1966, the National Education Association (NEA) issued *The Invisible Minority*, which documented the educational challenges that Mexican American children faced in Southwestern schools: family poverty, low academic achievement, and high dropout rates. In contrast to the deficit assumptions that drove many compensatory education programs (Valencia, 2010), the report also highlighted school practices by asking, "Is there something inherent in our system of public education that impedes the education of the Mexican American child?" (NEA, 1966, p. 7). *Invisible Minority* argued that the "watered-down" English-dominant curriculum taught in most schools and prohibitions against speaking Spanish increased the achievement gap between Mexican American students and their Anglo-American peers, lowered students' self-esteem, and reinforced negative stereotypes about Mexican American students. The report showcased model programs in the Southwest aimed at developing students' Spanish proficiency alongside English.

After the report was issued, the NEA held a planning conference in Tucson to promote the report and its findings to policymakers. In January 1967, Senator Ralph Yarborough of Texas introduced the Bilingual Education Act (BEA) in Congress, which amended the Elementary and Secondary Education Act by adding Title VII, Bilingual Education Programs, to address the needs of ELLs (San Miguel, 2004). Some of the NEA staff members involved in the report and conference worked with Yarborough's staff to draft the bill, which was signed by President Johnson in December 1967.[9]

Compared to the bill that became law, Yarborough's original bill departed from the language-as-problem orientation in important ways. The earliest version of the BEA proposed programs targeted at Spanish speakers, and had a relatively expansive conceptualization of language rights. When Yarborough introduced the bill in Congress, he framed it by highlighting the school experiences of Mexican American students (113 Cong. Rec., 1967):

Little children, many of whom enter school knowing no English and speaking only Spanish are denied the use of their language. Spanish is forbidden to them and they are required to struggle along as best they can in English. . . . Thus the Mexican-American child is wrongly led to believe from his first day of school that there is something wrong with him, because of his language. (p. 599)

Yarborough's bill reflects the language-as-barrier orientation, which was shaped by emerging civil rights law. Some policymakers felt that some forms of discrimination that prevented individuals from fully participating in educational and other settings would not be addressed by removing formal barriers and that more proactive efforts were needed (Skrentny, 2002). Whereas claims based on the language-as-problem orientation view the student as the primary problem, the language-as-barrier orientation suggests that school practices hinder student progress (Moran, 2005). More specifically, in the school segregation cases that exemplify the language-as-problem orientation, district officials used language to rationalize racially discriminatory practices. In contrast, the BEA was a language policy aimed at supporting and encouraging schools to create or expand programs and change their instructional practices to support ELL students.

The law proposed by Yarborough also drew on the language-as-resource orientation because it endorsed and would have provided financial support for programs that taught Spanish as a native language. Another provision would have amended the National Defense Education Act to support the training of teachers of bilingual students. Evoking the language-as-resource orientation in his remarks on the Senate floor, Yarborough described this latter proposal as a way to develop bilingual speakers with the cultural knowledge to advance U.S. foreign policy goals in Latin America (113 Cong. Rec., 1967).

The version of the BEA that became law was more firmly rooted in the language-as-barrier orientation rather than the language-as-resource orientation. The final bill targeted low-income ELL[10] students who spoke any language rather than Spanish speakers of any income level (BEA, 1968). Although it provided funds to support bilingual education programs, the BEA as passed did not address native language instruction. Instead, the funds awarded to schools for compensatory education could be used to support the more neutral goal of "programs designed to impart to students a knowledge of the history and culture associated with their languages" (BEA, 1968, p. 817). Yarborough's provision for amending the National Defense Education Act was also dropped; the final bill provided funds aimed at improving the qualifications of teachers of students of "limited English-speaking ability" rather than teachers of bilingual students (p. 820).

According to Moran (1988), the BEA was "largely symbolic" because it was a "modest grant-in-aid program to support experimental educational projects" and did not impinge on states' and local districts' authority (pp. 1259, 1263). However, a 1970 memorandum issued by the Office for Civil Rights (OCR) represented a shift toward the language-as-right orientation because it extended the protections of Title VI of the Civil Rights Act to language minority students by directing districts that received federal funding to take "affirmative steps" to ensure that ELLs benefitted from the instruction they received (p. 929; Moran, 1988). Levin (1983) viewed the 1970 memorandum as significant because "it was the first expression of a legal requirement to provide special assistance to children with English-language deficiencies" (p. 35), and it applied to any district that received federal funds—not just those funded under the BEA. In practice, both were largely unenforced mandates (Moran, 1988; Skrentny, 2002). Although Congress authorized between $30 million and $135 million in funding per year for the BEA for the first 6 years of implementation, it appropriated a fraction of the allotted funds. Similarly the OCR "committed itself to regulatory protections in principle without considering whether enforcement resources were available" (Moran, 1988, p. 1249). However, the 1970 memorandum played a significant role in the first Supreme Court decision that directly addressed language policy in public schools, *Lau v. Nichols* (1974; Moran, 2007).

Lau v. Nichols (1974) was brought on behalf of non–English speaking Chinese students in the San Francisco School District who were not receiving academic support to help them learn English. The Supreme Court did not address the plaintiffs' equal protection claims. Instead, the Court drew on the provisions of the Civil Rights Act that prohibited any program or activity supported by federal funds from discriminating based on "race, color, or national origin" (p. 566), and the 1970 OCR memorandum to conclude that the lack of services for "national origin-minority group children" constituted a form of discrimination that was prohibited by the Civil Rights Act (*Lau v. Nichols*, 1974, p. 568). Reflecting the language-as-barrier orientation informed by the language-as-right orientation, *Lau* established ELL students' rights to benefit from instruction in public schools conducted in English. The court did not directly address the role of students' home languages in that process, although the court did observe that California allowed schools to offer bilingual education as long as "it does not interfere with the systematic, sequential and regular instruction of all pupils in the English language" (*Lau v. Nichols*, 1974, p. 565).

Congress codified *Lau* in the Equal Educational Opportunities Act (EEOA) of 1974 (20 USCS § 1703). The EEOA was largely concerned with segregation; most of the provisions prohibited districts from engaging in practices that would create or perpetuate school segregation. However, § 1703(f) defines inaction by educational agencies to address language barriers that prevent students' equal participation in instructional programs taught in English as another form of the denial of equal educational opportunity. Although statements by federal officials suggested that the EEOA would ensure that students had a right to bilingual education (Del Valle, 2003), the version of § 1703(f) that was approved by Congress remained firmly rooted in the language-as-barrier orientation, although it gave students the right to redress. The reauthorization of the BEA in 1974 contained a much more expansive view of the role of language and language rights.

Although a full discussion is beyond the scope of this chapter, the two goals of the EEOA—desegregating schools and addressing language barriers—can be in tension if pursued in tandem in districts. Indeed, *Lau* was litigated in the wake of a lawsuit that resulted in a court-ordered desegregation plan for the San Francisco Unified School District (Moran, 2007). Chinese families that opposed the desegregation plan because they saw neighborhood schools as important for maintaining their culture and language sought a court order preventing the plan from being enacted, which the Supreme Court denied. In a decision upheld by the Supreme Court, the district court ruled that the school district could continue to offer bilingual classes "in any manner which does not create, maintain or foster segregation" without acknowledging the implementation challenges this presented (*Johnson v. San Francisco Unified School District*, 1971, p. 1322).[11] Similarly, in the remedy phase of *Keyes v. School District* (1975), the Tenth Circuit Court held that Hispanic students could not be segregated for the purposes of receiving bilingual education and that "bilingual instruction must be subordinate to a plan of desegregation" (p. 480).

The BEA of 1974 is more squarely rooted in the language-as-rights orientation because it framed bilingual education as necessary for "establish[ing] equal educational opportunity for all students" (BEA of 1974, § 702(a)). The funds authorized under the act were not targeted at low-income students, which departed from the language-as-problem orientation of its predecessor (Ruiz, 1984). The BEA of 1974 also engaged the language-as-resource orientation to some degree. For example, the statement of legislative intent recognized that ELLs have different cultural backgrounds from their English-dominant peers and highlighted the need to support bilingual educational programs because "children of limited English-speaking ability benefit through the fullest utilization of multiple language and cultural resources" (BEA of 1974, § 702(a)). That said, the central focus of the legislation remained the use of students' native languages to support English acquisition; the law did not address the maintenance of native languages.

In 1975, the OCR issued a document outlining remedies districts could take to comply with *Lau v. Nichols* that represented a broader engagement with the language-as-resource orientation than the BEA of 1974. Known as the Lau Remedies, the document described formal procedures for districts to identify ELL students, diagnose students' needs, and select educational programs to meet those needs. The Lau Remedies recommended that elementary or middle school students receive a transitional bilingual educational (TBE) program, bilingual/bicultural program, or a multilingual/multicultural program. The latter two were defined as drawing on students' native languages and cultures for instruction with the goal of educating students so that they could "function, totally, in both languages and cultures" (OCR, 1975). A TBE program provided the same features as the bilingual/bicultural program until students were "fully functional" in English after which they would no longer receive instruction in their native languages (p. 940).[12] The Remedies also specified that elementary and middle school students should not be placed in English as a Second Language programs because they were not developmentally appropriate. If ELL students did not have the skills to succeed in classes taught in their native languages, districts must provide "compensatory education in the native language" (OCR, 1975, p. 937).

Perhaps because the document was meant to enforce *Lau*, which did not directly address language rights, the Lau Remedies did not explicitly frame learning their home languages as a right to which ELLs were entitled. Rather, the use of students' home languages was characterized as necessary to support their developmental needs. As a result, the Lau Remedies fell short of a robust instantiation of the language-as-resource orientation informed by the language-as-right orientation where students have a right to become fluent in English and their home languages. In practice, the Remedies were used to negotiate consent agreements for districts that were out of compliance with Title VI (Levin, 1983).[13] Between 1975 and 1980, HEW reached 500 compliance agreements with districts based on the Lau Remedies.

Although federal legislation and regulations began to engage the language-as-resource orientation, in the period after the Supreme Court's decision in *Lau*, the federal courts were more equivocal. For example, in *Serna v. Portales* (1974) the Tenth Circuit Court upheld the remedy the trial court devised to address the educational needs of Mexican American students, which suggested but did not mandate that the district provide bicultural education. The plaintiffs and the school district disagreed on the scope of the bilingual education plan for the elementary and junior high schools. The district's plan, which the Tenth Circuit Court characterized as a "token plan that would not benefit appellees" would have provided bilingual instruction for 30 minutes a day to 150 elementary school students in Grades 1 through 4; the plaintiffs proposed a "more expansive bilingual-bicultural program" (*Serna v. Portales*, 1974, p. 1154). The trial court ordered the district to (a) expand the amount of time bilingual instruction was offered in elementary schools, (b) offer it to all eligible students, and (c) institute a testing program to ensure that the bilingual instruction met students' needs. The court also required that the district's elementary schools incorporate "a bicultural outlook . . . in as many subject areas as practicable" (*Serna v. Portales*, 1974, p. 1151). Junior high students had to be tested for English proficiency and provided with bilingual classes if necessary. Whereas the district argued that the trial court overstepped its authority, the Tenth Circuit Court upheld the trial court's ruling, noting that the evidence presented at trial suggested that Mexican American students had been long underserved.

The Tenth Circuit Court drew heavily on *Lau* decided 6 months earlier. The goal of bilingual instruction was to "rectify English deficiencies" so that students could meaningfully benefit from the district's instructional programs (*Serna v. Portales*, 1974, p. 1153). The court did not explicitly address the maintenance of students' home languages, and bicultural education was suggested but not mandated. In the years that followed, few courts embraced the provision of bicultural education and the goal of home language maintenance suggested by the Lau Remedies. Many of the defendant districts had consent agreements with HEW. Although some of these districts offered instruction in students' home languages and cultures, the courts primarily saw this as a means to help students become English proficient. For example, in *Rios v. Reed* (1978), the court found that although the school district's bilingual program and placement procedures fell short of the requirements of *Lau* and federal regulations, it was "not obligated to offer a program of indefinite duration for instruction in Spanish art and culture. The bicultural element is necessary only to enhance the child's learning ability. The purpose is not to establish a bilingual society" (*Rios v. Reed*, 1978, p. 23). When school districts did not offer bicultural education, most courts, and in particular appellate courts, were reluctant, or, even resistant to requiring it (*Guadalupe Organization v. Tempe Elementary School District*, 1978; *Keyes v. Denver School District No 1*, 1975; *Otero v. Mesa County School District*, 1975).[14]

By the end of the 1970s, political support for bilingual education had significantly declined. In 1978, the reauthorization of the BEA defined a bilingual educational program as Structured English Immersion (SEI; Wiese & Garcia, 2001; see also

Gándara & Gómez, 2009). Students' native languages could be used "to the extent necessary to allow a child to achieve competence in the English language"[15] (BEA of 1978, § 703 (a)(4)). In 1978, HEW agreed to publish the Lau Remedies as proposed regulations after Alaska challenged HEW's efforts to enforce them (Levin, 1983). The proposed guidelines "moved away from the Remedies' emphasis on long-term enrichment through bilingualism and biculturalism to a narrower focus on short-term compensatory education" (Moran, 1988, p. 1294). HEW withdrew the proposed guidelines and the Lau Remedies after widespread and organized opposition (Del Valle, 2003; Levin, 1983; Moran, 1988; San Miguel, 2004).

In 1981, the Fifth Circuit Court addressed the legal merits of the Lau Guidelines in *Castañeda v. Pickard*. *Castañeda* was brought by parents in a school district in Texas in which HEW had unsuccessfully tried to enforce Title VI of the Civil Rights Act. The plaintiffs charged that the district's bilingual education program violated Title VI and the EEOA because they were inconsistent with the Lau Remedies. The court held that the district's program did not violate Title VI because the Remedies (a) were intended for districts that were not providing language remediation for ELL students and (b) were not developed using standard administrative procedures for rules and regulations, and as such should not be given deference by the court.

In addressing the plaintiffs' EEOA claim, the court noted that Congress did not intend the EEOA to prescribe a specific type of language remediation program; rather, it provided funds for districts to adopt model programs or develop their own. Because Congress did not provide guidelines for courts to evaluate districts' language remediation programs, the Fifth Circuit Court established a three-part inquiry that subsequent courts have used to assess if these programs adequately address the needs of ELL students. First, a school district's program must be "informed by a theory recognized as sound by some experts in the field" (*Castañeda v. Pickard*, 1981, p. 1009). Second, the district's program and practices must be consistent with this theory. Third, the district's must evaluate its programs after they have been implemented to ensure that they address students' language barriers, and change them as necessary. According to Bowman (2010), *Castañeda* allows districts a significant amount of latitude to choose instructional programs that comply with the EEOA, including SEI programs. The three-part inquiry established in *Castañeda* became the "seminal test for determining EEOA compliance" (Bowman, 2010, p. 930).[16]

For a brief period, the Lau Remedies legitimized aspects of the language-as-resource orientation by asserting that ELLs' home languages should be developed and maintained, although they fell short of framing the development of students' home language skills as a right. The BEA of 1978 and *Castañeda* repudiated this partial embrace of the language-as-resource orientation and reflected a belief that the use of ELL students' native languages in public schools should be focused on teaching students English. As a result, they are more closely aligned with the language-as-barrier orientation. Moreover, students' language rights were limited to the narrower right of participating and benefiting from instruction in English. Gándara et al. (2004) have observed that the amendments to the BEA after 1978 whittled away at the support for the use of students' home languages in instruction in earlier iterations of the legislation. When the Elementary and Secondary Education Act was reauthorized as the No Child Left Behind Act in 2001, Title VII (Bilingual Education, Language Acquisition, and Language Enhancement) was replaced by Title III, titled "Language Instruction, Limited English-Proficient and Immigrant Students" (Gándara et al., 2004, p. 40). The new law emphasized improving ELLs' English proficiency and transitioning them into all-English instructional settings with only a passing mention of the use of students' native language in instruction.

SCHOOL FINANCE

The case of *Flores v. Arizona* represents the third major phase in this trajectory. In *Flores*, language rights were intertwined with a legal approach aimed at increasing equity and access for poor and minority students—school finance litigation. Although generally race-neutral in its claims, school finance litigation was a strategy developed by scholars and civil rights advocates in the late 1960s to address de facto segregation and the effects of White flight on schools, or the more intractable patterns of racial and economic inequality that were outside the scope of *Brown v. Board of Education* (Liu, 2006; Minorini & Sugarman, 1999). Most states fund their public schools by requiring school districts to generate a significant proportion of their revenues via local property taxes. School districts with high property wealth can more easily raise revenues and thereby fund their public schools than school districts with low property wealth. School finance cases challenge state education financing methods with the goal of forcing state legislatures to more equitably distribute funding to school districts in order to improve the educational opportunities available to poor and minority students, who are often clustered in low-wealth school districts.

Initially, plaintiffs challenged school financing systems in both state and federal courts and had some early successes in state courts (e.g., *Serrano v. Priest*, 1971) and setbacks in federal courts (*McInnis v. Shapiro*, 1968). In *San Antonio School District v. Rodriguez* (1973), the Supreme Court rejected the claim that there was an identifiable class of poor people whose rights were denied by the state of Texas's funding scheme and declared that education was not a "fundamental right" guaranteed by the U.S. Constitution. As a result, the state's system of school funding did not have to meet the higher standard of judicial scrutiny associated with federal Equal Protection claims and was declared constitutional by the Supreme Court. *San Antonio School District v. Rodriguez* (1973) foreclosed subsequent challenges to state school financing systems in the federal courts. Most subsequent efforts to reform school funding systems turn on the provisions for education in state constitutions—state courts are the appropriate legal venue for these cases. *Flores v. Arizona* is an exception. I provide an overview of the history of Flores in the lower federal courts to provide context for my analysis of the Supreme Court's decision in *Horne v. Flores* (2009) and the federal district court's decision in *Flores v. Arizona* (2013).

Originally filed in 1992, the *Flores* plaintiffs alleged that Arizona violated Title VI and the EEOA because it did not provide ELL students in the Nogales Unified School District (NUSD) with "a program of instruction calculated to make them proficient in speaking, understanding, reading, and writing English, while enabling them to master the standard academic curriculum as required of all students" (*Flores v. Arizona*, 1999, p. 939). Because the central legal question in *Flores v. Arizona* involved the provision of services for ELLs, which is under the jurisdiction of federal law, the case has been tried in the federal courts. However, the plaintiffs also alleged funding disparities. After many delays, the case went to trial in 1999. In an initial order, the federal trial court judge informed the parties that he planned to use the holdings of the Arizona Supreme Court in a school finance case, *Roosevelt v. Bishop* (1994), to guide his analysis (*Flores v. Arizona*, 1999). In *Roosevelt*, the Arizona Supreme Court declared that the state's method of funding capital improvements for public schools was unconstitutional because it created "substantial disparities" in funding across districts and as such fell short of the requirement in the state constitution that the state shall provide a "general and uniform" public school system (*Roosevelt v. Bishop*, 1994, p. 815). In a subsequent decision at the remedy phase, the Arizona Supreme Court criticized the legislature's revised capital funding scheme "because the dollar amount chosen to cure inadequacies in public school facilities is arbitrary and bears no relation to actual need" (*Hull v. Albrecht*, 1997, p. 524). The Court required the state to create standards for adequate facilities and provide funds to ensure that schools would not fall below those standards.

In 2000, the U.S. District Court ruled in favor of the plaintiffs. It held that the state did not provide adequate funding for ELL programs in the NUSD. The court conducted a *Casteñeda* inquiry, which it elaborated using *Roosevelt v. Bishop* (1994). The court stated at the outset that the state and district's models for ELL instruction passed the first part of the *Casteñeda* inquiry. For the second part of the *Casteñeda* inquiry, the court determined that the state needed to adopt minimum standards for ELL funding and program monitoring because without such standards it could not assess whether or not the programs implemented by the state were reasonably related to the theory that guided the program. The district court's initial decision reflected both the language-as-barrier orientation and the emphasis on adequacy in contemporary school finance cases. In adequacy cases, plaintiffs' claims focus around the extent to which students—in this case ELL students—have access to the educational resources they need to meet state standards (Koski & Reich, 2006; Odden & Clune, 1998).

The district court held that the funding the state provided for ELLs was "arbitrary and capricious" and not substantially related to the level of spending needed to ensure ELL students have the resources that will enable them to meet state standards (*Flores v. Arizona*, 2000, p. 1239). The court attributed the district's inability to provide a high-quality program for ELLs to revenue shortfalls that resulted from the state's funding model. Arizona's public schools are funded primarily by state and local governments through a foundation program; the state provides districts with a minimum or base funding level per student. School districts can supplement the state-guaranteed minimum through voter-approved increases in property taxes. Compared to districts with low property values, districts with high property values can generate more revenue at lower tax rates through voter-approved property tax overrides. Although the state provided districts with an additional $150 per ELL student each year, this sum was well below the $450 per student suggested by a cost study of districts' spending on programs for ELLs the state had conducted more than 10 years earlier. ELL students tend to be concentrated in low–property wealth school districts like the NUSD. As a result, these districts have higher educational costs and less capacity to raise the funds they need to meet their students' needs.

The court concluded that because of these funding disparities, ELL students in NUSD were placed in overcrowded classrooms without sufficiently qualified teachers, aides, and materials. In essence, state funding and resource shortfalls prevented the district from putting its theory of ELL instruction into practice. As a result, the court held that the state's funding scheme failed the second part of the *Castañeda* test and thus violated the EEOA. The court ordered the state to (a) conduct a cost study of an adequate education for ELLs and (b) use the findings of the cost study to fund programs for ELLs at an appropriate level. In 2001, the court extended its order to address ELL funding for the entire state.

The state did not appeal or comply with the court's decision.[17] For example, in December 2001, the legislature increased funding for ELL students to match what the NUSD school district spent on its ELL programs. The district court rejected the revised funding model because it had already determined that the programs in NUSD were inadequate. The legislature also conducted a 2005 cost study that suggested the state needed to increase funding for ELL students considerably but did not use it to change its funding model (Office of the Auditor General, 2007). As the state's response to *Flores* was unfolding, Proposition 203 changed ELL education in Arizona. In 2000, Arizona's voters overwhelmingly approved Proposition 203, which requires ELL students to participate in SEI "for a temporary transition period not normally intended to exceed one year" (Arizona Secretary of State, 2000, p. 1). All of the books and instructional materials used in SEI classrooms have to be in English; teachers are limited to minimal use of students' home languages while speaking with students. Although Proposition 203 did not remove bilingual programs from public schools, it made SEI programs the default choice for families.

In January 2005, the district court ordered the state to comply with its decision or face an escalating series of fines, which it imposed in December. In March 2006, the legislature passed HB 2064, which increased yearly funding for ELL students to approximately $450 per student and established a task force charged with developing and adopting research-based models for teaching ELLs. When the district court determined that HB 2064 did not comply with its 2000 decision, the state appealed the decision to the Ninth Circuit Court. The state asserted that it should be released from the district court's 2000 order under Rule 60(b)(5) because "applying [the order] prospectively is no longer equitable" (*Flores v. Arizona*, 2008, p. 1162). The state claimed that since 2000, changes in state, local, and federal policies had altered conditions for ELLs so that the question of whether or not HB 2064 satisfied the court was no longer relevant. When the Ninth Circuit Court rejected the state's argument, it appealed to the Supreme Court. The Rule 60(b)(5) claim was the focus of the Supreme Court's decision in *Horne v. Flores* (2009).

The Supreme Court decided in favor of the state by a five to four majority and remanded the case to the lower court to conduct a Rule 60(b)(5) analysis based on the parameters it outlined in its opinion. Although the majority observed at the outset of its opinion that the state must "fulfill its obligation under the EEOA" (*Horne v. Flores*, 2009, p. 2), its central concern was local control. The majority's analysis was not focused on students' rights but on the right of state officials to make decisions. The Court viewed Rule 60(b)(5) as a means of checking the power of federal courts to enforce their orders. Deeply skeptical of federal control, the court took issue with the duration of the lawsuit. It viewed the lower court's order as "dictating state or local budget priorities" and as a result it "[bound] state and local officials to the policy preferences of their predecessors," which limited the authority conferred on them by their offices (*Horne v. Flores*, 2009, pp. 12, 13).

The majority held that the lower courts' focus on the funding directed at ELLs was too narrow and instead required the district court to assess if the state's programs and policies met the EEOA's "appropriate action" standard. According to the Court, "[I]f a durable remedy has been implemented, continued enforcement of the order is not only unnecessary, but improper" (*Horne v. Flores*, 2009, p. 13), because § 1712 of the EEOA "limits court-ordered remedies to those that 'are essential to correct particular denials of equal educational opportunities or equal protection of the laws'" (*Horne v. Flores*, 2009, p. 14). The court outlined four conditions that the district court had to consider in its analysis: (a) the new instructional model for ELLs, (b) increases in state funding for education, (c) reforms undertaken in NUSD that addressed some of the issues identified by the district court, and (d) the No Child Left Behind Act (NCLB). The first two are relevant for the discussion here.

First, the Supreme Court noted that ELL instruction in NUSD changed considerably because it had shifted from a bilingual model to a SEI model to conform to the requirements of Proposition 203. It also highlighted the provisions of HB 2064 that created a task force to develop models for SEI, professional development requirements for teachers, and provided state support for implementation. By the time *Flores* was heard by the Supreme Court, the state had adopted a model for SEI instruction under the auspices of HB 2064 that requires ELL students to be placed in separate classes for a 4-hour English Language Development (ELD) block focused on developing discrete language skills with little emphasis on academic content (Gándara & Orfield, 2012; T. Martinez, 2010).[18] This model was not evaluated by the Supreme Court. However, the majority clearly stated that it viewed research evidence suggesting that "SEI is significantly more effective than bilingual education" as more persuasive than research that supported the use of students' home language in instruction (*Horne v. Flores*, 2009, p. 24).[19]

Overall language issues were incidental to the court's decision. Indeed, the majority opinion does not cite *Lau*. To the extent that the court addressed language rights it drew on the EEOA or *Casteñeda v. Pickard* (1981). While the *Lau* court was reluctant to view language rights as raising constitutional questions, its decision is grounded in federal civil rights statutes. In *Horne* the majority is concerned with procedural issues. Likewise, whereas *Lau* suggested that students' home languages could be used to support instruction, *Horne* is hostile to that view. Not incidentally, this stance on language rights is aligned with the majority's stance on state's rights, although the state's ELD model constrains local school officials' decisions about ELL instruction (Brief for the Washington Lawyers' Committee for Civil Rights and Urban Affairs et al. in Support of Respondents, 2009).

Second, the majority viewed the lower courts' focus on targeted funding as misguided. They argued that overall funding for schools had increased in the decade since the complaint was filed, which they saw as meeting EEOA requirements. Although the majority conceded that it was "unfortunate" that schools might have to "divert money from other worthwhile programs" (*Horne v. Flores*, 2009, p. 33), they viewed these as decisions that local officials were empowered to make. The opinion did not address how the between-district inequalities in funding documented in the lower courts' decisions might constrain some district leaders' control over their programs and funding more than others.[20] As a result, the majority's engagement with the key concern that drives school finance litigation was also thin.

The federal district court's final decision in *Flores* was announced in March 2013. The district court was charged with assessing the instructional model implemented under HB 2064, the 4-hour ELD block. Although it observed that "the academic content [in the ELD block] provided to ELL students is not the same, and is less than, what is provided to English proficient students," and that the state does not have provisions to ensure that these students are not "deprived of academic content," it deferred to the judgment of the task force empowered by the state legislature under HB 2064 to determine the state's model for ELL instruction (pp. 9–10).

Drawing on *Casteñeda*, the court noted that its role was not to adjudicate research debates about ELL instruction. Rather, the court has to determine that the program in question meets a more basic standard, that is, it is "recognized as sound by some experts in the field, or at least deemed a legitimate strategy" (*Casteñeda v. Pickard*, cited in *Flores v. Arizona*, 2013, p. 20), and the 4-hour block met that minimal standard. Whereas in prior decisions, the court has deferred to the state regarding its choice of instructional models for ELL education (e.g., *Flores v. Arizona*, 2007), it also observed here that "[t]he Supreme Court made clear that the State has tremendous discretion and flexibility to design programs that meet local needs" (*Flores v. Arizona*, 2013, p. 19). The federal district court's final word suggests that the Supreme Court gave it extremely narrow parameters for assessing the state's programs and policies:

It appears that the state has made a choice in how it wants to spend funds on teaching students the English language. It may turn out to be penny wise and pound foolish, as at the end of the day, speaking English, and not having other educational gains in science, math, etc. will still leave some children behind.

However, this lawsuit is no longer the vehicle to pursue the myriad of educational issues in this state. (*Flores v. Arizona*, 2013, pp. 22–23)

The court also rejected the plaintiffs' claim under § 1703(a) of the EEOA that the 4-hour ELD block was a form of segregation, instead characterizing it as a form of ability grouping. Prior courts—including the *Casteñeda* court—have concluded that ability grouping is allowable under the EEOA (*Flores v. Arizona*, 2013).

CONCLUSION: BACK TO THE FUTURE

This review highlights how courts have been reluctant to engage language rights for ELL students attending public schools to any substantive degree, preferring instead to defer to the judgment of state and local officials. In many ways, *Horne v. Flores* (2009) and *Flores v. Arizona* (2013) bring us back to the policies and practices that predated *Lau* (see also Gándara & Orfield, 2012). In *Horne v Flores* (2009), the Supreme Court used a procedural rule to arrive at a conclusion that paralleled the decision of the Texas Court of Appeals in *Independent School District v. Salvatierra* (1930) almost 80 years earlier. Both courts privileged the judgment of state officials and declared evidence of possible inequalities in treatment as inconclusive and irrelevant. Although post-*Lau* courts have upheld ability grouping by language, the finding by the district court in *Flores v. Arizona* (2013) that districts could segregate based on language ability also echoes Judge McCormick's holding in *Mendez*. Although McCormick was critical of the districts' segregation practices because they were clearly a form of invidious segregation, he also concluded that school officials could segregate students in separate classrooms to address their language needs. Finally, the evidence reviewed by the district court suggests that ELL students in the 4-hour ELD blocks are students receiving "watered-down curricula," a concern raised by the NEA (1966) in *Invisible Minority*. Likewise, the 1970 OCR Memorandum cautioned that ability grouping based on language "must not operate as a dead end or permanent track" (p. 929), yet the state has no means in place to ensure that this will not occur.

This review also highlights how deeply the language-as-barrier orientation has shaped judicial decision making related to language policy in the post–Civil Rights era and suggests that the *Flores* decisions could be read as steps backward from what was an already limited understanding of language rights. The more expansive conceptualization of the role of language in society associated with the language-as-resource orientation has never been substantively engaged by appellate courts or federal policies. Language rights for ELLs in U.S. public schools have been, by default, left to state and local policymakers whose willingness to create policies that value and support multiple languages has been uneven at best, and always subject to reversal.

ACKNOWLEDGMENTS

William Koski's detailed and thoughtful comments helped improve this chapter considerably. I also benefited from Eleanor Brown's feedback. An earlier version of this chapter was presented at the 2013 Law and Society Association Annual Meeting.

NOTES

[1]Ruiz (1984) defines orientations as "dispositions towards language and its role, and toward languages and their role in society" (p. 16). Orientations provide a cognitive frame for understanding the role of language in societies.

[2]I use the term *home language* to refer to the dominant non-English language spoken in students' homes. When relevant I use *native language* and *primary language* interchangeably with *home language* to be consistent with the terms used in the policy documents I analyzed.

[3]Kloss (1971) described this as promotion-oriented language rights. Rodriguez (2006) proposed that multilingualism and language rights should go beyond maintaining ELLs' home language and address the use of the home language in social and political life.

[4]The language-as-barrier orientation closely parallels what Rodriguez (2006) describes as the remedial conception of language rights associated with the "immigrant seeking assimilation on non-discriminatory terms" (p. 705).

[5]Ruiz (1984) views the language-as-problem orientation as encompassing "malicious attitudes resolving to eradicate, invalidate, quarantine or inoculate or comparatively benign ones concerned with remediation and 'improvement'" (p. 21). I describe the latter as the language-as-barrier orientation to distinguish between these because there is a different moral valence between the two. I am indebted to William Koski for the latter point.

[6]Other language rights that might be relevant in educational settings are freedom from discrimination and freedom to use the home language without sanction (Ruiz, 1984).

[7]The Supreme Court's decision in *Meyer v. Nebraska* (1923) is often cited as a key precedent for minority language rights in the United States (Crawford, 1992; Del Valle, 2003). I begin with the segregation cases cited above because *Meyer* addressed language instruction in private schools: "[T]he State's power to prescribe a curriculum for institutions which is supports" was not at issue in the case (*Meyer v. Nebraska*, 1923, p. 402).

[8]As I explain elsewhere, McCormick's decision is complex (Powers & Patton, 2008). Because all parties agreed that racial discrimination was not at issue in the case, McCormick did not have to engage the main holdings in *Plessy v. Ferguson* (1896) and other decisions upholding segregation. Also, state law did not mandate the segregation of Mexican American students.

[9]Yarborough entered an excerpt from *Invisible Minority* into the Congressional Record as an exhibit in support of his bill.

[10]As a compensatory program, the BEA of 1968 also reflected the language-as-problem orientation (Ruiz, 1984).

[11]See also *Morgan v. Kerrigan* (1975) and *Evans v. Buchanan* (1976), both with Hispanic interveners. The courts held that the desegregation plans in question had to ensure that Hispanic students were placed at schools in sufficient numbers to allow bilingual programs to continue. These cases suggest that some parents of ELL students may have preferred maintaining ELL programs to desegregation.

[12]According to Gándara et al. (2004), TBE was the default program in the Lau Guidelines; districts were advised to offer the other programs "when feasible" (p. 29).

[13]Consent or compliance agreements are informal agreements between the Department of Education and school districts that are not meeting federal program requirements. If the districts agree to take steps to come into compliance, the Department will not withhold funds or pursue litigation against the district (Bowman, 2010).

[14]For an exception that predated *Lau*, see *United States v. Texas* (1971).

[15]This was a subtle shift from the definition outlined in the BEA of 1974, which stated that students' native languages could be used to help them "progress effectively through the educational system" (Pub. L. No. 93-380, § 703(a)).

[16]In *Casteñeda* the plaintiffs also argued that the school district's methods of ability grouping unlawfully segregated Mexican American students. The court held that ability grouping is

permissible even if it results in segregation if the ability grouping is "genuinely motivated by educational concerns and not discriminatory motives" (*Castañeda v. Pickard*, 1981, p. 986). However, ability grouping in districts with a history of discrimination that have not fully addressed the effects of discrimination should be subject to closer judicial scrutiny than districts without histories of discrimination. Because there was evidence that suggested the district was conflating language ability and general ability (e.g., the children in the "high" group were all English speakers), the Fifth Circuit Court remanded the case to the trial court to determine if the district's practices resulted in unlawful segregation.

[17]In August 2000, the state entered into a consent decree with the plaintiffs that addressed the methods of identifying ELLs, program quality, and monitoring but did not address the funding issues highlighted by the court (Arizona State Senate Research Staff, 2008).

[18]For research-based critiques of the state's SEI model, see the special issue of *Teachers College Record* on *Horne v. Flores* (introduced by Rios-Aguilar & Gándara, 2012) and Arias and Faltis (2012).

[19]For an overview of research that supports the efficacy of bilingual education, see Brief for the Washington Lawyers' Committee for Civil Rights and Urban Affairs et al. in Support of Respondents (2009) and Brief for the National School Boards Association et al. (2009). See also August and Shanahan (2006) more generally.

[20]In his dissent in *San Antonio School District v. Rodriguez* (1973), Thurgood Marshall characterized this as "the myth of local control" (p. 1346).

REFERENCES

113 Cong. Rec. 599–608 (daily ed. January 17, 1967).

Alvarez, R. R. (1986). The Lemon Grove incident: The nation's first successful desegregation court case. *Journal of San Diego History, 32*(2). Retrieved from http://www.sandiegohistory.org/journal/86spring/lemongrove.htm

Arias, M. B., & Faltis, C. (2012). *Implementing educational language policy in Arizona: Legal, historical and current practices in SEI.* Bristol, England: Multilingual Matters.

Arizona Secretary of State. (2000). *Proposition 203.* Retrieved from http://www.azsos.gov/election/2000/info/pubpamphlet/english/prop203.htm

Arizona State Senate Research Staff. (2008, August 27). Arizona State Senate issue paper: *Flores v. Arizona.* Phoenix: Author.

Arriola, C. (1995). Knocking on the schoolhouse door: Mendez v. Westminster—Equal protection, public education and Mexican Americans in the 1940s. *La Raza Law Journal, 8,* 166–207.

August, D., & Shanahan, T. (Eds.). (2006). *Developing literacy in second-language learners: Report of the National Literacy Panel on language-minority children and youth.* Mahwah, NJ: Lawrence Erlbaum.

Behnken, B. (2011). *Fighting their own battles: Mexican Americans, African Americans, and the struggle for civil rights.* Chapel Hill: University of North Carolina Press.

Bilingual Education Act of 1968, Pub. L. No. 90-247, 81 Stat. 783 (1968).

Bilingual Education Act of 1974, Pub. L. No. 93-380, 88 Stat. 503 (1974–1975).

Bilingual Education Act of 1978, Pub. L. No. 95-561, 92 Stat. 2268 (1978).

Blanton, C. K. (2006). George I. Sanchez, ideology and whiteness in the making of the Mexican American Movement 1930-1960. *Journal of Southern History, 72,* 569–604.

Bosworth, M. H. (2001). *Courts as catalysts: State supreme courts and public school finance equity.* Albany: State University of New York Press.

Bowman, K. L. (2010). Pursuing educational opportunities for Latino/a students. *North Carolina Law Review, 88,* 911–992.

Brief for the National School Boards Association, the American Association of School Board Administrators, the National Education Association, and the Arizona Education Association in Support of Respondent, Horne v. Flores, 129 S. Ct. 2579 (2009).

Brief for the Washington Lawyers' Committee for Civil Rights and Urban Affairs Immigrant and Refugee Rights Project, DC Language Access Coalition, and the Latin American Youth Center in Support of Respondent, Horne v. Flores, 129 S. Ct. 2579 (2009).

Brown v. Board of Educ., 347 U.S. 483 (1954).

Casteñeda v. Pickard, 648 F.2d 989 (5th Cir. 1981).

Cisneros v. Corpus Christi ISD, 324 F. Supp. 599 (S.D. Tex. 1970).

Civil Rights Act of 1964 § 7, 42 U.S.C. § 2000e *et seq.* (1964).

Crawford, J. (1992). *Hold your tongue: Bilingualism and the politics of English-only.* Reading, MA: Addison-Wesley.

Delgado v. Bastrop, No. 338 Civil (W.D. Tex 1948).

Del Valle, S. (2003). *Language rights and the law in the United States: Finding our voices.* Clevedon, England: Multilingual Matters.

Donato, R., & Hanson, J. S. (2012). Legally white, socially "Mexican": The politics of de jure and de facto segregation in the American Southwest. *Harvard Educational Review, 82,* 202–225.

Equal Educational Opportunities Act, 20 U.S.C. § 1703 (1974).

Evans v. Buchanan, 416 F. Supp. 328 (3rd Cir. 1974).

Flores v. Arizona, 48 F. Supp 2d 937 (D. Ariz. 1999).

Flores v. Arizona, 172 F. Supp. 2d 1225 (D. Ariz. 2000).

Flores v. Arizona, 480 F. Supp. 2d 1157 (D. Ariz. 2007).

Flores v. Arizona, 516 F.3d 1140 (9th Cir. 2008).

Flores v. Arizona, No. 92-CV-596-TUC-RCC (D. Ariz. 2013).

Foley, N. (1998). Becoming Hispanic: Mexican Americans and the Faustian pact with whiteness. In N. Foley (Ed.), *Reflexiones 1997: New directions in Mexican American studies.* Austin: University of Texas Press.

Foley, N. (2010). *Quest for equality: The failed promise of black-brown solidarity.* Cambridge, MA: Harvard University Press.

Gándara, P., & Gómez, M. C. (2009). Language policy in education. In G. Sykes, B. Schneider, & D. J. Plank (Eds.), *Handbook of education policy research* (pp. 581–595). New York, NY: Routledge.

Gándara, P., Moran, R., & Garcia, E. (2004). Legacy of Brown: Lau and language policy in the United States. *Review of Research in Education, 28,* 27–46.

Gándara, P., & Orfield, G. (2012). Why Arizona matters: The historical, legal, and political contexts of Arizona's instructional policies and U.S. linguistic hegemony. *Language Policy, 11*(1), 7–19.

Gonzales v. Sheely, 96 F. Supp. 1004 (D. Ariz. 1951).

Green v. County School Board of New Kent County, 391 U.S. 430 (1968).

Gross, A. J. (2007). "The Caucasian cloak": Mexican Americans and the politics of whiteness in the Twentieth century Southwest. *Georgetown Law Journal, 95,* 337–392.

Guadalupe Organization v. Tempe Elementary School District No. 3, 87 F.2d 1022 (9th Cir. 1978).

Haney López, I. F. (1997). Race, ethnicity, erasure: The salience of race to LatCrit theory. *California Law Review, 85,* 1143–1211.

Hernandez v. Driscoll, 1957 U.S. Dist. LEXIS 4784 (S.D. Tex. 1957).

Horne v. Flores, 129 S. Ct. 2579 (2009).

Horowitz, D. L. (1977). *The courts and social policy.* Washington, DC: Brookings Institution Press.

Hull v. Albrecht, 950 P. 2d 1141 (Ariz. 1997).

Independent School District v. Salvatierra, 33 S.W.2d 790 (Tex. Ct. App. 1930).

Johnson v. San Francisco Unified School District, 339 F. *Supp.* 1315 (Dist. Ct. N.D. Cal. 1971).

Keyes v. Denver School District No 1, 413 U.S. 189 (1973).

Keyes v. Denver School District No 1, 521 F.2d 465 (10th Cir. 1975).

Kloss, H. (1971). Language rights of immigrant groups. *International Migration Review, 5,* 250–268.

Koski, W. S., & Reich, R. (2006). When adequate isn't: The retreat from equity in educational law and policy and why it matters. *Emory Law Journal, 56,* 545–618.

Lau v. Nichols, 414 U.S. 563 (1974).

Levin, B. (1983). An analysis of the federal attempt to regulate bilingual education: Protecting civil rights or controlling curriculum? *Journal of Law & Education, 12,* 29–60.

Lippi-Green, R. (2011). *English with an accent: Language ideology and discrimination in the United States.* New York, NY: Routledge.

Liu, G. (2006). The parted paths of school desegregation and school finance litigation. *Law and Inequality, 24,* 81–106.

Martinez, G. A. (1994). Legal indeterminacy, judicial discretion and the Mexican-American litigation experience: 1930-1980. *UC Davis Law Review, 27,* 555–618.

Martinez, T. (2010). *English as a second language, middle school education, education policy, Hispanic American studies.* Available from ProQuest Dissertations and Theses. (UMI No. 1483411)

McInnis v. Shapiro, 293 F. Supp. 327 (N.D. Il. 1968).

Mendez v. Westminster, 64 F. Supp. 544 (Dist. Ct. S.D. Cal. Central Division, 1946).

Meyer v. Nebraska, 262 U.S. 390 (1923).

Minorini, P. A., & Sugarman, S. D. (1999). School finance litigation in the name of educational equity: Its evolution, impact, and future. In H. F. Ladd, R. Chalk, & J. S. Hansen (Eds.), *Equity and adequacy in education finance: Issues and perspectives* (pp. 34–71). Washington, DC: National Academies Press.

Moran, R. F. (1988). The politics of discretion: Federal intervention in bilingual education. *California Law Review, 76,* 1249–1352.

Moran, R. F. (2005). Undone by law: The uncertain legacy of Lau v. Nichols. *Berkeley La Raza Law Journal, 16,* 1–10.

Moran, R. F. (2007). The story of Lau v. Nichols: Breaking the silence in Chinatown. In M. A. Olivas & R. G. Schneider (Eds.), *Education law stories* (pp 111–157). New York, NY: Thomson West.

Morgan v. Kerrigan, 401 F. Supp. 216 (1st Cir. 1975).

National Education Association. (1966). *The invisible minority: Report of the NEA-Tucson survey on the teaching of Spanish to the Spanish-speaking.* Washington, DC: Author.

Odden, A., & Clune, W. H. (1998). School finance systems: Aging structures in need of renovation. *Educational Evaluation and Policy Analysis, 20,* 157–177.

Office of the Auditor General. (2007). *Financing Arizona's English language learner programs: Fiscal years 2002 through 2006.* Phoenix, AZ: Author.

Office for Civil Rights. (1970). Identification of discrimination and denial of services on the basis of national origin. 35 Fed. Reg. 11595 (1970). (Reprinted from *The encyclopedia of bilingual education,* pp. 929–930, by J. M. Gonzáles, Ed., 2008, Thousand Oaks, CA: Sage).

Office for Civil Rights. (1975). Task force findings specifying remedies available for eliminating past educational practices ruled unlawful under Lau v. Nichols. (1975). (Reprinted from *The encyclopedia of bilingual education,* pp. 935–940, by J. M. Gonzáles, Ed., 2008, Thousand Oaks, CA: Sage).

Otero v. Mesa County School Dist., 408 F. Supp. 162 (D. Colo. 1975).

Perea, J. F. (1992). Demography and distrust: An essay on American languages, cultural pluralism, and Official English. *Minnesota Law Review, 77,* 269–373.

Perea, J. F. (1997). The black/white binary paradigm of race: The "normal science" of American racial thought. *California Law Review, 85,* 1213–1258.

Plessy v. Ferguson, 163 U.S. 537 (1896).

Powers, J. M. (2008). Forgotten history: Mexican American school segregation in Arizona from 1900–1951. *Equity & Excellence in Education, 41,* 467–481.

Powers, J. M. (2012, November). *Parallel tracks with points of intersection.* Paper presented at the History of Education Society annual meeting, Seattle, WA.

Powers, J. M., & Patton, L. (2008). Between Mendez and Brown: Gonzales v. Sheely (1951) and the legal campaign against segregation. *Law & Social Inquiry, 33,* 127–171.

Rios v. Reed, 480 F. Supp. 14 (E.D. N.Y. 1978).

Rios-Aguilar, C., & Gándara, P. (2012). Horne v. Flores and the future of language policy. *Teachers College Record, 114*(9), 1–13.

Rodriguez, C. M. (2006). Language and participation. *California Law Review, 94,* 687–757.

Romero, M. (2005). Brown is beautiful. *Law & Society Review, 39,* 211–234.

Romo v. Laird, No. 21617 (Ariz. Super. 1925).

Roosevelt v. Bishop, 877 P. 2d 806 (Ariz. 1994).

Ruiz, R. (1984). Orientations in language planning. *Journal for the National Association for Bilingual Education, 8*(2), 15–34.

San Antonio School District v. Rodriguez, 411 U.S. 1 (1973).

San Miguel, G. (1987). *"Let them all take heed": Mexican Americans and the campaign for educational equality in Texas.* College Station: Texas A&M University Press.

San Miguel, G. (2004). *Contested policy: The rise and fall of federal bilingual education in the United States, 1960-2001.* Denton: University of North Texas Press.

Schott, R. L. (1982). *School desegregation in Texas: The implementation of United States v. Texas* (Policy Research Report No. 51). Austin: Lyndon B. Johnson School of Public Affairs, University of Texas at Austin.

Serna v. Portales, 499 F.2d 1147 (10th Cir. 1974).

Serrano v. Priest 487 P.2d 1241 (Ariz. 1971).

Sheridan, C. (2003). "Another white race": Mexican Americans and the paradox of whiteness in jury selection. *Law and History Review, 21,* 109–144.

Skrentny, J. D. (2002). *The minority rights revolution.* Cambridge, MA: Harvard University Press.

Stone, G. R., Seidman, L. M., Sunstein, C. R., Tushnet, M. V., & Karlan, P. S. (2005). *Constitutional law* (5th ed.). New York, NY: Aspen.

Strum, P. (2010). *Mendez v. Westminster: School desegregation and Mexican-American rights.* Lawrence: University Press of Kansas.

United States v. Jefferson County Board of Education, 372 F.2d 836 (5th Cir. 1966).

United States v. State of Texas, 342 F. Supp. 24 (E.D. Tex. 1971)

United States v. Texas Education Agency, 431 F. 2d 1313 (5th Cir. 1970).

U.S. Commission on Civil Rights. (1971). *Ethnic isolation of Mexican Americans in the public schools in the Southwest.* Washington, DC: U.S. Government Printing Office.

Valencia, R. (2005). The Mexican American struggle for equal educational opportunity in Mendez v. Westminster: Helping to pave the way for Brown v. Board of Education. *Teachers College Record, 107,* 389–423.

Valencia, R. R. (2008). *Chicano students and the courts: The Mexican American legal struggle for educational equality.* New York: New York University Press.

Valencia, R. R. (2010). *Dismantling contemporary deficit thinking: Educational thought and practice.* New York, NY: Taylor & Francis.

Wiese, A. M., & Garcia, E. (2001). The Bilingual Education Act: Language minority students and US federal educational policy. *International Journal of Bilingual Education and Bilingualism, 4,* 229–248.

Wiley, T. G. (2002). Accessing language rights in education: A brief history. In J. W. Tollefson (Ed.), *Language policies in education: Critical issues* (pp. 39–64). Mahwah, NJ: Lawrence Erlbaum.

Wilson, S. H. (2003). Brown over "other white": Mexican Americans' legal arguments and litigation strategy in school desegregation lawsuits. *Law and History Review, 21,* 145–194.

Wilson, S. H. (2005). Some are born white, some achieve whiteness, and some have whiteness thrust upon them: Mexican Americans and the politics of racial classification in the federal judicial bureaucracy, twenty-five years after Hernandez v. Texas. *Chicano-Latino Law Review, 25,* 201–225.

Wollenberg, C. (1976). *All deliberate speed: Segregation and exclusion in California schools, 1855-1975.* Berkeley: University of California Press.

Chapter 5

Reclaiming Indigenous Languages: A Reconsideration of the Roles and Responsibilities of Schools

TERESA L. MCCARTY
University of California, Los Angeles

SHEILAH E. NICHOLAS
University of Arizona

[W]herever there is a situation of domination and subordination between any two groups, whatever their color or religion, this will be reflected in the language relationship: one language dominating the other.

—wa Thiong'o (2011, p. 244)

INTRODUCTION

In this chapter, we offer a critical examination of a growing field of educational inquiry and social practice: the reclamation of Indigenous mother tongues. We use the term *reclamation* purposefully to denote that these are languages that have been forcibly subordinated in contexts of colonization (Hinton, 2011; Leonard, 2007). Language reclamation includes *revival* of a language no longer spoken as a first language, *revitalization* of a language already in use, and *reversal of language shift* (RLS), a term popularized by Joshua Fishman (1991) to describe the reengineering of social supports for intergenerational mother tongue transmission. All of these processes involve what Māori scholar Margie Kahukura Hohepa (2006) calls *language regeneration*, a term that speaks of "growth and regrowth," recognizing that nothing "regrows in exactly the same shape that it had previously, or in exactly the same direction" (p. 294).

Review of Research in Education
March 2014, Vol. 38, pp. 106-136
DOI: 10.3102/0091732X13507894
© 2014 AERA. http://rre.aera.net

As the epigraph that introduces this chapter suggests, the causes underlying shift from a community language to a dominating one are complex and power linked. Our goal is to peel back the layers of that complexity. To begin, we note that all languages change through time as a result of language-internal processes and as their speakers interact with other speech communities and cultural changes require new linguistic forms. Linguistic change of this sort is different from community-wide language shift, which occurs when the social structures supporting intergenerational transmission disintegrate as a result of dominant–subordinate linguistic encounters and the "often violent replacement of one linguistic code by another" (Meek, 2010, p. 4), leading to fewer language users, uses, and domains with each generation. Fishman (1991) describes this process:

> The destruction of languages is an abstraction which is concretely mirrored in the concomitant destruction of intimacy, family and community, via national and international . . . intrusions, the destruction of local life [and] of the weak by the strong. (p. 4)

Throughout the world, language education policies have been one powerful mechanism for the eradication of Indigenous and other minoritized mother tongues. By requiring education only in the socially dominant language, such policies aim to "erase and replace" linguistically encoded knowledges and cultural identifications with those associated with dominant-group speakers (Lomawaima & McCarty, 2006). The Kenyan literary scholar Ngugi wa Thiong'o (2009) refers to this as linguicide, "conscious acts of language liquidation"; its physical counterpart is genocide (p. 17; see also Skutnabb-Kangas, 2000; Skutnabb-Kangas & Dunbar, 2010). Restrictive language education policies have had cascading negative consequences for Indigenous children and youth, who experience some of the lowest rates of educational attainment and the highest rates of poverty, depression, and teen suicide (Castagno & Brayboy, 2008). Thus, the project of language reclamation is not merely or even primarily a linguistic one but is profoundly linked to issues of educational equity, Indigenous self-determination, and the (re)construction of community well-being via culturally distinctive worldviews, identities, and life orientations.

We organize this review around two foci. First, we concentrate on school-based language reclamation. It is well established that schools and their medium-of-instruction policies have been major catalysts for language shift (Hornberger, 1988; King, 2001; Reyhner, 2006; Wyman, 2012). What remains at issue is whether or how schools might be efficacious sites for language reclamation. Fishman (1991), for example, has long held that RLS requires fundamental social restructuring to restore family-based language transmission, insisting that schools "should be on tap and not on top of a language" (p. 194); and "nothing can substitute for the rebuilding of society at the level of . . . basic, everyday, informal life" (p. 112). Krauss (1998) goes further, arguing that "school programs can do more harm than good, insofar as they shift the responsibility for transmitting the language in the home, . . . to the school, at best such a poor alternative" (p. 17). And in a recent review of Hornberger's (2008) edited collection asking the question of whether schools can "save" Indigenous languages, Edwards (2012) claims that "educational programmes of language revitalization are the lamp-post in whose light we hope to recover things that were lost elsewhere" (p. 203).

Despite the fact that schools are "extremely contentious places" (Rockwell & Gomes, 2009, p. 105), the reality is that in settings around the world, schools—the single place where children spend much of their waking hours—are looked to as prime sites for language reclamation. As stated by the Hopi linguist, educator, jurist, and activist Emory Sekaquaptewa, "Someone must take the responsibility for language preservation, and the logical place is the school" (quoted in Nicholas, 2005, p. 34). We now have more than 25 years—fully a generation—of data on such efforts. It is time to take stock and to reconsider: What roles have schools played in reclaiming and revitalizing threatened Indigenous mother tongues? What approaches have been successful, and what have been some of the pitfalls, tensions, and challenges? As state-level instruments of socialization, do schools and their personnel bear a *responsibility* to act as agents of language reclamation?

Our second focus is geographic. We draw on an international literature but concentrate on the United States and Canada. We choose this geographic focus not only because it is one with which we have extensive firsthand experience but also because Native North America illuminates the wide range of language planning challenges and possibilities that attend the sociohistorical, educational, and sociolinguistic circumstances of diverse Indigenous peoples, as well as crosscutting themes of language education policy, sovereignty, and human rights.

We come to this discussion as scholar-practitioners who have worked in the field of Indigenous language education for many years. Sheilah Nicholas is a Hopi educator and scholar who has worked across national borders and with her own cultural community on its language reclamation efforts. Teresa McCarty is a non-Native educator and anthropologist who has worked at the local, national, and international levels with a variety of language revitalization and language rights initiatives.

We start by defining key concepts and terms. Sketching a brief portrait of Indigenous linguistic and cultural diversity in the United States and Canada, we then discuss the relationship of Indigenous languages to distinct knowledge systems and to official language policies in these two nation states. This sets the stage for a closer examination of four "telling" cases (cf. Hornberger, 1997): Mohawk in Canada and the United States, Hawaiian in the Pacific, and Hopi and Navajo in the U.S. Southwest. How has school-based language reclamation developed in each setting? Who are the stakeholders, and what are their goals? What have been the impacts of these reclamation projects? We close by returning to our key questions on the roles and responsibilities of schools in language reclamation, discussing the implications for Indigenous cultural continuance (Ortiz, 1992) and for educational, linguistic, and social justice.

INDIGENOUS LANGUAGE RECLAMATION:
WHAT IS DIFFERENT? KEY CONCEPTS AND TERMS

[Our] peoples are nations not only because they possess the legal and political attributes of nationhood according to European . . . definitions. We were—and remain—nations because of the undeniable fact of our distinctive languages, cultures, traditional forms of political organization, our inherent self-governing status and a collective desire to maintain our distinctiveness. (Task Force on Aboriginal Languages and Cultures, 2005, p. 27)

We use the terms *Indigenous, Native, American Indian, Alaska Native, Métis,* and *First Nations* to refer to peoples whose ancestry within the lands now claimed by the U.S. and Canada predates the colonial invasion and whose oral and written traditions place them as the original occupants of those lands. As Patrick (2012) explains, the term *Indigenous* "is a transnational category created in the twentieth century" in the context of United Nations human rights initiatives, which serves both to unite diverse Indigenous peoples and to "distinguish them from other ethnic minorities" (pp. 30–31). We therefore use initial capital letters when referring to Indigenous/Native American peoples and languages to recognize them as peoples with a singular legal-political status.

This usage signals the fact that indigeneity must be understood from the vantage point of tribal sovereignty: "the right of a people to self-government, self-determination, and self-education" (Lomawaima & McCarty, 2006, p. 10), including the right to linguistic and cultural expression according to local languages and norms. As the epigraph that begins this section suggests, tribal sovereignty is inherent, predating the U.S. Constitution and the 1867 British North American Act that established the Canadian confederation. From the first encounters between Native Americans and Europeans, the two groups operated on a nation-to-nation basis. This political relationship resulted in the signing of hundreds of treaties, many of which had education-related stipulations, and all of which forced the relinquishment of Native lands in exchange for certain federal guarantees, including education. The tribal–federal relationship has been formalized in legislation, court decisions, and official agencies such as the Bureau of Indian Affairs and the Department of Aboriginal Affairs and Northern Development Canada. These structures reflect and support the tribal–federal *trust relationship*, which entails the "federal responsibility to protect or enhance tribal assets [including linguistic and cultural assets] through policy decisions and management actions" (Wilkins & Lomawaima, 2001, p. 65).

Language rights, of which language reclamation is part, are fundamental to nation building and sovereignty. We use the terms *reclamation, revitalization, regeneration,* and *regenesis* to denote these processes, which are intended to "bring endangered languages back to some level of use within their communities (and elsewhere) after a period of reduction in usage" (Hinton, 2011, p. 291). All of this falls under the rubric of *language planning*: deliberate acts to alter the status, acquisition, development, and use of a language. Although many such activities involve schools, language planning takes place at the family and community levels as well, and indeed, it is these more intimate, everyday communicative contexts that school-based efforts ultimately hope to influence (for more on out-of-school language reclamation, see Hinton, 2013).

NATIVE AMERICAN LINGUISTIC AND CULTURAL DIVERSITY: A PORTRAIT OF PERSISTANCE

When Columbus made landfall in the Bahamas in October 1492, Indigenous peoples within the North American continent spoke hundreds of languages, representing a multitude of linguistic families and scores of linguistic isolates (Krauss, 1998; Yamamoto, 2007; see Figure 1).[1] Cree, for example, an Algonquian language, is as different from Mohawk, an Iroquoian language, as English is from Cantonese. Among the Puebloan peoples of the U.S. Southwest, 21 languages are still spoken, representing four linguistic families and one linguistic isolate. Within every language community, multiple dialects are spoken, which embody distinct identities and kinship groupings (Kroskrity & Field, 2009). Dialectal differences express and evoke strong sentiments in language reclamation work and add to the complexity of language planning.

Recent U.S. census data report 5.2 million people who identify as American Indian and Alaska Native (1.7% of the U.S. population) and 1.2 million people who identify as Native Hawaiian and "other Pacific Islanders" (0.4% of the population; Hixson, Hepler, & Kim, 2012; Norris, Vines, & Hoeffel, 2012). Among these cultural communities the U.S. census reports 170 Native American languages spoken by approximately 370,000 people, excluding languages spoken by peoples indigenous to Latin America and to American-affiliated Pacific Island territories (Siebens & Julian, 2011). In Canada, the 2006 census reports 1.2 million First Nations, Métis, and Inuit people (4% of the population), representing 196 First Nations reserves (Statistics Canada, 2009a, 2009b). Approximately 250,000 Canadian Indigenous people or 29% of the Indigenous population (1% of the total population) report speaking an Indigenous language, half of whom report using their language on a daily basis (Statistics Canada, 2008, 2009b).

These numbers highlight the two-sided situation of great linguistic diversity and mounting threats to that diversity. We urge caution, however, in taking census data at face value, as enumeration of this sort privileges a conception of languages as bounded and unitary, overlooks "new speakers" who are (re)learning their ancestral language as an additional language (many of whom live in nontribal urban areas), and obscures the power relations inherent in censusing (Hill, 2002; Moore, Pietikäinen, & Blommaert, 2010). Our intent with this demolinguistic portrait is instead to show Indigenous languages as diverse, performative, and dynamic (Field & Kroskrity, 2009, p. 26), defying the constraints of enumeration, objectification, and homogeneity. Viewing languages this way allows us to recognize the transformative ability of Indigenous languages and language users to adapt to sociocultural and sociolinguistic change, thus affirming the persistence, endurance, and continuance of Native American communities.

THE SOCIOHISTORICAL CONTEXT
FOR LANGUAGE RECLAMATION

Indigenous Languages as Part of Distinct
Knowledge and Education Systems

Our language holds our culture, our perspective, our history, and our inheritance. What type of people we are, where we came from, what land we claim, . . . all . . . are based on the language we speak. (Mary Siemens, Dogrib language specialist, quoted in Task Force on Aboriginal Languages and Cultures, 2005, p. 21)

We are our language. (Aboriginal Language Services logo in the Yukon Territory, cited in Meek, 2010, pp. 131, 150)

We begin this section with the role of Indigenous languages within situated systems of knowledge and meaning. As Lomawaima and McCarty (2006) write, all such systems "share the human goal of creating competent, caring adults who share core values" (p. 32). Despite persistent stereotypes of Native American students as "silent" or "nonverbal" learners (see Foley, 1996; McCarty, Wallace, Lynch, & Benally, 1991, for critiques), learning in Indigenous societies has always required "language-rich activities and instruction" to develop communicative, sociocultural, intellectual, and moral competencies (Lomawaima & McCarty, 2006, p. 32).

Historically and today, these competencies have been rooted in oral tradition—the stories, songs, prayers, and other oral media that carry a people's repository of knowledge (McCarty & Nicholas, 2012). This knowledge has traditionally been emplaced within physical landscapes that embody a close affective and spiritual attachment to the people who have occupied those landscapes over time. "The result," states the Task Force on Aboriginal Languages and Cultures (2005), "is a linguistically reinforced sense of intimate connection" to place, community, and worldview (p. 23). According to Acoma scholar and language activist Christine Sims (2005), these orally transmitted connections constitute the "core foundation of tribal languages" and are the means of representing and recreating Indigenous sociocultural, socioreligious, and sociopolitical life (p. 105).

We illustrate these processes with a few examples. Among the Hopi in northeastern Arizona, children continue to learn Hopi ways of "doing and being" through participation in ritualized practices, cultural institutions, and ceremonies conveyed via myriad language forms including songs, teachings, and prayers (Nicholas, 2008, 2009). The practice of growing corn by hand is one such cultural practice. While emphasizing the skill of farming, growing corn by hand also serves as a "metaphor for the work ethic of attaining the 'know-how' for making a living, *qatsitwi*, and survival in a harsh environment" (McCarty & Nicholas, 2012, p. 148). For Hopi men and women, planting corn by hand (a male role) and preparing food made from corn (a female role) "allows each generation . . . to participate in the ways of Hopi ancestors" (McCarty & Nicholas, 2012, p. 148). When Hopi people engage in these cultural

FIGURE 1
Geographic Portrait of Native American Language Groups

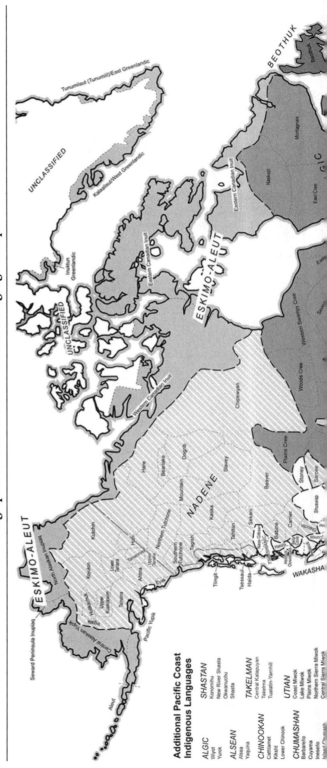

Additional Pacific Coast
Indigenous Languages

ALGIC
Wiyot
Yurok

ALSEAN
Alsea
Yaquina

CHINOOKAN
Cathlamet
Kiksht
Lower Chinook

CHUMASHAN
Barbareño
Cuyama
Island Chumash

SHASTAN
Konomihu
New River Shasta
Okwanuchu
Shasta

TAKELMAN
Central Kalapuyan
Takelma
Tualatin-Yamhill

UTIAN
Coast Miwok
Lake Miwok
Plains Miwok
Northern Sierra Miwok
Central Sierra Miwok

Source. Adapted from Goddard (1999). Graphics by Shearon Vaughn (2013).

Note. A full-color version of this map is available in the online journal at http://rre.aera.net.

practices, the Hopi language is reinforced alongside a distinctly Hopi identity and way of life (see Nicholas, 2005, 2009, for a detailed discussion).

Writing of traditional forms of education and language socialization among the Anishinaabe (Ojibwe) of the Great Lakes region, Ojibwe language educator and intellectual Basil Johnson (1976) explains that oral tradition expresses "the sum total of what people believe about life, being, existence, and relationships" (p. 7). This claim encompasses Indigenous epistemologies, ontologies, and cosmologies—the ways through which Anishinaabe people seek to establish a shared identity premised on distinctive knowledge systems and generations of life experiences. Among the Pomo of what is now northern California, Margolin (1981) notes that orality conveys a "practical" education in locally valued skills, as well as lessons for leading a "virtuous" life. Through oral tradition, children tacitly absorb culturally specific attitudes, manners, and values. Similarly, among the Lakota, oral tradition encompasses guidance (*wahohunkiye*) about Lakota values and virtues: *wantognaka*, generosity; *cante t'inza*, bravery; *wacintanka*, patience; and *ksabahan opiic 'iya*, wisdom (Powers, 1986).

The language-rich activities and instruction encompassed in oral tradition existed in what Wilson and Kamanā (2014) describe as "linguistically healthy communit[ies]" (p. 188). Prior to extensive Anglo-European contact, Indigenous languages were the medium of instruction as well as the "means of communication across internal-generational and peer-group boundaries" (Wilson & Kamanā, 2014, p. 188). Through oral tradition, the young came to learn what was needed and valued within their communities and were prepared to become competent, contributing members of their society and the wider world.

Today, Indigenous community members have "widely variable fluency in the ancestral language" (Wilson & Kamanā, 2014, p. 188). Moreover, the physical emplacements of linguistic traditions have changed as more Native people—approximately 7 in 10—reside in urban centers outside of tribally held lands (Norris et al., 2012; Williams, 2013). Importantly, in these urban settings "there is active demand for and interest in language revitalization" (Hermes & King, 2013, p. 127). Across these varied sociolinguistic and physical landscapes, customary cultural practices remain efficacious mechanisms for contemporary youth and families to "live their Indigenousness"—to "maintain continuity of identity" while adapting to modernity—thus enabling them to sustain "historical and metaphorical connections" to the past as well as "strong bonds between use of a language and a particular geographic location" (Wilson & Kamanā, 2014, pp. 189–191).

Nicholas (2008, 2009) theorizes these processes as "language as cultural practice." This notion recognizes that language resides in the ever-evolving cultural practices that convey the values, ideals, and principles unique to a particular society. This in turn unites individuals in a shared identity maintained through language across time and space. By refocusing on these culturally specific oral traditions, language reclamation efforts such as those discussed later in this chapter seek to instill in young people the knowledge and skills that continue to be needed and valued within their communities. These cultural experiences help cultivate in the young what Wilson and Kamanā (2014) call "great yearnings" to attain emotional, intellectual, and spiritual well-being within their communities, including a desire for "ancestral language survival" (p. 199). As we see in the cases that follow, such yearnings can serve as a catalyst for "positive language shift" (King, 2001) toward revitalization of the Indigenous mother tongue, and "affective enculturation"—an emotional commitment to cultural practices and ideals (Nicholas, 2014).

Colonial Language Policies and Indigenous Countermovements

With the coming of Europeans, Indigenous socialization systems, including the oral practices described above, came under attack. As former British colonies, the United States and Canada have followed parallel paths in their policies toward Indigenous peoples and languages. Following the American Revolution, the new federal government turned its attention to "pacifying" Native peoples in the quest for Native lands (Adams, 1995). Toward that end, in 1819 the U.S. Congress passed the Civilization Fund Act to support missionary schooling, with the goal of exterminating Indigenous languages and lifeways so as to literally clear the path for the takeover of Native lands. By the end of the 19th century, punitive, segregated schooling in English-only boarding schools became a primary mechanism for linguistic pacification.

In Canada, the country's two official languages, French and English, reflect a "two-founding people" ideology (Patrick, 2010) that has marginalized Indigenous peoples in their homelands and ignored the 70 Indigenous languages still spoken. In 1867, the British North American Act enshrined the new federal government's domination over Indigenous affairs. This was followed by the Indian Act of 1876, which began a deliberate course of genocide and linguicide through the removal of Indigenous peoples to reserves and the creation of a segregated residential school system. As the Canadian government took control over former mission schools, it adopted the industrial school model employed in the United States. Also like the United States, the medium of instruction was solely English (in some places, French), "accompanied by a derogation of, and often severe punishment for even the minimal use of indigenous languages" (Sachdev, Arnold, & Yapita, 2006, p. 118).

The residential school system had one highly significant if officially unanticipated effect: It provided fertile ground for uniting the survivors. Amid late–20th-century civil rights and progressive movements in the United States, these key alliances helped secure passage of the 1972 Indian Education Act, which funded Native language and culture programs, and the 1975 Indian Self-Determination and Education Assistance Act, which enabled Native American communities and tribes to operate their own schools. Together with the 1968 Bilingual Education Act, this legislation laid a legal and financial framework for placing Native American education under community control.

In Canada, Indigenous resistance came to a head in a 1972 policy brief published by the National Indian Brotherhood, *Indian Control of Indian Education*, a "clear and moving call for an education system based on Aboriginal values and priorities" (Fettes, 1998, p. 122). Concurrent with the Indigenous community-controlled school movement in the United States, Native communities in Canada began to assert greater control over local schools and to implement bilingual-bicultural education (Fettes, 1998).

Although these school programs have been a powerful force for Indigenous self-determination, they have not been sufficient to turn back the pressures for language shift. As Hermes, Bang, and Marin (2012) write,

> While there are communities in which English has not claimed ownership, in many of our communities, children and families have no choice about the language they use in everyday speech. School, work, and the majority of our routine daily practices occur in . . . English. (p. 398)

This situation has given rise to a widespread language reclamation movement, represented in the United States by the 1990/1992 Native American Languages Act (NALA) and the 2006 Esther Martinez Native American Languages Preservation Act (EM-NALPA), and in Canada by national initiatives such as the Aboriginal Language Task Force and language protections at the territorial level (e.g., the 2007 Nunavut Official Languages Act and the Inuit Language Protection Act). Nevertheless, Canada has no national policy recognizing Indigenous languages comparable to NALA or EM-NALPA in the United States. "Canada has no positive linguistic rights for [Indigenous] peoples," states Maliseet language educator Andrea Bear Nicholas (2009, p. 224).

This is one level of account in understanding Native American language education policy, but these same challenges and complexities exist at the level of tribal governments and local schools. Just as federal education policies have historically failed to engage parent and community voices in education decision making, so too does this occur in colonized settings in the interaction of tribal agencies with local communities and schools. The history of official language policy in Canada and the United States is thus fraught with continuing legacies of colonization. In both national settings, the project of language reclamation is intimately tied to decolonization, cultural autonomy, and identity. It is a passionate movement that is also "political, and deeply personal," write Hermes et al. (2012), "particularly for many Native people who are acutely aware that the federal government's attempted genocide was the direct cause of Indigenous language loss" (p. 383). We turn now to an in-depth examination of these processes through the lens of four cases.

LANGUAGE RECLAMATION CONTEXTS AND CASES[2]

The four cases in this section were selected to illustrate language regenesis processes across a range of educational, sociolinguistic, and geographic settings. Each case illuminates facets of school-based revitalization, and the possibilities and challenges entailed. In crafting the cases, we draw on the extant literature as well as our experience as researcher-participants in some of these settings. For each case, we begin with brief sociolinguistic, educational, and sociohistorical background and then discuss the ways in which individual communities have pried open what Hornberger (2006) calls "ideological and implementational spaces" for language reclamation.

The Mohawk Case: "Taking Control of Children's Education Was the Only Alternative"

Mohawk is a Northern Iroquoian language spoken by peoples indigenous to what is now upstate New York, southern Québec, and eastern Ontario. The Indigenous self-referential term is Kanienkehaka, People of the Flint, a reference to the flint deposits used for tool making in the Kanienkehaka homelands within present-day Mohawk Valley, New York (Mohawk Council of Kahnawà:ke, 2012). The Kanienkehaka were part of the six-nation Haudenosaunee (Iroquois) Confederacy, which long predates the European invasion. When Europeans entered Iroquois territory in the 17th century, the Haudenosaunee faced ongoing encroachment on their lands, missionization, and ravaging disease (Bragdon, 1997). The American Revolution brought more turmoil, fragmenting the Confederacy and leading some groups to relocate permanently to Canada (Bragdon, 1997).

Today, the Kanienkehaka reside in inland New York, along the St. Lawrence River, and in southern Ontario. Most Native speakers are older adults, although in some areas there are younger speakers (Gordon, 2005). Two such areas are Kahnawà:ke, a community of approximately 8,000 on the south shore of the St. Lawrence River 10 kilometers from Montréal, Québec, and Akwesasne (also known as St. Regis), a reserve of about 13,000 people straddling the international boundary between Canada and the State of New York. Here we consider language reclamation at each of these locales.

Kahnawake Survival School

Regeneration of Kanienkeha (the Indigenous term for the Mohawk language) began at Kahnawà:ke in 1970, when a small group of parents, aided by a non-Native elementary school principal, pushed for teaching Kanienkeha for 15 minutes each day. Prior to that time, writes Kaia'titahkhe Annette Jacobs (1998), "The only thing native in our schools was the children" (p. 117). Over the next several years, language revitalization was accelerated by a Native-language teacher preparation program established at the University of Québec in 1972. Mohawk student teachers in the program created a writing system for use in the schools, then constructed a curriculum designed to enable children to acquire the language naturally, with the goal of "teach[ing] children a way of thinking, not simply a translating skill" (Mithun & Chafe, 1987, pp. 27–28)

As these efforts got underway, the newly elected Parti Quebecois passed Bill 101, the French Language Charter, making French the sole official language of Québec and restricting education in other languages. Protesting the bill's violation of tribal sovereignty and historic treaty agreements, the Kahnawà:ke community established the Native-controlled Kahnawake Survival School and the Kanien'kehaka Raotitiohkwa

Cultural Center (KRCC) to ensure that "future Mohawk generations would . . . survive with their language, culture and traditions in tact" (Hoover & KRCC, 1992, p. 270). The Center began the first Indigenous-language immersion program in Canada, which grew incrementally from a full-immersion preschool to a preschool through Grade 4 immersion program followed by Grades 5 and 6 maintenance and a middle school and senior program that teaches Kanienkeha as part of the regular curriculum (Grenoble & Whaley, 2006).

Twelve years into the immersion effort, a community survey showed a dramatic reversal of language shift among young people in the 10- to 19-years age-group. As Hoover and the KRCC (1992) relate, "Through the control of its school system, which enabled the community to introduce a Mohawk immersion program . . . ., [t]he trend over the last 50 years of each succeeding generation speaking less Mohawk [was] reversed" (p. 281). Efforts at reversing language shift require eternal vigilance, however, and the Kahnawake Survival School continues as one of three community schools designed to enable students to "achieve pride and self sufficiency through a powerful curriculum based on Kaien'kehá:ka language, values, beliefs, and traditions along with sound academic [principles] and content, guided by innovative teaching methods" (http://kss.qc.com/).

Akwesasne Freedom School

The 41–square mile reserve at Akwesasne (Land Where the Partridge Drums) straddles the U.S.–Canadian border. As a consequence of assimilationist federal policies, only about 5% of those who live at Akwesasne are fluent speakers of Mohawk (White, 2009). The Akwesasne Freedom School, founded by Mohawk parents in 1979, grew out of activist movements by Native teachers determined to reverse this trend. According to Margaret Peters, a longtime Akwesasne educator,

A struggle between the U.S. government who wanted control and the Mohawk people who simply wanted to maintain their culture and save their language gave birth to the Freedom School. Taking control of the children's education was the only alternative there was. (quoted in Stairs, Peters, & Perkins, 1999, p. 45)

Situated in a facility built by parents and other volunteers to resemble a traditional longhouse, the Akwesasne Freedom School today has 12 teachers and enrolls 60 to 65 students in a year-round, pre-K through Grade 8 program. For many years, Kanienkeha was the sole language of instruction until the end of sixth grade, when English was introduced as students prepared to enter the public high school. In 2011, the school began to implement Mohawk immersion in Grade 7 (White, 2009).

The Haudenosaunee Thanksgiving Address or *Ohonten Kariwahtekwen*, "which teaches gratitude to the earth and everything on it" (Mohawk Nation Council of Chiefs, n.d.), and the *Kaianere:kowa* (Great Law of Peace or Charter of the Iroquois Confederacy) anchor the school curriculum. According to Mohawk scholar Louellyn White (2009), holistic and experiential learning, including participation in Mohawk songs, dances, and ceremonies, are key pedagogic practices. Each day begins and ends with a student delivering the *Ohonten Kariwahtekwa* from memory. The cultural knowledge and values embedded in this oral narrative are "to be understood and lived [internalized], not merely recited," White stresses, with the Thanksgiving Address providing "structure to the curriculum and allow[ing] students to explore . . . botany, fisheries, astronomy, and planting" (p. 116). The Indigenous language "is heard almost everywhere," White adds; "English is rarely heard or seen" (2009, pp. 175–176). At the same time, White's research suggests that the school is the primary and often the only place where children are likely to hear Kanienkeha spoken. "The only place that taught me the language was the Freedom School," an alumnus told White (2009, pp. 175–176).

The Freedom School is financed by parents, nongovernmental grants, donations, tuition, and fund-raisers such as a renowned annual quilt fair. The school "has never received direct funding from state, provincial, or federal governments," White states (2009); "to do so would undermine [parents'] sovereign rights to decide the type of education their children would receive" (p. 91). Although the school struggles with limited financial resources, parents comment that this "help[s] to keep the school united [because we are] required to do so much more" (p. 97).

As with other cases we discuss, the Freedom School has positively affected out-of-school language learning opportunities. White (2009) reports that three families, all Freedom School alumni, are raising their children as primary speakers of Kanienkeha. The community has established the Akwesāhsne Board of Education with three additional schools under its charge in Québec and Ontario as well as singing societies and summer language classes for adults (L. White, personal communication, April 28, 2012). All of these efforts are designed to repatriate Kanienkeha, or, as White (2009) puts it, to help Mohawk people "find our talk" (p. 177).

The Mohawk case illuminates the processes and outcomes of a long-term, determined effort by a small group of parents to take control of their children's education using the local language and culture as cornerstones of educational autonomy. According to White (2009), although some Mohawk-immersion students have experienced difficulty making the transition from Mohawk- to English-medium schooling, the students adjust and experience academic success. Equally important "is that these youth have an interest in learning their language, they take pride in the language, and they value the language" as "critical in Mohawk identity formation and continuance of Mohawk culture" (pp. 201, 202). Thus, schools such as Akwesasne and Kahnawake serve to unite and heal community fractures imposed by colonization (White, 2009). Although small in scale, they also serve as exemplars of the ways in which language reclamation can be central to reclaiming the schooling process itself.

The Hawaiian Case: Connecting Students to Practices That Have "Nurtured Their Culture for Generations"

A Polynesian language related to Māori and Samoan, Hawaiian is advantaged by a large corpus of written materials and a "long and rich oral literature" (Warner, 2001, p. 134). From the time of the initial populating of the islands in the 8th century CE, Hawaiian was the only language used and for generations, it developed with little outside influence (Wilson, 1998). Following the British arrival in 1778, the Hawaiian Kingdom grew under an Indigenous monarchy. During this time, "Hawaiian was spoken by hundreds of thousands of people," and 90% of the Hawaiian population was reported to be literate in Hawaiian—the highest literacy rate recorded in the world at the time (Grenoble & Whaley, 2006, p. 95).

At the same time, Native Hawaiians faced the devastation of European-introduced diseases, and the population of 800,000 in 1778 plummeted to 47,500 within 100 years (Warner, 2001). In 1893, backed by powerful U.S. businessmen, the U.S. military mounted an illegal takeover of the Hawaiian Kingdom, and a ban ensued on Hawaiian-medium instruction in public and private schools. According to Wong (2011), the "resulting stigma" attached to speaking Hawaiian "dramatically accelerated the process of language shift" (p. 4). By 1920, most Hawaiian children had begun speaking Hawaiian Creole English, which was "used as a marker for socioeconomic discrimination against its speakers—Hawaiians and immigrants" (Warner, 2001, p. 135).

In 1959, Hawai'i was incorporated as the 50th U.S. state. Over the next two decades, against the backdrop of the Civil Rights Movement, a "Hawaiian renaissance" took root, with a strong language revitalization component. "From this renaissance came a new group of second-language Hawaiian speakers who would become Hawaiian language educators," Warner states (2001, p. 135). In 1978, Hawaiian and English were designated co-official languages. By this time the "number of children speaking Hawaiian was less than 50 statewide" (Wilson, Kamanā, & Rawlins, 2006, p. 42).

With support from Māori language activists in Aotearoa/New Zealand, in 1983 a small group of parents and language activists established the 'Aha Pūnana Leo (Hawaiian language nest) nonprofit organization and then its family-run preschools. The preschools enable children to interact with fluent speakers entirely in Hawaiian with the goal of cultivating knowledge of Hawaiian language and culture in "much the same way that they were in the home in earlier generations" (Wilson & Kamanā, 2001, p. 151). As their children prepared to enter elementary school, Pūnana Leo parents lobbied for Hawaiian-medium elementary school tracks, and Hawaiian-medium schooling has spread horizontally to other communities and vertically by grade. In 1999, the first students educated totally in Hawaiian graduated from high school.

As one example of these language reclamation processes, Wilson and Kamanā (2001, 2006, 2011) report on the Nāwahīokalani'ōpu'u (Nāwahī) Laboratory School in Hilo, a full-immersion, early childhood through high school program affiliated with the University of Hawai'i Hilo's College of Hawaiian Language and 'Aha Pūnana Leo. The school teaches all subjects through Hawaiian, offering a college preparatory curriculum and "an explicit understanding that use of the Hawaiian language has priority over . . . English" (Wilson & Kamanā, 2001, p. 158). Students also learn a "useful" third language such as Japanese, which, in light of Hawaii's multiracial history, is for some students a heritage language as well.

Of special interest is Nāwahī's role as part of an integrated system of Hawaiian-medium structures called *honua*, which "develop, protect, nurture and enrich young adult and child fluency in Hawaiian along with the crucial disposition to use Hawaiian with Hawaiian speaking peers" (Wilson & Kawai'ae'a, 2007, p. 38). For example, in the school gardens, students "connect to traditional Hawaiian practices and the natural environment that has nurtured their culture for generations" (Wilson & Kamanā, 2008, para. 2). These structures also include the self-governing Ka Haka 'Ula O Ke'elikōlani College, which provides curriculum support to pre-K through Grade 12 laboratory schools (including Nāwahī) in partnership with 'Aha Pūnana Leo, and the college's Kahuawaiola Indigenous Teacher Education Program, which involves preservice teachers in designing lesson plans aligned with state standards and those developed specifically for Hawaiian-medium schooling. Additional supports include a PhD program in Hawaiian and Indigenous Language and Culture Revitalization and a master's degree in Indigenous Language and Culture Education (Wilson & Kawai'ae'a, 2007, p. 49).

Although language reclamation has been the priority in the Hawaiian case, Hawaiian-medium instruction has yielded impressive academic results. Nāwahī students surpass their nonimmersion peers on English standardized tests and have outperformed the state average for all ethnic groups on high school graduation, college attendance, and academic honors (Wilson & Kamanā, 2011). "Nāwahī demonstrates that programming that is highly focused on the [Indigenous language] and its heritage can produce exceptional [Indigenous language] results, without negatively affecting academic outcomes or English proficiency," Wilson and Kamanā state (2011, p. 53).

On a larger scale, the revitalization of Hawaiian is widely recognized as one of the most effective Indigenous-language reclamation movements in the world, with as many as 15,000 Hawaiians reporting they use or understand Hawaiian (Hinton, 2001, p. 8). Hawaiian-medium education now serves approximately 2,000 students statewide in a coordinated set of schools, beginning with the preschools and moving through full Hawaiian-medium elementary and secondary education (Wilson et al., 2006). The language is widely taught in Hawaiian universities and has extended into nonschool domains such as Hawaiian-speaking sports (Warner, 2001).

The important lessons in this case are threefold: First, Hawaiian-medium schooling demonstrates the proactive role that schools can play in language reclamation when parents and community members control the curriculum and its implementation. Second, the Hawaiian case shows the importance of sustained Indigenous-language schooling that incorporates cultural values and knowledge over the course of children's pre-K–12 education. And finally, the Hawaiian case makes clear that language reclamation is a long-term, multigenerational effort, often undertaken by small groups of people. Language reclamation requires enormous dedication and foresight, but the benefits can be transformative; as Wilson and Kamanā (2011, p. 53) write of these processes at Nāwahī, after a full generation of Hawaiian-immersion schooling, Nāwahī graduates are raising their own children as first-language speakers of Hawaiian.

The Hopi Case: *"Itam Qa Paysoq Yeese"*—"We (Hopìit) Do Not Merely Exist"

The Hopi are the westernmost of the Pueblos, who reside on 1.6 million acres of their aboriginal lands in northeastern Arizona. Approximately 7,000 of the population of 13,000 reside in and around 12 villages situated on Black Mesa. Although contemporary Hopi society has incorporated much of Western urban lifestyle— mobility, economy, and education—the traditional practices that follow an annual farming and ceremonial calendar remain a major aspect of village life.

Most Hopi speakers regard Hopi, a Uto-Aztecan language, as having four distinct dialects. While Hopi continues to be a viable medium of intergenerational interaction during cultural and ceremonial activities, and remains a language spoken by all generations, this is rapidly changing. A Hopi parent described the present linguistic situation to Nicholas (2008) as youth becoming "accustomed to speaking English," due to residence in off-reservation boarding schools and migrations to English-speaking towns for the benefits offered by the *Pahaana* (Anglo) world (p. 249).

Beginning in the mid-1990s, growing community awareness of language shift and its impact—"un-Hopi" behaviors and attitudes among younger Hopi and the ominous prospect of fading linguistic and cultural continuity—was being publicly voiced in community forums. One community member's words conveyed a worrying trajectory: "If we don't work on this language issue, we're just going to be Hopis in name only. There will be no meaning beyond that" (Nicholas, 2008, p. 35).

According to Hopi belief, the Hopi people exist with a preordained purpose to adhere to the Hopi way of life, planting corn by hand, which is not only a secular economic activity but also a religious duty—an act of faith in attending to the spiritual well-being of humankind (Nicholas, 2009). "That's how Hopis think about it. This is passed through the language," stated a community member at a village forum (Village of Munqapi Forum, 1997). This sense of responsibility remains indelible in the consciousness of the Hopi people; as such, it is to the Hopi way that the Hopi have (re)turned for understanding and guidance (E. Sekaquaptewa, personal communication, October 25, 2000).

For the past two decades, Hopi language reclamation efforts have been ongoing at the tribal, village, school, and individual levels. In 1994, the Hopi Tribal Council initiated successive policy initiatives mandating "the infusion of the Hopilavayi [Hopi language] and culture in the school system to meet the needs of Hopi children" (Hopi Tribal Council, 2005, para. 3), and the subsequent establishment of the Hopilavayi Program within the tribal Culture Preservation Office to support existing community- and school-based programs. In what follows, we draw from Nicholas's role in establishing the Hopi Tribe's Hopilavayi Summer Institute for teacher language education from 2004 to 2010.

The initial institute design was informed by a professional development project conducted at a local K–6 elementary school in the spring of 2004. This project provided groundwork for language education planning, premised on the following:

1. The vitality of the Hopi language continues to reside in Hopi cultural traditions, institutions, and ceremonial practices. Hopi thus remains primarily an oral language. Although a writing system exists, Hopi as a written language is not widely used.
2. Paraprofessionals (teacher assistants) responsible for language teaching are crucial resources for language reclamation. As active participants in the culture, they "live the curriculum" and possess the linguistic means to convey it to others. However, these paraprofessions need an effective approach—oral immersion similar to that discussed above for Hawaiian and Mohawk—to teach the language to children.
3. Student voices are essential to understand what to do and how to proceed. Student responses to a survey administered by the school's teacher supervisor emphasized the desire to "talk": "I want to *talk*, to know how to talk in Hopi." "We should *talk* Hopi every day." "*Talk* to us in Hopi and see if we understand."
4. Youth identified the program goal: helping them become speaker-users of Hopi.

The Institute also incorporated features of the internationally recognized American Indian Development Institute housed at the University of Arizona: a 4-week summer program of intensive, university-accredited coursework; hands-on work with instructors in the field; "microteaching" in which participants team-teach a language and culture lesson; and a focus on the community's ancestral language.

The first Summer Institute, held in 2004, represented a collaborative partnership between the Hopi Tribe, the University of Arizona, and the Hopi Day School, which provided physical facilities and equipment. Nicholas and the late Emory Sekaquaptewa offered participants—who included paraprofessional language teachers, certified teachers, and Head Start preschool teachers—coursework on language revitalization, the oral immersion approach, and basic Hopi language literacy. Subsequent institutes expanded on the previous summer's experience. The 2005 program, for example, engaged participants in developing and implementing an oral immersion language experience for community youth. In 2006 the focus was on curriculum development; the 2007 Institute gave attention to Hopi literacy for instructional purposes, community awareness, action research, and computer skills. With eight participants advancing to mentor teacher level, a mentor–apprentice approach was piloted in 2008 (see Hinton, 2011, for discussion of the master–apprentice language learning program on which this approach is based). Two of the eight participants completed their master's degrees in 2010, and five worked on the Hopi Word Book Project. A second cohort of potential language teachers was recruited for the 2009 program, and the 2010 Institute engaged adult language learners age 23 through 45 years.

Overall, the oral immersion event, *Naatuwpi* (self-[re]discovery through the Hopi language), proved to be efficacious for language learners and teachers. The mentor–apprentice approach was significant in helping apprentices make a connection between theory and practice. Team-teaching afforded teachers time to gain confidence in the methodology supported by team members and practice with a real audience. Institute participants regularly used the Hopi phrase, *qa tuvosi*, challenging, recognizing that language reclamation represents a personal commitment undertaken "from the heart" to confront the challenges that come from within and outside the community.

Importantly, over 7 years the Hopilavayi Institute created the opportunity and the space for Hopi paraprofessionals to redefine themselves as language teachers. These language teachers have made Hopi visible and heard in the school environment by using Hopi as the language of classroom routines and by preparing children to speak and sing in Hopi for school and public events, and in after-school programs. Although the impact on regeneration of the Hopi language among Hopi youth remains to be seen, the project has empowered paraprofessionals with new skills, knowledge, and confidence as self-described "caretakers of the language":

> We need to prioritize helping our youth; they cannot do this alone. They have found us to be the needed help they have been seeking. Language learners are in need of a comfort zone. We as caretakers of the language can be the ones to offer this space. (Institute participant, 2010)

"We are 'feeding' them [youth] with the nourishment they crave and need," another participant observed.

The Hopi example speaks to the importance of professional development opportunities within the language reclamation process. In this case, those opportunities created "ideological and implementational space" (Hornberger, 2006) for local educators to reconcile their sense of the language's viability and the role of schools as appropriate sites for Hopi language and culture with their personal histories of linguistic punishment and exclusion (McCarty, Nicholas, & Wyman, 2012, pp. 53–54). This raised consciousness about the role and responsibility of schools to support language reclamation, and enabled Hopi language teachers to make the language viable in the school setting. Through their self-empowerment these educators were able to create a school language policy in which the Native language has a revitalized role. "We must teach [the Hopi language] because children are not taught at home," a 2009 participant stated, adding that it is the children's "right to learn their own language." Another participant concurred: If teaching the Hopi language is not taking place at home, "then school seems to be the place."

The Navajo Case: "We Wanted These Children to Experience Success in School *Through* Navajo"

Despite a robust print literacy history and a relatively large number of Native speakers (almost half of all self-reported speakers of Native American languages in the United States are Navajo), the Navajo language "is at a crossroads,: . . . it can be revived [and] strengthened in daily use, or it can continue to decline" (Benally & Viri, 2005, p. 106). In this "crossroads" context, the Navajo Nation and individual Navajo (Diné) communities have launched a number of pre-K–12 language revitalization efforts. One of the most long-lived and successful is Tséhootsooí Diné Bi'ólta' (hereafter TDB), The Navajo School at the Meadow Between the Rocks, situated on the eastern border of the Navajo Nation in Fort Defiance, Arizona.

A century and a half ago, Fort Defiance was the epicenter of Anglo-American violence perpetrated against Navajo people, when, in the fall of 1863, Colonel Kit Carson used the fort as a base to launch a scorched earth campaign, forcing families to flee their homes. Starvation and desperate circumstances led thousands of Diné to surrender at Fort Defiance, from which they were forced to trek 300 miles to a federal concentration camp at Fort Sumner, New Mexico. Hundreds of people died along the way and thousands succumbed to starvation and foreign-borne diseases at Fort Sumner. In 1868, a treaty was signed, promising a schoolhouse and teacher for every 30 Navajo children between the ages of 6 and 16 years. Four years later, the first federal boarding school for Navajos opened at the original Fort Defiance military camp.

Fort Defiance is thus both a physical site and a symbol of genocide. Its historic significance makes contemporary language reclamation efforts there equally symbolic and momentous. By the mid-1980s, Fort Defiance had grown into a small town whose location 30 miles from the reservation border regularized contact with English speakers. These social and physical transformations, combined with the legacy of compulsory English-only schooling, are reflected in the fact that in this setting, most children enter school speaking English as a primary (and sometimes only) language.

In 1986, the Window Rock Unified School District launched a voluntary Navajo language immersion program at Fort Defiance Elementary School. "In this dynamic sociolinguistic situation," program cofounders Marie Arviso and Wayne Holm (2001) write, it "was becoming increasingly obvious that . . . [Navajo-language immersion] might be the only . . . program with some chance of success" (p. 205). The program began as a K–5 Diné immersion track in an otherwise all-English public elementary school. With the exception of two daily 20-minute periods in English, all instruction was in Navajo. By the time students reached second and third grades, the program included a half-day in Navajo and a half-day in English; fourth and fifth graders received an hour each day of Navajo instruction. An additional requirement was that an adult family member or caretaker "spend some time talking with the child in Navajo each evening after school" (Arviso & Holm, 2001, p. 210).

"We did not feel that we could claim . . . that these children would necessarily do better academically," Arviso and Holm (2001) reflect; instead, "we wanted to help these children experience success in school *through* Navajo" (p. 205). Nevertheless, after its first decade of operation, fourth-grade Navajo immersion students performed as well on local tests of English as nonimmersion students; immersion students performed better on English writing assessments and were "way ahead" in mathematics (A. Holm & Holm, 1995). On standardized tests of English reading, students were slightly behind, but catching up (A. Holm & Holm, 1995, p. 150). In short, the Navajo immersion students "were doing almost as well as, or better than, the [monolingual English] students" (Arviso & Holm, 2001, p. 211). Moreover, by fourth grade, the nonimmersion students scored *lower* on Navajo-language assessments than they had in kindergarten. These data show the powerful negative effect of the absence of Indigenous-language schooling and its potentially positive impact on language revitalization and academic achievement.

In 1999—the same year that the first cohort of Pūnana Leo students graduated from high school—the Fort Defiance immersion program saw some of its first students graduate from high school, and in 2003, the district's Diné immersion classes were consolidated at a single school, TDB. As with the initial program, in kindergarten and first grade, all instruction, including initial literacy, takes place in Navajo. English is introduced in second grade and gradually increased until a 50:50 distribution is attained by Grade 6. TDB's curriculum integrates Navajo tribal standards for language and culture with those required by the state, and the school emphasizes a "Diné language and culture rich environment . . . including lunch room, playground hallways and the bus" (F. T. Johnson & Legatz, 2006, p. 30).

Longitudinal data from TDB show that the benefits to language revitalization have not come at the cost of children's English language learning or academic achievement, as TDB students consistently outperform their peers in English-only classrooms on local and standardized assessments of English reading, writing, and mathematics, while also developing strong Navajo oral language and literacy skill (F. T. Johnson & Legatz, 2006). W. Holm (2006) summarizes a key lesson from the Fort Defiance/TDB case: "Schools cannot save a language or culture," but they can "make it possible for students to find new and more meaningful ways of being Navajo in the future" (p. 36).

LOOKING BACK AND MOVING FORWARD: LESSONS FROM A GENERATION OF INDIGENOUS LANGUAGE RECLAMATION

In this final section, we return to our original questions. What do the four case examined here suggest about the roles and responsibilities of schools and their personnel in Indigenous-language reclamation? What has worked well, what have been some of the tensions, and what challenges remain?

We start with the foundations of sovereignty and trust. Each case here illuminate the ways in which Indigenous interpretations of sovereignty, including educational sovereignty, are self-empowering and manifest in cultural and linguistic regeneration. As we have emphasized, this is part of a larger fight for cultural continuance and autonomy (Ortiz, 1992). In the pre-Columbian period, survival and continuance were premised on an intimate relationship with a particular geographic location in which oral tradition conveyed "a vast array of empirical knowledge" (Kawagley, 2011 p. 73), enabling people to survive and flourish in often extreme and harsh environments (MacLean, 2010). As a consequence of colonial policies, survival and continuance today are steeped in a political struggle to maintain distinctive identities and pursue the right to "remain Indian" (Lomawaima & McCarty, 2006). Inherent in this is personal and collective well-being and for children, the opportunity to experience academic success through their ancestral language.

In this decolonizing context, the circumstances are such that the home and community as ideal situations for sustaining Indigenous languages and lifeways have been eroded. In many places, schools have been appropriated as sites of regeneration of "the resourcefulness of those forebears and the cultural legacy that they have left as a source of pride to their descendants" (MacLean, 2010, p. 41). The reclamation of education control in these cases is coterminous with the reclamation of language. At Akwesasne, for instance, parents viewed "taking control of the children's education [as] the only alternative" to taking back "our talk" (Stairs et al., 1999, p. 45; White, 2009, p. 177). In Hawai'i, Hawaiian-medium schools have been instrumental in "fostering a distinctive self-reproducing community" of Hawaiian first-language speakers (Wilson & Kamanā, 2011, p. 48). On the Navajo Nation, Navajo-medium schooling has given young people access to their heritage language and culture in a modernizing multilingual world (W. Holm, 2006). Among the Hopi, extraschool professional development has fostered new knowledge, confidence, and skill among Hopi mentor teachers, who are bringing their linguistic and cultural knowledge into local schools, often against great odds.

These are but a few illustrative cases of a widespread grass roots revitalization movement being carried out within Indigenous nations and in urban centers throughout the world. As these efforts move to the schools, school-based programs often come to serve as supports for family language planning in the home and community (see, e.g., King, Logan, & Fogle-Terry, 2008). "For language revitalization efforts to be successful," Hermes and King (2013) observe, "they need not just to instruct the language in formal or school domains, but to promote its use and transmission . . . in informal contexts such as the home and family" (p. 127). "Those who dream of language revitalization," Hinton (2013) notes, "ultimately desire the natural transmission of the language from parent to child and its use in daily life" (p. xiv). This recognizes that family members are primary in any language reclamation effort. We see this reflected in the parent- and community-led schools at Kahnawake and Akwesasne, the parent-run Hawaiian Pūnana Leo preschools, the voluntary immersion program at TDB, and in Hopi language teachers' expressed desire to "feed" Hopi youth their ancestral language and culture, much as was traditionally done in the home. (For powerful personal accounts of family-based language reclamation, see Hinton, 2013.)

Finally, the cases here testify to the efficacy of "strong and long" language revitalization models whereby learners have sustained access to comprehensible input (Krashen, 1985) in the Indigenous language over the course of the school day and their school careers, and where language reclamation is viewed as a multigenerational process. "Success in developing high-level proficiency . . . in an indigenous language is directly proportionate to its level of use and supportive framing in the school," Wilson and Kamanā state (2011, p. 51). At Akwesase, Nāwahī, and TDB, students are immersed in the Native language for much (and sometimes all) of the school day, over a period of several years. Yet prioritization of the Indigenous language and culture does not come at the "cost" of learning English; the scholarly literature is unanimous that "strong" language revitalization programs produce students with high levels of Indigenous-language proficiency and "academic and majority language outcomes equal to or surpassing those of peers in nonimmersion programs" (Wilson & Kamanā, 2011, p. 46; see also W. Holm, 2006; May, Hill, & Tiakiwai, 2004; McCarty, 2003, 2013; Tedick, Christian, & Fortune, 2011).

At the same time, these Indigenous programs demonstrate the importance of taking a long-term view of the language regenesis process. "For us to reach a point where our language was no longer spoken," Daryl Baldwin states with reference to *Myaamia* (Miami), "was an intergenerational process of declining language and cultural use" (cited in McCarty, 2013, p. 104). Revitalizing an Indigenous/heritage language "is also an intergenerational process," Baldwin maintains (cited in McCarty, 2013, p. 104).

This discussion would be incomplete without addressing the formidable challenges that school-based language revitalization efforts face. Beyond the challenges of any revitalization effort—declining numbers of speakers and language-use domains, and the proverbial race against time—Indigenous school-based programs typically must "grow their own" teachers and curricula. This entails enormous corpus and acquisition planning, which, depending on the situation, is likely to include language documentation, the development and/or refinement (and sometimes standardization) of practical writing systems, the creation of teaching materials, technology development, and the preparation of language teachers (see Coronel-Molina & McCarty, 2011, for examples of these activities). None of these are simple, straightforward, or nonideological tasks, and all require significant investments of time, ingenuity, and human and material resources. Whereas in some settings institutional supports are in place for teacher preparation and materials development, in many places there are few resources for these purposes (see De Korne, 2013, for a discussion).

Language reclamation efforts also face contentious ideological issues. In ethnographic work with Navajo and Pueblo youth and young adults, for example, Lee (2009, 2014) found that young people's motivation to learn and use their Native language was often dimmed by the "mixed messages" they received about the value of their heritage language. Within "the hierarchical positioning of Native languages and English," Lee (2009) states, there is a continuous negotiation "to determine the place of Native languages in relation to the privileged position of English" (p. 310). Similarly, Meek (2010), in an ethnography of Kaska language revitalization in British Columbia, describes pervasive language-linked stereotypes of "rural" versus "urban," "traditionalist" versus "assimilated Indians," and associated stigmatized identities that can derail revitalization efforts (p. 5). Yet these and other ethnographers also document Indigenous resistance and agency; in Lee's (2014) research, for instance, youth countered denigrating societal messages by exercising a "critical Indigenous consciousness," interrogating "the historical and broad oppressive conditions that have influenced current realities in Indigenous people's lives" (p. 145). Importantly, school-based language classes were crucial supports in activating this critical consciousness and encouraging young people to learn and use their heritage mother tongue outside of school (Lee, 2014, pp. 141–143). (For additional qualitative accounts of youth-focused language revitalization across a range of Indigenous settings, see Wyman, 2012; Wyman, McCarty, & Nicholas, 2014; and Romero-Little et al., 2011.)

One of the greatest challenges to school-based revitalization is the hostile policy environment in which bi/multilingual education efforts of any kind often operate, particularly in the United States. In a study of language policy in Yup'ik-serving schools, Wyman et al. (2010) found that the current U.S. policy emphasis on high-stakes English-only testing "has strongly exacerbated local worries that Yup'ik 'holds children back' from achieving in English," threatening the viability of Yup'ik bilingual schooling and encouraging bilingual parents to use English with their children at home (p. 40). In some states No Child Left Behind (NCLB) Act–mandated testing is exacerbated by English-only constitutional amendments. In Arizona and California—states with some of the largest Native American populations in the United States—Propositions 203 and 227, respectively, require that "All children in . . . public schools shall be . . . placed in English language classrooms" (Arizona Proposition 203, Article 3.1, Sec. 15-752). As Combs and Nicholas (2012) write, with the advent of these state laws "enrollment in Indigenous language programs became, if not illegal, certainly more complicated" (p. 103).

Despite heightened federal and state "language policing" (Blommaert, 2013), school-based language revitalizers continue to find ways to work around and through the constraints. Wilson (2012), for example, describes a boycott by Nāwahī parents of federally mandated English-only testing. "Testing academic content through a language other than the one through which that content is learned is neither consistent with professional standards nor valid and reliable," he observes (p. 26). Furthermore, high-stakes English-only testing mandated under the federal NCLB Act violates NALA, which guarantees Native Americans the right "to use, practice, and develop their traditional language in public schools" (Wilson, 2012, p. 36). Unlike NCLB, NALA lacks enforcement mechanisms and is modestly funded. The Nāwahī protest nonetheless "is an example of Native American families being inspired by NALA to resist forced linguistic loss and assimilation" (Wilson, 2012, p. 42).

We close by returning to our overarching question: Given what we know from three decades of research and practice in Native American language revitalization, do schools and their personnel have a *responsibility* to act as agents of language reclamation? We are witness to the devastating impacts of the language and culture exclusionary policies of the past. In many ways, language-restrictive policies such as NCLB and Propositions 203 and 227 "stem from the same language policy that dictated how Native American children were to be schooled in…boarding schools" (Wong Fillmore, 2011, p. 28). All children have the right to develop competence in the national language and the broader culture, but not at the cost of the disintegration of their heritage-language relationships and identities. This either/or, subtractive approach is not simply bad pedagogy and bad public policy, it is also racially and linguistically discriminatory and a violation of Indigenous people's educational and linguistic human rights (see, e.g., May, 2011, chap. 8; Skutnabb-Kangas & Dunbar, 2010).

Our answer to the question, then, is a resounding *of course*! School-based programs are not the only means to reclaim a threatened language, nor are they necessarily the most efficacious. Further, because they are situated in historically assimilative institutions, school-based programs and their personnel face the monumental challenge of countering the hegemony of the state. Hence, such programs represent *one* important means—"strategic tools" for language reclamation (McCarty, 2008)—ideally employed in concert with family, community, and other governmental and nongovernmental supports. Where they are desired and Indigenous community members exercise authority over their development and implementation, such programs can be highly effective in promoting heritage-language revitalization simultaneously with children's academic success. Equally important, these efforts are transforming hegemonic expectations about Indigenous languages and cultures, from loss and extinction to resilience and self-empowerment (cf. Webster & Peterson, 2011). This is a victory of Indigenous self-determination in schooling, and it promises to yield new possibilities for social, linguistic, and educational justice for Indigenous communities worldwide.

ACKNOWLEDGMENTS

We thank the editors, Terrence Wiley, Kathryn Borman, Arnold Danzig, and David Garcia, for inviting this submission and for patience and support during its development. We express sincere gratitude to consulting editor Kendall A. King for immensely valuable and ever-timely feedback throughout the writing process and for steering us to key sources. Special thanks to Wayne Holm for detailed feedback on Navajo, Louellyn White of Concordia University for providing feedback on language reclamation efforts at Akwesasne/St. Regis and to William Wilson and Kauanoe Kamanā for extensive commentary over the years on language revitalization in Hawaiʻi.

NOTES

[1]Although geophysically and linguistically not part of North America, we include Hawaiʻi and Hawaiian, a Polynesian language, in Figure 1 because Hawaiian is a Native American language, recognized in U.S. state and federal law and in key language policies such as the 1990/1992 Native American Languages Act. As we discuss, the revitalization of Hawaiian has been a leading language reclamation "success story," serving as a model for other Native North American language groups and for Indigenous peoples around the world.

[2]Parts of this section are adapted from McCarty (2013, chap. 5), and used with permission of Multilingual Matters.

REFERENCES

Adams, D. W. (1995). *Education for extinction: American Indians and the boarding school experience*. Lawrence: University Press of Kansas.
Arizona Proposition 203. (2000). *English language education for children in public schools*. Retrieved from http://www.azsos.gov/election/2000/info/PubPamphlet/english/prop203.htm

Arviso, M., & Holm, W. (2001). Tséhootsooídi Ólta'gi Diné bizaad bíhoo'aah: A Navajo immersion program at Fort Defiance, Arizona. In L. Hinton & K. Hale (Eds.), *The green book of language revitalization in practice* (pp. 203–215). San Diego, CA: Academic Press.

Bear Nicholas, A. (2009). Reversing language shift through a Native language immersion teacher training programme in Canada. In T. Skutnab-Kangas, R. Philipson, A. K. Mohanty, & M. Panda (Eds.), *Social justice through multilingual education* (pp. 220–237). Bristol, England: Multilingual Matters.

Benally, A., & Viri, D. (2005). Diné bizaad (Navajo language) at a crossroads: Extinction or renewal? *Bilingual Research Journal, 29*, 85–108.

Blommaert, J. (2013). Policy, policing and the ecology of social norms: Ethnographic monitoring revisited. *International Journal of the Sociology of Language, 219*, 123–140.

Bragdon, K. J. (1997). The Northeast culture area. In M. R. Mignon & D. L. Boxberger (Eds.), *Native North Americans: An ethnohistorical approach* (2nd ed., pp. 113–158). Dubuque, IO: Kendall/Hunt.

Castagno, A. E., & Brayboy, B. M. J. (2008). Culturally responsive schooling for Indigenous youth: A review of the literature. *Review of Educational Research, 78*, 941–992.

Combs, M. C., & Nicholas, S. E. (2012). The effect of Arizona language policies on Arizona Indigenous students. *Language Policy, 11*, 101–118.

Coronel-Molina, S. M., & McCarty, T. L. (2011). Language curriculum design and evaluation for endangered languages. In P. K. Austin & J. Sallabank (Eds.), *The Cambridge handbook of endangered languages* (pp. 354–370). Cambridge, England: Cambridge University Press.

De Korne, H. (2013). Allocating authority and policing competency: Indigenous language teacher certification in the United States. *Working Papers in Educational Linguistics, 28*, 23–41.

Edwards, J. (2012). Book review of N. H. Hornberger (Ed.), *Can Schools Save Indigenous Languages? Policy and Practice on Four Continents* (New York: Palgrave Macmillan, 2008). *Language Policy, 11*, 201–203.

Fettes, M. (1998). Life on the edge: Canada's Aboriginal languages under official bilingualism. In T. Ricento & B. Burnaby (Eds.), *Language and politics in the United States and Canada: Myths and realities* (pp. 117–149). Mahwah, NJ: Lawrence Erlbaum.

Field, M. C., & Kroskrity, P. V. (2009). Introduction: Revealing Native American language ideologies. In P. V. Kroskrity & M. C. Field (Eds.), *Native American language ideologies: Beliefs, practices, and struggles in Indian Country* (pp. 3–28). Tucson: University of Arizona Press.

Fishman, J. A. (1991). *Reversing language shift: Theoretical and empirical foundations of assistance to threatened languages.* Clevedon, England: Multilingual Matters.

Fishman, J. A. (1996). Maintaining languages: What works and what doesn't. In G. Cantoni (Ed.), *Stabilizing Indigenous languages* (pp. 165–175). Flagstaff: Northern Arizona University Center for Excellence in Education.

Foley, D. (1996). The silent Indian as a cultural production. In B. A. U. Levinson, D. E. Foley, & D. C. Holland (Eds.), *The cultural production of the educated person: Critical ethnographies of schooling and local practice* (pp. 79–91). Albany: State University of New York Press.

Goddard, I. (Compiler). (1999). *Native languages and language families of North America* (revised and enlarged ed.). Retrieved from http://cpfx.ca/files/NatLangMap.jpg

Gordon, R. G., Jr. (2005). *Ethnologue: Languages of the world* (15th ed.). Dallas, TX: SIL International.

Grenoble, L. A., & Whaley, L. J. (2006). *Saving languages: An introduction to language revitalization.* Cambridge, England: Cambridge University Press.

Hermes, M., & King, K. A. (2013). Ojibwe language revitalization, multimedia technology, and family language learning. *Language Learning & Technology, 17*, 125–144.

Hermes, M., Bang, M., & Marin, A. (2012). Designing Indigenous language revitalization. *Harvard Educational Review, 82*, 381–402.

Hill, J. (2002). "Expert rhetorics" in advocacy for endangered languages: Who is listening, and what do they hear? *Journal of Linguistic Anthropology, 12*, 119–133.

Hinton, L. (2001). Language revitalization: An overview. In L. Hinton & K. Hale (Eds.), *The green book of language revitalization in practice* (pp. 3–18). San Diego, CA: Academic Press.

Hinton, L. (2011). Revitalization of endangered languages. In P. K. Austin & J. Sallabank (Eds.), *The Cambridge handbook of endangered languages* (pp. 291–311). Cambridge, England: Cambridge University Press.

Hinton, L. (Ed.). (2013). *Bringing our languages home: Language revitalization for families.* Berkeley, CA: Heyday Books.

Hixson, L., Hepler, B. B., & Kim, M. O. (2012). *The Native Hawaiian and Other Pacific Islander population: 2010. 2010 Census Briefs.* Washington, DC: U.S. Department of Commerce, Economics and Statistics Administration, U.S. Census Bureau.

Hohepa, M. K. (2006). Biliterate practices in the home: Supporting Indigenous language regeneration. *Journal of Language, Identity, and Education, 5,* 293–301.

Holm, A., & Holm, W. (1995). Navajo language education: Retrospect and prospects. *Bilingual Research Journal, 19,* 141–167.

Holm, W. (2006). The "goodness" of bilingual education for Native American children. In T. L. McCarty & O. Zepeda (Eds.), *One voice, many voices: Recreating Indigenous language communities* (pp. 1–46). Tempe: Arizona State University Center for Indian Education.

Hoover, M. L., & Kanien'kehaka Raotitiohkwa Cultural Center. (1992). The revival of the Mohawk language in Kahnawake. *Canadian Journal of Native Studies, 12,* 269–287.

Hopi Tribal Council. (2005). *Hopi Tribal Council Resolution H-010-2006.* Hopi Tribe, AZ: Author.

Hornberger, N. H. (1988). *Bilingual education and language maintenance: A southern Peruvian Quechua case.* Berlin, Germany: Mouton de Gruyter.

Hornberger, N. H. (1997). Literacy, language maintenance, and linguistic human rights: Three telling cases. *International Journal of the Sociology of Language, 127,* 87–103

Hornberger, N. H. (2006). *Nichols* to *NCLB:* Local and global perspectives on US language education policy. In O. García, T. Skutnabb-Kangas, & M. E. Torres-Guzmán (Eds.), *Imagining multilingual schools: Languages in education and glocalization* (pp. 223–237). Clevedon, England: Multilingual Matters.

Hornberger, N. H. (Ed.). (2008). *Can schools save Indigenous languages? Policy and practice on four continents.* New York, NY: Palgrave Macmillan.

Jacobs, K. A. (1998). A chronology of Mohawk language instruction at Kahnawá:ke. In L. A. Grenoble & L. J. Whaley (Eds.), *Endangered languages: Language loss and community response* (pp. 117–125). Cambridge, England: Cambridge University Press.

Johnson, B. (1976). *Ojibway heritage.* Lincoln: University of Nebraska Press.

Johnson, F. T., & Legatz, J. (2006). Tséhootsooí Diné Bi'ólta' [Fort Defiance Navajo Immersion School]. *Journal of American Indian Education, 45*(2), 26–33.

Kawagley, A. L. (2011). Alaska Native education: History and adaptation in the new millennium. In R. Barnhardt & A. O. Kawagley (Eds.), *Alaska Native education: View from within* (pp. 73–95). Fairbanks: Alaska Native Knowledge Network, Center for Cross-Cultural Studies, University of Alaska Fairbanks.

King, K. A. (2001). *Language revitalization processes and prospects: Quichua in the Ecuadorian Andes.* Clevedon, England: Multilingual Matters.

King, K. A., Logan, L., & Fogle-Terry, A. (2008). Family language policy. *Language & Linguistics Compass, 2,* 907–922.

Krashen, S. D. (1985). *Inquiries and insights.* Hayward, CA: Alemany Press.

Krauss, M. (1998). The condition of Native North American languages: The need for realistic assessment and action. *International Journal of the Sociology of Language, 132,* 9–12.

Kroskrity, P. V., & Field, M. C. (Eds.). (2009). *Native American language ideologies: Beliefs, practices, and struggles in Indian Country.* Tucson: University of Arizona Press.

Lee, T. S. (2009). Language, identity, and power: Navajo and Pueblo young adults' perspectives and experiences with competing language ideologies. *Journal of Language, Identity, and Education, 8,* 307–320.

Lee, T. S. (2014). Critical language awareness among Native youth in New Mexico. In L. T. Wyman, T. L. McCarty, & S. E. Nicholas (Eds.), *Indigenous youth and multilingualism: Language identity, ideology, and practice in dynamic cultural worlds* (pp. 130–148). New York, NY: Routledge.

Leonard, W. Y. (2007). *Miami language reclamation in the home: A case study* (Unpublished doctoral dissertation). University of California, Berkeley.

Lomawaima, K. T., & McCarty, T. L. (2006). *"To remain an Indian": Lessons in democracy from a century of Native American education*. New York, NY: Teachers College Press.

MacLean, E. (2010). Culture change for Iñupiat and Yup'ik people of Alaska. In R. Barnhardt & A. O. Kawagley (Eds.), *Alaska Native education: View from within* (pp. 41–58). Fairbanks: Alaska Native Knowledge Network, Center for Cross-Cultural Studies, University of Alaska Fairbanks.

Margolin, M. (1981). *The way we lived: California Indian reminiscences, stories, and songs*. Berkeley, CA: Heyday Books.

May, S. (2011). *Language and minority rights: Ethnicity, nationalism, and the politics of language* (2nd ed.). New York, NY: Routledge.

May, S., Hill, R., & Tiakiwai, S. (2004). *Bilingual/immersion education: Indicators of good practice. Final report to the New Zealand Ministry of Education*. Wellington: New Zealand Ministry of Education. Retrieved from http://www.educationcounts.govt.nz/publications/schooling/5079

McCarty, T. L. (2003). Revitalising Indigenous languages in homogenising times. *Comparative Education, 39*, 147–163.

McCarty, T. L. (2008). Schools as strategic tools for indigenous language revitalization. In N. H. Hornberger (Ed.), *Can schools save indigenous languages? Policy and practice on four continents* (pp. 161–179). New York, NY: Palgrave Macmillan.

McCarty, T. L. (2013). *Language planning and policy in Native America: History, theory, praxis*. Bristol, England: Multilingual Matters.

McCarty, T. L., & Nicholas, S. E. (2012). Indigenous education: Local and global perspectives. In M. Martin-Jones, A. Blackledge, & A. Creese (Eds.), *The Routledge handbook of multilingualism* (pp. 145–166). London, England: Routledge.

McCarty, T. L., Nicholas, S. E., & Wyman, L. T. (2012). Re-emplacing place in the "global here and now": Critical ethnographic case studies of Native American language planning and policy. *International Multilingual Research Journal, 6*, 50–63.

McCarty, T. L., Wallace, S., Lynch, R., & Benally, A. (1991). Classroom inquiry and Navajo learning styles: A call for reassessment. *Anthropology & Education Quarterly, 22*, 42–51.

Meek, B. A. (2010). *We are our language: An ethnography of language revitalization in a Northern Athabaskan community*. Tucson: University of Arizona Press.

Mithun, M., & Chafe, W. L. (1987). Recapturing the Mohawk language. In T. Shopen (Ed.), *Languages and their status* (pp. 1–34). New York, NY: Winthrop.

Mohawk Council of Kahanwá:ke. (2012). *Mohawks of Kahnawá:ke*. Retrieved from http://www.kahnawake.com/

Mohawk Nation Council of Chiefs. (n.d.). Akwesasne Freedom School. Retrieved from http://www.northnet.org/mohawkna/freedom.htm

Moore, R., Pietikäinen, S., & Blommaert, J. (2010). Counting the losses: Numbers as the language of endangerment. *Sociolinguistic Studies, 4*, 1–26.

Nicholas, S. E. (2005). Negotiating for the Hopi way of life through literacy and schooling. In T. L. McCarty (Ed.), *Language, literacy, and power in schooling* (pp. 29–46). Mahwah, NJ: Lawrence Erlbaum.

Nicholas, S. E. (2008). *Becoming "fully" Hopi: The role of the Hopi language in the contemporary lives of Hopi youth—A Hopi case study of language shift and vitality* (Unpublished doctoral dissertation). University of Arizona, Tucson.

Nicholas, S. E. (2009). "I live Hopi, I just don't speak it": The critical intersection of language, culture, and identity for contemporary Hopi youth. *Journal of Language, Identity, and Education, 8*, 321–334.

Nicholas, S. E. (2014). "Being" Hopi by "living" Hopi:—Redefining and reasserting cultural and linguistic identity: Emergent Hopi youth ideologies. In L. T. Wyman, T. L. McCarty, & S. E. Nicholas (Eds.), *Indigenous youth and multilingualism: Language identity, ideology, and practice in dynamic cultural worlds* (pp. 70–89). New York, NY: Routledge.

Norris, T., Vines, P. L., & Hoeffel, E. N. (2012). *The American Indian and Alaska Native Population: 2010.* Washington, DC: U.S. Department of Commerce Economics and Statistics Administration, U.S. Census Bureau.

Ortiz, S. J. (1992). *Woven stone.* Tucson: University of Arizona Press.

Patrick, D. (2010). Canada. In J. A. Fishman & O. García (Eds.), *Handbook of language and ethnic identity: Vol. 1. Disciplinary and regional perspectives* (pp. 286–301). Oxford, England: Oxford University Press.

Patrick, D. (2012). Indigenous contexts. In M. Martin-Jones, A. Blackledge, & A. Creese (Eds.), *The Routledge handbook of multilingualism* (pp. 29–48). London, England: Routledge.

Powers, M. N. (1986). *Oglala women: Myth, ritual, and reality.* Chicago, IL: University of Chicago Press.

Reyhner, J. (2006). *Education and language restoration.* Philadelphia, PA: Chelsea House.

Rockwell, E., & Gomes, M. R. (2009). Introduction to the special issue: Rethinking Indigenous education from a Latin American perspective. *Anthropology & Education Quarterly, 40*, 97–109.

Romero-Little, M. E., Ortiz, S. J., McCarty, T. L., & Chen, R. (Eds.) (2011). *Indigenous languages across the generations–Strengthening families and communities.* Tempe: Arizona State University Center for Indian Education.

Sachdev, I., Arnold, D. Y., & Yapita, J. (2006). Indigenous identity and language: Some considerations from Bolivia and Canada. *BISAL, 1*, 107–128.

Siebens, J., & Julian, T. (2011). *Native North American languages spoken at home in the United States and Puerto Rico: 2006-2010.* Washington, DC: U.S. Department of Commerce Economics and Statistics Administration, U.S. Census Bureau.

Sims, C. (2005). Tribal languages and the challenges of revitalization. *Anthropology & Education Quarterly, 36*, 104–106.

Skutnabb-Kangas, T. (2000). *Linguistic genocide in education: Or worldwide diversity and human rights?* Mahwah, NJ: Lawrence Erlbaum.

Skutnabb-Kangas, T., & Dunbar, R. (2010). Indigenous children's education as linguistic genocide and a crime against humanity? A global view [Special issue]. *Gáldu Cála: Journal of Indigenous Peoples Rights, 1.*

Stairs, A., Peters, M., & Perkins, E. (1999). Beyond language in Indigenous language immersion schooling. *Practicing Anthropology, 20*(2), 44–47.

Statistics Canada. (2008). *Census profile of federal electoral districts: Language, mobility and migration and immigration and citizenship.* Ottawa, Ontario, Canada: Statistics Canada. Retrieved from http://www.statcan.gc.ca/bsolc/olc-cel/olc-cel?catno=97-555-X2006027&lang=eng

Statistics Canada. (2009a). Aboriginal peoples. *Ottawa, Ontario: Statistics Canada.* Retrieved May 27, 2013 from http://www12.statcan.ca/census-recensement/2006/rt-td/ap-pa-eng.cfm

Statistics Canada. (2009b). *Table 23: Percentage of First Nations people who have knowledge of an Aboriginal language, by age groups, Canada, 2001 and 2006.* Retrieved from http://www12.statcan.ca/census-recensement/2006/as-sa/97-558/table/t23-eng.cfm

Task Force on Aboriginal Languages and Cultures. (2005). *Towards a new beginning: A foundational report for a strategy to revitalize First Nation, Inuit and Métis languages and cultures.* Ottawa, Ontario, Canada: Aboriginal Languages Directorate, Aboriginal Affairs Branch, Department of Canadian Heritage.

Tedick, D. J., Christian, D., & Fortune, T. W. (Eds.). (2011). *Immersion education: Practices, policies, possibilities.* Bristol, England: Multilingual Matters.

Village of Munqapi Forum. (1997, January 22). *Minutes of public orientation by the Hopi Tribe Culture Preservation Office on the Hopi Language Assessment Project (HLAP).* Hopi Tribe, AZ: Author.

Warner, S. N. (2001). The movement to revitalize Hawaiian language and culture. In L. Hinton & K. Hale (Eds.), *The green book of language revitalization in practice* (pp. 133–144). San Diego, CA: Academic Press.

wa Thiong'o, N. (2009). *Something torn and new: An African renaissance.* New York, NY: Basic Books.

wa Thiong'o, N. (2011). Linguistic feudalism and linguistic Darwinism: The struggle of the Indigenous from the margins of power. In M. E. Romero-Little, S. J. Ortiz, T. L. McCarty, & R. Chen (Eds.), *Indigenous languages across the generations—Strengthening families and communities* (pp. 241–246). Tempe: Arizona State University Center for Indian Education.

Webster, A. K., & Peterson, L. C. (2011). Introduction: American Indian languages in unexpected places. *American Indian Culture and Research Journal, 35*(2), 1–18.

White, L. (2009). *Free to be Kanien'kehaka: A case study of educational self-determination at the Akwesasne Freedom School* (Unpublished doctoral dissertation). University of Arizona, Tucson.

Wilkins, D. E., & Lomawaima, K. T. (2001). *Uneven ground: American Indian sovereignty and federal law.* Norman: University of Oklahoma Press.

Williams, T. (2013, April 13). Quietly, Indians reshape cities and reservations. *New York Times.* Retrieved from http://www.nytimes.com/2013/04/14/us/as-american-indians-move-to-cities-old-and-new-challenges-follow.html?_r=0

Wilson, W. H. (1998). I ka 'olelo Hawai'i ke ola, "Life is found in the Hawaiian language." *International Journal of the Sociology of Language, 132,* 123–137.

Wilson, W. H. (2012). USDE violations of NALA and the testing boycott at Nāwahīokalani'ōpu'u School. *Journal of American Indian Education, 51*(3), 30–45.

Wilson, W. H., & Kamanā, K. (2001). "Mai loko mai o ka 'i'ini: Proceeding from a dream": The 'Aha Pūnana Leo connection in Hawaiian language revitalization. In L. Hinton & K. Hale (Eds.), *The green book of language revitalization in practice* (pp. 147–176). San Diego, CA: Academic Press.

Wilson, W. H., & Kamanā, K. (2006). "For the interest of the Hawaiians themselves": Reclaiming the benefits of Hawaiian-medium education. *Hūlili: Multidisciplinary Research on Hawaiian Well-Being, 3,* 153–178.

Wilson, W. H., & Kamanā, K. (2008, February). Ke Kula 'O Nāwahīokalani'ōpu'u: An Indigenous language revitalization laboratory school. *ACIE Newsletter, 10*(2). Retrieved from http://www.carla.umn.edu/immersion/acie/vol11/No2/feb08_schoolprofile.html

Wilson, W. H., & Kamanā, K. (2011). Insights from Indigenous language immersion in Hawai'i. In D. J. Tedick, D. Christian, & T. W. Fortune (Eds.), *Immersion education: Practices, policies, possibilities* (pp. 36–57). Bristol, England: Multilingual Matters.

Wilson, W. H., & Kamanā, K. (2014). A Hawaiian revitalization perspective on Indigenous youth and bilingualism. In L. T. Wyman, T. L. McCarty, & S. E. Nicholas (Eds.), *Indigenous youth and multilingualism: Language identity, ideology, and practice in dynamic cultural worlds* (pp. 187–200). New York, NY: Routledge.

Wilson, W. H., Kamanā, K., & Rawlins, N. (2006). Nāwahī Hawaiian Laboratory School. *Journal of American Indian Education, 45*(2), 42–44.

Wilson, W. H., & Kawai'ae'a, K. (2007). I kumu I lālā: "Let there be sources; let there be branches": Teacher education in the College of Hawaiian Language. *Journal of American Indian Education, 46*(3), 37–53.

Wong, K. L. (2011). Language, fruits, and vegetables. In M. E. Romero-Little, S. J. Ortiz, T. L. McCarty, & R. Chen (Eds.), *Indigenous languages across the generations: Strengthening families and communities* (pp. 3–16). Tempe: Arizona State University Center for Indian Education.

Wong Fillmore, L. (2011). An ecological perspective on intergenerational language transmission. In M. E. Romero-Little, S. J. Ortiz, T. L. McCarty, & R. Chen (Eds.), *Indigenous languages across the generations: Strengthening families and communities* (pp. 19–48). Tempe: Arizona State University Center for Indian Education.

Wyman, L. T. (2012). *Youth culture, language endangerment, and linguistic survivance.* Bristol, England: Multilingual Matters.

Wyman, L. T., Marlow, P., Andrew, F. C., Miller, G. S., Nicholai, R. C., & Rearden, N. Y. (2010). Focusing on long-term language goals in challenging times: A Yup'ik example. *Journal of American Indian Education, 49*(1/2), 28–49.

Wyman, L. T., McCarty, T. L., & Nicholas, S. E. (Eds.). (2014). *Indigenous youth and multilingualism: Language identity, ideology, and practice in dynamic cultural worlds.* New York, NY: Routledge.

Yamamoto, A. Y. (2007). Endangered languages in USA and Canada. In M. Brenzinger (Ed.), *Language diversity endangered* (pp. 87–122). Berlin, Germany: Mouton de Gruyter.

Chapter 6

The Rediscovery of Heritage and Community Language Education in the United States

JIN SOOK LEE
University of California, Santa Barbara

WAYNE E. WRIGHT
University of Texas at San Antonio

INTRODUCTION

Language and cultural preservation efforts among different communities of language speakers in the United States have received increasing attention as interest in linguistic rights and globalization continues to deepen. In addition to mounting evidence of the cognitive, psychological, and academic benefits of heritage language/community language (HL/CL) maintenance for linguistic-minority children (see Lee & Suarez, 2009, for a summary of the research), scholars have advocated for the recognition, support, and utilization of the potentially rich pool of HLs/CLs as a resource for filling linguistic and cultural voids in professional and political sectors of our society (Brecht & Ingold, 1998; Peyton, Ranard, & McGinnis, 2001; Wiley, 2005b, 2007). Yet the maintenance of HLs/CLs even among children of first-generation immigrants has been difficult, and it has been nearly unattainable beyond the third generation (Fishman, 2001; Rumbaut, 2009; Veltman, 1983). Counter to popular beliefs that HLs/CLs can be easily maintained in the home if parents speak to their children in the HL/CL, studies have shown that home language use alone is an insufficient condition for producing highly proficient users of the language, particularly those who can function in professional domains. Some form of explicit instruction is needed (Fillmore, 1991, 2000; Lao & Lee, 2009; Lee, 2002; Wright, 2004).

Throughout U.S. history, the most significant efforts for HL/CL instruction outside the home have occurred in community-based HL/CL schools (Fishman, 2001;

Review of Research in Education
March 2014, Vol. 38, pp. 137-165
DOI: 10.3102/0091732X13507546
© 2014 AERA. http://rre.aera.net

137

Valdés, 2001). Although their history of existence in the United States stretches over 300 years, community-based HL/CL programs have typically existed away from the scope of mainstream society (Fishman, 2001). Within the past decade or so, however, there has been a reemergence of interest in HL/CL issues, as evidenced by the growth in conferences, books, journals, centers, and university programs dedicated to HL/CL education and research. This article examines the contributions of community-based HL/CL education programs to the promotion of language diversity in the United States. We begin by defining HL/CL and framing the boundaries of HL/CL education as distinct from language instruction programs offered in U.S. schools, where the attention has been primarily on English acquisition. Then, we review the history of HL/CL education in the United States, focusing on how educational language policy and politics have influenced the instructional models as well as the learning outcomes of HL/CL education. Next, we offer a synthesis of the challenges and needs faced by community-based HL/CL programs. Following this synthesis, we present contrastive examples of the different approaches to HL/CL education taken by two different communities, the Korean American and the Cambodian (Khmer) American. We conclude by arguing for a rediscovery of community-based HL/CL programs as an alternative but legitimate educational space, where critical discourses about and practices supportive of multilingualism and multiculturalism can flourish.

DEFINITION OF HL/CL EDUCATION

The terms *heritage language* and *community language* have been used mainly to refer to immigrant, indigenous, refugee, and ancestral languages other than English with which a speaker has a personal connection (Fishman, 2001) or some degree of proficiency (Valdés, 2001). *Heritage language* and *community language* can be defined in terms of individual or collective affiliation with a particular ethnolinguistic group or religion, as in the case of Korean ethnic students learning Korean or Muslim students learning Standard Arabic, which may not necessarily be a language spoken in their homes but is strongly tied to the religious heritage of Islam and the Koran (Aburumuh, 2012; Bale, 2010; Fishman, 2001; Lee, 2002; Wiley, 2001). They can also be defined in terms of the level of proficiency an individual has in the language (Hornberger & Wang, 2008; Valdés, 2001). Although some scholars favor the use of *community language* to signify an active and dynamic connection between the language and its speakers over the use of *heritage language*, which has been criticized for evoking images of the past and relegating languages to a powerless position (Baker & Jones, 1998; O. García, 2005; Hornberger, 2005), the use of *heritage language* has held its place in the literature because of its capacity to encompass also the nonusers of the language who may have a personal connection to the language based on their family's history, "even though the linguistic evidence of that connection may have been lost for generations" (Van Deusen-Scholl, 2003, p. 222). While there are still limitations and ambiguities associated with both terms, *heritage language* and *community language* present a better alternative to other terms that have been widely used in the literature. For example, *heritage/community language* captures more accurately the diversity of language connections that different people have in comparison to terms such as *primary language, home language, native language*, and *mother tongue*, which suggest some level of past or current proficiency in the language, as well as to labels such as *minority language, indigenous language, immigrant language*, or *ethnic language*, which are loaded with sociopolitical implications. According to Hornberger (2005, p. 102), *heritage/community language* represents a more "neutral" and "inclusive" option. Therefore, for the purposes of this chapter, we use *heritage/community language* (HL/CL) not only to preserve this neutrality and inclusiveness that embraces the full range of personal connections to languages but also to recognize the varied usages of these terms.

The education of HL/CL generally starts in the home with parents and/or grandparents and, in most cases, becomes formalized in community-based HL/CL schools. Community-based HL/CL programs are driven by the desire to transmit language and culture intergenerationally so that connections within families and ethnic communities through socialization into cultural values and practices can be maintained (Fishman, 2001). Based on Fishman's (1991) Graded Intergenerational Disruption Scale, which outlines eight sociolinguistic conditions that assess the status of a language's vitality, the survival of community-based language schools and the effectiveness of HL/CL instruction depend on the realization of intergenerational transmission of a language, which is determined not only by individual parental decisions but also by societal and institutional conditions that influence parental decisions about their children's language behavior. Thus, the involvement of parents may be the single most important factor for the success of HL/CL education as it is often the parents of the students themselves who organize and manage HL/CL programs. Unlike traditional schooling, without parent participation and commitment to program administration, teaching, and student recruitment, HL/CL programs would and could not exist.

Due to their local governance by families, community leaders, churches, and civic organizations within the individual ethnic communities they serve, HL/CL programs differ greatly in their instructional goals and services, structure and organization, and resources including staff qualifications and funding sources. For example, the presence of learners with different motivations and reasons for learning the HL/CL in particular community contexts makes it difficult to adopt a unified curricular or instructional approach. In some local contexts where there is a greater presence of learners who mainly desire a stronger connection to their ethnic identity, identity-based approaches that emphasize the sociopsychological needs of HL/CL speakers in their curricula and instruction may be more applicable. Community-based language schools provide opportunities for students to socially network with coethnic peers and to nurture cultural identities and ethnic pride that may otherwise weaken due to pressures to assimilate (Zhou & Kim, 2006). Thus, they have been an integral part of ethnic social structures by serving as the locus of social support, network building, and social capital formation (N. Liu, 2010; Zhou & Kim, 2006). On the other hand, in communities where use of the HL/CL is vibrant, proficiency-based approaches that call for a greater sensitivity toward sociolinguistic differences across HL/CL dialects may be better suited (Lee, 2005; Peyton, Carreira, Wang, & Wiley, 2008). Apart from language instruction, community-based HL/CL schools also typically offer lessons in culture-specific activities such as calligraphy, traditional dancing, or martial arts.

Because the availability of resources and funds vary from community to community, community-based HL/CL programs are operated through different organizations and in different kinds of spaces. Many programs are associated with religious organizations such as churches, temples, synagogues, and mosques, whereas others are more independently operated and are held in private homes, commercial buildings, or public spaces such as local schools or universities. Most community-based HL/CL programs are nonprofit organizations and can include nongovernment-sponsored programs, such as ethnic community language programs; homeland government–sponsored programs, such as Japanese schools for returnee children of expatriates, and U.S. government–sponsored programs, such as the Ka Haka ʻUla O Keʻelikōlani program, which provides outreach services through a local university to support indigenous languages throughout Polynesia and the United States (http://www.olelo. hawaii.edu/khuok/laeula.php). Such programs operate under a service model; they are either free or of nominal charge, attempting to make participation affordable for all families regardless of their economic means.

Records of community-based HL/CL schools are difficult to find and are incomplete, primarily due to a lack of centralized records and systemic governance of such schools (Kelleher, 2010). One of the most comprehensive attempts to document community-based HL/CL schools was undertaken by the sociolinguist Joshua Fishman in the early 1980s (Fishman, 1985). He identified over 6,000 HL/CL programs teaching 145 different languages, of which 91 were indigenous American languages. The majority of the schools taught immigrant languages such as Chinese, French, Hebrew, Italian, Japanese, Korean, Polish, Portuguese, Spanish, Ukrainian, and Yiddish. Since then there has been no comprehensive attempt to document existing HL/CL programs, with the exception of the efforts of the Center for Applied Linguistics and the National Foreign Language Center to support the Alliance for the Advancement of Heritage Languages (www.cal.org/heritage). One goal of the Alliance is to develop a centralized database for HL/CL programs in order to raise awareness of such programs and facilitate streamlined efforts that can better support their mission and implementation. Although only a limited number of all HL/CL programs in the country are represented, as of September 2013, the database included over 690 programs teaching about 70 languages; 417 of the programs included are community-based. The information provided is helpful for making HL/CL programs visible and for establishing a platform where challenges, successes, and resources can be shared.

There are also K–16 bilingual and foreign language educational programs, such as dual language immersion and language tracks for heritage or native speakers (e.g., Spanish for Spanish Speakers), which provide important opportunities for HL/CL development (see, e.g., Brinton, Kagan, & Bauckus, 2008; Christian, Howard, & Loeb, 2000; Gambhir, 2001; Kono & McGinnis, 2001; Lindholm-Leary, 2001; Peyton, Lewelling, & Winke, 2001; S. C. Wang & Green, 2001; Webb & Miller, 2000, for overviews of such programs). However, school-based or government-based programs are not discussed in this article, as our focus is on community-based programs.

HISTORY OF HL/CL EDUCATION IN THE UNITED STATES

Despite perceptions of past immigrants abandoning their native languages and quickly learning English, the reality is that many immigrant groups have sought to maintain their native languages and provide opportunities for their children to learn them through community-based schooling (Wiley, 2005a). German/English bilingual education was common in German communities throughout the United States from the 17th century until World War I (Kloss, 1998; Toth, 1990; Wiley, 1998), and Spanish/English bilingual programs were offered throughout the Southwest in the 19th century (Blanton, 2004; Kloss, 1998). Notably, the importance of English was never ignored in these educational settings. During this same period, there were also U.S. schools established by ethnic minority communities providing language instruction in Chinese, Japanese, French, Cherokee, Swedish, Danish, Norwegian, Italian, Polish, Dutch, and Czech, primarily for heritage speakers (Crawford, 2004; Kloss, 1998). Also, in certain regions, given the large numbers of HL/CL speakers of a particular language, there were official policies that called for French instruction in Massachusetts high schools and Spanish instruction in high schools across the territory of New Mexico, which at the time included Arizona and parts of Utah, Colorado, and Nevada (Crawford, 2004; Kloss, 1998; Wright, 2010). In addition, HL/CL courses were sometimes supported by foreign governments, as in the cases of the governments of France, Russia, and Hungary providing instruction in their national languages to students in New Orleans, Alaska, and Connecticut, respectively (Kloss, 1998).

Not all groups, however, enjoyed such linguistic tolerance (Wiley & Wright, 2004). English-only Indian boarding schools were established with the goal of eradicating Native American languages and culture, thus making it easier for Whites to take Native American land (Haynes, 2010). Similarly, prohibitions against the use of native languages by enslaved Africans were accompanied by "compulsory ignorance laws"—policies designed to suppress resistance and rebellion by making it illegal for slaves to be provided with English literacy instruction (Weinberg, 1995). Such restriction-oriented language policies began to rise in the context of the Americanization Movement during and after World War I, pushing the ideology that being American means speaking only English (McClymer, 1982). With Germany as a war enemy, heavy restrictions were placed on the teaching of German (Toth, 1990; Wiley, 1998). These restrictive policies had an impact on other languages as well, which drove many states to adopt English-only instructional policies for public and private schools.

A challenge to these restrictions came in the early 1920s. Roman Catholic and Lutheran German parochial schools contested the state of Nebraska's Simian Act (1919), which had outlawed foreign language instruction for students below Grade 8. The state court upheld the mandate for English-only instruction but declared that the Act could not prevent schools from offering German language instruction outside of the hours of regular school study. The parochial schools used this ruling to provide German instruction during extended recess periods. Policymakers seeking to close this loophole fined the parochial schoolteacher Robert Meyer $25 for teaching Bible stories to children in German (Wiley & Lee, 2009). The case *Meyer v. Nebraska* (1923) went to the U.S. Supreme Court and was consolidated with similar cases from Ohio and Idaho. The Supreme Court ruled that although states can legislate the language of instruction in schools, they may not pass laws preventing communities from offering private language classes outside of the regular school system.

In a similar case in Hawaii in 1927, *Farrington v. Tokushige*, the U.S. Supreme Court offered further protections of after-school HL/CL programs following attempts by education authorities to restrict Japanese, Korean, and Chinese programs (Wiley & Lee, 2009). However, during World War II, Japanese and Chinese language schools were shut down in California and Hawaii (Wiley & Wright, 2004). Chinese communities began to reestablish their schools following World War II, but Hawaii attempted to implement new restrictions through programs associated with the Act Regulating the Teaching of Foreign Languages to Children. The state argued that it needed to "protect children from the harm of learning a foreign language" (Del Valle, 2003). In *Stainback v. Mo Hock Ke Lok Po* (1947), the state court not only struck down this restrictive act but also argued that at least for "the brightest" students, the study of a foreign language can be beneficial (Del Valle, 2003).

Despite these legal victories, these court decisions were essentially about parents' rights under the 14th Amendment, rather than about language rights per se (Del Valle, 2003). Where attempts at language-restrictive legislation failed, wartime xenophobia largely succeeded. The number of schools providing instruction in the Japanese and German languages dropped dramatically in the context of World War II, mainly due to fears of community members that their loyalty to the United States would be questioned. Nevertheless, the legacy of the *Meyer, Farrington,* and *Stainback* cases is that the common practice today of language communities offering HL/CL programs after school and on weekends is protected by the U.S. Constitution (Wright, 2010). Yet these cases also made clear that states can mandate the language of instruction. By the mid-1900s, several states had established laws requiring English as the medium of instruction in public schools.

The Civil Rights Movement opened the way for more tolerance-oriented language policies (Gándara & Hopkins, 2010). The 1968 Bilingual Education Act was passed to provide support for schools in offering innovative programs that made use of both English and students' native languages. The U.S. Supreme Court case *Lau v. Nichols* in 1974 was brought forward by Chinese American students in the San Francisco Unified School District who had been placed in mainstream classrooms and left to sink or swim. The court ruled that such practices were unconstitutional and that school districts must take appropriate actions to address the linguistic and academic needs of English language learners. Although the court mentioned bilingual education as one possible remedy, it neither mandated any particular approach nor did it articulate the maintenance of the students' native languages as a goal (Wright, 2010). Most bilingual programs were transitional, their goal being to move students into English-only instruction as quickly as possible. However, the growth of bilingual education opened up spaces for stronger instructional models with goals of bilingualism and biliteracy for a wider range of students, including proficient English speakers who lacked proficiency in their HL/CL (Baker, 2011).

The general trend of tolerance-oriented policies began to shift as proponents of English-only policies succeeded in loosening mandates and support for bilingual education. A new wave of restriction-oriented policies began in the late 1990s when three key voter initiatives—California's Proposition 227 (1998), Arizona's Proposition 203 (2000), and Massachusetts' Question 2 (2002)—placed restrictions on bilingual education through mandates that English learners be instructed through structured English immersion programs (Gándara & Hopkins, 2010). Although interpretation and implementation of these initiatives have varied, each has resulted in a reduction of the number of bilingual programs.

The passage of the No Child Left Behind (NCLB) Act of 2001 has proven to be one of the biggest challenges to providing in-school bilingual and other HL/CL programs (Wright, 2007). Although previous versions of federal education law explicitly recognized the benefits of individual and societal bilingualism, these disappeared as Title III of NCLB replaced the Bilingual Education Act with an exclusive focus on English and stripped all direct references to bilingualism from the law. While bilingual education programs are not prohibited under NCLB, there is no encouragement of or direct support for them. Each state is free to determine which types of language education programs to support with Title III funds. Furthermore, NCLB's heavy emphasis on school accountability through high-stakes testing has been one of the biggest detriments to in-school foreign language and HL/CL programs (Menken, 2008; Rhodes & Pufahl, 2010; Wright & Choi, 2006). Pressure to raise test scores has resulted in efforts to ensure that students are taught only in the language of the test. Despite allowances for testing students in their native language, the reality is that most students are tested only in English (Wright & Choi, 2006). Thus, many of the remaining bilingual education programs have placed greater emphasis on test-focused instruction in English than on developing students' bilingual skills. Some after-school HL/CL programs have also been indirectly affected by NCLB, as in the case of a California school district where mandated after-school test preparation sessions conflicted with HL/CL classes (Wright, 2007). Although community-based HL/CL programs were not directly affected by NCLB, the push for English-only instruction has reinforced language minority children's and their parents' sense of urgency for native-like English acquisition and has indirectly dampened attitudes and motivation toward HL/CL education and programs (Jeon, 2008; Lee & Jeong, 2011).

Apart from the effects of NCLB-specific policies, efforts to provide multilingual instruction in K–12 schools have been minimal, and therefore K–12 education policy is out of sync with other federal efforts to increase the language capacity of the country by focusing on areas such as higher education and national security. The 1991 National Security Education Act provided financial support for study in over 70 critical needs and preferred languages that are less commonly taught (e.g., Arabic, Hindi, Korean, Mandarin, Russian, Swahili, Vietnamese) in American universities. Ironically, these are languages spoken by many young immigrant and American-born students when they first enter school, yet few of these students are given opportunities to further develop and maintain them at levels desperately needed by the country. Most efforts at building capacity in these languages focus on nonnative speakers. In recognition of this irony, increasing efforts are now being directed at supporting HL/CL speakers in this period of rediscovery of HL/CL education (Brecht & Ingold, 1998). For example, there are 15 Language Resource Centers funded by the U.S. Department of Education to promote foreign language study at the university level, including the National Heritage Language Resource Center, housed at the University of California, Los Angeles (http://www.nhlrc.ucla.edu).

Despite existing language restriction-oriented policies, allowances for waivers and other loopholes in these laws have left space for innovative programs, making possible bilingual and other in-school HL/CL programs within the limits of federal and state policies (see, e.g., Combs, Evans, Fletcher, Parra, & Jiménez, 2005; Freeman, 2004; Johnson & Freeman, 2010). The availability of such spaces is particularly important in the current climate of growing anti-immigrant sentiments and educational language policies that restrict the use of languages other than English in educational and public settings (Wiley & Wright, 2004). As O. García (2005) states,

[The] use of the term *heritage languages* in education . . . provides a way to "crack" today's homogenous monolingual schooling of very different children in the United States, providing a space for the use of languages other than English in educating children. (p. 602)

Thus, HL/CL learning has opened up alternative paths for language education of English-speaking children of language minority backgrounds.

CHALLENGES AND NEEDS OF COMMUNITY-BASED HL/CL PROGRAMS

Community-based HL/CL programs are a common experience in the lives of many U.S. children who speak a language other than English (Bradunas, 1988;

Fishman, 2001; Hinton, 1999; Portes & Rumbaut, 2006). According to Tran (2008), for example, whenever there are enough Vietnamese people living in close proximity of one another, Vietnamese language classes for children are typically organized through a Buddhist temple, church, or community organization. With increased immigration, the numbers of programs and students in community-based programs have grown. For instance, McGinnis (2005) reported that there are over 140,000 students in Chinese HL/CL programs, which is about a 59% increase from 1996. However, studies have found that community-based HL/CL programs have not led to significant improvements in HL/CL proficiency among the second generation (Hinton, 1999; H. Kim & Lee, 2011; Lee, 2002; P. Wang, 1996; You, 2011; Zhou & Kim, 2006). In this section, we survey the literature to identify common challenges faced by HL/CL programs and ways in which programs can become more successful. Although community-based programs differ greatly in their structure and organization, we focus on five factors that have been consistently noted as areas for improvement across studies on HL/CL programs. While these challenges are to a certain degree interconnected, we discuss each individually in terms of what the issues are and what is needed to address them.

Need to Cultivate Broad-Based Support

HLs/CLs and HL/CL programs within the private spheres of ethnic communities have generally been tolerated by mainstream society (Macías & Wiley, 1978/1998). Public awareness of and interest in HLs/CLs have been minimal. As such, societal efforts from outside academia to document the existence of such programs or to explore these venues as potential resources for building language capacity in the United States have been meager. The lack of acknowledgement and recognition from the wider society has contributed to the unofficial status of community-based HL/CL programs, making them less important in the eyes of program participants (Lee, 2002). Studies have reported that students and parents do not take attendance at community-based HL/CL programs as seriously as for their regular schools; the students see it as extra work that bears no relation to their formal schooling; and some students even perceive it to be a waste of time or a punishment because they are forced to go to school on Saturdays (Lao & Lee, 2009; Lee, 2002; Shin, 2005). Furthermore, most students do not receive any formal language credit for attending HL/CL programs, and more troublingly, public school teachers often neither have knowledge of the HL/CL programs in their community nor know which of their students attend such schools (Compton, 2001; Lee & Oxelson, 2006). In such an environment, productive connections across entities with similar interests and goals cannot be made, resources cannot be shared, and students' learning cannot be reinforced, validated, or valued. However, the potential for such positive connections exists, as documented by Pu (2008), who found evidence of the positive transfer of language and literacy skills developed in a Chinese HL/CL program on young students' development of English language and literacy skills in their public school classroom, and vice versa.

To cultivate broader support, public awareness of HL/CL programs must be raised by establishing a strong understanding of the local contexts of language communities and the relationship between the HL/CLs and the broader society. Based on Cooper's (1990) language planning and policy framework, S. C. Wang (2007) argued for a need to understand how HL/CLs are situated in the broader ecology of the U.S. context. We know from previous research that a range of factors, including the number of speakers, the economic and political power of the native country, the vitality of HL/CL programs, the social positioning of HL/CL speakers, and the perceived instrumental utility of the HL/CL, can influence the social position of a language (Baker, 2011; M. García, 2003; Lee & Suarez, 2009; Lo Bianco, 2008; Montrul, 2010; Shibata, 2000; Tannenbaum & Howie, 2002; Tran, 2008; Zentella, 1997). We also know that the status of an HL/CL can change over time as a result of the dynamics and connections among U.S. foreign policies, immigration policies, sociocultural ethnic group relationships inside the United States, educational concerns, economic factors, and national security issues (S. C. Wang, 2007). With informed understanding of the position of the HL/CL in the U.S. ecology, Edwards (2004) stated that local community members need to continue bottom-up efforts to support HL/CL education in homes and communities and assume a leadership role in developing top-down policies to create a stronger and broader infrastructure that can support HL/CL programs. The balance of top-down and bottom-up efforts is necessary so that the main goals of HL/CL programs do not get lost or transformed in the process of seeking collaborative relationships with larger organizations such as schools and universities, which can provide the broader infrastructure needed for survival and advancement (Hornberger, 2005). It is critical to understand that these efforts cannot be mutually exclusive, nor can they be accomplished by one entity alone.

Experience has shown that the more disconnected community-based HL/CL schools are from school systems and social institutions, the more difficult it is for them to be successful (Campbell & Christian, 2003; He, 2010). Therefore, it is important to connect relevant groups and institutions invested in HL/CL education and improve communication across them. S. C. Wang (2007) reported that in the case of Chinese, many entities are involved in the mission of Chinese HL/CL education, but there is hardly any articulation across the entities. McGinnis (1999) proposed that interinstitutional articulation is needed to connect the various HL/CL instructional settings, including K–12 public and private schools, HL/CL programs, colleges and universities, and study-abroad programs. Presently the resources in each sector are not optimally shared or leveraged, and articulation across programs is minimal. For example, according to Chao (1997), not many HL/CL programs have been able to give students foreign language credit for their participation; however, more recent efforts, such as the Seal of Biliteracy in California and New York, provide official recognition of proficiency in languages other than English on students' high school diplomas. Other local opportunities offer provisions for high school students to earn credit in nontraditional ways by demonstrating mastery of course content. Yet, to date, receiving credit for language skills acquired outside of regular K–12 schools is complicated and places the burden on individual students and their parents to negotiate a credit flexibility plan with the local school district. To better facilitate transfer of credit policies, curricula used in HL/CL programs and other educational institutions need to be standardized, and assessment practices that can accurately measure learner outcomes need to be developed. The complexities involved in addressing these needs can most efficiently be resolved through interinstitutional connections, where resources can be shared and curricula and goals can be aligned.

Need for More Resources

One of the greatest challenges in the implementation of a community-based HL/CL program is insufficient financial, spatial, and temporal resources. Because most programs operate independently of a larger organization that can provide a stable infrastructure, basic logistics and administrative planning are undertaken by individual programs. Over 95% of the programs in the database of the Alliance for the Advancement of Heritage Languages reported that they are in need of greater financial resources (N. Liu, Musica, Koscak, Vinogradova, & López, 2011). Most programs charge a nominal fee or offer free classes as community-based HL/CL programs have generally been considered a service to the community, and thus, it is difficult to sustain a program without active volunteerism, especially from parents, donations, and some sort of other financial support from businesses, ethnic community organizations, or homeland government. Some programs have reported conducting regular fund-raising events, applying for grants from homeland governmental agencies, and seeking business sponsorships as alternative means of raising funds for operation costs. However, these efforts have yet to alleviate the physical challenges that many programs face, such as the need for more space. For most programs, the number of classrooms is limited, which has implications for how many levels of classes can be offered. One consistent issue with HL/CL learners is that there are both age-developmental and proficiency-level needs; for example, it is discouraging to a sixth grader to be placed in the same classroom as first graders for reasons related to proficiency levels. There need to be multiple levels of classes based on both proficiency and age, which means that adequate classroom space and numbers of teachers are necessary. Although space costs and problems can be reduced when the programs are housed in religious institutions (Compton, 2001; N. Liu et al., 2011; Lee & Shin, 2008), in such cases instructional activities are often streamlined with religious teachings, which can dissuade nonbelievers from continuing their studies. Renting or requesting free use of classrooms from local schools during after-school hours is the preferable situation in terms of accessibility; however, it is difficult without local school district buy-in to support the efforts of community-based HL/CL schools.

Finally, the shortage of instructional hours appears to be another reason for less than ideal learning outcomes in HL/CL programs. A recent study conducted by

N. Liu (2010) indicates that 63% of the teachers and 72% of the parents in Chinese heritage language programs regard "not enough class time" as one of the chief problems in HL/CL education. Because of the nonalignment with mainstream education, HL/CL programs are generally scheduled only for a few hours per week, which is not enough time to achieve language proficiency and the kinds of learning outcomes that are desired. Furthermore, attendance is affected because the scheduling of HL/CL programs is often in competition with other extracurricular activities, such as sports, music, or community service activities, which are perceived to carry more weight in mainstream society and for college admission.

Unless HL/CL programs are formally recognized and instructional credit is granted for participating in these programs and/or achieving language proficiency, it will be difficult to increase the number of instructional contact hours in such programs (S. C. Wang, 2007). Although the use of technology and summer camps may provide alternative strategies to increase instructional hours (S. C. Wang, 1996), it is important to note that community-based HL/CL programs alone cannot provide the contact hours needed to develop or maintain productive skills in a language (Fishman, 2001). In other words, school-based programs are one setting needed for providing valuable linguistic input and literacy instruction, in particular for children from homes where parents do not have literacy skills; however, neither schooling nor home language use alone is sufficient for developing HL/CL language competence. To maximize opportunities for HL/CL development, varied methods of language input in formal, institutional settings such as schools (e.g., Byon, 2003; He, 2000; Lo, 2004), in homes and communities (Bayley & Schecter, 2003; Brinton et al., 2008; Kondo-Brown, 2006; Park, 2008; Xiao, 2008), and via technology and popular culture (Lam, 2008; Lee, 2006) are needed. Furthermore, HL/CL development cannot be limited to specific periods of time; thus, appropriate instructional programs and methods of delivery need to be made available across learners' life spans, as HL/CL competencies, choices, and ideologies change due to shifting motivations, social networks, and opportunities for language use (He, 2010).

Need for More Appropriate Curriculum, Materials, and Instruction

Studies have shown that the need to develop appropriate curricular and learning materials for HL/CL learners in the United States is critical (Lee, 2002; Lynch, 2008; X. Wang, 1996). It is not only the paucity of materials but also the lack of meaningful and appropriate curricula for different HL/CL age-groups and proficiency levels that present challenges. Many programs use textbooks that are provided by homeland government agencies. In many cases, however, the content of these books has little relevance to HL/CL learners in the United States. For example, P. Wang (1996) reported that about 80% of Chinese HL/CL schools use the Hua Yu series textbook, which teaches traditional values through folklore stories. Students raised in the United States perceived these stories to have little connection to their lives and found them to be difficult to understand. Such recognition has led to increasing efforts to meet the needs of students who live in the United States and identify with more current cultural trends. For example, N. Liu (2012) documented that many Chinese HL/CL programs are now offering a variety of choices in courses, textbooks, and program models and are attempting to align their assessment practices with those that are formally recognized in public schools, such as the SAT II Chinese. However, these efforts have not fully addressed the need for more authentic and engaging materials and more student-centered instructional approaches in the classrooms, all of which are recommended by the American Council on the Teaching of Foreign Languages Standards.

Some HL/CL programs, particularly those in public and private schools, have also adapted materials from the field of foreign language education (Valdés, Fishman, Chavez, & Perez, 2006). However, research has shown that the characteristics and learning needs of HL/CL learners differ from those of foreign language learners. For example, linguistic studies of HL/CL systems show that HL/CL grammars reveal processes of simplification that often are found in language contact situations as well as the emergence of new linguistic forms that are unlike the forms used by native speakers of the HL/CL and English (see Montrul, 2010, for a review). Due to reduced language input and output opportunities and influences of English on heritage language use, HL/CL speakers are likely to retain some core aspects of the HL/CL language but have grammatical and lexical gaps in their vocabularies and grammars. To compensate for limited access to language input in terms of frequency of exposure and use in restricted contexts such as the home, HL/CL instruction that provides rich opportunities to use the language is vital (Fishman, 2001; Montrul, 2010). Therefore, instruction needs to be based on a theory of HL/CL acquisition with use of curricular materials that are appropriate for the learning styles of HL/CL students and that can motivate and sustain their interest in learning and using the language (S. C. Wang & Green, 2001).

HL/CL education has focused primarily on issues of cultural identity of HL speakers and on pedagogical and practical questions, including what to teach and how to best instruct HL/CL learners so that their personal, cultural, and linguistic needs are appropriately addressed (Brinton et al., 2008; Hornberger & Wang, 2008; Montrul, 2010; Wiley, 2008). The goal of community-based HL/CL programs should not be to mark a divide between HL/CL and English but to support children in effectively integrating their languages and cultures as rich resources in their lives.

Need to Recruit and Provide Professional Development for HL/CL Teachers

Most teachers in heritage community language schools are volunteers from the community (often parents of students in the program) who provide language and cultural instruction for a few hours a week. It is rare to have a trained language educator in HL/CL classrooms. Furthermore, most teachers are native speakers of the language who have received the majority or all of their formal education in their native land, as opposed to proficient HL/CL speakers who may be familiar with the needs and learning styles of the HL/CL students. Problems arising from mismatches in expectations and in teaching and learning styles between teachers and students have been documented in several studies (Jia, 2006, 2009; Lee, 2002; Shin, 2005; Tran, 2008; X. Wang, 1996). To improve learning outcomes in community-based HL/CL schools, strategies to recruit qualified teachers and efforts to develop professional training programs for HL/CL teachers warrant greater attention.

Professional development opportunities and certification are necessary to provide teachers with pedagogical knowledge and strategies that are effective in HL/CL settings and to establish a professional identity for HL/CL teachers. Wu, Palmer, and Field (2011) found that teachers in community-based HL/CL programs had a weak sense of professionalism because they viewed their teaching to be a voluntary or secondary job. They reported that low to no pay, insufficient pedagogical training, and limited collegial interactions have contributed to teachers' low sense of professional identity. The teachers in the study commented that they chose to become Chinese teachers as part of a personal mission to contribute to the maintenance of Chinese language and culture. P. Liu (2006) found that Chinese heritage language teachers in California believed that professional training fosters effective heritage language instruction. Thus, it seems that a teaching certificate and professional development can validate HL/CL teachers' roles, enable them to feel empowered, and promote their effectiveness as teachers in these programs.

Although collaboration with foreign language teacher training programs to develop a specialty track for HL/CL educators would seem to be a sensible solution, the greater underlying issue is related to teacher incentives. That is, how can community-based HL/CL education attract talented teachers to the profession? Better incentives (e.g., monetary pay) for teachers to be motivated to pursue a teacher certification program or professional development opportunities in a specialized track such as HL/CL education are needed. It would be unrealistic to expect volunteer teachers to invest money and time in taking up these opportunities; however, if formal training and certification were available at no cost through better funded programs, more individuals might be recruited to the profession and to teach in community-based schools.

Need for Strategies to Recruit and Retain Students

The recruitment and retention of students is also an important concern in community-based HL/CL programs. Many HL/CL programs have closed or are on the verge of closing because there are not enough students to sustain their continuation. Schedule conflicts, the programs' status as representing supplemental and informal learning, the belief that the HL/CL can be learned exclusively in the home, and a lack of interest and motivation seem to be some reasons that HL/CL speakers do not attend or stay in HL/CL programs (Lao & Lee, 2009; Lee & Shin, 2008; N. Liu et al., 2011).

Stronger partnerships between home and school may increase the chances of sustained enrollment in the programs. Throughout history, parents have always had a central role in the implementation of community-based HL/CL schools ranging from administration to classroom teaching, yet there has been a lack of clear articulation between home and community-based HL/CL programs. It is important that family language-planning decisions be aligned with the goals of community-based HL/CL programs. However, there is often a mismatch between what parents and children report with regard to their attitudes toward and commitment to heritage language learning and their behavior in pursuing HL/CL learning opportunities (King, 2000). For example, Lee and Jeong (2011) found that first-generation Korean immigrant parents stated that it was very important for their children to know how to speak Korean, yet they placed priority on their children's regular school and extracurricular activities over HL/CL school attendance. Parents mentioned that after fourth grade it became difficult to send their children to HL/CL schools not only because of their competing schedules but also because of their dissatisfaction with HL/CL programs, teachers, and curricula. Therefore, positive attitudes alone do not seem to be a determining factor for participation in HL/CL education opportunities; other competing factors and tensions appear to play a role as well.

In addition to a stronger home-school partnership, more innovative curricula and pedagogical approaches are necessary to sustain interest in HL/CL education. Leeman, Rabin, and Román-Mendoza (2011) argued that one of the most important aspects of sustaining motivation and desire to continue learning the HL/CL is to fuel students' sense of pride about their community and their own linguistic expertise. HL/CL education curricula need to show students how useful their knowledge can be for social use, social change, and other opportunities. Leeman et al. (2011) proposed the incorporation of critical pedagogy to promote students' agency as HL/CL speakers outside the classroom. Their research project examined the effects of a critical service learning model in which university students taught Spanish literacy to HL/CL children in local after-school programs. The activities focused on social activism to promote HL/CL maintenance in the larger society, which opened up a unique space for the university students to create change in the community as expert instructors of the HL/CL. Service learning projects such as the Prospera Hispanic Learners Program (http://prosperaleads.org) are examples of how to increase students' desire to learn and speak the HL/CL by creating opportunities to use the HL/CL for authentic purposes and integrating HL/CL learning into issues concerning the wider society. It is important to develop approaches that integrate the societal utility of the HL/CL and demonstrate to students the value of and need for developing proficiency in the HL/CL.

In sum, the success of community-based HL/CL programs rests on the effective collaboration of parents, community leaders, school administrators, teachers, organizations, and universities to build a consortium that will create pipelines for feeding resources into the system and make use of the language and cultural competencies produced within the system (S. C. Wang, 2007). With better articulation of the goals, purposes, and plans for HL/CL development and maintenance across the entities of such a consortium, HL/CL education can be greatly enhanced to achieve outcomes that will be beneficial to individuals, families, communities, and the nation.

HL/CL EDUCATION IN THE KOREAN AND KHMER COMMUNITIES

In this section, we examine how community-based language programs have contributed to increasing language diversity in the United States. The following cases describe the pathways taken by two different communities in building HL/CL language capacity outside of public education. We selected the Korean and Khmer communities as contrastive examples to depict varied immigration histories, community characteristics, and economic and political resources held by local ethnic communities. These two communities also highlight the different approaches to and challenges of providing HL/CL education for their community members given their local community resources.

Korean HL/CL Education in the United States

In the United States, Korean is spoken as an HL/CL by over 1 million Koreans, who represent the country's fifth-largest Asian American subgroup (U.S. Census Bureau, 2010). The majority of Koreans in the United States are upper middle-class professionals and college graduates that arrived after the Hart-Cellar Act of 1965 (H. Kim & Min, 1992) to seek better economic and educational opportunities and a stable political landscape in a new land. Since 1987, however, Korean immigration has gradually declined due to improvements in the economic, political, and social conditions in South Korea. However, the main factor promoting immigration among Koreans continues to be better educational opportunities for their children (H. Kim & Min, 1992). Today, the Korean American community is diverse, comprising a growing group of Korean ethnics from countries such as China and Brazil, mixed-race Koreans, Korean adoptees, and nearly 90,000 foreign students and temporary exchange visitors from Korea (Batalova, 2006).

Community-based HL/CL schools have been the backbone of HL/CL maintenance for the Korean American community since the beginning of Korean immigration to the United States in 1903. The first HL/CL program was established by community members of the First Presbyterian Korean Church soon after their settlement as plantation workers in Hawaii. With over 70% of Korean Americans attending churches—a surprising statistic given that Koreans come from a culture deeply rooted in Shamanism, Buddhism, and Confucianism influences—churches have played an important role in organizing and supporting Korean language education by offering a central and stable location for Koreans to convene, establish social networks, and develop HL/CL education and other programs for their children (Hurh & Kim, 1984). To date, the majority of Korean HL/CL programs and schools are operated by local Korean churches, although there are many independent non–religious-affiliated Korean HL/CL schools in larger Korean communities (H. Kim & Lee, 2011; You, 2011).

According to the Los Angeles Korean Education Center 2010 survey, there are 1,052 registered Korean language schools in the United States, with 9,589 teachers and 57,525 students (H. Kim & Lee, 2011). Approximately 260 of these schools are in the Los Angeles area, and 210 are in New York. Some schools, like the Korean School of Southern California, which recently celebrated its 40-year anniversary, are well-established and have approximately 400 students, whereas other programs are short-lived and operate with fewer than 10 students. Various models of HL/CL programs in the Korean community exist, ranging from short informal language classes to institutionalized HL/CL schools that operate on weekends with language and culture-based classes such as Korean dance, traditional music, calligraphy, and Tae Kwon Do. However, most Korean HL/CL schools are managed with limited resources and are not able to provide multiple classes to accommodate the wide range of proficiency and age levels (Shin, 2005).

In general, HL/CL schools have catered to K–12 children of first-generation Korean immigrants who have access to Korean-speaking parents and whose futures are positioned in the United States, whereas HL/CL classes in Korean cultural centers and agencies have offered classes for adults, including both Koreans and non-Koreans. Previously held assumptions about students' language needs, language backgrounds, identities, attitudes, and motivations toward HL/CL maintenance are changing. For example, in the past, it could be easily assumed that students came to HL/CL schools with some exposure to oral Korean language; however, the increasing numbers of third- and fourth-generation Korean children, Korean adoptees, and children from mixed racial backgrounds, who grow up in non–Korean-speaking homes, challenge this assumption. Furthermore, parents', teachers', and children's goals for learning Korean were assumed to be related to developing sufficient proficiency to communicate with family members. Now, recognition of greater career opportunities in Korea and the United States afforded to those with high levels of proficiency in Korean has prompted learners to want to achieve advanced proficiency levels.

Despite the strong presence of community-based HL/CL programs in the Korean American community, they are perceived by parents and children as a competing force rather than a complementary educational space. To address these challenges and integrate community-based HL/CL opportunities into the larger academic schema of Korean American children, the Korean American community, with the support of the South Korean government and conglomerates such as Samsung, has created professional organizations to provide better structural support for Korean language education and heritage language schools since the 1980s. One of the most prominent attempts to integrate community-based HL/CL education into the mainstream educational system is the creation of The Foundation for Korean Language and Culture in USA (http://www.klacusa.org), a nonprofit organization established to develop Korean language and culture courses in K–12 schools. The foundation raised funds to cover the cost of developing the Scholastic Aptitude Test II (SAT II) Korean test as a foreign language elective. Since 1997, when Korean was first offered as part of the SAT II, there has been a gradual increase in Korean foreign language class enrollments and a steady rise in the number of test takers, putting Korean among the top five languages in which the test is taken (Silva, 2007). Presently, the foundation is also pursuing the creation of an Advanced Placement Korean language program for U.S. secondary schools. The Advanced Placement exam is likely to ensure a complete high school curriculum with teacher training workshops and credentialed teachers and, more important, a heightened sense of legitimacy and importance as a school subject (Silva, 2007).

Other organizations are also dedicated to supporting Korean language community schools. Most Korean community language schools are members of either the National Association for Korean Schools or the Korean School Association in America. In larger Korean American communities such as Chicago, Houston, Los Angeles, New York, San Francisco, and Washington, D.C., regional centers have been created to boost Korean language and cultural education (H. Kim & Lee, 2011), and homeland foundations, such as the International Korean Language Foundation (www.glokorean.org), have been established to support the global spread of Korean instruction. The availability of such organizations has contributed to the vitality and preservation of the Korean language among future generations of Korean Americans.

To enhance the impact that community-based HL/CL has had on increasing the linguistic diversity of the United States, greater efforts to cultivate broader based support for Korean learning beyond the Korean ethnic community are required. For example, the media can play a significant role in raising public awareness of Korean HL/CL schools and their activities. Furthermore, the branding of Korean as a useful and valuable language is essential. Recent trends show that one of the most effective promoters for Korean culture and language is Korean popular culture, known as *Hallyu* (Korean wave; D. Kim & Kim, 2011). A desire to access Korean drama and K-pop music has motivated younger generation Korean Americans as well as those from other ethnic groups, most notably Taiwanese, Vietnamese, Chinese, and Japanese, to learn Korean. More recently, crossover Korean pop groups like Girls Generation and the craze for "Gangnam Style," a music video by Korean rapper PSY, have fueled unprecedented worldwide interest in the Korean language and culture. The attractiveness of *Hallyu* as well as the surge of lucrative employment opportunities for bilingual speakers in the financial, science, and business sectors of Korea are some changes that are likely to give Korean as an HL/CL more recognition as a valuable commodity in the eyes of mainstream society.

Khmer (Cambodian) HL/CL Education in the United States

Khmer is the national language of Cambodia and an HL/CL to approximately 307,888 Cambodian Americans in the United States. The American Community Survey (2010) estimated that 77% of Cambodian Americans age 5 years and older speak a language other than English, presumably Khmer for the vast majority. In addition to being a much smaller and relatively more recent ethnic minority group in the United States than Korean Americans, the Cambodian population differs substantially from the Korean population in many important ways. Most Cambodian families first arrived in the United States after 1975 as political refugees in the aftermath of the Vietnam War. The majority were survivors of the genocidal Khmer Rouge regime in power from 1975 to 1979, during which time approximately one third of the population perished. The first wave of refugees included 4,600 members of the urban educated classes, who fled just prior to the Khmer Rouge takeover. The next waves followed the fall of the Khmer Rouge in 1979, when over 100,000 Cambodians fled to refugee camps along the Thailand border. From there many resettled in other countries, with most coming to the United States. Refugee resettlement peaked in the mid-1980s and came to an end by the early 1990s. The majority of these refugees were from rural areas with limited access to formal education. Under the Khmer Rouge, all schools and universities were shut down, and teachers, students, and their families were forced into the fields to perform agricultural labor under the harshest of conditions. In the refugee camps, schooling options were limited. Thus, refugee students experienced significant disruptions in their education prior to their arrival in the United States, resulting in a lack of Khmer literacy skills for many youths and adults. By 1990, approximately 147,700 Cambodian refugees had resettled in the United States (Wright, 2010). Since 1993, limited immigration opportunities have been available through sponsorship by relatives, marriage, and international adoptions. A small number of Cambodians now arrive in the United States on student, business, tourist, or missionary visas.

According to the American Community Survey (2010), just over half of Cambodian Americans (54%) are foreign born; 68% of foreign-born Cambodians arrived before 1990, whereas only 32% arrived after 1990. Despite substantial progress during the first 35 years since initial refugee resettlement (Wright & Boun, 2011), Cambodian Americans "have some of the lowest socioeconomic indicators among the Asian American population" (Asian and Pacific Islander Health Forum, 2006, p. 1). In 2007, the American Community Survey reported that approximately 23% of Cambodian families with children younger than age 18 lived in poverty, compared to only 15% of the total U.S. population. About 58% of Cambodian Americans worked in low-paying jobs in factories, restaurants, hotels, and retail stores. With regard to education, 38% of Cambodians age 25 years and older had less than a high school diploma, only 11% had completed a bachelor's degree, and only 3% had completed a graduate or professional degree (Wright, 2010).

In contrast to the Korean American population, Cambodian Americans have far fewer human and economic resources to promote HL/CL programs. There are no national networks of Khmer HL/CL schools and teachers. There is no support from the Cambodian government, which relies heavily on foreign aid and is still struggling to rebuild its own education system. There are no wealthy multinational Cambodian corporations that can provide funding for Khmer HL/CL programs. In addition, it is highly unlikely that advanced placement exams will be developed for Khmer.

Nonetheless, Cambodian American parents and community leaders believe strongly in the link between the Khmer language and Cambodian ethnic identity, arguing that to be Khmer (Cambodian) is to speak Khmer (Smith-Hefner, 1990). Thus, in small, medium, and large Cambodian communities across the country, there have been many attempts by parents and community leaders to establish Khmer HL/CL programs. Community-based programs have been held after school or on weekends at Buddhist temples, Christian churches, community organizations, public libraries, or public schools or on college campuses. Echoing many of the challenges identified in the review of the research outlined above, Khmer programs struggle with a lack of appropriate and interesting teaching materials, volunteer teachers' lack of training, and ineffective teaching methods (Needham, 2003). Most programs struggle with sporadic attendance and student retention. Thus, many programs are short-lived, but they continue to persevere in the communities.

Given the lack of a national network, the number of Khmer HL/CL programs is unknown. In the early 2000s, Wright (2003) estimated that in California—home to 40% of Cambodian Americans—less than 3% of Cambodian American students were participating in school- or community-based Khmer HL/CL programs. In a national survey of Southeast Asian American college and university students conducted by Wright and Boun (2011), respondents included 69 Khmer HL/CL speakers, 81% of whom were American born, and all but 2 of whom had begun schooling in the United States in preschool or kindergarten. Seventy-two percent reported having good or very good Khmer listening skills, but only 25% reported having good or very good Khmer speaking skills. Most reported poor or no ability in reading (84%) and writing (88.4%) in Khmer. Lao and Lee (2009) found similar ratios of high Khmer oral language skills and low Khmer literacy skills among 93 Cambodian American college students. Wright and Boun (2011) found that only 12% of the Cambodian American respondents had participated in a Khmer community-based HL/CL program. About 46% reported there were no programs where they lived, or at least they were not aware of any.

In Long Beach, California, home to the largest population of Cambodian Americans, there have never been any large, well-organized community-based Khmer HL/CL programs, though there have been several small programs. Needham (1996) spent 6 years in the late 1980s and early 1990s documenting the practices of three such community programs, one at a Buddhist temple, one at a Catholic church, and one at a Cambodian community organization. Although the temple and community organization programs continued sporadically for many years after Needham's (1996) study, neither currently offers Khmer HL/CL classes. The only remaining community-based program in Long Beach began about 4 years ago at a public library in a section of the city recently designated as "Cambodia Town." About 20 students attend Khmer classes for 90 minutes on Saturday mornings. Although it may appear to be a Cambodian community initiative, the program is actually run by the city government through its Neighborhood Services Bureau. The Cambodian American Bureau employee responsible for the program explained that his drive to start the program is based on his strong passion for the Khmer language and culture and his desire to pass it on to the next generation (personal communication, October 5, 2012). This program faces similar challenges of sporadic attendance, especially among students who rely on their parents for transportation.

Interestingly, the longest lasting and most stable community-based Khmer HL/CL programs are found in smaller communities in northern and central California. The Cambodian American Resource Agency in San Jose reports that their Cambodian Saturday School has served hundreds of Cambodian (and non-Cambodian) students age 7 to late 20s throughout Santa Clara County since the early 1990s. Its classes at three levels (beginning, intermediate, and advanced) take place for 2 hours each Saturday at a public library in San Jose, but currently, attendance is low: only 10 to 20 students come each week (personal communication, October 14, 2012). One of the best known programs is the Khmer Emerging Education Program (Project KEEP) in Fresno, California, which began by offering Cambodian art and music classes at a local Cambodian Buddhist Temple as well as language and literacy instruction (Olsen, 2001). Local Cambodian American university students founded this after-school program in 1992. Later the program received support from the Fresno Unified School District, which provided space and some materials support (Multilingual/Multicultural Office, 2001). Although the program once served over 300 students, today the number has dropped to around 40. Busy schedules of parents and students as well as competition with other after-school programs have contributed to decreasing participation (Wright, 2007). One of the program's directors also noted with discouragement that "the younger generations are not acquiring enough of the native language" at home, leading parents to feel their children have not acquired enough Khmer-speaking ability at home to be able to participate in Khmer literacy instruction through Project KEEP (personal communication, October 6, 2012).

Although the numbers of Khmer HL/CL programs and student participants are declining, there are still signs that Cambodian American students wish to learn their HL/CL. For example, there have been slight increases in the number of HL/CL students participating in the few existing Khmer language programs at the higher education level (Wright, in press). Wright and Boun (2011) found that 76% of the college students in their study expressed dissatisfaction with their Khmer language proficiency, and 97% wanted more opportunities to improve it. In lieu of formal HL/CL programs, many Cambodian Americans are turning to the growing number of popular websites and YouTube videos for learning Khmer. High interest among youth in Khmer popular music has led many to develop their Khmer reading skills by singing Khmer karaoke. There are over 100,000 such videos on YouTube alone. Some Karaoke video producers even provide a Romanized script under the Khmer script, clearly to accommodate Cambodian Americans and others who want to sing along but who cannot yet read the Khmer script. As of September 2013, the keywords "learn Khmer" returned over 176,000 results on YouTube. Khmer language-learning videos produced by a Cambodian American teenager who calls himself "Khmer Guru

Kimheng" have over 114,000 views. From the comments left by viewers, it is clear that many, if not most, are Cambodian Americans looking to improve their HL/CL.

CONCLUSION

Community-based HL/CL programs have a long history in the United States. Despite early efforts to pass policies that restricted the promotion and use of ethnic languages for instruction in schools, the highest court of the land reaffirmed the rights of ethnic minorities to establish community-based schools to help their children develop and preserve their HLs/CLs. Community-based HL/CL programs are also somewhat protected from official language and education policies that affect language education programs in K–12 public schools. Thus, they hold immense potential to contribute to the building of multilingual and multicultural capacity in our nation, particularly in languages that are less commonly taught in public schools.

In this recent period of rediscovery, community-based HL/CL programs should be positioned as an ideal setting where points of linguistic and cultural tension frequently experienced by language minority children in English-dominated social settings can be bridged and integrated. They present an opportunity for the creation of a validated third space that can generate new possibilities and challenge existing boundaries set by the dominant discourse of mainstream society (Bhabha, 1990). That is, as a third space in which "alternative and competing discourses and positionings transform conflict and difference into rich zones of collaboration and learning" (Gutiérrez, Baquedano-López, & Tejada, 1999, p. 286), HL/CL educational programs can serve to promote linguistic and cultural diversity and respect for both HL/CL and English. They can foster discourses and practices that challenge binary oppositions that would otherwise force individuals to choose between either English or their HL/CL. Thus, community-based HL/CL programs open up possibilities for learning and working in multiple languages, exploring alternative educational possibilities, and promoting multiple linguistic identities in this current climate of English-only and anti-immigration policies. Yet, to realize the full potential of community-based HL/CL programs, ideological alignment and concerted efforts toward the goal of multilingualism among students, parents, teachers, schools, and policymakers in addition to community support are mandatory requirements.

To facilitate the rediscovery of community-based HL/CL schools as an official educational space, their status as a supplementary rather than a complementary addition to formal schooling needs to be transformed by improving the articulation between HL/CL programs and other educational institutions as well as the conditions in HL/CL programs (Zhou & Kim, 2006). HL/CL programs currently face a number of challenges, including the need for better broad-based support; additional financial resources; more appropriate curricula, materials, and instructional approaches; teachers who speak the language and have teaching credentials; professional development for teachers; and improved strategies to recruit and retain students and teachers. Addressing these challenges can best be accomplished through joint efforts between community-based HL/CL programs and formal school institutions to align goals in ways that will produce meaningful outcomes for HL/CL learners.

With the validation and rediscovery of community-based HL/CL programs as dynamic alternative spaces for learning and promoting linguistic diversity in the nation, they are likely to provide a space where students can foster both individual agency and the collective agency as an ethnic group to develop their proficiency and competence in their HL/CL. The cases of the Korean and Khmer (Cambodian) American communities demonstrate that despite substantial differences of internal resources, they are both driven by a strong desire and commitment to preserving their HLs/CLs. Although there is still much more room for improvement, community-based HL/CL schools continue to play a vital role in providing the means (e.g., formal instruction, access to effective curricula and teachers) to develop language and cultural proficiency, opportunities to make use of that proficiency, and the motivation and encouragement to continue building HL/CL competence that contribute to increasing the linguistic diversity and capacity of our country.

ACKNOWLEDGMENTS

We are grateful to Joy Peyton, the editors of this volume, and the reviewers of our chapter for their invaluable comments. We also thank Meghan Corella for her assistance in the preparation of this chapter.

REFERENCES

Aburumuh, H. (2012). *Enrolling Arabic heritage language learners in Texas community-based schools: Examining the attitudinal and motivational factors impacting parental choices* (Unpublished doctoral dissertation). University of Texas at San Antonio, San Antonio.

American Community Survey. (2007). *American fact finder*. Washington, DC: U.S. Census Bureau. Retrieved from http://factfinder2.census.gov

American Community Survey. (2010). *American fact finder*. Washington, DC: U.S. Census Bureau. Retrieved from http://factfinder2.census.gov

Asian and Pacific Islander Health Forum. (2006). *Cambodians in the United States* (APIAHF Health Brief). Retrieved from http://www.apiahf.org/sites/default/files/APIAHF_Healthbrief08b_2006.pdf

Baker, C. (2011). *Foundations of bilingual education and bilingualism* (5th ed.). Bristol, England: Multilingual Matters.

Baker, C., & Jones, S. (1998). *Encyclopedia of bilingualism and bilingual education*. Clevedon, England: Multilingual Matters.

Bale, J. (2010). International comparative perspectives on heritage language education policy research. *Annual Review of Applied Linguistics, 30*, 42–65.

Batalova, J. (2006). *Spotlight on foreign students and exchange visitors*. Washington, DC: Migration Policy Institute. Retrieved from http://www.migrationinformation.org/USfocus/display.cfm?ID=489

Bayley, R., & Schecter, S. R. (2003). *Language socialization in bilingual and multilingual societies.* Clevedon, England: Multilingual Matters.

Bhabha, H. (1990). The third space. In J. Rutherford (Ed.), *Identity, community, culture and difference* (pp. 207–221). London, England: Lawrence & Wishart.

Blanton, C. K. (2004). *The strange career of bilingual education in Texas, 1836-1981.* College Station: Texas A&M University Press.

Bradunas, E. (1988). Introduction. In E. Bradunas & B. Topping (Eds.), *Ethnic heritage and language schools in America* (pp. 13–27). Washington, DC: Library of Congress.

Brecht, R. D., & Ingold, C. W. (1998). *Tapping a national resource: Heritage languages in the United States.* Washington, DC: Center for Applied Linguistics. Retrieved from http://www.cal.org/resources/digest/0202brecht.html

Brinton, D. M., Kagan, O., & Bauckus, S. (Eds.). (2008). *Heritage language education: A new field emerging.* New York, NY: Routledge.

Byon, A. S. (2003). Language socialisation and Korean as a heritage language: A study of Hawaiian classrooms. *Language, Culture and Curriculum, 16,* 269–283.

Campbell, R., & Christian, D. (2003). Directions in research: Intergenerational transmission of heritage languages. *Heritage Language Journal, 1,* 1–44.

Chao, T. H. (1997). *Chinese heritage community language schools in the United States.* Washington, DC: Center for Applied Linguistics. Retrieved from http://www.cal.org/resources/digest/chao0001.html

Christian, D., Howard, E. R., & Loeb, M. I. (2000). Bilingualism for all: Two-way immersion education in the United States. *Theory Into Practice, 39,* 258–266.

Combs, M. C., Evans, C., Fletcher, T., Parra, E., & Jiménez, A. (2005). Bilingualism for the children: Implementing a dual-language program in an English-only state. *Educational Policy, 19,* 701–728.

Compton, C. (2001). Heritage language communities and schools: Challenges and recommendations. In J. K. Peyton, D. A. Ranard, & S. McGinnis (Eds.), *Heritage languages in America: Preserving a national resource* (pp. 145–165). Washington, DC: Center for Applied Linguistics.

Cooper, R. L. (1990). *Language planning and social change.* Cambridge, England: Cambridge University Press.

Crawford, J. (2004). *Educating English learners: Language diversity in the classroom* (5th ed.). Los Angeles, CA: Bilingual Education Services.

Del Valle, S. (2003). *Language rights and the law in the United States: Finding our voices.* Clevedon, England: Multilingual Matters.

Edwards, J. D. (2004). The role of languages in a post-9/11 United States. *Modern Language Journal, 88,* 268–271.

Fillmore, L. W. (1991). When learning a second language means losing the first. *Early Childhood Research Quarterly, 6,* 323–346.

Fillmore, L. W. (2000). Loss of family language: Should educators be concerned? *Theory Into Practice, 39,* 203–211.

Fishman, J. A. (1985). Ethnicity in action: The community resources of ethnic languages in the USA. In J. A. Fishman (Ed.), *The rise and fall of the ethnic revival: Perspectives on language and ethnicity* (pp. 195–282). Berlin, Germany: Mouton De Gruyter.

Fishman, J. A. (1991). *Reversing language shift.* Clevedon, England: Multilingual Matters.

Fishman, J. A. (2001). 300-plus years of heritage language in the United States. In J. K. Peyton, D. A. Ranard, & S. McGinnis (Eds.), *Heritage languages in America: Preserving a national resource* (pp. 81–97). Washington, DC: Center for Applied Linguistics.

Freeman, R. (2004). *Building on community bilingualism: Promoting multiculturalism through schooling.* Philadelphia, PA: Caslon.

Gambhir, S. (2001). Truly less commonly taught languages and heritage language learners in the United States. In J. K. Peyton, D. A. Ranard, & S. McGinnis (Eds.), *Heritage languages in America: Preserving a national resource* (pp. 207–228). Washington, DC: Center for Applied Linguistics.

Gándara, P., & Hopkins, M. (Eds.). (2010). *Forbidden language: English learners and restrictive language policies.* New York, NY: Teachers College Press.

García, M. (2003). Recent research on language maintenance. *Annual Review of Applied Linguistics, 23*, 22–43.

García, O. (2005). Positioning heritage languages in the United States. *Modern Language Journal, 89*, 601–605.

Gutiérrez, K. D., Baquedano-López, P., & Tejada, C. (1999). Rethinking diversity: Hybridity and hybrid language practices in the third space. *Mind, Culture, and Activity, 6*, 286–303.

Haynes, E. (2010). *What is the difference between indigenous and immigrant heritage languages in the United States?* (Heritage Brief). Washington, DC: Center for Applied Linguistics. Retrieved from http://www.cal.org/heritage/pdfs/briefs/what-is-the-difference-between-indigenous-and-immigrant-heritage-languages-in-the-united-states.pdf

He, A. W. (2000). Grammatical and sequential organization of teachers' directives. *Linguistics and Education, 11*, 119–140.

He, A. W. (2010). The heart of heritage: Sociocultural dimensions of heritage language learning. *Annual Review of Applied Linguistics, 30*, 66–82.

Hinton, L. (1999). Trading tongues: Loss of heritage languages in the United States. *English Today, 15*(4), 21–30.

Hornberger, N. H. (2005). Heritage/community language education: US and Australian perspectives. *International Journal of Bilingual Education and Bilingualism, 8*, 101–108.

Hornberger, N. H., & Wang, S. C. (2008). Who are our heritage language learners? Identity and biliteracy in heritage language education in the United States. In D. M. Briton, O. Kagan, & S. Bauckus (Eds.), *Heritage language education: A new field emerging* (pp. 3–38). New York, NY: Routledge.

Hurh, W., & Kim, K. (1984). *Korean immigrants in America: A structural analysis of ethnic confinement and adhesive adaptation.* Cranbury, NJ: Associated University Press.

Jeon, M. (2008). Korean heritage language maintenance and language ideology. *Heritage Language Journal, 6*, 54–70.

Jia, L. (2006). *The visible and the invisible: Language socialization at the Chinese heritage language school* (Unpublished doctoral dissertation). University of Texas at San Antonio.

Jia, L. (2009). Contrasting models in literacy practice among heritage language learners of Mandarin. *Journal of Asian Pacific Communication, 19*, 56–75.

Johnson, D. C., & Freeman, R. (2010). Appropriating language policy on the local level: Working the spaces for bilingual education. In K. Menken & O. Garcia (Eds.), *Negotiating language policies in schools: Educators as policymakers* (pp. 13–31). New York, NY: Routledge.

Kelleher, A. (2010). *What is a heritage language?* (Heritage Brief). Washington, DC: Center for Applied Linguistics. Retrieved from http://www.cal.org/heritage/pdfs/briefs/What-is-a-Heritage-Language.pdf

Kim, D., & Kim, M. (2011). *Hallyu: Influence of Korean popular culture in Asia and beyond.* Seoul, Korea: Seoul National University Press.

Kim, H., & Lee, N. (2011, December). 미주지역 한국어 교육에 대한 인식 및 현황 [The perception and status of Korean language education in the US]. Conference proceedings from the 2nd conference on the Globalization of the Korean Language (pp. 3–36), Los Angeles, CA

Kim, H., & Min, P. (1992). The post-1965 Korean immigrants: Their characteristics and settlement patterns. *Korean Journal of Population and Development, 21*, 121–143.

King, K. (2000). Language ideologies and heritage language education. *International Journal of Bilingual Education and Bilingualism, 3,* 167–184.

Kloss, H. (1998). *The American bilingual tradition.* Washington, DC: Center for Applied Linguistics. (Original work published 1977)

Kondo-Brown, K. (Ed.). (2006). *Heritage language development: Focus on East Asian immigrants.* Amsterdam, Netherlands: John Benjamins.

Kono, N., & McGinnis, S. (2001). Heritage languages and higher education: Challenges, issues and needs. In J. K. Peyton, D. A. Ranard, & S. McGinnis (Eds.), *Heritage languages in America: Blueprint for the future* (pp. 197–206). Washington, DC: Center for Applied Linguistics.

Lam, W. S. E. (2008). Language socialization in online communities. In P. Duff & N. H. Hornberger (Eds.), *Encyclopedia of language and education: Vol. 4. Language socialization* (pp. 301–312). New York, NY: Springer.

Lao, R., & Lee, J. S. (2009). Heritage language maintenance and use among 1.5 generation Khmer college students. *Journal of Southeast Asian American Education & Advancement, 4.* Retrieved from http://jsaaea.coehd.utsa.edu/index.php/JSAAEA/article/view/50/59

Lee, J. S. (2002). The Korean language in America: The role of cultural identity and heritage language. *Language, Culture and Curriculum, 15,* 117–133.

Lee, J. S. (2005). Through the learners' eyes: Reconceptualizing the heritage and non-heritage learner of the less commonly taught languages. *Foreign Language Annals, 38,* 554–567.

Lee, J. S. (2006). Exploring the relationship between electronic literacy and heritage language maintenance. *Language Learning and Technology, 10,* 93–113.

Lee, J. S., & Jeong, E. (2011). *A study of parents' attitudes toward bilingualism and heritage language maintenance.* Paper presented at the Globalization of the Korean Language Conference. California State University of Los Angeles, Los Angeles.

Lee, J. S., & Oxelson, E. (2006). "It's not my job": K–12 teacher attitudes toward students' heritage language maintenance. *Bilingual Research Journal, 30,* 453–477.

Lee, J. S., & Shin, S. (2008). Korean heritage language education in the United States: The current state, opportunities and possibilities. *Heritage Language Journal, 6,* 1–20.

Lee, J. S., & Suarez, D. (2009). A synthesis of the roles of heritage languages in the lives of immigrant children. In T. Wiley, J. S. Lee, & R. Rumberger (Eds.), *The education of linguistic minority students in the United States* (pp. 136–171). Bristol, England: Multilingual Matters.

Leeman, J., Rabin, L., & Román-Mendoza, E. (2011). Identity and activism in heritage language education. *Modern Language Journal, 95,* 481–495.

Lindholm-Leary, K. J. (2001). *Dual language education.* Clevedon, England: Multilingual Matters.

Liu, N. (2010). *The role of Confucius Institutes in Chinese heritage language-community language (HL-CL) schools: Stakeholders' views* (Unpublished doctoral dissertation). Arizona State University, Tempe.

Liu, N. (2012). *Curriculum and assessment in Chinese heritage language programs.* Paper presented at the American Council on the Teaching of Foreign Languages, Philadelphia, PA.

Liu, N., Musica, A., Koscak, S., Vinogradova, P., & López, J. (2011). *Challenges and needs of community-based heritage language programs and how they are addressed* (Heritage Brief). Washington, DC: Center for Applied Linguistics. Retrieved from http://www.cal.org/heritage/pdfs/briefs/challenges-and%20needs-of-community-based-heritage-language-programs.pdf

Liu, P. (2006). Community-based Chinese schools in Southern California: A survey of teachers. *Language, Culture and Curriculum, 19,* 237–247.

Lo, A. (2004). Evidentiality and morality in a Korean heritage language school. *Pragmatics, 14,* 235–256.

Lo Bianco, J. (2008). Organizing for multilingualism: Ecological and sociological perspectives. In *Keeping language diversity alive: A TESOL symposium* (pp. 1–18). Alexandria, VA: Teachers of English to Speakers of Other Languages. Retrieved from http://www.tesol.org/attend-and-learn/symposiums-academies/upcoming-symposiums/symposiums/a-tesol-symposium-on-keeping-language-diversity-alive

Lynch, B. K. (2008). Locating and utilizing heritage language resources in the community: An asset-based approach to program design and evaluation. In D. M. Briton, O. Kagan, & S. Bauckus (Eds.), *Heritage language education: A new field emerging* (pp. 331–326). New York, NY: Routledge.

Macías, R. F., & Wiley, T. G. (1978/1998). Introduction to the second edition. In H. Kloss (Ed.), *The American bilingual tradition* (pp. vii–xiv). Washington, DC: Center for Applied Linguistics.

McClymer, J. (1982). The Americanization movement and the education of the foreign born adult, 1914-1925. In B. J. Weiss (Ed.), *Education and the European immigrant: 1840-1940* (pp. 96–116). Urbana: University of Illinois Press.

McGinnis, S. (1999). Articulation. In M. Chu (Ed.), *Mapping the course of the Chinese language field* (Vol. 3, pp. 331–344). Milwaukee, WI: Chinese Language Teachers' Association.

McGinnis, S. (2005). More than a silver bullet: The role of Chinese as a heritage language in the United States. *Modern Language Journal, 89,* 592–594.

Menken, K. (2008). *English learners left behind: Standardized testing as language policy.* Clevedon, England: Multilingual Matters.

Montrul, S. (2010). Current issues in heritage language acquisition. *Annual Review of Applied Linguistics, 30,* 3–23.

Multilingual/Multicultural Office. (2001). *Project KEEP* [Motion picture]. Fresno, CA: Fresno Unified School District.

Needham, S. A. (1996). *Literacy, learning and language ideology: Intracommunity variation in Khmer literacy instruction* (Unpublished doctoral dissertation). University of California, Los Angeles.

Needham, S. (2003). "This is active learning": Theories of language, learning, and social relations in the transmission of Khmer literacy. *Education and Anthropology Quarterly, 34,* 27–49.

Olsen, L. (2001). Khmer emerging education program. In L. Olsen, J. Bhattacharya, M. Chow, A. Jaramillio, D. P. Tobiassen, J. Solorio, & C. Dowell (Eds.), *And still we speak: Stories of communities sustaining and reclaiming language and culture* (pp. 22–29). Oakland: California Tomorrow.

Park, E. (2008). Intergenerational transmission of cultural values in Korean American families: An analysis of the verb suffix–ta. *Heritage Language Journal, 6*(2), 21–53.

Peyton, J. K., Carreira, M., Wang, S., & Wiley, T. G. (2008). Heritage language education in the United States: A need to reconceptualize and restructure. In K. A. King, N. Schilling-Estes, L. W. Fogle, J. J. Lou, & B. Soukup (Eds.), *Sustaining linguistic diversity: Endangered and minority languages and language varieties* (pp. 173–186). Washington, DC: Georgetown University Press.

Peyton, J. K., Lewelling, V. W., & Winke, P. (2001). *Spanish for Spanish speakers: Developing dual language proficiency.* Washington, DC: Center for Applied Linguistics. Retrieved from http://www.cal.org/resources/digest/spanish_native.html

Peyton, J. K., Ranard, D. A., & McGinnis, S. (2001). *Heritage languages in America: Preserving a national resource.* Washington, DC: Center for Applied Linguistics.

Portes, A., & Rumbaut, R. G. (2006). *Immigrant America: A portrait.* Berkeley: University of California Press.

Pu, C. (2008). *Learning your heritage language while learning English: Chinese American children's bilingual and biliteracy development in heritage language and public schools* (Unpublished doctoral dissertation). University of Texas, San Antonio.

Rhodes, N. C., & Pufahl, I. (2010). *Foreign language teaching in U.S. schools: Results of a national survey.* Washington, DC: Center for Applied Linguistics. Retrieved from http://www.cal.org/projects/archive/flsurvey.html

Rumbaut, R. G. (2009). A language graveyard? The evolution of language competencies, preferences and use among young adult children of immigrants. In T. G. Wiley, J. S. Lee, & R. Rumberger (Eds.), *The education of language minority immigrants in the United States* (pp. 35–71). Bristol, England: Multilingual Matters.

Shibata, S. (2000). Opening a Japanese Saturday school in a small town in the United States: Community collaboration to teach Japanese as a heritage language. *Bilingual Research Journal, 24,* 465–474.

Shin, S. (2005). *Developing in two languages: Korean children in America.* New York, NY: Multilingual Matters.

Silva, D. (2007). Issues in Korean language teaching in the United States: Recent facts and figures. *Korean Language in America, 12,* 106–125.

Smith-Hefner, N. J. (1990). Language and identity in the education of Boston-area Khmer. *Anthropology & Education Quarterly, 21,* 250–268.

Tannenbaum, M., & Howie, P. (2002). The association between language maintenance and family relations: Chinese immigrant children in Australia. *Journal of Multilingual and Multicultural Development, 23,* 408–424.

Toth, C. R. (1990). *German-English bilingual schools in America: The Cincinnati tradition in historical contexts.* New York, NY: Peter Lang.

Tran, A. (2008). Vietnamese language education in the United States. *Language, Culture and Curriculum, 21,* 256–268.

U.S. Census Bureau. (2010). *2010 Census data.* Retrieved from http://www.census.gov/prod/cen2010/briefs/c2010br-11.pdf

Valdés, G. (2001). Heritage language students: Profiles and possibilities. In J. K. Peyton, D. A. Ranard, & S. McGinnis (Eds.), *Heritage languages in America: Preserving a national resource* (pp. 37–77). Washington, DC: Center for Applied Linguistics.

Valdés, G., Fishman, J., Chavez, R., & Perez, W. (2006). *Towards the development of minority language resources: Lessons from the case of California.* Clevedon, England: Multilingual Matters.

Van Deusen-Scholl, N. (2003). Toward a definition of heritage language: Sociopolitical and pedagogical considerations. *Journal of Language, Identity & Education, 2,* 211–230.

Veltman, C. (1983). *Language shift in the United States.* Berlin, Germany: Mouton de Gruyter.

Wang, P. (1996). Academic curriculum. In X. Wang (Ed.), *A view from within: A case study of Chinese heritage community language schools in the United States* (pp. 21–27). Washington, DC: National Foreign Language Center.

Wang, S. C. (1996). Improving Chinese language schools: Issues and recommendations. In X. Wang (Ed.), *A view from within: A case study of Chinese heritage community language schools in the United States* (pp. 63–67). Washington, DC: National Foreign Language Center.

Wang, S. C. (2007). Building societal capital: Chinese in the US. *Language Policy, 7,* 27–52.

Wang, S. C., & Green, N. (2001). Heritage language students in the K-12 education system. In J. K. Peyton, D. A. Ranard, & S. McGinnis (Eds.), *Heritage languages in America: Blueprint for the future* (pp. 167–196). Washington, DC: Center for Applied Linguistics.

Wang, X. (Ed.). (1996). *A view from within: A case study of Chinese heritage community language schools in the United States.* Washington, DC: National Foreign Language Center.

Webb, J., & Miller, B. (Eds.). (2000). *Teaching heritage language learners: Voices from the classroom.* Yonkers, NY: ACTFL.

Weinberg, M. (1995). *A chance to learn: The history of race and education in the United States.* Long Beach: The University Press, California State University, Long Beach.

Wiley, T. G. (1998). The imposition of World War I era English-only policies and the fate of Germans in North America. In T. Ricento & B. Burnaby (Eds.), *Language and politics in* the United States and Canada: Myths and realities (pp. 211–241). Mahwah, NJ: Lawrence Erlbaum.

Wiley, T. G. (2001). On defining heritage languages and their speakers. In J. K. Peyton, D. A. Ranard, & S. McGinnis (Eds.), *Heritage languages in America: Blueprint for the future* (pp. 29–36). Washington, DC: Center for Applied Linguistics.

Wiley, T. G. (2005a). *Literacy and language diversity in the United States* (2nd ed.). Washington, DC: Center for Applied Linguistics.

Wiley, T. G. (2005b). The reemergence of heritage and community language policy in the U.S. national spotlight. *Modern Language Journal, 89,* 594–601.

Wiley, T. G. (2007). The foreign language "crisis" in the United States: Are heritage and community languages the remedy? *Critical Inquiry in Language Studies, 4,* 179–205.

Wiley, T. G. (2008). Chinese "dialect" speakers as heritage language learners: A case study. In D. M. Briton, O. Kagan, & S. Bauckus (Eds.), *Heritage language education: A new field emerging* (pp. 91–106). New York, NY: Routledge.

Wiley, T. G., & Lee, J. S. (2009). Introduction. In T. G. Wiley, J. S. Lee, & R. W. Rumberger (Eds.), *The education of language minority students in the United States* (pp. 1–34). Bristol, England: Multilingual Matters.

Wiley, T. G., & Wright, W. E. (2004). Against the undertow: The politics of language instruction in the United States. *Educational Policy, 18,* 142–168.

Wright, W. E. (2003). Khmer (Cambodian) heritage language programs in California. *Multilingual Educator, 4,* 28–31.

Wright, W. E. (2004). What English-only really means: A study of the implementation of California language policy with Cambodian American students. *International Journal of Bilingual Education and Bilingualism, 7,* 1–23.

Wright, W. E. (2007). Heritage language programs in the era of English-only and No Child Left Behind. *Heritage Language Journal, 5,* 1–26. Retrieved from http://www.international. ucla.edu/languages/heritagelanguages/journal/article.asp?parentid=56454

Wright, W. E. (2010). *Foundations for teaching English language learners: Research, theory, policy, and practice.* Philadelphia, PA: Caslon.

Wright, W. E. (in press). Khmer. In T. G. Wiley, J. K. Peyton, D. Christian, & S. Moore (Eds.), *Handbook of heritage and community languages in the United States: Research, educational practice, and policy.* New York, NY: Routledge.

Wright, W. E., & Boun, S. (2011). Southeast Asian American education 35 years after initial resettlement: Research report and policy recommendations. *Journal of Southeast Asian American Education and Advancement, 6.* Retrieved from http://jsaaea.coehd.utsa.edu/ index.php/JSAAEA/article/view/114/89

Wright, W. E., & Choi, D. (2006). The impact of language and high-stakes testing policies on elementary school English language learners in Arizona. *Education Policy Analysis Archives, 14*(13), 1–56. Retrieved from http://epaa.asu.edu/ojs/article/view/84

Wu, H. P., Palmer, D. K., & Field, S. L. (2011). Understanding teachers' professional identity and beliefs in the Chinese heritage language school in the USA. *Language, Culture and Curriculum, 24,* 47–60.

Xiao, Y. (2008). Home literacy environment in development. In A. W. He & Y. Xiao (Eds.), *Chinese as a heritage language: Fostering rooted world citizenry* (pp. 151–166). Honolulu, HI: University of Hawaii Press.

You, B. (2011). *Korean heritage language schools in the United States* (Heritage Brief). Washington, DC: Center for Applied Linguistics. Retrieved from http://www.cal.org/ heritage/pdfs/briefs/korean-language-schools-in-the-us.pdf

Zentella, A. (1997). *Growing up bilingual.* Oxford, England: Blackwell.

Zhou, M., & Kim, S. S. (2006). Community forces, social capital, and educational achievement: The case of supplementary education in the Chinese and Korean immigrant communities. *Harvard Educational Review, 76*(1), 1–29.

Chapter 7

Heritage Language Education and the "National Interest"

JEFF BALE

Michigan State University

On May 1, after more than a decade, the search for Osama bin Laden came to an end. It took patience and perseverance. And it took not only military prowess, but also intelligence that depended on a solid understanding of that region of the world and capabilities in a number of foreign languages that are not widely known in the United States. . . . Specifically, the United States' ability to both confront challenges and exploit opportunities relies heavily on Americans being able to understand and speak less commonly taught languages.

—Madeline Albright and Chuck Hagel (2011)[1]

In May 2011, university language and area studies programs under the Title VI and Fulbright-Hays umbrellas sustained a 40% cut in federal funding (Wilhelm, 2011). The epigraph above is taken from one of many public responses to these budgets cuts. Given the cantankerous relationship at present between the two major political parties, it is perhaps noteworthy that a Clinton-era Secretary of State collaborated with a former Republican Senator to coauthor an appeal on behalf of Title VI. Less noteworthy, however, is its logic, specifically the claim that U.S. national security and the national interest more broadly "rely heavily" on U.S. language capacity in less commonly taught languages.

Indeed, for as long as the federal government has been involved in language education policymaking, in almost every instance the stated goal of these policies has been to bolster U.S. geopolitical and economic security. To wit: In his written testimony to Congress during the hearings in 1958 that first authorized Title VI language and area studies programs within the National Defense Education Act (NDEA), Kenneth Mildenberger advocated for these programs in terms almost identical to those of Albright and Hagel (2011). Not only is language capacity directly tied to

Review of Research in Education
March 2014, Vol. 38, pp. 166-188
DOI: 10.3102/0091732X13507547
© 2014 AERA. http://rre.aera.net

the U.S.'s world position, he maintained, but also there are not enough proficient speakers of non-English languages to sustain that position. Mildenberger, then of the Modern Language Association but soon to become the first federal administrator of Title VI, wrote,

Although it is a commonplace that the United States now occupies a position of world leadership, it is still not sufficiently recognized that in order to meet, on a basis of mutual understanding and cooperation, not only the diplomats and military men but also the common people of the other nations of the globe, the United States does not yet have nearly enough persons adequately trained in the languages. (*Scholarship and Loan Program*, 1958, p. 1824)

Over a decade later, the future of Title VI was unclear: Congress had reauthorized the legislation in 1968, but the Nixon administration proposed to eliminate all funding for it in 1970.[2] The administration maintained that war spending coupled with President Johnson's Great Society programs had emptied federal coffers (see Scarfo, 1997). However, testimony given before Congress that year suggests it was political turmoil surrounding the Vietnam War that undermined the legitimacy of such programs. In particular, student protests against covert federal agents working inside Vietnamese studies programs at Michigan State University and Southern Illinois University were cited as reasons to cancel program funding (see *Office of Education Appropriations, FY71*, 1970, p. 302). Nevertheless, Harvard Sinologist John K. Fairbanks used his testimony that year to argue for continued Title VI funding in particularly acute terms:

Not only have we been caught with our pants down [in Vietnam], but with our pants off. . . . We have this terrific fire power, and we tear things up. But we don't know what the people are saying. . . . It's absolutely incredible to me that the American academic community has responded so slowly to such a clear need. The net result is a scandal. (*Office of Education Appropriations, FY71*, 1970, p. 301)

This two-pronged claim (i.e., that the United States is a world leader but that its status is threatened by insufficient language capacity) continued well after the first generation of federal language education policies was initiated, a continuity to which I have referred elsewhere as the "refrain" (see Bale, 2011b). Shortly after the first Gulf War in 1991, former Senator Paul Simon (D-IL) echoed this refrain in his book on foreign language education. Implying that the United States could pursue its interests by means other than war if sufficient language capacity existed, Simon (1992) wrote,

During the Iraqi invasion of Kuwait, our military had only forty-five linguists with any knowledge at all of Iraqi dialect—and only five of them were trained in intelligence. International understanding is a fundamental component of national security. Perhaps war would not have been necessary if we had communicated more effectively with the Iraqis in the months preceding the conflict. (p. x)

During the second Gulf War, which started in 2003, the issue of insufficient language capacity and the threat it posed to U.S. interests surfaced yet again. In this instance, the refrain was taken up by the Iraq Study Group, a bipartisan commission convened by then-President G. W. Bush to examine the catastrophe unfolding in U.S.-occupied Iraq. The group concluded,

All of our efforts in Iraq, military and civilian, are handicapped by Americans' lack of language and cultural understanding. Our embassy of 1,000 [in Baghdad] has 33 Arabic speakers, just six of whom are at the level of fluency. (Iraq Study Group, 2006, p. 92)

We thus return to the epigraph that opens this article; in the midst of yet another budget battle over Title VI and related federal policies supporting language and area studies, a bipartisan voice added itself to the steady refrain that U.S. national security is directly tied to language education and language capacity.

In this article, I review empirical research, policy analysis, and other forms of scholarly commentary on this long-standing rationale of framing language education in service of U.S. geopolitical and economic security. As I argue below, this synthesis directly calls into question the commonsense view that national security and economic competitiveness are the most expedient, if not the most effective, rationales for framing and implementing foreign and/or heritage language education policy in the United States. To substantiate this argument, I have structured this chapter in three parts. First, I provide an historical overview of formal (and sometimes informal) language education policies tied to U.S. geopolitical and economic security. Second, I identify and synthesize three analytical stances within scholarship about this connection between language education policy and the "national interest," namely, technocratic, pragmatic, and critical approaches. I conclude the chapter by identifying several gaps in the literature on this complicated relationship between language learning and national security.

HISTORICAL OVERVIEW

This section presents a brief narrative of major policy initiatives targeting foreign and/or heritage language education in the United States over the past century. A preliminary word about terminology is required; although this chapter aims to focus on policies related to heritage language education, this field is a fairly recent development within applied linguistics (see Brinton, Kagan, & Bauckus, 2007). Thus, it would be inappropriate to apply the term to discuss policies in historical eras before this distinct field (heritage language education) emerged. Consequently, in this overview I refer to policies using terminology appropriate to the respective era, while keeping an analytical eye on how these historical policies attended to (or not) people whom we might refer to nowadays as *heritage learners*.[3]

Policy in the Negative: The Americanization Movement

Without accounting for the lasting consequences of the Americanization era in U.S. schools, it is difficult to understand the hurdles that foreign and/or heritage language education policies must overcome. The term *Americanization* is used in the literature in somewhat imprecise ways. At times, it refers to a formal federal program administered after World War I designed primarily to assimilate adult immigrants by means of citizenship and English-language classes (see McClymer, 1980). More often, it refers to a broad historical era, roughly the 1880s-1920s,[4] during which both formal and informal policies shifted in U.S. schools to exclude non-English languages from the curriculum and to assimilate immigrant children and the children of immigrants into Anglo linguistic and cultural practices. This era corresponds to the historical moment at which the United States completed its westward expansion and attendant conquest of Native nations, became the world's largest economy, and engaged in its first extracontinental colonial expeditions. In this sense, the Americanization project was one that tacked between new U.S. ambitions abroad while consolidating, indeed enforcing, a specific American national identity at home in a society experiencing historic levels of immigration from Eastern and Southern Europe, Mexico, and East Asia (see Bale, 2011c).

Interpretations of this era in educational historiography have changed dramatically over time; it is important to note, however, the consistent and predominant focus in the literature on European immigration during this era. Mirel (2010) notes, "For most of the twentieth century these Americanization efforts, especially those of the public schools, were viewed as a welcome and positive contribution to the making of American society" (p. 3). By the 1970s, this assessment had come under sharp critique from revisionist historians, who argued that Americanization was in fact a program that forced immigrant children and the children of immigrants to sacrifice their home language and cultural practices as the price of admission to the (Anglo-)American mainstream (e.g., Karier, 1975; Olneck, 1989; Weiss, 1982). Carlson (1987) characterized this process most sharply as "cultural genocide" (p. 12). However, what had been a revisionist perspective has since become the "standard view of Americanization education" (Ramsey, 2011, p. 491). More recent historiography has challenged the revisionist read, both by questioning how exclusively negative or oppressive the era was in all instances and by highlighting immigrant agency in choosing which (Anglo-)American practices they adopted and which linguistic and cultural practices from their heritage they maintained (e.g., Mirel, 2010; Ramsey, 2010; Zimmerman, 2002; see Spack, 2002, for analysis regarding Native Americans and English-language practices).

It is beyond the scope of this chapter to evaluate these historiographical developments, although it merits mention that most applied linguistic research of language planning and policy continues to adopt the revisionist perspective (e.g., Bale, 2011c; Herman, 2002; Lomawaima & McCarty, 2006; Ricento, 2003; Wiley, 1998, 2002, 2007). Irrespective of the extent to which Anglo linguistic and cultural practices were imposed, negotiated, and/or appropriated, there is little dispute as to the outcomes of this era: (a) It marked the end of German as the most prominent non-English community language, as well as the extensive tradition of German–English bilingual schooling in many areas of the United States (Ramsey, 2010; Wiley, 1998); (b) it led to the wholesale removal of non-English language study from the elementary school curriculum; and (c) as secondary enrollments began to increase dramatically after World War I, it led to the codification of secondary-level foreign language study in the curriculum as an elite project for English-speaking, college-bound students (see Watzke, 2003). This constellation has not fundamentally changed in U.S. public schools, even if the predominant non-English language studied has (i.e., from German to Spanish). As García (1992) noted, U.S. language education policy since this era can best be described as a "schizophrenic double-bind" (p. 15): on one hand, a set of policies whose objectives are to replace immigrants' home language with English, on the other, a set of policies whose objectives are to expand proficiency in certain "foreign" languages in service of the national interest. It is from within this double bind that a number of specific policy efforts have been made since World War I to promote the study of foreign and/or heritage languages.

Informal Policy in the Positive: The Campaign for Spanish Between the Wars

The first of these efforts focused on promoting Spanish language education between 1914 and 1945. Advocates were successful in soliciting public support for this campaign from high-ranking political figures such as three U.S. presidents and various cabinet members (including a Secretary of the Treasury). Nevertheless, this advocacy is best characterized as informal insofar as high school and university Spanish educators, school district administrators, representatives of the Pan American Union (forerunner of the Organization of American States), and various ambassadors worked outside the formal legislative process to increase access to Spanish language education and proficiency in the language. Advocacy for Spanish language education took place in three main venues: in the official publications of the American Association of Teachers of Spanish (founded in 1917); in the media, such as a 1935 radio address on WNYC made by Lawrence Wilkins, founding president of the American Association of Teachers of Spanish and the former director of modern language programs for New York City public schools; and pedagogical materials, such as teaching methods textbooks whose introductions included rationales for the study of Spanish as a foreign language.

Bale (2011a, 2013) analyzed three main features of this advocacy for Spanish. First, advocates explicitly justified the need for Spanish language education in terms of U.S. economic interests in Latin America and its growing political influence in the region. Writing in the pages of the *Yale Review* in 1915, for example, the Yale professor Frederick Luquiens (1915) noted that the war then underway among European powers provided new opportunities for U.S. economic interests in the Western hemisphere. However, those opportunities would only be realized if more Americans spoke Spanish. He argued,

There is a familiar rhyme about an old woman whose pig wouldn't jump over the stile until water quenched fire, and fire burned stick, and stick beat dog, and dog bit pig—whereupon all turned out as it should. In like manner we may achieve success in our South American trade through a series of agencies.

It will come through machinery [of trade], markets, and money, which will come through public opinion, which will come through Spanish, which will come through our educators and our teachers of Spanish. Upon them rests the ultimate responsibility. (p. 711)

Rarely has the claim been more clearly made that language educators are directly implicated in bolstering U.S. geopolitical and economic interests.

Second, because this campaign developed concurrent to the highpoint of Americanization education, advocates had to reckon with public opinion and formal policy that simultaneously favored English-only education and viewed heritage language maintenance at school as suspect, if not outright seditious (in the case of German). Spanish language advocates navigated this terrain by arguing that (a) there should be no foreign language study in elementary school; (b) Americans are right to fear the inroads that German propaganda might make through German language study; and (c) Spanish language study was in fact patriotic, as it supported U.S. geopolitical and economic interests across Latin America (see Bale, 2013). Finally, this campaign focused almost exclusively on the study of Spanish as a foreign language (i.e., designed for English-only students to acquire the language at school). Across some 30 years of advocacy, native speakers of Spanish living in the United States or its territories merited almost no mention at all. When they were mentioned, advocates argued that the primary goal for Spanish speakers should be to master English first (see Bale, 2011a).

First-Generation Formal Policies

The final two parts of this historical narrative focus in turn on what I call first- and second-generation policies to support language education in service of the national interest. Besides chronology, three features distinguish one generation from the other. First, the earlier generation of policies supported language education under the broader umbrella of international education. They emerged in the late 1950s and 1960s and were primarily designed to convene interdisciplinary centers on university campuses to enhance U.S. understanding of specific geopolitical regions; language education was supported primarily as an instrument to facilitate such studies. By contrast, second-generation policies, implemented after the first Gulf War in 1991, have specifically funded language education programs with the express intent of developing advanced proficiency in certain languages among a wider cadre of U.S. professionals and academics. Second, there was no explicit mention of using first-generation policies to target native or heritage speakers of the respective languages, whereas second-generation policies have been more intentional in recruiting such speakers to their programs; "tapping" this "hidden resource," for example, is a common metaphor used to convey this intention (e.g., Brecht & Ingold, 2002; Crawford, 1999). Finally, whereas the U.S. Departments of Education (and its forerunner, the Office of Education) and State have administered most first-generation policies, various defense and intelligence agencies have had direct or indirect oversight over most second-generation policies.

The first major federal intervention into secondary and tertiary foreign language study was Title VI of the NDEA of 1958. It is widely acknowledged that NDEA was legislated in response to the Soviet's launch of their Sputnik satellite the previous year. However, this was not the first time that formal policies and government programs had funded language study in the name of national defense. Shortly after the United States entered World War II, it initiated the Army Specialized Training Program (ASTP) to prepare military personnel with the requisite language skills for their pending service. In the 2 years of the program's existence, it would grow in scope to train some 15,000 personnel at over 55 higher education institutions nationwide (Gumperz, 1970; Spolsky, 2002). Although the program's audience was English-only servicemen, Walker (1943) described the auxiliary role that native speakers of the respective target languages played in ASTP instruction:

What strikes one about this new American adventure in language learning is the morale of students. It's as high as that of pre-flight cadets, and for the same reason: There is a consuming purpose behind the assignment; the men know why they are studying. Also, the presence of native speakers gives a dramatic sense of reality. "I'm actually talking to an Arab, a Jap, or a Russian. Not my professor, but a native who will answer back in his own language." . . . Last summer the boys at the University of Pennsylvania took their Moroccan on a tour of Philadelphia, explaining the mysteries of Independence Hall and of an American night club to him in Arabic. (p. 372)

In addition to the short-lived ASTP, the Ford, Carnegie, and Rockefeller Foundations contributed throughout the 1950s to a number of international education programs, many of which included language study components. The most consequential of these was the Modern Language Association's Foreign Language Program (FLP). The program was designed to assess the state of language study across the K–16 system and, by 1966, led to the founding of the American Council on the Teaching of Foreign Languages (Gumperz, 1970). The FLP employed both Kenneth Mildenberger and William Parker, who would be central in designing and administering Title VI programs after passage of NDEA in 1958. In addition to this genealogical connection between the FLP and Title VI, the program is relevant to this discussion in two ways: (a) It was the first instance of private foundations, professional scholarly organizations, and government agencies working in tandem to support foreign language study in terms of national security; and (b) FLP publications regularly interpreted the brief upsurge in foreign language study in elementary schools in the 1950s as evidence that the U.S. population understood the importance of language study for maintaining the U.S.'s status as a world leader (see Parker, 1961).

It was on the basis of these previous policies and advocacy efforts that Title VI was designed and integrated into NDEA. Title VI contained two main parts, focusing on the K–12 and higher education systems, respectively, that together authorized four basic activities: the establishment of language and area centers at colleges and universities, the funding of modern foreign language fellowships, the funding of research to improve foreign language instruction and instructional materials, and the establishment of summer language institutes for professional and language development programs for teachers. Title VI relied on a list created by the American Council of Learned Societies to identify which languages it would target. This list distinguished six primary languages (viz., Arabic, Chinese, Hindi/Urdu, Japanese, Portuguese, and Russian) from 18 languages of "secondary priority," and a third set of 59 "additional" languages (Scarfo, 1997). Fellowship recipients were expected to use their knowledge of these languages gained through Title VI programs to pursue careers in public service, in particular, to take academic positions and continue to teach the language.

It is widely understood how national security concerns facilitated the passage of NDEA in the context of a burgeoning Cold War. However, what has been lost in this pragmatic interpretation of NDEA is the role this national security framework played in meeting two other major Congressional goals for public education: (a) keeping the federal government out of racial desegregation efforts as mandated by *Brown vs. Board of Education* (1954) and (b) marginalizing the progressive education movement as much as possible (Clowse, 1981; Ruther, 1994; Spring, 1989; Valenti, 1959). In 1956, for example, 101 Democratic Congressmen (including then-Senator Lyndon Johnson) signed the Southern Manifesto, which decried *Brown* and pledged to resist any school desegregation efforts. Just 2 years later, two signatories from Alabama (Senator J. Lister Hill and Representative Carl Elliot) would count among the central players pushing for NDEA (Clowse, 1981; Ruther, 1994; Urban, 2010). As Clowse (1981) noted,

Senator Hill was also acutely sensitive to the prevailing fears in Alabama and throughout the South over school desegregation. He knew, therefore, that in the 1958 session [of Congress], any educational-aid plan he might sponsor should not seem to be part of that explosive situation. He notified his staff from the start to use the national-security emphasis to assist, if possible, all levels of education. He ordered them to draft titles, however, that would be technically free of latency as desegregation weapons. Hill was hopeful that a bill directed toward national-defense needs might well succeed in steering a course "between the Scylla of race and the Charybdis of religion." (p. 67)

In other words—and to foreshadow a debate in contemporary language policy analysis described below in greater detail—it was not the case that there existed multiple rationales for federal education policies such as NDEA and Title VI, each employed to various degrees in the policymaking process. Instead, one rationale in particular was intentionally pursued *at the expense of* the others.

By the end of the mid-1970s, despite the budget battle described in the introduction to this chapter, Title VI had grown into what Hines (2001) characterized as a "modest but stable program" (p. 8). It was supplemented in 1961 by passage of the Mutual Education and Cultural Exchange Act (more commonly known as Fulbright-Hays), part of which specifically funded language study abroad (Scarfo, 1997). In 1966, moreover, Congress passed the International Education Act (IEA), which stood out in this period as having no explicit connections to national security rationales. Nevertheless (or perhaps, consequently), the IEA was never funded, and its modest language education components were rolled into subsequent reauthorizations of Title VI (see Vestal, 1994, for a full history of the IEA). In 1980, NDEA was not reauthorized; instead, its K–12 programs were rolled into the Elementary and Secondary Education Act, with the remaining programs moved to the Higher Education Act, both of 1965. Throughout the 1980s and 1990s, Title VI continued to expand its scope, providing funding for distinct business and language resource centers in addition to the area studies centers (now known as national resource centers). The inclusion of business resource centers, in particular, reflected an expanding definition of the *national interest* at that time to include economic competitiveness. As one long-standing policy advocate based in Washington, D.C., described it, "So through the '80s what I started arguing was that Toyota was the Sputnik of the 80s, and what we should tie ourselves to—and what Congress was buying—was economic competitiveness" (quoted in Bale, 2008, p. 190).

In sum, Brecht and Rivers (2000) distilled six debates that have framed Title VI and followed it since its inception in 1958: (a) whether the primary focus of Title VI should be on language or area study, (b) whether funding should support less commonly or more commonly taught languages, (c) whether the goal of Title VI programs should be to produce specialized knowledge for advanced scholars or generalized knowledge for wider segments of higher education students, (d) whether subsequent Title VI funding should work to refine the expertise already developed or to expand it, (e) whether Title VI centers should be organized around world regions or around themes of study, and (f) whether the primary target for Title VI funding should be at the higher education or K–12 levels.

Second-Generation Formal Policies

In a sense, second-generation formal policies developed in response to the first of the debates that Brecht and Rivers (2000) categorized. That is, they specifically support language education independently from area or other interdisciplinary studies, with the express intent of developing advanced proficiency in specific languages among greater numbers of professionals. Many of these policies are an outgrowth of the National Security Education Act (NSEA) of 1991. Much like NDEA, NSEA was formulated in reaction to a geopolitical crisis, namely, the first Gulf War in 1991. Its sponsor, Senator David Boren (D-OK), convened hearings on the proposed legislation in order "to address some of the problems" in military competency, logistics, and communication "revealed by Desert Storm" (Edwards, Lenker, & Kahn, 2008, p. 5). NSEA is the legislation behind the National Security Education Program (NSEP), which sponsors a number of language education programs across the K–16 system, including the Language Flagships and the Boren Scholarships and Fellowships, as well as programs such as English for Heritage Language Speakers and the National Language Service Corps.

In addition to NSEA, the other significant "umbrella" legislation sponsoring language education is the National Security Language Initiative (NSLI) of 2006. Consistent with earlier federal policies, NSLI was also motivated by a constellation of geopolitical crises, namely, the events of September 11, 2001, and the subsequent

U.S.-led wars in Afghanistan and Iraq. Indeed, then-President Bush explained his initiative to an audience of university presidents in 2006 in no uncertain terms: "This program is part of a strategic goal, and that is to protect this country in the short term and protect it in the long term by spreading freedom. We're facing an ideological struggle and we're going to win" (quoted in Capriccioso & Epstein, 2006). NSLI has functioned primarily to reorganize and streamline the administration of many federal agencies involved in funding language education programs, although it has also created new programs, such as STARTALK. One consequence of this reorganization is that language education policies that hitherto had no connection to national security rationales, such as the Foreign Language Assistant Program or the Gilman Scholarships for study abroad, now place competitive priority on those applications that focus on what are often called *critical* languages (e.g., Arabic [all dialects], Chinese [all dialects], Indic languages, Japanese, Korean, Persian languages, [Brazilian] Portuguese, Russian, Swahili, and Turkic languages).

As mentioned above, one defining characteristic of these second-generation language policies is that their administration is housed in a broader range of federal agencies, not only in Education (as with Title VI) or State (as with Fulbright-Hays). The Language Flagships serve as a key example in that they are formally tied to the Department of Defense. This NSEP program began in 2002 and supports universities in developing innovative and ambitious language education programs that produce what the program calls "professionally proficient" graduates. The program has grown to include K–12 flagships, which partner with local school districts to support curriculum development and to create a pipeline for students to begin language study in grade school and continue with it at university. In addition, STARTALK is a second-generation policy formally sponsored by the Office of the Director of National Intelligence. STARTALK funds two kinds of summer programs, one focusing on language teacher professional development and the other on summer language learning opportunities for students.

Congressional oversight for second-generation policies has shifted, as well. Whereas the respective subcommittees in the House and Senate for education policies have been responsible for Title VI and Fulbright-Hays, it is defense-related subcommittees that oversee second-generation policies. For example, David Boren was a long-standing chair of the Senate Committee on Intelligence, through which NSEA became law. One important consequence of this administrative shift is the difficulty of getting these modest language education policies noticed at all, as they are dwarfed by the size, scope, and financing of the other defense programs for which these Congressional committees are responsible (T. Ricento, personal communication, December 17, 2012).

The direct connections between these programs and defense and/or intelligence agencies, as well as the original stipulation that their fellows or graduates later work for a federal agency directly involved in national security, have made them more controversial than first-generation policies have been. Partly in response to pushback from university-based policy stakeholders, the requirements for employment have become more flexible. For example, recipients of the Boren Scholarships and Fellowships must now only document that they sought work in a federal agency related to national security, not that they actually accepted such a position. In addition, third parties are now more likely to carry out day-to-day administration of these programs, not the federal agencies themselves. For example, the National Foreign Language Center and the University of Maryland collaborate to oversee STARTALK, even though it is formally an Office of the Director of National Intelligence program. Likewise, the Institute of International Education now administers many of the NSEP programs, such as the Language Flagships and the Boren programs. This has helped alleviate some faculty resistance to participating in these programs given their connections to defense and intelligence agencies (see Bale, 2008).

Finally, these second-generation policies are more explicit in their orientation to heritage language speakers and thus qualify to a certain extent as heritage language education policies. Several of the Language Flagships, such as the Arabic Language Instruction Flagship at Michigan State University, have specific "heritage tracks" as distinct from language classes designed for true beginners or otherwise nonnative speakers. Moreover, many second-generation policies explicitly aim to recruit native and/or heritage speakers. The STARTALK programs, for example, actively recruit native and/or heritage speakers for their summer teacher training and professional development workshops and thus make a vital contribution to broadening the pool of language teacher professionals in the United States (Ingold & Wang, 2010; Wang, 2009).

PATTERNS OF SCHOLARLY INQUIRY AND ANALYSIS

As the chapter turns to synthesize the literature on federal foreign and/or heritage language education policies, it is important to acknowledge at the outset how little scholarship there is at all. One reason, perhaps, is that language planning and policy has only existed as a discrete field within applied linguistics for a relatively short period of time. In addition, as the historical narrative in the previous section suggested, these policies only tend to appear in relation to major geopolitical crises, which is to say that scholarly analysis of them also only tends to follow in the wake of these geopolitical crises. This irregular rhythm has contributed to normalizing the policy connections between foreign and/or heritage language education policies and U.S. geopolitical and economic security, insofar as there has not been a consistent or extensive research agenda about them. Finally, I should note that there does exist a historiography of federal policies such as NDEA and Fulbright-Hays (e.g., Clowse, 1981; Ruther, 1994; Urban, 2010). However, its focus is neither on the language education aspects of these policies nor on analysis of them as language policies, per se. As such, I have not included them in this synthesis of the literature.

Nevertheless, the scholarship on foreign and/or heritage language education policy in service of the "national interest" that does exist tends to adopt one of three stances: technocratic, pragmatic, and critical. This section takes up each in turn.

Technocratic Approaches

The first of these analytical trends, technocratic approaches, reflects the normalization to which I referred above; that is, studies adopting this approach accept at face value, if not endorse, the national security rationale behind such policies, and thus focus attention on the technical and logistical features of them. In some cases (e.g., Brecht & Rivers, 2000; Lambert, 1984; O'Connell & Norwood, 2007), these studies are federally funded, or commissioned by a federal agency as part of the legislative review process to assess the impact of international education and language education policies over time. In other cases (e.g., O'Meara, Mehlinger, & Newman, 2001), this analysis takes the form of proceedings from conferences organized to acknowledge important anniversaries and other benchmarks in the history of international education and language education policies.

The scope of these studies has been fairly similar, in that they include narrative histories of the policies in question, descriptive statistics on the number and type of programs, the number and (more recently) the demographic background of participating students, and the career paths they pursue after graduation. Their conclusions have been equally similar, insofar as they acknowledge the vital role that federal support has played in creating the cadre of language experts that does exist in the United States, and then enumerate various recommendations to extend and deepen this impact. There are two features that distinguish these studies among all those included in this synthesis. On one hand, they are among the few examples of empirical research on language education policies tied to the national interest. On the other, it is noticeable that none has questioned why their basic structure and conclusions are so similar over time. In other words, if the federal government has been in the business of supporting language education in service of the national interest for some 60 years, and yet the recommendations for improving such policies have remained fairly consistent (i.e., recall the "refrain" to which I alluded above), it seems self-evident, then, that a different set of research questions is required to better *explain*—not just *describe*—why these policies continue to fall short of their stated goals.

In addition to empirical studies, there are more explicit advocacy texts that take a technocratic stance to foreign and/or heritage language education policies tied to the national interest. These advocacy texts reflect the generational divide I described above. For example, Lambert (1986) made a compelling argument for a national foundation for international studies that could coordinate policymaking, program and curriculum development, and program evaluation to enhance the expertise that already existed by the mid-1980s. As with most first-generation policies, his argument sees language education as part of the broader project of international education. By contrast, more recent policy advocacy from this perspective (e.g., Edwards, 2004; Brecht, 2007; Brecht & Ingold, 2002) has focused specifically on developing advanced proficiency in critical languages and the role that heritage speakers can play in achieving this goal. In some instances, this advocacy constitutes a strong endorsement of U.S. geopolitical and economic interests. As Richard Brecht, the former executive director of the Center for the Advanced Study of Language at the University of Maryland, clarified, "Our motivation is national security, not to improve education necessarily" (quoted in Hebel, 2002, p. A26).

Pragmatic Approaches

Another approach in scholarly inquiry and analysis takes a decidedly pragmatic stance toward the policy connections between foreign and/or heritage language education and U.S. geopolitical and economic interests. This pragmatism aims to reconcile the needs and ambitions of heritage language communities while operating under the assumption that national security concerns will inevitably play a central, if not dominant, role in the policymaking process. Spolsky (2002), for example, drew on his extensive experiences working with the Navajo Nation to explore the connections between heritage languages and national security. He specifically contrasted the Navajo Code Talker program during World War II and the ASTP, described above, to argue that advanced proficiency in critical languages is best achieved when people begin to learn the language at home, versus starting as true beginners in school. Spolsky (2004), who identifies himself elsewhere as a "pragmatic liberal" (p. ix), expanded on Haugen's (1972) ecological framework to identify three domains of language policy (viz., practice, ideology, and maintenance; see Spolsky, 2004, for extensive discussion of this model). This ecological model per se is neither motivated by nor explicitly concerned with U.S. geopolitical and economic security. However, he concluded by noting the potential efficacy of this model for addressing such concerns.

Arguably, the most developed—and most widely accepted—pragmatic model for understanding foreign and/or heritage language education policies is Ruiz's (1984, 2010) resource orientation to language and language policy. The resource orientation is one of three (along with language-as-problem and language-as-right), which taken together reflect underlying ideological assumptions about language and its place in society (Ruiz, 1984). Insofar as the language-as-problem orientation facilitates (in) formal policies that restrict development of heritage and immigrant languages, the resource orientation is clearly beneficial in that it serves to reframe heritage language proficiency as an asset to cultivate, not a deficit to redress. However, the resource orientation is also premised on a critique of the language-as-right framework, namely, that the latter leads to conflict. Because rights are typically defined in terms of "compliance," "enforcement," and "entitlement," they can "create an automatic resistance to whatever one is talking about" (p. 24). In this way, the resource orientation can work to recast heritage language practice as broadly beneficial, that is, of value to the heritage language community in maintaining and extending their linguistic practices, and of value to English-only speakers in terms of acquiring a new linguistic skill set.

This understanding of the resource orientation has been widely taken up in applied linguistics scholarship due to its social justice implications for resolving conflict between heritage language and English-only communities. However, already in the original explication of this framework, Ruiz (1984) argued that the resource orientation also allows for defining heritage languages as a resource for meeting U.S. geopolitical, military, diplomatic, and economic aims. More recently, Ruiz (2010) revisited the resource orientation in light of multiple critiques of his original thesis. In his discussion of the relationship between the rights and resource orientation, however, the links between the latter and national security concerns and the potential consequences thereof are not addressed. In short, the balance of his comments reaffirmed that language-as-resource will mean different things to different people.

McGroarty (2006) has made the most compelling argument that this ambiguity is, in fact, a benefit in the policymaking process. Because of the cyclical nature of policy discussions as they "spike" (p. 4) into and out of public discourse, she argued that language policy advocates need to employ a number of rationales in order to be effective:

[Indeed] a logical implication for those who consider themselves pragmatists or political realists is that advocates for positive language-in-education policies must constantly articulate the value of bilingualism, and be able to do so in varied terms that respond to a protean environment of public discussion. (pp. 5–6).

From this perspective, then, articulating the need for language education policy as a function of U.S. geopolitical and economic ambitions is one among these multiple rationales, even when the ultimate goal is expanded social bilingualism for its own sake.

Critical Approaches

As compelling as McGroarty's (2006) argument is, it reinforces the tension between political principle and pragmatism at the heart of the resource orientation, namely, if language is a resource, then to what ends and in whose interests? Furthermore, can we employ language education to meet multiple ends and serve multiple interests at once, or do some interests in fact predominate (Ricento, 2005)? The final trend in scholarly analysis to be discussed, namely, critical approaches, interrogates this tension more explicitly. One type of analysis uses the concept of hegemony to explore the extent to which some policy interests in fact dominate the formation, implementation, and practice of foreign and/or heritage language education policy. For example, Ricento (2005) questioned not the resource metaphor itself but rather how scholars, practitioners, and policymakers employ it. He challenged language education advocates to clarify "hegemonic ideologies associated with the roles of non-English languages in national life" (p. 350) in how they frame their advocacy. Petrovic (2005) linked his analysis of the resource metaphor to the conservative restoration of U.S. power. With respect to language education, this neoconservative offensive centers on antibilingual education initiatives. Petrovic acknowledged that the resource approach hopes to counter these attacks on bilingual education. But because such an approach identifies with national economic and political needs, it bolsters the same ideological framework that it aims to challenge. Like Ricento, Scollon (2004) addressed his argument primarily to language policy scholars and advocates. Referencing the "paradox" that the "idea of one nation—one language—one culture is a mainstay of the hegemony of nation-state power" (p. 273), he noted the potential for language education scholarship and advocacy to be misused for extending that hegemonic power. He argued,

> Scholars and students of language who take a multiple and variable resource view of language and culture are most often those who also take a sociopolitical position of opposition to the hegemony of the First World, its nation-state apparatuses, and its monolingual/monocultural view of human life. When their work begins to fall within the ever-searching spotlight of hegemonic attention, they are sometimes startled to discover that what can be used for the good of encouraging diversity, grassroots opposition, and genuine democracy can also be used for surveillance and hegemonic intervention. (p. 274)

The logical implication is that such "multiple and variable" resource views are inconsistent with the goals of "sociopolitical opposition."

Another critical approach in understanding the policy connections between foreign and/or heritage language education and the national interest historicizes the question. Wiley (2007), for example, discussed the historical tension of language policies in the United States tacking between restrictive, tolerant, and promotional goals to reveal the ideological connotations of the term *heritage language*, and to question whether heritage speakers can in fact be called on to "resolve" the *foreign language* crisis for national security needs. He concluded,

> Given the hegemony of the English monolingualist ideology and the fear of foreignness that dominate language policy debates in the US [historically], it is unlikely that the narrow focus on national security and "strategic" languages in the national interests will do much in the long term to promote the study of languages in the US. (p. 200)

Building on an empirical policy analysis of Title VI programs between 1958 and 1991 and their impact on Arabic language education (see Bale, 2008), Bale (2011c) synthesized classical Marxist theories of nationalism and imperialism to identify an inverse correlation between the status of the United States as a world power and the prospects for foreign and/or heritage language education. Namely, those moments in U.S. history in which U.S. imperialism has been ascendant and powerful correlate with those moments in which Anglo cultural and linguistic practices have been most sharply enforced to the exclusion of heritage, immigrant, and Native language practices. Conversely, those historical moments in which U.S. imperialism has suffered defeat or otherwise been pushed back from the world stage, social space has opened "at home" to extend the practice of and education in minoritized languages. The logical implications of this correlation is that language education policies that explicitly aim to bolster U.S. geopolitical and economic power internationally have the paradoxical effect of contributing to the very material and ideological forces that constrict the social space required to develop and extend proficiency in non-English languages.

To be sure, critical approaches to the policy connections between foreign and/ or heritage language education and the national interest are not without their own inconsistencies and contradictions. For example, in a critical discussion of the historical intersection between foreign language research and economic, cultural, and national defense interests, Kramsch (2005) scrutinized how linguists have found themselves entangled in such interests. As her analysis turned to the post-9/11 context, however, the argument shifts. Specifically,

[Recent national policy initiatives regarding foreign language] are still under construction, but they do raise the relation of knowledge and power in applied linguistics. No one would deny that it is the prerogative of a nation state to rally the expertise of its scientists for its national defense. After all, linguists have always served the interests of their country in times of war and much good has come out of it both for the theory and practice of language learning and teaching. But the current appropriation of academic knowledge by state power in the name of a security problem that is as ill-defined as the current one runs the risk of redefining what it means for an applied linguist to "respond to real-world" problems. (p. 557)

There is a key contradiction at play here: How can we at once scrutinize "the current appropriation of academic knowledge by state power" if "no one would deny that it is the prerogative of a nation state to rally the expertise of its scientists for its national defense?" If such a right is in fact undeniable, then on what basis can we evaluate what makes one appropriation of academic knowledge in the name of national defense reasonable and another risky?

A second example, Reagan (2002), relates more specifically to critical languages (although the author uses the term *less commonly taught languages*). The overall focus of the argument is on acknowledging the profound impact that race, class, and language variation have on language education. Nevertheless, as Reagan turned to the topic of critical languages, he invoked "the geopolitical aspect" of language education and argued that it is in society's interest to develop linguistic capacity "in the various national and regional languages that are used in areas of national political, economic, and strategic concern" (p. 42). Referencing the events of September 11, 2001, Reagan continued,

Our [italics added] need to understand others in the world provides another justification for studying the less commonly taught languages, since the languages themselves play an essential role in *our* [italics added] ability to understand the speech communities that use them. (p. 42)

The sharpness of Reagan's (2002) earlier discussion dulls once the conversation turns to critical languages and national security. Now, it seems there exists a set of undifferentiated interests—*our* interests—at play. Because *our* is not defined, it is unclear whether the racial, class, and linguistic differences at the heart of Reagan's analysis are again subordinated to the dominant national identities and interests that he had criticized earlier.

CONCLUSION

Each of these three stances in the scholarship on foreign and/or heritage language education in service of the national interest presents its own set of theoretical or analytical inconsistencies that require further investigation. The most important issue, as alluded to above, is the need for a more consistent, empirical approach to the question. I raise this point not to disregard the useful insights gleaned from commentary and policy advocacy, such as the semiannual *Perspectives* section of *The Modern Language Journal*, which has convened discussion on various aspects of language education policy and the national interest in some six issues between 2003 and 2009. Clearly, the geopolitical crises of September 11 and the two subsequent wars provided a key impetus to organize and sustain this discussion. However, the question arises whether such attention to foreign and/or heritage language education policy will again fade—or indeed, perhaps, already has—now that the advent of those geopolitical crises is more than a decade behind us. In much the same way that many technocratic studies have concluded that the United States requires stable and well-planned language education policies and programs, not ones that rise and fall in haste with the latest geopolitical crisis, my read of the scholarship on this policy connection is largely the same: We need to move beyond the tendency to engage in scholarly analysis of this policy connection only as it relates to the latest geopolitical crisis and instead evaluate it more consistently on its own terms. That is, we need an ongoing, empirical research agenda from various theoretical and methodological positions that can better test the efficacy and explain the consequences of policy connections between foreign and/or heritage language education and the national interest.

One potentially fruitful avenue of research is comparative historical analysis of language education policies in the United States (see Wiley, 1999, 2006). With respect to the specific case of heritage language education, García (2005) noted the implications of the term *heritage* in conceding the political defeat of *bilingual* education as a positive educational model. Although I share that concern, one potential benefit of this term is that it can be used to undermine the historically rigid boundaries between additive, often elite, language education programs meant for English-only students on one hand and those programs, often subtractive and compensatory, meant for immigrant children and the children of immigrants on the other. This blurring can be operationalized methodologically to design historical studies comparing, for example, the formal and informal policy advocacy on behalf of bilingual-bicultural education in the Southwestern United States in the 1950s and 1960s with similar advocacy on behalf of security-oriented foreign language education policies of the same period. The rich historiography of the former, typically conducted by trained historians in the field of Chicano Studies (e.g., Navarro, 1995; San Miguel, 2001; Trujillo, 1998; Vargas, 2005), has not yet been brought into systematic conversation with the (admittedly less rich) historiography of the latter. Recall the point made earlier about interpretations of the brief upsurge in elementary-level FLPs in the 1950s as "evidence" that Americans understood their position in the world and the attendant need for foreign language competency. That interpretation has developed its own sort of common sense since then but is worth comparing to the growing activism within Mexican American and other heritage language communities for greater access to their own language and cultural practices at school that had their roots immediately before World War II and peaked in the late 1960s to early 1970s. Another generative avenue of blurring the lines between various language education models would be to extend the development of ethnographic analysis of Native and immigrant language policy and practice (see McCarty, 2011) by including such analysis of foreign and/or heritage language policies on a comparative basis. The potential benefit of such comparison, whether between historical cases or ethnographic accounts of contemporary ones, is empirically testing the efficacy of different orientations to language policy advocacy, whether they are the orientations developed by Ruiz (1984) or altogether new orientations generated by this comparative approach.

As the previous point suggests, there is also a dire need for interdisciplinary approaches to the policy connection between foreign and/or heritage language education and U.S. geopolitical and economic interests. The fact that educational historiography has begun to raise sharp debates about features of the Americanization era that most applied linguistic policy research takes for granted is one small indication of this need. Another is a conspicuous detail about language policy advocacy in service of the national interest that has gone almost entirely unmentioned in the literature reviewed here. I would argue that one reason for the heightened and sustained controversy over the 2006 NSLI, the most recent round of language education policies tied to national security, is that a controversial Republican president proposed them in the wake of the controversial wars he initiated. What has been lost in the extensive analysis of this and other security-oriented language policies is that in every case—*except for NSLI*—such policies have been sponsored and advocated by Democrats. This presents a complicated but key question: On what grounds is it more palatable for one political party to use U.S. geopolitical and economic concerns to frame heritage language education versus another? The distinction between *soft* and *hard* geopolitics that has been theorized in critical approaches to international relations and political science (see Callinicos, 2009; ten Brink, in press) can be helpful in understanding the complexity of the fact that although both parties at times take different approaches to enforcing and extending U.S. power on the world stage, they are in fundamental agreement that the United States has the right and obligation to do so. In other words, drawing from other academic disciplines to develop clearer conceptions of the "national interest" within applied linguistic study of language policy helps us both to rethink dominant assumptions about the policy process and the stakeholders in it and to uncover new ways to frame policy advocacy in the first place.

Whereas the previous points describe an empirical research agenda on heritage language education policy, the final point suggests a more normative project. As mentioned above, García (2005) has raised an important objection to the term *heritage* language insofar as it "signals a losing of ground for language minorities that was gained during the civil rights era" (p. 602). Although this objection may seem focused on terminology, I read her point as raising a more fundamental concern with an ostensibly zero-sum approach that dominates contemporary language education policy: Languages education is *either* an economic and political resource to bolster the national interest *or* essential for the expression and extension of the rights of minoritized language communities. As this research review has argued, however, this either–or approach has characterized language education policy advocacy fairly consistently for almost 100 years: Recall the silence of Spanish language education advocates regarding native speakers living in U.S. territories as they positioned Spanish as a resource for U.S. economic interests in Latin America; recall Clowse's (1981) story of how Congressional actors used national security rationales to "succeed in steering a course 'between the Scylla of race and the Charbydis of religion'" (p. 67); recall the fundamental distinction between language-as-right and language-as-resource in Ruiz's (1984) foundational notion of language orientations. The consistency of this either–or approach stands in stark contrast to the fairly limited historical moment (i.e., the 1960s and 1970s) during which language education was conceived of as a right for minoritized language communities. An essential, if also normative, research agenda thus needs to recover rights-based policy advocacy from that highpoint of the civil rights era and renew it in a context of a contemporary United States that is even more linguistically diverse than it was during that era. It needs to pose such questions: Is it enough to advocate heritage language education policy using a variety of political and ideological rationales? What do rights mean in multilingual settings (i.e., in settings where bilingual models are not possible)? What historical models do we have for rights-based advocacy and to what extent would they apply in the future?

In sum, because the policy connections between foreign and/or heritage language education policy and the national interest have an almost 60-year history, there is both analytical room and a dire need for empirical assessments of this policy connection. Sustained historical, comparative, and interdisciplinary research that is willing to question in normative terms what indeed is pragmatic, logical, and realistic can help scholars to reconceptualize which language policies are needed to maintain and extend the sort of multilingual practice that policy advocates and applied linguistic policy scholars advocate.

NOTES

[1]Note the factual inaccuracies here on two counts. First, news media widely reported that Bin Laden was killed on May 2, 2011, not May 1. Second, the "search" for Bin Laden did not begin until after the events of September 11, 2001. This search, then, could not have begun "more than a decade" ago. My point is not to nitpick at such details but rather to highlight the rhetorical strategies typically used to advocate for federal language education policies. Such rhetoric rarely misses an opportunity to invoke the most recent respective geopolitical crisis (e.g., Sputnik, the rise of Japan's auto industry in the 1980s, the Iraqi invasion of Kuwait

[Saddam = the new Hitler], September 11, etc.). These events are thus taken from the realm of objective fact and transformed into ideological referents in such policy discussions.

[2]Any analysis of federal policymaking has to account for the two-step legislative process in the United States: A given policy is first authorized (or reauthorized), and then it is funded (or not). In this case, Title VI and its related programs were in fact reauthorized by Congress in 1968 for 4 years, but the Nixon administration proposed a zero budget in 1970 (see Bale, 2008, pp. 190–192).

[3]Among the important discussions about who qualifies as a heritage language learner, I generally follow Valdés (2001) in viewing heritage learners as those who grow up in homes and communities in the United States in which the non-English language is spoken and thus bring some proficiency in the language to the classroom.

[4]Mirel (2010) has recently made a convincing argument for expanding this era temporally to the end of World War II. His argument is that efforts to implement intercultural education curriculum reforms in the 1930s represent an important, although understudied, corollary to earlier Americanization reforms and thus offer a more rounded picture of how European immigrants (were) integrated into the American mainstream.

REFERENCES

Albright, M., & Hagel, C. (2011, July 15). Language cuts endanger U.S. *USA Today*. Retrieved from http://usatoday30.usatoday.com/news/opinion/forum/2011-07-15-albright-hagel-foreign-languages-budget-cuts_n.htm

Bale, J. (2008). *When Arabic is the "target" language: National security, Title VI and Arabic language programs, 1958-1991* (Unpublished doctoral dissertation). Arizona State University, Tempe.

Bale, J. (2011a). The campaign for Spanish language education in the "Colossus of the North," 1914-1945. *Language Policy, 10*, 137–157.

Bale, J. (2011b). Language and imperialism: The case of Title VI and Arabic, 1958-1991. *Journal for Critical Education Policy Studies, 9*, 376–409.

Bale, J. (2011c). Tongue-tied: Imperialism and second language education in the United States. *Critical Education, 2*(8), 1–25.

Bale, J. (2013). *Patriotic duties: The campaign for Spanish language education in the Americanization era*. Manuscript submitted for publication.

Brecht, R. D. (2007). National language educational policy in the nation's interests: Why? How? Who is responsible? *Modern Language Journal, 91*, 264–265.

Brecht, R. D., & Ingold, C. W. (2002). *Tapping a national resource: Heritage languages in the United States*. Washington, DC: Center for Applied Linguistics. Retrieved from http://www.cal.org/resources/Digest/0202brecht.html

Brecht, R. D., & Rivers, W. P. (2000). *Language and national security for the 21st century: The role of Title VI and Fulbright-Hays in supporting national language capacity*. Dubuque, IA: Kendall/Hunt.

Brinton, D. M., Kagan, O., & Bauckus, S. (2007). *Heritage language education: A new field emerging*. New York, NY: Routledge.

Callinicos, A. (2009). *Imperialism and global political economy*. Cambridge, England: Polity Press.

Capriccioso, R., & Epstein, D. (2006, January 6). Bush push on "critical" foreign languages. *Inside Higher Ed*. Retrieved from http://www.insidehighered.com/news/2006/01/06/foreign

Carlson, R. A. (1987). *The Americanization syndrome: A quest for conformity*. London, England: Croom Helm.

Clowse, B. B. (1981). *Brainpower for the Cold War: The Sputnik crisis and National Defense Education Act of 1958.* Westport, CT: Greenwood Press.

Crawford, J. (1999). *Heritage languages: Tapping a "hidden" resource.* Retrieved from http://www.elladvocates.org/heritage/Crawford_Heritage_Languages.pdf

Edwards, J. D. (2004). The role of languages in a post-9/11 United States. *Modern Language Journal, 88,* 268–271.

Edwards, J. D., Lenker, A. L., & Kahn, D. (2008). National language policies: Pragmatism, process, and products. *NECTFL Review, 63,* 2–42.

García, O. (1992). Societal multilingualism in a multicultural world in transition. In H. Byrnes (Ed.), *Languages for a multicultural world in transition* (pp. 1–27). Lincolnwood, IL: National Textbook Company.

García, O. (2005). Positioning heritage languages in the United States. *Modern Language Journal, 89,* 601–605.

Gumperz, E. M. (1970). *Internationalizing American higher education: Innovation and structural change.* Berkeley: University of California, Center for Research and Development in Higher Education.

Haugen, E. I. (1972). *The ecology of language.* Palo Alto, CA: Stanford University Press.

Hebel, S. (2002, March 15). National-security concerns spur Congressional interest in language programs. *Chronicle of Higher Education,* p. A26.

Herman, D. M. (2002). "Our patriotic duty": Insights from professional history, 1890-1920. In T. Osborn (Ed.), *The future of foreign language education in the United States* (pp. 1–29). Westport, CT: Greenwood.

Hines, R. (2001). An overview of Title VI. In P. O'Meara, H. D. Mehlinger, & R. M. Newman (Eds.), *Changing perspectives on international education* (pp. 6–10). Bloomington: Indiana University Press.

Ingold, C. W., & Wang, S. C. (2010). *The teachers we need: Transforming world language education in the United States.* College Park: National Foreign Language Center at the University of Maryland. Retrieved from http://www.nflc.org/publications/the_teachers_we_need.pdf

Iraq Study Group. (2006). *The Iraq Study Group report: The way forward—A new approach.* Retrieved from http://bakerinstitute.org/Pubs/iraqstudygroup_findings.pdf

Karier, C. J. (1975). *Shaping the American educational state, 1900 to the present.* New York, NY: Free Press.

Kramsch, C. (2005). Post 9/11: Foreign languages between knowledge and power. *Applied Linguistics, 26,* 545–567.

Lambert, R. D. (with Barber, E. G., Jorden, E., Merrill, M. B., & Twarog, L. I.). (1984). *Beyond growth: The next stage in language and area studies.* Washington, DC: Association of American Universities.

Lambert, R. D. (1986). *Points of leverage: An agenda for a national foundation for international studies.* New York, NY: Social Science Research Council.

Lomawaima, K. T., & McCarty, T. L. (2006). *To remain an Indian: Lessons in democracy from a century of Native American education.* New York, NY: Teachers College Press.

Luquiens, F. B. (1915). The national need for Spanish. *Yale Review, 4,* 699–711.

McCarty, T. L. (Ed.). (2011). *Ethnography and language policy.* New York, NY: Routledge.

McClymer, J. F. (1980). *War and welfare: Social engineering in America, 1890-1925.* Westport, CT: Greenwood Press.

McGroarty, M. (2006). Neoliberal collusion or strategic simultaneity? On multiple rationales for language-in-education policies. *Language Policy, 5,* 3–13.

Mirel, J. E. (2010). *Patriotic pluralism: Americanization education and European immigrants.* Cambridge, MA: Harvard University Press.

Navarro, A. (1995). *Mexican American Youth Organization: Avant-garde of the Chicano movement in Texas*. Austin: University of Texas Press.

O'Connell, M. E. & Norwood, J. L. (Eds.) (2007). *International education and foreign languages: Keys to securing America's future*. Washington, DC: National Academies Press.

Office of Education Appropriations, FY71: Hearings before the Subcommittee on Departments of Labor and Health, Education and Welfare, of the Senate Committee on Appropriations, 91st Cong. 301(1970d) (Insertion of article by William H. Jones).

Olneck, M. R. (1989). Americanization and the education of immigrants, 1900-1925: An analysis of symbolic action. *American Journal of Education, 97*, 402–405.

O'Meara, P., Mehlinger, H. D., & Newman, R. M. (Eds.). (2001). *Changing perspectives on international education*. Bloomington: Indiana University Press.

Parker, W. R. (1961). *The national interest and foreign languages: A discussion guide prepared for the U.S. National Commission for UNESCO, Department of State* (3rd ed.). Washington, DC: U.S. Government Printing Office.

Petrovic, J. E. (2005). The conservative restoration and neoliberal defenses of bilingual education. *Language Policy, 4*, 395–416.

Ramsey, P. J. (2010). *Bilingual public schooling in the United States: A history of America's "polyglot boardinghouse."* New York, NY: Palgrave Macmillan.

Ramsey, P. J. (2011). A review of "Patriotic pluralism: Americanization education and European immigrants." *Educational Studies, 47*, 490–494.

Reagan, T. (2002). *Language, education, and ideology: Mapping the linguistic landscape of U.S. schools*. Westport, CT: Praeger.

Ricento, T. (2003). The discursive construction of Americanism. *Discourse & Society, 14*, 611–637.

Ricento, T. (2005). Problems with the "language-as-resource" discourse in the promotion of heritage languages in the U.S.A. *Journal of Sociolinguistics, 9*, 348–368.

Ruiz, R. (1984). Orientations in language planning. *NABE Journal, 8*, 15–34.

Ruiz, R. (2010). Reorienting language-as-resource. In J. E. Petrovic (Ed.), *International perspectives on bilingual education: Policy, practice and controversy* (pp. 155–172). Charlotte, NC: Information Age Publishing.

Ruther, N. L. (1994). *The role of federal programs in internationalizing the U.S. higher education system from 1958-1988* (Unpublished doctoral dissertation). University of Massachusetts, Amherst.

San Miguel, G., Jr. (2001). *Brown, not white: School integration and the Chicano movement in Houston*. Houston, TX: The University of Houston.

Scarfo, R. D. (1997). The history of Title VI and Fulbright-Hays. In J. N. Hawkins, C. M. Haro, M. A. Kazanjian, G. W. Merkx, & D. Wiley (Eds.), *International education in the new global era: Proceedings on a national policy conference on the Higher Education Act, Title VI and Fulbright-Hays Programs* (pp. 23–25). Los Angeles: UCLA International Studies and Overseas Programs.

Scholarship and loan program, Part 3: Hearings before the Subcommittee on Special Education and the Subcommittee on General Education, of the House Committee on Education and Labor, 85th Cong. 1814 (1958) (Testimony of Kenneth W. Mildenberger).

Scollon, R. (2004). Teaching language and culture as hegemonic practice. *Modern Language Journal, 88*, 271–274.

Simon, P. (1992). *The tongue-tied American: Confronting the foreign language crisis*. New York, NY: Continuum.

Spack, R. (2002). *America's second tongue: American Indian education and the ownership of English, 1860-1900*. Lincoln: University of Nebraska Press.

Spolsky, B. (2002). Heritage language and national security: An ecological view. In S. J. Baker (Ed.), *Language policy: Lessons from global models* (pp. 103–114). Monterrey, CA: Monterrey Institute for International Studies.

Spolsky, B. (2004). *Language policy.* Cambridge, England: Cambridge University Press.

Spring, J. (1989). *The sorting machine revisited: National educational policy since 1945.* New York, NY: Longman.

ten Brink, T. (in press). *Geopolitics and global political economy* (J. Bale, Trans.). Leiden, Netherlands: Brill. (Original work published 2008)

Trujillo, A. (1998). *Chicano empowerment and bilingual education: Movimiento politics in Crystal City, TX.* New York, NY: Garland.

Urban, W. J. (2010). *More than science and Sputnik: The National Defense Education Act of 1958.* Tuscaloosa: The University of Alabama Press.

Valdés, G. (2001). Heritage language students: Profiles and possibilities. In J. K. Peyton, D. A. Ranard, & S. McGinnis (Eds.), *Heritage languages in America: Preserving a national resource* (pp. 37–80). Washington, DC: Center for Applied Linguistics.

Valenti, J. J. (1959). The recent debate on federal aid to education legislation in the United States. *International Review of Education/Internationale Zeitschrift für Erziehungswissenschaft/ Revue Internationale de l'Education, 5,* 189–202.

Vargas, Z. (2005). *Labor rights are civil rights: Mexican American workers in twentieth-century America.* Princeton, NJ: Princeton University Press.

Vestal, T. M. (1994). *International education: Its history and promise for today.* Westport, CT: Praeger.

Walker, C. R. (1943). Language teaching goes to war. *School & Society, 57,* 369–373.

Wang, S. (2009). Preparing and supporting teachers of less commonly taught languages. *Modern Language Journal, 93,* 282–287.

Watzke, J. L. (2003). *Lasting change in foreign language education: A historical case for change in national policy.* Westport, CT: Praeger.

Weiss, B. J. (Ed.) (1982). *American education and the European immigrant: 1840-1940.* Urbana: University of Illinois Press.

Wiley, T. G. (1998). The imposition of World War I-era English-only policies and the fate of German in North America. In T. Ricento & B. Burnaby (Eds.), *Language policies in the United States and Canada: Myths and realities* (pp. 211–241). Philadelphia, PA: Lawrence Erlbaum.

Wiley, T. G. (1999). Comparative historical analysis of U.S. language policy and language planning: Extending the foundations. In T. Huebner & K. A. Davis (Eds.), *Sociopolitical perspectives on language policy and language planning in the U.S.A* (pp. 17–37). Amsterdam: John Benjamins.

Wiley, T. G. (2002). Accessing language rights in education: A brief history of the U.S. context. In J. W. Tollefson (Ed.), *Language policies in education: Critical issues* (pp. 39–64). Mahwah, NJ: Lawrence Erlbaum.

Wiley, T. G. (2006). The lessons of historical investigation: Implications for the study of language planning and policy. In T. Ricento (Ed.), *An introduction to language policy: Theory and method* (pp. 135–152). Malden, MA: Blackwell.

Wiley, T. G. (2007). The foreign language "crisis" in the U.S.: Are heritage and community languages the remedy? *Critical Inquiry in Language Studies, 4,* 179–205.

Wilhelm, I. (2011, April 13). Language and international-studies programs face devastating cuts under budget deal. *Chronicle of Higher Education.* Retrieved from http://chronicle. com/article/Language-and/127122/

Zimmerman, J. (2002). Ethnics against ethnicity: European immigrants and foreign-language instruction, 1890-1940. *Journal of American History, 88,* 1383–1404.

II. International Context

Chapter 8

Language Diversity and Language Policy in Educational Access and Equity

JAMES W. TOLLEFSON
AMY B. M. TSUI
The University of Hong Kong

This article examines the role of language policies in mediating access and equity in education. By examining a range of research and case studies on language policies, we explore how educational language policies serve as a central gatekeeper to education itself, as well as to quality education that may fundamentally depend on language ability, not only for literacy and classroom interaction but also for textbooks, materials, assessment, and other language-related aspects of education. Our analysis offers an argument for placing language policies at the center of debates about educational access and equity, as well as a broad range of sociopolitical processes that shape learners' educational achievement.

We begin with the principles of the concept of "Education for All," based on the key organizing document (UNESCO, 1990) in the worldwide movement to improve educational access and equity. Then we focus on the role of globalization in the economy and politics, particularly its profound consequences for language learning and language use and its multiple implications for language policies in education. We specify three processes of globalization—migration, urbanization, and changes in the nature of work—that place language policies in education at the center of the processes shaping language learning. Then we examine specific cases in Asia and Europe in which language policies affect educational access and equity. Our emphasis in these cases is primarily on policies and practices of state institutions; due to space limitations, we do not examine the policy implications of important research on micro-level classroom practices (e.g., Pérez-Milans, 2013). Finally, we offer suggestions for how language policies may be used to open greater access and reduce inequalities in education.

Review of Research in Education
March 2014, Vol. 38, pp. 189-214
DOI: 10.3102/0091732X13506846
© 2014 AERA. http://rre.aera.net

LANGUAGE POLICIES AND EDUCATION FOR ALL

The international education framework established by UNESCO's World Conference on Education for All in Jomtien, Thailand (UNESCO, 1990), prioritizes access and equity in primary education. Since the Jomtien meeting, a commitment to universal access and equity in the quality of educational provision is being extended to other levels of education worldwide, including secondary, tertiary, and lifelong adult education. Although the main goal of the Declaration—universal access to quality primary education—has yet to be achieved, governments have responded with programs that acknowledge the central role of language policies in schools, especially medium of instruction (MOI) policies. Tanzania and Ethiopia, for example, have expanded the use of African languages in education to open access for students who were largely blocked from education when colonial languages were used as the MOI (Alidou, 2004). The value of such policies is well documented, as in the Language of Instruction in Tanzania and South Africa project, which spells out the harmful impact on learning and school participation of the policy of using a colonial language rather than an African language as MOI (Brock-Utne, 2006). Although there are important counterexamples where mother tongue MOI is a component in systems of repression (e.g., apartheid South Africa), there is widespread evidence internationally that mother tongue MOI can significantly reduce barriers to educational access and equity (see Baker, 2011).

In the United States, federal law generally does not address the importance of language in determining access to quality education, although there are exceptions in important court cases, such as the *Lau v Nichols* decision in 1974 and the Ann Arbor decision in 1979, both of which required schools to provide educational accommodations for students facing the challenge of using a new variety as MOI (Baron, 2011). In many other countries, the language of the classroom has long been recognized as a central factor in educational access and equity. Accordingly, many international agreements and declarations encourage education authorities to use learners' home languages as MOI. Such documents include the European Charter for Regional and Minority Languages, which encourages states "to make available primary education in the relevant regional or minority languages," and the United Nations Universal Declaration on Indigenous Rights, which declares that indigenous people should have "the right to all forms of education, including in particular the right of children to have access to education in their own languages." Such declarations, however, are usually vague in their requirements and include many qualifications that exempt state authorities from legally binding commitments. For example, the European Charter encourages but does not require mother tongue MOI, and it limits its application to "the territory in which such languages are used, according to the situation of each of these languages" only when the number of children "is considered sufficient" (see Skutnabb-Kangas, 2008; Skutnabb-Kangas & Phillipson, 1994).

Nevertheless, many national education authorities specifically acknowledge the impact of language on access and equity. Among these are countries in the Andean region, such as Bolivia, Ecuador, and Peru, where languages other than Spanish have gained increasing support as MOI (Coronel-Molina, 2013); Nicaragua, where state programs promote language rights for people in the Caribbean Coast region (Freeland, 2013); Wales, particularly in the Welsh–English bilingual schools, which express an ideological commitment to bilingual MOI (Jones & Martin-Jones, 2004); Native America, most prominently in Navajo-medium schools (McCarty, 2013); New Zealand, where Māori MOI has spread from primary to secondary education (Benton, 2007); and Niger, Burkina Faso, and Mali, where experimental bilingual programs have been undertaken as part of a long-term effort to change the MOI in primary education (Alidou, 2004). In contexts in which students are forced to acquire a new language for schooling, efforts to achieve access and equity as prioritized by Education for All present a fundamental challenge to education authorities: "Can quality education for all be achieved when it is packaged in a language that some learners neither speak nor understand?" (UNESCO Bangkok, 2007, p. 1).

Research addressing this question is extensive and widely known. In Hong Kong, for example, following the change from English MOI (EMI) to Chinese MOI (CMI) for most schools in 1997-1998, follow-up studies found that graduates of Chinese-medium schools significantly improved scores on standardized exams at the end of secondary school, and improved as well on other measures of learning such as class participation and the quality of verbal interaction (Tsui, 2007). Similarly, following on the Jomtien Declaration, a major study of primary schools in Ethiopia found that MOI is a central factor in children's achievement, with mother tongue classes proving superior to English MOI during the primary years. MOI for teacher training also has a major impact on children, with teachers whose training takes place in the mother tongue more likely to have the technical and pedagogical vocabulary for teaching school subjects and the necessary confidence in their own language ability. As the final report on Ethiopia states,

[C]lassroom observation and assessment data demonstrate that English MOI does not necessarily result in better English learning; in fact, those regions with stronger mother tongue schooling have higher student achievement levels at Grade 8 in all subjects, including English.... These findings are fully supported by international literature on language learning and cognitive development, which show clearly that investment in learning through the mother tongue has short, medium and especially long term benefits for overall school performance and for the learning of additional languages. (Heugh, Benson, Bogale, & Yohannes, 2007, p. 6)

Too often, however, education policymakers do not adequately consider the consequences of language policies for learning, and when they do, they are often faced with difficult decisions when educational and political agendas are in competition (Tsui & Tollefson, 2004). In particular, although there is clear evidence that mother tongue MOI can provide significant educational advantage in most contexts, policymakers often resist this approach for political reasons. When it offers greater educational access to excluded groups, mother tongue MOI may reduce the social, political, and economic advantages enjoyed by privileged groups that control major educational institutions and have easy access to quality education. As a result, policymakers may offer economic rationales (e.g., mother tongue MOI is too expensive) as well as pedagogical ones (e.g., lack of textbooks and materials) for maintaining policies that systematically privilege some groups over others (Tollefson, 2002; UNESCO Bangkok, 2007).

An additional issue of access and equity is whether all learners have the opportunity to acquire dominant languages necessary for higher education and employment. Mother tongue MOI in primary and secondary education may need to be paired with high-quality instruction in additional languages used in higher education and the workplace. Lack of access to such instruction is an important source of economic, social, and political inequality in many settings, such as Bangladesh (Hossain & Tollefson, 2004) and India (Annamalai, 2013).

In addition, standardized tests in a dominant language in which students are not fluent often result in tracking such students into remedial, vocational, or special education programs, due to test scores that do not accurately measure students' aptitude or achievement. In the United States, the federal No Child Left Behind Act of 2001 means that most linguistic-minority children must take standardized examinations in English, a language in which some students are not proficient. As a result, their ability to meet statewide assessment standards often trails the performance of English-speaking students by 30% to 50% (Abedi & Dietel, 2004).

The distinction between "additive" and "subtractive" bilingual education is relevant here.[1] Many supporters of mother tongue MOI, recognizing that its benefits for subject area learning and educational achievement may be insufficient if higher education and employment require additional languages, argue that equitable education for all must include second-language instruction. Thus high-quality instruction in English aimed at adding English proficiency to individuals' linguistic repertoire is crucial for educational equity in South Africa, Singapore, Hong Kong, the United States, the United Kingdom, and much of Europe, if all students are to have the opportunity to gain the full benefits of educational provisions (see Fang, 2011).

GLOBALIZATION AND LANGUAGE POLICIES IN EDUCATION

Since the 1980s, language policies have become more important than ever in rationing educational access, due to the triumph of global capitalism and its major social consequences. In the economy, globalization entails a transnational system of corporations with no specific territorial base, finance that is largely unregulated, and weakened nation-states that have lost much of their traditional control over exchange rates and the money supply (Hobsbawm, 1994). In education, globalization has meant the movement toward uniform ("globalized") curricula that emphasize science and technology rather than humanities and the arts; replacement of teachers' classroom-based tests with high-stakes standardized assessment; the "deskilling" of teachers (Baumann, 1992) within curriculum-driven programs in which teachers lose control over goals, methods, materials, and assessment; the dominance of commercially prepared materials; the replacement of liberal education with education for employment; the expanding use of English and other standardized and colonial languages as MOI; and the subjugation of education policy to labor policy and national security (cf. the "educational security state"; Spring, 2006). These developments are rationalized by discourses that foreground the instrumental value of "global" languages (especially English), language learning for the national interest, and the opportunities globalization offers for those with education and specific language and literacy skills.

The educational consequences of the global economic crisis that began in 2008 have varied from one context to another. A few states have increased funding for education. In Hong Kong, for example, public funding for higher education grew by 41% from 2007-2008 through 2008-2009 as part of a major transformation of the educational system (in particular, expanding from a 3-year to a 4-year undergraduate degree) and in line with Hong Kong's commitment to education as a strategic industry (UNESCO Bangkok, 2012). In contrast, the United States and the United Kingdom have reduced public education funding and imposed a variety of neoconservative policies, including shifting costs from the state to individuals, permitting the use of public funds for private schooling, and expanding the number of for-profit schools (Union of Colleges and Universities, 2011). Such changes have had serious educational consequences for the poor, working class, and middle class, specifically limiting access to education. Although employment opportunities have been reduced due to the economic crisis, and increasingly restricted to individuals with secondary and higher education, deep reductions in public funding for education make it more difficult than ever for families to pay for schooling. Moreover, as part of funding cuts and increasing costs to individuals (often rationalized with reference to the economic crisis and monoglossic ideologies of language[2]), many programs designed to provide educational access for linguistic-minority students have been reduced or eliminated, such as bilingual education, literacy programs, and various forms of classroom support such as bilingual aides (McGroarty, 2013).

Restrictions on access to high-quality education must be understood within the context of three major social changes associated with globalization that specifically affect language policies in education: the migration of labor, urbanization, and the increase in demand for workers with secondary or higher education and with specific skills in language and literacy. First, the migration of labor has been one of the most important social phenomena since the early 20th century. Until the 1980s, migration was largely regulated by the state, and especially in Europe and North America, it was a state-sponsored mechanism for managing labor shortages (Hobsbawm, 1994). More recently, however, migration has not only increased dramatically in scale but also taken place to a growing extent outside state regulation, and although it remains primarily from poor regions toward North America and Europe, it also includes substantial movements into the oil-producing countries of the Middle East and North Africa, city-states such as Singapore and Hong Kong, and special economic zones in many countries worldwide. Second, a major consequence of migration is urbanization, resulting in a major shift in the geographical distribution of the population. In Japan, for example, the proportion of the population involved in farming declined from 52.4% in 1947 to less than 10% by the 1980s. This trend is not only evident in wealthy states, as similar declines have taken place in Latin America and Southeast Asia (International Labour Organization, 1990). Thus, language policies in urban schools have an increasingly important impact on access and equity among the growing population of urban students, particularly as available employment in urban areas requires skills that are normally learned in school. Third, as hundreds of millions of people worldwide have moved to the cities, employment involves new categories of work in business and finance, service industries (e.g., call centers; see Friginal, 2009), government bureaucracy, and aid agencies or other nongovernmental organizations (Clayton, 2006). Many of these jobs require English or other dominant languages (e.g., Chinese in East and Southeast Asia, French in North Africa), as well as literacy and other skills normally learned in school. In addition, since the 1960s, many countries have adopted a policy of universal primary education, thereby dramatically increasing the proportion of the population enrolled in schools (see Eurostat, 2008).

These profound social changes have major consequences for educational language policies that affect equity and access. (a) Migration from rural areas to cities means that rural language varieties are often lost, replaced by dominant varieties spoken by the middle class, government functionaries, and (in some settings such as Pakistan) military officers (Rahman, 2007). (b) These dominant urban varieties are often former colonial languages used for intergroup communication in multilingual cities and as MOI in urban schools. (c) The new categories of work mean that languages of the capital or business become essential for employment, and therefore there is increased pressure to use them as MOI; often this means the use of English, even in contexts where a major national language is dominant (e.g., Japan and China). (d) Although such varieties are important for intergroup communication and MOI in schools, urban centers are also characterized by the phenomenon of superdiversity (Vertovec, 2007), which leads to the emergence of hybrid forms of heteroglossia that do not correspond with traditional conceptions of linguistic boundaries implicit in many language policies and of pidgins, local varieties of English, regional lingua francas, and "cool" urban mixed varieties that signal what Maher (2005) calls "metroethnicity." (e) In the context of the contraction of the labor market since 2008, the intense competition for places in schools and for new jobs that require literacy and fluency in English (and in other regional and former colonial languages) may lead to the repression of linguistic minorities, with language policies in education an important mechanism of repression (Tollefson, 2013). Such repressive policies have been adopted in the United States, including English proficiency rules in proposals for immigration reform, the loss of bilingual education programs through state measures such as Proposition 227 in California and Proposition 203 in Arizona, and testing policies requiring English-only under the No Child Left Behind law (Wiley & Wright, 2004), as well as in England (including restrictions on the use of immigrants' languages in education; see Lanvers, 2011), and elsewhere. Thus, with the growing importance of schooling, the implicit language policies and practices of the extended family, which has been the primary institution for intergenerational transmission of languages (Fishman, 2000), have been increasingly overshadowed by the regulatory framework of language policies in schools that favor dominant languages (especially English).

In addition to its impact on learners seeking education in a language in which they are not fluent, globalization also has consequences for speakers of dominant languages in some nation-states with varieties that are almost universally learned in childhood. In Japan, China, and many states in Europe, for example, English promotion policies have been adopted in secondary and higher education; many parents seek to enroll their children in secondary or even elementary schools with English MOI (e.g., international schools in Japan, China, and South Korea). In such settings, one result may be a sense of insecurity about the future of the national language and its associated national identity, leading to ambivalence or resistance to English. In Japan, for example, the promotion of English is mediated by deep suspicion of globalization itself, especially its consequences for Japan, such as increased immigration, wider use of languages other than Japanese, and a perceived loss of security and belonging (Hashimoto, 2013).

Moreover, the claimed link between language and national identity, along with the associated denial of the linguistic complexity of multilingual communities, is often the basis for suppressing minority languages. Many scholarly analyses have not understood well the heteroglossic nature of many environments (both urban and rural), the hybrid linguistic repertoires that are commonplace worldwide, and the sociolinguistic ecology of multilingual regions where cultural groups meet in complex relations of domination and subordination (Freeland, 2013). Thus, schoolchildren may be faced with a new language variety as MOI, in addition to their fluency in multiple, overlapping varieties that do not match well with policymakers' assumptions about their linguistic repertoire. Often, MOI policies assume a clear demarcation between fixed, distinct standardized varieties, and thus policies may be inappropriate for the complex linguistic ecology of urban neighborhoods (cf. Blommaert, 2012). Indeed, despite recent research that clearly demonstrates highly complex, variable, and fluid language–identity relationships, fundamental assumptions about the direct connection between distinct languages and identities that emerged from 19th century European nationalism continue to underlie language policies in most educational contexts worldwide (Freeland, 2013; McCarty, 2013).

We now turn to cases in which language policies in education—especially policies promoting the use of English as MOI—have important consequences for educational access and equity. We begin with Hong Kong, where debates about the use of Chinese and English as MOI have continued since the resumption of sovereignty by the People's Republic of China over Hong Kong in 1997.

"FINE-TUNING" MOTHER TONGUE EDUCATION POLICY IN HONG KONG

For several years following the implementation of the "mother tongue" Chinese-medium instruction (CMI) policy in Hong Kong in 1998, the Government Education Bureau publicized the results of the Hong Kong Certificate of Education

Examination (a Secondary 5 school–leaving examination) to provide evidence that mother tongue education had helped students to achieve better academic results compared to the days when English or mixed code was used as MOI. For example, in 2005, 7 years after the implementation of the mother tongue policy, the Education Bureau released the following figures: The proportion of all CMI students obtaining five or more subject passes (including Chinese Language and English Language) increased by 5.6% compared with that in 2002, the year when the last cohort sat for the examination before the MOI policy change. Out of more than 200 schools that switched from English-medium instruction (EMI) to CMI in 1998, the number of schools showing an improvement in student attainment increased from 40 schools in 2003 and 80 schools in 2004, to 120 in 2005. Moreover, compared to 2003, 75% (or 150 schools) of the CMI schools attained higher pass rates in English Language (Syllabus B) or credit rates in English Language (Syllabus A; Education and Manpower Bureau [now Education Bureau, Hong Kong SAR], 2005). These results confirmed the findings of an independent study conducted by Marsh, Hau, and Kong (2000) and were subsequently borne out by Li and Majhanovich (2010). However, the picture was somewhat different in the results of the Hong Kong Advanced Level Examination, a preuniversity public examination. According to Li and Majhanovich (2010), although there were variations in the passing rates of subjects irrespective of whether or not they were language intensive, the Chinese language showed a steady improvement, with the passing rate reaching the highest ever (94.2%) in 2006, whereas the English language showed a continuous decline after 2005. That result was a great cause for concern, particularly among parents. Although contextual factors contributed to the decline in English, such as the impact on student learning of switching to EMI after 5 years of CMI and the effect of mixed-mode teaching (i.e., teaching materials in English but oral interaction in class in Cantonese, a spoken dialect of Chinese), there was a strong demand from the general public for reinstating EMI in all schools at all secondary levels.

This demand persisted despite the fact that the policy provided better access to higher education for students in CMI schools. According to a large-scale survey conducted by the University of Hong Kong in 2006-2007 on second-year students, who were the first cohort of university entrants since the implementation of the mother tongue policy, out of the 811 respondents, the percentage of students who took Hong Kong A-Levels in Chinese were 12% for science, 14% for mathematics, and 20% for humanities. These percentages, though still the minority, were considerably better than the past, when very few students from CMI schools attained the requisite scores for admission into this university. In other words, the adoption of CMI did allow more students to gain access to a prestigious university education, which in the past was restricted to the English-medium elite.

This outcome notwithstanding, in mid-2009, 10 years after implementation of the mother tongue MOI policy, the Hong Kong SAR government succumbed to political pressure and announced the elimination of the bifurcation of schools into CMI and EMI. Starting from the 2010-2011 school year, at Secondary 1 level, schools were allowed to use EMI or CMI for nonlanguage subjects. Schools that were previously classified as CMI schools are now allowed to adopt EMI for a particular class if 85% of its students are in the top 40% in academic ability. The government emphasized on a number of occasions that this was not a reversal but a "fine-tuning" of the mother tongue education policy. To justify this modification, the Education Bureau (2009) wrote, "Schools are in the best position to keep track of students' learning progress and teach according to diverse abilities. Accordingly, schools meeting the above criteria should be allowed to determine their professional school-based MOI arrangements."

This policy has resulted in a diversified mode of MOI in schools: CMI in all nonlanguage subjects for all classes, CMI/EMI in different subjects in different classes, or EMI in all nonlanguage subjects for all classes. This is tantamount to reverting to the practices before the 1998 implementation of the mother tongue education policy (except for closer monitoring by the Education Bureau in implementation of the policy). It is interesting to note that in the 2009 circular announcing the new policy, the discourse of schools exercising their own professional judgment was prominent, in stark contrast to the discourse in the 1998 documents, where the efficacy of mother tongue MOI on student learning was first and foremost (Education Bureau, 2009).

In a study conducted in 1999 on the problems encountered by CMI schools after the implementation of the mother tongue policy, out of 131 CMI schools that responded, 52.7% reported that their better performing students were withdrawing, 32% claimed that the standards of their incoming students were declining, and 25% reported a decline in the number of applicants for Secondary 1 entry (Tsui et al., 1999). Therefore, in 2009, CMI schools were quick to reinstate English-medium teaching in as many classes as possible and to publicize (especially in student recruitment) the number of classes and the subjects taught in English, although no statistics have been disclosed by schools or the Education Bureau regarding the correlation between the academic standards of student intake and the number of EMI classes offered. The situation is paradoxical: On one hand, there was clear evidence that the mother tongue education policy had enabled more students, who were hitherto disadvantaged by learning through English, to have better access to quality higher education. Yet on the other hand, this policy was frowned upon by CMI schools for excluding them from participation in EMI, a much desired model of education, and for the stigmatization they suffered; it was criticized by parents of CMI students for unjustly denying their children access to English; it was denounced by the business sector as aggravating the already declining English standards and hence undermining the competitiveness of Hong Kong; and it was viewed with suspicion by the community as well as by democratic political parties as part of the exercise of sovereignty by the Chinese central government.

Finally, it is important to note that the debate between EMI and CMI ignores hybrid varieties and code mixing commonplace in Hong Kong. At the policy level, the Education Bureau proscribes mixed-code teaching, although students and teachers often ignore this regulation. As in many contexts worldwide, policy-level language instruction assumes rigid boundaries between language varieties, despite the widespread use of creative and complex forms of heteroglossia among teachers and students (Lin, 1996).

MEDIUM OF INSTRUCTION IN BASIC AND HIGHER EDUCATION IN ASIA

The past two decades have witnessed a sea change in the landscape of higher education in Asia. First, there is rapid expansion of publicly and privately funded higher education in Asian countries, spurred by the need to produce university graduates with knowledge and skills to meet the needs of economic development. This is achieved partly by upgrading postsecondary education institutions into universities and partly by importing higher education from destination countries. Since the 1990s, "transnational education," which used to take the form of students completing part of their study in their home countries and part in the degree-offering universities, has taken the form of the latter setting up branch or joint campuses overseas, which is much cheaper than sending students overseas. For example, from 2009 to 2011 there was a 50% increase to 18 campuses in Singapore and a 17% increase to 17 schools in China (Rosenfeld, 2012). In 2012, there were 10 campuses in Malaysia, with 5 more opening soon ("Get to Know," 2012).

Second, a number of Asian countries aspire to be the educational hub of the region and to achieve high ranking in the various world university rankings. Because internationalization, measured by the percentages of international faculty and students, is one of the major criteria in the ranking metrics, Asian universities have tried to attract as many international students as possible, particularly from the region. For example, the number of international students in Malaysia increased from over 5,600 in 1997 to over 45,600 in 2008. In China, the number of international students reached a record high of over 292,000 in 2011, representing a 10% growth compared to the previous year ("Over 290,000 Foreign," 2012).

These two major changes resulted in a dramatic increase in the number of English-medium courses and programs in universities. Consequently, the English proficiency level of the secondary school graduates has become increasingly important for students to gain access to prestigious universities.

"Bilingual Education" in China

In recent years, there has been a strong promotion of EMI at all educational levels in China, spearheaded by the Ministry of Education. It is widely known as "bilingual education/teaching" (*shuangyu jiaoyu/jiaoxue*; Hu, 2009), which means that some or all content subjects are taught in English. In 2002, the Higher Education Department of the Ministry of Education announced that one of the criteria for assessing higher education institutions is that the number of bilingual programs offered in a discipline should be no less than 10%. It also specified that a "bilingual program" is defined as using EMI for no less than 50% of the curriculum time (Ministry of Education, PRC, 2002). Since then, there has been a dramatic increase in the number of bilingual courses/

programs offered by universities. Special funding from the Ministry of Finance was provided for universities to develop exemplar "bilingual" courses at 100,000 yuan per course. For example, in 2010, 151 exemplar courses were selected for funding and listed online (Ministry of Education, PRC, 2010). It also provided on the web a list of institutions that offer English-medium programs (updated in 2013; see Ministry of Education, PRC, 2013).

Faced with a shortage of teachers who can teach through the medium of English, schools must provide incentives to attract teachers with high English proficiency, such as higher salary, bonuses, subsidies, promotion, sponsored training, and more favorable workload. Hence, only schools that are well resourced can afford to do so. The resources come not only from government funding but also from charging higher fees and donations from parents. Hence, middle-class parents who are prepared to pay higher fees and donate to the school are much more likely to get their children into bilingual schools than working-class parents who cannot afford to do so (Feng, 2005). In addition, to deal with the shortage of "bilingual" teachers, many local governments and schools have defined the ability to teach content subjects through a foreign language, which is essentially English, as an attribute of a "qualified" teacher in bilingual schools (Feng, 2005). In some schools in Shanghai, for example, teachers are classified as "probationary," "prospective," or "qualified" according to their readiness to teach through the medium of English (Shen, 2004). The consequences of these practices are dire: They widen the gap between schools that are well resourced and those that are not within the same city; they exacerbate the chasm between the affluent coastal cities and the poorer inland cities where resources for education are scarce, as well as between the urban and the rural areas; they lead to inequity of access to a mode of education that has been touted by authorities as "quality" education; and they create two classes of teachers, those who possess the symbolic capital, English, and those who do not (Feng, 2009).

English-medium education has also created tension between the majority group, the Han, and the ethnic minority groups, because of inequitable access to English. For the majority group, English is learned as a subject as early as Primary 1 or Primary 3, and for some, even used as an MOI for some subjects. For most minority students, however, English is not taught in the 9-year compulsory education, and for some, English is not taught until university. This is because for these students, Mandarin Chinese is taught as a second language and used as the MOI for content subjects. Therefore, even when English is taught, Mandarin Chinese (referred to as *zhongjieyu*; "mediating language"), rather than the mother tongue, is used as the medium of teaching and of textbooks (Olan, 2007; see also Xiao, 2003, Xu, 2000, cited in Feng, 2009). This means that ethnic minority students are less likely than Han students to achieve a high level of proficiency in English and hence are less competitive in getting into top universities in China. For example, despite a positive discrimination policy in university admission through the *gaokao* (the university entrance examination), the increase of minority students' enrolment in universities is very small compared to the overall growth rate. From 2005 to 2010, the increase for minority students enrolled in universities was around 37% (90,000), compared to the much larger overall growth rate of around 75% (from around 4.7 million in 2005 to 6.3 million in 2010) in undergraduate students in China's universities (Ives, 2010). Minority students have always been disadvantaged because the MOI in universities has been Chinese, and they have had to take a 1-year remedial course in Chinese. With the rapid increase in the number of English-medium courses and programs, ethnic minority students are further disadvantaged.

Another consequence of the spread of EMI is that in minority regions, minority languages that were previously taught to Han students, to enhance interethnic communication and understanding, are being replaced by English, because Han parents are more interested in their children learning English than a minority language. The displacement of the Uyghur language by English for the Han students in the school curriculum (Tsung & Cruickshank, 2009) and the consistent marginalization of the Uyghur language in universities in Xinjiang is a case in point. This policy accentuates "Han-Chinese ethno-centrism" (Jia, Lee, & Zhang, 2012, p. 177), exacerbates the imbalance in the power relationship between the Han majority and the ethnic minorities, and aggravates the tension and segregation between the Han majority and the ethnic minorities, as evidenced by the widely reported ethnic conflicts in Xinjiang and Tibet.

Access to English and the Social Divide in India

India is a divided society in a number of respects, and the English language has contributed significantly to the divide. English was the language of the elite in the colonial period and is widely seen as a "passport" to the future. However, it is also viewed with suspicion, particularly by the lower caste, as the English-educated elite has marginalized the non–English speaking grassroots. With a rapidly growing middle class able to afford expensive English-medium education and a strong grassroots push for access to English, the teaching of English has been advanced from secondary level to primary level and in public schools to Primary 1. Public policy also avows universal access to English. Nevertheless, access to English is by no means universal, despite the fact that English is now considered a basic skill for children and integrated into the curriculum even in vernacular-medium schools. Only 60% of the 14- to 16-year-old age-group reach secondary education where a second language is used as the MOI, either a regional language, Hindi or English. However, the dropout rate is very high, with only 28% completion rate at Grades 11 and 12. At college or university, a much higher proportion of courses is taught through English, but only 12% of the students can get into universities (Graddol, 2010). Thus, even with much wider access to English in the past 10 years or so, English is still the language of the elite. According to a poll conducted by the Indian television channel CNN-IBN in August 2009, 87% of the respondents felt that English was very important to success in life, but over 80% felt that knowing the state language was also very important, over 60% felt that jobs should be reserved for those who speak the state language, and close to 60% felt that English made them forget their mother tongue (see Graddol, 2010).

In other words, although English is still a much-desired commodity, the tension between English and the vernacular languages has not attenuated.

English often enters political debates in India and is used by politicians as a platform to gain the support of their constituencies. Aware of the tension between English and the regional languages, most politicians will not address a rally in English, which is seen as not the language of the "commoners." On the other hand, within the English-speaking circle, politicians who are not able to speak English fluently are often ridiculed. For example, in a recent report in *Wall Street Journal-India* headlined "Mamata Banjeree on the Great English Language Divide," it was reported that Mamata Banjeree, the vocal West Bengal Chief Minister, in response to criticisms of her opposition to key policy initiatives of the central government, pointed out that the English-educated "Delhi people" did not understand local issues and that her English was poor because she was a "commoner": "We are from the very middle class family. We have not come from the English-medium school. We came from our regional languages school" (Stancati, 2012). She further pointed out that because her English was poor, she was often misinterpreted and harshly treated by critics and the press. It is worth noting that although English is pitched against regional languages in political debates, it is also used as a tool to resist domination of one vernacular language over another. Some of the southern states have chosen English rather than Hindi as the official language as a form of resistance against domination by the northern states.

Medium of Instruction in Malaysia

Whereas in China and India English-medium education has created tension between the ethnic groups because of inequitable access to English, in Malaysia, the switch to English MOI at all three levels of the education system in 2002 created tension of a different kind. After independence from British colonial rule in 1957, Bahasa Malaysia was adopted as the national language. However, a mother tongue education policy was adopted under the 1957 Education Ordinance (Ministry of Education, 1957) for all ethnic groups, so that the language and culture of ethnic groups other than the Malays would be preserved and sustained. Hence the national education system comprised two types of schools, the Malay-medium national schools and the vernacular-medium "national type schools." This system allowed Chinese-medium and Tamil-medium schools to grow, with the former flourishing because of the high-quality teaching and outstanding academic achievements of their graduates. However, after the Education Act in 1961 mandated that the national language, Malay, be adopted as the MOI for all schools, funding for schools that retained the vernacular as an MOI was greatly reduced. According to the Centre for Public Policy Studies (2012) in Kuala Lumpur, the recent budget allocation for vernacular schools was only 2.4% to 3.6% of the entire education budget. This step created grave concern among the Chinese, the second largest ethnic group in Malaysia (with a quarter of the population). Keen to ensure that their culture, language, and ethnic identity were maintained and confident that Chinese-medium education was best for their children, the Chinese raised funds from their own community to support Chinese-medium schools. There are now 1,293 Chinese-medium primary schools (Centre for Public Policy Studies, 2012) and 60 Chinese independent secondary schools in Malaysia (Arifin, 2012).

The consequence of the implementation of the Malay-medium education policy was contrary to what the Malaysian government had intended. Instead of raising the status of the Malay language and uniting the nation through its use, the policy led to further tension between the Malays and the ethnic minorities. The publicly funded universities in Malaysia were Malay medium, whereas the privately funded universities had the autonomy to use English as the MOI. As a result, graduates of English-medium universities, because of their high proficiency in English, were keenly sought by the private sector, which offers much higher pay and better career prospects. The overwhelming majority of graduates of Malay-medium public universities, because of their poor English, ended up with less well-paid jobs in the government, where English skills were not as crucial. Even though Malays make up 65% of the population, Chinese 26%, and Indians 7.7%, the jobs in the private sector have gone mainly to the Chinese and the Indians, whereas 94% of the jobs in the government have been taken by Malays, and only 3.7% by Chinese and 1.7% by Indians (Gill, 2007). To ensure that the Malays would not continue to be disadvantaged, then–Prime Minister Mahatir Mohammed decided that English-medium education should be adopted in publicly funded schools for the teaching of science and mathematics starting with Primary 1, Secondary 1, and Lower 6 in the first year and moving up to higher levels in the following years.

This reversal of MOI policy provided greater access to English, but it was not welcomed by the Chinese community, where it was perceived as a threat to the mother tongue education system and to the distinctiveness of Chinese-medium schools. It was argued that science and math were best learned through the mother tongue, as evidenced by the outstanding academic achievements of Chinese children. Consequently, after intense negotiations between the leaders of the Chinese community and the Malaysian government, a compromise was reached in which CMI would be used predominantly for mathematics and science and English MOI only for a couple of hours in the total lesson hours per week.

In Hong Kong, working-class and middle-class parents, whether English speaking or non–English speaking, even those who know that their children would learn better through their mother tongue, have fought vehemently for English-medium education. Similarly, in China and India, access to English is given priority over quality of learning. By contrast, in Malaysia, Chinese parents fought to maintain mother tongue education because it guarantees high-quality learning. What appears to be contradictory is not really so, however, if we see it from the perspective of whether the choice of MOI restricts or facilitates access to further education and future careers. The Chinese community in Malaysia—middle class and with the resources to send children to private universities in Malaysia or prestigious overseas universities—can ensure that their children are able to cope with English-medium higher education, and thus Chinese-medium schooling is seen as pedagogically superior.

Globalization and English in Japan

The spread of English also has consequences for educational equity in contexts characterized by nearly universal access to education. One such case is Japan, where, in 2002, Japan's Ministry of Education, Culture, Science, Sports and Technology adopted its "strategic plan to cultivate Japanese with English abilities" (Ministry of Education, Culture, Science, Sports and Technology, 2002). Since then, the study of English has spread into primary schools and the use of English as MOI has been extended to English language classes in secondary schools, to a system of elite "super-English high schools" and to a growing number of programs in higher education (Hashimoto, 2013). An increasing body of evidence, however, suggests that the promotion and use of English provide significant educational and employment advantage only for a small proportion who have access to high-quality instruction and to opportunities to use English outside school, whereas most students gain little benefit from their many hours of study of English.

As in many contexts, English in Japan (particularly in higher education) is rationalized with an elite discourse of "globalization-as-opportunity" (Yamagami & Tollefson, 2011), which often appears in university promotional materials for English MOI programs. Promotion of English-medium higher education is also aimed at attracting more students from abroad, yet public discussion about globalization and international student enrollment is often embedded in a discourse of "globalization-as-threat" that focuses on immigration, such as manufacturing workers of Japanese descent from Brazil and Peru, health care providers from Indonesia and Philippines, students from China, and unskilled workers in "three-K jobs" (*kitsui, kitanai,* and *kiken*; hard, dirty, and dangerous) from China and elsewhere (see Tabuchi, 2009). This nationalist counterdiscourse is skeptical of English promotion policies rationalized by a discourse of globalization-as-opportunity (Yamagami & Tollefson, 2011).

One reason for resistance to English may be the growing recognition that the promotion of English offers economic advantages mainly to a small number of middle- and upper middle-class individuals who gain employment in transnational corporations, international organizations such as the United Nations, and nongovernmental organizations (Kobayashi, 2007). The high wage structure of Japan severely limits the growth of domestic industries that might offer expanded employment for other English learners in fields such as medical transcription and call centers (see Friginal, 2009). Thus, the case of Japan suggests that the impact of language policies on equity and access in different settings must be understood within the specific economic context (also see Nakanishi, 2006).

The Rise of China and the Learning of Mandarin Chinese

The rise of China as a major economic power has led to important changes in language policies and language curriculum in many parts of the world. In Hong Kong, many schools have incorporated the teaching of Putonghua in the curriculum, although it is not mandated, and many school activities have used Putonghua as a medium of communication alongside English. Universities in Hong Kong have set up centers for administering the official tests of Putonghua on behalf of the Ministry of Education in China, and the number of students taking these tests (and studying privately) has increased substantially (Tian, 2007).

In Malaysia, there have been increasing cultural exchanges between Malaysian and Chinese universities, and a growing number of non-Chinese students attend schools that use Chinese as an MOI in morning sessions and Malay in the afternoon. In the year 2000, more than 60,000 non-Chinese students, mostly Malays, enrolled in Chinese-medium primary schools because of the importance of Chinese, the excellent results in math and science in Chinese schools, and better job opportunities on graduation. Whereas the older generation of teachers in Chinese schools speak Chinese as a second language, the younger generation of teachers speak Chinese as their mother tongue (Hashim, 2009).

In Singapore, promotion of English as the lingua franca and English-medium education have led to a drastic reduction of the number of Chinese-medium schools. In 1980, the merging of Nanyang University, a Chinese-medium institution, with the University of Singapore to form the National University of Singapore, which is an English-medium university, led to the demise of Chinese-medium schools in the 1980s. Since then, the percentage of the population who speak English as a home language has risen dramatically from 9% in 1980 to 32% in 2010. Among school-age children (5-14 years old), close to half (48%) spoke English as a home language in 2010 compared to 32% in 2000. The trend for speaking Mandarin as a home language is the reverse: 42% of school children spoke Mandarin at home in 2000, but the percentage dropped to 31% in 2010. In other words, English is becoming the dominant home language.

Although Chinese is a compulsory subject at school and passing the subject is a prerequisite for college and university entrance, because there is little or no need to use the language in everyday life and it is not an MOI at university, there is little incentive for students to achieve a high level of proficiency. In 1999, a review led by then–Deputy Prime Minister Lee Hsien Loong acknowledged that many so-called mother tongue Chinese children had little or no exposure to Chinese at home. Therefore, an alternative examination syllabus, Syllabus B, requiring a lower level of proficiency, was designed for the majority of the students, whereas the Higher Chinese Language Syllabus was retained for the elite. To ensure that schools produce graduates with high proficiency not only in English but also in Chinese, the government has designated a small number of elite schools (11 in total) where both English and Chinese are used as an MOI for some subjects. In 2011, a Language Review Committee led by the Director General of Education made recommendations to improve the proficiency levels of Chinese and the teaching of Chinese, including a proposal to make it "a living language" that is not just used in the classroom and examinable but also used to communicate effectively in real-life settings (Singapore

Ministry of Education, 2011, p. 14).

Since the 1990s, the question of whether Mandarin Chinese will overtake English as the global lingua franca has often been raised. Reported figures about the number of learners of Mandarin Chinese suggest a sharply rising worldwide trend that has created unease, especially in the English-speaking countries. In 2006, it was estimated that 30 million people were studying Mandarin Chinese and that the number would grow to 100 million in a few years' time. Observing that Mandarin Chinese has emerged as a "must-have" language in Asia and elsewhere, Graddol (2006) compares the rush to learn Chinese in South Korea to the earlier rush to learn English.

Nevertheless, English continues its domination. In a speech in 2009, Chinese Premier Wen Jia Bao claimed that in China there were 300 million learners of English (Bardsley, 2011). According to Graddol (2010), the number of speakers of English in India is estimated to be between 55 million and 350 million. Given that the U.S. economic and geopolitical power is unlikely to decline precipitously, Bruthiaux (2009) argues that it is highly unlikely that Mandarin Chinese will become the dominant language of global communication, although it is likely to provide better access to educational opportunities and increasing economic advantages to middle- and upper-class learners able to develop fluency in it.

INTERNATIONALIZATION OF HIGHER EDUCATION AND MOI POLICY IN CONTINENTAL EUROPE

In Europe, more than 60 regional and minority languages are currently spoken. With 23 official languages, the European Union's official language policy claims to protect linguistic diversity and promote multilingualism for preservation of cultural identity, social cohesion, and intercultural understanding. The member states of the European Union are required to commit themselves to teaching the languages of the other states and to encouraging their citizens to learn at least two languages other than their mother tongue. The European Commission (2000) declares that all languages in Europe are "equal in value and dignity from the cultural point of view and form an integral part of European cultures and civilization." In 2003, a detailed plan consisting of 45 actions was adopted by the European Commission to extend the learning of languages to all educational levels, including adult education; to improve the quality of language education; and to create an environment favorable to language learning (European Commission, 2004). In 2008, the European Commission specified actions that need to be taken to make linguistic diversity an asset for solidarity and prosperity.

Within this context, the use of English as a dominant MOI has become a major phenomenon only in the past 20 years (Bruthiaux, 2009). When the policy was first mooted in some countries, strong objections were raised (e.g., in 1990, when the Dutch Minister of Education proposed making English the official language of instruction at Dutch universities; see Brock-Utne, 2007; Höglin, 2002).

Despite objections to such policies, the number of programs switching to English has increased dramatically, especially since the launch of the Bologna Process in 1999 to create a European Higher Education Area to facilitate the transferability of credits and degree qualifications among universities in continental Europe. The need to have a common language to facilitate staff and student mobility, particularly the latter, has led to an explosion of the number of courses and programs delivered through the medium of English. Indeed, as Phillipson (2009) observed, in the Bologna Process, "internationalization" means English-medium higher education. The move to English-medium education is further accelerated by the fact that internationalization of higher education is one of the key profile indicators in international rankings of universities, including the Times Higher Education University Ranking and the QS World Ranking. To obtain higher scores in these international rankings, the recruitment of staff and students outside the home country has become an essential part of the strategic plan of nearly all universities.

The result is an exponential growth of the number of English-medium programs in the past 10 years. In 2001-2002, according to a survey conducted by the Academic Cooperation Association (reported in Coleman, 2006), among the 1,558 higher education institutes in 19 continental European countries, only 30% had one or more English-medium program (Maiworm & Wächter, 2002; also see Wächter, 2008), but in a follow-up study in 2006-2007 in 27 European countries, 2,400 degree programs were taught in English (Wächter & Maiworm, 2008; see also Gill & Kirkpatrick, 2013). The consequence is that English is even used to teach courses that would be better taught in the mother tongue (e.g., a German student studying Kant in English).

Another significant impact of internationalization in higher education is on the language of research and scholarship, which increasingly favors English. In the Times Higher Education ranking, publishing with researchers outside the home country accounts for one third of the scores for international outlook. Moreover, in the scores for research and publication, the citation of published work and journal quality are largely based on impact factors as reflected in a citation index, which favors publications in English, which have the largest readership. Research assessment exercises and promotion and tenure also increasingly favor English-language publication. To encourage more publications in English, European universities have various incentive measures in place. In Norway, for example, the Norwegian Association of Higher Education Institutions proposed in 2004 a reward system that ranked journals and publishing companies according to three levels (UHR, 2004). According to Brock-Utne (2007), of the 486 ranked publishing companies listed on the Internet, more than 80% ranked at Level 2 (the highest level) were U.S. publishing companies, and no Norwegian publishing house was given similar ranking; and out of some 170 journals (of 1,700 total) that were ranked Level 2, only 4 were published in Norwegian. This situation has also affected research students' work. In the University of Iceland, for example, doctoral theses in the Faculties of Social Sciences and Medicine are required to be written in English whereas those in the Humanities can be written in English or Icelandic (Hilmarsson-Dunn, 2009). Monetary incentive is also provided to doctoral students for writing their theses in English (e.g., the University of Oslo; see Brock-Utne, 2007).

The effect of English-medium higher education on secondary education is that English has to be taught at a higher level of proficiency and students must be prepared to deal with academic texts in English. Hence, the learning of English has been advanced to the beginning of primary education. The teaching of a foreign language through content subjects, referred to as Content and Language Integrated Learning, has been strongly promoted by the European Commission for all levels of school education. Although the languages taught through Content and Language Integrated Learning in principle include national, regional, and minority languages, English is far ahead of all other languages in all countries (European Commission, 2006).

In sum, it is clear that English has become a basic skill that must be mastered and a daily necessity that one cannot do without. Thus, the educational achievement of anyone with limited access to high-quality English learning will be restricted. However, with increased mobility across the globe, with the emergence of multiple centers of political and economic power, and with the increasingly porous boundaries of all kinds, it is no longer enough to be proficient only in English. Knowledge of a third or fourth language, and an understanding of the culture associated with it, will soon be a basic necessity across the globe. With unequal access to high-quality instruction in multiple languages, inequities in educational opportunities and outcomes are likely to increase in the years ahead.

CONCLUSION: REDUCING INEQUALITY AND IMPROVING ACCESS

MOI policies increasingly affect educational access and equity, especially in light of the growing importance of language policies in schools and the processes of globalization that have increased the importance of language-related skills for education and employment. Although in many contexts MOI policies exacerbate problems of access and equity in education, we end our analysis with ways that MOI policies may improve educational opportunities and outcomes, briefly illustrated with the cases of New Zealand, Solomon Islands, and Native America.

New Zealand is a rare case of a suppressed indigenous language adopted as an official language at the national level. This achievement was the result of efforts made by the Māori working outside the official educational system, to develop independent Māori-medium preschools in the early 1980s (see May, 2004). The success of this movement in revitalizing Māori knowledge and cultural practices led to the spread of Māori-medium education to other levels of schooling and, in 1990, to official recognition of the Māori schools as part of the state education system.

In the case of Solomon Islands, where more than 70 indigenous languages compete with English and Solomons Pijin, the failure of rural education has been intensified by the spread of English MOI and by the recent violence and civil war (1998-2003), which has led to the collapse of education in some areas and the migration of thousands of Kwara'ae-speaking Malaitans from the island of Guadalcanal back to their native island of Malaita (Gegeo & Watson-Gegeo, 2002, 2013). With local schools failing to respond to the educational needs of Malaitan children (many of whom were traumatized by violence and forced migration), the Malaitan community has responded with revitalized community education based on indigenous Malaitan culture and epistemology.

Education in Native American schools, particularly in Navajo communities in the U.S. Southwest, includes indigenous languages used as MOI. Schools using Navajo as MOI have been particularly successful, with the Rough Rock Community School in Chinle, Arizona, founded in 1966, gaining recognition as a model for indigenous MOI schools worldwide (McCarty, 2013).

The cases of New Zealand, Solomon Islands, and Native America suggest five generalizations about MOI policies that can help achieve greater access and equity in education:

1. *The importance of self-determination in school administration and MOI policymaking*: Māori MOI in New Zealand was a direct result of the community's efforts to create and control schools that only later gained official support. In Solomon Islands, central education authorities failed to understand or support policies that would serve the needs of Kwara'ae-speaking Malaita youth; only after community leaders took control of educational policies have these needs begun to be addressed. In the Southwest United States, Navajo-medium schools are community institutions, largely controlled by the community for the community's benefit.

2. *The value of an ideology and discourse to support mother tongue MOI*: In New Zealand, the recent discourse of bilingual and bicultural Aotearoa/New Zealand identity has provided an ideological and discursive framework for the promotion of Māori MOI. This framework includes appeals to the dominant non-Māori, English-speaking population. In Solomon Islands, a commitment to indigenous praxis provides a powerful framework for promoting Kwara'ae-medium education. In the United States, Navajo MOI has been articulated within the framework of Native American self-determination, which provides some protection against the powerful English-only ideology that is directed primarily against speakers of Spanish and African American Vernacular English.

3. *The importance of using the legal context to promote MOI policies for access and equity*: In New Zealand, the Treaty of Waitangi and the Māori Language Act of 1987 provide a legal framework for the spread of Māori MOI. In the United States, among other laws, the Indian Self-Determination and Education Assistance Act of 1975, the Native American Languages Act of 1990, and the Native American Housing and Self-Determination Act of 1996 provide a legal framework for the promotion of Native American MOI.

4. *The value of historical precedents*: In New Zealand, early mission schools offered Māori MOI. In Solomon Islands, the development of indigenous pedagogy, in

response to the abysmal condition of education on the island of Malaita, can be traced to the 1980s, long before the recent conflict. In Native America, the history of Native-language MOI, disrupted by the period of American conquest, means that Navajo MOI schools are, in a sense, a return to a long tradition of Navajo MOI.

5. *The importance of MOI policies that fill specific, identifiable needs*: In New Zealand, Māori preschools emerged from the need for quality child care services; as preschool children moved into primary schools, parents wanted to continue Māori language learning and use, and thus Māori MOI at the primary level was adopted. In Solomon Islands, the failure of traditional schools to confront the disruption of war and migration offered an opening for new forms of community education for children from Malaita. In Native America, isolated communities require local institutions that offer a broad range of social services and support. In that context, indigenous MOI is an obvious policy approach.

Thus, despite ample evidence of educational inequities associated with MOI policies worldwide, these cases suggest that policies can be adopted to open access and reduce inequities in education.

NOTES

[1]Additive bilingual education refers to programs in which the first language continues to be developed along with the second language. In subtractive bilingual education, learning the second language restricts first-language development, potentially resulting in language loss (Roberts, 1995).

[2]According to García and Torres-Guevara (2010), a monoglossic ideology "values only monolingualism and ignores multilingualism" and views language "as an autonomous skill that functions independently of the context in which it is used" (p. 182).

REFERENCES

Abedi, J., & Dietel, R. (2004). *Challenges in the No Child Left Behind Act for English language learners* (CRESST Policy Brief). Los Angeles: UCLA Center for the Study of Evaluation.

Alidou, H. (2004). Medium of instruction in post-colonial Africa. In J. W. Tollefson & A. B. M. Tsui (Eds.), *Medium of instruction policies: Which agenda? Whose agenda?* (pp. 195–214). New York, NY: Routledge.

Annamalai, E. (2013). India's economic restructuring with English: Benefits versus costs. In J. W. Tollefson (Ed.), *Language policies in education: Critical issues* (2nd ed., pp. 191–207). New York, NY: Routledge.

Arifin, L. J. (2012). Dr. M: More Chinese independent schools will divide people. *The Malaysian Insider*. Retrieved from http://www.themalaysianinsider.com/malaysia/article/dr-m-more-chinese-independent-schools-will-divide-people/

Baker, C. (2011). *Foundations of bilingual education and bilingualism* (5th ed.). Bristol, England: Multilingual Matters.

Bardsley, D. (2011, August 22). English the lingua franca in China. *The National*. Retrieved from http://www.thenational.ae/business/industry-insights/economics/english-the-lingua-franca-in-china

Baron, D. (2011). Language and education: The more things change. In A. Curzan & M. Adams (Eds.), *Contours of English and English language studies* (pp. 278–297). Ann Arbor: University of Michigan Press.

Baumann, J. F. (1992). Basel reading programs and the deskilling of teachers: A critical examination of the argument. *Reading Research Quarterly, 27,* 390–398.

Benton, R. A. (2007). Mauri or mirage? The status of the Māori language in Aotearoa New Zealand in the third millennium. In A. B. M. Tsui & J. W. Tollefson (Eds.), *Language policy, culture and identity in Asian contexts* (pp. 163–181). New York, NY: Routledge.

Blommaert, J. (2012). *Chronicles of complexity: Ethnography, superdiversity, and linguistic landscapes* (Tilburg Papers in Cultural Studies 29). Tilburg, Netherlands: Tilburg University.

Brock-Utne, B. (2006). Language and democracy in Africa. In D. B. Holsinger & W. J. Jacob (Eds.), *Inequality in education: Comparative and international perspectives* (pp. 172–189). Hong Kong: Springer & the Comparative Education Research Centre of the University of Hong Kong.

Brock-Utne, B. (2007). Language of instruction and research in higher education in Europe: Highlights from the current debate in Norway and Sweden. *International Review of Education, 57,* 367–388.

Bruthiaux, P. (2009). Multilingual Asia: Looking back, looking across, looking forward. *AILA Review, 22,* 120–130.

Centre for Public Policy Studies. (2012). *Vernacular schools in Malaysia: "A heritage to be celebrated or a hindrance to nation building?"* Kuala Lumpur, Malaysia: Author. Retrieved from http://www.cpps.org.my/upload/VERNACULAR%20SCHOOLS%20IN%20 MALAYSIA%20REPORT%202012.pdf

Clayton, T. (2006). *Language choice in a nation under transition: English language spread in Cambodia.* New York, NY: Springer.

Coleman, J. A. (2006). English medium teaching in European higher education. *Language Teaching, 39,* 1–14.

Coronel-Molina, S. M. (2013). New functional domains of Quechua and Aymara. In J. W. Tollefson (Ed.), *Language policies in education: Critical issues* (2nd ed., pp. 278–300). New York, NY: Routledge.

Education and Manpower Bureau. (2005, August 10). *SEM pleased with HKCEE results* (Press Release). Retrieved from http://www.info.gov.hk/gia/general/200508/10/08100203.htm

Education Bureau, Hong Kong SAR. (2009, June 5). *Fine-tuning the medium of instruction for secondary schools* (Education Bureau Circular No. 6/2009). Retrieved from http://www.edb. gov.hk/attachment/en/edu-system/primary-secondary/applicable-to-secondary/moi/support-and-resources-for-moi-policy/lsplmfs-sch/d-sch/ow/sp/edbc09006e.pdf

European Commission. (2000). *Decision No. 1934/2000/EC of the European Parliament and of the Council of 17 July 2000 on the European Year of Languages 2001.* Retrieved from http://eur-lex.europa.eu/LexUriServ/LexUriServ.do?uri=OJ:L:2000:232:0001:0005:en: PDF

European Commission. (2004). *Promoting language learning and linguistic diversity: An action plan 2004-06.* Luxemburg: Office for Official Publications of the European Communities.

European Commission. (2006). Eurydice report. *Content and language integrated learning (CLIL) at school in Europe.* Brussels, Belgium: Eurydice European Unit.

European Commission. (2008). *Multilingualism: An asset for Europe and a shared commitment.* Communication from the Commission to the European Parliament, the Council, the European Economic and Social Committee and the Committee of the Regions. Retrieved from http://eur-lex.europa.eu/LexUriServ/LexUriServ.do?uri=CELEX:52008DC0566:EN: NOT

Eurostat. (2008). *Students in tertiary education, 2008.* Retrieved from http://epp.eurostat. ec.europa.eu/portal/page/portal/eurostat/home/

Fang, G. (2011). Linguistic capital: Continuity and change in educational language policies for South Asians in Hong Kong primary schools. *Current Issues in Language Planning, 12,* 251–263.

Feng, A. (2005). Bilingualism for the minor or the major? An evaluative analysis of parallel conceptions in China. *International Journal of Bilingual Education and Bilingualism, 8,* 529–551.

Feng, A. (2009). English in China: Convergence and divergence in policy and practice. *AILA Review, 22,* 85-102.

Fishman, J. A. (Ed.) (2000). *Can threatened languages be saved?* Clevedon, England: Multilingual Matters.

Freeland, J. (2013). Righting language wrongs in a plurilingual context: Language policy and practice in Nicaragua's Caribbean Coast region. In J. W. Tollefson (Ed.), *Language policies in education: Critical issues* (2nd ed., pp. 91–115). New York, NY: Routledge.

Friginal, E. (2009). Threats to the sustainability of the outsourced call center industry in the Philippines: Implications for language policy. *Language Policy, 8,* 51–68.

García, O., & Torres-Guevara, R. (2010). Monoglossic ideologies and language policies in the education of Latinas/os. In E. Murillo, S. Villenas, R. T. Galván, J. S. Muñoz, C. Martínez, & M. Machado-Casas (Eds.), *Handbook of Latinos and education: Research, theory and practice* (pp. 182–193). New York, NY: Routledge.

Gegeo, D. W., & Watson-Gegeo, K. A. (2002). The critical villager: Transforming language and education in Solomon Islands. In J. W. Tollefson (Ed.), *Language policies in education: Critical issues* (1st ed., pp. 309–325). New York, NY: Routledge.

Gegeo, D. W., & Watson-Gegeo, K. A. (2013). The critical villager revisited: Continuing transformations of language and education in Solomon Islands. In J. W. Tollefson (Ed.), *Language policies in education: Critical issues* (2nd ed., pp. 233–251). New York, NY: Routledge.

Get to know the new and upcoming Malaysia branch campuses. (2012, October 24). *After School Higher Education Advisor.* Retrieved from http://afterschool.my/get-to-know-the-new-and-upcoming-malaysia-branch-campuses/

Gill, S. K. (2007). Shift in language policy in Malaysia: Unravelling reasons for change, conflict and compromise in mother-tongue education. *AILA Review, 20,* 106-122.

Gill, S. K., & Kirkpatrick, A. (2013). English in Asian and European higher education. In C. A. Chapelle (Ed.), *The encyclopedia of applied linguistics* (pp. 1916–1920). Oxford, England: Blackwell. Retrieved from http://onlinelibrary.wiley.com/store/10.1002/9781405198431/asset/homepages/3_English_in_Asian_and_European_Higher_Education.pdf?v=1&s=4c49dc8642113e36a4e3bf192876688ba8addaa2

Graddol, D. (2006). *English next: Why global English may mean the end of "English as a foreign language."* Retrieved from http://www.britishcouncil.org/learning-research-english-next.pdf

Graddol, D. (2010). *English next: India.* Retrieved from http://www.britishcouncil.org/learning-english-next-india-2010-book.htm

Hashim, A. (2009). Not plain sailing: Malaysia's language choice in policy and education. *AILA Review, 22,* 36–51.

Hashimoto, K. (2013). The Japanisation of English language education: Promotion of the national language within foreign language policy. In J. W. Tollefson (Ed.), *Language policies in education: Critical issues* (2nd ed., pp. 175–190). New York, NY: Routledge.

Heugh, K., Benson, C., Bogale, B., & Yohannes, M. A. G. (2007). *Final report: Study on medium of instruction in primary schools in Ethiopia.* Addis Ababa, Ethiopia: Ministry of Education.

Hilmarsson-Dunn, A. M. (2009). The impact of English on language education policy in Iceland. *European Journal of Language Policy, 1,* 39-59.

Hobsbawm, E. (1994). *The age of extremes: A history of the world, 1914-1991*. New York, NY: Vintage.

Höglin, R. (2002). *Engelska språket som hot och tillgång i Norden* [The English language as a threat and an asset in the Nordic countries]. Copenhagen, Denmark: Torkil Sørensen.

Hossain, T., & Tollefson, J. W. (2004). Language policy in education in Bangladesh. In A. B. M. Tsui & J. W. Tollefson (Eds.), *Language policy, culture and identity in Asian contexts* (pp. 241–257). New York, NY: Routledge.

Hu, G. (2009). The craze for English-medium education in China: Driving forces and looming consequences. *English Today, 25*(4), 47–54.

International Labour Organization. (1990). *ILO yearbook of labour statistics: Retrospective edition on population censuses 1945-1989*. Geneva, Switzerland: Author.

Ives, M. (2010, December 19). CHINA: Time to reassess minority education policy? *World University News, 152*. Retrieved from http://www.universityworldnews.com/article.php?story=20101217223320655

Jia, W., Lee, Y. T., & Zhang, H. (2012). Ethno-political conflicts in China: Towards building interethnic harmony. In D. Landis & R. D. Albert (Eds.), *Handbook of ethnic conflict: International perspectives* (pp. 177–196). New York, NY: Springer.

Jones, D. V., & Martin-Jones, M. (2004). Bilingual education and language revitalization in Wales: Past achievements and current issues. In J. W. Tollefson & A. B. M. Tsui (Eds.), *Medium of instruction policies: Which agenda? Whose agenda?* (pp. 43–70). New York, NY: Routledge.

Kobayashi, Y. (2007). Japanese working women and English study abroad. *World Englishes, 26*, 62–71.

Lanvers, U. (2011). Language education policy in England: Is English the elephant in the room? *Apples: Journal of Applied Language Studies, 5*(3), 63–78.

Li, V., & Majhanovich, E. S. (2010). Marching on a long road: A review of the effectiveness of the mother-tongue education policy in post-colonial Hong Kong. *GiST Education and Learning Research Journal, 4*, 10–29.

Lin, A. M. Y. (1996). Bilingualism or linguistic segregation? Symbolic domination, resistance and code-switching in Hong Kong schools. *Linguistics and Education, 8*, 49–84.

Maher, J. (2005). Metroethnicity, language and the principle of cool. *International Journal of the Sociology of Language, 175/176*, 83–102.

Maiworm, F., & Wächter, B. (2002). *English-language-taught degree programmes in European higher education: Trends and success factors*. Bonn, Germany: Lemmens.

Marsh, H. W., Hau, K. T., & Kong, C. K. (2000). Late immersion and language of instruction in Hong Kong high schools: Achievement growth in language and non-language subjects. *Harvard Educational Review, 70*, 302–346.

May, S. (2004). Māori-medium education in Aotearoa/New Zealand. In J. W. Tollefson & A. B. M. Tsui (Eds.), *Medium of instruction policies: Which agenda? Whose agenda?* (pp. 21–42). New York, NY: Routledge.

McCarty, T. L. (2013). Language planning and cultural continuance in Native America. In J. W. Tollefson (Ed.), *Language policies in education: Critical issues* (2nd ed., pp. 255–277). New York, NY: Routledge.

McGroarty, M. (2013). Multiple actors and arenas in evolving language policies. In J. W. Tollefson (Ed.), *Language policies in education: Critical issues* (2nd ed., pp. 35–58). New York, NY: Routledge.

Ministry of Education, Culture, Science, Sports and Technology. (2002). *Developing a strategic plan to cultivate "Japanese with English abilities"—plan to improve English and Japanese abilities*. Tokyo, Japan: Author. Retrieved from http://www.mext.go.jp/english/news/2002/07/020901.htm

Ministry of Education, Malaysia. (1957). *Malaysia Education Ordinance*. Retrieved from http://blogs.wsj.com/indiarealtime/2012/03/21/mamata-banerjee-on-the-great-english-language-divide/

Ministry of Education, PRC. (2002). *Putong gaodeng xuexiao benke jiaoxue gongzuo shuiping pinggu fang'an (shixing)* [Assessment of quality of undergraduate teaching in higher education institutions (pilot)]. Retrieved from http://jw.zzu.edu.cn/glwj/new_page_2.htm

Ministry of Education, PRC. (2010). *Jiaoyubu Caizhengbu Guanyu Pizhun Erlingyiling Niandu Shuangyu Jiaoxue Shifan Kecheng Jianshe Xiangmu di Tongzhi* [Ministry of Education and Ministry of Finance Circular on Approval of 2010 Exemplar Bilingual Courses Development Project]. Retrieved from http://www.gov.cn/zwgk/201007/27/content_1664810.htm

Ministry of Education, PRC. (2013). *List for English-taught programmes in Chinese higher education institutions*. Retrieved from http://www.moe.edu.cn/publicfiles/business/htmlfiles/moe/moe_2812/200906/48835.html

Nakanishi, S. (2006, May 25). Primary school English: An opponent responds. *The Daily Yomiuri (Edition A)*, p. 12.

Olan, M. (2007). An investigation of the status quo of minority college students learning English. *Xinjiang Daxue Xuebao, 35*, 156–160. (In Chinese)

Over 290,000 foreign students study in China. (2012, March 1). *People's Daily Overseas Edition*. Retrieved from http://english.peopledaily.com.cn/203691/7745000.html

Pérez-Milans, M. (2013). *Urban schools and English language education in late modern China: A critical sociolinguistic ethnography*. New York, NY: Routledge.

Phillipson, R. (2009). English in higher education: Panacea or pandemic? *Angles on the English-Speaking World, 9*, 29–57.

Rahman, T. (2007). The role of English in Pakistan, with special reference to tolerance and militancy. In A. B. M. Tsui & J. W. Tollefson (Eds.), *Language policy, culture and identity in Asian contexts* (pp. 219–239). New York, NY: Routledge.

Roberts, C. A. (1995). Bilingual education program models: A framework for understanding. *Bilingual Research Journal, 9*, 369–378.

Rosenfeld, E. (2012, August 22). Universities look east: Fuelling branch-campus boom. *Time World*. Retrieved from http://world.time.com/2012/08/27/universities-look-east-fueling-branch-campus-boom/#ixzz2O2VUH5pE

Shen, Z. Y. (2004). Yiyi zai shijian mubiao zai chengxiao [Implementation and effectiveness of bilingual education]. *Zhongguo Jiaoyubao, May*, 2.

Singapore Ministry of Education. (2011). *Nurturing active learners and proficient users: 2010 Mother Tongue Languages Review Committee report*. Retrieved from http://www.moe.gov.sg/media/press/files/2011/mtl-review-report-2010.pdf

Skutnabb-Kangas, T. (2008). Human rights and language policy in education. In S. May & N. H. Hornberger (Eds.), *Encyclopedia of language and education: Vol. 1. Language policy and political issues in education* (pp. 107–11). New York, NY: Springer.

Skutnabb-Kangas, T., & Phillipson, R. (Eds.). (1994). *Linguistic human rights: Overcoming linguistic discrimination*. Berlin, Germany: Mouton.

Spring, J. (2006). *Pedagogies of globalization: The rise of the educational security state*. New York, NY: Routledge.

Stancati, M. (2012, March 21). Mamata Banjeree on the great English language divide. *India Realtime-Wall Street Journal-India*. Retrieved from http://blogs.wsj.com/indiarealtime/2012/03/21/mamata-banerjee-on-the-great-english-language-divide/

Tabuchi, H. (2009, April 23). Japan pays foreign workers to go home. *The New York Times*. Retrieved from http://www.nytimes.com/2009/04/23/business/global/23immigrant.html?pagewanted=all&_r=0

Tian, X. L. (2007). The tenth year of the National Putonghua Proficiency Test in Hong Kong. In *Disanjie Quanguo Putonghua Shuiping Ceshi Xueshu Yantaohui Lunwenji* [Proceedings from the 3rd National Putonghua Proficiency Test Symposium] (pp. 261–269). Fuzhou, China: Institute of Applied Linguistics, Ministry of Education. (In Chinese)

Tollefson, J. W. (Ed.). (2002). *Language policies in education: Critical issues* (1st ed.). New York, NY: Routledge.

Tollefson, J. W. (2013). Language policy in a time of crisis and transformation. In J. W. Tollefson (Ed.), *Language policies in education: Critical issues* (2nd ed., pp. 11–34). New York, NY: Routledge

Tsui, A. B. M. (2007). Language policy and the construction of identity: The case of Hong Kong. In A. B. M. Tsui & J. W. Tollefson (Eds.), *Language policy, culture, and identity in Asian contexts* (pp. 121–141). New York, NY: Routledge.

Tsui, A. B. M., & Tollefson, J. W. (2004). The centrality of medium-of-instruction policy in sociopolitical processes. In J. W. Tollefson & A. B. M. Tsui (Eds.), *Medium of instruction policies: Which agenda? Whose agenda?* (pp. 1–18). New York, NY: Routledge.

Tsui, A. B. M., Tse, S. K., Shum, M. S. K., Ki, W. W., Wong, C. K., & Kwong, W. L. (1999). *Implementing mother-tongue education in schools: Problems encountered and support needed.* Hong Kong: Department of Curriculum Studies, University of Hong Kong.

Tsung, L. T. H., & Cruickshank, K. (2009). Mother tongue and bilingual minority education in China. *International Journal of Bilingual Education and Bilingualism, 12,* 549–563.

UHR (Norwegian Association of Higher Education Institutions). (2004). *A bibliometric model for performance-based budgeting of research institutions.* Retrieved from http://www.uhr.no/documents/Rapport_fra_UHR_prosjektet_4_11_engCJS_endelig_versjon_av_hele_oversettelsen.pdf

UNESCO. (1990). *World declaration on education for all and framework for action to meet basic learning needs* (Adopted by the World Conference on Education for All Meeting Basic Learning Needs, Jomtien, Thailand 5-9 March 1990). Paris, France: Author.

UNESCO Bangkok. (2007). *Advocacy kit for promoting multilingual education: Including the excluded.* Bangkok: UNESCO, Asia and Pacific Regional Bureau for Education.

UNESCO Bangkok. (2012). *The impact of the economic crisis on higher education.* Bangkok: UNESCO, Asia and Pacific Regional Bureau for Education.

Union of Colleges and Universities, United Kingdom. (2011). Draft resolution on higher education and research and the global financial crisis. In *Congress Book 5: Draft Congress Resolutions, Education International 6th World Congress* (p. 43). Brussels, Belgium: Education International.

Vertovec, S. (2007). Super-diversity and its implications. *Ethnic and Racial Studies, 30,* 1024–1054.

Wächter, B. (2008, May). *Internationalisation and the European higher education area.* Report prepared for the Bologna Process Seminar Bologna 2020: Unlocking Europe's Potential—Contributing to a Better World, Ghent, Belgium. Retrieved from http://www.ond.vlaanderen.be/hogeronderwijs/bologna/BolognaSeminars/documents/Ghent/Ghent_May08_Bernd_Waechter.pdf

Wächter, B., & Maiworm, F. (2008). *English-taught programmes in European higher education.* Bonn, Germany: Lemmens.

Wiley, T. G., & Wright, W. E. (2004). Against the undertow: The politics of language instruction in the United States. *Educational Policy, 18,* 142–168.

Yamagami, M., & Tollefson, J. W. (2011). Elite discourses of globalization in Japan: The role of English. In P. Seargeant (Ed.), *English in Japan in the era of globalization* (pp. 15–37). Houndsmills, England: Palgrave Macmillan.

Chapter 9

Justifying Educational Language Rights

STEPHEN MAY

The University of Auckland

INTRODUCTION

Not so long ago, we seemed to be making progress on the question of how to incorporate meaningfully the cultural and linguistic backgrounds of our increasingly diverse school student population. In the 1990s, multicultural and bilingual educational approaches were becoming commonplace in modern liberal democracies (Banks & Banks, 2004; May, 1999, 2009). Similarly, multiculturalism appeared to be gaining widespread acceptance as a public policy response to the burgeoning diversity of state populations in an era of rapid globalization and related transmigration (Kymlicka, 2001, 2007; Parekh, 2000). Both developments built on a history of nearly 50 years of advocacy of multicultural and bilingual education, and wider state policies of inclusion for minority groups, which had its genesis in the U.S. Civil Rights movement but had extended to other Western countries, including Canada, Britain, Australia, and New Zealand. Even critics of multiculturalism conceded its impact on public policy at that time, particularly within education—a wearied resignation most notably captured in Nathan Glazer's (1998) phrase, "We are all multiculturalists now." Multiculturalism, at least in Glazer's view, had finally "won" because the issue of greater public representation for minority groups was increasingly commonplace in discussions of democracy and representation in the civic realm—including, centrally, within schools (see, e.g., Goldberg, 1994; Kymlicka, 1995; Taylor, 1994).

How times have changed. Over the past decade, and particularly post-9/11, we have seen a rapid and significant retrenchment of multiculturalism as public policy, particularly within education. In the United States, a burgeoning standards and testing movement, spearheaded by the No Child Left Behind (NCLB) Act of 2001, has replaced earlier attention to racial and ethnic diversity (May & Sleeter, 2010). Decades of affirmative action and related civil rights advances for African

Review of Research in Education
March 2014, Vol. 38, pp. 215-241
DOI: 10.3102/0091732X13506694
© 2014 AERA. http://rre.aera.net

Americans have been dismantled, most notably in relation to access to higher education (Kellough, 2006). The related provision of bilingual education, particularly for Latino/Latina Americans, has also been severely circumscribed, and in some U.S. states actually proscribed, by legislation promoting a monolingual English language philosophy as a prerequisite for U.S. citizenship (Crawford, 2008; May, 2012, chap. 6). Meanwhile, across Europe, multiculturalism as public policy is in apparent full retreat, as European states increasingly assert that minority groups "integrate" or accept dominant social, cultural, linguistic, and (especially) religious mores as the price of ongoing citizenship (Modood, 2007). Again, education has been a key focus, with bilingual and multicultural education programs facing significant retrenchment across Europe as a result (Modood & May, 2001).

LANGUAGE, COSMOPOLITANISM, AND MOBILITY

This apparent retrenchment of multiculturalism as public policy has been bolstered by parallel arguments for a more "cosmopolitan" approach to education within an increasingly globalized world (Archibugi, 2005; Barry, 2001; Waldron, 1995). In these accounts, globalization is sometimes viewed as primarily a geocultural consequence of late capitalism (e.g., Cox, 1996) or, alternatively, as a geopolitical phenomenon, linked to previous forms of social and political organization, most notably the nationalism of the previous few centuries (Held, McGrew, Goldblatt, & Perraton, 1999; Hobsbawm, 2008; Robertson, 1992, 1995).[1] However, in both accounts, as the sociologist Craig Calhoun (2003, 2007) argues, globalization is linked with new global (and hybrid) forms of identity that allow one to "escape" the "confines" of more localized (and, by extension, fixed) identities, including linguistic ones. In this view, globalization constitutes both the basis of individual transformation—the ability to adopt hybrid, cosmopolitan forms of identity that transcend both local and national borders—and, more broadly, is seen as the next stage of the modernization process. Martha Nussbaum's (1997) notion of "citizen of the world," a global form of citizenship that is no longer rooted in, or confined to, local, ethnic, or national identities, but specifically transcends them, highlights this clearly.

Closely allied with this generalist cosmopolitan view is an advocacy of languages of wider communication, and particularly English as the current world language, as the new means of global interchange and the basis of social mobility. A related argument is that the ongoing use of "local languages," via language rights or the broader politics of multiculturalism, simply entrenches social, cultural, and political isolationism, as well as socioeconomic disadvantage. A recent example of this position can be seen in the work of the Italian political theorist, Daniele Archibugi (2005). He argues that the answer to the "problem" of increasing linguistic diversity is not the multiculturalist recognition of language rights but rather a global cosmopolitanism based on a language of wider communication. This is because, for Archibugi, a democratic politics requires "the willingness of all players to make an effort to understand each other" and thus a "willingness to overcome the barriers of mutual understanding, including linguistic ones" (p. 537). Following from this, he maintains that "linguistic diversity is an *obstacle* [italics added] to equality and participation" (p. 549; see also Blommaert, Peppännen, & Spotti, 2012). Although he uses the metaphor of the artificial language, Esperanto, to illustrate his normative arguments, and perhaps also to create some cover for their implications, it is nonetheless still abundantly clear that the "common language" he has in mind here is English (Ives, 2010). We see this in the case study examples he uses to illustrate his position: In one—a state school in an increasingly mixed Anglo/Latino neighborhood in California—Archibugi (2005) outlines a hypothetical scenario of increasing tension between the two groups with respect to the school's future direction:

The Hispanic students do not speak English well and their parents speak it even worse. School parents-students meetings end in pandemonium, with the Anglos complaining that their children are starting to make spelling mistakes and the Hispanics protesting because their children are bullied. At the end of a stormy meeting, an Anglo father, citing Samuel Huntingdon, invites the Hispanic community to dream in English. In return, an outraged Mexican slaps him in the face. (p. 547)

Meanwhile, Archibugi (2005) also assumes in his scenario that the Anglo parents are middle-class and that most of the Latino parents are "cleaners" but with aspirations "to enable their children to live in conditions that will avoid perpetuating the [existing] class division based on different ethnic groups" (p. 548). In offering potential solutions going forward, he contrasts a multiculturalist response of parallel English and Spanish instruction within the school for the respective groups—bilingual or dual language education, in effect—with, in his view, a clearly preferable cosmopolitan solution of English language instruction for all. This cosmopolitan solution is predicated on the basis that "American citizens with a good knowledge of English have (1) higher incomes; (2) less risk of being unemployed; (3), less risk of being imprisoned and (4) better hopes for a longer life" (p. 548). As a salve to the Latino population, however, the cosmopolitan proposal also includes compulsory courses in Spanish language and culture for all, while encouraging Latino parents to learn English in night school and Anglo parents "salsa and other Latin American dances" (p. 548).

The underlying presumptions about language and mobility in Archibugi's (2005) scenario are also clearly echoed in comparable accounts. Another prominent political theorist, Thomas Pogge (2003), for example, begins his discussion on the language rights attributable to Latinos in the United States—or, more accurately, in his view, the lack thereof—by asserting unequivocally that English is the predominant language of the United States and has been so for much of its (colonial) history.[2] He then proceeds to observe, in close accord with Archibugi's (2005) hypothetical example, that many Latinos "do not speak English well" (Pogge, 2003, p. 105). Accordingly, to best serve the educational interests of Latino children, Pogge specifically endorses an English "immersion"[3] educational approach so as to ensure that Latino students gain the necessary fluency in English to succeed in the wider society. He argues,

The choice of English as the universal language of instruction is justified by reference to the best interests of children with other native languages, for whom speaking good English (in addition to their native language) will be an enormous advantage in their future social and professional lives. (p. 120)[4]

But Pogge (2003) does not end his arguments there. He also suggests that those (Latino) parents who opt instead for bilingual education may well be "perpetuating a cultural community irrespective of whether this benefits the children concerned" (p. 116). For him, this amounts to an illiberal "chosen inequality" for those children because it "consigns" them to an educational approach that, in maintaining Spanish (or other languages), willfully delimits their longer term mobility in U.S. society. This position is made even starker by Pogge's intimation that such a choice could possibly warrant the same constraints applied to parents as other child protection laws; equating bilingual education, in effect, with child abuse, a trope much used by the wider "English-only" movement in the United States (Crawford, 2008; May, 2012, chap. 6; see below for further discussion).

Two other political theorists, David Laitin and Rob Reich (2003), argue much the same position, asserting that "forcing" bilingual education on children will curtail "their opportunities to learn the language of some broader societal culture" (p. 92). Relatedly, they fret that these "individuals have no influence over the language of their parents, yet their parents' language if it is a minority one . . . constrains social mobility." As a result, "those who speak a minority (or dominated) language are more likely to stand *permanently* [italics added] on the lower-rungs of the socio-economic ladder" (p. 92). Indeed, they proceed to observe that if minority individuals are foolish enough to perpetuate the speaking of a minority language, then they can simply be regarded as "happy slaves," having no one else to blame but themselves for their subsequent limited social mobility.

Setting aside, if one can, the clearly racialized paternalism that pervades all these accounts, a key additional problem with them is that they are substantively wrong. This is so both with respect to the links between English and social mobility and in terms of the apparent efficacy of English-only language instruction for learning English as an additional language. I will return, in due course, to the latter issue of the most effective pedagogies for bilingual students. But first let me, briefly, address the former presumption that knowledge of English automatically leads to increased educational, social, and economic mobility for linguistic-minority students. Quite simply, this is not nearly so often the case as advocates of a cosmopolitan education in English might presuppose. Why this is so is because what is often (willfully) overlooked in such cosmopolitan accounts are the ongoing structural inequalities that necessarily delimit access and opportunities—particularly for minoritized populations. For example, in many postcolonial countries, small English-speaking elites have continued the same policies as their former colonizers to ensure that (limited) access to English language education acts as a crucial distributor of social prestige and wealth (Heugh, 2008; Ives, 2010). Pattanayak (1969, 1985, 1990) and Dasgupta (1993) describe exactly this pattern in relation to India, where English remained the preserve of a small high-caste elite until at least the 1990s. The impact of globalization has changed this somewhat in India since then, particularly with the increasing use by multinational companies of business process outsourcing and information technology outsourcing requiring English language expertise (Graddol, 2007). Examples here include call centers and publishing, both of which India has benefited directly from in the past decade. However, these developments also highlight the significant differentials and inequalities in pay and conditions for workers in India and other comparable contexts when compared with "source" countries—indeed, these conditions are the principal raison d'être for the outsourcing in the first place. Meanwhile, the necessary English language expertise is still closely related to existing social class and related educational hierarchies in India, as elsewhere (Morgan & Ramanathan, 2009; Sonntag, 2009).

A similar scenario is evident in Africa, where, despite English being an official or co-official language in as many as 15 postcolonial African states, the actual percentage of English speakers in each of these states never exceeds 20% (Heugh, 2008; Ngũgĩ, 1993; Schmied, 1991). Indeed, Alexandre (1972) has gone as far as to suggest that in postcolonial Africa, social class can be distinguished more clearly on linguistic than economic lines. Although this observation willfully understates the coterminous nature of linguistic and social class stratification—in Africa, as elsewhere—it does usefully underscore how these class/linguistic distinctions can extend to the *types* of English language varieties (often agglomerated in cosmopolitan arguments for access to English) also used in these contexts. For example, the English acquired by urban Africans may offer them considerable purchase and prestige for their middle-class identities in African towns, where it often acts as a trade lingua franca, but the same variety of English may well be treated quite differently if they moved to London, identifying them as stigmatized, migrants, and from the lower class. Blommaert (2010) describes the latter as context-specific, "low-mobility" forms of English (p. 195) that do little to change social and economic trajectories in contexts of transmigration.

Returning to the question of Latinos learning Spanish in the United States, canvassed earlier, we see a similar disconnection with empiricism in relation to the leitmotif that the obverse—the maintenance of Spanish—entrenches ghettoization and/or immobility. First, there is the question of context. If Spanish is demonstrably a language of social prestige and mobility in other contexts (as in Spain or Latin America), why cannot it also be so in the United States? And then there is the inconvenient fact of demographics. After all, African Americans have been speaking English for 200 years in the United States and yet many still find themselves relegated to urban ghettos (Macedo, 1994). Racism and discrimination are far more salient factors here than language use. Likewise, English is almost as inoperative with respect to Latino social mobility in the United States as it is with respect to Black social mobility. Twenty-five percent of Latinos currently live at or below the poverty line, a rate that is *at least twice as high* as the proportion of Latinos who are not English speaking (García, 1995; San Miguel & Valencia, 1998).

All this points to the fact that the lofty advocacy of English as the basis for a new global cosmopolitanism is significantly overstated. Rather, it is *existing* elites who benefit most from English—or, more accurately, those prestigious varieties of English to which they have preferential access (high-status varieties with normative accents and standardized orthographies). For the majority of other linguistic-minority speakers, the wider structural disadvantages they consistently face, not least poverty, racism, and discrimination, limit, even foreclose, any beneficial effects (Blommaert, Muyllaert, Huysmans, & Dyers, 2006). Acquiring English is thus more often a palliative than a cure, masking rather than redressing deeper structural inequalities. As Peter Ives (2010) concludes,

Learning English, or any dominant language, is not inherently detrimental in the abstract, but the context in which it occurs often means that it helps to reinforce psychological, social and cultural fragmentation. Thus a "global language" like English can never fulfill the role cosmopolitanism sets for it, that of helping those marginalized and oppressed by "globalization" to be heard. (p. 530)

If such accounts are demonstrably wrong factually, why do they still hold such sway in discussions of language and education for minority students? The answer lies in the wider sociohistorical and sociopolitical conceptions that still frame what it means to be a citizen in modern liberal democracies. Ironically, this also returns us to the significance of the social and political organization of the modern nation-state system and the role of public education therein. This is ironic because of the almost de rigueur assumption by advocates of cosmopolitanism that the nation-state is in permanent decline and/or already irremediably passé: that we have moved on, in effect, to the next level of social and political organization.[5] Of course, nation-states *are* clearly subject to wider trends toward greater economic and political interdependence in this age of late capitalism. To suggest otherwise would be foolish. But the idea that this is an entirely new phenomenon, the recent product of globalization in effect, would also appear to be misplaced. After all, nation-states have always been subject to wider economic and political forces of one form or another. As Hinsley (1986) observes, the idea of complete economic and political sovereignty is a "situation to which many states may have often aspired, but have never in fact enjoyed" (p. 226). Meanwhile, for the majority of us, the nation-state model remains the *primary* social, political, *and linguistic* frame of reference for our everyday public lives including, crucially, within education (see R. Bauman & Briggs, 2003; Blommaert et al., 2012). In light of this, it behooves us to examine more closely the underlying presumptions that still so influence the more specific debates on language and education before we turn to an examination of possible alternatives.

THE NATION-STATE AND THE "PLURALIST DILEMMA"

Debates over citizenship in modern liberal democracies have often focused on the significance of language to both national identity and state citizenship. These debates have addressed, in particular, two key issues:

1. Whether speaking the state-mandated or national language—that is, the majority or dominant language of the state—is, or should be, a *requirement* of national citizenship and a demonstration of both political and social integration by its members (especially for those who speak other languages as a first language [L1])
2. Whether this requirement should be at the *expense* of, or in *addition* to the maintenance of other languages—minority, or nondominant languages, in effect—within the state: or to put it another way, whether public monolingualism in the state-mandated language should be enforced on an often-multilingual population or whether some degree of public as well as private multilingualism can be supported (see May, 2008b for further discussion)

Needless to say, how these two issues are addressed has significant implications for the development of language policy and the provision of language education in modern nation-states. In particular, they require modern nation-states to address the balance between social *cohesion*, a key concern of all such states, and the recognition (or lack thereof) of cultural and linguistic *pluralism*. This often-difficult balancing act between maintaining cohesion on the one hand and recognizing pluralism on the other within modern nation-states has been termed by Brian Bullivant (1981) as *the pluralist dilemma*. As Bullivant observes, it is "the problem of reconciling the diverse political claims of constituent groups and individuals in a pluralist society *with the claims of the nation-state as a whole* [italics added]" (p. x); what he elsewhere describes as the competing aims of "civism" and "pluralism." In an earlier analysis, Schermerhorn (1970) described these countervailing social and cultural forces as *centripetal* and *centrifugal* tendencies:

Centripetal tendencies refer both to cultural trends such as acceptance of common values, styles of life etc., as well as structural features like increased participation in a common set of groups, associations, and institutions . . . Conversely, centrifugal tendencies among subordinate groups are those that foster separation from the dominant group or from societal bonds in one way or another. Culturally this most frequently means retention and presentation of the group's distinctive tradition in spheres like language, religion, recreation etc. (p. 81)

How then can the tensions arising from the pluralist dilemma best be resolved in the social and political arena? Drawing on political theory, two contrasting approaches have been adopted in response to this central question, which Gordon (1978, 1981) has described as "liberal pluralism" and "corporate pluralism." Liberal pluralism, exemplified in the seminal contribution of John Rawls (1971), is characterized by the absence, even prohibition, of any national or ethnic minority group[6] possessing separate standing before the law or government. Its central tenets can be traced back to the French Revolution and Rousseau's conception of the modern polity as comprising three inseparable features: freedom (nondomination), the absence of differentiated roles, and a very tight common purpose. On this view, the margin for recognizing ethnic, cultural, and linguistic differences within the modern nation-state is very small (Taylor, 1994). In contrast, corporate pluralism or multiculturalism, as it is now more commonly described, involves the recognition of minority groups as legally constituted entities, on the basis of which, and depending on their size and influence, economic, social, and political awards are allocated.

It is clear, however, that for most commentators the merits of liberal pluralism significantly outweigh those of a group rights or multiculturalist approach. In effect, the answer to the pluralist dilemma has been consistently to favor civism over pluralism. On this basis, the "claims of the nation-state as a whole"—emphasizing the apparently inextricable interconnections between social cohesion and national homogeneity—have invariably won the day over more pluralist conceptions of the nation-state where ethnic, linguistic, and cultural differences *between different groups* are accorded some degree of formal recognition. As such, formal differentiation within the modern nation-state on the grounds of minority group association is rejected as inimical to the individualistic and meritocratic tenets of liberal democracy. Where countenanced at all, alternative ethnic, cultural, or linguistic affiliations should be restricted solely to the private domain since the formal recognition of such alternative collective identities is viewed as undermining personal and political autonomy and fostering social and political fragmentation. As the political philosopher Will Kymlicka (1989) observes of this, "The near-universal response by liberals has been one of active hostility to minority rights . . . schemes which single out minority cultures for special measures . . . appear irremediably unjust, a disguise for creating or maintaining . . . ethnic privilege" (p. 4). Any deviation from the strict principles of universal political citizenship and individual rights is seen as the first step down the road to apartheid. Or so it seems. The resulting liberal consensus is well illustrated by Brian Bullivant (1981) himself:

Certain common institutions essential for the well-being and smooth functioning of the nation-state as *a whole* must be maintained: common language, common political system, common economic market system and so on. Cultural pluralism can operate at the level of the *private*, rather than public, concerns such as use of ethnic [*sic*] language in the home . . . But, the idea that maintaining these aspects of ethnic life and encouraging the maintenance of ethnic groups almost in the sense of ethnic enclaves will assist their ability to cope with the political realities of the nation-state is manifestly absurd. (p. 232)

These emphases on civism at the expense of pluralism help to explain the fragility of the apparent gains for multicultural and bilingual education initiatives up until the 1990s and the significant retrenchment they have since faced internationally. They also undergird many of the presumptions that inform the arguments against the maintenance of minority languages via public education on the basis of social mobility (and integration), as outlined in my earlier discussion of cosmopolitanism. How, then, can one respond effectively (if at all) to this confluence of opinion, and associated ideological and structural imperatives, arraigned against language education provision for linguistic-minority students? In two ways: via the promotion of language rights, particularly in relation to both international and national law, and by an associated exposition and defense of the efficacy of minority language educational approaches for linguistic-minority students. Moreover, these need to be deployed in conjunction if they are to have any immediate—let alone, lasting—effect in shifting the locus of debate in favor of such provision. Let me outline each of these crucial, interconnected, elements in turn.

THE ARGUMENT FOR LANGUAGE RIGHTS

International Law

Much of the post–Second World War era has been largely antipathetic to the notion of language rights for linguistic minorities. This is because the prevailing emphasis in international law, most clearly encapsulated by the 1948 United Nations (UN) Universal Declaration of Human Rights, has been on a view of human rights as primarily, even exclusively, *individual* rights. In similar vein to the notion of civism, discussed above, what follows from this is a view of rights that addresses the person *only* as a political being with rights and duties attached to his or her status as a *citizen*. Such a position does not countenance private identity, including a person's communal membership, as something warranting similar recognition. These latter dimensions are excluded from the public realm because their inevitable diversity would lead to the complicated business of the state mediating between different conceptions of "the good life" (Dworkin, 1978, 2000; Rawls, 1971, 1999). On this basis, personal *autonomy*—based on the political rights attributable to citizenship—always takes precedence over personal (and collective) *identity* and the widely differing ways of life that constitute the latter. In effect, personal and political participation in liberal democracies, as it has come to be constructed post–Second World War, ends up denying group difference and posits all persons as interchangeable from a moral and political point of view (Young, 1993, 2000).

This poses immediate difficulties for the advocacy of language rights because the right to the maintenance of a minority language within any given context presupposes that the particular language in question constitutes a *collective* or communally shared good of a particular linguistic community (de Varennes, 1996, 2001; Thornberry, 1991). Or, put more simply, arguments for maintaining a language necessarily require a wider language community with which to interact in the first instance. An additional challenge is that language rights are often linked directly, as we have seen above, with the (unnecessary) promotion of ethnic particularism at the perceived expense of wider social and political cohesion. The prominent sociolinguist Joshua Fishman (1991) ably summarizes this view:

Unlike "human rights" which strike Western and Westernized intellectuals as fostering wider participation in general societal benefits and interactions, "language rights" still are widely interpreted as "regressive" since they would, most probably, prolong the existence of ethnolinguistic differences. The value of such differences and the right to value such differences have not yet generally been recognised by the modern Western sense of justice. (p. 72)

Even so, there is a nascent consensus within international law on the validity of minority language and education rights. This is predicated on the basis that the protection of minority languages does fall within generalist principles of human rights (May, 2011; see also Kymlicka, 2001, 2007). Following from this, there is a growing acceptance of differentiated linguistic and educational provision for minority groups within some national contexts. These developments, which I will discuss in more detail shortly, can first be usefully referenced by a distinction that another prominent sociolinguist, Heinz Kloss (1971, 1977), has made between what he terms *tolerance-oriented* rights and *promotion-oriented* rights (see also Macías, 1979).[7]

Tolerance-oriented rights ensure the right to preserve one's language in the private, nongovernmental sphere of national life. These rights may be narrowly or broadly defined. They include the right of individuals to use their L1 at home and in public; freedom of assembly and organization; the right to establish private cultural, economic, and social institutions wherein the L1 may be used; and the right to foster one's L1 in private schools. The key principle of such rights is that the state does "not interfere with efforts on the parts of the minority to make use of [their language] in the private domain'" (Kloss, 1977, p. 2).

In contrast, promotion-oriented rights regulate the extent to which minority rights are recognized within the *public* domain, or civic realm of the nation-state. As such, they involve "public authorities [in] trying to promote a minority [language] by having it used in public institutions—legislative, administrative and educational, including the public schools" (Kloss, 1977, p. 2). Again, such rights may be narrowly or widely applied. At their narrowest, promotion-oriented rights might simply involve the publishing of public documents in minority languages. At their broadest, promotion-oriented rights could involve recognition of a minority language in all formal domains within the nation-state, thus allowing the minority language group "to care for its internal affairs through its own public organs, which amounts to the [state] allowing self government for the minority group" (p. 24). The latter position would also necessarily require the provision of state-funded minority language education *as of right*.

It is this notion of promotion-oriented rights that most concerns us here since it impinges directly on the issue of the provision of minority language education. And there are increasing examples in international law that support this position, albeit with the proviso that individual nation-states may still choose to ignore such laws, or apply them in only limited ways. One of the most significant of these developments is the UN Declaration on the Rights of Persons Belonging to National or Ethnic or Religious Minorities, adopted in December 1992. This UN Declaration recognizes that the promotion and protection of the rights of persons belonging to minorities actually contributes to the political and social stability of the states in which they live (Preamble). Consequently, the Declaration asserts,

Persons belonging to national or ethnic, religious and linguistic minorities . . . *have the right* [italics added] to enjoy their own culture, to profess and practise their own religion, and to use their own language, in private *and in public* [italics added], freely and without interference or any form of discrimination. (Article 2.1)

In addition, and significantly, Article 2.1 recognizes that minority languages may be spoken in the public as well as the private domains, without fear of discrimination—a clear, promotion-oriented language right. That said, the 1992 UN Declaration remains a recommendation and not a binding covenant—in the end, it is up to nation-states to decide if they wish to comply with its precepts. In a similar vein, the actual article that deals with minority language education (Article 4.3) qualifies the more general positive intent of Article 2.1 considerably: "States *should* take *appropriate* measures so that, *wherever possible*, persons belonging to minorities have *adequate* opportunities to learn their mother tongue *or* to have instruction in their mother tongue [italics added]" (see Skutnabb-Kangas, 2000, pp. 533–535, for an extended discussion).

Another example where exactly the same question applies can be found in the 2007 UN Declaration on the Rights of Indigenous Peoples (UNDRIP). The UNDRIP was formulated over a 25-year period. This included the development over more than 10 years of the 1993 Draft Declaration by the Working Group on Indigenous Populations, in turn a part of the UN's Sub-Commission on the Prevention of Discrimination and Protection of Minorities. The merits of the Draft Declaration were subsequently debated for nearly 15 years, with many UN member states raising substantive and repeated objections to its promotion of greater self-determination for indigenous peoples (see Xanthaki, 2007, for a useful overview). Despite these objections, UNDRIP retained its strong assertion of indigenous rights, *including* specific promotion-oriented language and education rights. Article 14.1 states, for example, "Indigenous peoples have the right to establish and control their educational systems and institutions providing education in their own languages, in a manner appropriate to their cultural methods of teaching and learning." The key question remains though: Given many nation-states' reservations about the document, what likelihood is there of its meaningful implementation within those states?

Other developments in pan-European law also reflect these competing tensions between, on the one hand, a greater accommodation of promotion-oriented minority language and education rights, and on the other, the ongoing reticence of nation-states to accept such a view. The 1992 European Charter for Regional or Minority Languages is another such example. It provides a sliding scale of educational provision for national and regional minority languages (but not immigrant languages), which ranges from a minimal entitlement for smaller groups—preschool provision only, for example—through to more generous rights for larger minority groups such as elementary and secondary/high school language education. Again, however, European nation-states have discretion in what they provide, on the basis of both local considerations and the size of the group concerned. These nation-states also retain considerable scope and flexibility over which articles of the Charter they actually choose to accept in the first place. In this respect, they are only required to accede to 35 out of 68 articles, although 3 of the 35 articles must refer to education. The process here is twofold. A state must first sign the Charter, symbolically recognizing its commitment to the Charter's values and principles. Following this, states can ratify the treaty—formally recognizing, in this case, which particular regional or minority languages within the state are to be recognized under the treaty's auspices. On this basis, 33 European states have since signed the Charter, although only 24 of these have actually since ratified it (Council of Europe, 2008; Grin, 2003; Nic Craith, 2006).[8]

A similar pattern can be detected in the 1994 Framework Convention for the Protection of National Minorities, which was adopted by the Council of Europe in November 1994 and finally came into force in February 1998. The Framework Convention allows for a wide range of tolerance-based rights toward national minorities, including language and education rights. It also asserts at a more general level that contributing states should "promote the conditions necessary for persons belonging to national minorities to maintain and develop their culture, and to preserve the essential elements of their identity, namely their religion, language, traditions and cultural heritage" (Article 2.1). That said, the specific provisions for language and education remain sufficiently qualified for most states to avoid them if they so choose (Gilbert, 1996; Thornberry, 1997; Trenz, 2007; Troebst, 1998).

Territorial Language Principle

Despite the ongoing potential for noncompliance at the level of the nation-state, the increasing endorsement of promotion language rights in international law has also been reflected in some national and regional contexts. Where this has occurred, it has usually been based on one of two organizing principles. The first is the "territorial language principle," which grants language rights that are limited to a particular territory in order to ensure the maintenance of a particular language in that area (see Williams, 2008, for a useful overview). The most prominent examples of this principle can be found in Catalonia, Wales, and Québec, as well as in Belgium and Switzerland. Taking one of these examples, Catalonia has since 1979 used the territorial language principle to (re)establish Catalan as the working language of regional government and of education. Prior to this time, Catalan had been publically banned by the 40-year dictatorship of Franco's Spain (1936–1975) in favor of Castilian Spanish—this despite (or perhaps because of) Catalan boasting over 9 million speakers in Catalonia and throughout Europe (see May, 2012, chap. 7, for further discussion). With the advent, post-Franco, of the 1978 Spanish Constitution, however, a far greater emphasis was placed on the recognition of Spain's cultural and linguistic pluralism—granting specific cultural and linguistic rights, as well as a considerable degree of political autonomy, to the different national minorities within the Spanish state. The result was the establishment of 17 "autonomias," or autonomous regions within Spain, of which Catalonia was the first, as formalized by the 1979 Catalan Statute of Autonomy. The 1979 statute asserts that Catalan is "la llengua pròpia de Catalunya" (Catalonia's own language) and that "Catalan is the official language of Catalonia as Castilian is the official language of the whole of the Spanish state" (Article 3.2; see Artigal, 1997, p. 135; Guibernau, 1997, p. 96). The statute also stipulates a specific plan of action:

The Generalitat [Catalan regional government] . . . will guarantee the normal and official use of both languages, adopt whatever measures are deemed necessary to ensure both languages are known, and create suitable conditions so that full equality between the two can be achieved as far as the rights and duties of the citizens of Catalonia are concerned. (Article 3.3; cited in Strubell, 1998, p. 163)

The reestablishment of Catalan as a civic language since 1979 has been achieved by embarking on an extensive language policy program within Catalonia itself. The principal instrument of this program, at least initially, was the 1983 Llei de Normalització Lingüística (Law of Linguistic Normalization), also known as the "Charter of the Catalan Language." Linguistic normalization in the Catalonian context was first described by the Congress of Catalan Culture (1975–1977) as "a process during which a language gradually recovers the formal functions it [has] lost and at the same time works its way into those social sectors, within its own territory, where it was not spoken before" (cited in Torres, 1984, p. 59). In this light, and following Fishman (1991), the process of linguistic normalization subsequently embarked on in Catalonia can be described as having three broad initial aims:

1. To achieve the symbolic promotion and functional institutionalization of Catalan in all key public and private language domains, including, crucially, within schools
2. To redress illiteracy in Catalan, and any remaining sense of inferiority attached to Catalan, both legacies of the Franco years
3. Via a "policy of persuasion" (Woolard, 1989), to gain the commitment of first-language Spanish speakers to Catalan, while at the same time countering any hostility toward Catalan as a perceived "threat" to Spanish as the language of the Spanish state

Over the course of the past 30 years, Catalonia has been largely successful in achieving the first two objectives, although the third remains contested, with conservative elements elsewhere in Spain still viewing Catalan autonomy as a potential threat to the Spanish state (DiGiacomo, 1999; May, 2011). Nonetheless, as a result of these language policy developments, today Catalonian citizens have the right to use Catalan on all (public and private) occasions, while virtually all written and oral work in the Generalitat and local authorities is now undertaken in Catalan. More pertinently for our purposes, Catalan is also now the language of education. The latter was crucially facilitated by the 1998 Catalan Linguistic Policy Act, which supported the legal consolidation of Catalan language policies in schools and the wider civil service. The former was achieved by fully implementing unified Catalan immersion education, the latter by further strengthening formal Catalan language requirements for civil servants working in the Catalonian Generalitat and in local authorities. A second objective of the 1998 Act was to increase the presence of Catalan in the media and commerce fields (in which Castilian Spanish remains dominant), principally via the introduction of minimum Catalan language quota systems in the media and the requirement of bilingual service provision in the commercial sector (Pujolar, 2007). In this latter respect, the Act specifically called for private companies to implement programs and measures in support of the further use of Catalan at work. The third objective of the Act was a more broad-based one, to achieve full equality or comparability between Catalan and Spanish in all formal language domains. This included not only the devolved areas of administration regarded as the responsibility of the Catalonian Generalitat but also those areas that still remained under the jurisdiction of the Spanish central government, notably the judicial system, law and order, and tax administration (Costa, 2003).

More recently, an updated (2006) Catalan Statute of Autonomy further emphasizes the separate regional identity of Catalonia, as distinct from the wider Spanish state, and Catalan as its territorial language. As Colino (2009) summarizes it,

Following the notion that Catalan is Catalonia's only "proper" language, considering Spanish as simply the official state language, the new statute establishes Catalan as the language of preferential use in public administration bodies, in the public media and as the language of normal use for instruction in the education system, now extending this to university education . . . [it requires citizens] to know the regional language . . . thus equalizing its status with that of Spanish in the constitution. It also introduces the so-called obligation of linguistic availability, which imposes the obligation for businesses and establishments of answering its users or consumers in the language of their choice. (p. 275)

In addition, the 2006 statute extends promotion-oriented language rights within the region to the Aranese variant of Occitan, spoken in the subregion of Val d'Aran, and to Catalan sign language, both of which are elevated to co-official languages alongside Catalan and Castilian. The new statute also directly addresses the rights of other language speakers, particularly the growing number of Arabic and Urdu speakers who have migrated to the region in increasing numbers over the past decade. Specific tolerance-oriented language rights are now provided so that other language speakers can maintain these languages privately, if they so choose, as well as ensuring access to key services and opportunities to learn the official languages of the region (París, 2007).

Personality Language Principle

The second approach to the promotion of minority language rights is predicated on the "personality language principle," which attaches language rights to individuals, irrespective of their geographical position. This provides greater flexibility than the territorial language principle in the apportionment of group-based language rights, although it also has its strictures. The most notable of these is the criterion "where numbers warrant"—that is, language rights may be granted only when there are deemed to be a *sufficient* number of particular language speakers to warrant active language protection and the related use of such languages in the public domain. Canada adopts the personality language principle, where numbers warrant, in relation to French speakers outside of Quebec, via the 1982 Canadian Charter of Rights and Freedoms. A similar approach is adopted in Finland with respect to first-language Swedish speakers living there. Swedish speakers can use their language in the public domain in those local municipalities where there are a sufficient number of Swedish speakers (currently, at least 8%) for these municipalities to be deemed officially bilingual. With over 200 language varieties spoken across 30 states and five Union territories, India though, provides perhaps the best example of this principle in operation. On one hand, we have seen in India the long-standing promotion of English, and more recently Hindi, as the state's elite, pan-Indian, languages. On the other hand, there are 18 languages recognized in India as "principal-medium languages," which, in addition to English and Hindi, include 16 official state languages. The division of India's states along largely linguistic grounds means that local linguistic communities have control over their public schools and other educational institutions. This, in turn, ensures that the primary language of the area is used as a medium of instruction in state schools (see Daswani, 2001; Schiffman, 1996). Indeed, dominant regional language schools account for 88% of all elementary schools in India (Khubchandani, 2008). But not only that, the Constitution of India (Article 350A) directs every state, and every local authority within that state, to provide "adequate" educational facilities for instruction in the L1 of linguistic minorities, at least at elementary school level. As a result, over 80 minority languages are employed as mediums of instruction in elementary schools throughout India.

Recent developments in both international and national law are, then, at once both encouraging and disappointing. The principle of separate minority recognition in language and education is legally enshrined at least as a minimal tolerance-oriented right—that is, unhindered ongoing language use when restricted to the private domain—in almost all modern nation-states[9] and is reinforced by clear intent in instruments of international law. However, more liberal interpretations of tolerance-oriented rights (involving some state support where numbers warrant), and certainly more promotion-oriented rights, are less secure and remain largely dependent on the largesse of individual nation-states in their interpretation of international (and national) law with respect to minorities. As a result, there are as yet no watertight legal guarantees for the recognition and funding of minority language and education rights, although there is a clearly articulated basis for them.

At the very least though, there is an increasing recognition within both international law, and in a growing number of national contexts, that significant minorities within the nation-state have a *reasonable* expectation to some form of state support (Carens, 2000; de Varennes, 1996). In other words, although it would be unreasonable for nation-states to be required to fund language and education services for all minorities, it is increasingly accepted that where a language is spoken by a significant number within the nation-state, it would also be unreasonable not to provide some level of state services and activity in that language. In combination, this provides an ever-strengthening basis for minority language education rights.

THE CASE FOR (AND AGAINST) BILINGUAL EDUCATION

Having addressed the basis for language rights in both international and national law, let me now turn to the key educational tenets underpinning a more linguistically diverse approach to language learning within schools. This is crucial, because contra to the oft-stated position that the best means of learning English is via English-only instruction, the best means of learning English (or any additional language) is actually via one's L1. Indeed, it has long been demonstrated that English-only education programs are the *least* effective means of successfully acquiring (bi)literacy for bilingual learners (May, 2010; see also below). The reason for this, of course, is that such programs demonstrably fail to build on the *existing* linguistic repertoires of bi/multilingual learners—instead, willfully ignoring and/or excluding them from the teaching and learning process (May, 2014). Moreover, their principal aim is usually for learners eventually to become monolingual in English at the specific expense of their bi/multilingualism—as the earlier accounts of Archibugi (2005), Pogge (2003), and the like would clearly seem to suggest.

In contrast, extensive international research on bilingual education consistently finds that long-term or "late-exit" bilingual programs are the most effective educationally for bilingual students, followed by short-term or "early-exit" bilingual education programs. The academic literature supporting these conclusions is voluminous and I am not able to explore it in detail here (see C. Baker, 2011; García, 2009; May, 2008a, for useful recent overviews). But I will discuss briefly, by way of example, two major studies, both conducted in the United States, which clearly support these general conclusions.

Ramírez, Yuen, and Ramey (1991) compared English-only programs with early-exit and late-exit bilingual programs, following 2,352 Spanish-speaking students over 4 years. Their findings clearly demonstrated that the greatest growth in mathematics, English language skills, and English reading was among students in late-exit bilingual programs where students had been taught predominantly in Spanish (the students' L1). For example, students in two late-exit sites that continued L1 instruction through to Grade 6 made significantly better academic progress than those who were transferred early into all-English instruction. Ramírez et al. conclude,

Students who were provided with a substantial and consistent primary language development program learned mathematics, English language, and English reading skills as fast or faster than the norming population in this study. As their growth in these academic skills is atypical of disadvantaged youth, it provides support for the efficacy of primary language development facilitating the acquisition of English language skills. (pp. 38–39)

In contrast, the Ramírez et al. (1991) study also confirmed that minority language students who receive most of their education in English rather than their L1 are *more* likely to fall behind and drop out of school. In fact, it is important to note here that the English-only programs used for comparison in the Ramírez study were not typical to the extent that although the teachers taught in English, they nonetheless understood Spanish. This suggests that in the far more common situation where the teacher does not understand the students' L1, the trends described here are likely to be further accentuated.

In the largest study conducted to date, Thomas and Collier (2002) came to broadly the same conclusions. Between 1996 and 2001 Thomas and Collier analyzed the education services provided for over 210,000 language minority students in U.S. public schools and the resulting long-term academic achievement of these students. As with the Ramírez et al. (1991) study, one of Thomas and Collier's (2002) principal research findings was that the most effective programs—"feature-rich" programs as they called them—resulted in achievement gains for bilingual students that were above the level of their monolingual peers in English-only classes. Another key conclusion was that these gains, in both L1 *and* second language (L2), were most evident in those programs where the students' L1 was a language of instruction for an extended period of time. In other words, Thomas and Collier found that *the strongest predictor of student achievement in L2 was the amount of formal L1 schooling they experienced*: "The more L1 grade-level schooling, the higher L2 achievement" (p. 7). Thomas and Collier also found that students in English-only classes performed far less well than their peers in late-exit bilingual programs, as well as dropping out of school in greater numbers. Students in early-exit, transitional, bilingual programs demonstrated better academic performance over time but not to the extent of late-exit bilingual programs. In both these major studies, then, length of L1 education turned out to be more influential than *any* other factor in predicting the educational success of bilingual students, *including* socioeconomic status.

There are a wide range of other studies, both from the United States and from other national contexts, that broadly corroborate these findings.[10] Suffice it to say, these findings, when taken cumulatively, unequivocally support the efficacy of late-exit bilingual education[11] and thus stand in direct contradiction to Archibugi (2005), Pogge (2003), and Laitin and Reich's (2003) conclusions about bilingual education for Latino students, discussed earlier. English-only instruction ensures neither "fluency in English" (Pogge, 2003) nor participation in "broader societal culture" (Laitin & Reich, 2003). Indeed, it is most often the *cause* of, rather than the solution to, the educational failure of bilingual students. Why then, given the widely attested efficacy of bilingual education, does it still so seldom translate into policy and practice in the language education provision for linguistic-minority students? Again, the answer is primarily a sociopolitical/sociohistorical one, rather than an educational one per se. Returning to the pluralist dilemma, the imperative of civism, which, in this case, requires the linguistic assimilation of minority students as the "price" of citizenship, outweighs any arguments for the educational efficacy of bilingual education and/or the educational and wider benefits that would result for those students. Or, to put it another way, research evidence that appears to contradict the dominance of English and/or the related ideology of public monolingualism is not a welcome feature for those wishing to buttress or ensure them. As Thomas Ricento (1996) observes of the U.S. context, for example, in spite of an impressive amount of both qualitative and quantitative research now available on the merits of bilingual education, "The public debate (to the extent that there is one) [still] tends to focus on perceptions and not on facts" (p. 142). Or as Joshua Fishman (1992) despairingly asks of the same context, "Why are facts so useless in this discussion?" (p. 167). This laissez-faire approach to the facts is no more starkly demonstrated than in the ideology and political advocacy of the so-called official English movement in the United States—or, as I prefer to term it, the *English-only* movement.

The English-Only Movement

Since its inception in the early 1980s, the English-only movement has been preoccupied with achieving an English Language Amendment (ELA) to the U.S. constitution that would recognize English as the official language of the United States.[12] The aim of an ELA is to ensure that English is the only language of government activity (see Crawford, 2000, 2008) and to "require" immigrants to the United States—and here Latinos are particularly targeted—to learn English (with an implicit, sometimes explicit, agenda that this should be *at the specific expense* of their L1). To date, all ELA proposals at the federal level have failed. However, the English-only movement has increasingly turned to the state level to enact its political aims. As Daniels (1990) observes of the latter, "The overall strategy [here] seems to be to get some official-English law on the books of a majority of states and to continually fan public resentment over schooling policies that 'degrade English' and 'cater' to immigrants" (p. 8). This state-level approach has also included specifically targeting existing bilingual education programs. For example, in a U.S. English advertisement in 1998, the tagline read,

Deprive a child of an education. Handicap a young life outside the classroom. Restrict social mobility. If it came at the hand of a parent it would be called child abuse. At the hand of our schools . . . it's called "bilingual education" (cited in Dicker, 2000, p. 53).

This has also been the leitmotif of Ron Unz, a prominent software entrepreneur and conservative public figure, and his organization, English for the Children. Targeting four key U.S. states that allow for citizens-initiated referenda, Unz has successfully promoted public propositions delimiting or dismantling bilingual education in three of these states. The most prominent of these is California's Proposition 227 (1998), which saw 61% support the measure overall, *including* 37% of Latino voters. However, Unz was also successful in sponsoring similar measures in Arizona (2000; 63%) and Massachusetts (2002; 68%). Only in Colorado (2002; 44%) was a comparable measure defeated, although, controversially, this was because those opposing the measure played on the fears of Anglo parents that this would result in the reintroduction of too many Latino students into mainstream classrooms (Crawford, 2007). Suffice it to say, in none of the referenda did research evidence in support of the educational efficacy of bilingual education inform wider public debate. Prior to the Arizona referendum (Proposition 203), for example, the *New York Times* ran a front-page story in August 2000 strongly supporting the apparently incontrovertible educational merits of its precursor, Proposition 227. Subsequently, it was revealed that the claims made in the article simply repeated key talking points in Unz's campaign, although, not surprisingly, it still had a powerful effect on strengthening public support for Proposition 203 (Wiley & Wright, 2004; Wright, 2005).

This pattern of deliberate misrepresentation and obfuscation by proponents of English-only continues to the present largely unabated. For example, George W. Bush's flagship NCLB (2001) saw the revocation of the 1968 Bilingual Education

Act on the premise that English language instruction and assessment is best for all students.[13] Subsequent advocacy of NCLB has touted its positive effects for bilingual students. However, research evidence again suggests the opposite is true. Menken (2008) has documented the clearly negative educational effects that NCLB testing policies are having on bilingual students. She found in New York City, for example, that, as a result of NCLB's requirement to be assessed in English, with no recourse to one's L1, bilingual students ranged from 20 to 50 percentage points below native English speakers.

Insisting on the merits of English-only education for bilingual students in the face of research evidence that clearly suggests otherwise demonstrates a remarkable degree of cynicism. But this cynicism becomes breathtaking when measured against another variable: the funding of English-only programs. In this respect, the English-only movement is again clearly found wanting. Many who supported the establishment of official state-level English policies, for example, including the Unz-led referenda against bilingual education, logically assumed that a principal concern of the legislation was to expand the opportunities for immigrants to learn English. However, logical or not, this has proved not to be the case. Although the English-only movement spent lavishly to get ELA measures on the ballot, in 1988 it declined to support legislation creating a modestly funded federal program for adult learners of English (Crawford, 1992). As a result of public criticism, the English-only movement did make some subsequent effort to fund similar ventures, but these efforts have remained largely desultory and continue to constitute only the barest minimum of their total funding efforts (Dicker, 2000).

CONCLUSION

The example of the English-only movement in the United States, and its ongoing political effectiveness in delimiting bilingual education there, should remind us why there has been such an effective retrenchment of more plurilingual approaches to language education over the past two decades, as discussed at the outset of this article. Indeed, my aim in (necessarily) covering so much ground in this account is precisely to highlight how difficult it is to make the case for minority language rights, despite the positive developments in international law and (some) national contexts. This is because of a confluence of ongoing forces arraigned against such rights being recognized and enacted—the predilection toward civism (and a related public monolingualism) at the level of the nation-state, as well as the valorization of English as the new language of cosmopolitanism and of social mobility in an increasingly globalized world. Add to this a lingering antipathy to minority linguistic identification that is, more often than not, constructed by opponents as antediluvian and/or as an attempt at willful ghettoization by minorities, and one can see just what is at stake. These difficulties also explain why bilingual education approaches, despite their attested educational efficacy, are potentially so fragile and easily dismantled as a result of the wider social and political vicissitudes described above.

Even so, as this account also makes clear, much too has been achieved since the advent of multiculturalism in the 1960s/70s, and not all these accomplishments have been retrenched over the past 20 years. Indeed, there is a nascent consensus that suggests that the long-held practice of making no accommodations to linguistic-minority demands is not so readily defensible in today's social and political climate. Ignoring such demands is also unlikely to quell or abate the question of minority rights, as it might once have done. Indeed, it is much more likely to escalate them, not least because minority groups are far less quiescent about the injustices attendant on their long-standing cultural and linguistic marginalization as the price of civic inclusion in the (monolingual) nation-state (May, 2012). Under these circumstances, as de Varennes (1996) outlines,

> Any policy favouring a single language to the exclusion of all others can be extremely risky . . . because it is then a factor promoting division rather than unification. Instead of integration, an ill-advised and inappropriate state language policy may have the opposite effect and cause a levée de bouclier. (p. 91)

As for bilingual education, so often the frontline in these wider debates, there is the related responsibility of those well versed in the research literature to articulate clearly and consistently the benefits of more plurilingual approaches to the education of bi/multilingual students—in both academic and the wider public domains. As McGroarty (2006) argues,

> It is the job of [those] interested in policies that include attention to bilingualism to keep the value of bilingualism in the public consciousness, to continue to demonstrate that bilingual approaches to education are not only feasible but, in fact, actually exist. (2006, p. 5)

In order to achieve this, McGroarty (2006) continues, "Advocates for positive language and education policies must constantly articulate the value of bilingualism, and to be able to do so in varied terms that respond to a protean environment of public discussion" (pp. 5–6). A failure to do so will mean that the clearly attested educational effectiveness of bilingual/immersion programs will continue to be (conveniently) overlooked in these wider public debates, to the inevitable cost of bilingual students. More broadly, it is only from an informed research base, which in turn directly influences language educational policy development, that further progress can be made on realigning the predilection to monolingualism that still so dominates public policy on language education—particularly, but not exclusively, when the language in question is the new global juggernaut of English.

NOTES

[1]Although these two positions presuppose significantly different historical trajectories for globalization, they are not necessarily incompatible. Blommaert (2010), for example, argues that geopolitical globalization has clearly emerged from earlier historical antecedents such as capitalist expansion in the 19th century. Meanwhile, geocultural globalization is linked to the more recent features of late capitalism, such as new technologies, business process outsourcing (e.g., establishing multinational company call centers in developing countries), and related

changes in migration patterns; the division of labor; migration; and wider social and economic inequalities.

[2]This is, in fact, a wildly historically inaccurate assertion—amounting to what I have elsewhere described as deliberate "historical amnesia" (May, 2005). Indeed, the United States has had both a bi/multilingual population and a related accommodation (albeit limited) in its legislative history of public bilingualism since its inception as a modern nation-state (see Dicker, 2003; May, 2012, chap. 6, for an extended discussion).

[3]This is more accurately described as "submersion" in English or an English-only educational approach (see below for further discussion).

[4]Although this might suggest that Pogge (2003) is not, ipso facto, opposed to ongoing bilingualism, the parentheses are a telling example of where the priorities still lie. Moreover, the underlying premises of English-only educational instruction specifically militate against the maintenance of students' bilingualism, a point I will return to in more detail in due course.

[5]See, for example, Z. Bauman (1998), Held (1995), Held et al. (1999), Heller (2003, 2008, 2011), Hobsbawm (2008), Kraidy (2005), Pieterse (2009), and Robertson (1992).

[6]Drawing on Will Kymlicka's (1995) seminal work, national and ethnic minority groups can be distinguished as follows. National minorities are those groups that have always been associated historically with a particular territory but have been subject to colonization, conquest, or confederation and, consequently, now have only minority status within a particular nation-state. These groups include, for example, the Welsh in Britain, Catalans and Basques in Spain, Bretons in France, Quebecois in Canada, and some Latino groups (e.g., Puerto Ricans) in the United States, to name but a few. National minorities also include the world's indigenous peoples who have been subject to the same historical processes, but often at much greater cost. Ethnic minorities, in contrast, have migrated from their country of origin to a new host nation-state, or in the case of refugees have been the subject of forced relocation. For further discussion of the implications of this distinction for language rights, see May (2012, chap. 3).

[7]Macías (1979) distinguishes between two broadly comparable sets of rights: the right to freedom from discrimination on the basis of language, and the right to use your language(s) in the activities of communal life.

[8]As of 2013, eight European states have signed the Charter but not ratified it: Azerbaijan, France, Iceland, Italy, Malta, Moldova, Russia, and the Former Yugoslav Republic of Macedonia.

[9]Nonetheless, there remain a few rogue states in this regard. The ongoing state-sanctioned proscriptions of Kurdish in Turkey and Tibetan in China are two contemporary examples of states that continue to flout this human rights' principle.

[10]See, for example, Cummins (2000), Fortune and Tedick (2008), Genesee (2008), May (2013), May and Aikman (2003), Tedick, Christian, and Fortune (2011), and Tollefson and Tsui (2004) for national and international examples of the effectiveness of bilingual education. For ethnographic accounts of highly successful bilingual schools, see also Freeman (1998, 2004), May (1993, 1994), McCarty (2002), and Pérez (2003).

[11]There are a few studies that have apparently contradicted these broad findings on the efficacy of late-exit bilingual education—most notably, K. Baker and de Kanter (1981, 1983) and Rossell and Baker (1996)—and which, as a result, have been used prominently in arguments for the disestablishment of bilingual education programs, particularly in the United States (see below). However, these studies have since been widely discredited (see May, 2008a, for further discussion).

[12]The fact that it is not may be surprising to some. However, the United States, at the time of confederation, followed the British laissez-faire language policy model, recognizing English as the dominant language but rejecting the need to make it official (see Dicker, 2003).

[13]The remit of the 1968 Bilingual Education Act was to rectify the poor educational performance of "limited English-speaking ability" students, rather than dealing with issues of bilingualism per se (Shannon, 1999). Nonetheless, it was a consistent target of the English-only movement because it ostensibly allowed for the development of both transitional (early-exit) bilingual programs and late-exit bilingual approaches, the latter being a particular anathema to English-only proponents. The reality, as always with the English-only movement, was somewhat different. The Act was a modest, consistently underfunded, grant-in-aid program that focused almost solely on transitional bilingual programs over its 30-year history (Ricento & Wright, 2008). Moreover, the increasing hostility generated toward bilingual education over that period meant that each time the Act came up for reauthorization, its remit was further delimited. In short the Act's influence was far less than its opponents proclaimed. This also, perhaps, explains why it was so easily dispensed with in the end by the then–Bush administration.

REFERENCES

Alexandre, P. (1972). *Languages and language in Black Africa.* Evanston, IL: Northwestern University Press.

Archibugi, D. (2005). The language of democracy: Vernacular or Esperanto? A comparison between the multiculturalist and cosmopolitan perspectives. *Political Studies, 53,* 537–555.

Artigal, J. (1997). The Catalan immersion program. In R. Johnson & M. Swain (Eds.), *Immersion education: International perspectives* (pp. 133–150). Cambridge, England: Cambridge University Press.

Baker, C. (2011). *Foundations of bilingual education and bilingualism* (5th ed.). Bristol, England: Multilingual Matters.

Baker, K., & de Kanter, A. (1981). *Effectiveness of bilingual education: A review of the literature.* Washington, DC: U.S. Department of Education.

Baker, K., & de Kanter, A. (Eds.). (1983). *Bilingual education: A reappraisal of federal policy.* Lexington, MA: Lexington Books.

Banks, J., & Banks, C. (Eds.). (2004). *Handbook of research on multicultural education* (2nd ed.). San Francisco, CA: Jossey-Bass.

Barry, B. (2001). *Culture and equality: An egalitarian critique of multiculturalism.* Cambridge, MA: Harvard University Press.

Bauman, R., & Briggs, C. (2003). *Voices of modernity: Language ideologies and the politics of inequality.* Cambridge, England: Cambridge University Press.

Bauman, Z. (1998). *Globalization: The human consequences.* London, England: Sage.

Blommaert, J. (2010). *The sociolinguistics of globalization.* New York, NY: Cambridge University Press.

Blommaert, J., Muyllaert, N., Huysmans, M., & Dyers, C. (2006). Peripheral normativity: Literacy and the production of locality in a South African township school. *Linguistics and Education, 16,* 378–403.

Blommaert, J., Peppännen, S., & Spotti, M. (2012). Endangering multilingualism. In J. Blommaert, S. Leppänen, P. Pahta, & T. Raisanen (Eds.), *Dangerous multilingualism: Nordic perspectives on order: Purity and normality* (pp. 1–21). London, England: Palgrave Macmillan.

Bullivant, B. (1981). *The pluralist dilemma in education: Six case studies.* Sydney, New South Wales, Australia: Allen & Unwin.

Calhoun, C. (2003). Belonging in the cosmopolitan imaginary. *Ethnicities, 3,* 531–553.

Calhoun, C. (2007). Social solidarity as a problem for cosmopolitan democracy. In S. Benhabib, I. Shapiro, & D. Petranovic (Eds.), *Identities, affiliations, and allegiances* (pp. 285–302). Cambridge, England: Cambridge University Press.

Carens, J. (2000). *Culture, citizenship and community: A contextual exploration of justice as evenhandedness.* Oxford, England: Oxford University Press.

Colino, C. (2009). Constitutional change without constitutional reform: Spanish federalism and the revision of Catalonia's Statute of Autonomy. *Publius, 39,* 262–288.

Costa, J. (2003). Catalan linguistic policy: Liberal or illiberal? *Nations and Nationalism, 9,* 413–432.

Council of Europe. (2008). *The European Charter for Regional or Minority Languages: Legal challenges and opportunities.* Strasbourg Cedex, France: Author.

Cox, R. (1996). A perspective on globalization. In J. M. Mittelman (Ed.), *Globalization: critical reflections* (pp. 21–30). Boulder, CO: Lynne Rienner.

Crawford, J. (1992). *Hold your tongue: Bilingualism and the politics of "English only."* Reading, MA: Addison-Wesley.

Crawford, J. (2000). *At war with diversity: US language policy in an age of anxiety.* Clevedon, England: Multilingual Matters.

Crawford, J. (2007). Hard sell: Why is bilingual education so unpopular with the American public? In O. García & C. Baker (Eds.), *Bilingual education: An introductory reader* (pp. 145–161). Clevedon, England: Multilingual Matters.

Crawford, J. (2008). *Advocating for English learners: Selected essays.* Clevedon, England: Multilingual Matters.

Cummins, J. (2000). *Language, power and pedagogy: Bilingual children in the crossfire.* Clevedon, England: Multilingual Matters.

Daniels, H. (1990). The roots of language protectionism. In H. Daniels (Ed.), *Not only English: Affirming America's multilingual heritage* (pp. 3–12). Urbana, IL: National Council of Teachers.

Dasgupta, P. (1993). *The otherness of English: India's auntie tongue syndrome.* London, England: Sage.

Daswani, C. (Ed.). (2001). *Language education in multilingual India.* New Delhi, India: UNESCO.

de Varennes, F. (1996). *Language, minorities and human rights.* The Hague, Netherlands: Kluwer Law International.

de Varennes, F. (2001). Language rights as an integral part of human rights. *International Journal on Multicultural Studies, 3,* 15–25.

Dicker, S. (2000). Official English and bilingual education: The controversy over language pluralism in US society. In J. K. Hall & W. Eggington (Eds.), *The sociopolitics of English language teaching* (pp. 45–66). Clevedon, England: Multilingual Matters.

Dicker, S. (2003). *Languages in America* (2nd ed). Clevedon, England: Multilingual Matters.

DiGiacomo, S. (1999). Language ideological debates in an Olympic city: Barcelona 1992–1996. In J. Blommaert (Ed.), *Language ideological debates* (pp. 105–142). Berlin, Germany: Mouton de Gruyter.

Dworkin, R. (1978). Liberalism. In S. Hampshire (Ed.), *Public and private morality* (pp. 113–143). Cambridge, England: Cambridge University Press.

Dworkin, R. (2000). *Sovereign virtue: The theory and practice of equality.* Cambridge, MA: Harvard University Press.

Fishman, J. (1991). *Reversing language shift: Theoretical and empirical foundations of assistance to threatened languages.* Clevedon, England: Multilingual Matters.

Fishman, J. (1992). The displaced anxieties of Anglo-Americans. In J. Crawford (Ed.), *Language loyalties: A source book on the Official English controversy* (pp. 165–170). Chicago, IL: University of Chicago Press.

Fortune, T., & Tedick, D. (Eds.). (2008). *Pathways to multilingualism: Evolving perspectives on immersion education.* Clevedon, England: Multilingual Matters.

Freeman, R. (1998). *Bilingual education and social change.* Clevedon, England: Multilingual Matters.

Freeman, R. (2004). *Building on community bilingualism*. Clevedon, England: Multilingual Matters.

García, O. (1995). Spanish language loss as a determinant of income among Latinos in the United States: Implications for language policies in schools. In J. Tollefson (Ed.), *Power and inequality in language education* (pp. 142–160). Cambridge, England: Cambridge University Press.

García, O. (2009). *Bilingual education in the 21st century: A global perspective*. Malden, MA: Blackwell.

Genesee, F. (2008). Dual language in the global village. In T. Fortune & D. Tedick (Eds.), *Pathways to multilingualism: Evolving perspectives on immersion education* (pp. 22–45). Clevedon, England: Multilingual Matters.

Gilbert, G. (1996). The Council of Europe and minority rights. *Human Rights Quarterly, 18*, 160–189.

Glazer, N. (1998). *We are all multiculturalists now*. Cambridge, MA: Harvard University Press.

Goldberg, D. (1994). Introduction: Multicultural conditions. In D. Goldberg (Ed.), *Multiculturalism: A critical reader* (pp. 1–41). Oxford, England: Basil Blackwell.

Gordon, M. (1978). *Human nature, class and ethnicity*. New York, NY: Oxford University Press.

Gordon, M. (1981). Models of pluralism: The new American dilemma. *Annals of the American Academy of Political and Social Science, 454*, 178–188.

Graddol, D. (2007). *English next: Why global English may mean the end of "English as a Foreign Language."* London, England: British Council.

Grin, F. (2003). *Language policy evaluation and the European Charter for Regional or Minority Languages*. London, England: Palgrave Macmillan.

Guibernau, M. (1997). Images of Catalonia. *Nations and Nationalism, 3*, 89–111.

Held, D. (1995). *Democracy and the global order: From the modern state to cosmopolitan governance*. Cambridge, England: Polity Press.

Held, D., McGrew, A., Goldblatt, D., & Perraton, J. (1999). *Global transformations: Politics, economics and culture*. Cambridge, England: Polity Press.

Heller, M. (2003). Globalization, the new economy, and the commodification of language and identity. *Journal of Sociolinguistics, 7*, 473–492.

Heller, M. (2008). Language and the nation-state: Challenges to sociolinguistic theory and practice. *Journal of Sociolinguistics, 12*, 504–524.

Heller, M. (2011). *Paths to post-nationalism: A critical ethnography of language and identity*. Oxford, England: Oxford University Press.

Heugh, K. (2008). Language policy in Southern Africa. In S. May & N. Hornberger (Eds.), *Encyclopedia of language and education (2nd ed.): Vol. 1. Language policy and political issues in education* (pp. 355–367). New York, NY: Springer.

Hinsley, F. (1986). *Sovereignty*. Cambridge, England: Cambridge University Press.

Hobsbawm, E. (2008). *Globalisation, democracy and terrorism*. London, England: Abacus.

Ives, P. (2010). Cosmopolitanism and global English: Language politics in globalisation debates. *Political Studies, 58*, 516–535.

Kellough, J. (2006). *Understanding affirmative action: Politics, discrimination, and the search for justice*. Washington, DC: Georgetown University Press.

Khubchandani, L. (2008). Language policy and education in the Indian subcontinent. In S. May & N. Hornberger (Eds.), *Encyclopedia of language and education (2nd ed.): Vol. 1. Language policy and political issues in education* (pp. 369–381). New York, NY: Springer.

Kloss, H. (1971). The language rights of immigrant groups. *International Migration Review, 5*, 250–268.

Kloss, H. (1977). *The American bilingual tradition*. Rowley, MA: Newbury House.

Kraidy, M. (2005). *Hybridity, or the cultural logic of globalization*. Philadelphia, PA: Temple University Press.

Kymlicka, W. (1989). *Liberalism, community and culture*. Oxford, England: Clarendon Press.

Kymlicka, W. (1995). *Multicultural citizenship: A liberal theory of minority rights*. Oxford, England: Clarendon Press.

Kymlicka, W. (2001). *Politics in the vernacular: Nationalism, multiculturalism, citizenship*. Oxford, England: Oxford University Press.

Kymlicka, W. (2007). *Multicultural odysseys: Navigating the new international politics of diversity*. Oxford, England: Oxford University Press.

Laitin, D., & Reich, R. (2003). A liberal democratic approach to language justice. In W. Kymlicka & A. Patten (Eds.), *Language rights and political theory* (pp. 80–104). Oxford, England: Oxford University Press.

Macedo, D. (1994). *Literacies of power: What Americans are not allowed to know*. Boulder CO: Westview Press.

Macías, R. (1979). Language choice and human rights in the United States. In J. Alatis & G. Tucker (Eds.), *Language in public life: Georgetown University round table on language and linguistics* (pp. 86–101). Washington, DC: Georgetown University Press.

May, S. (1993). Redeeming multicultural education. *Language Arts, 70*, 364–372.

May, S. (1994). *Making multicultural education work*. Clevedon, England: Multilingual Matters.

May, S. (Ed.). (1999). *Critical multiculturalism: Rethinking multicultural and antiracist education*. London, England: Routledge Falmer.

May, S. (2005). Language rights: Moving the debate forward. *Journal of Sociolinguistics, 9*, 319–347.

May, S. (2008a). Bilingual/immersion education: What the research tells us. In J. Cummins & N. Hornberger (Eds.), *Encyclopedia of language and education (2nd ed.): Vol. 5. Bilingual education* (pp. 19–34). New York, NY: Springer.

May, S. (2008b). Language education, pluralism and citizenship. In S. May & N. Hornberger (Eds.), *Encyclopedia of language and education: Language policy and political issues in education* (2nd ed., Vol. 1, pp. 15-29). New York, NY: Springer.

May, S. (2009). Critical multiculturalism and education. In J. Banks (Ed.), *Routledge international companion to multicultural education* (pp. 33-48). New York, NY: Routledge.

May, S. (2010). Curriculum and the education of cultural and linguistic minorities. In B. McGraw, E. Baker, & P. Peterson (Eds.), *International encyclopedia of education* (3rd ed., Vol. 1, pp. 293–298). Oxford, England: Elsevier.

May, S. (2011). Language rights: The "Cinderella" human right. *Journal of Human Rights, 10*, 265–289.

May, S. (2012). *Language and minority rights: Ethnicity, nationalism and the politics of language* (2nd ed.). New York, NY: Routledge.

May, S. (2013). Indigenous immersion education: International developments. *Journal of Immersion and Content-Based Education, 1*, 34–69.

May, S. (Ed.). (2014). *The multilingual turn: Implications for SLA, TESOL and bilingual education*. New York, NY: Routledge.

May, S., & Aikman, S. (Eds.). (2003). Indigenous education: New possibilities, ongoing restraints. *Comparative Education, 39*, 139–145.

May, S., & Sleeter, C. (Eds.). (2010). *Critical multiculturalism: Theory and praxis*. New York, NY: Routledge.

McCarty, T. (2002). *A place to be Navajo*. New York, NY: Routledge.

McGroarty, M. (2006). Neoliberal collusion or strategic simultaneity? On multiple rationales for language-in-education policies. *Language Policy, 5*, 3–13.

Menken, K. (2008). *English learners left behind: Standardized testing as language policy*. Clevedon, England: Multilingual Matters.

Modood, T. (2007). *Multiculturalism: A civic idea.* Cambridge, England: Polity Press.

Modood, T., & May, S. (2001). Multiculturalism and education in Britain: An internally contested debate. *International Journal of Educational Research 35*(3), 305-317.

Morgan, B., & Ramanathan, V. (2009). Outsourcing, globalizing economics, and shifting language policies: Issues in managing Indian call centers. *Language Policy, 8,* 69–80.

Ngũgĩ, w. T. (1993). *Moving the centre: The struggle for cultural freedoms.* London, England: James Currey.

Nic Craith, M. (2006). *Europe and the politics of language: Citizens, migrants, and outsiders.* London, England: Palgrave-Macmillan.

Nussbaum, M. (1997). *Cultivating humanity.* Cambridge, MA: Harvard University Press.

Parekh, B. (2000). *Rethinking multiculturalism: Cultural diversity and political theory.* London, England: Macmillan.

París, M. (2007). *Language policy as social policy: The role of languages in an open society.* Retrieved from http://www20.gencat.cat/docs/Llengcat/Documents/Publicacions/Publicacions%20en%20linea/Arxius/conf_spl2007_ang.pdf

Pattanayak, D. (1969). *Aspects of applied linguistics.* London, England: Asia Publishing House.

Pattanayak, D. (1985). Diversity in communication and languages; Predicament of a multilingual nation state: India, a case study. In N. Wolfson & J. Manes (Eds.), *Language of inequality* (pp. 399–407). Berlin, Germany: Mouton de Gruyter.

Pattanayak, D. (Ed.). (1990). *Multilingualism in India.* Clevedon, England: Multilingual Matters.

Pérez, B. (2003). *Becoming biliterate: A study of two-way bilingual immersion education.* Mahwah, NJ: Lawrence Erlbaum.

Pieterse, J. (2009). *Globalization and culture: Global mélange* (2nd ed.). Lanham, MA: Rowman & Littlefield.

Pogge, T. (2003). Accommodation rights for Hispanics in the US. In W. Kymlicka & A. Patten (Eds.) *Language rights and political theory* (pp. 105–122). Oxford, England: Oxford University Press.

Pujolar, J. (2007). The future of Catalan: Language endangerment and nationalist discourses in Catalonia. In A. Duchêne & M. Heller (Eds.), *Discourses of endangerment: Ideology and interest in the defence of languages* (pp. 121–148). London, England: Continuum.

Ramírez, J., Yuen, S., & Ramey, D. (1991). *Final report: Longitudinal study of structured English immersion strategy, early-exit and late-exit transitional bilingual education programs for language-minority children.* San Mateo, CA: Aguirre International.

Rawls, J. (1971). *A theory of justice.* Oxford, England: Oxford University Press.

Rawls, J. (1999). *The law of peoples.* Cambridge, MA: Harvard University Press.

Ricento, T. (1996). Language policy in the United States. In M. Herriman & B. Burnaby (Eds.), *Language policies in English-dominant countries* (pp. 122–158). Clevedon, England: Multilingual Matters.

Ricento, T., & Wright, W. (2008). Language policy and education in the United States. In S. May & N. Hornberger (Eds.), *Encyclopedia of language and education (2nd ed.): Vol. 1. Language policy and political issues in education* (pp. 285–300). New York, NY: Springer.

Robertson, R. (1992). *Globalization: Social theory and global culture.* London, England: Sage.

Robertson, R. (1995). Globalization: Time-space and homogeneity-heterogeneity. In M. Featherstone, S. Lash, & R. Robertson (Eds.), *Global modernities* (pp. 25–44). London, England: Sage.

Rossell, C., & Baker, K. (1996). The effectiveness of bilingual education. *Research in the Teaching of English, 30,* 7–74.

San Miguel, G., & Valencia, R. (1998). From the Treaty of Guadalupe Hidalgo to Hopwood: The educational plight and struggle of Mexican Americans in the Southwest. *Harvard Educational Review, 68,* 353–412.

Schermerhorn, R. (1970). *Comparative ethnic relations.* New York, NY: Random House.

Schiffman, H. (1996). *Linguistic culture and language policy.* London, England: Routledge.

Schmied, J. (1991). *English in Africa: An introduction.* London, England: Longman.

Shannon, S. (1999). The debate on bilingual education in the US: Language ideology as reflected in the practice of bilingual teachers. In J. Blommaert (Ed.), *Language ideological debates* (pp. 171–199). Berlin, Germany: Mouton de Gruyter.

Skutnabb-Kangas, T. (2000). *Linguistic genocide in education—or worldwide diversity and human rights?* Mahwah, NJ: Lawrence Erlbaum.

Sonntag, S. (2009). Linguistic globalization and the call center industry: Imperialism, hegemony or cosmopolitanism? *Language Policy, 8,* 5–25.

Strubell, M. (1998). Language, democracy and devolution in Catalonia. *Current Issues in Language and Society, 5,* 146–180.

Taylor, C. (1994). The politics of recognition. In A. Gutmann (Ed.), *Multiculturalism: Examining the politics of recognition* (pp. 25–73). Princeton, NJ: Princeton University Press.

Tedick, D., Christian, D., & Fortune, T. (Eds.). (2011). *Immersion education: Practices, policies, possibilities.* Bristol, England: Multilingual Matters.

Thomas, W., & Collier, V. (2002). *A national study of school effectiveness for language minority students' long-term academic achievement.* Santa Cruz, CA: Center for Research on Education, Diversity and Excellence. Retrieved from http://crede.berkeley.edu/research/llaa/1.1_final.html

Thornberry, P. (1991). *International law and the rights of minorities.* Oxford, England: Clarendon Press.

Thornberry, P. (1997). Minority rights. In Academy of European Law (Ed.), *Collected courses of the Academy of European Law* (Vol. 6, Book 2, pp. 307–390). The Hague, Netherlands: Kluwer Law International.

Tollefson, J., & Tsui, A. (Eds.). (2004). *Medium of instruction policies: Which agenda? Whose agenda?* Mahwah, NJ: Lawrence Erlbaum.

Torres, J. (1984). Problems of linguistic normalization in the Països Catalans: From the Congress of Catalan Culture to the present day. *International Journal of the Sociology of Language, 47,* 59–63.

Trenz, H.-J. (2007). Reconciling diversity and unity: Language minorities and European integration. *Ethnicities, 7,* 157–185.

Troebst, S. (1998). *The Council of Europe's Framework Convention for the Protection of National Minorities revisited.* Flensburg, Germany: European Centre for Minority Issues.

Waldron, J. (1995). Minority cultures and the cosmopolitan alternative. In W. Kymlicka (Ed.), *The rights of minority cultures* (pp. 93–119). Oxford, England: Oxford University Press.

Wiley, T., & Wright, W. (2004). Against the undertow: The politics of language instruction in the United States. *Educational Policy, 18,* 142–168.

Williams, C. (2008). *Linguistic minorities in democratic context.* Basingstoke, England: Palgrave Macmillan.

Woolard, K. (1989). *Double talk: bilingualism and the politics of ethnicity in Catalonia.* Stanford, CA: Stanford University Press.

Wright, W. (2005). The political spectacle of Arizona's Proposition 203. *Educational Policy, 19,* 662–700.

Xanthaki, A. (2007). *Indigenous rights and United Nations Standards.* Cambridge, England: Cambridge University Press.

Young, I. (1993). Together in difference: Transforming the logic of group political conflict. In Judith Squires (Ed.), *Principled positions: Postmodernism and the rediscovery of value* (pp. 121–150). London, England: Lawrence & Wishart.

Young, I. (2000). *Inclusion and democracy.* Oxford, England: Oxford University Press.

Chapter 10

The Lightening Veil: Language Revitalization in Wales

Colin H. Williams
Cardiff University

INTRODUCTION

The Welsh language, which is indigenous to Wales, is one of six Celtic languages. It is spoken by 562,000 speakers, 19% of the population of Wales, according to the 2011 U.K. Census, and it is estimated that it is spoken by a further 200,000 residents elsewhere in the United Kingdom. No exact figures exist for the undoubted thousands of other Welsh speakers beyond the United Kingdom who are able to communicate in Welsh as migrants to other European countries, members of the Welsh diasporas in North and South America, Australia, and Southern Africa; and language learners elsewhere.

The subject of this chapter is a sometimes mysterious, often idiosyncratic process, which always involves struggle, sacrifice, and tension.[1] Language revitalization is an attempt to counter trends that have influenced decline in the use and learning of the language. The pressures typically are a combination of historical conquest, political and economic control, and deep psychological hurt whereby a former relatively autonomous group are subjugated into a dependent people whose prime markers of distinction, such as language or religious differentiation, are eroded, made illegal, or otherwise eradicated from formal public life. At various periods in West European history, this has been the fate of Welsh, Irish, Gaelic, Breton, Basque, and Catalan, among others.[2]

Thus, at root, language revitalization speaks of a much deeper and significant historical trend, the attainment of an element of cultural and popular autonomy within salient historical domains such as public education, local government, and community development.[3] Language revitalization is a conscious effort to change ideas, values, attitudes, and behaviors.

Review of Research in Education
March 2014, Vol. 38, pp. 242-272
DOI: 10.3102/0091732X13512983

Political Agitation in Favor of Language Revitalization

In the United Kingdom, many of the worthwhile initiatives in support of the promotion and recognition of the Welsh language have been achieved as a result of direct action and stealth politics, often in the face of considerable opposition and hostility by agencies of the hegemonic state and its local representative institutions. It is now the National Assembly for Wales (NAW) that determines the shape of some 20 devolved policy areas, of which the Welsh language is one.

Over the past century, the Welsh language movement has been marked by increasing sophistication, specialization, and breadth of approach.[4] Three distinct phases may be identified. In the period 1912–1962, the concern was with gaining public recognition for the language and with establishing a designated Welsh language education system. The second stage, around 1962–1980s, witnessed a period of mobilization linked to a wider sustained protest at the perceived unfair treatment of Welsh in public and civic life.[5] Its main ambitions were to promote the growth of Welsh-medium education, to ensure bilingual public services, and to secure the establishment of a Welsh-medium television channel, S4C. The third and current stage is preoccupied with two different sets of challenges. The first is the spatial and geolinguistic impact of differential migration on predominantly Welsh-speaking communities and the attempts to "normalize" Welsh through expanding the demo-linguistic base of pupils who attend Welsh-medium schools. The challenge here is to construct a sociolinguistic context that reinforces Welsh language skills outside the school-based socialization experience. Although essentially a phenomenon of the anglicized southeast and northeast, there is growing evidence that this is becoming a more prevalent issue throughout Wales. The second political, administrative, and legal challenge has to do with constructing a national infrastructure that embeds the current opportunities to use Welsh more deeply within the fabric of society. The focus here has been on the articulation of language policy, citizen services, and rights; the passage of new language legislation; the role of information technology; and the need to secure a greater presence for Welsh language skills within the economy.

Let us look at the first challenge in more detail. The sociolinguistic stability of communities is the bedrock on which the discourse regarding successful language revitalization process has been based. In the coalfield areas of the south and the slate-quarrying districts of the north, the Welsh language and its associated culture were heavily influenced by the penetration of advanced capitalism, globalization, and the increasing internationalization of social mores, political ideologies, popular culture, and leisure pursuits. Although Anglicization characterized the eastern coalfield area, the mass and density of Welsh-speaking communities in the west and north were sufficiently robust as to withstand the acculturating effects of rapid industrialization, at least for two generations.

By the 1960s, this was no longer feasible, as the Welsh-speaking communities began to shrink and atrophy. A crisis mentality in relation to the survival of Welsh necessitated new ideas and forms of action to resist language decline. A major concern of language campaigners, and a consideration in government policy, has been the condition of Heartland communities in the informal designated area known as "Y Fro Gymraeg." Initially associated with *Adfer* in the 1960s and 1970s, the foundation of this appeal is territorial recovery, initially through private economic and community endeavors. The stimulus for this movement was the economic and social undermining of rural Wales by undifferentiated state policies, the uneven effects of regional development and capitalist penetration, tourism, and the growth of second-home ownership. A modern variant of this anxiety over loss of local control, housing policies, inadequate employment, in-migration, and creeping Anglicization resurfaced in Gwynedd with the formation of Cymuned (community) in the early part of this century. Coupled with this has been a progressively spiraling housing market, which disadvantages local purchasers and forces younger families to move from the community to less attractive locations in market terms. As a consequence of these demographic forces, the sociolinguistic nature of many predominantly Welsh-speaking communities, including their social networks, is undergoing a profound transition.[6] All of these concerns were made far more acute by the publication of the 2011 Census headline results on the Welsh language (Welsh Government, 2012b), which revealed a decline in Welsh speakers from 20.8% in 2001 to 19% in 2011. Thus, despite an increase in the size of the population, the number of Welsh speakers decreased from 582,000 in 2001 to 562,000 in 2011.

In this chapter, I want to focus on four pillars of language revitalization, namely, language policy and sociolegal developments, formal education, the family, and community life. A more comprehensive analysis would include interpretation of economic diversification, regional development in United Kingdom, global commercial trends, IT and software initiatives and their impact on behavior and language choice, and the U.K. devolution process and constitutional change, together with European Union (EU) influences in myriad domains.[7]

GOVERNMENTAL SUPPORT FOR LANGUAGE REVITALIZATION

Wales represents a distinct variant within U.K. public policy in that the U.K. central government has been crucially involved in supporting Welsh language initiatives since the early 1960s and in establishing a distinct language regime. Critical reforms such as the establishment of the Welsh television channel S4C, a Welsh national curriculum following the passage of the Education Act 1988, the Welsh Language Act in 1993 (Her Majesty's Stationery Office, 1993), and the establishment of the NAW in 1999 as a result of constitutional reform and devolution have their origin in Westminster legislation. The underlying reason why such reforms were instituted has much to do with the pressure exerted by civil society, a powerful and well-placed language lobby, the internal dynamics of the party political system, and the differential response to nationalism, both cultural and political. A cogent argument could be constructed that these lobby capacities have been piecemeal, contingent, nonpermanent, and powerful only in the sense that they have been relative to the capacities of individuals in a given location. Be that as it may, a central feature of the 1993 legislation was the creation of a language promotion agency, the Welsh Language Board (WLB), which was set to be the determining influence on the contours of Welsh language policy for almost 20 years.

The Welsh Language Act of 1993

The passage of the Welsh Language Act of 1993 provided a statutory framework for the treatment of English and Welsh on the basis of equality[8] and was a turning point in the history of Welsh language promotion. The Act established a statutory WLB and ushered in a system whereby named public organizations were required to specify, by means of a language scheme, what range of bilingual services they would offer to the public (Her Majesty's Stationery Office, 1993). Within a decade, the WLB had established itself as the principal agency for the promotion of Welsh in public life and had adopted several far-reaching programs of action in the field of community development, language transfer within the family, educational strategies, IT, and private sector initiatives (Campbell, 2000; C. H. Williams, 2000).

The 1993 Act details key steps to be taken by the WLB and by public sector bodies in the preparation of Welsh language schemes, which are designed to implement the central principle of the Act, that is, to treat Welsh and English on the basis of equality. However, this obligation is not absolute; public bodies need only implement the principle "so far as is both appropriate in the circumstances and reasonably practicable." The Act provides that the Board must issue guidelines as to the form and content of schemes each public body must regard in preparing their scheme, that the public body must carry out consultations in the preparation of the scheme, and that the scheme must be submitted to the Board for approval. The guidelines require details on how the body's scheme will deal with the Welsh-speaking public in terms of correspondence, telephone communication, and the conduct of meetings, together with the organization's identity, iconography, signage, publishing and printing material, official notices, press notices, publicity, and advertising.

The Board also had the right to extend its remit in other sectors covered by the Act, and had given priority to education and training. By June 1998, the Welsh education schemes of 2 local authorities had been approved, and a further 15 were being developed. Further and higher education colleges, together with Welsh-medium preschool provision, have also received attention. Starting in 1998, Education Learning Wales, with input from the Board, had coordinated a national strategy for Welsh for Adults, and this sector has benefited from a more robust and systematic provision of service, accreditation of adult tutors, resource development, and strategic intervention related to skills acquisition in key areas of the economy, such as insurance and banking, retail sales, and the legal profession. In total, grants of £2,027,000 were distributed in the year 1997–1998 to local authorities to promote Welsh language education.

The WLB was a public body sponsored by the Welsh Assembly Government (WAG). Total grant in aid for the year April 1, 2009, to March 31, 2010, was

£13,653,000.The net expenditure for the year was £13,781,000 (2008–2009: £13,512,000). On March 31, 2010, the general reserve was £596,000 (2008–2009: £701,000). By 2010, a total of 487 public sector language schemes had been approved, with a further 76 approved in the voluntary sector (WLB, 2010). By 2011, over 565 Welsh language schemes had been validated, including all Education Authorities and Tertiary Education Institutes in Wales, and the annual grant expenditure of the WLB had risen to £7,522 million in 2009–2010.

The Welsh Language Board and Language Management

In successive strategy documents (WLB, 1995), the Board set itself four priorities[9]:

1. To increase the numbers of Welsh-speakers
2. To provide more opportunities to use the language
3. To change habits in relation to language use
4. To strengthen Welsh as a community language

However, the WLB did not have a real statutory remit to achieve all this; rather, through the local action plans and language schemes the WLB was able to develop a working relationship with county authorities in relation to their Welsh-medium education and service provision (WLB, 2005, 2006, 2008a). The Welsh language scheme system put the onus on the public bodies to discuss and shoulder responsibility for Welsh language services for the first time; this was a major step forward for the language revitalization program.[10]

The WLB had become the key agency in language revitalization for it now created a discourse and set an agenda for process and action.[11] In 1996, following local government reform, the eight counties became 22 local authorities, and this provided an opportunity to create new Welsh language schemes that opened up new possibilities. This was realized in 1996–1997 when a new system of language schemes was created with the first being Carmarthenshire County Council. The language scheme system was extended to other local authorities, universities, and further and advanced education colleges. For the first time public bodies had to conform to a statutory language scheme and had to report regularly on how they were adhering to an agreed scheme. Language schemes also created a discourse within institutions that had never previously been required to discuss the needs of Welsh speakers. Now they were required to consider how they were going to service the interests of Welsh into the medium-term future, and this led to elements of mainstreaming Welsh through the establishment of 558 Welsh language schemes that have totally transformed the role of Welsh within public administration. However, as reported in C. H. Williams (2010, 2013), the delivery of the services was inconsistent and difficult and has led to a reform of the system in favor of a set of service delivery standards as discussed below.

An important influence in the process is the cumulative impact and role of civil society (C. H. Williams, 2008). Whatever the difficulties and challenges posed by civil society to the direction or decisions of the WLB Board, there were at the very least access points for dialogue, discussion, and disagreement. Formally these were provided in the shape of regular public meetings of the WLB, hosted somewhere in Wales every 6 weeks or so. The general public were thus afforded an opportunity to air their grievances, interrogate and challenge the decisions of public officials and WLB personnel, and give early advance warning of several issues on the horizon. WLB data and evidence on trends affecting the Welsh language in, for example, education, health, housing, and the like often grounded the discussions in locally related context and within a regional or national perspective also, so as to gauge how the local community was faring with regard to the rest of the nation.

At another step removed from such public fora was the intense networking the WLB undertook both with its partners, public organizations in the United Kingdom and the EU, and with, of course, professional societies, lobby groups, and special interest groups, concerned, for example, with the media, education, translation, tourism, skills development, housing, and so on. These meetings afforded the collection of additional data and perspectives and often acted as a precursor to the development of WLB strategy in specific domains. They also built up a certain degree of trust and complicit understanding that the promotion of Welsh was a concern of both civil society and responsible agencies. This is not to say that there was necessarily ready agreement or that the WLB was not the subject of intense criticism and scrutiny, especially in the allocation of grant awards. But these channels of informed opinion did add to the general intelligence displayed in and around the implementation of language policy.

This was an undoubted strength in terms of networking and in furthering the influence of the Board within different regions and interest groups. A conscious strategy was pursued whereby the Board would instigate initiatives and then promote the ideas and activities under the banner of the partner. A good example is the TWF initative that arose from the WLB Community Research Project (C. H. Williams & Evas, 1998),[12] although in the long term this approach to language management may have damaged the Board as the political authorities and the general public did not appreciate or value the extent to which the WLB was actually both the principal actor and the main driver in coordinating the movement to revitalize Welsh. This, together with its status as a quango, one step removed from direct government control, was the reason why the Government of Wales announced that it was of the mind to abolish the WLB, which duly happened in March 2012.

The Legacy of the Welsh Language Board

Doubtless in international comparative terms the WLB will be hailed as one of the few genuine innovative language-planning agencies. It has earned its respect in Welsh public policy circles in terms of its effectiveness as a promotional body and as an asset to the long-term fortunes of the Welsh language. It operated at a pivotal time in the development of Welsh governance and civil society and had a very constructive role to play in transforming the Welsh language from a political football to a public good.

There are grounds for arguing that the WLB was not given a sufficient opportunity to fulfill its complex and challenging remit. It embarked on approving Welsh language schemes only in 1996, and this was followed by a 7-year preparatory period when the supporting infrastructure was put in place. There were two critical features of this period. One was the educational aspect of the Board's work whereby it tutored named institutions and local government officers and helped manage their expectations as to how to implement the statutory obligations contained within the Welsh Language Act of 1993. The second feature was its partnership with the Welsh Government and its successive ministers, some of whom were far better than others in extending the remit of the Board and in securing additional resources for it to staff its increasingly ambitious program of action.

One of the chief virtues of *Iaith Pawb* (WAG, 2003), the first Action Plan of the WAG, was that it allocated sufficient resources to allow the Board to monitor performance, and this came to full fruition in 2006, ironically a full 2 years after it had been announced that the WLB was to be incorporated directly within the Government. There is a bittersweet irony in the timing of all this for Board members and staff. In consequence, several of them were led to ask whether it was really necessary to abolish such a relatively young organization when the legislation had not been fully tested and the Welsh language schemes were still finding their operative role within the public sector. However, in several submissions made to the NAW Legislation Committee scrutiny process of 2010, a consistent criticism was made of the WLB that it either lacked teeth or failed to use the powers it had in a sufficiently robust manner until its later years. In consequence within the new system it was assumed that "regulated bodies (would) take compliance with language obligations seriously" (Lewis, 2010).

That will depend to a great extent on the nature of the new language service standards currently being developed and how rigorous the Welsh Language Commissioner will enforce compliance by named bodies.

EDUCATION

A significant feature of Welsh-medium and bilingual education is that it has grown in an organic manner, largely as a result of parental power, rather than purposive planning by either central or local authorities save for the pioneering work of Glamorgan, Clwyd, and Gwynedd local Education Authorities.[13] The result is that parts of the education system are innovative and engaging, whereas others are inadequate; for despite understanding the nature of bilingualism in detail, there have been too few attempts to develop a holistic approach to educational provision that encompasses the whole range of required outcomes. Currently there are signs of a more strategic approach to constructing a bilingual educational sector, but it is still too early to talk of a comprehensive Welsh model. More critically socioeconomic and political developments in society threaten to undermine, or at least weaken, some of the progress made to date, as will be reported below.[14]

The range of issues includes the lack of consistency in terms of the linguistic provision in different types of schools, the specific challenges posed to Welsh-speaking communities by the presence of pupils who possess radically different capacities in terms of their Welsh language skills, the need for the sector to increase its capacity to foster adequate skill sets so as to prepare pupils both for external examination assessment and the world of work, the enduring challenge of "managing" linguistic continuity trends, and the growing role of Welsh-medium provision within the Higher Education sector so as to realize the full range of the current education and language strategy. Until recently the various stages of education were not planned in an integrated manner and are still not resourced in an effective and mutually supportive way (Baker & Jones, 1999). Beyond the formal statutory sectors of the education system, consideration also needs to be given to broader socioeconomic elements, including greater capacity building, language awareness, and in-service retraining, all of which are crucial elements in the development of a bilingual economy and workforce (Cwmni Iaith, 2008; Welsh Local Government Association, 2004).

Educational Experiments

Throughout the period 1948–1988, the statutory education system was largely unilingual English in character. In the early part of this period, namely, 1948–circa 1972, the growth in the number of Welsh-medium schools offered an opt-in choice for parents in some areas who wished their children to pursue a bilingual education. As far as the U.K. government was concerned, Welsh was to be promoted primarily through the education system, and the Welsh Office and local Education Authorities adopted a rather laconic and laissez-faire approach to the provision of Welsh-medium education in toto, although there were significant individual initiatives taken by some of Her Majesty's Inspectors of Schools and local authorities such as Flint and Glamorgan in the late 1950s and early 1960s.[15] The scholastic, social, and sporting standing of the first Welsh-medium schools were of such a high order that they established Welsh-medium education as a credible alternative for many parents who hitherto were apprehensive about committing their children's education to an unproven, minority, and somewhat differentiated education pattern. The 1966 Education Act defined Welsh-medium schools as those that taught over half their foundation subjects, excluding Welsh, English, and Religious Education, either wholly or partly through the medium of Welsh.

In 1971 the establishment of *Mudiad Ysgolion Meithrin* (The Welsh Medium Nursery Schools Movement) formalized a close confederation of voluntary and non-statutory nursery schools that had been growing in numbers since the late 1940s. This new movement was a significant step forward, opening up Welsh-medium education to a new cohort of parents who did not necessarily speak Welsh and providing the first entry point into the Welsh-medium system, while simultaneously providing a boost to community development and refreshing the system with many new ideas regarding language transmission and child care.

The gains made in the provision of Welsh-medium education were almost entirely as a result of the pressure exerted by parental demand in specific locations usually championed by tireless articulators of the cause.[16] In the north and west of Wales, local Education Authorities such as Gwynedd pursued a comprehensive approach whereby the vast majority of primary schools and a large proportion of secondary schools delivered a bilingual curriculum. Clwyd formulated the idea of specialist Welsh language supply teachers, Athrawon Bro, and diffused the idea to the rest of Wales. In the period 1980–1996 there developed a comprehensive Ancillary Teacher service, Gwasanaeth Bro, which went some way toward remedying a long-term lack of supply of trained Welsh teachers.

In the second part of this period, circa 1974–1988, despite these initiatives, in many parts of Wales, 45% of pupils did not receive regular lessons in Welsh. This was changed following the Education Act of 1988, which made Welsh one of four Core Subjects in the National Curriculum in schools that taught through the medium of Welsh and a compulsory subject in all other schools within the statutory education age range of 5 to 16 years.[17] Since its implementation in 1989, all children had an opportunity to develop bilingual skills, and a substantial minority could develop real fluency in Welsh. Previously some Education Authorities had concentrated their efforts on the teaching of Welsh as a second language (L2) during the years 3 to 6. With the implementation in 1989/1990 of the National Curriculum, Education Authorities and schools started to teach Welsh in English-medium schools through-out the entire age range, from Reception classes onward, and this development may in part be responsible for the upturn in the 2001 census. Both the numbers and attitude to Welsh changed markedly.

The single most important feature of the Education Act was the steady growth in L2 delivery, and this approach to bilingualism through statutory educational policy remains an important element of the government's strategy as articulated in the language policy *Iaith Pawb* (WAG, 2003) and various educational strategies.[18]

During the early 1980s, incremental reforms in education, the legal system, public administration, and local government had increased the opportunities to use Welsh in society. However, these were regarded as piecemeal, insufficient, and rudimentary. The challenge of the 1980s was to realize a fully functional bi/multilingual society through creating new opportunities for language choice within the public, voluntary, and private sector of the economy. Single-issue educational organizations such as Mudiad Ysgolion Meithrin, RhAG (Rhieni Dros Addysg Gymraeg), and CYDAG (Cymdeithas Ysgolion Dros Addysg Gymraeg), together with civil society action movements such as Cymdeithas yr Iaith Gymraeg and Cefn, had raised the language issue to a national concern, and indeed, the three formative decades 1963 to 1993 had been significant in terms of articulating the chief causes of language decline, identifying areas of growth in education and public administration, and mobilizing sections of society in defense of the language as detailed in the contributions of Jenkins and Williams (2000).

Yet all this energy and pressure had been sporadic, largely uncoordinated, and one step removed from government policy and resourcing. Having gained a victory in the establishment of S4C in 1983, the two remaining unfulfilled demands at the start of the nineties were political devolution and legislative recognition of the right to use Welsh in the widest possible spheres of public life.

The National Profile of Welsh-Medium Education

In 1999, as a result of U.K. constitutional change, a devolved NAW took over responsibility for educational policy. After the first decade of devolution by 2010, there were 464 mainly Welsh-medium primary schools, representing 30.7% of all primary schools, an increase of 18 schools over the previous decade. These provided education for 53,479 children (20.8% of the national total), an increase of 9,495 pupils on the 1991 figure of 43,984. At the secondary level, there were 55 Welsh-speaking schools (as defined by the 1996 Education Act), an increase of three over 10 years. The most significant change within the decade was the increase in the number of secondary pupils learning Welsh as an L2, up from 122,112 (67.8%) in 1999 to 146,656 (83.1%) in 2009.

Currently the Welsh-medium education system is characterized by four strengths: the professional commitment of highly motivated teaching staff, very strong parental support, high academic achievement, and a supportive cultural and community basis to the educational provision that promotes a meaningful and rich school experience and rewards innovation and engagement.[19] This profile is tempered by a number of weaknesses that, as the system has grown, have generated a good deal of reconsideration regarding the aims and achievements of the sector. The weaknesses are inconsistency in the nature of the educational experience, far too much fragmentation in the sector, and a general uncertainty as to what counts as a Welsh-medium and/or a bilingual school, for there are at least four working models in operation. An overriding complicating factor is that these trends and patterns vary geographically. Thus, in some areas there are poor succession rates in the transfer of Welsh-medium pupils from the primary to the secondary and tertiary stages of education.[20] In other areas, such as southeast Wales, progression rates from Key Stage 2 to Key Stage 3 are high, with little loss.[21] Progression from first language at Key Stage 2 to first language in secondary in the Welsh hinterland lead to further attrition and the creation of the WLB's Continuity and Progression Project, which had initial success. Thus within the Welsh medium, as opposed to the bilingual categorization, there is less by way of fragmentation, uncertainty as to linguistic nature, or clarity of outcome and ambition. Designated Welsh-medium secondary schools are to be found both in the predominantly Welsh-speaking areas of west Wales (Carmarthen and Ceredigion) and in the predominantly English-speaking eastern parts of Wales. In the north and west, the most important demolingusitic variable is the rate and scale of persistent non–Welsh-speaking migration (largely English) over the past decades. This demographic influx threatens the long-term viability of national language and educational policies, such as *Iaith Pawb* (WAG, 2003; C. H. Williams, 2004) and the degree to which county education authorities can maintain the primacy they have given to Welsh as a medium of both education and examination. One element of success is the *Canolfannau Hwyrddyfodiaid* (latecomer centers), which are centers designed to accelerate the linguistic integration of in-migrant pupils at primary level into the education systems of predominantly Welsh-speaking counties such as Gwynedd and Môn.[22]

Redknap (2006) has argued that the 1966 Education Act definition of Welsh medium no longer offers a sufficiently precise description of the extent of the Welsh-medium teaching in a school, nor does it fully reflect the degree to which immersion education works. "By now, this statutory definition is not sufficiently robust to meet the needs required for the collation and analysis of meaningful statistical information" (p. 11). Consequently, greater emphasis has been placed on identifying a range of bilingual experiences along a continuum, and in some county education authorities, schools have been categorized into models that reflect the proportion and range of subject taught through the medium of Welsh.

Lewis (2010) has drawn attention to several underlying difficulties that face predominantly Welsh-speaking local authorities, most critically that Welsh learners who do not perform satisfactorily are not given more intense, supportive Welsh language tuition (e.g., *gloywi iaith* = language improvement lessons) but are rather encouraged to pursue their studies and formal examinations in English. Although at times pragmatic, this seems to be a self-defeating outcome of an ostensibly Welsh-medium education system. Lewis has identified seven structural weaknesses that characterize the current practice of schools and education authorities in predominantly Welsh-speaking regions of Wales. The first concerns the language of instruction and the language of formal assessment. At times, for very specific subjects the whole of the instruction may be in Welsh but the external assessment may be in English, sometimes because the only examinations offered by schools are ones provided by examination boards outside Wales and are therefore not in Welsh. Also, it is argued that the proportion of Welsh-medium assessment is low in comparison with the Welsh-medium schools in the more Anglicized areas of northeast and southeast Wales. Thus, two issues interact, the first are continuity and succession rates, the second is the language of assessment versus the language of instruction debate. A third situation arises where the formal assessment may occur in English whereas the teaching may have followed bilingual precepts.

A second trend, as identified by Estyn (the office of Her Majesty's Inspectorate for Education and Training in Wales; Menter a Busnes, 2010) and educational specialists such as Redknap (2006), is for pupils who have followed a first-language Welsh program at primary school to switch to study Welsh as a second language in some secondary school clusters or counties. Redknap (2006) observes that "this loss of ground is apparent in the transition period between Key Stage 2 and Key Stage 3, and even more ground is lost as pupils move to Key Stage 4 and beyond" (p. 12). Thus, linguistic continuity is a consideration for all ranges. There are some puzzling tendencies though. Redknap details the decline as indicated by Assembly Government statistics (2000–2003) whereby 17.6% of pupils were assessed in Welsh at the end of Key Stage 2 in 2000. Only 13.9% of the same student cohort were assessed in Welsh 3 years later at the end of Key Stage 3. She indicates that the language loss is most acute in the traditionally Welsh-speaking counties of the north and west.

As a consequence, some L2 pupils have tended to not demonstrate a mastery or real confidence in the use of either or both languages, and this has implications for their ability to integrate fully into predominantly Welsh-medium social networks and to take up bilingual employment opportunities. However, recent evidence and debates surrounding the language delivery and acquisition rates of L2 have been far more encouraging than is generally acknowledged, and this pattern seems set to continue.

Lewis (2010) confirms Redknap's (2006) analysis and argues that some secondary schools in predominantly Welsh-speaking areas, such as the counties of Carmarthenshire and Ceredigion, do not cater for the full potential of L2 students. Consequently, a great deal of solid, preparatory work undertaken in honing language acquisition skills at the primary level is not realized or fulfilled by the secondary-level experience. As a result, this particular variety of education tends not to be "cost-effective." Because such schools do not always succeed in integrating pupils from a non-Welsh-speaking background, it is possible that English becomes the default language of social exchange among the first-language Welsh speakers. The advantage of Category 1 and 2a models is that they can adopt robust and unambiguous language policies that are not a characteristic of the other so-called Welsh-medium schools. In consequence, non–Welsh-speaking migrants to such areas can demand English-medium education for their children at the expense of the provision made for local Welsh-speaking families (Lewis, 2010).

The Current Welsh-Medium Education Strategy

In May 2009, the WAG published its plans for Welsh-medium education. This was a very welcome development as previously the Education Department had been criticized for not contributing in a detailed manner to the preparation of the *Iaith Pawb* strategy document (C. H. Williams, 2004). The Government outlined six strands by which it will implement its Welsh-medium educational strategy in the pre–statutory age range of 3 to 5 and the statutory age range of 5 to 16 (WAG, 2011):

1. Improve provision planning (prestatutory and statutory)
2. Improve provision planning (post-14)
3. Develop language skills and continuity
4. Ensure numbers and train practitioners
5. Center support to improve qualifications, resources
6. Contribute toward informal use

As with all such strategies, the long-term impact will be felt only when local author-ities and educational institutions fully implement the government's vision. But there is also the critical issue as to how the government will honor its own involvement in this strategy and allocate sufficient resources to realize the declared aims. How these targets are to be met is, as yet, unclear, for a persistent problem with bilingual educa-tion is its inconsistent implementation. Within this long history of fragmentation, fresh initiatives, and radical proposals, one feature stands out—namely, the patterned inconsistency between what was practiced by local authorities and what was recom-mended in the policy documents of the government. Indeed a persistent criticism has been the very lack of government leadership and policy clarification in this field.

Wales has not lacked good ideas or champions in the field of Welsh-medium education. Quite the opposite, for in the period 1939 to 1988, Wales was a pioneer in Europe of bilingual education (I. W. Williams, 2003). What Wales has lacked is a universal set of standards by which educational provision could be measured and improved on.[23] The current degree of planning, resourcing, and strategic oversight is far greater than that obtained in predevolution days.[24] This augurs well for the medium-term future, but as with so many other fields of public policy, much depends on external influences: the political calculations and machinations of government, local, national, and U.K.; the fiscal policies adopted by successive Chancellors of the Exchequer; and the manner in which certain budgetary requirements are interpreted and implemented at the local level.

The prevailing discourse is an admixture of evidence, propaganda, and hype. What are needed are clear well-reasoned messages that advance the cause of Welsh-medium education within an increasingly plural and multilingual context, both within Wales and globally. Typically, such arguments have been made in relation to parental choices and to prospective students, but this message needs to be rearticulated so that it is also aimed at politicians and decision makers and businesspeople, the probable employers. Much of the discourse reflects a post-Thatcher, quasi-Blairite concern with meeting demand, viewing education as a free choice exercised by customers in a relatively closed market. There is little discussion of measuring need or considering the logical questions that arise in post-18 education if a larger proportion of the statu-tory 5 to 16 age-group receive a Welsh-medium education. A small glimmer of hope is the realization that civil society needs to be engaged in these detailed discussions, and not just as parents, so that Welsh may be treated increasingly as a public good and not as a political football.[25]

There is also a belated recognition that the balance between the various educa-tional sectors needs to be recalibrated. One consideration is the trend for parents to decide on a Welsh-medium education for their children at primary level, only for different patterns to emerge at the secondary level due to such children being trans-ferred by some parents from Welsh-medium to bilingual or English-medium schools. A more positive trend is the additional emphasis on Welsh for Adults in the current education and learning strategy, which is welcomed as it provides language skills and confidence for both young parents and those who are required to use Welsh in the workplace. One lacuna is the skills development and training for the workplace, which needs urgent attention if the aim of creating a bilingual society is to be realized in any meaningful way. Thus, greater capacity building, language awareness, and in-service re-training are all urgent and crucial priorities.[26]

Tertiary-Level Bilingual Education

One of the chief difficulties facing language planners in building capacity and improving language skills throughout the system is the lack of succession as students progress from primary, through secondary, to tertiary education.[27] Wales has a poor record of tertiary-level Welsh-medium provision. In June 2009, the WAG produced a *Statistical Bulletin on Welsh in Higher Education Institutions* (HEI) 2007/08, whose key results were as follows:

- The number of students studying some of their course through Welsh increased again—continuing the upward trend of recent years, as around 3.5% of all enrollments were studying some of their course through Welsh.
- In all, 3.5% of student enrollments at Welsh HEIs had some teaching through the medium of Welsh, compared with 3.2% in 2006/2007.
- There were 4,445 student enrollments at Welsh HEIs with some teaching through the medium of Welsh, 9.1% greater than the number in 2006/2007 (4,075).
- There were 4,050 Welsh domiciled students at Welsh HEIs with some teaching through the medium of Welsh, 7.9% greater than the number in 2006/2007 (3,755).
- Of those students with some Welsh teaching, 26% of full-time students and 62% of part-time students received all their teaching through Welsh.
- There were 620 academic staff able to teach through the medium of Welsh, but only 390 academic staff teaching through the medium of Welsh actually do so.

In February 2009, the higher education sector agreed to establish a national electronic resources portal and a virtual learning environment for the Welsh-medium higher education sector. This consists of a central repository of Welsh-medium web-based resources that can be used by all Welsh-medium students and practitioners, and includes a virtual learning environment to host learning materials for collaborative modules and to guide the learner in an effective way. The 2009 Welsh-medium Education Strategy proposed that three subgroups be established to support the work of the HE Sector Group. These would focus on aspects of the National Development Plan, namely, Marketing, Progression, and Stimulating Demand; Staff Development; and E-Learning and Blended Learning. There are 12 network panels that enable institutions to collaborate on developing new resources and provision for Welsh-medium higher education in particular subject areas. Significant investment has been made to provide Welsh-medium lecturers via the Postgraduate Scholarship Scheme and the Welsh-Medium Teaching Fellowships Scheme, which are administered by the Centre for Welsh-Medium Higher Education.

Y Coleg Cymraeg Cenedlaethol

Conscious that there was a need for a national level initiative to promote Welsh-medium university education, the Minister for Education and Skills announced the establishment of a Federal College Planning Board, chaired by Professor Robin Williams. This was a policy promise of the coalition government in line with the commitment in *One Wales*. Its report, released in 2009, envisaged a "spoke and hub" arrangement among all the stakeholders: the HEIs, including the staff and students; the Higher Education Funding Council for Wales (HEFCW); and the WAG. By August 2011, the College had become an independent legal entity with its own constitution and an independent decision-making structure but "owned" by the HEIs as a group. Its first student enrollment was in September 2011. There has been a formal agreement between Y Coleg and HEFCW to guarantee that the funds channeled through the Coleg are directed in accordance with its constitution, the accountability requirements of HEFCW, and the wishes of the Welsh Government. This administrative structure, based on a small central hub together with branches in the HEIs, should ensure efficient communication and a rapid decision-making process. Staff and students participating in Welsh-medium teaching and learning are able to be members of the Coleg and have representation on its National Council.

Historically, Welsh-medium provision was concentrated at Aberystwyth and Bangor, Trinity College, and Lampeter; consequently, any attempt to build up provision within the rest of the HEI sector is faced with some severe difficulties related to patterns of expectation and capacity issues. This is because there has been a tendency to treat Welsh-medium education in many universities as an add-on feature and not integral to the institute's remit and mission. Farsighted institutions, such as Trinity Saint David, had recognized the element of growth and opportunity for developing a distinct profile that such policy initiatives offer. However, other institutions were sanguine about committing a great deal of energy, not to say resources, to the pursuit of bilingual teaching and research. This reticence has been met to a large extent by the appointment of well-qualified and dynamic staff in several hitherto underdeveloped fields in terms of tertiary Welsh-medium education such as the Law, Health Education, Engineering, and the Social Sciences. The Coleg displays a great deal of ambition and augers well for the future development of the sector.

New Challenges in a Changing Context

Clearly, the contours of Welsh language revitalization are shaped by wider considerations. I want to draw attention to three currents of change that are likely to have an impact on the direction bilingual education will take over the medium term. The first is the legislative rights turn. In March 2010, the Welsh Government announced a new Welsh Language Measure, which included the following commitments: (a) the replacement of Language Schemes by new national standards of language service delivery, (b) the establishment of a Welsh Language Commissioner, (c) the abolition of the WLB. In December 2010, the details of these reforms were included in a draft Welsh Language Measure.

What legislative devolution occasions is a different constitutional configuration within the United Kingdom as a multilevel state. In terms of education, it is quite likely that a more integrated set of Welsh models will emerge, distinct from their English, Scottish, and Northern Irish counterparts. But the ability to sustain a separate educational system that is at least equal to that which obtains in other parts of the United Kingdom is a constant challenge given the scale of the fiscal settlement from the U.K. Treasury. Current complaints by business leaders about the relatively poor skill levels of Welsh students and the underperformance of the regional economy together with lower rates of inward investment all suggest that new ways of promoting excellence and entrpreneurship have to be found. National Assembly politicians and many within the educational system would favour Welsh-grown answers to specific Welsh problems. Others argue for a greater transfer of knowledge from other contexts and more harmonization of policies within the EU.

Between December 2010 and February 2011, consultation took place on the Government's wider strategy for the Welsh language. *A Living Language: A Language for Living* (Welsh Government, 2012a). The document provides a strategic framework for the support and promotion of the Welsh language within the family, in the community, at work, and at leisure. Successful implementation of numerous proposals in this Strategy will complement both the principles and objectives of the Welsh-medium Education Strategy. These strategies should make a valuable contribution to the linguistic experiences and opportunities of children and young people, as they progress through their educational careers and extend their use of the Welsh language into the wider community. In February 2011, the granting of Royal Assent to the Welsh Language (Wales) Measure, passed in December 2010, marked another milestone in the history of the Welsh language. In terms of policy and legislation, therefore, one can justifiably argue that the Welsh language has never been in such an advantageous position.

The developments reported on suggest that although there is a firmer commitment to improving bilingual education at the statutory school level, the promotion of Welsh-medium teaching and scholarship at the level of HEIs remains fragmented, idiosyncratic, and inadequate. The response is driven largely by national government finance and authorization, which is in itself periodic and often short term rather than structural and integral to educational planning and policy. In consequence, many of the initiatives described herein have yet to realize their full potential, let alone be accepted as part of the normal provision of university-level education and training. Yet the signs are promising, and much of this is related to the determination of committed individuals and lobby groups who long ago recognized that the foundations of a bilingual society are built not only within the statutory education sector but critically within the Higher Education sector also if real skills development at a professional level is to be achieved.[28] The delivery of bilingual services by a wide range of professional bodies in Wales, as elsewhere in Europe, presupposes a capacity-building period, not just a language rights regime and improved opportunities to use the language in a wider set of domains. The promotion of Welsh within the work place and the economy more generally remains a major challenge that currently seems to be ranked fairly low down in the "list of things to do" order, being subordinate to initiatives in the Welsh for Adults sector, language legislation, and a new set of statutory educational strategies. Yet, without this structural transformation in the instrumental value of Welsh in day-to-day real life, so many of the other gains will remain as potential assets to be realized someday in society rather than being fundamental features of the modern way of earning a livelihood and of serving customers in many "banal" situations.[29]

The deeper question is where does power lie within the education system, and whose interests are best served by current strategies and reforms? If elements of the promising plans and strategies are realized as fact, and not just in rhetorical terms, then some of the constraints that curtail current ambitions will have been lifted, but if past experience is any guide, they will soon be replaced by a different set of constraints—such is the lot of minorities struggling to navigate into the mainstream.

COMMUNITY LANGUAGE DEVELOPMENT

The third pillar of language revitalization I wish to discuss is community development. This is the essential context for giving life to a language, for no matter how proficient the education system is in producing capable speakers, it is in the socioeconomic reality of daily life that a language gains purchase and demonstrates vitality. Two central questions drive the community language revitalization program:

How may endangered communities mobilize their own resources and those of external official agencies to promote language revitalization efforts?

How may such communities engage in the politics of language mobilization without running the risk of alienating the very people in whose name language revitalization efforts are conducted?

These are cardinal issues because all too often community-level initiatives become trammeled by the conventions of government bureaucracy, and what starts out as the politics of recognition soon becomes the politics of compulsion and regulation.

It is generally agreed that community language planning practice should be predicated on a thorough understanding of the local context, which involves gathering information about the social practices, language use and values of specific individuals and social groups, and sociolinguistic and socioeconomic processes and trends.

To realize its fourth objective of community development, the WLB was involved in the following planning initiatives:

- Undertaking research into the linguistic makeup of Welsh-speaking communities and the social and economic factors that affect them
- Identifying the main threats to the Welsh language within Welsh-speaking communities and formulating action plans for addressing potential problems in conjunction with key players across all sectors
- Discussing and developing with local government unitary authorities, especially those in the traditional geographically distinct Welsh-speaking strongholds, their role in terms of administering language initiatives and coordinating language policies
- Promoting cooperation between communities to foster mutual support, encouragement, and understanding
- Assessing the effectiveness of existing community-based initiatives (e.g., "Mentrau Iaith") as a means of promoting the use of Welsh, and evaluating their usefulness as a model for facilitating the creation of new locally run initiatives
- Facilitating the establishment of local language fora to promote Welsh language initiatives, to create opportunities for using Welsh, and to motivate and encourage people to do so
- Promoting the learning of Welsh by adults (including the provision of worthwhile opportunities to use Welsh outside the classroom and other ancillary support)
- Providing grants to support activities to strengthen Welsh within the community

Mentrau Iaith: The Community's Response

How are such aims and initiatives to be realized and coordinated by community-based organizations? A promising answer concerns the development of the 23 community language enterprise agencies, the Mentrau Iaith, which operate as community regeneration organizations with a linguistic cutting edge. Wales comprises 22 County Authorities, and by today, almost all local authorities contain or share a Menter Iaith. In addition, a Menter Iaith was established in Patagonia, Argentina, in 2008, to serve the needs of the Welsh diaspora and their descendants.

In the first period of incremental growth (1991–2001), two compelling reasons were given for supporting Mentrau Iaith, namely, that in situations characterized by strong language potential but a weak sociolinguistic network, Mentrau Iaith were deemed to offer a significant sociopsychological fillip for Welsh maintenance. Second, as local language planning bodies, they could function as a focus to create a new set of partnerships between the central government in the form of the National Assembly, the WLB, local government, statutory public bodies, health trusts, and a variety of other voluntary agencies and private companies, so as to extend the domains within which it would be possible to use Welsh.

Between 1993 and 2012, Mentrau Iaith were funded mainly by an annual grant from the WLB, at some £1.3 million per annum, together with ancillary funding by Local Authorities, which amounted to about £310,384 per annum. They are now funded directly by the Welsh Government.

A Menter (pl. Mentrau) Iaith is a local organization that offers support to communities to increase and develop their use of Welsh in a variety of ways. Advice is provided to parents on raising their children bilingually, to public and voluntary organizations on how to increase their use of Welsh, to businesses eager to begin to offer a bilingual service to their customers, and to those who wish to know more about Welsh-medium education. Typically their activities would include social and leisure opportunities for children and young people to use their Welsh, opportunities for Welsh learners to use their language outside the classroom, short translation work or putting clients in touch with a translator, and partnership with local organizations to offer social activities.

The first venture, Menter Cwm Gwendraeth, was established in January 1991. It acted as a pioneering program to promote Welsh at the community level and to provide a model for language planning that could be adapted to other parts of Wales. Its initial strategy aimed at the following:

- To create social conditions that will nurture positive attitudes toward Welsh and an increase in its general use
- To normalize the use of Welsh as a medium of social and institutional communication
- To highlight the close relationship between language and attitudes that relate to quality-of-life issues, the environment, and the local economy

Understandably, as each Menter is designed to serve a local area with quite varying socioeconomic needs and strengths, there will be variants on the original model described above. One such variant is the second Menter established, namely, Menter Aman Tawe, whose goals were to act as a program to promote the Welsh language in the Tawe and Aman Valleys.

Menter Aman Tawe functioned as a coordinating forum for Welsh in a relatively depressed region ravaged by the twin effects of deindustrialization and high levels of out-migration. It focused its activities on youth work and on adopting Welsh as a natural extension of daily life, including the creation of social activities, games, and cultural events, as the conventional social networks, having broken down, were less able to support Welsh-medium vitality. In its early days, it placed a great emphasis on direct social involvement with people and paid far less attention to structural planning than did other mentrau. Some might argue that Menter Aman Tawe's impact was thus more immediate and direct, adopting an essentially pragmatic mode of action. However, this style also reflected the social class and occupational structure of the area, which is predominantly working class and relatively poor.

Initially some 25 village committees were established to expedite the work of the Menter. By 1997, many had ceased to function due to a lack of sustained enthusiasm on the part of the volunteers. After the initial enthusiasm abated, Menter Aman Tawe was faced with the lack of social leaders who could advance its cause. There was no lack of commitment or initiative displayed by its staff; what was lacking was a sense of community ownership of the Menter, as opposed to a community interest in its success. As the national network of Mentrau Iaith themselves developed, it was recognized that the needs of the Aman valley could be better served by amalgamating the initial Menter organizations so as to produce economies of scale and build capacity from within the broader area covered by the County of Neath Port Talbot.

The principal consequence of linguistic intervention in the postindustrial valleys of Gwendraeth and Aman was an upsurge in community confidence and pride as residents experienced the regenerative impulse of more dynamic sociolinguistic activity in the locality. It has also contributed to the re-formation of cultural and socioeconomic networks on a limited scale. This observation holds true for many of the other 20 Welsh mentrau established in the intervening period. In tandem with national language strategies, the Mentrau Iaith have prompted many of their local region's institutions to offer a practical language choice in their service provision. These new opportunities have led to the strengthening of Welsh-medium activities in the spheres of popular culture, sport, health care, children's activities, and so on.

Evaluation of the Mentrau and Community Language Planning

Today the Mentrau Iaith continue to refine their national framework and core mission, having become significant agencies for tackling linguistic fragmentation. Another advantage is that mentrau can encourage the use of Welsh in limited domains and without them constituting part of the official administration of any district. To maximize this autonomy, mentrau staff have to display political acumen and demonstrate interpersonal skills, for they must operate as respected coordinating bodies, without necessarily accruing any political status or institutional power.

The better developed mentrau possess a great deal of experience and have adopted earlier policy recommendations made by WLB-sponsored reviews such as the Community Language Project (C. H. Williams & Evas, 1997), which sought to outline a strategic framework for the development of mentrau. The Community Language Project also recommended concentrating on how social leaders are nurtured and integrated into the language regeneration process. Three other means of revitalizing Welsh within the context of community language planning proposed by Williams and Evas (1997, 1998) included Local Action Plans, which have been adopted; by contrast, the establishment of resource centers at county and national levels and developing the role of linguistic *animateurs* have not yet been supported.

A second review *Venturing Onwards* (Jones & Ioan, 2000) contained two significant recommendations:

The WLB's statutory functions, funding and staffing levels must be extended in order to guarantee its influence and effectiveness in co-ordinating language planning initiatives both nationally and at community level; and secondly that any local language planning must be backed by national institutional power; otherwise, members of the local communities do not have sufficient power to achieve any change themselves. (p. 123)

As a result of implementing these recommendations, the mentrau witnessed a period of sustained growth, becoming an integral element of Welsh language policy and planning. By 2008, a network of 22 Mentrau Iaith had been established, with support from the WLB totaling £1,450.537. This was a 122.3% increase on the level of support for the 18 mentrau who in 2001/2002 received £652,425. The mentrau also attract funding from other sources such as Local Authorities, the European Commission, and the National Lottery. In comparative spending terms, the WLB in 2007–2008 allocated £2,844,820 to promote Welsh language education, £1,123,601 to Mudiad Ysgolion Meithrin (the Welsh-medium nursery school organization), £663,754 to Urdd Gobaith Cymru (the Welsh League of Youth), and £478,839 to the National Eisteddfod of Wales (WLB, 2008b).

The mentrau continue to attract a wide variety of external funding so as to pursue their collective aims, thus they become a more integral element of community life and service provision. For example, in 2012, Menter Iaith Sir Ddinbych gained Heritage Lottery Funding for developing their Memories Museum project, while neighboring Menter Iaith Conwy attracted project finance from the Rural Development Plan to fund a County Translation service, an Outdoor Pursuits Agency, and to subsidize attendance for adult learners of Welsh at the National Language Centre in Nant Gwrtheyrn.

Outstanding Challenges

How have the Mentrau Iaith responded to successive changes in the welfare state, the neoliberal, and the emergent Welsh tradition? Having initially been largely dependent on the WLB for their finance, direction, and legitimacy, the mentrau were in a precarious position as a grassroots language regime. The neoliberal concern with regulation, target setting, value for money, and accountability increased the pressures on the mentrau to be institutionalized and brought into conformity with the dictates of a semistate agency, which they sought to resist. This brought on disagreements with the WLB over directions of strategy, issues of funding, and accountability. One common source of tension was that several mentrau, to secure additional finances, had extended their original brief and became service providers in a range of fields, such as tourism, social services, Welsh language teaching, and translation, and so on. But this was a predictable response to the neoliberal pressures as they responded both to market demands and to the various sources of funding, both local and EU, that were available.

A further criticism is that some mentrau at some stages in their development lacked ambition and were far too isolated from the national network and the sponsoring bodies, often disorganized and financially prone to short-term disasters for lack of accurate and professional planning. Again this is a feature of being reliant on local volunteers, many of whom are engaged in winning the soft targets or engaging in the more "fun" aspects of youth work, or cultural activities, rather than the management and control aspects of administration. Consequently, the WLB had difficult periods when it sought to exercise the strictures of fiscal probity, regular accounting procedures, and good local governance practice.

Issues of finance, remit, and responsibility have also reflected a wider set of tensions between the emergent Welsh tradition and the prevailing U.K. state tradition that at times has complemented and/or been "hegemonized" by that state tradition. Although the mentrau are more reflective of the Welsh tradition, they are not immune to these shifts in the state tradition.

In relation to community development, the Welsh Government has inherited the WLB's staff expertise and is responsible for continued financial support, which in 2012–2013 involved a £1.5 million contribution to the costs of the mentrau. The mentrau adhere to the aims enunciated in the Welsh Language Strategy 2012–2017 (Welsh Government, 2012a), which is a product of a more distinct autochthonous Welsh tradition. One of the two operational changes of note is that the mentrau now make a bid for finance in their annual grant application, which may also involve them in undertaking to do more diversified work for additional finance. The second reform is that the Welsh Government now funds Mentrau Iaith Cymru directly to undertake part of the responsibilities the WLB discharged. This involves the diffusion of information, community best practice, and innovative ideas; the production of a monthly bulletin; the arranging of seminars, workshops, and conferences; and the in-service training of staff and volunteers, together with direct support for individual mentrau. It would seem sensible to enhance the role of Mentrau Iaith Cymru as the national agency responsible for delivering an overall strategy, training, and capacity building within the field; engaging in economies of scale with respect to human resource issues, insurance, police, and security vetting of new staff; the cocreation of new projects; and specializing in large grant applications that several of the smaller mentrau find daunting and beyond their resources.

For these developments to bear fruit, there would have to be a corresponding strengthening of the capacities of the core civil staff within the Welsh Government who are responsible for community language policy, especially as they relate to the much larger Community First project and the reconfigured Welsh language policy directorate, which since June 2013 is answerable directly to the First Minister of Wales.

Given that these changes will involve a more direct, interventionist approach the future development of the mentrau raises some intriguing questions. First, should any additional mentrau be conceived primarily as a language or community or economic development enterprise, or a combination thereof? Second, are there too many mentrau and would some rationalization along subregional lines be a more effective use of staff, resources, and energy? Third, what should be the relationship between the mentrau and the local authorities? In time, one can anticipate that selected local authorities be asked to shoulder more responsibility for supporting the needs of any new, refashioned or existing mentrau iaith. In political terms, this may be a positive move as it is far more likely to enable mentrau iaith to coordinate their myriad activities *within* a variety of well-established statutory and voluntary organizations, enabling them to operate as cost-effective interventionist agencies engaged in the process of community regeneration. However, as a result of a number of structural reforms and fiscal cutbacks, the capacity of local government to take on more and more responsibilities is open to question.

If mentrau are meant to be interventionist agencies, should they be a short-term or a medium-term venture? One of the paradoxes facing mentrau is that they are destined to lose their catalytic element by becoming incorporated into the institutional system they were designed to effect through intervention. Thus, need mentrau necessarily be temporary adjuncts to other community initiatives as was the original WLB approach? Or given that the current Welsh Government has taken direct responsibility for the language, should they become permanent agencies within the linguistic regime charged with the coordination and encouragement of Welsh-medium activities initiated by others? Governments tend to wish to fund such initiatives only for a relatively short life span so as to encourage self-sufficiency through the search for new core funding, but they often find themselves unable to jettison the financial guarantees they provide. Although financial autarchy may be a viable ambition, there is still a tendency to treat the mentrau as an extension of government language policy. Theoretically the menter employees are answerable to their local committee, but in several cases government bodies have treated them as proxy civil servants and in the most extreme cases have stepped in, suspending their grant-in-aid and foreclosing on failing mentrau.

However, herein lies a major conundrum for planners and activists alike. Unless there is a clearer definition of the role of mentrau and a shared operational conception of basic terms like *community, empowerment,* and *partnership,* there is every possibility that this type of language planning will be challenged periodically. As public finances become more limited, attempts will be made to "return" or "transfer" to the community the power and responsibility for the reproduction of Welsh without also releasing the necessary political and economic investment to realize this wish fulfillment as social practice.

Finally, three trends need to be taken into account. First the costs of community support have risen considerably, but the initial financial dependence on the WLB has given way to a more diverse basis that includes central government and local authority finance, private finance, and EU support. Second, the range of mentrau activities is growing and cumulative. Consequently there is a need for economies of scale and for prioritizing where language-related investment is located so as to support the increasing demands on the provision of new software, IT, translation, terminological innovations, best practice work programs, templates, and so on. This calls for a careful central control of corpus and status planning (currently within the purview of the Welsh Language Commissioner), so that unnecessary duplication in a fairly limited market is reduced. Third, the support of the Welsh Government has been critical in terms of setting out language policy in its strategic document *Iaith Pawb* (2003) and later related policy statements, particularly the Welsh Language Strategy (2012a). It was recognized in 2003 that to deliver this policy, the central language planning agency, the WLB, needed to build up its staff and resource capacity so as to manage and fund these initiatives, and this expansion was achieved. Consequently, although much of the potential for community language planning has been based on the willingness of committed volunteers and professionals, the case for the development of the various policies has been grounded in evidence-based evaluations and regular monitoring of the programs. This has provided a robust argument for the promotion of Welsh and has consequently been far less susceptible to accusations that such programs fail to satisfy community needs and long-term improvements in social welfare, skills acquisition, economic diversification, and leisure activities. In fact, quite the opposite case can be made with confidence, for such initiatives appear to work and are thus worthy of continued development in the Welsh context.

LANGUAGE POLICY REFORM IN CONSTITUTIONAL PERSPECTIVE

The transition from administrative to legislative devolution in Wales has demonstrated many of the complexities inherent in U.K. constitutional reform. Issues of legislative competence, joint scrutiny of draft bills, and the interdependence of senior civil servants in briefing on common issues are all critical to the success of the manner in which both Westminster and Cardiff legislation apply to Wales. I want to argue that in terms of the prevailing discourse, we have moved inexorably during the period 1993–2013 from a misplaced faith in language promotion to a misplaced faith in language regulation as the contours of Welsh language policy have been shaped by successive official strategies, legislative initiatives, and profound organizational change.

In May 2011, the NAW election saw the Labour Party returned to power with 30 of the 60 available National Assembly Members.[30] The First Minister, Carwyn Jones, renamed the Wales Assembly Government as the Welsh Government and with a slimmed-down cabinet transferred responsibility for the Welsh language from the Heritage Department to the Education Department, headed by Leighton Andrews, Assembly Member. Although this aligned the interests of the Welsh language far closer to the main statutory responsibility of education, it did not necessarily reduce the crosscutting relevance of bilingualism for all policy matters of the Government of Wales. With the resignation of Leighton Andrews, the Minister for Education and Skills, on June 25, 2013, Welsh language policy was transferred to the remit of First Minister Carwyn Jones with immediate effect.

Having abolished the WLB in March 2012, some of its functions were transferred to government and some to a Welsh Language Commissioner, which became operative in April 2013.

The Welsh Language Commissioner

How might the Welsh Language Commissioner's duties and basic operation be developed? The development of a robust system could be a major step forward in implementing language standards, especially if specific attention were paid to the sociolinguistic condition of various types of community contexts. Of major interest is just how the new set of Standards, particularly those concerned with service delivery that are the core of the Language Measure, will play out in society.

It is evident that the Measure should be as clear and unambiguous as possible in its application, so it must be able to answer the doubt of cynics as to what exactly the legislation is purporting to achieve. A common complaint of the Measure in its formative stages was that this was a piece of framework legislation that did little to specify the exact nature of language responsibilities in Wales, and even less for members of the public to know what exactly they could claim as an unconditional expectation in the provision of language services and national standards. Recent debates over the setting of standards, the government's rejection of the Commissioner's proposed version in the March 2013, and government's insistence that a new, simpler, and more operational set be codified had delayed but not damaged the idea of a comprehensive set of standards.

In related fashion, some may argue that the Measure militates against the principle of equal treatment and application to a far greater extent than does the Welsh Language Act of 1993. They would argue that the one cardinal obligation of the 1993 Act is that it requires all organizations to prepare a common core legally binding document, namely, the Welsh Language Scheme. However, much of the strength of the new set of standards is that they are more binding and subject to far greater regulatory control than the Language Scheme, so that the principle of equal treatment and consistency should be well served if the new system is implemented rigorously.

Among the institutional challenges the Commissioner will face is the issue of legitimizing the role and the office. It could be argued that a timely investigation of the Welsh Government's noncompliance would certainly demonstrate the independence of the office, but with what medium-term implications? A related institutional issue is how to keep the "best" of the WLB process and experience while demonstrably active in a new context.

It seems evident that some additional work will have to be undertaken in order to define and finesse the relationship between the *promotion* of Welsh as an official language and its *regulation* in terms of the compliance functions of the Welsh Language Measure, that is, the statutory regulation. Additionally, one may legitimately ask how the Welsh Language Commissioner will influence behavior and initiate reform within the public administration system and with the Welsh public writ large. Part of the answer will undoubtedly be influenced by the style, authority, and character of the prime officeholder and senior colleagues, and in consequence, one may ask what weighting should be given to advocacy and a proactive stance in operationalizing the remit of the post?

Doubtless, when the revised Welsh system is fully operational there will be some additional challenges.[31] The most critical in both conceptual and operational terms is to make the new system work in a timely and professional fashion. A real consideration must be to guard against the temptation to spend an inordinate amount of time establishing the new system, and thus lose momentum or public engagement. A related medium-term challenge is to determine how best to develop additional legislative measures in relation to language policy and the creep toward defining "rights" in this field. If such rights are to be realizable they must also be resistant to challenge, else the edifice will crumble.

One of the effects of constitutional reform in the United Kingdom is that we are evolving toward a variable geometry of legislative outcomes as a result of the increasing competence in devolved fields being demonstrated by parliaments and assemblies in Scotland, Wales, and Northern Ireland. An underlying thread in the discussion, which has influenced the progress toward the establishment of a Welsh Language Commissioner, is the proposition that in time the Commissioner would be charged with putting forward draft proposals by which the notion of language rights might be realized as legislative fact by the NAW.[32] This proposition goes far beyond the adjudicative role of an ombudsman or auditor general and aligns the Commissioner far closer to the Welsh Language Policy Unit and NAW clerks as they seek to reflect law advances in policy development. In that respect, the Commissioner will have a more proactive rights role than that currently exercised by all the other subject Commissioners in Wales, whose mandates derive from an earlier period and have not been determined by primary legislation with an express obligation to develop a rights agenda.

The Emergence of a Welsh Tradition?

Revitalization elements have depended on a lucid exposition of the role of the former semiautonomous WLB in the process of stimulating practical developments in language planning. Now that the Welsh Government has taken direct control over Welsh language policy, consideration should be given to additional variables that influence language revitalization efforts. In some senses, this may be reflective of an emerging third state tradition, namely, the Welsh tradition. Having been so long dominated by the Labour Party and socialist principles, there remains in Wales an uncompromising attachment to distinct interventionist politics, to the Welfare State, the National Health Service, and universal benefits, in the form of "free" medical prescriptions, transport and bus passes for the over-60s, and nonpunitive university fees for Welsh residents or those from Wales who have opted to study at other U.K. universities. The fiscal pressures may emanate from a neoliberal U.K. Treasury, but within the Barnett Formula budget the Welsh government exercises a considerable amount of discretion. As a result, it has given priority to community regeneration, the up-skilling of the work force, and backing local initiatives for self-sustaining growth.

CONCLUSION

The driver for language revitalization has been the unstinting commitment of individuals acting as parents, local sociopolitical activists, or decision makers. The initial domain they targeted was the formal education system, and the platform this created for subsequent developments in creating a partial bilingual society should not be underemphasized. It is significant that the contours of language revitalization have not followed a national plan or strategy in a slavish manner; they have been largely ad hoc, if innovative. Having been initiated as an organic, ground-up movement, language revitalization shows increased signs of top-down language planning and professional direction. For the first time in Welsh history, the government has shouldered responsibility for language policy and operates within a potentially robust promotional and regulatory context. In that respect, although the demolingusitic reality may continue to disappoint, given that so many of the Welsh speakers produced by the education system inevitably migrate, those who remain face a more positive future where increased opportunities to learn, live, and work in Welsh are being realized. If the Welsh example of language revitalization teaches us anything, it is that stubborn collective action by the community must be stimulated before government language policy responds in a reactive manner, but having so responded, that community engagement must also be maintained, for fear of losing direction and long-term momentum (Williams, 2007a, 2007b).

ACKNOWLEDGMENTS

I am grateful to Meirion Prys Jones and Joy Penton for their critical comments that helped improve the structure and logic of this chapter.

NOTES

[1]The darkening veil might have categorized the predicament of the Welsh language from around 1871 to 1971. In this chapter, I argue that gradually the colonial and relatively pessimistic darkened veil of the previous generations is being lifted and replaced by a more constructive, purposive, and outcome-oriented set of actions so as to restore Welsh to its role as a national language.

[2]The category of language revitalization referred to tends to be subsumed under substate nationalism.

[3]I will not rehearse the historical process of state integration. For accounts, see C. H. Williams (2000) and Jenkins and Williams (2000).

[4]The initial concern with devising an official policy for Welsh language education within the Welsh Department of the Education Board may be traced to 1907; thereafter, a small number of highly influential central government reports drew attention to the desirability of increasing the provision of Welsh language teaching. For details, see Morgan (2003).

[5]The most influential actors were Cymdeithas yr Iaith Gymraeg (The Welsh Language Society), Cefn, RhAG, CYDAG, and more episodically Cymuned (Cymdeithas yr Iaith Gymraeg, 2005).

[6]Groups such as Adfer and Cefn in the past, and Cymuned, CYD, Dyfodol, and RhAG today, have augmented the pressure brought to bear by the Welsh Language Society in terms of a collective movement to advocate reforms in the field of civil rights, housing, tourism, planning, education, language legislation, a Property Act, and the deepening of the bilingual character of the National Assembly.

[7]An element of this approach may be seen in C. H. Williams (2013).

[8]The Welsh Language Act of 1993, passed by the U.K. Parliament on October 21, 1993, repealed several of the historically significant pieces of legislation that had shaped the contours of Welsh life, not least the Laws in Wales Acts of 1535 and 1542, the so-called Acts of Union of England and Wales, which incorporated the territory of Wales into the English Crown system and state.

[9]The Welsh Language Board, a semistate agency was created by the Welsh Language Act of 1993 and functioned between 1993 and March 2012 when it was abolished and some of its functions were divided between the Welsh Government and the newly created office of the Commissioner for the Welsh Language.

[10]Of the eight county authorities at the time, only six had a language plan.

[11]In the period 1994–1999, John Walter Jones, the Chief Executive of the WLB, had a firm and robust view of how the organization should be run and what its immediate remit should be. Within the education section, a more creative and free hand was allowed, which brought dividends in terms of a strategic oversight and innovative action/intervention. Rhodri Williams as Chair of the WLB secured some internal rearrangements, Meirion P. Jones became responsible for Language Planning, and Prys Davies became responsible for Language Schemes; as a consequence of these appointments, a more integrated approach was adopted toward thematic development, innovation, and forging new partnerships.

[12]For details of this Transfer Within Family initiative, please visit http://twfcymru.com/?skip=1&lang=en

[13]The two terms *Welsh-medium* and *bilingual* are often used interchangeably in general discourse; however, the former term refers to designated schools whereas the latter is a more loose term incorporating a range of contexts, situations, and practices.

[14]This is in many ways a sketch of the current system and is offered as a summary overview and interpretation of selected issues only.

[15]The three pioneering high schools were Ysgol Glan Clwyd (1956) and Ysgol Maes Garmon, (1961) in Flintshire and Ysgol Uwchradd Rhydfelen in Glamorganshire (1962).

[16]Active participants in southeast Wales included Dorothy Rees, Member of Parliament; Gwyn Daniel; Cassie Davies; Maxwell Evans; Lily Richards; and Raymond Edwards, whereas pioneering teachers at nursery and primary level in one location, Barry, included Ceinwen Clarke, Irene Williams, Rachel Williams, W. R. Evans, and Elwyn Richards.

[17]In one of the repeating dualisms of language policy in Wales, the Education Reform Act of 1988 removed responsibility for Further Education from Gwynedd's direct control just as it was about to launch a major push in bilingual education within that sector. I am grateful to Dr. Carlin for this observation.

[18]For a comprehensive account of the growth of Welsh-medium schools, 1939–2000, see I. W. Williams (2003).

[19]WAG (2003).

[20]Piecemeal and infrequent research has been undertaken on several aspects of Welsh-medium education, largely in the form of snapshot surveys or more sustained PhD theses, such as that completed by H. S. Thomas in 2009 and elaborated on in Thomas and Williams (2013), which is replete with acute insights and evidence-based policy recommendations.

[21]Succession is a major problem at all levels after primary education is completed. Thus, were the same number of pupils to be enrolled in senior secondary and post-18 courses as are enrolled as 5- or 7-year-olds in the educational system, the capacity to use Welsh as a real language of choice within social and commercial life would be revolutionized.

[22]In Wales, England, and Northern Ireland, a Key Stage is a stage of the education system that identifies the educational knowledge expected of pupils at various ages.

[23]A more general point is that in many respects the education system works reasonably well, and thus the reflections presented here deal only with those "problem areas" or issues that need far more robust government leadership and clearer strategies.

[24]The Department of Education and its Minister have a crucial role, but the relationship with Local Authorities is often tense when it comes to sanctioning or disallowing the establishment of Welsh-medium schools, for example, Caerffili, Cardiff, and Carmarthenshire.

[25]The WLB had a statutory duty to provide strategic oversight in the policy area of bilingual education but little real power to direct the internal deliberations of HEIs. Some would argue that the WLB had not exercised its duty for strategic planning, as the lack of cross-border local authority cooperation has shown: Ysgol Gyfun Llangynwyd is an obvious example.

[26]It is recognized that a great deal of tension is inherent in the structural transformation Welsh is undergoing in its progress from a political football to a public good; perhaps this is a necessary creative stage, but for how long should it endure and why has not the political

system conformed to a more mature representation of Welsh as a national resource? These are deep and troubling questions that go to the heart of the power relationship between the linguistic minority and the state.

[27]Other considerations that I do not investigate here are the following: Are we developing a linguistic underclass? What is the link between language of home, school, community, media, and society? Despite warnings, are we continuing to overburden the education system in order to deliver solutions to largely identity and sociolinguistic issues? How are we to deal with the growing discrepancy between the official institutional perspective and the "street" perspective on Welsh language rights, behavior, and achievements?

[28]I recognize that progression from the statutory sector to the higher education sector relates to a different type of succession and opens up a greater deal of choice in terms of discipline specialization. Nevertheless, the overall point regarding continuity of both language of instruction and language of assessment remains pertinent.

[29]This includes start-up investment in Welsh-medium lectureships in a range of nontraditional subjects and pressure to recognize skills qualifications and training for the professions, for example, the Law, Pharmacy, Optometry, Accountancy, and so on.

[30]I use the term *banal* in the same manner as many have used it to describe *banal nationalism*—that is, the taken-for-granted, everyday reality of eking out an existence in this all-too-fraught and fragile world.

[31]For the short term, they governed alone, but they had to strike an accord with the Liberal Democrats to get their first budget through. If the Government adopts a heavy legislative and policy program, they will likely seek a junior coalition partner to ensure a relatively stable period of office.

[32]Legal experts have suggested to me that if the Scottish precedent holds true, there will be far less instances than expected as civil society tends to be "tolerant" of the need for devolved powers to bed in and be given time to work and adapt to a new legal system.

[33]Prior to the details of the Language Measure being known I would have said that this would seem to be an incongruous role for the Commissioner's Office, even if the temptation to boost the NAW's competence and capacity might favor close cooperation between the Parliamentary drafters and the Language Commission. When confronted by unclear authority in unchartered waters, prudence suggests a strict separation of the functions of the lawmakers and the law regulators.

REFERENCES

Baker, C., & Jones, M. P. (1999). *Dilyniant mewn Addysg Gymraeg* [Succession in Welsh education]. Cardiff, Wales: Welsh Language Board.

Campbell, C. (2000). Menter Cwm Gwendraeth: A case study in community language planning. In C. H. Williams (Ed.), *Language revitalization: Policy and planning in Wales* (pp. 247–290). Cardiff, Wales: University of Wales Press.

Cwmni Iaith. (2008). *Creating a truly bilingual Wales: Opportunities for legislating and implementing policy.* Newcastle Emlyn, Wales: Author. Retrieved from http://www.iaith.eu/uploads/report_on_welsh_langugae_legislation.pdf

Cymdeithas yr Iaith Gymraeg. (2005). *Deddf Iaith Newydd—Dyma'r Cyfle, Papur Trafod* [A new language law—Here is the opportunity]. Aberystwyth, Wales: Author.

Her Majesty's Stationery Office. (1993). *Welsh Language Act.* London, England: Author.

Jenkins, G., & Williams, M. (Eds.). (2000). *Let's do our best for the ancient tongue: The Welsh language in the twentieth century.* Cardiff, Wales: University of Wales Press.

Jones, K., & Ioan, G. (2000). *Venturing onwards.* Cardiff, Wales: Welsh Language Board.

Lewis, H. G. (2010, December 9). A yw ysgolion dwyieithog yn llwyddo? [Do bilingual schools succeed?]. *Golwg*, p. 11.

Menter a Busnes. (2010). *Communities first & bilingualism: Meeting the challenge*. Aberystwyth, Wales: Author. Retrieved from http://estynllaw.org/uploads/meeting_the_challenge.pdf

Morgan, I. (2003). The early days of Welsh-medium schools. In I. W. Williams (Ed.), *Our children's language* (pp. 21–44). Talybont, Wales: Y Lolfa.

Redknap, C. (2006). Welsh-medium and bilingual education and training: Steps towards a holistic strategy. In W. G. Lewis & H. G. F. Roberts (Eds.), *Welsh-medium and bilingual education* (pp. 1–20). Gwynedd, Wales: Bangor University, School of Education.

Thomas, H., & Williams, C. H. (Eds.). (2013). *Parents, personalities and power*. Cardiff, Wales: University of Wales Press.

Welsh Assembly Government. (2003). *"Iaith-Pawb": National action plan for a bilingual Wales*. Cardiff, Wales: Author.

Welsh Government. (2011). *Review of the Welsh Language Support Service for Schools*. Cardiff, Wales: Author. Retrieved from http://dera.ioe.ac.uk/13165/1/110701athrawonbroen.pdf

Welsh Government. (2012a). *A living language: A language for living—Welsh Language Strategy 2012–2017*. Cardiff, Wales: Author. Retrieved from http://wales.gov.uk/docs/dcells/publications/122902wls201217en.pdf

Welsh Government. (2012b). *Headline results: 2011 Census*. Cardiff, Wales: Author.

Welsh Language Board. (1995). *Strategic review*. Cardiff, Wales: Author.

Welsh Language Board. (2005). *The future of Welsh: A strategic plan*. Cardiff, Wales: Author.

Welsh Language Board. (2006). *Response by the Welsh Language Board to the Consultation by the Welsh Assembly Government on the merger with the Welsh Language Board*. Cardiff, Wales: Author.

Welsh Language Board. (2008a). *Language awareness training pack*. Cardiff, Wales: Author.

Welsh Language Board. (2008b). *Annual review 2007–08*, Cardiff, Wales: Author.

Welsh Language Board. (2010). *Annual report 2010*. Cardiff, Wales: Author.

Welsh Local Government Association. (2004). *The role of local authorities in a post quango Wales*. Cardiff, Wales: Author.

Williams, C. H. (Ed.). (2000). *Language revitalization: Policy and planning in Wales*. Cardiff, Wales: University of Wales Press.

Williams, C. H. (2004). Iaith-Pawb: The doctrine of plenary inclusion. *Contemporary Wales*, 17, 1–27.

Williams, C. H. (2007a). Deddfwriaeth Newydd a'r Gymraeg [New legislation and the Welsh language]. *Contemporary Wales*, 19, 217–233.

Williams, C. H. (Ed.). (2007b). *Language and governance*. Cardiff, Wales: University of Wales Press.

Williams, C. H. (2008). *Linguistic minorities in democratic context*. Basingstoke, England: Palgrave.

Williams, C. H. (2010). From act to action in Wales. In D. Morris (Ed.), *Welsh in the twenty first century* (pp. 36–60), Cardiff, Wales: University of Wales Press.

Williams, C. H. (2013). *Minority language promotion, protection and regulation*. Basingstoke, England: Palgrave.

Williams, C. H., & Evas, J. (1997). *The Community Research Project*. Cardiff, Wales: Welsh Language Board.

Williams, C. H., & Evas, J. (1998). *Community language regeneration: Realising the potential*. Cardiff, Wales: Welsh Language Board.

Williams, I. W. (2003). *Our children's language*. Talybont, Wales: Y Lolfa.

FURTHER READING

Ahmed, T. (2011). *The impact of EU law on minority rights*. Oxford, England: Hart.

Loughlin, J. (2009). The "hybrid" state: Reconfiguring territorial governance in Western Europe. *Perspectives on European Politics and Society*, 10, 51–68.

Marquand, D. (2004). *The decline of the public.* Oxford, England: Polity Press.

National Assembly for Wales. (1999). The National Assembly (Transfer of Function) Order 1999 (S.I. 1999/672). Cardiff, Wales: National Assembly for Wales.

National Assembly for Wales. (2009). *Legislative Committee No 5.* Retrieved from http://www.assemblywales.org/bus-home/bus-legislation/bus-leg-legislative-competence-orders/bus-legislation-lco-2009-no10.htm

Rawlings, R. (2003). *Delineating Wales.* Cardiff, Wales: University of Wales Press.

Richard Commission. (2004). *Report of the Commission on the powers and electoral arrangements of the National Assembly for Wales.* Cardiff, Wales: National Assembly for Wales.

Welsh Assembly Government. (2006). *Consultation by the Welsh Assembly Government on the merger with the Welsh Language Board.* Cardiff, Wales: Author.

Welsh Assembly Government. (2007). *Defining schools according to Welsh-medium provision* (Information Document 023/2007). Cardiff, Wales: Author.

Welsh Government. (2012). *School census results, July 2012.* Cardiff, Wales: Author. Retrieved from http://wales.gov.uk/docs/statistics/2012/120711sdr1082012en.pdf

Welsh Language Board. (1991). *Recommendations for a new Welsh Language Act, February.* Cardiff, Wales: Author.

Welsh Language Board. (2001). *Annual report and accounts, 2000–01.* Cardiff, Wales: Author.

Welsh Office. (1997). *A voice for Wales, Llais dros Gymru* (Cm. 3718 of July 1997). Cardiff, Wales: Author.

Williams, C. H. (1989). New domains of the Welsh language: Education, planning and the law. *Contemporary Wales, 3,* 41–76.

Williams, C. H. (1998). Operating through two languages. In J. Osmond (Ed.), *The National Assembly agenda* (pp. 101–115). Cardiff, Wales: Institute of Welsh Affairs.

Williams, C. H. (2000). Governance and the language. *Contemporary Wales, 12,* 130–154.

Williams, G., & Morris, D. (2000). *Language planning and language use: Welsh in a global age.* Cardiff, Wales: University of Wales Press.

Chapter 11

The Weight of English in Global Perspective: The Role of English in Israel

Elana Shohamy

Tel Aviv University

INTRODUCTION

Similar to most countries in the world today, English in Israel plays a major role, both as a global and a local language in multiple domains such as business, academia, media, and education, as well as in daily interactions. English is the language of texts that students are required to read in academia in most disciplines; it is a language frequently "peppered" in Hebrew oral interactions, especially by youth in urban spaces; it is a language widely used in the cyber space and the one used in global corporations and high-technological companies; it is also a language heard in most films and television programs accompanied by translations but no dubbing. Finally, it is a language that all students are required to learn from a very early age of elementary school and through the end of secondary school; in addition, a high level of English proficiency is required for admission into higher education institutions. English is the language that is widely displayed in public spaces, at times along with Hebrew and more rarely with Arabic; English is to be found also as a single language in names of shops, advertisements, names of buildings, commercials, announcements, and instructions. According to a study by Ben Rafael, Shohamy, Amara, and Trumper-Hecht (2006) that documented the languages displayed in public spaces (e.g., linguistic landscape), in Israel English is displayed almost as frequently as Hebrew, the dominant and official language, in areas where Jews reside. This is in stark contrast to the absence of English in public places in towns and villages where Arabs live; in these areas, Arabic, the other official language of Israel, is the main language of communication as well as the medium of instruction in all Arab schools. Arabic in these areas is dominant in public spaces, along with Hebrew; yet English is hardly to be found. The patterns

Review of Research in Education
March 2014, Vol. 38, pp. 273-289
DOI: 10.3102/0091732X13509773
© 2014 AERA. http://rre.aera.ne

that emerge indicate that English, a nonofficial language in Israel, plays an important role mostly in Jewish areas but in Arab communities, which make up 20% of the Israeli population, Hebrew is viewed as a "global" language; English, a compulsory language for all Arab students in schools from a very early age, is only minimally represented in public spaces. Furthermore, the level of English proficiency reached by Arab students is substantially lower than that of the Jews. Arabs invest most of their "language-learning energies" in learning Hebrew and in Modern Standard Arabic (MSA); English comes last.

Thus, although English plays a central role among those born into Hebrew families, it does not have the same status, role, and priority among groups who are born into different languages such as Arabs as well as immigrants, whose first priority is to acquire Hebrew, the lingua franca within Israel. Countries are not homogenous entities, and a theme such as "the role of English in Israel" needs to be analyzed and interpreted within the diverse communities and spaces in varied sociolinguistic realities. Indeed, current views of language policy do not view policies in homogenous terms but rather as complex phenomena embedded in multiple factors and layers (Johnson, 2010) that require a deeper level of study about the interconnections among languages, communities, and spaces. Thus, a study of English in a nation such as Israel requires a focus into the multiple complexities associated with history, ideology, politics, religion, economics, education, law, and geography. English, the "foreign visitor" and the "current player" in Israeli society, is embedded in those complex factors and realities. It is within this complexity that I will address here a set of factors regarding the multiple roles of English in Israeli education and society in an attempt to understand the following issues: How did it come to be? How is English connected to other languages? How does it relate to different groups, communities, and people? How accessible is English to all? To what extent does the presence of English support and/or challenge multilingualism? In our book, *The Languages of Israel* (Spolsky & Shohamy, 1999), we referred to English as "everybody's second language"; yet in this chapter I raise doubts as to whether English is in fact "everybody's language." If it is not, who are those who are left behind, who are those who cannot connect to English and whose access to education and employment is being denied? Does English perpetuate justice and equality? How is it manifested in the education systems? How does the dominance of English affect the linguistic diversity of minorities and immigrants? How do the ideologies, policies, and practices associated with the revival of Hebrew affect or how are they affected by the power of English and its high status.

The aim of this chapter then is to point to the complexities of the English language in Israel from a critical perspective, its global language status, and the manners in which it affects and interacts with a variety of local issues. The main focus is on how the presence of a global language, like English, affects a given sociolinguistic reality, bringing about specific consequences in terms of people's participation, equality, justice, and rights. Addressing these questions and issues will proceed along two main themes: The first is a historical and current perspective of the phases that English went through in Israel parallel to the revival of Hebrew and its accompanying ideologies; the second is the impact of the power of English on other languages and people, especially on Arabs, who use a different community language, and on immigrants, who arrive in Israel with home languages other than Hebrew. These groups are expected to acquire both Hebrew and English in order to participate and function in the society in education and employment.

ENGLISH AND HEBREW: COMPLEMENTARY RIVALRY

The relationship between English and Hebrew has been complex and dynamic and hence needs to be interpreted within the history of Israel. At the end of the 19th century, when Jews started to immigrate to the area, still under the Othman regime, Hebrew was constructed as an ideological language as a symbol of a new national collective identity. This continued during the years that the British ruled over Palestine, from 1917 to 1947, the *mandate* era. During most of these years, English was accepted as a language of the British government, whereas those who immigrated used the various languages of the places and communities from where they came in Europe, the United States, as well as Middle Eastern countries—German, Polish, Russian, Arabic, Turkish, and a variety of Jewish languages such as Yiddish, Ladino, Jewish Arabic, and so on. In those days, English was not viewed as a meaningful rival to the revival of Hebrew like some of the other languages of the immigrants, especially Yiddish, German, and Polish. The British implemented a trilingual official language policy with English as the government language, Hebrew as the language of the Jewish community, and Arabic for the Arab communities. Still, given that English was the language associated with the British regime that Jews wanted to overthrow in the process of reaching independence, it was viewed by some as a symbol of colonialization. It is mostly toward the end of the mandate years that the English language became more closely associated with the British rule. Indeed, one of the first acts of the Israeli Government after reaching independence was to remove English from the official list as an overt act of independence from the colonial rule, leaving Hebrew and Arabic as the two official languages. Although English in the 1950s was constructed negatively as the language of the colonializer and as a threat to the revival of Hebrew, it regained prestige, mostly in the 1960s, when it became associated with the United States and globalization; in all these years it has been continued to be taught in schools. Yet the widespread use and power of English have been perceived in those years as endangering the status, vitality, and revival of Hebrew. English today is accepted as a legitimate and essential language in schools and society but "up to a point" only. This means that there is still fear in many Hebrew language planners and ideologues that English will sweep away the great accomplishment achieved by the revival of Hebrew. A detailed description of this process is described below.

As noted, the early years of migration of Jews to Palestine took place in the Othman era at the end of the 19th century. These influxes continued more intensively during the years of the British mandate when Palestine became a British mandate in 1917 and the League of Nations approved the Balfour Declaration to grant Jews the right to a homeland. One of the major ideologies of many of the leaders of the time, although not of Hertzel, the main visionary of Zionism, was the revival of the

Hebrew language and associating it with the creation of nationhood and collective national identity. The ideology then was to turn Hebrew from a written language, used mostly in prayer books, to a living language, a vernacular that will be used by all and in all domains of life—homes, education, and public spaces. The main agenda was to introduce the Hebrew language as a replacement to the many languages spoken and used by the Jewish immigrants who arrived in Palestine at the time. The Hebrew ideology was sweeping and oppressive and was targeted against both Jewish languages such as Yiddish and other territorial languages used by immigrants such as Polish, Russian, and especially German, given its high status as the language of science and literature at the time and a home language for many German Jews who arrived during the 1930s and who openly refused to give up German for the sake of Hebrew (Shohamy, 1994, 2008). Still, in 1923, Zionist activists who supported Hebrew managed to convince the British authorities to recognize Hebrew as an official language of the Jews in Palestine, resulting in the trilingual policy of English, Hebrew, and Arabic, mentioned above. Although in those years Hebrew had already become the language of instruction in school, only a relatively small number of people were proficient in the language, whereas Yiddish and other immigrant languages continued to be used at home and in public spaces (Segev, 1999). English in those days was mostly used by British officials as the language of government, but it was not viewed as a strong competition to Hebrew as the two languages were expected to live harmoniously with one another, serving complementary functions. Various documents of the time point to active campaigns promoting the use of Hebrew as the "only" language while rejecting all other languages. In some of these documents, English is mentioned as an exception, and the British are portrayed as those helping the Jews protect Hebrew from other languages, especially Yiddish (Shohamy, 2008). However, throughout most of these years English was taught in both Hebrew and Arab schools as an additional language.

Some groups, such as the Germans, resented the ideology of the sole rule of Hebrew, insisting that their newspapers should continue to appear in German; immigrants from Poland continued to send their children to Polish-speaking schools, and many others continued to use Yiddish at home, often unable or unwilling to learn Hebrew. English was not viewed in competition until the end of the 1930s and the beginning of the 1940s, when a number of activist groups marked English as the language of colonialization and called for its removal as a symbol of the British regime in the move to independence. This was especially reenforced when the British put a limit on the number of Jews who would be permitted to immigrate to Palestine so as to not change the demographic balance of the Jewish and Arab communities in Palestine. During this period, the British government came to be viewed as a rival instead of an ally, which brought about violent acts by extreme Jewish groups against the British rule. In those years, the English language became viewed as "the language of the enemy."

Below is an interview with Mr. Gabriel who was active in the *Gdud Maginei Ha-Safa* ("battalion for the defense of Hebrew"; quoted in Shohamy, 2008, p. 214):

> **Interviewer:** *Do you think it could have been done in another way?*
> **Mr. Gabriel:** *Maybe, if there was a government, then. But this was the time when the British were here, a very hating government. They would do anything they could to hurt us. Had they not been so much against us, things could have been different. So, we had no choice but to establish organizations such as the "gdud" and to take the authority into our own hands. These groups had to be established to ensure that we can revive and maintain the beauty of the Hebrew language, and especially the use of correct speech. The British and the English language were viewed as occupiers of the language.*

The partition policy by the United Nations in 1947 was followed by the war that led to the creation of the state of Israel, resulting in a change of the demographic balance so that a substantially lower number of Arabs remained in Israel and the Jews became the majority. As noted, one of the first acts of the newly formed Israeli government was to drop English as an official language, a symbolic act of "getting rid of the British." The removal of English was also an ideological act giving prime importance and centrality to Hebrew as the sole language, especially in the context of the vast migration at the time of immigrants who did not know Hebrew and the need to create a cohesive collective national identity.

The 1950s can be viewed as times when major government policies were introduced to spread Hebrew as a homogenous language, a language of instruction in all schools, accompanied by widespread education policies for teaching the language to adults as well as the establishment of the *Ulpans*, intensive schools for teaching Hebrew to professional immigrants. This included inventing new Hebrew words, establishing the Hebrew Language Academy, and introducing strong policies of language purity and language correction, directed mostly to the huge flow of new immigrants arriving in Israel after the Second World War. The negative attitudes toward English continued both in private and public spaces, but English continued to play a central role in the curriculum being taught in schools in both elementary and secondary levels and in higher education. This is an important policy given the taboo imposed on all other languages of the Jews such as German or Yiddish, which were totally banned at universities until the 1960s (Harshav, 1993; Spolsky & Shohamy, 1999).

Major political changes took place in the 1960s, with the closer affinity of Israel with the United States; the vast migration of Jews from English-speaking countries, especially North America; and the status of English as a global and international language. English was no longer associated with the British colonial regime but rather with the United States, especially since English has become not only the world's lingua franca but also the main language of communication for the Jews, substituting Yiddish, a language that almost vanished among secular Jews after the holocaust and the migration of Jews from Europe. English has become a major language in schools and universities, with substantial expansion of teaching hours in schools and the adoption of a communicative curriculum to fit the new role of English as a major international language of communication. English since then has become a highly desired language by most of the Jewish population in Israel and a requirement for university enrollment, given its role as the language of science and academia.

In spite of these developments or perhaps because of that, English has been viewed by many Hebrew language leaders as a threat to Hebrew. Voices of resistance to the growing power of English have been echoed frequently in the media and at academic conferences. There are cases when the head of the Hebrew Language Academy banned the proposed policy of the Minister of Education to use English as a medium of instruction in two content areas (crafts and gymnastics). The reason given was that such a policy will threaten Hebrew and lead to its decline. The Minister of Education gave in to the request, and no content-based instruction has been introduced in Israeli Jewish schools ever since. (No such objection was made with regard to teaching content in English for Arab schools.)

The power of English as a global language, its broad use among Jewish speakers, and especially its attraction to youth were framed as posing a major threat to the dominance of Hebrew. It is the combination of the global status of English along with Hebrew paranoia associated with national existential fear that positioned English in competition to Hebrew and its symbolism. Yet, along with that, there have been ample initiatives by parents, schools, and municipalities to develop programs to teach English at an earlier age, hoping that it would bring about higher proficiency in the language and greater mobility and status. Currently, most schools teach English from first grade, and often even earlier, defying the official education policy of later grades. Municipalities initiate programs to teach English by homeroom teachers in first grade, and some universities offer prestigious programs where English is the medium of instruction as part of internationalization of higher education and as an economic source drawing students from countries worldwide.

The resentment to such programs by Hebrew leaders and ideologues continues in this day and age and is always framed as a threat to the existence of Hebrew, that is, the fear that English might take over and eclipse the achievement of the revival of Hebrew and hence threaten collective national identity. The Hebrew Academy views its role as a source to not only introduce new words in Hebrew but also guard and protect Hebrew from English. As late as 2012, Professor Bar Asher, the head of the Hebrew Language Academy, stated that English poses a threat to Hebrew, especially in higher education. He expressed fears that it will become the medium of instruction that will rule the academic scene entirely. The battle against the use of English as a subject of academia is expressed in Paragraph 1 below, along with the response of universities' speakers who argue that English is needed as the language of science and academic prestige, presented in Paragraph 2; both have been taken from the Israeli newspaper *Haaretz* (Nesher, 2012).

Paragraph 1: *The Academy of the Hebrew Language has declared war against the increasing use of English in the country's institutions of higher learning. The academy says students have a right to speak and study in Hebrew in all course work. Academy President Moshe Bar-Asher has met with Education Minister Gideon Sa'ar and demanded that he takes action immediately. The academy called on Sa'ar to annul any ban on the use of Hebrew at any university or college department around the country. "That in the State of Israel there could be such a ban against Hebrew, as in the dark days of our people's existence, is inconceivable," said the academy. The academy called on Sa'ar to collect data and set clear criteria for the use of English in academic work. Tali Ben Yehuda, the academy's director-general, said "demands that students study in English represent the gravest expression of the trend" of minimizing Hebrew's role in academia. Demands that students speak or study in English constitute a phenomenon "that is expanding considerably." Unless steps are taken, she warned, "academic departments will instruct solely in English, and this will spread to the high schools, because a conscientious parent will not send his or her child to a high school that doesn't prepare the youngster for university study. According to Ben Yehuda, "We understand pressures faced by the universities regarding the world at large, but as far as I know, the State of Israel has not decided to endorse academic study in English. This isn't a private matter on which each academic department can reach its own decision to forgo studies in Hebrew. We want Hebrew to be spoken in Israel and used in undergraduate and graduate studies, and in every school around the country."* (Nesher, 2012)

Paragraph 2: *Yehuda Band, the head of the university's chemistry department, said last night that this English-use requirement did not apply to undergraduates. He said that "if someone tries to record research results in Hebrew, that consigns his or her work to oblivion—nobody will read the research summary. Every person who deals in science today in Israel reads English." According to Band, written work in English "adds prestige to the institution and departments where a graduate student writes his thesis. Whatever the language of the dissertation, the researcher will have to proceed to publish his work in English." According to Band, another argument in favor of English is Ben-Gurion University's desire to recruit foreign students. The moment there's a student in a class who doesn't speak Hebrew, the lesson has to be conducted in English. "Of course, these circumstances make things harder for people whose native tongue is Hebrew, and yet the use of English is something that any scientist has to master to advance in his or her work," Band said. "If a researcher doesn't know English, he's finished. If he doesn't know how to write in English, he won't be able to publish on his own and will depend on the largesse of others."* (Nesher, 2012)

Opposition to English occurs also in terms of displays in the public space. In 2006, Professor Zohar Shavit, a member of the Tel Aviv council, introduced a city provision that it will be compulsory to include Hebrew in all signs around the city of Tel Aviv.

In spite of this rivalry and the opposition of Hebrew language leaders, the situation at all universities in Israel is that they practice bilingual Hebrew-English policies since almost all academic texts that students read are in English whereas classes are taught in Hebrew. In some universities, there are provisions that require that at least one subject be taught in English. Still, the rivalry between Hebrew and English continues, which has a major impact on the education policy on English, as well as on the level of proficiency achieved by Israeli students. The Ministry of Education still opposes the early start of English, so only private funding is available to teach English in earlier grades; thus, only affluent schools can afford it. There is still no content-based instruction programs such as the CLIL (Content and Language Integrated Learning), widely used in Europe, at any Israeli schools. Many university students have great difficulties in reading academic texts in English, and a large number of students have to study in special English courses before they are accepted to the universities as high schools do not prepare them sufficiently for dealing with high-level English academic texts. English texts are almost never used in Hebrew classes in high schools, not even in subjects such as history, science, and literature. However, high proficiency in English serves as the main criterion for admission to universities, and students need to incur great financial expenses and spend a lot of time in order to prepare for these courses before they are accepted into universities. Thus, the lack of effective content-based teaching at schools and the strict separation of Hebrew from English in academic content prevent many students from entering universities. Thus, although Hebrew and English are intermingled in many domains of life in Israel and in virtual spaces, they are kept totally apart in the education systems of elementary and high schools. The fact that schools do not provide sufficient levels of English teaching means that many wealthy families have to send their children out of Israel to acquire higher levels of English and parents initiate programs that they finance rather than rely on the public education system. The current policies have a detrimental impact on English proficiency.

The rivalry between Hebrew and English can be observed in other places as well as in attitudes to immigrants who come from English-speaking countries. In a study by Blumstein and Shohamy (2012), titled "Do Speakers of Powerful Language Need to Be Empowered?" it was shown that immigrants from English-speaking countries, in opposition to immigrants from non–English speaking countries, are discriminated against in terms of public services. Although most immigrants to Israel obtain special services, like translation services for accommodation especially for Russians, French, and Ethiopian immigrants, no such services are provided to English speakers. It was found that immigrants who are proficient in English, the powerful language that most Israelis are eager to acquire, are being "penalized" as they do not obtain such services in English. In a series of interviews, English-speaking immigrants protested against the absence of language services in public life, especially in health services.

The main argument here is that proficiency in a powerful language (English) causes them to be overlooked as people, as immigrants, who are in need for services as any other immigrants: Their status as English speakers marks them as different. Most of the people in the study were senior citizen immigrants from North America, who despite their use of a powerful language, English, are not powerful enough in terms of their status as immigrants and hence do not demand language services in English such as those obtained by immigrants from other countries. English, even today, is not viewed as an immigrant language but rather as a powerful language in competition with Hebrew, resulting in discrimination against users of the language.

Yet, in spite of such strict top-down policy toward English as in competition with Hebrew, there is a strong bottom-up pressure demanding more English. The ongoing trend is for students to begin studying English in a much earlier age than the policy of the ministry permits, and store owners bypass the regulation regarding public signs by putting signs in English and include Hebrew in tiny letters, just to comply with municipal laws.

In conclusion, it is clear that the status of English in Israel is between high prestige and dominance to rejection and opposition by those who fear that English will become more dominant than Hebrew. There is the realization that English is important, global, international, and functional, but this realization is accompanied by questions and doubts as to the future of Hebrew, especially since the latter has only "recently" been revived and has become a vital national language. English in Israel is held captive by Hebrew: There is still lack of confidence about the future of Hebrew, and the price paid is the low level of English achieved by Israeli students and especially the fact that English serves as a gatekeeping device to higher education and the workplace. Bilingualism in the two languages in spite of the reality of university studies and the public spaces is still viewed as a threat to the great achievement of Hebrew revival, and any mixture and trans-languaging among the two languages is viewed negatively, although it is very common. There is wide acceptance of English as a global language and ample use of the two languages in public spaces and certainly on the Internet, but there is still the notion that English "should know its limits" and that Hebrew should always come first and certainly not as a medium of instruction. The policies demand that Hebrew should be the only language of instruction in all schools and subjects and English should never be allowed to surpass Hebrew. This does not mean that there is no resistance to these restrictions "on the ground" and that alternative policies are not created and circumvented, usually with additional costs to the learners. After all, people see great value in English for mobility and are eager to acquire it at a younger age as they view the advantages that come with knowing the language and hence seek other venues and channels to learn it. The tension originates mostly from the fear of "otherness" as a threat to the continued existence of Hebrew ideology. Multilingualism is not accepted for English; Hebrew and English are taught in schools in total separation. Hebrew is the only medium of instruction in all Israeli Jewish schools and English is still viewed as a "foreign" language, as opposed to its use "on the ground" in society.

ENGLISH FOR ARABS AND IMMIGRANTS

Whereas the first part of this chapter focused on the relationship between Hebrew and English in Israel, this section addresses the impact and inequalities resulting from the power of the English language for those who were not born into Hebrew—Arabs and immigrants. In Israel, Jewish immigrants are expected to acquire Hebrew as it is the dominant language and the only medium of instruction in all Israeli Jewish schools. As was noted above, for Arabs, who make up 20% of the Israeli population, the Arabic language is the medium of instruction in Arab schools and a vital community language; Hebrew, though, is the language of power that Arabs are expected to acquire in order to function in most places in Israeli society as it is de facto the national language in spite of the official status of both languages (Amara & Rahman, 2002). For both Arabs and Jewish immigrants, English is a third language. English is a compulsory language in both Arab and Jewish schools, and students learn it from the third grade. Yet for Arabs English is not a top priority given the dominance of Hebrew in Israel and its role as a societal mobilizer needed for academic participation as Hebrew is the sole language of instruction in all universities. Although a number of Arab higher education institutions exist, these are all in the field of education and not in other disciplines. The inequality results from the fact that whereas English is a top priority for Jews, it does not occupy the same priority for Arabs as well as for immigrants, who invest most of their language efforts in learning Hebrew. Already in the higher grades of Arab secondary schools, Hebrew has become the language used to learn mathematics and sciences, and most textbooks are in fact in Hebrew, given the realization that Hebrew is the main language of instruction at universities. Another complexity emerges from the fact that spoken Arabic is drastically different from MSA; the latter considered of higher status in the Arab community and the variety being promoted in all schools. Yet MSA is drastically different from the spoken language, so students invest a lot of time and resources in learning MSA; English then can be considered a fourth language. The inequality also results from the fact that immigrants and Arabs are expected to reach identical levels of proficiency in English as Jews, and they are in fact being compared on the same English tests at the end of High School; the scores on these tests are used as the main criteria for acceptance to all Israeli universities. The different conditions of learning English in the different communities are not taken into account, although the results of these tests have a direct impact on the outcomes of being accepted or rejected by the universities. For Arab students, the lack of high proficiency in English poses a major obstacle, and it is detrimental to their participation in higher education. It is no surprise then that the scores of the Arab students on those final tests are substantially lower than those of the Jewish students. Yet, if one examines the total linguistic repertoire of Jews versus Arabs and immigrants, the latter two groups have a broader linguistic repertoire. The overlooking of the rich linguistic repertoire can be viewed as an act of marginalization, exclusion, and injustice. It is the need to fit into hegemonic Jewish ideologies of Hebrew, a powerful ideological language in Israel, *and* of English, a global and powerful language, while marginalizing home languages, that contributes to the continued policy of colonialization perpetuating "otherness," which is also accompanied by the negative consequences of limited access to higher education, limited academic success, and lack of equal opportunities and participation.

To counteract this discriminatory policy, a new trend that is currently emerging among Arabs is the enrollment of Arab students at Universities in Jordan where the language of instruction is Arabic. In a number of studies on the topic, Arar and Haj-Yehia (2010) point to the costs and benefits that motivate this trend, such as the lack of Hebrew and English proficiency. At the same time, the studies show that although these students gain a linguistic advantage, they suffer from the social and psychological difficulties of being "the others" in Jordan as well as having to pay substantially higher tuition payments than in Israeli universities. Furthermore, these studies also show that after the students return to Israel on graduation, they have great difficulties in finding employment.

This phenomenon is important to examine within the current trend toward the development of multilingual competencies. Both immigrants and Arabs develop multilingual skills as they all are far more proficient, to various degrees in multiple languages, than the majority of the Israeli Jewish population, who are proficient in two languages only—Hebrew and English. Yet, although the opportunity to learn two additional languages is much appreciated, there are serious consequences of not having high levels of proficiency in the *very* languages that are most valued and appreciated in the Israeli society. Most of the views that promote multilingualism somehow treat all languages as if they have identical values so that the more languages one knows the better. Yet these policies fail to delve deeper into the meaning of multilingualism, with questions such as "multilingual in what"? For Arabs in Israel, learning Hebrew as the only medium of instruction at universities is not neutral as it is associated with a linguistic phenomenon that has been imposed on them since 1948; it is a language that occupied them. This may involve deep emotions, hostility, threats for collective identity, historical events, a feeling of marginalization, as well as lack of personal and language rights. The learning of the language may introduce a complex set of emotions that touch the very essence of being a minority in Israel that is further magnified by the official status of Arabic, which is mostly on paper but has no meaningful manifestation. This may be similar to English, a language that is accompanied by a complex set of emotions (Shohamy, 2007). Whereas Israeli Jews view English as a desirable language, related to the United States, a symbol of progress, advancement, globalization, and the "West," Arab students tend to view it as a "Jewish" lingual franca, especially given the large number of Jewish immigrants in Israel who come from English-speaking countries (e.g., about half of Israeli English teachers come from English-speaking countries, mostly from North America). Thus, English can assume different meanings for different people, in different contexts, at different points in time. In some contexts, a global language such as English is learned as an instrumental and mobilizing tool and/or one that is associated with imperialism or the West, as a cultural and linguistic occupation; loss of identity; and a mark of marginality. Multilingualism then does not come free, but different languages are associated with and related to multiple meanings, layers, and levels that are embedded in historical, political, ideological, and emotional contexts (Pavlenko, 2006).

Take, for example, the study by Abu Ghazaleh-Mahajneh (2009), who showed in his research that for Arabs the need to learn Hebrew and English at the University of Haifa lowered their perceptions of the status of their home and community language, Arabic. He found that for Arab students, who at the beginning of the academic year viewed their language as prestigious, valuable, and important, this perception changed after 7 months of studying at the university where Hebrew and English had strong salience whereas Arabic had no visibility and functionality on campus. Thus, at the end of the year, their perceptions drastically changed—the students admitted that since the university was dominated exclusively by Hebrew and English, this led them to undervalue their own language, Arabic, viewing the learning of Arabic in their schools previously to attending the university as useless and "a waste of time," that is, they felt betrayed by the system. In a follow-up study (Shohamy & Abu Ghazaleh-Mahajneh, 2012), Arab students at that same university expressed feelings of frustrations and lack of respect given that their home languages had no representation on campus, especially in the linguistic landscape; they therefore felt that they were forced to *surrender* to Hebrew and English ideologies and overlook their own language.

CONCLUSIONS AND DISCUSSION

In analyzing the role of English in Israel, two main themes were brought up: One is the competition between English and Hebrew, two powerful languages between which there has been continuous rivalry over the years, and this continues in different degrees until today. Both languages are learned in schools, but language planners still fear that English is threatening the continued existence of the revival of Hebrew. It was claimed that this rivalry has a negative impact on the level of English teaching and learning in Israel, especially in higher education. English is rarely taught with Hebrew in the same space as there is total separation of the two languages in schools, unlike the more complementary role in public in Israel and in cyberspace. The second theme addressed the cost of English for Arabs and immigrants, pointing to the inequality of the comparison in English proficiency between students for whom English is a second language and those for whom it is the third or even fourth language. The results of equivalent English tests for all groups regardless of the conditions of learning have a major impact on access, participation, and rights.

These issues led to a critique of current views about the promotion of multilingualism; being multilingual for Arabs and immigrants not only does not provide any academic advantage but also penalizes them as they are not knowledgeable in the languages that the society values the most, overlooking their whole linguistic repertoire. The current movement toward multilingualism needs to delve deeply into such issues. In the case of Arab and immigrant students in Israel who are multilingual in a number of language, this is not viewed as an asset, as they are multilingual in the "wrong" languages, as multilingualism varies by the very contexts in which people function at a given point in time. Arab students do not view the multilingualism they share as an advantage as while studying at the university, they do not see any advantage in terms of mobility. In fact, in each political context there is a hierarchy of languages that are perceived as having high and/or low values, depending on a complex set of political, social, economic, and historical factors. This means that students would rather be bilingual in the languages that society values highly than be multilingual in a number of languages that do not hold meaningful values and that have limited economic currency. In the case of Arabic, the language is very powerful and prestigious in most countries in the Middle East; yet in Israel today, Arabic is marginal and stigmatized. At the same time, although Hebrew is considered prestigious in Israel today, it is not used anywhere else out of Israel as a vernacular. Hebrew and English are the most valued languages, whereas Arabic, Russian, or any other immigrant languages, apart from English, have very limited value, and proficiency in these languages is not appreciated. These languages are neither used widely in the media or as medium of instruction in any of the prestigious academic institutions in Israel, nor are they languages that Hebrew users seek to acquire as they do not provide any societal and academic benefits, at this point in time.

The main conclusion is that categorizing languages as global or national does not capture the scope, depth, and complexity of factors that are associated with language engagements. There is a need to focus more seriously on what it means to expect students to learn global languages and to examine the ramifications of specific languages in contexts such as the cost of learning other languages that may in the short and long run serve as assets and of value. As was shown above, learning Hebrew and English by Arabs in Israel is not identical to learning global and national languages in other places in Israel. The long-term effects of such policies are far-reaching. Accompanying the academic marginality, there is also a message about the marginal position of the very people whose home languages are not valued as the loss of prestige, respect, and honor. For example, these policies lead Arab students to develop low motivation for sustaining their home languages as no practical and symbolic values are associated with them especially in the bastion of higher education, which often serves as the index of the prestige of languages. In fact, in a number of Arab communities in Israel, there is a growing demand by school administrators, parents, and students to introduce Hebrew and English as early as possible, often on the account of Arabic. More recently, many school subjects are no longer taught in Arabic but rather in Hebrew and English as both are perceived to be more rewarding and leading to greater economic benefits. In mixed towns with closer contacts between Hebrew and Arabic speakers, many Arab students seek to enroll in Hebrew-speaking schools, and the proficiency in academic Arabic is rapidly declining. In a study by Goldstein-Havazki

(2011), it was shown that Arabs in mixed towns such as Jaffa, even in areas where most residents are Arabs, prefer to use Hebrew and English on signs in their shops and businesses and to remove Arabic. A number of high school students who participated in the study documented the linguistic landscape in Jaffa's public spaces and found that Arabic has given way to Hebrew and English; this led them to develop a critical awareness of the phenomenon of the loss of Arabic. As a result, they became activists in trying to bring back Arabic to Jaffa; they then held conversations with their parents demanding greater representations of Arabic in public spaces.

It is the role of language policy specialists to recommend language policies that can even out the inequalities that exist in societies, such as by creating a need for the majority students to acquire minority languages so to boost the prestige and value of these languages (Shohamy, 2006). This is especially important given research findings indicating that learning of the languages "of the others" can become tools for bridging political conflicts and ethnic tensions. In a study on the learning of Arabic by Hebrew speakers in Israel (Donitsa-Schimdt, Inbar, & Shohamy, 2004), it was demonstrated that even a short time of learning spoken Arabic by Jews could change their attitudes about Arabs, viewing them as people and not as political objects. In other words, although there may be compelling reasons to acquire global languages, it is of utmost importance not to overlook the other values of learning languages, specifically for coexistence, for bridging political conflicts, and for creating more equal and democratic societies where people feel they can participate and be included in societies so they have the right to participate in *any* language. Education policies cannot be limited to mobility and economic achievements but must consider a variety of other important values such as inclusion, participation, representation, respect, honor, and connections—let alone personal rights. Language is a very powerful tool that can be most useful in creating close and meaningful contacts among people. It therefore requires paying close attention to its role as bridging divides, repairing inequalities, empowering different languages, and redistributing power.

HOW UNIQUE IS ENGLISH IN ISRAEL?

Although this chapter focused on the role of English in Israel, one wonders about the extent to which the phenomenon described above is typical to other non-English countries in this day and age or is it unique to Israel given the revival of Hebrew. The revival of Hebrew and the competition with English may be unique to Israel in the sense that in other countries languages have not been revived in such ways; yet the idea of one common language that is ideological, dominant, and viewed as a unifying factor for diverse groups has been around since the end of the 19th century (and in some cases even before) when national homogenous languages replaced multilingualism and many language varieties in nations such as in Italy, Spain, France, China, Japan, and Germany, and this continues till today. In most countries, national single languages were perpetuated, standardized, and imposed as the only "correct" languages of instruction in schools and in society; China and other countries are promoting one single language that serves the dominant groups in societies, and certainly English is promoted in many English countries as a national language and not necessarily as a global language. The process in Israel may have been somewhat different, as a whole country made up of immigrants and other ethnolinguistic groups who lived there before was forced to acquire a new language, Hebrew, for creating a collective national identity. The situation with Arabs after 1948 was somewhat different as they were "allowed" to continue to use Arabic as the language of the community and the language of instruction in school especially in homogenous areas where the only residents were Arabs (unlike Jewish immigrants who are forced into Hebrew from the day of their arrival). Yet, as shown above, Arabs have no choice but to adopt Hebrew for functionality purpose, while Arabic vitality continues and needs to be guarded and cultivated. Thus, the fact that all universities use Hebrew as the only language of instruction and English as the language of texts is detrimental for Arabs, who often feel "forced" to drop Arabic especially as there is a growing number of Arabs who participate in higher education.

As to the competition with English, Israel is not unique, as newly standardized languages that were recognized by nation-states were poised in competition and fear with "the other" language, English. English and other national languages are still viewed as competitors in many countries such as Japan, Germany, Spain, and France. It is also not unique to Israel where English becomes a marginalizing language as immigrants and minorities are forced to acquire national languages and reach only low levels of proficiency in the language, yet are being compared with the those for whom English is a second language, leading to multiple inequalities and injustices as noted above.

As a final note, it is important to realize that one outcome from the focus on multilingualism in the past few years has been greater recognition and legitimacy on trans-languaging, that is, the use of a number of languages together and moving harmoniously from one language to the next according to needs. It is realized now that speakers of first languages do not leave their first languages behind and use these languages in the acquisition of their second and third languages (Haim, 2013). Thus, both Arabs and the immigrants living in Israel and in other places worldwide continue to rely and use their home languages as valuable resources, especially in processing content in schools. Similar studies are emerging across many multilingual contexts today especially in Africa, where students are required to use English in schools along with their first language, which used to be taboo in the past; the new trend to mix languages and to legitimize multiple languages in the same space may be helpful in reducing the fear from English in some places and empowering other languages for immigrants and minorities. Together, these can lead to multilingual policies that are more just and inclusive and use English more harmoniously.

It is the role of language policy experts to demonstrate these trends and to take activist steps in order to challenge these inequalities and marginalization as a result of English and promote the uses of first languages in more integrated ways. First, it is important to point to the phenomenon of victimization of people as a result of language globalization and the high price paid for globalization and promotion of English language as well as other powerful languages, as in the case of national languages speakers of minority languages. Then, there is a need to point to the several years it takes to acquire second languages; to the fact that people should be given opportunities to demonstrate their knowledge through a variety of means and not only through national or global languages (Levin & Shohamy, 2008; Levin, Shohamy, & Spolsky, 2003; Shohamy, 2011). Finally, to legitimate and then encourage the use of various varieties and mixture of languages, hybrids, fusions, and trans-languaging, as native-like proficiency is not possible to achieve, nor it is desired. Language participation is part of freedom of speech and can be enhanced with various forms of translation. Also it is important to note that although English is considered a global language, the real meaning of globalization is multilingualism—it is about diversities, options, and possibilities where a variety of languages are used in many shapes and forms and even within the different Englishes. English may be the beginning, but it is not the end. We need to point out that schools that serve governments and turn multilingual realities into monolingual islands in the interest of political reasons work against a just society; instead, teachers should work on developing and cultivating the knowledge with which students come to school and not marginalize it. It is important to show how languages are used as manipulative tools with the pretense of quality education, standards, and correctness; yet in fact, these approaches suppress the wealth of knowledge that gets filtered when other languages interact. True globalization is the acceptance, inclusion, and participation in local, national, and global societies in Israel and in other places where these phenomena occur.

REFERENCES

Abu Ghazaleh-Mahajneh, M. (2009). *Attitudes towards the status of the Arabic, Hebrew and English languages among Arab students at the university* (Unpublished master's thesis). Tel Aviv University, Tel Aviv, Israel. (In Hebrew)

Amara, M. H., & Rahman, M. A. (2002). *The Arab minority in Israel*. Dordrecht, Netherlands: Kluwer Academic.

Arar, K., & Haj-Yehia, K. (2010). Emigration for higher education: The case of Palestinians living in Israel studying in Jordan. *Higher Education Policy, 23*, 358–380.

Ben Rafael, E., Shohamy, E., Amara, M. H., & Trumper-Hecht, N. (2006). Linguistic landscape as symbolic construction of the public space: The case of Israel. *International Journal of Multilingualism, 3*, 7–30.

Blumstein, M., & Shohamy, E. (2012). Do speakers of power language need to be empowered? *Hed Ha-Ulpan, 99*, 99–105. (In Hebrew)

Donitsa-Schmidt, S., Inbar, O., & Shohamy, E. (2004). The effects of teaching spoken Arabic on students' attitudes and motivation in Israel. *Modern Language Journal, 88*, 217–228.

Goldestein-Havazki, R. (2011). *A travel diary in Jaffa: Development of linguistic landscape awareness and attitudes among teenagers* (Master's thesis, Tel Aviv University).

Haim, O. (2013). Factors predicting academic success in second and third language among Russian-speaking immigrant students studying in Israeli school. *International Journal of Multilingualism*. Advance online publication. doi:10.1080/14790718.2013.829069

Harshav, B. (1993). *Language in time of revolution*. Berkeley, University of California Press

Johnson, D. C. (2010). The relationship between applied linguistic research and language policy for bilingual education. *Applied Linguistics, 31*, 72–93.

Levin, T., & Shohamy, E. (2008). Achievement of immigrant students in mathematics and academic Hebrew in Israeli school: A large scale evaluation study. *Studies in Educational Evaluation, 34*, 1–14.

Levin, T., Shohamy, E., & Spolsky, B. (2003). *Academic achievements of immigrants in schools* (Report submitted to the Ministry of Education). Tel Aviv, Israel: Tel Aviv University. (In Hebrew)

Nesher, T. (2012). *Israel's Academy of the Hebrew Language declares war—on English*. Retrieved from http://www.haaretz.com/print-edition/news/israel-s-academy-of-the-hebrew-language-declares-war-on-english-1.415431

Pavlenko, A. (2006). *Bilingual minds: Emotional experiences, expression and representation*. Clevedon, England: Multilingual Matters.

Segev, T. (1999). *Yemei Ha-Kalaniyot: Palestine under the British*. Jerusalem: Keter. (In Hebrew)

Shohamy, E. (1994). Issues of language planning in Israel: Language and ideology. In R. Lambert (Eds.), *Language planning around the world: Contexts and systemic change* (pp. 131–142). Washington, DC: National Foreign Language Center.

Shohamy, E. (2006). *Language policy: Hidden agendas and new approaches*. London, England: Routledge.

Shohamy, E. (2007). Reinterpreting globalization in multilingual contexts. *International Multilingual Research Journal, 1*, 127–133.

Shohamy, E. (2008). At what cost? Methods of language revival and protection: Examples from Hebrew. In K. King, N. Schilling-Estes, L. Fogle, J. Lou Jia, & B. Soukup (Eds.), *Sustaining linguistic diversity: Endangered and minority languages and language varieties* (pp. 205–218). Washington, DC: Georgetown University Press.

Shohamy, E. (2011). Assessing multilingual competencies: Adopting construct valid assessment policies. *Modern Language Journal, 95*, 418–429.

Shohamy, E., & Abu Ghazaleh-Mahajneh, M. (2012). Linguistic landscape as a tool for interpreting language vitality: Arabic as a "minority" language in Israel. In D. Gorter, H. F. Marten, & L. Van Mensel (Eds.), *Minority languages in the linguistic landscape* (pp. 89–108). Basingstoke, England: Palgrave-Macmillan.

Chapter 12

Overcoming Colonial Policies of Divide and Rule: Postcolonialism's Harnessing of the Vernaculars

Vaidehi Ramanathan
University of California, Davis

This chapter[1] offers a situated account of English and vernacular literacy practices from a postcolonial perspective. Postcolonial scholarship in disciplines such as cultural studies and English literature has alerted us to the extent to which colonial rule partially created and reproduced negative images regarding "natives" so as to be better able to govern. Within applied linguistics, this awareness provides a necessary sociohistorical background against which to understand current grounded realities around language teaching and learning. Colonial policies in South Asian education—especially the policy of Divide and Rule—created schisms between the English medium (EM) and vernacular medium (VM) of education (Phillipson, 1992). This breakdown assumes neocolonial hues and dovetails directly with local societal stratifications (of caste and class) that exacerbate unequal conditions between those who are educated in the two tracks. Situated in ongoing endeavors in a variety of local contexts in Ahmedabad, Gujarat, India, where I was raised and schooled, this chapter calls attention to some key educational sites through which these policy-related inequities are reproduced, and some ways in which individual teachers and institutions assume the responsibility to make conditions more just and equal. The chapter concludes with a discussion of how a postcolonial research framework allows us to understand not only grounded inequities around language policies in terms of historical colonial pasts but also how fellow humans draw on particular rationalizations to harness the veranaculars and work toward moving us all to more equal footings (Canagarajah, 1997).

Increasing discussions around English being a "world" language (Brutt-Griffler, 2002) and the instrumental role it plays in globalization force us now to take stock of the "dominating" role that English seems to be assuming. Scholarship in this realm ranges from researchers questioning mediums-of-instruction policies, to ways in

Review of Research in Education
March 2014, Vol. 38, pp. 290-311
DOI: 10.3102/0091732x13511049
© 2014 AERA. http://rre.aera.net

which English operates to create inner and outer circles in different countries, to how it gets positioned vis-à-vis local, "vernacular" languages (Alidou, 2004). Regardless of how scholars are positioned in the debate, much of the research seems to draw from and is connected to issues in implicit and explicit English language policies—statewide, nationwide, and institutional—and the ways in which they affect a variety of teaching and learning contexts. Such views, although valuable, can be seen to run the risk of rendering language policies around English and local languages as abstract entities partially formulated behind closed doors, and formalized in documents without paying much heed to local realities. In the area of postcolonial scholarship, issues of language policies around English and the vernaculars assume particular hues, given historical, political, cultural, and geographic tropes, with colonial policies still in place.

However, grounded perspectives of postcolonial engagements—everyday engagements by teachers and learners—prod us to consider ways in which policies are not just top-down mandates that happen to us humans, shaping our engagements in the world, but live, dynamic forces that find their viability and articulation in the most local of spaces: in institutions, pedagogic practices, school settings, teacher education programs, and disciplinary orientations (Ramanathan, 2005a, 2005b; Tollefson, 1991; Tollefson & Tsui, 2004; Wiley & Wright, 2004). Such views have tended to remain largely marginalized in West-based applied linguistic research, but they are crucial to consider since many of our students in (West-based) English as a Second Language classrooms are from formerly colonized countries (India, Sri Lanka, Pakistan, Bangladesh, Nigeria, South Africa, and Zimbabwe, to name a few) and bring with them learning experiences that need to be a part of our MA in Teaching English to Speakers of Other Languages and other teacher education programs. In what follows, I offer a few grounded sketches of postcolonial realities based in key educational sites in the city of Ahmedabad, Gujarat, India, where I completed my K–12 and some of my graduate school education. Two overarching research questions frame this exploration:

Research Question 1: What is the postcolonial framework?
Research Question 2: In what ways does the postcolonial framework inform English and vernacular debates in applied linguistics?

WHAT IS POSTCOLONIALISM?

In simple terms, postcolonialism refers to the points of view of people from formerly colonized countries regarding their colonial past. In terms of scholarship, it manifests itself as "speaking back" to colonial powers, often in the language of the colonizer (Canagarajah, 1997). European colonial powers had assumed the right to take over entire countries—almost all of them non-Western—and sought to rationalize their takeover in terms of prevailing discourses that viewed non-Western peoples as "inferior, child-like or feminine, incapable of looking after themselves (despite of having done so perfectly well for millennia) and requiring the paternal rule of the west for their own interests (today they are deemed to require 'development')" (Young, 2003, p. 2). Atrocities committed by colonial powers in the defense of building Empires varied in different countries, with some cataclysmic events spurring local "subjects" toward fighting for independence. Within the Indian context, the Jallianwalla Bagh massacre of 1919, when General Dyer opened fire on an unarmed crowd of 20,000 people, was a pivotal moment for freedom fighters such as Gandhi, Tagore, and Andrews (see Ramanathan & Morgan, 2009, for details), who sought to overturn more than 500 years of colonial rule (Indian independence was won in 1947).

The policies and mandates that the English colonial powers set in place especially in the field of education were, in many instances, in the South Asian context (of India, Pakistan, Sri Lanka, and Bangladesh), ones of "Divide and Rule." This was a mode of operating that the Raj (as the English colonial power is known in South Asia) devised so as to rule more effectively. The Raj needed Indians to run their Empire and so offered English education to small numbers of Indians as it would help them in this endeavor. This one colonial policy took root and went very deeply into the South Asian ideological space to where EM education was deemed as having more cultural capital and symbolic power than an education in the vernaculars (Gee, 1990; Hawkins, 2004; Kalantzis & Cope, 2002; McCarty, 2002, 2005), an ideology that is very visible, enacted, and real today. Phillipson (1992) aptly terms such ideologies *linguistic imperialism* and speaks of the extent to which they inform and affect linguistic diversity. The colonizing impact that English has on local languages manifests itself in extremely obvious and sometimes very nonobvious ways, aspects that, as we will see later in the chapter, crucially inform the "speaking-back" agenda of the postcolonial framework.

The general importance accorded to English and the extent to which it pervades the everyday life of the postcolonial person, have, from the point of view of some scholars, rendered the postcolonial identity "hybrid." Indeed, authors such as Verma (2010) write about "forked tongues" and the general deracination a person educated in EM might feel because he or she does not have as intimate a connection with their local vernacular as they do with English (and so by extension may be seen to feel "less Indian"). Postcolonial scholarship often refers to this amalgam as being "hybridized" because a variety of colonial and vernacular resources inform personal identities. (Formerly colonized countries have also been called the "subaltern" since they have remained on the margins of dominant hegemonic power structures.[2])

I began my project in Ahmedabad by going back to the college where I received my undergraduate degree. I knew the principal and the teachers, I was familiar with the curriculum, and the hallways, canteens, and basketball courts were old haunts of mine. Being immersed again in this context not only allowed me to address policies that had changed but also enabled me to start relating issues that came up in this one institution to others in the city, and before long to those in nonformal educational domains as well. The project is most multifaceted and has, over the years, assumed a propelling energy for which I could take little credit, since it emerged from the collective ideas of teachers, principals, students, textbooks, exam responses, media write-ups, interviews, field notes, and documentaries. It is snapshots of this endeavor to which I now turn.

ENGLISH AND VERNACULAR-MEDIUM EDUCATION IN INDIA: COLONIAL VESTIGES, NEOCOLONIAL LAMINATIONS

Issues of Data and Method

My extended endeavor with EM and VM teachers and students in Ahmedabad, Gujarat, has to do with partially addressing ways in which colonial policies assume neocolonial laminations in current postcolonial India. Sixty-five years as India is from independence from the Raj, the country has begun to rethink and change colonial education policies. But many colonial mandates remain, and my engagements in this space have been about addressing how everyday lived realities get negotiated.

My data—accumulated over a decade now—comprise a range of materials gathered in and with a variety of peoples in different institutions in Ahmedabad, Gujarat, India. Ahmedabad's population is approximately 4.5 million, and almost everybody speaks at least two languages. The official languages in the state and city are Gujarati, Hindi, and English (although there are sizeable pockets of populations speaking a variety of other Indian languages), and all three are taught at the K–12 level (more on K–12 language policies presently). In the space of formal learning is my work in three institutional sites: (a) a middle-class, EM Jesuit liberal arts institution (where I attended college); (b) an upper-class, EM business college that encourages only English language use in its classes; and (c) a very poor, VM women's college where instruction is predominantly in Gujarati, including the teaching of English literature.[3] Data from these institutions included extensive interviews with students, faculty, and administrators; copies of pedagogic materials, texts, and exams; student responses; and countless hours of classroom observations and field notes. I have also gathered pedagogic materials used in the K–12 level so as to better understand what students are bringing with them as they transition to college. Also part of this project are occasional individual and group meetings with both EM and VM teachers to discuss concerns about curriculum, especially the adapting of West-based English language teaching materials partially made available by the British Council and some of which I supply (when asked) in the Indian setting.

My data from nonformal educational domains come from two sites, both of which embody Gandhian notions of "noncooperation": (a) an extracurricular program run out of the women's college (mentioned above) that caters to addressing concerns of civic change and (b) the Gandhi Ashram (which was historically Gandhi's home/office and continues to engage in Gandhian projects and be a source of Gandhianism in the state). Data from these sites include extended interviews with key people running various civic projects in the city, field notes on workshops, and a variety of historical material written by and to Gandhi (letters, memos, bulletins) that is available in the Ashram and at the Rhodes House library in Oxford University (see Ramanathan & Morgan, 2009, for a discussion of some of this correspondence).

My seeking out people at the Ashram has been intentional and is propelled in part by the increasingly rabid Hindu nationalistic rhetoric emanating from the Gujarat state government (and until recently the central government as well).[4] My sustained engagement with one of the VM teachers (discussed here) prompted me into seeking other pockets of practice that countered some of the dangerous political ideologies threatening secularism, and the workshops at the Gandhi Ashram seemed, in many ways, ideal. Not only do they have Gandhi's larger philosophy of noncooperation against political hegemonies at their core (more on this presently), they also opened up for me a way of understanding both how Gandhianism is situated and how particular dimensions of the identities of participants get laminated.

My juxtaposing of data from formal and nonformal domains of education is deliberate as is my juxtaposing of some K–12 materials with college-level concerns. The general inequity between the EM and VM that is so obvious at the formal K–12 level gets sharply contested when we turn our gaze to issues in the community.

Sites That Reproduce the English–Vernacular Divide: Tracking Policies, Inequities in Textbooks

Most K–12 students in India get slotted into what are called "vernacular-medium" (Gujarati in the present case) and "English-medium" tracks of schooling (see Ramanathan, 2005a, for a detailed discussion of inequities perpetuated by such tracking). Constitutionally, the Indian government promises the availability of an education in the mother tongue (in the 21 official languages) as well as an education in English (where English is the medium of instruction). In Gujarat, English is introduced as a foreign language in Grade 5 in the Gujarati-medium classes, and Gujarati is introduced at the same grade level in EM classes. Hindi is introduced in Grade 4 and Sanskrit in Grade 7 in both mediums, and all EM and VM students have learned these through Grade 12. If policies existed in vacuums, this scene might be regarded as reasonably egalitarian; after all, students in both streams are becoming literate in several languages, with multilingualism being institutionally validated and legitimized.

However, as we know, educational policies, and enactments of and around them, have rings of divisiveness and exclusionism that surround them (Hornberger & Johnson, 2007; King, 2001; McCarty, 2005; Shohamy, 2006). Equity in this context, as indeed in many parts of the world, is directly tied to which kind of student is ready for college. Colleges in India, for the most part (except for a few liberal arts colleges), are in EM, which of course means that students with VM backgrounds (where they have had access to a few hours of English instruction a week) have to compete with their EM counterparts (for whom English is almost a first language) in colleges and beyond. And given our globalizing world and inequities relating to who has access to English (Gee, 2003) and how access to it opens other communal doors (jobs, interviews), this plays itself out in most differentiated ways (Morgan & Ramanathan, 2009).

One key site where this gulf is very evident is in the English-language textbooks that are available to students in the two different tracks. Toward underscoring how the two tracks of education produce two very different "literate in English" candidates, I offer Table 1, which lays out the "minimal levels of learning" (somewhat comparable to what in the California context is referred to as K–12 "standards") for English-language learning in the two mediums.[5] (I do need to note here that there has been a concerted effort to change statewide educational policies so that English might now be introduced in the first grade instead of the fifth.) For now, though, the present policies are still the norm.

Two noticeable writing-related differences in Table 1 are that (a) writing for VM students is presented as a discrete skill and is addressed separately from reading, a feature that contrasts with writing and reading being presented as conjoined entities for EM students, and (b) writing for EM students is essayist in orientation from early on: "writing paragraphs on given topics" (vs. "gaining the basic mechanics of English writing . . . with proper spacing" for the VM student) or writing essays based on texts (vs. learning to write words and sentences neatly for the VM student).

These unequal levels of literacy across the two mediums are evident in the very divergent kinds of English language readings for the two tracks for students. Table 2 offers a partial list of topics addressed in the English language textbooks used in each track.

Several interesting features emerge from a close comparison of the partial list of contents in the two sets of textbooks. VM texts with their general focus on survival English emphasize how language is used in particular Indian contexts (at the park, at the zoo, or sending a telegram). The readings in EM texts, in contrast, are more cosmopolitan, drawing as they do from a variety of texts, including essays and short readings on Abraham Lincoln in Grade 6, to those by Stephen Leacock and Tolstoy in Grade 8, to ones by Hemmingway and Tagore in Grade 10. Poetry, a genre that draws heavily on metaphorical use of language, is relegated to the "optional" category in VM texts (indeed, prefaces to the textbooks say that poetry for VM students is to be regarded as "supplementary reading"). Poetry is part of the mandated EM curriculum.[6]

At a somewhat superficial level the above tables could be read as snippets of "evidence." However, it is their positioning in larger cultural and political interlocking chains (that include snobberies, pedagogies, ideologies) that contributes to sedimenting these inequities in the formal realm.[7]

NONFORMAL EDUCATION, CIVIC ENGAGEMENTS, EFFORTS AT EQUALITY

Such instances of the "divide" necessarily force one to raise the question: What can be done to make language education issues more equitable? Is it the case that

TABLE 1
Divergent MLLs for VM and EM Students

	Excerpts From MLL From English Textbooks Used in the Gujarati Medium	Excerpts From MLL From English Textbooks Used in the English Medium
Grade 5	*Writing*	*Reading and writing*
	Gains control of the basic mechanics of writing in English like capital letters, small letters, punctuation, writing neatly on a line with proper spacing	Reading textual material and writing answers to questions based on and related to the text
	Transcribes words, phrases, and sentences in English	Reading and interpreting and offering comments on maps and charts
	Produces words and spells them correctly	Reading children's literature and talking about it
	Writes numbers up to 50, telephone numbers, road signs	Writing paragraphs on given topics
		Reading and writing simple recipes
Grade 6	*Reading*	*Reading and writing*
	Reads aloud simple sentences, poems, dialogues, and short passages with proper pauses	Reading textual material and writing answers to questions based on the text
	Reads and follows given directions	Reading and interpreting simple abbreviations
	Reads numbers up to 100	Reading narrative prose and adventure stories and talking about them
	Writing	
	Writes with proper punctuation marks	Writing/building stories based on given questions/points
	Writes words and sentences neatly on a line with proper spacing, punctuation marks, and capitalization	Reading and using the telephone directory
	Writes answers to questions based on text material	

(continued)

TABLE 1 (CONTINUED)

	Excerpts From MLL From English Textbooks Used in the Gujarati Medium	Excerpts From MLL From English Textbooks Used in the English Medium
Grade 7	*Reading* Reads aloud simple sentences Finds key words and phrases from a text *Writing* Writes words and sentences and paragraphs dictated with correct spellings, proper punctuation marks Learns to write words and sentences neatly on a line with proper spacing and punctuation Writes answers to questions based on the text From Purani, Salat, Soni, and Joshi (1998, pp. 1–3; for Grades 5, 6, and 7)	*Reading and writing* Reading textual material and writing answers based on the text Writing essays based on the text Reading literary stories and prose lessons Reading simple passages of reflective prose Reading and interpreting common instructions such as railway timetables From Purani, Salat, Soni, and Joshi (1998, p. 2; for Grades 5, 6, 7)

Note. MLL = minimal level of learning; EM = English medium; VL = vernacular medium.

as researcher I am focusing only on inequities? Have I been blind to how ordinary, everyday shifts happen and to what extent did my EM background keep me from seeing transformations? Teachers, although heavily influenced by policies and mandates, are thinking agents who make choices, who choose to act in ways that are sometimes diametrically opposed to official rules, and who are motivated by codes of individual ethics—sometimes rationalized in religious terms, sometimes philosophic—and who stare fearlessly back at inequity and move toward dissolving it one very small grain at a time. It was when one of the teachers at the low-income women's college introduced me to some of his students working in nonformal education projects that I realized the extent to which the EM part of my background had superseded the vernacular parts of me (at least as far as this research endeavor was concerned), and kept me myopic. I turn now to addressing Gandhianism and nonformal learning, and ways in which grassroots efforts at empowerment happen by drawing on the most local and available of resources, namely, the vernaculars. As we will see, both instances laminate "learning" differently from the formal realm and make us pay heed to institutionalized schooling policies that supply us with only the narrowest understandings about inequity and learning. Although it may seem as if I am taking a major detour in the following section, it is necessary background by

TABLE 2
A Partial List of Contents: Grades 6, 8, and 10

	Vernacular Medium List of Contents	English Medium List of Contents
Grade 6	Welcome, Friends A Fancy Dress Show A Seashore A Park A Village Fair In the School Compound What Time Is It Now? The Environment Day	A Voyage to Lilliput Farewell to the Farm The Changing World Abraham Lincoln (Parts 1 and 2) Don Quixote Meets a Company of Actors The Poet's House Woodman, Spare That Tree! City Streets and Country Roads
Grade 8	*GM (no authors provided)* *Poetry (optional)* 　Rhyme 　Rhyme 　Rhyme 　Only One Mother 　The Picnic 　Two Birds *Prose* 　Let's Begin 　Hello! I Am Vipul 　A Railway Station 　At the Zoo 　On the Farm 　Good Manners 　In the Kitchen	*Poetry* 　Under the Greenwood Tree: William Shakespeare 　She Dwelt Among the Untrodden Ways: William Wordsworth 　To a Child Dancing in the Wind: W. B. Yeats 　The Listeners: Walter de la Mare 　Coming: Phillip Larkin 　A Blackbird Singing: R. S. Thomas *Prose* 　Little Children Wiser Than Men: Leo Tolstoy 　Do You Know? Clifford Parker 　My Financial Career: Stephen Leacock 　The Lady Is an Engineer: Patricia Strauss 　The Judgment Seat of Vikramaditya: Sister Nivedita
Grade 10	*Poetry (optional)* 　Laughing Song: Blake 　In the Night: Naidu 　Wander Thirst: Gerald Gould 　The Secret of the Machines: Rudyard Kipling	*Poetry* 　Blow, Blow, Thou Winter Wind: Shakespeare 　London: Blake 　Upon Westminster Bridge: Wordsworth 　To . . .: Shelley 　La Belle Dame Sans Merci: Keats

(continued)

TABLE 2 (CONTINUED)

Vernacular Medium List of Contents	English Medium List of Contents
Prose (no authors provided)	The Professor: Nissim Ezekeil
An Act of Service	The Fountain: Lowell
Strange But True	*Prose*
Have You Heard This	Ramanujam: C. P. Snow
One?	On Saying Please: A. G. Gardener
Vaishali at the Police	The Home Coming: Tagore
Station	Andrew Carnegie: E. H. Carter
Prevention of Cruelty to	A Day's Wait: Hemmingway
Animals	After Twenty Years: O. Henry
The Indian Village—	Vikram Sarabhai: M. G. K. Menon
Then and Now	From Vamdatta, Joshi, and Patel (2000, p. 44)

which to understand civic engagement, alternate literacies, and the value of nonformal education.

Some Communal Issues in Ahmedabad: Setting the Backdrop for Nonformal Education

In 2001 and 2002, two devastating events occurred that affected the city of Ahmedabad in traumatic ways.[8] The first was a 7.9 earthquake in 2001, and the second, gory Hindu–Muslim riots in 2002. The earthquake of 2001, which occurred around 9:00 a.m. on January 26 (about the time that most educational institutions in the city were holding Republic Day celebrations), had its epicenter in the small town of Bhuj, about 200 miles from Ahmedabad. An estimated 17,000 bodies were recovered, more than 30,000 people were reported dead or missing, 166,000 or more were injured, and over a million homes were destroyed. The devastation in Ahmedabad, needless to say, was extensive, with school buildings crushing little children, flats and apartments coming down on families getting ready to start their day, and businesses being decimated.

As if this were not enough, the following year, on February 27th, 2002, the city broke out into the worst Hindu–Muslim riots in recent years. The events allegedly unfolded like this (there is a lot of room for debate here about how planned or accidental the whole scenario was. Indeed, the case is still pending the courts): 58 Hindu pilgrims returning from Ayodhya (a Hindu holy site) had their train cabin set ablaze outside Ahmedabad. The train had made a scheduled stop, during which a scuffle between some of the pilgrims and a tea vendor began, started to escalate, and eventually culminated in the train compartment going up in blazes and the pilgrims being burnt to death (allegedly by a group of Muslims). This led to a vicious collective anger on the part of the hardline Hindus that resulted in a horrendous week of rioting during which Muslim homes were burnt, businesses looted, women raped, and children killed. More than 1,000 Muslims died.

Although I cannot come close to accounting for the numerous local ways in which various groups in the city of Ahmedabad leapt into action,[9] including the group of teachers I work with, I shall devote myself to explaining in some detail the work of two endeavors committed to communal and educational change in very different ways (see Ramanathan, 2006a, for a detailed discussion). My point here is to underscore how vernacular resources—typically seen as "backward," rabid, fundamentalist, nativist—a colonial legacy that the EM press has tended to assume become a most valuable well of means for reconstructing lives and communities. Learning and teaching in these contexts assume very different hues that complicate our collective notions of devaluing the vernacular.

Gandhian Ideologies in Two Settings: Gandhi's Views on Nonformal Education, Community Service, and Noncooperation

Because both institutions echo Gandhian views in a variety of direct and indirect ways, I would like to provide in this section a brief and interconnected understanding of those aspects of noncooperation that are most relevant to the issues at hand. Whereas world history documents noncooperation in terms of civil disobedience, Satyagraha, and nonviolence, there are a host of details in this philosophy that are pertinent to the present discussion: (a) the value of harnessing the vernaculars (including those of promoting VM education), (b) the importance of community service being an integral part of a basic education, and (c) promoting nonformal education that encourages a healthy development of civic citizenship.

Each of these ideals gets encased in the larger rhetorical strain of "noncooperation," which Gandhi advocated during his struggles for Indian independence (see Ramanathan, 2006b, for a detailed discussion), and which people at the two institutions interpret and enact differently. The following table displays some excerpts from his writings on this topic.

On vernacular (and English) education
1. I hold it to be as necessary for the urban child as for the rural to have the foundation of his development laid on the solid work of the mother-tongue. It is only in unfortunate India that such an obvious proposition needs to be proved. (Gandhi in *Harijan*, September 9, 1939, edited by Kumarappa, 1954)
2. "The only education we receive is English education. Surely we must show something for it. But suppose we had been receiving during the past fifty years education through our vernaculars, what should we have today? We should have a free India, we should have our educated people, not as if they were foreigners in their own land, but speaking to the heart of the nation; they would be working amongst the poorest of the poor, and whatever they would have gained during the past fifty years would be a heritage for the nation. (Gandhi in *Harijan*, September 9, 1939, edited by Kumarappa, 1954)

(continued)

On (non-) formal education

3. "But unless the development of the mind and body goes hand in hand with a corresponding awakening of the soul, the former alone would prove to be a poor lop-sided affair. By spiritual training I mean education of the heart. A proper and all-around development of the mind, therefore, can take place only when it proceeds pari passu with the education of the physical and spiritual faculties of the child. They constitute an indivisible whole. According to this theory, therefore, it would be a gross fallacy to suppose that they can be developed piecemeal or independently of one another. (Gandhi, 1954, p. 25)

4. By education I mean all-round drawing out of the best in children—body, mind, and spirit. [Formal] Literacy is not the end of education nor the beginning. It is only one of the means whereby men and women can be educated. (Gandhi, 1954, p. 25)

5. [Non formal education] . . . will check the progressive decay of our villages and lay the foundation for a juster social order in which there is no unnatural division between the "haves" and the "havenots" and everybody is assured a living wage and the rights to freedom . . . It will provide a healthy and a moral basis of relationship between the city and village and will go a long way towards eradicating some of the worst evils of the present social insecurity and poisoned relationship between the classes. (Gandhi, 1954, p. 25)

6. *Fundamentals of basic education*

   1. All education to be true must be self-supporting, that is, it will pay its expenses excepting the capital.

   2. In it the cunning of the hand will be utilized even up to the final stage, that is to say, hands of pupils will be skillfully working at some industry for some period during the day.

   3. All education must be imparted through the medium of the provincial language.

   4. In this there is no room for giving sectional religious training. Fundamental universal ethics will have full scope.

   5. This education whether it is confined to children or adults, male or female, will find its way to the homes of the pupils.

   6. Since millions of students receiving this education will consider themselves as of the whole of the India, they must learn an interprovincial language. This common interprovincial speech can only be Hindustani written in Nagari or Urdu script. Therefore, pupils will have to master both scripts. (Gandhi, 1954, p. 56)

Gandhi's views have to be interpreted in the political context in which they were made. From approximately 1920 to 1947, Gandhi's views were decidedly nationalistic, since he and his allies were trying to rally the country toward destabilizing the Raj and gaining Indian independence. Because his views on the above issues were directly anti-English—since he felt that the language divided the country—his championing of the vernaculars sits in a polarized position (somewhat simplistic by today's standards) vis-à-vis English. Although Gandhi's message of nonviolence seems to be ironically completely forgotten in Gujarat, given the recent horrific riots, the larger strain of noncooperation still resonates. As we will see, noncooperation in the two endeavors discussed presently is directed against perceived social forces that preserve inequities. The steadfast way in which both projects work at bridging perceived gulfs is reminiscent of Gandhi's insistence on being "civil" and of responding to tyranny by searching for nonviolent, effective alternatives.

The Two Endeavors: Drawing on Noncooperation to Expand "Education" and Civic Engagement

The National Social Service Scheme at the Women's College

Located in the inner city, the women's college is a low-income Gujarati-medium liberal arts college in downtown Ahmedabad where much of the rioting of 2002 occurred. In my previous writing (Ramanathan, 2006b) regarding this college, I have discussed ways in which the National Social Service (NSS)—a nationwide, Gandhian, social service organization, a chapter of which is in this school—engages many of the institution's female students in extracurricular activities that directly target community needs. Begun in commemoration of Gandhi's centennial year in 1969, the organization encourages students to volunteer time toward social projects, including those relating to literacy, health, sanitation, women and children's welfare, AIDS awareness, drug addiction awareness, human rights, and national integration.[10] Added to this list are the recent projects that address the needs of families most affected by the two events. Although I have addressed the ways in which this extracurricular project harnesses a variety of vernacular resources in some detail elsewhere (Ramanathan, 2006a), I will for the purposes of the present discussion attempt to make this point by drawing primarily on interview data with Mr. P., the key person who runs this project endeavor (I do need to note here that all my interviews were in Hindi and Gujarati and that I have translated the excerpts below for the present argument; see Ramanathan, 2006b, for a discussion on tensions with translations).

Mr. P., a teacher of 19th-century British literature, began this project more than 15 years ago, with a commitment to translating the best of Gandhi's ideals—of service, self-respect, valuing the vernacular backgrounds of his students—to specific contexts of practice.[11] Realizing that he operates in a space where speaking openly of sociopolitical issues is most incendiary—in downtown Ahmedabad where much of the rioting occurred, in a very poor, diverse college with students from both Hindu and Muslim (as well as other) backgrounds—this man works toward expanding his view of education by connecting it to issues of "citizenship," taking pride in being "Gujarati," and relying on what is currently within one's reach to ply instruments of change. When asked about why the classroom was not a viable sphere for his message, he said,

The classroom is the most incendiary place to raise community issues . . . you see, the students come from such different backgrounds, with such divergent points of view, how can I bring up political and community issues, especially now when everyone, but everyone is reeling from the riots? Some of my students have lost their homes, some family members. *But I will say this: I know that I want to address these issues somehow; I want them to know that education is not only about what they learn and what we teach in classes about Dryden and Congreve, it is about participating in the community.* It is about taking the best of literary values—connecting to other humans—and living them. So rather than be overtly political about it, I channel their and my energy in my projects where the focus is on the community, regardless of who the members of the community are, and I have both Muslim and Hindu students working in these projects. (FI, 2: 2, June 2, 2004)[12]

When the earthquake hit, he organized his students into groups that went out and worked in the community: working in communal kitchens for people left homeless, contacting municipal authorities for clean drinking water, and getting blankets and warm clothes because it was winter. Because the riots occurred around the time that many of the students were to take their final university exams, and because the exam centers were far away and there was curfew in town, he organized buses that would take students from riot-affected areas to the exam centers.

As he explains in the excerpt above, "education" for him is more about "connecting to other humans" than it is about what is taught and learned in the classroom, and moving toward this end without engaging in divisive political rhetoric is instrumental in his mission, since his focus is on "what needs to get done, what the reality in front of me is like" (FI, 2: 5). One way that he works toward this goal is by emphasizing in his workshops (for NSS volunteers) what being "Gujarati" means: its diversity (that fact that it is a native language for a diverse set of people including Hindus, Sikhs, Muslims, Parsis, Christians, and Jews), the fact that it is home to other migrant Indians (like my family who are originally Tamilian but who have settled in Gujarat), and the fact that it is the birthplace of Gandhi who represented the last word on community service, nonformal education, and above all Hindu–Muslim unity. As he says,

My job is to create a space whereby such sentiments and values about community participation can flourish. The last 3 or 4 years have been so painful for so many people in this state. I want to be able to say that when my students graduate they do so with some pride and awareness of the ties that bind them to their fellow citizens. That the riots should have happened here in Gandhi's home state, when his life's actions centered around Hindu–Muslim unity—how do I not get my Gujarati students to see that irony? My problem is: how do I get them to realize this inductively? How can I make that realization happen quietly, without dogma, without saying too much? (FI, 2: 7)

One way he communicates his message indirectly is by not speaking about NSS issues in the classroom, or in corridors where students abound, but by relying on his NSS student-volunteers to "spread the word" as indeed they do. As he explains,

It is crucial that this work not become a dogma . . . given my position, my speaking of it directly runs that risk. I speak of it in workshops, I organize their camps, I attend the training sessions with them; I want to do all that, but I will not seek students out by speaking of it directly. They have to want to do

this work. The value of non-formal education is that it remain "nonformal." You take it into the classroom and it is gone. Pfff . . . like that! They have to hear of this community work from other involved
students; they have to see their classmates being fulfilled by this. (FI, 2: 13)

Echoes of Gandhi's views on nonformal education are obvious here, as indeed is
the Gandhian insistence on proceeding with such work diligently and without fuss.
Although nonformal education has traditionally been conceived of as an educational
alternative operating outside the constraints of the classroom, the changes that such
education seems to seek eventually make their way to classrooms.

Education and Community at the Gandhi Ashram

This theme of quietly working on community problems and of viewing such work
as integral to larger understandings of education is most resonant in the Gandhi
Ashram, which houses a program called Manav Sadhna (MS; human improvement).
The Gandhi Ashram in Ahmedabad is the largest of Gandhi's ashrams, since this
particular one served as his headquarters during the struggle for independence. On
the banks of the river Sabarmati, the ashram is located on spacious grounds. One side
holds his library and archival materials about him, and on the doorway to this section
is a huge tribute to Martin Luther King. The other side of the ashram is what used to
be his living quarters, with his spinning wheel, his desk, and the rooms of his closest
allies. The ashram, even today, is a place that welcomes the poorest of the poor and
offers a haven and rehabilitation for those seeking it.

All work that goes on in the Gandhi Ashram seems to embody quintessential
"Gandhian" ideals of self-reliance, cross-religious unities, and nonformal and basic
education, coupled with a thick strain of quiet noncooperation. Begun by three people—Jayesh Patel, Anar Patel, and Viren Joshi—in 1991, MS today runs more than
20 well-developed community-oriented programs. Born and raised in the ashram
because his father was a staunch Gandhian follower, the first of the three has Gandhi
"in his bones," so to speak, and much of what follows in this section is drawn from
my interviews with him, from participating in workshops he has led, and from interviews with other people at the ashram with whom he has put me in touch.

Although there are several similarities between the NSS work of Mr. P and the
projects of MS—both have strong Gandhian strains, both enhance the vernaculars,
both are community oriented—there are interesting differences. Unlike the project
run by Mr. P., where civic engagement is parallel to formal, classroom-based learning, the focus of the projects at the Gandhi Ashram is on interpreting all education as
"civic education" and on attending to the most basic of human needs (food, clothing,
shelter) before addressing any issues related to formal learning. Also, unlike the NSS
project, the children the Ashram caters to are the extremely poor. When I spent time
at the ashram in May and June 2004, Jayesh recalled how the three of them began
their program with the explicit aim of working with the poorest persons they could
find. He narrated this to me in Gujarati; I am presenting it below in translation.
(I need to note here that I am deliberately choosing to present extensive, fuller quotes

to mitigate the loss already encountered in translation, a process that necessitates the adding of more layers of "distance" from the very first layer of the narrator's recounting and my interpreting in Gujarati, to my then presenting and interpreting this narrative in academic English.)

The three of us had noticed that a lot of village people, because of a scarcity of resources in villages—equipment, money, water—migrate to the cities and they live in slums. And we found that mothers work as cleaners/maids in people's homes, fathers work in pulling handcarts, and they send their children out to pick rags. The childhoods of these children are completely lost. Middle-class children have all they could possibly have but these others have no opportunities and we decided we wanted to work with these children. Think globally, act locally, so the three of us started our work. The three of us took along biscuits, chocolates, some clothes, and we set out in a rickshaw and went to the Naranpura crossroads. I still remember this, and there we saw 2 children working in a tea stall, making tea, and serving it to customers. We asked the tea-stall owner if we could sit with the children and chat with them. Hope you don't mind. We started talking to the children who were clearly suspicious of us. "Who are these people who are asking me all these questions," they thought. We told the children, "we came to be friends with you. Will you share a meal with us?" The children said yes . . . and when we got to know them, we gave them clothes, cut their nails, shampooed their hair, got them shoes. We went again in a few days, and by then, these children had talked about what we had done for them with their friends and before long they would wait for us to come, calling "Jayeshbhai Virenbhai" . . . We soon realized it was getting very difficult for us to cater to all the children there and so asked, "Will you come to the Gandhi Ashram? We have a campus there and we can introduce you to people there. Can you come once a week?" Our very first program was "Back to Childhood" in '91. While we had each done work with children before this, but this was our first Manav Sadhna project. Soon thereafter, the children started coming, first 10, then 15 . . . they seemed to enjoy coming here. We used to give them baths, clothes and then began helping them with their homework. You'll see some of them today . . . they've grown but are still here. They were dirty, unbathed, with unwashed clothes . . . we showered them with care, told them stories, prayed with them, showed them films and sang songs with them. We did a lot through play and then would eat together with them . . . (Jayesh Patel, GA, p. 2, June 3, 2004)

As Jayesh explained to me, "For us education is community work; if schooling does not teach you to connect with your fellow humans, then what good is it?" (June 3, 2004).

Like the NSS-related work at the women's college, MS is committed to working with and around social stratifications, including Hindu–Muslim tensions, some of which were exacerbated during the quake (and very definitely during the riots; indeed, there had been reports that particular groups of peoples, including Muslims, did not get the aid they needed). Jayesh, Viren, Anar, and the MS volunteers began working with some very poor destitute villages in a corner of Kutch (not far from the epicenter), with 80% of its population being Muslim, and with the Hindu population migrating. Almost all the homes had been decimated. As Jayesh explains,

There was almost nothing left there. We wanted to do something about this. *We did an initial analysis and educated ourselves of their needs*: broken-down homes, no resources, no fodder or water for livestock, the general geographical conditions of the place (frequent cyclones and hurricanes). Over the last few years we have reached a point where it is self-sufficient, stopped migration, worked out Hindu–Muslim tensions to where during the recent riots, not one of these 47 villages reported anti-Hindu, anti-Muslim incidents. (Jayesh Patel, GA, p. 4, June 3, 2004)

This close attention to "educating oneself," of figuring out and questioning one's own default assumptions, has echoes of Gandhi's noncooperation and finds interesting articulation in the idea that we each need to "not cooperate" with our default views but attempt to step outside them by "educating ourselves" by learning from others. A point that illustrates this best has to do with MS's work in a set of villages after the massive earthquake and the ways in which they went about educating themselves about the lives of the villagers after paying close attention to the needs of the local people, and by drawing extensively on their valued, vernacular ways of living. Robin Sukhadia, with who I have been in e-mail contact, and who has worked with MS in some of these villages, explains on his website the conflicts many of the villagers experienced between the modern kinds of houses that were being built for them after the quake and the "traditional" homes they were used to and wanted:

> There has been tremendous financial and infrastructural support pouring into Kutch after the earthquake, and so many NGOs and international agencies and religious organizations have come here to build homes and rebuild this area . . . new hospitals have been built, new roads, new homes, but sadly, it seems to me, that many of these projects (which are funded mainly from abroad) have very insensitively proceeded with building living "communities" without much thought as to the traditional way of life here . . . and it seems that many of the villagers and farmers who lost everything here, do not wish to live in homes that resemble city homes and pre-fabricated enclaves . . . the villagers, who have lived off the land for generations, have no where to put their cattle, to grow their crops, or to stay connected to the land in these new homes . . . sadly many of the homes are empty because the villagers have decided it is better to be homeless than succumb to these imposed forms of living which are being built in the name of service to the poor but . . . MS's approach here, thankfully, has been very different. They have, instead of imposing designs and architects, rather empowered the local communities to design their own homes in their traditional methods . . . they have built *Bhungas*, beautiful, mud-based round buildings that have been in use for hundreds of years here . . . not surprisingly, these structures were the only ones that survived the earthquake . . . they are very practical and make sense for this environment. So, *Manav Sadhna* provided the guidance for the reconstruction of their homes, and the community . . . [look at] what happens in the name of service . . . (Robin Sukhadia, quoted in Ramanathan, 2006b, p. 245)

The idea of drawing on, listening to, and educating oneself about what a community needs permeates all aspects of MS's projects and is a key issue in the orientation workshops (for MS volunteers) that I participated in. Not only are the volunteers— all of whom are Gujarati—reminded of and educated in Gandhi's ideals in the workshops—but they are also encouraged to make connections between the work they do and the specific Gandhian ideals they are enacting. So, whether it is working in a very poor Urdu-medium Muslim school (that municipal authorities have largely ignored), or finding clothes and food supplies for a very poor farmer who is suffering the consequences of a bad crop and little rain, or organizing the celebrations of a key religious holiday (Hindu, Muslim, Christian, Jewish, Sikh, Parsi), among others, the volunteers are provided platforms and contexts whereby both their conceptual understanding of Gandhi and their practice are extended and looped into each other. As one of the volunteers tells me, "These workshops are not just about educating ourselves about Gandhi, but about bringing our work back to Gandhi . . . we go out and do Gandhi's work, but we each have to come back to Gandhi . . ."(V2: 2, June 11, 2004).

Interestingly, politically and community oriented as all of this work by MS is, there is little or no reference to political events and to the ways in which they have exacerbated social/religious stratifications in the city. When discussing the work done by MS volunteers after the riots, no overt mention was made of Gujarat's chief minister (who has been accused of not doing enough to protect the Muslims) or of the incendiary rhetoric of the ruling BJP state government. The idea that "there is a job to be done" and "I have to do it" (Jayesh Patel, p. 5, June 10, 2004) seems to be a dominant theme, and noncooperation during this time was and still is enacted in terms of steadfastly engaging in the opposite of all riot-related acts: of making shelter, finding lost relatives, distributing food and clothes, finding employment for the numerous widowed women, and providing a haven for orphaned children. Although all of the volunteers at MS are engaged in various riot-related projects, it is with the children that they are most concerned. As Jayesh explains,

If we wish to reach the parents, we have to start with children. It is only through our work that we pass on our message. We cannot formally teach anybody anything; we can only do. In the end, everything we learn goes back to the community. Why not start with the community in the first place? Why not start with children? (Jayesh Patel, p. 6, June 3, 2004)

Clearly, distinctions between "civic engagement" and "education" have blurred here; they are in this context almost synonymous.

WINDING DOWN: ARTICULATING IMPLICATIONS

Moving away from the locality of these scenes to the more generalized space of research frameworks, we can see that juxtaposing skeins of formal and nonformal education permits hues around the vernaculars that otherwise tend to remain hidden. The vernaculars, although devalued in the formal realm, become the very resources by which communities heal themselves. This irony is a subtext that flows thickly through many issues around English and the vernaculars in South Asia and is integrally tied to the postcolonial research framework, which casts interesting light on issues of linguistic diversity. It is to the specifics of this framework and how it has helped my endeavor that I now turn.

First, since this framework involves "speaking back" to colonial powers, it ushers in history, a discipline that has been generally regarded as marginal to applied linguistics. After all, to gain a fuller sense of how I am today—where I fit, how I see myself, others, our planet—I had to gain a fuller sense of historical conditions that brought me to my present, a historical sense that exceeded the history I was taught in K–12. I had to educate myself about colonial documents, especially as they pertained to language teaching, largely separatist schooling policies for Indians and the English, ways in which Indian history until 1947 was told to Indians by British historians (which, as I mentioned earlier, was, by and large, unkind), the efforts of

Indian historians writing Indian history, and how my own family background had differing relations vis-à-vis the English (both of my grandfathers worked for the Raj, but one was a staunch Gandhian, the other an Anglophile). History, then—personal, national, international—is crucial in the postcolonial endeavor.

The second key point that this framework implies is a deep commitment to recognizing how history plays itself out in contexts of inequity. Within applied linguistics, this could mean identifying ways in which unjust conditions get reproduced in everyday interactions (the consistent use of a certain dismissive or patronizing tone in interactions with poorer VM students, for instance), ways in which various cultural institutions work together to elevate one language above others (thus stifling linguistic diversity), connections between these "smaller" contexts and other structural inequities (reproduced in textbooks, or in the low expectations on the part of teachers regarding VM students), and then further out into the larger culture (ideologies perpetuated by the media that equates EM people with "sophistication" and the VM with being "backward"). These issues are directly tied to understanding linguistic inequity in the present and permits insights into colonizing policies that still hold sway. Being alert to cross-questioning our own assumptions permits us to see and acknowledge local efforts at changing power equations (Rampton & Charalambous, 2012)

Growing into this multipronged awareness also raises consciousness regarding disputes and conflicts around ownership and claiming the right to speak for one's self about one's past. And this is where the third point about this research framework comes in. On the one hand is the wresting back of historiography from "colonial powers" and assuming the right to claim reception; on the other, it is also about recognizing that there are others who are already doing so (VM teachers and students in this case) but are doing so in ways, languages, and forms to which we have remained blind because we have collectively bought into status quo ways of being, thinking, believing, living that keep our vision blinkered. In my own case, it was not until I turned my gaze to issues in the community that I began to connect to the vernacular part of me. Doing so allowed me to acknowledge the efforts of Mr. P and MS, whose efforts are as much about claiming the right to claim a space and understanding of one's history—through enactments of Gandhianism—as is my own writing about these issues. The workshops with these teachers have, over the years, made me ever conscious of how critical work happens on the sidelines, in unexpected ways, and in manners that defy definition or categorization. It is in not cooperating with our own default assumptions that we render ourselves open to seeing the hierarchies in languages, peoples, and literacies, and it is in this way that this framework is ultimately ethical, since its focus is integrally on changing our own perspectives as it validates those of others that are waiting to be acknowledged and heard.

NOTES

[1]Versions of this chapter appear in Hawkins (2013) and Martin-Jones, Blackledge, and Creese (2012).

[2]My entry into my long-term endeavor in my home town ironically began in the United States when I was taking a seminar by Professor James Paul Gee at the University of Southern California. In 1989, we were reading his book *Social Linguistics and Literacies* (in proof form since his book had not yet emerged in print) wherein he seemed to crystallize for me something I knew to be unerringly correct but had not been able to articulate. I was working on a project for one of my qualifying papers—on two stories, one told by a little White child called Sandy, and another by a little Black child called Leona—wherein I argued that mainstream listeners were able to parse and comprehend Sandy's story with more ease than Leona (see Ramanathan-Abbott, 1993), thereby underscoring a point that Gee (1990) himself was making regarding mainstream U.S. teachers not being able to hear their nonmainstream students. Professor Gee was my mentor through my doctoral work (which I did in an area unrelated to literacy; on the sociolinguistic dimensions of Alzheimer discourse, as a matter of fact), and his views on narrative, literacy, and sociopolitics heavily shaped my thinking. When I introduced a couple of chapters of his book to teachers in Ahmedabad, their responses were similar to mine, and that contributed to the impetus for starting my project.

[3]Liberal Arts colleges in Gujarat are typically 3-year colleges. States like Maharashtra, on the other hand, include the last 2 years of high school—11th and 12th grades—as part of college. The institutions in the chapter have 11th and 12th grades as part of high school.

[4]There has been much discussion (in newspapers, among people, in schools, and in the group of teachers I work with) about the state having "forgotten Gandhi" and his teachings in the wake of the recent Hindu–Muslim violence in the city. Gandhi's views on Hindu–Muslim unity have generally been anathema to some factions of the right-wing Hindu BJP party in the state, since he was seen as supporting Muslims too much and as espousing a view of Hinduism that was generally deemed "effeminate."

[5]MMLs are mandated by the state board of education and in that sense do not vary from textbook to textbook. They serve as a guideline and get reinforced in teacher education programs.

[6]I do need to note here that the MMLs are quite different for literacy in the VM; the focus here is similar to the EM in that it too emphasizes acquiring academic literacy.

[7]English serves a strong gatekeeping function for college admissions in India. Students schooled in the vernacular are offered bridge programs in some colleges to get them ready for content-based instruction in English.

[8]Some of what follows has appeared in Ramanathan (2005a, 2006a, 2013).

[9]Some activist groups in Ahmedabad include the following:

   a. Janvikas: an organization that focuses on the empowerment and development of non-governmental organizations in Gujarat
   b. Janpath Citizens Initiative: a coalition of over 200 local grassroots nongovernmental organizations coming together in the days following the Gujarat quake
   c. Navasarjan Trust: led by Martin Macwan, an organization representing Dalit rights in India
   d. Rishta: A Gujarat Jesuit writers' cell engaged in a series of workshops for the development of vernacular media, especially for Christian and Muslim youth
   e. Manav Sadhna: Run out of the Gandhi Ashram

[10]Early camps and training are offered for all volunteers for minimal fee as well as extended camps for college-going youth. Themes of some camps in the past few years have been "Youth for Sustainable Development," Youth for Wasteland Development," and "Youth for Greenery."

[11]All instruction in all subjects at the VM college is in the vernacular.

[12]FI refers to faculty interview; GA to Gandhi Ashram.

REFERENCES

Alidou, H. (2004). Medium of instruction in postcolonial Africa. In J. Tollefson & A. Tsui (Eds.), *Medium of instruction policies: Which agenda? Whose agenda?* (pp. 195–216). Mahwah, New Jersey.

Brutt-Griffler, J. (2002). *World English: A study of its development.* Clevedon, England: Multilingual Matters.

Canagarajah, S. (1997). *Resisting linguistic imperialism in English teaching.* Oxford, England: Oxford University Press.

Gandhi, M. K. (1954). Medium of instruction (B. Kumarappa, Trans.). Ahmedabad, India: Navjivan.

Gee, J. (1990). *Social linguistics and literacies: Ideologies in discourses.* Bristol, PA: Falmer Press.

Gee, J. P. (2003). Opportunity to learn: A language-based perspective on assessment. *Assessment in Education, 10,* 27–46.

Hawkins, M. (Ed.). (2004). *Language learning and teacher-education.* Clevedon, England: Multilingual Matters.

Hawkins, M. (2013). *Framing languages and literacies: Socially situated views and perspectives.* New York, NY: Routledge.

Hornberger, N., & Johnson, D. (2007). Slicing the onion ethnographically: Layers and spaces in multilingual language education policy and practice. *TESOL Quarterly, 41,* 509–532.

Kalantzis, M., & Cope, B. (2002). Multicultural education: Transforming the mainstream. In S. May (Ed.), *Critical multiculturalism: Rethinking multicultural and antiracist education* (pp. 245–276). Philadelphia, PA: Falmer Press.

King, K. A. (2001). *Language revitalization processes and prospects: Quichua in the Equadorian Andes.* Clevedon, England: Multilingual Matters.

Martin-Jones, M., Blackledge, A., & Creese, A. (Eds.). (2012). *The Routledge handbook of multilingualism.* New York, NY: Routledge.

McCarty, T. (2002). Between possibility and constraint: Indigenous language education, planning, and policy in the United States. In J. Tollefson (Ed.), *Language policies in education: Critical* issues (pp. 285–307). Mahwah, NJ: Lawrence Erlbaum.

McCarty, T. (Ed). (2005). *Language, literacy and power in schooling.* Mahwah, NJ: Lawrence Erlbaum.

Morgan, B., & Ramanathan, V. (2009). Outsourcing, globalizing economics, and shifting language policies: Issues in managing Indian call centers. *Language Policy, 8,* 69–80.

Phillipson, R. (1992). *Linguistic imperialism.* Oxford, England: Oxford University Press.

Purani, T., Salat, J., Soni, P., & Joshi, S. (1998). *English readers.* Gandhinagar, India: Gujarat State Board of Textbooks.

Ramanathan, V. (2005a). *The English-vernacular divide: Post-colonial language policies and practice.* Cleveland, England: Multilingual Matters.

Ramanathan, V. (2005b). Situating the researcher in research texts: Dilemmas, questions, ethics, new directions. *Journal of Language, Identity, and Education, 4,* 291–297.

Ramanathan, V. (2006a). Gandhi, non-cooperation and socio-civic education: Harnessing the vernaculars. *Journal of Language, Identity, and Education, 5,* 229–250.

Ramanathan, V. (2006b). Of texts AND translations AND rhizomes: Postcolonial anxieties AND deracinations AND knowledge constructions. *Critical Inquiry in Language Studies, 3,* 223–244.

Ramanathan, V. (2013). A postcolonial perspective in applied linguistics: Situating English and the vernaculars. In M. Hawkins (Ed.), *Framing language and literacies: Socially situated views and perspectives* (pp. 84–105). New York, NY: Routledge

Ramanathan, V., & Morgan, B. (2009). Global warning: West-based TESOL, class-blindness and the challenge for critical pedagogies. In F. Sharifian (Ed.), *English as an international language: Perspectives and pedagogical issues* (pp. 154–168). Clevedon, England: Multilingual Matters.

Ramanathan-Abbott, V. (1993). An examination of the relationship between social practices and the comprehension of narratives. *Text & Talk, 13,* 117–141.

Rampton, B., & Charalambous, C. (2012). Crossing. In M. Martin-Jones, A. Blackledge, & A. Creese (Eds), *The Routledge handbook of multilingualism* (pp. 482–498). London, England: Routlege.

Shohamy, E. (2006). *Language policies: Hidden agendas and approaches.* New York, NY: Routledge.

Tollefson, J. W. (Ed.). (1991). *Planning language, planning inequality.* London, England: Longman.

Tollefson, J. W., & Tsui, A. (Eds.). (2004). *Medium of instruction policies: Which agenda? Whose agenda?* Mahwah, NJ: Lawrence Erlbaum.

Vamdatta, D., Joshi, P., & Patel, Y. (Eds.). (2000). *English, Standard 10.* Gandhinagar, India: Gujarat State Board of Textbooks.

Verma, P. (2010). *Becoming Indian: The unfinished revolution of culture and identity.* New Delhi, India: Penguin India.

Wiley, T., & Wright, W. (2004). Against the undertow: Language-minority education policy and politics in the "age of accountability." *Educational Policy, 18,* 142–168.

Young, R. (2003). *Postcolonialism: A short introduction.* Oxford, England: Oxford University Press.

Conclusion

A Cerebration of Language Diversity, Language Policy, and Politics in Education

JOSEPH LO BIANCO

University of Melbourne

During the more vitriolic moments of the 1980s "culture wars" in the United States, the "culture warrior" E. D. Hirsch made a clarion call in defense of universal study of the masterworks of the English literary canon. In this work, he conceded space to the canonical literature of prestige foreign languages but drew a very firm line against linguistic pluralism, which he contrasted to all the virtuous promise of standards as follows: "Linguistic pluralism enormously increases cultural fragmentation, civil antagonism, illiteracy, and economic-technological ineffectualness" (Hirsch, 1988, p. 91).

In similar vein, Bernstein (1994) saw language questions as a direct and immediate proxy for a political project aiming to destabilize U.S. civil and political unity and a deliberate and purposive act of subversion expressive of the connection between language education policy and the wider social compact. Treating the idea that Cherokee might be taught in public schools to incredulous ridicule, Bernstein saw its teaching as an "act of rebellion against white, Anglo-cultural domination" with a "multicultural animus against European culture and its derivatives" (p. 245). This critique of relativist multicultural lobbying conflates language education questions with nonlanguage educational sociopolitical claims just as surely as Hirsch's (1988) claim that subaltern and marginal peoples can attain educational equality only through access to core cultural content, selected from the canonical achievements over time.

Whether it is the more limited scope of assessable academic standards (Hirsch) or the wider scope of stability of the entire American polity (Bernstein), the 1980s and 1990s were a period during which technical/scientific and pedagogical evidence in favor of multilingualism would not be permitted to determine the communicative code selected as medium and object of instruction of small children in elementary schools. Today, although there is no shortage of opponents lining up against

Review of Research in Education
March 2014, Vol. 38, pp. 312-331
DOI: 10.3102/0091732X13511050
© 2014 AERA. http://rre.aera.net

minority languages and linguistic pluralism, we can allow some space to celebrate that there has been a lessening of these earlier levels of hyperbole. Indeed, *The New York Times* reported recently that Hirsch is "gaining ground" as the New York City Department of Education recommends Hirshean modes of curriculum construction (Baker, 2013). Although less journalistically inclined judgment would find this resurgence rather less impressive than what newspaper articles typically suggest, it must also mean, as the article implies, that the tone and some of the content of earlier positions have mellowed with time.

A wider acceptance that diversity and pluralism do not threaten the very sinews of American life can be identified despite and against the persistence of opposition, not least represented by the political success of Barack Obama's election. This creates space for more sanguine conversations and modes of reasoning that can foster a kind of language education planning informed better and more securely by pedagogical, linguistic, and sociolinguistic evidence. This is not a claim for a rationalist language planning, like the technicism that dominated an earlier phase of language planning in which it was believed that academic researchers would conduct studies using unimpeachable methodologies, apply these to practical problems, and produce widely shared if perhaps not universally endorsed programs of action. The optimistic phase of language policy, reflecting its "parent" public policy phase in which democratic politics would be perfected by injection of science-based policymaking and eliminate ideology and interests, has passed into history as surely as its technicist language-planning counterpart of the 1960s, 1970s, and early 1980s. Nevertheless, there is a need, and an urgent one, for scholarly research to be more and better used within policymaking.

During the bitterest years of the "culture wars," conflict about minority children was often only collateral damage in the central battle between progressives and traditionalists, but in some ways, it was the central question. This was inevitable given the growing presence of diverse worldviews, languages and life experiences. All these were naturally present in the community and automatically transmitted within homes and families, but they linked to demonstrably unequal educational and occupational prospects of minority language children, as pluralism contrasted with the dominant presence of English and the wider cultural patterns of American public and cultural life.

In addition, as the numbers of immigrants continue to grow rapidly their presence imposes adjustment on the epistemological assumptions of all education. What has been taken for granted becomes increasingly untenable as educators must engage in acts of teaching and learning in which more of what is taught requires negotiation between them, with continual checking and adjusting of perspective, and acknowledgment of inevitable dealing with difference.

The content of the present issue of *Review of Research in Education* (RRE) is therefore timely and important, allowing considered, multiperspectival active reflection, what I am calling cerebration, on language diversity as well as a call for concerted action for linking better the findings of research to the imperatives of teaching. For one of the central claims of proponents of serious bilingual education—of serious examination of the cognitive and social dimensions of difference—was precisely not the romantic delusion that Hirsch imagined he was attacking.

The turn to the critical in sociolinguistics has not always been kind to the interests and needs of minority populations (Lo Bianco, 2009). What is required is a critically disposed sociolinguistics that is at the same time engaged and productive, pushing for practical improvement and radical change in the way minority language and cultures are regarded, in the interests of reconfigured democratic and participatory citizenships. In any case, Hirsch's theories are contestable from diverse perspectives, several unimaginable when he first proposed them, such as whether a normalized standard, indeed a fixed and universal number of concepts, is productive in a globalized and rapidly ever more deeply enmeshed world. What can be appropriate in all education, for all learners, under such circumstances, since so little of the postschooling world is predictable? In a world of great flux in unpredictable directions, "pluralism" is hardly rare or radical; it is instead the common condition. What used to be "foreign" can scarcely be conceived this way any longer (Lo Bianco, in press).

Conceiving minorities as participants in a projected metareconstruction of the new senses of "community" in an age of instantaneous global contact, shorn of limitations of geography and locality is likely to inject their particular language and cultural knowledge as productive active resources into educational activity. In a more tightly globalized world, mainstream and periphery, as conceived in the past, will overlap and shape each other. Future education can be conceived only as investment in fostering student creativity, achievement, and thinking, and this remit for learning can ill afford to deny existing stocks of knowledge, skill, awareness, and behavior that are present in different parts of the world.

Specifying stocks of concepts and knowledge that all must acquire outside of the process of education is a risky activity. It lends itself too readily to the imposition of externally conceived and generated formulae of what is to be learned and how what is to be learned is to be taught, becoming too readily available in turn for commodification, rote practice, and validation through standardized examination. This, needless to say, would dispose of the need for the critical, which has been the preoccupation of many language planners for two decades but has yielded too little by way of change and improvement.

The critical turn in the languages sciences was premised on the assumption or belief that exposing inequalities, interests, and ideologies would be socially emancipatory. This is scarcely credible any longer and in any case neglects equally important principles in educational research and practice aimed at the creative and imaginative domain, for learners and learning. And what, ultimately, is the place of pluralist difference itself, as a phenomenon of existence? No "'cerebration" on language diversity, language policy, and politics in education can be considered complete if it fails to ask fundamental questions about difference.

The choice to address language diversity in education in *RRE* comes therefore at a propitious time, during which the United States faces deep social, cultural, and economic challenges as globalization gives effect to changes of great historic importance with the shift in the locus of the world's productive center away from North Atlantic, European, and North American locales toward an increasingly China-dominated Asia.

In conceiving this volume, the editors have designed four pedestals, serving as a kind of ontology, of the philosophical categories and their relations as the entities that constitute the domain of language pluralism. Exploring the efficacy and the function of education language policies involves asking questions about the concrete policies and practices in imparting communicative skill in the secondary socializing domain of the public school. Here children are deprived of their freedom to wander the streets and spend time with friends and social media and instead are compelled to surrender their temporal and spatial liberty for fixed hours of the day, fixed days of the week, fixed weeks of the year, and fixed years of their adolescence. This project of socialization in the interests of the formation of a consolidated state and nation, an economy and a citizenry, has always depended on the lingual behavior of teachers.

It is salutary and important to recall that education as it arose and was systematized as compulsory and universal through the 19th-century process of national consolidation, at least in European and Westernized polities, invested heavily in literate education. The "literacy economy" is therefore also a moral economy, a project of investing in skilled practice for purposes of consolidation of national identity and public order (Collins, 1999). Four category points organize this field:

- Educational access, equity, and achievement
- Native-language literacy as an educational right
- The paradox of majority and minority languages
- Emerging global demographic shifts

Terrence Wiley's chapter proceeds through long-term historical research from 16th-century U.S. society drawn on U.S. Census data, a reading of a question-and-answer sequence from a popular "Jeopardy" television game show (April 11, 2013), and a literature review. The author focuses on recent claims that transnational migrations and globalization are creating exceptional levels of ethno-linguistic "super diversity." By way of a thorough historical analysis of language policies in the United States, their impact on various ethno-linguistic groups, and the evolution of English-only ideology, he argues that the extent to which present configurations of diversity are "super" and unprecedented depends on how notions of past diversities are constructed and how they relate to presumed antecedent majority groups.

This is an important corrective to a tendency in research to inadequately, if at all, recognize the different form or value that historical events or phenomena take, a tendency which can mask as well as reveal developments. History is made of continuities and discontinuities with the present, and Wiley's important contribution is to ground current analysis in an interpretively stronger and data-rich evidence base. Examination of U.S. Census data and historical documents demonstrates that all past periods of U.S history could be seen as illustrative of "super diversities," and he goes on to contest claims made by Kloss (1971, 1977) of the "tolerant traditions" of U.S. society toward linguistic diversity. Instead what Wiley finds is that within U.S. history there has always prevailed an expectation of linguistic assimilation into English.

Kloss had argued that with the exception of the period associated with World War I, a policy climate of linguistic tolerance had been prevalent over the course of U.S. history, but this claim appears to be undermined by distinguishing activity and behavior that are merely *behavioral assimilation* from *structural incorporation*: effectively between education for domestication and education for full economic participation. In Wiley's reasoning, Kloss employed a reductive mode of questioning, and the question of whether throughout its colonial and national periods U.S. language policies have been largely tolerant or intolerant toward ethno-linguistic minorities is better answered contextually, based on the initial mode of incorporation of each group and their subsequent treatment in formal law as well as in informal social, educational, economic, and political contexts. Most recently, this has manifested as an "acceptability of prejudice on the basis of language," which operates as a "surrogate for other forms of prejudice."

The "Jeopardy" game show question analysis used by Wiley is around the first city in the United States: Is this Santa Fe, New Mexico, or San Juan, Puerto Rico? This interesting angle is used by Wiley to show how the question/answers reflect underlying and naturalized ways of thinking about the United States and its antecedent history during which prior Spanish colonization of areas long preceded the English founding of Jamestown. The Wiley contribution addresses the overview sections of the *RRE* volume related to native-language literacy as an educational right, the paradox of majority and minority languages, and emerging global demographic shifts. It constitutes a persuasive and thorough analysis demonstrating the value of grounding interpretations of the present in a secure footing of historical evidence.

Specifically addressing diachronic and synchronic analysis of Spanish as the "second national language" of the United States is the article by Reynaldo F. Macías. It is well known that the contiguous Spanish-speaking countries of the Americas supply a continually replenished speaker population to the already large and multiple forms of Spanish in the United States and that, according to census data, this replenishment stems rates of intergenerational language attrition for Spanish not unlike other language loss rates.

As a result of this demographic communicative reality, Spanish is a language of permanent and growing importance to U.S. education and society alike, in addition to its evident importance as a "foreign" language, a language spoken in (many) foreign places, many of which are proximal or close.

These multiple and multiplying realities for and about Spanish create its uniqueness, and these as they are surveyed and discussed by Macías provide the warrant for his claim that Spanish should be accorded exceptional standing in public and symbolic life in the United States. The author makes eight claims for Spanish that align with diachronic and synchronic axes in public life, consciousness, institutional operations, and demography. These are, essentially, that Spanish precedes English by a century in the North American continent; that some two thirds of the current landmass of the United States was under official Spanish polity for much or all of this period; that these conditions were disrupted through forcible incorporation of many of these peoples into the United States; that this resulted in official U.S. recognition of the status of Spanish at various levels of jurisdiction; that Spanish has grown and is projected to continue growing; and that it is a popular second language of choice in U.S. education. The final claims are synchronic ones, related to the world standing and importance of Spanish and the possibility of speaking of the United States as a Spanish-speaking country.

Drawing on statistical, historical, and legal data and instruments, ranging from 15th- and 16th-century Papal Bulls, to British monarchical edicts (Henry VIII's 1496 Discovery Doctrine), to the 2011 Universal Declaration of Linguistic Human Rights, Macías constructs a case for Spanish exceptionalism or primacy, within the context of linguistic pluralism of the United States. Within the logic and purpose of this volume, Macías's argument resides firmly within the discursive argumentative realm, proposing lines of questioning of existing understandings of what I will call the politics of language regimes.

In essence, Macías is defining a metapolicy for U.S. language planning in which Spanish resides in a hypercentral position, ranked above other non-English languages and reaching toward institutional incorporation within the U.S. polity as complementary, in a slightly subsidiary way, to English. This ordering of English, Spanish, and other languages appears to constitute what Aronin and Singleton (2012) call the Dominant Language Constellation: the spatial distribution of communication forms that organizes other languages in relation to itself because it prevails politico-communicatively.

In effect, this establishes for the United States what European sociolinguistics are coming to define as the distinction between polyglottism at the societal level and multilingualism at the level of individuals. In this way of understanding the sociolinguistics of the distribution of language capabilities, we see permanent and diffuse presence of multiple languages within territorially bounded states that were originally conceived as having single preeminent languages. Linguistic pluralism of this kind is today becoming the reality for ever-greater numbers of countries and practically all people on earth.

Macías's contribution expands the scope of consideration of the *RRE* volume to include, though still only suggestively, a politico-narrative and specifically a story, replete with facts and claims, of how Americans might come to talk of their home as a bilingual one. The deep cultural challenge this represents is well understood by the author, since no national narrative emerges without struggle and over long duration. America is readily recognized and its national formative story acknowledges itself as an *immigrant nation*, but a dominant element of that narrative is the sacrifice of difference entailed in becoming American. Is it imaginable, and will "facts" or "evidence" suffice in fostering moves toward an enriched narrative, in some foreseeable time, where polyglottism, or more specifically Spanish, will be admitted into the national register and achieve iconic presence within the American self-understanding? Macías opens a line of imagination that a hierarchical diglossia in which most Americans will have knowledge of, encounters with, and a normalized experience of Spanish will be naturalized as a cultural characteristic. The paradox of majority and minority languages and their relations and cultural/economic/education and political functions are all deeply affected by what future history makes of the cultural information assembled by Macías.

In the chapter by Ofelia García, attention is directed toward the presence of Spanish within U.S. education and its local and global intersections. She argues, essentially, that Spanish language education policies in the United States have failed to educate Latinos and non-Latinos alike due to three interlinked reasons: (a) English is characterized by educational authorities as the unique and powerful lingua franca, (b) Spanish is defined by the language authorities in Spain and Latin America as a global language of influence, and (c) the language is lived and practiced by bilingual Latino speakers.

In her historical account of the linguistic formation of Spanish, García isolates and discusses enduring ideological content within Spanish that can be traced to its teaching in the United States with the policies of language and culture agencies controlled by Spain. This consideration is a premise for the claim that a fluid bilingual practice, "translanguaging," understood as distinct from code-switching and also distinct from both "academic Spanish" and "academic English," is critical for future successful Spanish teaching in the United States.

The inevitable and permanent bilingualism that surrounds Spanish use in the United States is clear from the fact that Latinos represent 16% of the entire U.S. population, the world's greatest promoter of global English, making the country the fourth-largest Spanish-speaking country. U.S. Spanish is characterized by its proximity to English, both geographically and within homes and family conversations. García points out that 89% of U.S. Spanish speakers are completely bilingual and that only 11% do not speak English. Within the conversations that constitute regular language use, these demographic realities stand in stark contrast to the bounded language formulations inherited by institutions, discourses, and official agencies of government, both in Spain and in Latin America. Spanish and English reside close to each other, and the reach therefore of Spanish must be considerably greater within U.S. economic, public, and cultural life than it would be elsewhere—so proximity to American English acts as a kind of multiplier for the projection of Spanish worldwide or at least outside of Spanish-speaking countries.

García points out that U.S. Latino consumer purchase, the traction that Spanish speakers have, is significantly greater than the rest of the Spanish-speaking world, regardless of the relative economic position of Latinos within the United States, so the volume of Spanish-associated cultural output is greater than that of other Spanish-speaking nations.

In light of all this, it appears both ironical and counterproductive that U.S. language education policy should be restrictive in its orientation, as if fearing the consequences of the deep changes underway rather than imagining their future-enriching prospects and their importance in supporting improved educational outcomes and occupational futures for young Americans. In her research, the author finds that teachers themselves choose a flexible bilingual pedagogical approach to engage and challenge their bilingual Latino students, and therefore they enact translanguaging as pedagogy.

It is important, within the framing of the volume, to recognize and account for the ways in which teachers have language-planning agency (Lo Bianco, 2010) and are able to sustain or subvert regimes of language policy that are decided beyond the classroom and the school. García provides evidence of this. The prospects for realization of her call that Spanish must be taught as *U.S. Spanish*, as the language of Latinos rather than as a hegemonic global language, will be enhanced by an appreciation by teachers and researchers that they are indeed language-planning agents, capable of relatively autonomous action, rather than dependent practitioners of top-down language orders. If teachers and researchers already enact translanguaging pedagogies, as pragmatic response to the lived bilingual life of Latinos in the everyday bilingual reality of cities and schools, they have made themselves agents of direct-action language planning.

Jeanne M. Powers's chapter is a valuable introduction to and concise overview of critically important recent legal cases, the *Flores* cases, and their most recent findings, from March 2013, pertinent to the prospects of supporting long-term educational access, equity, and achievement and the volume theme of native-language literacy as an educational right.

Powers addresses the legal context for language rights in the United States, from "segregation to school finance." This contribution stands alone in the volume, dealing with the enabling/permitting domain of the law in relation to language rights in U.S. public schools, rather than educational, linguistic, or sociolinguistic matters. The author reviews the history of policy priorities and opinions from court cases focused on increasing access and equity for minority students through desegregation and school finance. Her analysis is structured by Ruiz's (1984) model for analyzing "orientations" in language policy. Ruiz defined three such orientations: language-as-problem, language-as-right, and language-as-resource. In his original formulation, Ruiz had argued that underlying public policies to minority languages was one or other of these orientations, structuring the choices made by the policy and the reasoning it adopts. Powers proposes a fourth orientation derived from court opinions and policy documents: *language-as-barrier*. She locates this orientation between language-as-resource and language-as-problem as an intermediate category to capture a shift in value in the aftermath of the Civil Rights Act and the significance of the 1974 *Lau v. Nichols* case, which partially addressed language from a resource orientation.

Powers organizes her legal review according to a matrix positioning these four "orientations" along the continua of (a) the goals of the language policy and (b) the use of the home language in instruction. The study is important in clarifying assumptions about language responsible for legal and policy arguments about how well English Language Learners should learn and be taught and the involvement of their "home languages." Powers has chosen the legal focus because legal decisions play an important cultural role in legitimizing and institutionalizing racial inequality and the legal framework for communication rights in the United States was an extension of Civil Rights era polices. To provide full historical grounding for her analysis, she discusses policies and legal cases dating back to the 1930s.

U.S. courts have been reluctant to engage language rights for English Language Learners attending public schools to any substantive degree, preferring to leave this to policymakers, while some rulings, specifically *Horne v. Flores* (2009) and *Flores v. Arizona* (2013), are regressive to policies and practices that predated the *Lau v. Nichols* (1974) case. Powers highlights the pervasive presence of the language-as-barrier orientation in these cases, a tendency that compounds a general societal-cultural reluctance to sustain multiple languages.

Judicial decision making related to language post–Civil Rights era is interpreted as providing limited and limiting comprehension of the notion of language rights, which the *Flores* decisions threaten to damage and weaken further. The language-as-resource orientation has struggled to be accommodated within appellate courts and in federal policies alike, and reversal of the small gains made is rendered more likely by the widespread belief that minority languages represent a barrier to civic participation and economic progress. Hence language is conceived as a barrier to equal participation in society and access to education.

In a 2010 publication, Richard Ruiz returned to the "orientations" theme after criticism of its adoption in some policy statements. Critics had alleged that advocating for minority languages as a resource for learning, culture, and public participation was all too easily diverted by policymakers into narrow economistic thinking. Critics alleged that in this process minority languages tended to be devalued, coming to be regarded as unimportant and subject to denigration, simply useful to an end, rather than important within the life and culture of a community. Finally, critics alleged that the language-as-resource orientation to multilingualism tended to diminish rather than enhance the recognition of language rights of minority populations.

These criticisms arose in response to how the language-as-resource orientation had been appropriated by policymakers seeking to involve minority language communities to service agendas antithetical to language rights. Much of this occurred after 9/11 and the newfound need of the United States for language skills in a large number of small-speaker languages, to support the national security agenda. In his 2010 reconsideration of the "orientations," Ruiz includes the international approach, similar to his own, of analyzing policy according to its underlying orientations, and this important paper should be read in conjunction with Powers's addition of a fourth policy orientation. Ruiz traces a different origin for the notion of language-as-resource from his 1984 use and underscores from international literature that the effective responses to the criticisms can be identified in the expanded notions of "language-as-resource," seeing multiple languages as sustaining diverse intellectual, social, citizenship, economic, and other purposes. This is helpful in advancing language rights in public policy and provides support to the case made by Powers that new ways to dislodge the domination of *language-as-barrier* thinking are needed.

Teresa McCarty and Sheilah Nicholas turn attention to the challenge and prospects of reclaiming indigenous languages in the U.S. context and specifically toward a reconsideration of schools, their roles, and their responsibilities. Reviewing international literature, U.S. Census data, and historical policy developments, and adding original qualitative research, the writers, McCarty, an anthropologist, and Nicholas, Hopi "educator and scholar," produce a nuanced collaborative reflection on the distinctive role of schools and schooling on language reclamation efforts.

This chapter is focused on indigenous language regeneration efforts in the United States and Canada and specifically how schools function as sites for language reclamation. Valuable effort is expended in a close and helpful definition of terms, concepts, and historical policy context setting followed by close examination of four case studies: Mohawk in Canada and in the United States, Hawaiian in the Pacific, and Hopi and Navajo in the U.S. Southwest. Each case study informs the key question on the role and responsibilities of schools in language reclamation and revitalization processes, including maintenance of cultural heritage and developing autonomy.

Indigenous languages are part of distinct knowledge and education systems, and as a result reclamation of education control is coterminous with reclamation of language. The revitalization of Hawaiian is widely recognized as one of the most effective indigenous-language reclamation movements in the world. The Hawaiian case shows the importance of sustained indigenous-language schooling that incorporates cultural values and knowledge of the course of children's preK–12 education. The Hopi example speaks to the importance of professional development opportunities within the language reclamation process for local educators. Scholarly literature is unanimous that "strong" language revitalization programs produce students with high levels of indigenous-language proficiency and "academic and majority language outcomes equal to or surpassing those of peers in non-immersion programs." School-based programs also often operate in hostile policy environments, and such programs have the potential to transform hegemonic expectations about indigenous languages and cultures from loss and extinction to recovery and regeneration. These themes and conclusions enlighten a long-standing discussion about schools and schooling, and their contribution to revitalization of language, one clearly shaped by what precisely is done within the school and its actors and the specifics of the policy environment within which they operate. Schools can be equally agents and institutions and forces for language rights, opportunity, and justice, but there is no guarantee other than the actions of the key actors and their purposes and effectiveness that these aims will be achieved or even attempted. McCarty and Nicholas show concretely how the responsibility that rests with schools derives precisely from the fact that they can be very effective in language reclamation and revitalization processes.

Lee and Wright direct our attention to the vast number and extraordinary diversity of languages that constitute the world of heritage and community language (HL/CL) education in the United States, which they title a "rediscovery." The essential reason for this characterization is that Lee and Wright are proposing a radical reconceptualization of the place and standing of HL/CL as an alternative but legitimate educational space. Through policy analysis and qualitative original research with schools delivering HL/CL education, the authors wish to reconstitute the spoken languages of Americans as distinct from the official language programs in schools.

In formal school education, English prevails, if not always overtly then at least in the overall trajectory and destination of the educational endeavor. This is invariably aimed at acquisition of literate standard educated English. In contrast, there is a tangential but immense network of autonomously functioning schools of language and culture, reliant on the effort, resources, energy, and institutional organization at the community level, whose trajectory and intended destination are intergenerational retention and use of an HL/CL. The world of HL/CL, represented by institutions and the diverse experiences they supply to learners, resides independently beside and in addition to official public day schools. Of course, the same learners experience both, since the HL/CL schools are mostly part-time, after-hours, and supplemental sites where learners encounter radically different language socialization.

The overriding aim of the HL/CL is not just language maintenance but also transmitting culturally authentic experiences of identity, belonging, and attachment, all contextualized and modified by their physical and temporal presence within American life. Lee and Wright offer a refreshing analysis of the HL/CL domain from a historical perspective with a view to the influence of policy and politics on HL/CL teaching models and outcomes. The challenges that HL/CL programs face are many and serious, and the authors describe how small communities, Korean American and Cambodian (Khmer) American in particular, respond to and reconcile the demands on them from learners, from the official sector of schooling, and from the wider society's expectations.

It is useful to keep in mind that the 2001 No Child Left Behind Act practically obliterated references to bilingualism from the legislative framework governing U.S. school education, leaving the development of bilingualism among young Americans increasingly within the efforts of the HL/CL school. If U.S. policymakers were to reimagine the gift, the private donation, represented by the HL/CL system and were sufficiently wise to foster its success without intruding on its autonomous operations of community ownership and management, they would stimulate a wider stream of effective, mass language-learning and language maintenance efforts than the public system could ever arrange within its own operational mode.

In Australia, we have grappled with precisely this same challenge for 40 years, with some successes and some disappointments, but what are increasingly called "complementary providers" regularly feature within public policy as allies in the effort to encourage multiple-language learning, in multiple modalities, using complementary but diverse approaches. The independent operational context of the HL/CL schools is a counter to the dominant focus on audit and accountability in high-stakes testing that is likely to be detrimental to public school foreign-language education.

It is of course ironical, an irony that researchers, teachers, and community organizations are enjoined to continually remind politicians about, that K–12 education policy tends to operate out of kilter with higher education, economic policy, and national security, where federal government calls for the need to raise American language capabilities are continually reiterated. Policies to include HL/CL programs within integrated national language education plans must tread a delicate path. Although many improvements are needed in HL/CL programs, such as upgrading curriculum design, instructional quality, materials, and teacher skill and supporting richer and more effective student engagement, such goals must be pursued without intruding excessively into the control and management of the schools by communities. The latter is what makes the sector both unique and possible.

HL/CL schools operate in a context radically different, for the most part, from that described by Macías and García for Spanish, where the future projection for Spanish use in the United States is of long-term viability and expansion. Most HL/CL communities face serious pressure of language attrition and loss, and many programs rely too much on a model of language maintenance that underplays the importance of sociological patterning so that the minority language can find unique domains for its use, and so learners can be encouraged to develop desire to acquire, use, and identify with the language of their parents but not their society. Instead, most HL/CL schools simply teach, they engage in "capacity building" to the relative neglect of fostering opportunity and desire (see Lo Bianco & Peyton, in press), and this model of intergenerational language maintenance may not be sufficient for minority language intergenerational vitality.

Jeff Bale's chapter discusses the role of heritage language education in the context of the "national interest." He focuses on U.S. domestic policy and the promotion of heritage language education for purposes of national geopolitical and economic security.

Bale reviews 60 years of empirical research, policy analysis, and other forms of scholarly commentary to argue that the regular conflation of heritage language learning with U.S. economic and security priorities is questionable and ineffective. The argument is structured in three parts: first, a historical review of language education policy in U.S. geopolitical and economic security (starting with the "Americanization" movement/era and mentioning Title VI of the National Defense Education Act of 1958).

Second, he identifies and synthesizes three analytical stances within scholarship about this connection between language education policy and the "national interest" (technocratic, pragmatic, and critical approaches). His conclusion notes gaps in the literature on the interplay between language learning and national security. Key evidence in Bale's analysis is 60 years of historical policy review, discussion of cases including *Brown v. Board of Education* (1954), consideration of informal policies, and first- and second-generation formal policies, that is, the National Security Education Act of 1991 and STARTALK, and their privileging focus on "critical languages."

Bale makes the important point that tying language policy directly to the national interest exposes policy, which for maximum effectiveness needs to be stable and well planned, to regular adjustment, chopping and changing, and rising and falling tendencies and priorities, in response to geopolitical crises. Compounding this problem of continual shifting and changing of policy settings that need to be stable and sustained to achieve their goals, since language learning is cumulative and time demanding, is the risk of erosion of identification of languages, specifically HL/CL with their communities, some of which are unwilling to be drawn into national planning processes for purposes they might not share or might even fear.

Bale also references Ruiz as a key example of "pragmatic approaches to reviews of language policy," in the context of his own three-part schema of *technocratic, pragmatic,* and *critical,* representing the lenses through which policies can be analyzed and interpreted. Although not linked to the four volume-overview sections directly, the chapter demonstrates how conflation of heritage language education with geopolitical, "national" interest detracts from language rights and educational access, equity, and achievement. It serves to show how emerging global demographic shifts tend to unconstructively drive language education policy, all essential points of reflection and lines of questioning for the theme of the volume.

Tollefson and Tsui bring international case studies and international research to the discussion, specifically addressing the appropriate medium of instruction. Their consideration of this question is focused on the effects that medium of instruction choices can have in relation to access to curriculum content, the skills it imparts, and principally and most important, literate capability and the consequent effects of particular choices on decreasing palpable and very large inequities in educational attainment.

The authors address the question of international instruments, and specifically what in international education circles is known as the EFA principle, "Education for All." This principle is espoused in UNESCO's *World Declaration on Education for All and Framework for Action to Meet Basic Learning Needs* (1990) and operates as a kind of shorthand in international development education, EFA signifying an overarching aim of many small initiatives and large government programs alike.

In my own work for UNESCO, and now for UNICEF, I appreciate the attention that Tollefson and Tsui dedicate to this critical question, which underscores an issue not particularly discussed in their piece but very important nonetheless, which is to do with how social context deeply influences efficacy of language choices.

Elites and mainstream children in the United States, Canada, Europe, and Singapore, as well as in other parts of the world, are immersed in second-language programs by choice and not because of constraint or absence of alternatives. The aim of immersion education is to gain publicly admired and affirmed language skills, and it is well known that such children are able to profit from having a language other than the mother tongue as a medium of instruction. However, for minoritized populations within the United States, immigrant and indigenous alike, as elsewhere, first-language initial literacy at least, and preferably an extended opportunity to develop intellectualized conceptual range in the mother tongue, is an essential premise for successful participation in education. The apparent contradiction between these two exists only if we see what happens in instruction as separate from the world of communication, economy, social relations, politics, and inequality that surrounds and conditions the micro world of the classroom.

Tollefson and Tsui remind us that across the world large numbers of children experience, many "endure," schooling with no prospect of developing educated standard knowledge of their mother tongue, and are subjected to subtractive bilingualism that restricts their first language of learning to ever narrower domains of meaning and potential in their lives. EFA is hampered by this, with deep and serious economic, health, and social effects.

The authors then identify three specific processes of globalization that affect language education: migration, urbanization, and changes in the nature of work. The pervasive effects of these metaprocesses that occur transnationally and intranationally destabilize a large number of the assumptions on which curriculum has been constructed and scramble the *one language–one nation* homogenizing assumptions on which so much of the division of the world proceeds. Tollefson and Tsui proceed to discuss a range of African, Asian, and European case studies, in both school settings and "transnational" university campuses, where language polices affect access to education and equity, before providing suggestions for how policies can be used effectively. They go on to discuss the implications of the rise of China and the new-found prominence of Chinese.

These premises lead the authors to claim that promotion and use of English, intimately associated with globalization, advantage only small and strategically located groups, usually elite urban students whose home cultural capital predisposes them to acquire prestige English and renders them able to access high-quality education and capitalize on out-of-school opportunities. They conclude that educational inequity is often associated with policies of medium of instruction, particularly when these favor use of English as the medium over local, and sometimes over national, languages and cite examples from New Zealand, Solomon Islands, and Native America from which they claim these disadvantages are mitigated.

Stephen May's chapter turns to the question of how educational language rights are actually or can potentially be justified, specifically in the context of language minority rights in modern liberal democracies. He reviews developments in international law in various national contexts (including the United States, South Africa, India, Spain, and Europe) to define how language rights in education are established and maintained and how the process of establishing rights affects provision of language education.

In this process, May discusses what he terms *ongoing skepticism* toward language rights in the context of seeing communication or language rights as "collective rights" that can be seen as inimical to the principles of individual human rights that are foundational in the legal systems of common law–influenced countries. Two key challenges and obstacles facing the case for minority language rights are "civism" and global English. A tendency toward "civism" at the level of the nation-state can be difficult for multiple-language advocacy because multilingualism is often seen to make participatory citizenship, the incorporation of all citizens in civic life, unfeasible or at least practically difficult. English as the language of globalization and its related attribution as essential to social mobility also represent a brake on language education rights.

May provides an extensive literature and policy review, including key historical declarations in international law over the past 60 years. He quotes campaign discourse against bilingual education in the United States, balanced against an analysis of results from two key U.S. research projects proving the efficacy of bilingual education (Ramírez, Yuen, & Ramey, 1991; Thomas & Collier, 2002).

In posing the argument for language rights, May asks how to respond effectively to the confluence of opinion and associated ideological and structural imperatives, arraigned against language education provision for linguistic-minority students. He responds by offering two ways to proceed: via the promotion of language rights in relation to both national and international law and by an associated exposition and defense of the efficacy of minority language educational approaches for linguistic-minority students. Specifically, May discusses the concepts of tolerance-oriented rights and promotion-oriented rights as proposed by Heinz Kloss (1971, 1977), favoring promotion-oriented rights, and provides a detailed related study of the case of Catalan in Spain (specifically in relation to territorial language rights) and the English-only movement in the United States.

Of special importance is the reference to the protection of English by the elite as part of the protection of their own interests, and as an instrument to marginalize the majority of the population, which complements the arguments made in Bale's chapter. May provides a broad overview of the possible normative and empirical arguments that might support educational language rights in arguments attached to the native-language literacy as an educational right and the paradox of majority and minority languages components of the *RRE*.

Colin Williams turns the focus of discussion toward Wales and its long-standing language revitalization efforts. Offering a largely historical review, the author uses census data and discusses legislation and policy documents such as the Welsh Language Act of 1993.

The Welsh case is important and useful because the focus is a single uncontested language within a single relatively benign polity over a long period of sustained effort. The Welsh language revitalization movement has developed through three identifiable phases. From 1912 to 1962, the focus was on gaining public recognition for the language and establishing a designated Welsh language education system. The second stage (1962–1980s) saw the growth of Welsh-medium education, the ensuring of bilingual public services, and the establishment of a television channel, S4C, also in Welsh medium. Two different sets of challenges mark the third and current phase, which are the influence of migration on communities that are primarily Welsh speaking and the attempts to "normalize" Welsh through expansion of the student base attending Welsh-medium schools (through to higher education).

Williams also notes the importance of building a national infrastructure in which to develop the use of Welsh in society more broadly. Each of these challenges is discussed in detail, leading the author to make the point that highly committed individuals are the reason Welsh language revitalization has continued to burgeon and that this community drive has been essential to prompt strategic language policy from government. This crucial observation underscores arguments elsewhere about the agentive possibilities available to language activists, since language is not the exclusive or private possession of particular institutions, bodies, disciplines, or other interests. The capability for individual-driven or -influenced change and betterment in language conditions, however, creates the ultimate challenge of long-term sustainability and maintenance of community engagement and the need for institution creation.

Wales is unique in U.K. public policy in that the central government has been involved in supporting Welsh-language initiatives since the early 1960s and establishing a language regime, including the *Mentrau Iaith*—multifaceted community-based organizations (including in Patagonia, Argentina), which were established first in 1991 for the growth and maintenance of Welsh in community life. The Welsh experience and its achievements as much as its current and future challenges suggest that educational access, equity, and achievement; native-language literacy as an educational right; and the paradox of majority and minority languages are all domains of interest enriched by comparative international evidence, even when the contextual differences are significant.

Elana Shohamy addresses the question of English and of its "weight" in global perspective, and specifically within Israel. The chapter examines multilingualism in Israel, including what the author describes as the Government's nationalistic preference for Hebrew over English and Arabic in schools, universities, and public life. Shohamy examines the history of Jewish nationalism and the related fear-driven preference for Hebrew and what she describes as official historical distaste for English. The multiplicity of multilingual communication domains in Israeli society make it possible to have such differing realities, separate from the evident utility and utilitarian usage of English within national official life, and with its presence in the daily life of most young Jewish Israelis and the country's numerous English-speaking immigrants. From premises laid down in this contrast, the argument goes on to examine the standing and place of Arabic, mother tongue Arabic, designated as one of Israel's official languages. Looking at this question against what she calls the discriminatory nature of Israeli education for mother tongue Arabic, Shohamy argues that the value of multilingualism in Israel needs urgent reassessment to disassemble the power- and status-driven question of "multilingual in what languages?" and enable equitable social access for all. These challenging proposals and this interesting critique are buttressed by sourcing primary documents in newspaper articles, what might be called the agitational space of language policy, where debate, arguments, and contestation about the purposes and nature of language education alternatives are highlighted as are policy laws and reports. Shohamy also cites her own research conducted both recently and over many years of sustained thinking about Israel's education futures and its linguistic configuration.

English is a powerful nonofficial language in Israel and plays an important role, mostly in Jewish areas. In Arab communities, which make up 20% of the Israeli population, Hebrew plays the role of the dominant "global" language, after Arabic, whereas English, which all Arab students are required to study from their earliest years of schooling, is only minimally represented in public spaces and the level reached by Arab students is substantially lower than that of Jewish counterparts.

Multilingualism in itself is not necessarily an asset or ticket to social mobility in Israel—the searing question is "multilingual in what languages?" For most Jewish Israelis, English is a (an unofficial) second language, whereas for Arabs, it is likely to be a fourth language. In a fascinating demonstration of the scrambling of domains, immigrants from English-speaking countries, in opposition to immigrants from non–English speaking countries, are discriminated against in terms of public services, such as health and transportation, essentially because English, despite its prominence, is seen as a threat to the Hebrew revival achievement. Shohamy shows how Israeli Jews view English as a desirable language linked to the United States and as a symbol of progress, advancement, globalization, and the "West," whereas Arabs tend to view it as a "Jewish" lingua franca.

This chapter offers an interesting international perspective highlighting how language policies and attitudes are complexly related, coexisting at times even when their tendencies are contradictory, and underscoring that language questions are highly situated and historically forged. What is possible in one setting might be scarcely portable to an ostensibly similar setting. Shohamy's chapter speaks to the aims of "educational access, equity, and achievement," particularly in relation to Arab students at university, and "native-language literacy as an educational right," in relation to immigrants to Israel and Hebrew ideological dominance. It also addresses "the paradox of majority and minority languages" in relation to Israel's especially complex and (recent) historical composition.

The article by Ramanathan is an excellent accompaniment to Tollefson and Tsui, departing from the analysis of their wide policy context and delving deeply into practices and processes within schools to expose the subtle workings of language dynamics within the uneven power dynamics of meaning potential. Tollefson and Tsui limit their analysis to the broad sweep of public policy and dominant practice in international comparative mode, rather than the detail of how access and equity are manifested in achievement/results for cohorts, populations, or individual students. They show, however, that public policy is a deeply conditioning reality, that there are inseparable connections between them, and that the conditions of what is possible in schools, but also, and more subtly, the understandings and ideologies with which teachers and school administrators operate, are drawn from what policy makes available. The domain of language planning and policymaking is therefore crucial for language educators concerned with exposing inequity in education, but the practices of the past few decades in which language-planning theory has been in thrall to the critical show that critique is insufficient. To foster and make possible productive change, new modes of thinking about language planning, which see teachers and communities as active protagonists capable of affecting the institutions and practices of education, are urgently needed.

The bottom-up processes of language policy change identified by Tollefson and Tsui point us to this more productive, active, agentive dimension. With the compelling indications and powerful orientation offered by the authors, the capacity for undertaking a critical language-planning analysis in international perspective is enhanced, and in doing this we should also reflect on the relative imbalance in the critical academic language-planning literature on "languages," that is, codes of communities, rather than individual learners and cohorts of students. The collective decisions and behaviors of the latter, communicatively speaking, shape and determine the fate of the former, a risk and occasionally a serious omission in macro language-centered analysis. Also important is for critical language-planning studies to address situations where the power language is not English but other national languages that have primacy over local indigenous/immigrant minority populations and their distinctive communication forms, and indeed intralanguage dialect repertoires where standard or prestige/power forms of a language prevail over spoken stigmatized dialects and varieties. These would serve to show whether and how inherited and nation-specific language ideologies predispose to different solutions to the mother tongue + national language + English formula that appears to be evolving in some parts of the world in an effort to reconcile the needs of subnational populations, national interests, and international communication.

In this light and with these considerations, the chapter by Vaidehi Ramanathan provides a nuanced micro and learning-centered account of colonial policies of Divide and Rule and the array of strategies they deploy. In her discussion of how postcolonialism in the site of her analysis has harnessed the vernaculars, with what purposes and which methods, a mix of original research data, contemporary teaching materials, and historical documents are scrutinized to provide a really interesting bottom-up analysis of vernacular and English mediums of instruction in various local contexts in Ahmedabad, Gujarat, India. In the educational sites analyzed, sites known intimately to her as student as well as researcher, policy-related inequities endure and are recycled continually, often in new guise and representation, in firsthand accounts of ways in which various individual teachers and institutions are taking initiatives to empower students and restore equity in line with the principles associated with India's great liberation figure, Mahatma Gandhi.

The author begins by discussing the colonial legacy of "divide and rule" through language education in India and its current neocolonial manifestations in Indian schooling. She then provides an analysis of data consisting of a range of interviews with key people running civic projects in Guajarat, field notes on workshops, a review of pedagogic materials used at the K–12 level, policy documents, and various historical materials written by and to Gandhi. The collective effect and force of the multiple sources of reinforcing reasoning show a kind of language policy diffused across actors, sites, and events. Ramanathan's chapter speaks powerfully to the question posed by *RRE* related to educational access, equity, and achievement and native-language literacy as an educational right. That it is an Indian/international and postcolonial setting rather than in the United States enhances its force since the processes of schooling, teaching, and planning are identifiably common to education practice and the various actors involved in it. In comparing the expected and produced minimal levels of learning for students engaged in vernacular medium contrasted to English medium, the shaped inequity is illustrated. Her analysis demonstrates how English language education becomes remedial in the vernacular institutions, whereas it assumes an "enrichment" approach in English institutions. All these categories of schooling are vestiges of colonial practice, but their recycled and reconstituted presence today indicates the capillary procedural manner in which old and large ideas persist.

The broader implications for language education policy reside in the critical need to fuse action for linguistic and expressive rights at all levels simultaneously; the autonomous operation of school choices can subvert progressive policies from outside or entrench and reinforce them. The chapter does not reference wider political debates about "linguistic imperialism" in which the dominance of English is maintained by structural and cultural inequalities between English and vernaculars; instead it opens up space for postcolonial perspectives in institutional life that can help us think about language diversity in situ.

In conclusion, despite multilingualism being well established as the predictable condition of all human society, historically nation-states have absorbed and legitimized discourses and self-understanding as homogenous and unilingual states. The discrepancy between the historical condition and its contemporary ideological representation gives rise to politics of language and policies in and for language education. The four theme points of *access, equity, and achievement in education; native languages and literacy as right; paradoxical relations between minority and majority languages;* and *emerging patterns and shifts of the global age* establish an enduring remit for consideration of language policy from multiple perspectives. Productive conversations across all these perspectives are likely from the arguments and data in the current volume. These should gravitate to how to reconcile the facts of multilingualism with official preferences for monolingualism. Demographically we see everywhere on-the-ground linguistic pluralism in all our societies. This is a pluralism in which languages, dialects, and genres of expression are not bounded and compartmentalized but fused and combined. Yet this daily and ubiquitous linguistic pluralism clashes with the official declarations and preferences for monolingualism, a monolingualism that privileges dominant languages and pushes education systems to promote secure, bounded, hierarchically ranked languages with uncontested literary canons. These are immense challenges whose depth and importance will be with us for decades into the future even as they are transformed further by migration, technology, and new understandings of communication. We need a new optimism that education language planning can be put to the service of multiliterate, multicultural, and multilingual future global citizens. If there is to be a new culture war, it should be one in which pluralism is granted central consideration as an overarching human right for justice and productivity, a true cause of cerebration.

REFERENCES

Aronin, L., & Singleton, D. (2012). *Multilingualism.* Amsterdam, Netherlands: John Benjamins.

Baker, A. (2013, September 27). Culture warrior, gaining ground. E. D. Hirsch sees his education theories taking hold. *New York Times.* Retrieved from http://www.nytimes.com/2013/09/28/books/e-d-hirsch-sees-his-education-theories-taking-hold.html?pagewanted=2&_r=0&smid=tw-share

Bernstein, R. (1994). *Dictatorship of virtue: Multiculturalism and the battle for America's future.* New York, NY: Knopf.

Collins, J. (1999). The ebonics controversy in context: Literacies, subjectivities, and language ideologies in the United States. In J. Blommaert (Ed.), *Language ideological debates* (pp. 201–235). The Hague, Netherlands: Mouton de Gruyter.

Hirsch, E. D. (1988). *Cultural literacy: What every American needs to know.* New York, NY: Vintage.

Kloss, H. (1971). Language rights of immigrant groups. *International Migration Review, 5,* 250–268.

Kloss, H. (1977). *The American bilingual tradition.* Rowley, MA: Newbury House.

Lo Bianco, J. (2009). CDA and LPP: Constraints and applications of the critical in language planning. In T. Le, Q. Le, & M. Short (Eds.), *Critical discourse analysis: An interdisciplinary perspective* (pp. 101–119). New York, NY: Nova Science.

Lo Bianco, J. (2010). Language policy and planning. In N. H. Hornberger & S. L. McKay (Eds.), *Sociolinguistics and language education* (pp. 143–176). Bristol, England: Multilingual Matters.

Lo Bianco, J. (in press). Domesticating the foreign: Globalization's effects on the place/s of languages. *Modern Language Journal,* 98(Suppl.).

Lo Bianco, J., & Peyton, J. K. (Eds.). (in press). Language vitality in the United States [Special issue]. *Heritage Language Journal.*

Ramírez, J., Yuen, S., & Ramey, D. (1991). *Final report: Longitudinal study of structured English immersion strategy, early-exit and late-exit transitional bilingual education programs for language-minority children.* San Mateo, CA: Aguirre International.

Ruiz, R. (1984). Orientations in language planning. *Journal for the National Association for Bilingual Education,* 8(2), 15–34.

Ruiz, R. (2010). Reorienting language-as-resource. In J. Petrovic (Ed.), *International perspectives on bilingual education: Policy, practice, and controversy* (pp. 155–172). Charlotte, NC: Information Age.

Thomas, W., & Collier, V. (2002). *A national study of school effectiveness for language minority students' long-term academic achievement.* Santa Cruz, CA: Center for Research on Education, Diversity and Excellence. Retrieved from http://crede.berkeley.edu/research/llaa/1.1_final.html

About the Editors

Kathryn M. Borman is professor emerita in the Department of Anthropology, University of South Florida. She received her doctorate in sociology of education from the University of Minnesota in 1976. She has extensive experience in educational reform and policy as well as evaluation studies. Recently, she worked as a consultant to the U.S. Department of Education and National School to Work Office for the project "Preparing Teachers to Use Contextual Teaching and Learning Strategies to Enhance Student Success in and Beyond School." Currently, she directs a $1.2 million evaluation study for the National Science Foundation titled "Assessing the Impact of the NSF's Urban Systemic Initiative." As co-principal Investigator of the NSF project, "Addressing National Addressing National Needs for Skilled Technical Graduates," she investigated policy issues related to national standards and the training of skilled technical workers. In 1992-1993, she worked on the Evaluation Projects for Cincinnati Public Schools using funds from the Cincinnati Public Schools to carry out eight projects with College of Education faculty. She also participated in the Evaluation of Cincinnati Youth Collaborative (1992), assessing ongoing school-based support activities for youth. Additionally, she has been involved in training graduate students for research and teaches a variety of courses, including anthropology, education, and methods in qualitative analysis.

Arnold B. Danzig is professor of educational leadership and policy studies and founding director of the educational leadership doctoral program at San José State University. He is professor emeritus at Arizona State University and prior to coming to SJSU served as professor and associate director of the School of Public Affairs at Arizona State University. He previously served as associate dean and director of the Division of Policy, Leadership, and Curriculum in the Mary Lou Fulton Institute and Graduate School of Education at Arizona State University. He is author and editor of books, chapters, and articles on school leadership and education policy including *Research on Learning and Teaching in Educational Leadership* (2014); *Review of Research in Education*, "Education, Democracy, and the Public Good" (Volume 36, 2012); *Learner-Centered Leadership: Research, Policy, and Practice* (2007) and his research appears in multiple journals including *International Studies in Educational Administration, Education Policy, Journal of Educational Administration, Educational Leadership and Administration*, and the *Journal of Educational and Psychological Consultation*. His research offers a humanistic vision of democratic leadership for schools with deep and practical commitments to individual and community betterment.

Review of Research in Education
March 2014, Vol. 38, pp. 332-333
DOI: 10.3102/0091732X14523729
© 2014 AERA. http://rre.aera.net

David R. Garcia is an associate professor in the Mary Lou Fulton Teachers College at Arizona State University. His professional experience includes extensive work in state and national education policy development and implementation. His research interests include school choice, accountability, and the study of factors that facilitate or distort policy implementation in public education. His research has appeared in numerous journals, including *Teachers College Record, Educational Policy*, and the *Journal of School Choice*. He received his doctorate from the University of Chicago in Education Policy, Research, and Institutional Studies.

Terrence G. Wiley is president of the Center for Applied Linguistics (CAL) and professor emeritus at Arizona State University, where he served as executive dean of the former Mary Lou Fulton Institute and Graduate School of Education and Director of the Division of Educational Leadership and Policy Studies. Among his numerous publications are *The Handbook of Heritage, Community, and Native American Languages Research, Policy, and Practice* (coeditor, CAL-Routledge, 2014), *The Education of Language Minority Immigrants in the United States* (coeditor, Multilingual Matters, 2009), and *Literacy and Language Diversity in the United States* (CAL, 2005). He has cofounded two international journals, the *Journal of Language Identity and Education* (currently coeditor, Routledge) and the *International Multilingual Research Journal* (Routledge), and he has served on numerous editorial boards. He has lectured and served as a visiting professor at a number of international universities, most recently at Renmin (People's) University of China.

About the Contributors

Jeff Bale is an assistant professor in the Department of Teacher Education at Michigan State University. His research focuses on three broad areas: sociohistorical analysis of language education policies in the United States; comparative study of neoliberalism and education policy in Germany, with a particular focus on the impact of such policy on students with a migration background; and second language teacher education. He taught English as a Second Language to newcomer immigrants and German for about 10 years in Washington, D.C.; Chicago, Illinois; and Tempe, Arizona, public secondary schools. His work has appeared in *Teachers College Record, Annual Review of Applied Linguistics*, and *Language Policy*, and he is coeditor of the book *Education and Capitalism: Struggles for Learning and Liberation* (Haymarket Books, 2012).

Ofelia García is a professor in the PhD programs of Urban Education and of Hispanic and Luso-Brazilian Literatures and Languages at The Graduate Center, City University of New York. She has been Professor of Bilingual Education at Columbia University's Teachers College, Dean of the School of Education at the Brooklyn Campus of Long Island University, and Professor of Education at The City College of New York. Among her recent books are *Bilingual Education in the 21st Century: A Global Perspective; Bilingual Community Education and Multilingualism* (with Z. Zakharia and B. Otcu); *Handbook of Language and Ethnic Identity, Vols. 1 and 2* (with J. A. Fishman); *Educating Emergent Bilinguals* (with J. Kleifgen); *Additive Schooling in Subtractive Times* (with L. Bartlett); *Negotiating Language Policies in Schools* (with K. Menken); *Imagining Multilingual Schools* (with T. Skutnabb-Kangas and M. Torres-Guzmán); and *A Reader in Bilingual Education* (with C. Baker). She is the associate general editor of the *International Journal of the Sociology of Language*.

Jin Sook Lee is a professor of education in the Gevirtz Graduate School of Education at the University of California, Santa Barbara. A former teacher of English as a second language, she earned her PhD in language learning and policy from Stanford University in 2000. Her research focuses on the cultural, sociopolitical, and sociopsychological factors that shape the language learning process among children of immigrants. She is currently working on a longitudinal ethnography examining the social and academic trajectories of Latino and Korean students in dual-language immersion programs and English-only schools. Her work has been published in journals at the intersections of linguistics and education including *International*

Review of Research in Education
March 2014, Vol. 38, pp. 334-340
DOI: 10.3102/0091732X14523727
© 2014 AERA. http://rre.aera.net

Journal of Bilingual Education and Bilingualism, Foreign Language Annals, Bilingual Research Journal, Language Learning and Technology, and *Language, Culture and Curriculum.* In 2009, she coedited (with Terrence Wiley and Russ Rumberger) *The Education of Linguistic Minority Students in the US* (Multilingual Matters) and was awarded an outstanding article of the year award from the *Bilingual Research Journal* in 2011. She serves on the editorial board of the *International Multilingual Research Journal, Language Arts, and The Journal of Asia TEFL.* She is a 2008 recipient of the Foundation for Child Development Scholars Award and a 2011 recipient of the Fulbright Scholars Research Award in Applied Linguistics for which she conducted a study on the English language teaching programs and policies in South Korea.

Joseph Lo Bianco is a professor of language and literacy education at the University of Melbourne, immediate past president of the Australian Academy of the Humanities, and Research Director, UNICEF Language and Peacebuilding, Myanmar, Burma; Malaysia; and Thailand. He wrote the National Policy on Languages for the Australian Federal Government, adopted in June 1987 as the first multilingual policy in an English-speaking society. He is a practitioner of language policy and planning, having been commissioned as a consultant in Asian, African, and European countries; he is also a researcher and writer on China–Western intercultural relations and language and intercultural education in general. He is currently preparing for publication a work on language ideologies in Tunisia, with Dr. Fethi Helal, a fiction-based intercultural study on Chinese–Western mutual representations and knowledge. He has more than 120 publications, and his most recent book, with Renata Aliani, is *Language Planning and Student Experiences: Intention, Rhetoric and Implementation* (Multilingual Matters).

Reynaldo F. Macías is currently professor of Chicana and Chicano studies, education, and applied linguistics in the César E. Chávez Department for Chicana and Chicano Studies at University of California, Los Angeles. He has joint faculty appointments in the departments of Education and Applied Linguistics and is an affiliated faculty member to the African American Studies Programs and the Civic Engagement minor. He received his PhD from Georgetown University in linguistics, specializing in sociolinguistics and minoring in theoretical linguistics and language policy and planning, and his master's in early childhood education from University of California, Los Angeles. He was director of the University of California's Linguistic Minority Research Institute between 1992 and 1998 and assistant director of the National Institute of Education, in charge of reading and language studies between 1979 and 1981. He was a Presidential appointee to the Advisory Board for the National Institute for Literacy, serving from 1996 until 2003. His research interests are in the politics of language policy, language demography, and educational sociolinguistics, including bilingual education, educational history and policy analysis, literacy, teacher preparation, and multicultural curricular education. He was intimately involved in the 1992 National Adult Literacy Survey that reported for the first time a representative estimate of literacy (including biliteracy and non-English literacy, measures he defined), along with bilingualism, for the nation's ethno-linguistic populations: *English Literacy and Language Minorities in the United States* (NCES 2001-464; with E. Greenberg, D. Rhodes, and T. Chan, 2001). He is currently writing a book on the history of language groups and politics in the United States.

Stephen May is professor of education in Te Puna Wananga in the Faculty of Education, The University of Auckland, New Zealand. He is also an honorary research fellow in the Centre for the Study of Ethnicity and Citizenship, University of Bristol, United Kingdom. Stephen has written widely on language rights, language policy, and language education, including bilingual education, indigenous language education, and multicultural education. To date, he has published nine books and over 90 academic articles and book chapters in these areas. His key books include *Language and Minority Rights* (2nd ed.; Routledge, 2012), the first edition of which received an American Library Association Choice's Outstanding Academic title award (2008). His latest book is a significant new edited collection, *The Multilingual Turn* (Routledge, 2014). He has previously edited, with Nancy Hornberger, *Language Policy and Political Issues in Education*, Volume 1 of the *Encyclopedia of Language and Education* (2nd ed.; Springer, 2008); and with Christine Sleeter, *Critical Multiculturalism: Theory and Praxis* (Routledge, 2010). He is general editor of the third edition of the multivolume *Encyclopedia of Language and Education* (Springer, 2016), a founding editor of the interdisciplinary journal, *Ethnicities* (Sage), and associate editor of *Language Policy* (Springer). His homepage is http://www.education.auckland.ac.nz/uoa/stephen-may.

Teresa L. McCarty is the George F. Kneller Chair in Education and Anthropology in the Graduate School of Education and Information Studies at the University of California, Los Angeles, and the Alice Wiley Snell Professor Emerita of Education Policy Studies at Arizona State University. Her research, teaching, and outreach focus on educational language policy, Indigenous/multilingual education, youth language, critical literacy studies, and ethnographic studies of education. A fellow of the American Educational Research Association, the Society for Applied Anthropology, and the International Centre for Language Revitalization, she has edited and coedited *Anthropology and Education Quarterly, American Educational Research Journal,* and the *Journal of American Indian Education.* Her books include *A Place to Be Navajo: Rough Rock and the Struggle for Self-Determination in Indigenous Schooling* (Erlbaum, 2002), *"To Remain an Indian": Lessons in Democracy From a Century of Native American Education* (with K. T. Lomawaima, Teachers College Press, 2006), *Ethnography and Language Policy* (Routledge, 2011), *Language Planning and Policy in Native America: History, Theory, Praxis* (Multilingual Matters, 2013), and *Indigenous*

Youth and Multilingualism: Language Identity, Ideology, and Practice in Dynamic Cultural Worlds (with L. T. Wyman and S. E. Nicholas, Routledge, 2014).

Sheilah E. Nicholas is a member of the Hopi Tribe and an assistant professor in the Language, Reading and Culture Program, Department of Teaching, Learning and Sociocultural Studies, at the University of Arizona (UA). She received her PhD in American Indian studies from UA in 2008. Her scholarly work focuses on Indigenous/Hopi language maintenance and revitalization, Hopi language literacy, Indigenous language ideologies and epistemologies, and cultural and linguistic issues in American Indian education. Her current research investigates the impact of educational policies, particularly the No Child Left Behind Act, on indigenous language programs and includes a schoolwide self-study regarding the role of schools in language revitalization efforts. She is also currently coordinator of the UA Bureau of Applied Research and Anthropology Hopi Children's Word Book Project. A former classroom teacher, she has served as coordinator of the American Indian Language Development Institute; director of Project NATIVE, a U.S. Department of Education–funded Native American teacher training program at Tohono O'odham Community College; and field researcher on Native American language revitalization for the Indigenous Languages Institute in Santa Fe, New Mexico. She has also served as a consultant to the Hopi Tribe for the Hopilavayi Program in planning and implementing Hopi language teacher training at the Hopilavayi Summer Institute. Her research has been published in numerous edited volumes and in *American Indian Culture and Research Quarterly, Journal of Language, Identity, and Education, Language Policy,* and *International Multilingual Research Journal.* Her recent edited volume (with L. T. Wyman and T. L. McCarty) is *Indigenous Youth and Multilingualism: Language Identity, Ideology, and Practice in Dynamic Cultural Worlds* (Routledge, 2014).

Jeanne M. Powers is an associate professor in the Mary Lou Fulton Teachers College, at Arizona State University. She received her PhD in sociology from the University of California, San Diego. Her research focuses on school segregation, school choice, and school finance litigation. One line of research draws from and extends her historical analysis of Mexican American school segregation cases in the Southwest. In another line of research she is examining how social science research shapes judicial decision making in school finance cases. Her research has been published in *Law and Social Inquiry,* the *American Educational Research Journal, Educational Policy, The Journal of School Choice,* and *Equity and Excellence in Education.* In addition, she has written a book on charter school reform: *Charter Schools: Reform Imagery, Reform Reality* (Palgrave Macmillan). She is an associate editor of *Education Policy Analysis Archives,* an open-access peer-reviewed scholarly journal.

Vaidehi Ramanathan (vramanathan@ucdavis.edu) is a professor of applied socio-linguistics in the linguistics department at the University of California, Davis. Her research interests span all domains of literacy, including teacher education, minority languages, language policies, and unequal power relations between English and the vernaculars in postcolonial contexts. She is also interested in aging, health, and disability studies as well as language learning and literacy studies. Her publications include *Language, Body and Health* (coedited, 2011, Mouton de Gruyter), *Bodies and Language: Health, Ailments, Disabilities* (2010, Multilingual Matters), *The English-Vernacular Divide: Postcolonial Language Politics and Practice* (2005, Multilingual Matters), *The Politics of TESOL Education: Writing, Knowledge, Critical Pedagogy* (2001, Routledge), and *Alzheimer's Discourse: Some Sociolinguistic Dimensions* (1997, Lawrence Erlbaum). She has also edited a special issue of *Language Policy* with a focus on health and coedited a special issue of *TESOL* Quarterly with a focus on language policies. Her most recent publication is an edited volume titled *Language Policies and (Dis)Citizenship: Rights, Access, Pedagogies* (2013, Multilingual Matters).

Elana Shohamy is a professor of language education at the School of Education, Tel Aviv University, Israel. Her research, teaching, writings, and plenary talks focus on a variety of topics related to language testing within a political and social framework; language policy in terms of multilingualism, empowerments, and mechanisms; academic achievements of immigrants in school within the perspectives of using multilingual repertoire and multilingual assessment; and linguistic landscape referring to representation, contestations, and justice of languages in public spaces. She has published extensively in journals and edited books: *The Languages of Israel: Ideology, Policy and Practice* (with B. Spolsky, Multilingual Matters, 1999); *The Power of Tests: Misuses of Language Tests* (Longman, 2001); *Language Policy: Hidden Agendas and New Approaches* (Routledge, 2006); *Encyclopedia of Language and Education: Vol. 7. Language Testing and Assessment* (edited with N. Hornberger, Springer, 2008); *Linguistic Landscape: Expanding the Scenery* (edited with D. Gorter, Routledge, 2009); and *Linguistic Landscape in the City* (edited with E. Ben Rafael & M. Barni, Multilingual Matters, 2010). She is the editor of the journal *Language Policy*. In 2010, she was granted the International Language Testing Association lifetime academic achievement award.

Monica L. Stigler is a PhD candidate in the Mary Lou Fulton Teachers College at Arizona State University. Her research focuses on the relationship between schools and communities and the extent to which education can lead to social transformation. Her research has also examined issues of school choice and equity. Professionally, she has worked as a policy analyst for Morrison Institute for Public Policy, a nonpartisan think tank, and as development director for a leading housing and human services nonprofit organization.

James W. Tollefson is currently a professor in the Faculty of Education at The University of Hong Kong. Before joining The University of Hong Kong in 2012, he taught at the University of Washington in Seattle and in Japan, the Philippines, and Slovenia in the former Yugoslavia. His research interests include language policy, sociolinguistics, language and inequality, second-language education, and language and ideology. His most recent books are *Language Policies in Education: Critical Issues; Power and Inequality in Language Education; Planning Language, Planning Inequality*; and (with Amy B. M. Tsui) *Medium of Instruction Policies: Which Agenda? Whose Agenda?* and *Language Policy, Culture and Identity in Asian Contexts*. His current research critically examines mass media coverage of language policy issues, language and nationalism in East Asia, and research methods in language planning.

Amy B. M. Tsui is pro-vice-chancellor and vice president (teaching and learning) of The University of Hong Kong and chair professor in the Faculty of Education. She has published and presented numerous keynotes on language policy, teacher learning and teacher development, classroom discourse, classroom-centered research, and conversational analysis. Her more recent major publications include *Understanding Expertise in Teaching: Case Studies of ESL Teachers* (2003), (with Ference Marton) *Classroom Discourse and the Space of Learning* (2004), (with James Tollefson) *Medium of Instruction Policy: Which Agenda? Whose Agenda?* (2004) and *Language Policy, Culture and Identity in Asian Contexts* (2007), and (as lead author) *Learning in School-University Partnership: Sociocultural Perspectives* (2009).

Terrence G. Wiley is president of the Center for Applied Linguistics (CAL) and professor emeritus at Arizona State University, where he served as executive dean of the former Mary Lou Fulton Institute and Graduate School of Education and Director of the Division of Educational Leadership and Policy Studies. Among his numerous publications are *The Handbook of Heritage, Community, and Native American Languages Research, Policy, and Practice* (coeditor, CAL-Routledge, 2014), *The Education of Language Minority Immigrants in the United States* (coeditor, Multilingual Matters, 2009), and *Literacy and Language Diversity in the United States* (CAL, 2005). He has cofounded two international journals, the *Journal of Language Identity and Education* (currently coeditor, Routledge) and the *International Multilingual Research Journal* (Routledge), and he has served on numerous editorial boards. He has lectured and served as a visiting professor at a number of international universities, most recently at Renmin (People's) University of China.

Colin H. Williams is a research professor in the School of Welsh, Cardiff University, Cardiff, United Kingdom. His main scholarly interests are in sociolinguistics and language policy in multicultural societies, ethnic and minority relations, and political geography. He has previously taught in universities in Canada, England, and the United States. Between 2000 and 2010 he was a National Assembly for Wales–appointed member of the Welsh Language Board, where he concentrated on language policy, intergovernmental strategy, and international aspects of language planning.

He continues to advise government agencies in the United Kingdom and elsewhere. His latest publications are *Minority Language Promotion, Protection, and Regulation* (2013, Palgrave) and *Parents, Personalities and Power: Welsh-Medium Schools in South East Wales* (as coeditor with H. Thomas; 2013, University of Wales Press).

Wayne E. Wright, PhD, is an associate professor of applied linguistics in the Department of Bicultural-Bilingual Studies at the University of Texas at San Antonio, where he directs the Teaching English as a Second Language Program. A former bilingual (Khmer), English as a second language, and structured english immersion teacher in southern California, he received his PhD in educational leadership and policy studies from Arizona State University in 2004. He is author of the widely used textbook *Foundations for Teaching English Language Learners: Research, Theory, Policy, and Practice* (Caslon, 2010) and of numerous published articles in leading academic journals and books on policy and practices in language minority and heritage language education. In 2009 he was a Fulbright scholar at the Royal University of Phnom Penh in Cambodia. He is editor of the *Journal of Southeast Asian American Education and Advancement* and book review editor of the *International Multilingual Research Journal*. He is currently coediting (with Sovicheth Boun and Ofelia García) the forthcoming *Handbook of Bilingual and Multilingual Education* (Wiley-Blackwell).